Tudor and Stuart Britain

Tudor and Stuart Britain 1485–1714

THIRD EDITION

Roger Lockyer

Harlow, England • London • New York • Boston • San Francisco • Toronto
Sydney • Singapore • Hong Kong • Tokyo • Seoul • Taipei • New Delhi
Cape Town • Madrid • Mexico City • Amsterdam • Munich • Paris • Milan

Pearson Education Limited

Edinburgh Gate
Harlow CM20 2JE
United Kingdom
Tel. +44 (0)1279 623623
Tel. +44 (0)1279 431059
Website: www.pearsoned.co.uk

First published 1964
Second edition 1985
Third edition published in Great Britain 2005

©Pearson Eduction Limited 2005

ISBN-10: 0-582-77188-9
ISBN-13: 978-0-582-77188-8

British Library Cataloguing in Publication Data
A CIP catalogue record for this book can be obtained from the British Library

Library of Congress Cataloging in Publication Data

Lockyer, Roger.
    Tudor and Stuart Britain, 1485–1714 / Roger Lockyer. – 3rd ed.
        p. cm.
    Includes bibliographical references and index.
    ISBN 0-582-77188-9 (pbk.)
        1. Great Britain–History–Tudors, 1485–1603. 2. Great Britain–History–Stuarts,
1603–1714. I. Title.

DA300.L6 2004
941.05–dc22   2004048631

10 9 8 7 6 5 4 3
08 07 06

Set by 3
Printed and bound in Malaysia, PJB

The Publisher's policy is to use paper manufactured from sustainable forests.

Contents

Preface

In the twenty years that have passed since the publication of the second edition of *Tudor and Stuart Britain* the pace of historical research has not slackened. My aim, in producing this third edition, has been to take full account of recent work without weakening the basic chronological structure of the book. I hope it will serve as a guide not only for those who are new to the period but also for those who have some knowledge of it but wish to keep abreast of current interpretations. It is obviously impossible, in the space available, to cover every topic at appropriate length, but I have provided a comprehensive section on 'Further Reading' to help anyone who wishes to delve more deeply into specific topics.

Roger Lockyer
London 2004

CHAPTER ONE

The new monarchy

The end of the Wars of the Roses

Edward, Duke of York, claimed the English throne and began his reign as Edward IV in 1461. Nine years later he was driven out of his kingdom by a Lancastrian coup, but after only a few months in exile he returned to England, crushed the Lancastrians at the battle of Tewkesbury in May 1471, and thereafter kept a firm hold on power until his death in 1483. He was succeeded – in name at least – by his twelve-year-old son, Edward V, but given that the new King was too young to rule, the royal authority was exercised by his uncle, Richard, Duke of Gloucester, Edward IV's brother. Whether or not Richard, as the Tudors later asserted, murdered Edward V and his brother – 'the Princes in the Tower'– he was certainly capable of it. Yet as Richard III he showed himself to be an effective monarch. Indeed, it could be argued that he seized the throne in order to continue Edward IV's firm rule and prevent England from slipping back into anarchy, which was often the consequence of a royal minority.

Henry Tudor, Earl of Richmond, who had inherited the Lancastrian claim to the throne, defeated and killed Richard III at the battle of Bosworth on 22 August 1485, but he had to struggle to keep his crown, for the Yorkists did not regard the verdict of Bosworth as final. In 1487 they put forward Lambert Simnel, the son of an organ-builder, as Edward IV's nephew, the Earl of Warwick. Henry, who was holding the real Earl of Warwick prisoner in the Tower of London, paraded him through the streets of the capital, but this gesture could not, of itself, end the Yorkist threat. Simnel's promoters took him to Ireland, where they had consider-able support, and in May 1487 the boy was solemnly crowned in Dublin Cathedral as Edward VI. A month later Simnel, accompanied by a Yorkist army, landed in Lancashire, hoping to spark off a general rising, since Richard III had been a popular ruler in northern England. His hopes were not fulfilled, but his army, numbering some eight thousand men, marched south-east and by 16 June had reached East Stoke, not far from Newark in Nottinghamshire. There Henry was waiting for him, with a larger force, and in a hard-fought engagement the Yorkists were utterly defeated. Simnel himself was taken prisoner and spent the remainder of his life as a turnspit in the royal kitchen.

The Yorkists were not rendered impotent by this defeat, nor were they impressed by Henry's gesture of reconciliation in marrying Edward IV's daughter. Elizabeth of York. In 1491 they put forward another pretender. This time it was Perkin Warbeck, the son of a Customs official at Tournai, who claimed to be Richard, Duke of York – Edward V's brother and one of the 'Princes in the Tower'. Warbeck, who called himself Richard IV, was pronounced genuine by no less an authority than Edward IV's sister, Margaret, dowager Duchess of Burgundy – who, as a leading Yorkist, had no love for the Lancastrian Henry. She supplied a small force of mercenaries with which 'Richard IV' hoped to make good his claim. In July 1495 he sent some of them ashore at Deal to spark off a rebellion in Kent, but no supporters materialised and the unfortunate soldiers were quickly rounded up by the sheriff. Warbeck made good his escape to Ireland and thence to Scotland, where he was welcomed by James IV, who feared that a resurgent England might threaten his own independence. James gave his blessing to a marriage between his cousin, Lady Catherine Gordon, and Warbeck, and agreed to provide men and money for the pretender. Warbeck's initial attempt to invade England, in September 1496, was a fiasco; nor was James IV more successful the following year, when he led his troops across the border. In September 1497 peace was concluded between the two states, but by that time Warbeck had left Scotland.

The pretender hoped for better luck in Cornwall, whose inhabitants had risen in revolt when Henry levied taxation on them in order to pay for the defence of his northern border. But although recruits flowed in to Warbeck he could not capture the key town of Exeter. News that Henry's forces were advancing towards them disheartened Warbeck's followers, and as they deserted him he was left with no alternative but to surrender and throw himself on the King's mercy. Henry kept him in prison for two years, until another imposter appeared, claiming to be the Earl of Warwick. The King realised he would have no peace while the Yorkist claimants remained alive, since their mere existence was a spur to rebellion. In November 1499, therefore, Warwick and Warbeck, the real earl and the false duke, were both tried for treason and condemned to death. Warbeck, as a commoner, was hanged, but Warwick, who had the blood royal in him, was beheaded.

Henry defeated all attempts to unseat him, but he could never relax, for the Yorkists remained unreconciled and there was no certainty that the Tudor regime would survive. In 1503, when the King was unwell, it was reported from Calais (an English possession) that a number of important officials gathered there had discussed what would happen if he were to die. 'Some of them', said the informant, 'spake of my lord of Buckingham, saying that he was a noble man and would be a royal ruler. Other there were that spake . . . of Edmund de la Pole. But none of them spake of my lord prince.' The Duke of Buckingham and Edmund de la Pole, Earl of Suffolk, both had hereditary claims to the throne, and it is significant that even at this late date, nearly twenty years after Henry's accession, they were considered as more serious contenders than the King's son, Prince Henry. Nevertheless, when Henry VII eventually died, in April 1509, the Prince succeeded him without any problems. The smooth transfer of power symbolised Henry VII's achievement in restoring order to England and establishing the Tudor dynasty securely on the throne.

The royal administration

In the early Middle Ages the expansion of royal government had led to specialisation, and departments emerged within the King's household to deal with finance and secretarial business. These departments, the Exchequer and Chancery, gradually acquired their own routines and ceased to be part of the royal court, although they remained under the monarch's control. That control was threatened, however, when the increasingly assertive and politically ambitious barons attempted to curb royal power. One way in which they did this was by imposing their own nominees on the Exchequer and Chancery, thereby, as they thought, taking over the administration. But the King's household was perpetually fecund. As the barons took over the outer ring of government, an inner ring came into being. The royal Chamber and Wardrobe by-passed the older offices and left them only the trappings of power. In times of emergency a determined King could use his household offices to govern the country. They were flexible and informal, not hamstrung by the formal routines that made the Exchequer, for instance, so ponderous and long-winded in its functioning.

The mainspring of royal government was the King's Council, but from the early fourteenth century onwards the magnates increased their representation on this body and eventually dominated it. Asserting their natural right to counsel the King, they made him accept them whether he wanted to or not. By the time Edward IV came to the throne, the Council was a largely aristocratic body, operating more or less independently of the crown. Such an institution was of little use to Edward. He wanted something much more tightly under his control, and he therefore created a Council very similar in its composition to that which Henry VII was later to use.

The names survive of some 225 persons who were called 'Councillors' in Henry VII's reign, but they never all met together. More than forty of them failed to put in any appearance, and it seems that the title was granted as a reward or an inducement to the King's supporters throughout the length and breadth of the country. Yet if the Council is considered as a whole, 27 per cent of its members were clerics, 22 per cent office-holders, 20 per cent courtiers, 19 per cent peers, and 12 per cent lawyers – though these categories are not, of course, mutually exclusive.

Clerics, who formed the largest group in Henry VII's Council, played as important a part as their medieval predecessors. The King's principal adviser was John Morton, who had shared Henry's exile. He was nominated Archbishop of Canterbury in 1486 and appointed Lord Chancellor the following year. Morton died in 1500, but his eventual successor as archbishop was William Warham, whom Henry appointed Lord Chancellor in 1504. Another former exile and prominent Councillor was Richard Fox, whom Henry chose as his Secretary. In 1487 Fox became Bishop of Exeter as well as Lord Privy Seal, and was frequently employed on diplomatic missions to European courts.

There was little indication under Henry VII, any more than there had been under Edward IV, of a deliberate policy to exclude members of the aristocracy from the royal administration. Several key positions were held by men who came from long-established noble families. The Lord Great Chamberlain was John de Vere, thirteenth Earl of Oxford, whom Henry appointed Lord Admiral. The Lord Steward of the Household was Lord Willoughby de Broke, another companion of Henry in exile. While those who had committed themselves to Henry when he was merely a pretender to the throne were duly rewarded once he obtained it, service to the Yorkist monarchy was not of itself a bar to office. Some thirty of Henry's Councillors had held a similar position under Richard III or Edward IV, for experienced and efficient administrators were not in such abundant supply that Henry could afford to deprive himself of their services. The same applied to soldiers. The Earl of Surrey had fought for Richard at

Bosworth, alongside his father, the sixth Duke of Norfolk, who had been killed on the battlefield, but once it became clear that he was willing to transfer his allegiance to the first Tudor sovereign he was appointed to the Council and became one of Henry's most trusted commanders.

While Henry was not, in principle, anti-aristocratic, he was obviously aware of the key role played by overmighty nobles in fomenting discontent during the turbulent years that preceded his accession. Edward IV had made matters worse by creating new titles, but Henry took the contrary course. At his accession there were twenty dukes, marquises and earls, but by the time he died there were only one duke and nine earls. This decline was largely the result of natural causes, but Henry made no effort to fill the gaps in the ranks of the peerage. Giles Daubeny, who had been in exile with the King and was appointed Lord Chamberlain of the Household, was made a baron in 1486, but the few other peerages that Henry conferred were re-creations of dormant titles. Henry preferred to reward his faithful servants by appointing them to the Order of the Garter – a great honour, of course, but not hereditary; nor did it entail a grant of lands from the crown to uphold the dignity, which was frequently the case with peerages.

While Henry placed considerable reliance on clerics and nobles, the influence of these two groups in the Council was undoubtedly diminished during his reign, for the King came to rely increasingly on lesser landowners and professional men whom he appointed to office. These were the men whom Warbeck denounced as 'caitiffs and villeins of low birth', but this was true only in the sense that they did not come from the handful of great families which had dominated English life in the preceding century. The majority were country gentlemen who had been trained in either common or civil law. Sir Reginald Bray, who was Henry's chief adviser on financial matters and one of his few close friends, was an exception in that his father was a citizen of Worcester, where he may have practised as a doctor. Daubeney, however, traced his descent from Norman ancestors who had come to England with William the Conqueror; Sir Richard Guildford, Comptroller of the Household, was the son of a Kentish knight; while Sir Thomas Lovell, Chancellor of the Exchequer and Speaker of the House of Commons in Henry's first Parliament, came from a family of Norfolk landowners. Among Councillors who rose to prominence later in Henry's reign, Edmund Dudley was the grandson of a peer, and Sir Edward Poynings the son of a Kentish squire. Only Sir Richard Empson, like Bray, came from an urban background, since his father was a leading citizen of Towcester in Northamptonshire. But the Empsons also owned land in the surrounding countryside, and the same may have been true of the Brays.

The number of members present at Council meetings varied from four to forty, with seven as the most frequent. A handful of Councillors were regular attenders and formed, in effect though not in name, an inner circle. They were full-time administrators and attended the King not only in the law terms, when most of the business was transacted, but during vacations as well. This 'Council attendant' was a skeleton staff which merged into the larger body when a full meeting took place. Its members included the great officers of state – the Lord Chancellor, Lord Treasurer and Lord Privy Seal – and officials such as Bray, Daubeney and Guildford who had the King's entire confidence. The King himself was the heart of the Council, giving it a cohesion and continuity that it would not otherwise have enjoyed. Henry, like Edward before him, was a frequent attender, and the Council is best regarded as an extension of the royal personality.

Because it reflected the King's will, the Council's competence was virtually unlimited. It sat regularly during the law terms and used for its meetings the room known as the Star Chamber. Its advisory and administrative functions were probably the most important part of its work, although much of this can only be inferred, since the Council had no seal of its own and had to use the signet or privy seal to authenticate its decisions. Councillors offered advice to the King on matters of policy, and framed letters, warrants, proclamations and all other documents necessary to execute the royal will.

Since the Council had the ultimate responsibility for maintaining law and order, it could act as a court. Occasionally it summoned offenders to appear before it, but most of the time it merely responded to complaints brought by private persons. It was forbidden by statute to deal with cases affecting property rights, but many litigants evaded this limitation by accusing their opponent of being involved in rioting, which was a prime concern of the Council. Such charges were often little more than a legal fiction, but litigants were prepared to strain the truth in order to get a hearing from the most powerful men in the kingdom. Even if the Council did no more than remit the case to the appropriate common-law court it would thereby speed up the judicial process, which was otherwise clogged by long delays. Henry may have hoped that the Council sitting as a court would take the lead in imposing order upon a turbulent society, but it had neither the time nor the staff to do so. It could deal with judicial business only at the expense of its other functions.

The Council tried to meet its multifarious obligations by setting up specialised tribunals. One of these was a court, established by statute in 1487, charged with the responsibility for putting down 'unlawful maintenances, giving of liveries, signs and tokens, and retainders'. It consisted of the three principal members of the Council – the Chancellor, Treasurer, and Keeper of the Privy Seal – as well as the two Chief Justices, and later in the sixteenth century the statute was given the heading *Pro Camera Stellata*, which implied that the court which it had created was Star Chamber. In fact, the 1487 tribunal was quite distinct from the Council sitting to do justice in Star Chamber, apart from the overlap in membership, and there is no reason to believe that it was particularly effective in dealing with the problems raised by retaining.

On the face of it, retaining was a major cause of lawlessness, for a lord with liveried followers had what one of Henry's judges described as 'a great company at his command. And for this [reason] men do not dare to execute the law on any of them.' However, Henry never attempted to outlaw retaining altogether, for it had its positive as well as negative side. Retainers could be usefully employed as police forces in local areas, and also provided the King with a reserve of soldiers when an emergency arose. Henry's aim, therefore, was not to abolish retaining but to make sure, so far as he could, that it was under his ultimate control. He took a big step in this direction with a statute of 1504 requiring all those who had retainers to give him a list of their names and obtain a royal licence. No exceptions were permitted, as became plain when charges of illegal retaining were brought against the King's mother, Lady Margaret Beaufort, and his close friend the Earl of Oxford. The problems associated with retaining could not be solved overnight, but Henry had begun the process, which his successors completed, of bringing the practice within the orbit of the royal government.

Another of the specialised tribunals which Henry VII's Council developed was the 'Council Learned in Law', though this, unlike the 1487 tribunal, was based upon the royal prerogative, not statute. It was a small body, with a maximum membership of twelve members – though they never all came together at any one time. The majority were 'learned in law', which explains the tribunal's name. The Council Learned was in existence from at least 1495 but only became a separate institution from 1499. It had close links with the Duchy of Lancaster, now an apanage of the crown, and Reginald Bray, who was Chancellor of the Duchy, played a leading role in it. Bray was known for his unswerving commitment to the King's service, which he put above all other considerations, but it was under his successors, Richard Empson and Edmund Dudley, that the Council Learned became notorious for its ruthlessness. Empson and Dudley were friends and colleagues of Bray, from whom they presumably learnt many of their methods, and from 1504 onwards Empson held Bray's former office of Chancellor of the Duchy.

The Council Learned acted as a debt-collecting agency for the crown, and undertook prosecutions on its behalf. It was also involved in the drawing up of bonds and recognisances, binding those involved to good behaviour under threat of a financial penalty. Henry used these on an unprecedented scale, as a means of controlling the disorderly propensities of his more important subjects, especially during the last seven years of his reign, when the death of his eldest son, Prince Arthur (1502), followed by that of his wife, Elizabeth of York (1503), made him fearful about the prospects of a peaceful succession for his surviving son, Prince Henry. Avarice may also have been a factor, though Dudley's account book for 1504–08 shows that out of a total of £220,000 which was owed the King, only £30,000 had actually been collected. Henry, in effect, put more than two-thirds of the peerage on probation, with fines and penalties hanging over them like the sword of Damocles. Dudley later declared that it had been the King's express objective 'to have many persons in his danger at his pleasure', and following Henry's death some two hundred recognisances were cancelled on the grounds that they were unjust.

The penalties which the Council Learned imposed on the King's behalf could be substantial. In 1504, to take one example, the Earl of Northumberland and the Archbishop of York, whose retainers had been involved in violent clashes, were each required to give bonds of £2,000, to be forfeited if they failed to keep the peace. Another noble, the Earl of Shrewsbury, was made to take out so many bonds that by the time of Henry VII's death he was 'endangered' for more than £5,000. Bonds and recognisances were undoubtedly an effective instrument for maintaining order, but the nobles who were brought under restraint in this manner bitterly resented them. There was nothing they could do while Henry VII was alive, but after the accession of Henry VIII Empson and Dudley were convicted of treason and executed. This was intended as a signal that the harsh regime of Henry VII was over and that the second Tudor monarch intended to win the love of his greater subjects rather than cow them into obedience.

Though the maintenance of the King's peace could never be taken for granted, even in England, the situation was particularly bad in the remote Welsh and Scottish border regions. In 1471 Edward IV created his baby son Prince of Wales and appointed a council to look after his estates in the area. This council subsequently acquired judicial functions and supervised the enforcement of law and order throughout the principality and the marcher lordships that guarded the border with England. It lapsed at Edward's death, but Henry VII appointed a similar council for his son, Prince Arthur. The young prince was subsequently given most of the crown's marcher lordships, including the great earldom of March, as well as the principality itself, and thereby became direct ruler over a substantial part of Wales. Even after Arthur's death the council continued its work, and the marcher lords, who had previously been semi-independent magnates, were forced to acknowledge the authority of the crown.

It may well be that Henry, as the Spanish ambassador reported in 1498, would have liked 'to govern England in the French fashion', but the ambassador's further comment, that 'he cannot', was an accurate summary of the situation. The only standing army in England consisted of some two hundred Yeomen of the Guard, whose duties were largely ceremonial. In times of crisis, when Henry needed soldiers, he had to issue commissions of array to his leading subjects requiring them to furnish men for his service. Even when there was no crisis, Henry was dependent upon the magnates for governing the localities. In Essex and East Anglia he relied upon his Lord Great Chamberlain, the Earl of Oxford, while in the south-west he gave his trust to Lord Daubeney. In the north-east he had virtually no choice, for this area had long been dominated by the Percy family, whose head was the Earl of Northumberland. The earl had been present at Bosworth on Richard's side, though he took no part in the battle, but Henry restored him to his position as Lord Warden of the East and Middle Marches which controlled the approaches to Scotland. Northumberland proved a loyal subject. Indeed, it was while he was engaged in the King's service, collecting the parliamentary subsidy granted in 1489, that he was set on by an angry mob and killed.

Northumberland's heir was a minor, so Henry took the boy into his guardianship and brought him up at court. In due course, the young earl took over his father's role as the King's man in the north, but in the interim Henry relied on the Earl of Surrey, acting under the nominal authority of Prince Arthur who, although still a baby, had been appointed Warden-General of the Marches. Surrey was given a council to advise him, similar to that which Richard III had set up. This provided a basis for the Council of the North that was formally established under Henry VIII, but in the short term the royal authority was exercised by Surrey. He was not a major landowner in the north, but he commanded respect by his lineage and rank, and also, of course, by the fact that he had the King behind him.

Adjoining the county of Northumberland, to the south, was County Durham, where the principal magnate was the Earl of Westmorland, formerly a close associate of Richard III. Henry never seems to have trusted him as he did Surrey, and it is significant that in 1494 he appointed one of his closest advisers, Richard Fox, as Bishop of Durham. Not all areas had resident magnates, and in these Henry relied on members of the leading gentry. Sometimes, though not invariably, these were courtiers or office-holders. Shropshire and Herefordshire, for example, were dominated by Sir Richard Croft, who was Henry's Treasurer of the Household. In south-west England the gentry had shown themselves to be particularly committed to Henry at his accession, but the King preferred to place his trust in three peers, Daubeney, Willoughby de Broke, and the Earl of Devon. This was a misjudgement, as was shown in 1497 when a major revolt broke out in the area, for many of the gentry either joined the rebels or held conspicuously aloof from attempts to suppress them. The Cornish Rising began as a tax revolt but grew into a major challenge to Henry's authority. With their numbers swollen to fifteen thousand, the rebels marched to the outskirts of London and camped on Blackheath. Henry had to cancel a planned expedition against the Scots and bring his troops back south to meet the Cornish threat. A pitched battle took place in which a thousand of the rebels were killed. The rest fled, and their ring-leaders were captured and executed.

No outline of late Yorkist and early Tudor administration would be complete that left out the personality of the monarch. Much of the achievement of Edward IV and Henry VII was a direct result of their energy and determination. When East Anglia was passing through a turbulent period, Edward appointed one of his household officers as sheriff and publicly declared that though he could ill spare so valuable an adviser he had sent him down 'to set a rule in the country'. He followed this up, in 1464, by touring the most disturbed areas to make sure that order was being enforced and justice administered. Richard III and Henry VII were likewise constantly on the move, asserting the royal authority simply by virtue of their presence.

Henry was only twenty-eight when he triumphed at Bosworth, and he had spent much of his life in exile. Portraits of him show a clean-cut face with a Roman nose, but they also suggest what his contemporaries remarked about him – a watchful reserve that allowed little or no intimacy. Francis Bacon, in his *Life of King Henry VII*, observed that if he had been a 'private man he would have been termed proud; but in a wise prince it was but keeping of distance'. The 'kingship of distance' was reinforced in the early 1490s when Henry decided to confine his public appearances at court to the Presence Chamber and turn the Privy Chamber into a truly private sphere, with a small staff of its own, directed by the Groom of the Stool. Here the King could be free from the press of courtiers and suitors and come as near to relaxing as Henry ever did.

Because he was a good judge of men, Henry was not jealous of ability and was therefore served as well, if not better, than any of his Tudor successors. He did not have the streak of vindictiveness that was to emerge in his son, and although he would not shirk killing his enemies he preferred taking their money instead. After the failure of Warbeck's rising in the west country, for instance, Henry appointed commissioners not to execute but to fine all those who had taken part, and thereby added close on £15,000 to his treasury. The legend of the miser King obscures the true image of a ruler who consciously emulated the Dukes of Burgundy, whose court was regarded as an exemplar, where the ruler's 'magnificence' was always on display. In the words of Polydore Vergil – an Italian humanist whom the King commissioned to write the history of his reign – Henry's 'hospitality was splendidly generous . . . He knew well how to maintain his royal majesty and all which appertains to kingship at every time and in every place'.

When the old royal palace at Sheen, in Surrey, was destroyed by fire, Henry replaced it with a new one named in honour of his northern earldom of Richmond. It cost a fortune, but it was designed to impress both his subjects and foreign visitors, which it certainly did. A great deal of money was also spent on remodelling the palace of Placentia on the banks of the Thames at Greenwich. Neither of these buildings survives, but King's College Chapel at Cambridge, with its elaborate fan vaulting and lavish use of royal symbols, gives some idea of Henry's lofty ambitions, as does the jewel-like Henry VII Chapel in Westminster Abbey, where he is buried in a fine Renaissance tomb. Henry was not simply a builder. He became a discerning collector of books and tapestries, and turned the royal library into a separate department of his household, with its own keeper. Between 1491 and 1503 the King also spent more than £100,000 on the purchase of jewellery, which was one of the most evident symbols of 'magnificence'. Henry, then, was not a miser, in the sense that he loved money for its own sake. He was quite prepared to spend it on a massive scale in order to glorify the Tudor monarchy. Yet he could not have done so unless and until he had restored the royal finances.

The royal finances

Since at least the reign of Henry I English public finances had been managed by the Exchequer, which collected revenues, made payments, and operated a sophisticated method of auditing to ensure that the King was not cheated. Over the centuries the Exchequer had developed routines that enabled it to keep track of the constant flow of lands into and out of the King's hands, but it was not primarily concerned with cash. In periods of emergency, such as war or rebellion, when the King needed to lay his hands on large sums of money at short notice, its painstaking methods proved a hindrance. Edward IV, as Earl of March, had become familiar with the very different techniques of management practised on large estates, and he applied these to the royal finances when he secured the throne. The most significant change consisted in making the King's Chamber, which was responsible for funding the royal household, an alternative national treasury.

Henry VII, surprisingly, allowed the older Lancastrian system to resume its traditional role in the opening years of his reign, but that was because his attention was focused on security problems. However, defeating the various Yorkist challenges required money as well as men, and Henry became aware of the Exchequer's deficiencies in this respect. After the battle of Stoke in 1487 he therefore began transferring revenues to the Chamber, but this was a gradual process and not until the mid-1490s did the Chamber replace the Exchequer as the principal financial department of government. By the end of the reign it was handling about 90 per cent of the King's income. Rents from crown lands were paid into it, as were feudal dues and the profits of justice. The Exchequer was left with the Customs duties and the 'ancient revenue', comprising the *firma comitatus* and the *firma burgi*, long-established annual payments made by counties and boroughs. The only other significant financial institution was the Duchy of Lancaster, which retained control of its own revenues.

The distinction between Chamber and Exchequer was one of institutions, not personnel, for administrators who were skilled in financial matters were in short supply, and they would move between departments. They were also a relatively small group, who knew each other and shared many of the same assumptions and methods. What happened under Henry, far more than under Edward, was that the Chamber became a genuine national treasury, taking under its purview, if not direct control, virtually all the crown's sources of revenue, including those which belonged to Henry as a landholder in his own right. But as the Chamber expanded its role and developed its procedures, it became less adept at fulfilling its original function of supplying large sums of cash for the King's immediate needs. Henry resolved this problem by setting up what Bacon called 'secret places' which were, in effect, mini-treasuries where money could be inconspicuously stored and dispensed. These 'privy coffers' were so private that they left little mark in the records, but it seems probable that they contained a great deal of money and that Henry, by the time of his death, was indeed as rich as he was reputed to be.

The Exchequer's bureaucratic auditing methods could not easily be extended to the Chamber. Edward IV therefore appointed *ad hoc* auditors to oversee the Chamber and Henry continued this practice, though he took such a close personal interest in the royal finances that he became his own principal auditor. He carefully inspected the accounts submitted to him by John Heron, Treasurer of the Chamber from 1492 onwards, and until 1503 initialled each entry to show his approval. Henry was aided in his self-imposed task by Sir Reginald Bray, who developed the practice of holding regular meetings at which the Chamber accounts were brought under a detailed survey. This practice survived his death in 1503, and the 'general surveyors', as they were called, eventually emerged as a separate body, or court, early in the reign of Henry VIII.

Henry VII paid particular attention to his income from land, since the royal estates were the foundation of the crown's wealth. He was fortunate, in that he held more property than any monarch since the Norman Conquest. He was Earl of Richmond in his own right, and by becoming King he acquired the duchies of Cornwall and Lancaster as well as the earldom of Chester. Furthermore, when he married Edward IV's eldest daughter, Elizabeth, in January 1486, he added the greater part of the dukedom of York to his possessions. Henry used Parliament to pass two acts of resumption, one in 1485 and the other in 1487, giving him the legal right to all lands owned by the crown in October 1455, even though by that date a great deal of property had already been alienated by the weak and incapable Henry VI. Henry VII's aim in securing this legislation was not to grab back all alienated property but to ensure that as disputes about ownership – the inevitable consequence of years of disorder – came before the courts for settlement, the crown would be well placed to assert its own claims.

Henry also added to the royal endowment by using acts of attainder against his enemies. Just under 140 individuals suffered in this way, and although a third of the attainders were reversed, the remaining two-thirds were enforced and resulted in a significant profit to the crown. Henry dealt ruthlessly with any suspicion of disloyalty. When, in 1495, the Lord Chamberlain of the Household, Sir William Stanley, was found guilty of treasonable correspondence with the pretender Perkin Warbeck, he was sent to the block and his property transferred to the crown. By this single operation Henry netted £9,000 in cash and lands worth £1,000 a year.

Land brought money into the King's coffers even when it was not under his direct ownership. Ever since the Norman Conquest a great deal of property throughout England had been held on a feudal tenure by 'tenants-in-chief' of the crown, in return for providing knights to serve in the royal armies. By the late fifteenth century feudalism as a military and social system was in decay, but Henry took good care to exact the financial dues that were an integral part of it. He could demand extraordinary 'aids' – as he did for the knighting of his eldest son and the marriage of his eldest daughter – but a more regular source of income was provided by the feudal 'incidents', which were paid every time a death occurred in a landholding family. If the landowner left no heir, then the crown exercised the right of escheat and took over his estates. When the heir was a woman, the crown either made her pay for freedom to choose a husband, or else married her off to the highest bidder. If the heir was a boy he became a royal ward, and although the crown sometimes took control of his property for its own benefit, it more commonly sold off the wardship for a substantial sum of money to purchasers who recouped their costs by ruthlessly exploiting the ward's estates. Even when the unfortunate heir at last came of age he had to pay an incident called 'livery' before he could resume possession of his lands and begin the slow process of restoring them to viability.

Landholders resented wardship as, in effect, an arbitrary tax and one that could undo years of careful work in maintaining and improving their property. They frequently tried to evade it by concealing information about their children. Edward IV appointed commissioners to enquire into feudal tenures and make sure he was not being cheated of his dues. Henry VII did the same, and some idea of the passive resistance to which landed families resorted is given by the fact that of the last fifty 'Inquisitions post-mortem' for Henry's reign, no less than twenty-eight revealed the existence of under-age heirs whose presence had been concealed. Henry was ruthless in enforcing his feudal rights, for he needed the money to make the crown once again the dominant force in English government and society. In 1487 wardship had brought in under £300, but by 1494 this figure had increased to more than £1,500 and by 1507 to almost £6,000. Much of the work of administering wardships had devolved upon Bray, but after his death Henry appointed Sir John Hussey as Master of Wards, charged with 'overseeing, managing and selling the wardships of all lands which may be in the King's hands'.

As a result of enlarging the royal estates and also of enforcing feudal 'incidents' Henry increased his land revenues, both direct and indirect, by some 45 per cent, from £29,000 to £42,000. He also increased the yield of Customs duties on trade, of which the most important were tonnage and poundage, voted to Henry for life by the first Parliament of his reign. The Book of Rates, which set out the tariffs on various items, was revised upwards in 1507, and the yield from this source was also increased by the fact that the restoration of order and stability throughout England encouraged the expansion of commerce. By 1509 Customs were bringing in some £40,000 a year – an increase of more than 20 per cent over the course of Henry's reign.

Edward and Henry each dabbled in trade on his own account. Edward's agents bought up wool and tin and shipped them to markets on the continent, while in 1505–06 Henry made £15,000 from the sale of alum – an essential component in the cloth-dyeing industry. Both kings were also active borrowers. Edward turned to Italian financiers for money, as well as the City of London, but had repaid most of his debts by the time he died. Henry took forced loans from those who could afford them in 1486 and 1489, but they aroused little or no protest, and he preserved his credit rating by repaying them. 'Benevolences' were another matter. These outright 'gifts' were so called because they were supposed to spring from the *benevolentia* or goodwill of the King's richer subjects, but Edward's benevolences were deeply resented, and Richard III made a bid for popularity by accepting a statute outlawing them. This did not prevent Henry VII from demanding them, on the grounds of pressing military need. He was accused of extortion, but the tax system was rigged in favour of the wealthier elements in society, and benevolences were a way of making them contribute a fairer share towards the King's expenses.

What is remarkable about the 'new monarchy' from a financial point of view is the way in which it clung to old practices. Henry VII was perhaps strong enough to have reformed the entire financial system, even at the risk of alarming and offending the landowners and merchants whose support he needed, but he was content to consolidate his revenues and manage them through his Chamber. Since he had more than enough for his own needs he was under no pressure to embark on fundamental reform, but during the course of the sixteenth century inflation was to play havoc with the royal finances, and the system of financial management which Henry passed on to his successors proved to be a strait-jacket, inhibiting their freedom of action.

Henry VII and Parliament

For extraordinary supplies of money Henry turned to Parliament, but he did this as rarely as possible, preferring to follow the example of Edward IV, who told the Commons in 1467: 'I purpose to live upon mine own, and not to charge my subjects but in great and urgent causes concerning the weal of themselves and also the defence of them and of this my realm'. Even taxation voted by the representatives of the nation in Parliament could arouse discontent and occasionally open rebellion, as in the case of the Cornish rising. This may account for the fact that Edward, who reigned for twenty-two years, only met six parliaments, while Henry, who reigned for twenty-four years, was content with seven. Both kings used Parliament to buttress their authority in their early years on the throne, and then left it in abeyance. In the last five years of his reign Edward IV summoned only one Parliament, which lasted a mere five weeks. Similarly, Henry VII called Parliament together only once after March 1497, and even then for a short session, lasting nine weeks. The total time taken up by Henry's parliaments was sixty-nine weeks, which is the equivalent of twenty days a year, but during the second half of his reign this figure dropped to nine days. Clearly Parliament was neither a regular nor an essential part of Edward IV's or Henry VII's government.

Parliaments were a valuable means of communication between the King and his subjects, but they were not unique in this respect. Between 1487 and 1502 Henry summoned five Great Councils, consisting of peers and Councillors, though on two occasions representatives of urban communities were also present. Great Councils were not legislative bodies, but this made them all the more useful to Henry, since they could concentrate on the issues which he put before them. If, as was frequently the case, he accepted their recommendation to summon a Parliament, the members of the Great Council would take their places in the Lords or Commons, where – because they were already well versed in the topics to be discussed – they could guide debates and ensure that the King's business was expedited.

When Parliament assembled, the Lords, as the upper house, held their debates in a room in the royal palace at Westminster, where they were grouped around the throne. The King himself frequently presided, but when he was absent his place was taken by the Lord Chancellor. The Lords consisted of two estates, spiritual and secular. Only thirteen bishops and seventeen abbots attended Henry's first Parliament, but in a full house the spiritual peers numbered forty-eight. Lay lords were thinner on the ground, only eighteen being present at the opening of the 1485 session. This was in part the consequence of the bitter struggle between York and Lancaster in which many nobles had lost their lives – not so much on the battlefield as by execution following their defeat and capture. A number of noble families had died out in the male line; others had been incorporated into the crown. Furthermore, those families which had survived were often headed by minors. Yet as Henry's reign went on, minors came of age, attainders were reversed, and the number of writs sent out to lay peers reached forty-three. This figure did not exactly reflect the size of the peerage, since Henry exercised his right to exclude those nobles who, for whatever reason, were out of favour.

The Commons had long been a House, both in fact and in name, but they met separately, not in the royal palace but in the nearby chapter house of the Abbey of Westminster. In theory they took no part in the proceedings of Parliament except at the beginning and end of sessions, when they were crammed into a small space at one end of the Lords' chamber, beyond the bar which marked its entrance, and made a report of their proceedings through their presiding officer, aptly named the Speaker. This official was 'elected' by the Commons but only after the King had indicated whom he wished to be so honoured. Speakers were invariably chosen from among the two knights elected for every shire except Cheshire and County Durham. This group of members had a higher social standing than the more numerous 'burgesses' who represented the boroughs, but not all the burgesses were in fact townsmen. Country gentlemen had already begun the process of putting themselves forward as candidates for local boroughs, since a parliamentary seat was becoming a sign of distinction.

Further evidence of the increasing importance of the House of Commons came from the fact that many of the King's non-noble Councillors, even though they had the right to attend the Lords as observers, preferred to stand for election to the Lower House, where they could take a full part in the proceedings. Another sign of change came in the procedure whereby bills were passed. It was a convention that public bills, affecting the country generally, began their passage in the Lords, and, when they reached the Commons, took precedence over bills that had originated in the Lower House. This was still the case in 1497, but not in 1504 and thereafter. Henry VII exercised the right to amend bills after they had passed both Houses, but unlike his successors he never needed to use his

other right to veto proposed legislation. It seems that members of the
Lords and Commons, even if they had reservations about the bills placed
before them, would not openly oppose the King's will.

Parliament's principal – and, indeed, unique – function was the passing
of statutes, which were the highest form of man-made law and commanded obedience from all the King's subjects. There were more than 190
statutes passed during Henry VII's reign, of which many are likely to have
originated from the Commons, for its members took advantage of a parliamentary session to promote legislation designed to remedy the
grievances of their constituents. A number of statutes, however, were
clearly the result of government initiatives. These included acts of
attainder, designed to cripple the King's enemies by depriving them of their
property. Henry had frequent resort to such acts throughout his reign, and
138 people suffered in this way. Statutes were also used to reinforce the
authority of Justices of the Peace, who were the King's agents in governing
the local communities. In 1495, for instance, they were authorised to
determine a range of minor offences without waiting for formal presentation by a grand jury. They were also instructed to supervise local officials
and to make sure that sheriffs did not show partiality when they set up jury
panels. Other statutes were designed to bring corporations and franchises
under closer royal control, to improve the coinage, and to establish
uniform weights and measures. Attempts were also made to stimulate the
economy and, at the same time, to prevent economic developments from
radically changing established ways of life. An example of this came in
1489, with the first general statute against depopulating enclosures.

Another important function of Parliament was granting the crown
extraordinary supply. The standard parliamentary grant, the tenth and
fifteenth, had originally been a charge on moveable property, but over
the years it had ossified into a fixed levy of some £30,000. Each county
knew how much it would be expected to pay, and the incidence of the
tax took little account of changes in the distribution of wealth. The
Lancastrian monarchs had made occasional attempts at a new assessment, and Henry pursued the same course in 1489. In that year
Parliament voted him an estimated £10,000 to stop the French from
taking over the independent duchy of Brittany, and Henry proposed that
the greater part of this should be raised from the laity through an income
tax of ten per cent as well as a property levy, to be assessed by royal commissioners. Such an innovation was deeply resented, and in a number of
places anger flared into violence. After a brawl at Thirsk, in Yorkshire, in
which the Earl of Northumberland was killed while acting as one of the

commissioners, the rebels laid siege to York, and Henry had to raise an army to restore order.

Fear of disorder may explain why in 1491, when Henry decided once again to intervene in Brittany, he resorted to a benevolence. This proved difficult to collect, however, and when a new crisis arose in 1496, this time over Scotland, Henry had recourse to Parliament. He was voted two fifteenths and tenths, as well as further 'aid and subsidy' based on a fresh assessment, but fiscal innovation once more led to rebellion, this time in the west country, whose inhabitants did not see why they should be taxed in order to pay for the defence of the remote northern borders of the kingdom. They were also making a general protest against the sheer size of Henry's demands. In 1497 he levied more than £88,000 in taxation – the largest amount in any year of his entire reign.

Henry's last request for financial assistance from his subjects came in 1504, when he was threatened by another Yorkist pretender, the Earl of Suffolk. He asked for the payment of two feudal aids – one for the knighting of Prince Arthur and the other for the marriage of Princess Margaret. These demands were within the letter of the law, even though the knighting of Prince Arthur had taken place fifteen years earlier and the young man was now dead, while Princess Margaret had been married in 1503. Members of Parliament, however, feared (perhaps with good reason) that the request for feudal aids was the cover for a detailed enquiry into the nature of landholding which would expose them to yet higher taxation. They therefore made Henry an offer of a subsidy worth £40,000, of which the King graciously remitted a quarter. This was an indication of Henry's success in shifting the basis of taxation away from the inflexible fifteenth and tenth towards the subsidy, which was to become the standard parliamentary tax under his successors.

The Church

From an ecclesiastical viewpoint England was a jigsaw of some nine thousand pieces of unequal size, each representing a single parish. Incumbents were maintained by tithes – a compulsory levy of a tenth of their produce on every parishioner – but during the course of the Middle Ages many of the principal landowners who dominated the local communities and appointed their priests had transferred their rights to a monastery in return for the saying of prayers for the release of their souls from purgatory. The monastery would impropriate the tithes and use the major part for its own purposes, paying the remainder to a curate who carried out the essential parochial duties The consequence of impropriate tithes was that some half of all parishes now provided too little for the adequate maintenance of a full-time priest.

One solution to this problem would have been the amalgamation of poorer parishes, but this was carried out only on a limited scale, partly because of innate conservatism but also because it involved non-residence – since one priest could not live simultaneously in two parishes – and this was regarded as undesirable. Yet even where amalgamation did take place it did not necessarily improve the situation. The Church was run by clerical administrators who needed an income from tithes if they were to carry out their task but had little time to spare for the performance of parochial functions. They were often given two or more wealthy livings rather than poor ones, which made the overall problem worse by creating a non-resident hierarchy of officials who battened upon the richer parishes while the poorer ones were served by an impoverished clerical proletariat.

Significant financial differences were also to be found among the bishops who governed the Church in England and Wales. The Welsh sees were notoriously poor, but eleven of the English ones were worth more than £1,000 a year – at a time when a parish priest was well provided for if he received £15 – and some a great deal more. The Bishop of Winchester, for instance, had an annual income in the region of £3,500. Although bishops were appointed by the King and Pope acting together, in practice the Pope did little more than ratify the King's choice. Henry VII broke with recent precedent by choosing his bishops on grounds of merit rather than birth, and only three of them came from noble families. But merit, in his eyes, depended upon administrative abilities rather than pastoral or spiritual qualities, and promotion to and within the episcopate was usually a reward for service in the royal government. Of the thirty-three bishops Henry appointed during the course of his reign, only eight had degrees in theology, compared with fifteen who had legal qualifications. Although a number of bishops had degrees in canon law, the law of the Church, Henry preferred men who had been given a training in Roman or civil law, such as John Morton, whom he chose as Archbishop of Canterbury.

While there were clearly benefits, both moral and financial, to be derived from using bishops as the King's principal ministers, these have to be set against the absence of firm spiritual leadership in the dioceses concerned. Many bishops regarded royal service as not only a burden but also a diversion from their primary pastoral task. Richard Fox, who was both Lord Privy Seal and Bishop of Winchester, served Henry VII faithfully, but was only too glad to lay down secular office after Henry VIII came to the throne. He confessed to Wolsey that although he had held four bishoprics he had never set foot in two of them, and he spoke remorsefully of 'being by the space of thirty years so negligent' of his spiritual functions.

Fox was one of the few members of Henry VII's episcopal bench to be touched by the 'new learning' of the Renaissance (*see* pp. 29–30), and founded Corpus Christi College at Oxford, to increase the supply of graduate clergy for the Church. Another episcopal patron of learning was John Fisher, whom Henry nominated to the see of Rochester in 1504. Fisher was confessor to Henry's mother, Lady Margaret Beaufort, a deeply pious woman, and it was at his suggestion that she refounded Christ's College in Cambridge and provided funds to endow chairs in divinity at both universities.

If the number of humanist bishops was small, the same is true of the clergy as a whole. Although many of them owned books, they tended to be conventional works of piety – books of hours and lives of the saints – but rarely included the Bible, let alone the Church fathers. One reason for this was the absence of any authorised version of the Bible in English. Translations had been made, and circulated from hand to hand, but they were associated with the heretical movement of the Lollards, the spiritual descendants of the fourteenth-century English reformer John Wycliffe. Lollards maintained that the Bible was the sole source of authority and that the entire structure of the Church, from Pope and bishops downwards, as well as much of its doctrine, were irrelevant to salvation. Savage repression had driven the Lollards underground, and Henry VII, who was entirely orthodox in his religious beliefs, continued this process. More than seventy persons suspected of Lollardy were prosecuted in Henry's reign. Most of them made public confession and repentance, but the handful who refused to abjure were burnt at the stake – Henry himself participating on at least one occasion.

While he was an exile Henry had cultivated good relations with Rome, and his efforts paid off when he captured the throne, for Pope Innocent VIII issued a bull threatening to excommunicate anyone who challenged Henry's claim. In 1492 Henry asked one of the cardinals resident in Rome to act as his agent in English affairs, and relations between England and the papacy remained harmonious throughout the reign. This was despite the fact that Henry taxed the Church heavily and kept most of the money for himself, remitting only a token sum to Rome. Papal co-operation enabled Henry to restrict the scope of clerical privileges, particularly where they affected the operation of the common law. One of these privileges concerned sanctuaries. These were areas, usually in or around a sacred building, in which criminals could take refuge and be free from arrest. The judges had decided early in Henry's reign that sanctuaries could not provide immunity for traitors, and the Pope promptly issued a bull designed to put an end to the abuse of these refuges and authorising the King to station guards outside them.

Another potential area of dispute between crown and Church concerned 'benefit of clergy.' This was the right enjoyed by everyone in holy orders to claim exemption from trial in a secular court. In practice, clerical status was claimed by those in minor orders – who were clergy only in name – and even by laymen, as long as they could demonstrate their literacy by reading a 'neck verse,' usually taken from one of the psalms. The system was widely abused, and in 1489 Parliament passed a statute which preserved the existing privilege for the first offence but decreed that for any subsequent offences the defendant would have to prove he really was in holy orders. Those convicted of a single offence were to be branded on the thumb to ensure that they could not claim exemption twice. The 1489 statute was not prompted by anticlerical feeling, but in taking action to curb the clergy's traditional privileges Parliament had indicated that if the Church failed to reform itself the state might be compelled to do so. This had significance for the future.

When accused persons were granted benefit of clergy they were handed over to a Church court to have their cases heard and determined. Church courts, however, were notorious for their leniency, and could not impose capital or corporal punishment. Henry had little respect for them, and made far greater use than his predecessors had done of the praemunire laws. The Statute of Praemunire, originally passed in 1353 but re-enacted, in stronger terms, in 1393, stated that 'anyone drawing the King's subjects out of the realm on pleas, the cognisance whereof belongs to the King's courts . . . shall be put out of the King's protection, his lands and goods forfeited and his body imprisoned at the King's pleasure'. The statute had been designed to preserve the King's authority by limiting appeals to Rome, but its wording was so broad that it could be used to restrict the Church's right to operate its own legal system. Under Henry, the law officers of the crown took the initiative in bringing praemunire actions against ecclesiastical judges. Writs of prohibition were also issued to defendants before Church courts, requiring their case to be heard at common law. Henry, in condoning such action, made plain that the Church, to which he was deeply attached, would not be allowed to impede his government or the operations of the common law.

Henry's piety showed itself in his concern for the religious orders in England. These were causing problems throughout Europe because laxity and worldliness had crept in to the monasteries and corrupted their integrity. In 1487 Henry asked the Pope for assistance in dealing with the religious orders, many of which were exempt from episcopal or royal control, and Innocent VIII responded with a bull empowering Archbishop Morton to take all appropriate steps. This could have been the prelude to a thorough reform of the English monasteries which, if it had taken place, would have left them better prepared to confront the onslaught of Henry VIII and Thomas Cromwell. However, little of substance was done. Much the same was true of the friaries, but Henry, who had what he described as a 'long continued devotion towards St Francis', made plain his preference for the Observant Franciscans – so-called because they observed the strict rule of their order, unlike the Conventuals, who had relaxed it. Henry took under his protection the Franciscan Observants whom Edward IV had settled at Greenwich, and in 1501 he established a new Observant foundation in the grounds of Richmond Palace. The Franciscans continued to benefit from his patronage even after his death, for he left the Observant communities several hundred pounds each, as witness of the fact that 'we always have had a special confidence and trust in the devout prayers of the Friars Observants of this our royaume'.

Henry VII clearly found the doctrine and ceremonies of the *Ecclesia Anglicana* – the English branch of the catholic Church – sufficient for his spiritual needs, and the same seems to have been true of the great majority of his subjects. The Church played a central part in the activities of the English people at all levels. Daily attendance at mass was not uncommon, especially in urban areas, and guilds and brotherhoods dedicated to Jesus or Corpus Christi or a particular saint were widespread. The English enjoyed and took for granted a rich religious culture which had as its focus the parish churches, and they showed their commitment by embellishing, enlarging and rebuilding these on a massive scale in the late fifteenth and early sixteenth centuries. The Church had serious faults, of which pluralism and non-residence were glaring examples, but it seemed to be firmly rooted in the affection and respect of its congregations. At the time of Henry VII's death there was little to suggest that the *Ecclesia Anglicana* was about to undergo radical transformation

Foreign policy

One of the main reasons for the collapse of the medieval English monarchy had been the cost of the Hundred Years War against France. Neither Edward IV nor Henry VII could afford to implement the English kings' claim to the French throne, yet they were under pressure from public opinion to maintain their honour and adopt a suitably bellicose posture. Edward IV showed how to resolve this dilemma. In 1474 he allied with the Duke of Burgundy against Louis XI of France, called on Parliament to vote supply, and took an army across the Channel. Louis, fortunately, had no more desire than Edward to be caught up in a real war and offered terms which Edward was happy to accept. By the Treaty of Picquigny, 1475, the English King, while still affirming his hereditary right to the crown of France, agreed to withdraw his troops from French soil. Louis, in return, agreed to pay him a substantial lump sum and an annual pension.

Edward's demonstration of how to make money out of war – or, at least, the threat of war – provided a model which Henry VII was happy to follow. In 1489 he sent an army to Brittany to try and prevent Louis' successor, Charles VIII, from annexing the strategically important seaboard duchy. However, the French proved too strong for the Bretons, and the reigning duchess, Anne, surrendered her independence, and that of her duchy, by marrying Charles in December 1491. Charles threw fuel on the flames of English discontent by welcoming the Yorkist pretender, Perkin Warbeck, to his court and offering him support. Henry could have chosen to ignore this provocation, but instead he raised a large army and took it over to Calais – though only late in the year, when the campaigning season was almost at an end. The last thing Charles VIII wanted was a protracted struggle with England, for his eyes were now fixed on Italy. In November 1492, therefore, he accepted the Treaty of Etaples, by which he agreed to withdraw support for pretenders to the English throne and to increase the pension paid to Henry, as long as the latter took his troops back to England. Overall, this was a good deal for Henry. Military intervention had cost him just under £50,000, but the 1491 benevolence and the parliamentary grants of 1489 and 1491 brought him in more than £180,000. Henry was able to return to England with his honour intact and his coffers full.

As the Tudor dynasty settled itself firmly on the English throne it came to be accepted by other ruling families and marriage negotiations were initiated. As early as 1489 it had been agreed, in principle, that Henry's eldest son, Prince Arthur, should marry Catherine of Aragon, daughter of Ferdinand of Aragon and Isabella of Castile, the rulers of Spain. There was no urgency about concluding the marriage, for Arthur was not yet three years old and Catherine not yet four. It eventually took place in 1501, but was probably never consummated, for both parties were still very young, and in any case Arthur died the following year, before reaching sixteen. By this time Ferdinand was anxious to retain the alliance with England, and Henry was reluctant to lose the dowry which Catherine had brought with her, so negotiations were started for a marriage between Catherine and Henry's second son, now heir, Prince Henry. There were difficulties to be overcome, including the fact that a papal dispensation would be required to set aside the biblical prohibition of marriage between a man and his brother's widow. Agreement was eventually reached, but by the time the marriage took place Henry VII was dead. Before his death he had arranged another dynastic alliance that was to have great significance for the future. In an attempt to put an end to the perpetual tension between England and Scotland, he married his eldest daughter Margaret to James IV, King of Scotland, in January 1503. The marriage treaty, concluded a year earlier, had been accompanied by a treaty of perpetual peace between the two kingdoms.

A new monarchy?

By the time he died, Henry was enjoying what Francis Bacon later described as 'the felicity of full coffers', which was no small achievement in the light of the collapse of royal finances under Henry VI. His revenues from all sources amounted to some £133,000 a year, which was three times what Henry VI had been receiving in the mid-1430s but significantly below Edward III's income. In other words, Henry, building on the foundations laid by Edward IV, had restored the crown's finances to something approaching their level under the later Plantagenets. But although he was rich by English standards he was relatively poor when compared with the Holy Roman Emperor, whose annual income was more than a million pounds, or the King of France, who received about £800,000 a year. In financial terms the Kings of England were minor players in the European power game.

Solvency was one of the most novel aspects of the 'new monarchy' of the Yorkist and early Tudor period, but from the institutional viewpoint there was little that was truly new. The Council was medieval in origin; Chamber finance was similar in essentials to the Wardrobe administration of the fourteenth century; and as for the use of 'new men' this was as old as monarchy itself. There were elements of despotism in Yorkist and early Tudor government, to be found mainly in the Council and its various off-shoots, but there were other elements, such as the continuing supremacy of the common law and the reliance on country gentlemen for local govern-ment, that pulled in the opposite direction. Edward and Henry could conceivably have created – or at least tried to create – a more autocratic monarchy on the French pattern, but instead of remodelling the English system of government they took the easier, and less risky course of pumping new blood and vigour into it. The significance of the new monarchy, therefore, lies rather in what it preserved than in what it changed.

CHAPTER TWO

King and Cardinal

Wolsey's rise to power

The accession of Henry VIII, a handsome, energetic young man, not yet eighteen, effectively closed the Wars of the Roses. While, through his father, Henry was the heir of Lancaster, he was also, through his mother, the heir of York, and as John Skelton, his tutor and later poet laureate, declared:

'*The Rose both white and red*
In one Rose now doth grow.'

Henry's looks attracted widespread and favourable comment. The Venetian ambassador reported that the new King was 'the handsomest potentate I ever set eyes on ... with auburn hair combed straight and short in the French fashion, and a round face so very beautiful that it would become a pretty woman'. Henry was also praised for his warmth and openness, the complete antithesis of his father's cold and calculating reserve.

In fact, Henry VIII was a far more complex character than his appearance suggested. For the first twenty years of his reign he devoted his days to hunting and his nights to feasting and love-making, leaving both the formulation of policy and day-to-day government in the hands of his principal adviser, Thomas Wolsey. Yet in the late 1520s he suddenly emerged as the dominant figure in English politics and remained so for the rest of his reign. He relied on able men, like Wolsey and Thomas Cromwell, to carry on the government in his name, but when, in a dark mood of anger or suspicion, he chose to assert himself, he swept his advisers out of the way with a ruthlessness unrestrained by gratitude or fear.

For the first few years of his reign Henry VIII was guided by Councillors he had inherited from his father, and although he had his own chosen companions they were without political significance. Only when Wolsey appeared on the scene did Henry find an adviser whose endeavour, in the words of his first biographer, 'was directed towards satisfying the King's mind, knowing right well that it was the very vein and right course to bring him to high promotion'. Wolsey, born in 1472, was the son of a butcher in the Suffolk town of Ipswich. For a talented and ambitious boy who did not come from the propertied elite, the Church offered the best career prospects, and by the time he was fifteen Wolsey was an undergraduate at Magdalen College, Oxford. He made such an impression that he was elected a fellow in 1497 and in the following year became a priest. Wolsey's duties included teaching in the school attached to Magdalen College, and among his pupils were the sons of the Marquis of Dorset, an influential nobleman who presented Wolsey to his first living and facilitated his entry into the governing circles of the kingdom. Henry VII appointed the young clergyman one of his chaplains and sent him on a number of diplomatic missions.

What looked like the beginning of a flourishing career was cut short by the death of Henry VII in 1509, but Wolsey was given the post of almoner to the young Henry VIII, who was quick to notice that 'he was the most earnest and readiest among all the Council to advance the King's mere will and pleasure, without any respect to the case in question'. The older Councillors urged restraint upon Henry, who was determined to follow the path set by his namesake and predecessor, Henry V, and regain the crown of France, but Wolsey took quite the opposite approach. If war was what the King wanted, then Wolsey would help him win it. An expedition despatched to south-west France in 1512 accomplished nothing, but Wolsey took it upon himself to organise another, this time to northern France. Henry went over in person to command the army of thirty thousand men assembled at Calais, and in August 1513 led it to victory in the 'Battle of the Spurs' – so called because of the speed with which the French retreated. Tournai was captured by the English, as was Thérouanne – neither of them towns of much significance, but valued by Henry as tangible evidence of his military prowess. This was not the only triumph achieved by Henry's forces. The Scots – who traditionally looked to France for protection against their stronger English neighbour – took advantage of Henry's absence to launch a massive raid into England. In September 1513 they crossed the border south-west of Berwick, but an army under the Earl of Surrey was waiting for them and at the Battle of Flodden the

Scots were routed. Their king, James IV, and many of his nobles were left dead on the field.

Henry had good reason to be satisfied. His enhanced standing in Europe was demonstrated in 1514 when Louis XII not only accepted peace terms which included the doubling of the pension payments made under the terms of the Treaty of Etaples (1492) but also agreed to marry Henry's sister, Mary. Wolsey, who had been the organiser of victory as well as the architect of the peace, was rewarded with the bishopric of Tournai. This was little more than a gesture, but it was followed almost immediately by his elevation to the rich and powerful see of Lincoln. However, he held this for little more than seven months, because in September 1514 Henry nominated him as Archbishop of York. Wolsey was now the second most important man in the English Church, but as long as William Warham remained alive he could never attain the primacy as Archbishop of Canterbury. However, a legate *a latere*, theoretically sent 'from the side of' the Pope, could override the existing hierarchy, and although he had never been to Rome and there were no exceptional circumstances which would justify such an appointment, Wolsey, with Henry's encouragement, pressed the Pope to make him legate *a latere*. The Pope did not wish to offend so valuable and loyal an ally as the King of England, and he eventually complied. Wolsey had already been made a cardinal, in 1515. Nine years later he was appointed *legatus a latere* for life.

Wolsey and the Church

Wolsey, as the Pope's viceroy, now had authority to intervene in every diocese, overriding the authority of bishops and archbishops alike. He had demanded his exceptional legatine powers on the grounds that the Church was badly in need of reform, and there was, indeed, a growing volume of complaint from the laity against its shortcomings – in particular, pluralism and non-residence, and the high fees charged for probate and mortuary. But the demand for reform did not come solely from outside the Church. There was an active and swelling movement within it, and this was given new impetus by the Christian Renaissance, spread throughout Europe by Erasmus of Rotterdam.

Desiderius Erasmus, born in 1466, came to maturity in a Europe that was being transformed by the Italian Renaissance. The 'rebirth' in question was that of the ancient world, many of whose written treasures had remained lost to sight for centuries in monastic libraries and other repositories. As Renaissance scholars sought out and published unknown or forgotten works of Latin and Greek authors, they created an intellectual ferment which paralleled the creative stimulus given to contemporary artists and sculptors with whom the term 'Renaissance' is more usually associated. These scholars were known as humanists, for like the classical writers they so admired they made the study of man their principal concern. Since the ancient world during its heyday had been pagan, the Renaissance appeared to have little relevance to Christianity, but Erasmus was among the first to realize that during the later Roman world the fundamental Christian texts – the Bible and the works of the early fathers of the Church – had made their appearance and were waiting to be rediscovered. He began collating manuscripts and produced editions of these texts that set a new standard of accuracy and rapidly circulated throughout the entire Christian world.

England had its own humanist scholars, of whom the most distinguished were William Grocyn, Thomas Linacre, Thomas More and John Colet. They, like Erasmus, saw the recovered learning of the ancient world as the key to the understanding of man and his relationship to God. Colet visited Italy, where he studied the early fathers, and returned to Oxford to lecture on the epistles of St Paul. It was there that Erasmus met him when, in 1499, he paid his first visit to England. The two men had much in common, and Colet took pleasure in introducing the Dutch reformer to his circle of friends at the university. Erasmus was delighted with his new acquaintances. 'I have lost little,' he wrote, 'in not going to Italy. When Colet speaks, I might be listening to Plato. Linacre is as deep and acute a thinker as I have ever met with. Grocyn is a mine of knowledge. And nature never formed a sweeter and happier disposition than that of Thomas More.'

The English humanists were in an optimistic mood, for there were indications that the new King, Henry VIII, shared their interests and aims. It was at Henry's insistence that Thomas More accepted appointment as a Councillor in 1517, and shortly before this More's friend and fellow humanist, Cuthbert Tunstall, had been appointed Master of the Rolls. Another humanist, Richard Pace, became the King's secretary in 1516. The ecclesiastical hierarchy also included a number of advocates of the new learning. The King's confessor, John Longland, who became Bishop of Lincoln in 1521, was one of these. The saintly John Fisher, Bishop of Rochester, was another. In short, the elements of reform were present in both state and Church. What was needed to combine them into an effective pressure group was a lead from above, and the humanists would have given their full support to Wolsey if only he had provided it.

Wolsey cannot be dismissed merely as someone who used the language of reform to advance his career, but had no real commitment to it. On the contrary, he showed his humanist preferences by choosing Colet to preach the sermon at the ceremony in which he was presented with the red hat of a cardinal, and his genuine interest in education led him to found a major new college at Oxford. But Wolsey was engaged in such a wide range of activities – diplomatic, judicial and administrative, as well as ecclesiastical – that he never had time to formulate and carry through a coherent reform programme. Furthermore, he believed that his elevated position as the Pope's representative, quite apart from the need to uphold the dignity of the Church, made it essential for him to live like a prince. This demanded sums of money on such a scale that the search for new sources of revenue took priority over his other objectives and drove him to exploit those very abuses which, as a reformer, he condemned. He extended the evil of pluralism into the ecclesiastical hierarchy, for he always held one other bishopric in addition to the archbishopric of York. Moreover, he continued Henry VII's practice of appointing non-resident Italians to English sees, paying them a fixed stipend, and pocketing the surplus. He had himself elected Abbot of St Albans, one of the richest monasteries in England, even though he was not a monk. He interfered in every diocese, appointing his own protégés regardless of the rights of patrons, and set up legatine courts to which he summoned men from all over England. He turned non-residency into a way of life, never setting foot in three of his sees and only entering the diocese of York sixteen years after he had been appointed archbishop.

In an age when the laxity of clerical morals was under growing criticism, Wolsey provided ammunition for the Church's critics by flouting the obligation to live chastely. He had two illegitimate children – one of them a son, on whom he showered lucrative ecclesiastical offices, and the other a daughter, whom he placed in a nunnery. Colet had complained of the clergy's 'pride of life', but he could hardly have envisaged the pomp and ceremony that were the hallmarks of Wolsey's lifestyle. George Cavendish, who was one of the cardinal's gentlemen-ushers and wrote his first biography, spends several pages merely listing the members of his household and estimates that there were at least five hundred of them, which put Wolsey on a par with Henry VIII. Wolsey lived in regal state at Hampton Court, which was his own creation, and at York Place, which Henry subsequently took over and turned into the palace of Whitehall. Cavendish describes how, when Wolsey made his way to Westminster Hall to do justice, he had 'two great pillars of silver, and his Sergeant-at-Arms with a great mace of silver-gilt. Then his gentlemen-ushers cried and said "On, my lords and masters. Make way for my lord's grace".'

Wolsey's major contribution to the cause of reform consisted in the foundation of Cardinal College (now Christ Church) at Oxford. In order to endow this and a smaller college in his home town of Ipswich, Wolsey dissolved twenty-nine monasteries on the grounds that they were too small to be of any practical use. This redistribution of the Church's wealth from sterile into creative activities was very much in tune with the demands of the Christian humanist reformers, and Wolsey made another gesture in their direction when he provided funds for distinguished scholars to give public lectures on classics and theology in the university of Oxford. Wolsey had many other plans, both for Cardinal College and the wider world. He expressed an intention to reform the monasteries and turn a number of them into the cathedrals of new sees, since the existing diocesan system, created centuries beforehand, took no account of changes in the distribution of population. He also intended to impose further limits on benefit of clergy and the right of sanctuary. His plans, if carried into effect, would have blunted criticism of the Church and made it better prepared to meet the challenge of the Reformation. But too many of his schemes failed to progress beyond the stage of aspirations. This may seem surprising, given the fact that Wolsey was renowned for his energy and administrative capacity. But even his exceptional abilities could not cope with all the demands he made upon himself, and the desire for self-aggrandisement was at odds with his reforming zeal. Not surprisingly, the high hopes that had been pinned on him turned to despair and contempt when, instead of leading the attack on the abuses which were undermining the authority of the Church, he multiplied and exploited them to his own advantage.

While the Church as a whole was popular, and many parish priests were loved and respected figures in their local communities, there was resentment at the charges imposed by the clergy for their services. In 1514, for example, a wealthy London merchant named Richard Hunne refused to pay the mortuary fee which the parson demanded for burying his infant son, on the grounds that it was excessive. The parson thereupon sued Hunne in a Church court, but Hunne countered this by bringing an action against him in King's Bench for a breach of praemunire. Hunne's case collapsed, but by this time he was in an ecclesiastical prison, charged with giving shelter to a convicted heretic. Hunne confessed to the offence, but before he could perform public penance he was found dead in his cell, hanging from a beam.

Hunne probably committed suicide, but a coroner's jury of London citizens returned a verdict of murder and indicted the Bishop of London's principal legal adviser or chancellor. The bishop wrote to Wolsey, asking for the case to be dealt with by the royal Council, on the grounds that 'if my chancellor be tried by any twelve men in London, they be so maliciously set in *favorem haereticae pravitatis* ['in favour of heretical depravity'] that they will cast and condemn my clerk, though he were as innocent as Abel'. Before the matter could go further, Parliament met early in 1515. The Commons had under consideration the renewal of the Criminous Clerks Act of 1512 which had been designed to exclude clerics in minor orders from benefit of clergy. However, in 1514 the Pope had defended the right of clergy not to be tried by lay courts, and when the Commons attempted to extend the operation of the 1512 act, the House of Lords, in which the bishops and abbots were in a majority, stifled their initiative.

At the same time as Parliament met, the Church's equivalent assembly, known as Convocation, was also assembling, and the Abbot of Winchcombe, Richard Kidderminster, used the occasion of his opening sermon to insist on clerical immunity. The outraged Commons called on the temporal lords – a significant conjunction – to join with them in appealing to the King, and a conference was held at Blackfriars in Henry's presence, at which the case against Kidderminster was presented by a doctor of divinity named Henry Standish. Convocation thereupon summoned Standish before it to answer charges of heresy, but Standish appealed to the King. He was joined in this by the Commons and temporal lords, still smarting under the rejection of the Criminous Clerks Act and with the Hunne scandal very much in their minds. They called upon the King to maintain his jurisdiction, which the clergy, they claimed, were seeking to invade.

A second conference then took place at Blackfriars, at which the judges gave their verdict that the clergy who had taken part in the citation of Standish had derogated the King's rights and infringed the Statute of Praemunire. At a subsequent assembly of the Lords and Commons, with the King again present, Wolsey, as representative of the English clergy, knelt before Henry and pleaded for royal favour, on the grounds that Convocation had never intended to invade his prerogative. He also requested that the whole case should be transmitted to Rome for final judgement. Henry rejected this request, and in a speech full of significance, because it seems to have expressed his own feelings and not those of his advisers, he declared that 'by the ordinance and sufferance of God we are

King of England, and the Kings of England in time past have never had any superior but God alone. Wherefore know you well that we shall maintain the right of our crown and of our temporal jurisdiction as well in this point as in all others'.

Despite the ominous tone of Henry's declaration the leaders of the Church had good reason to be satisfied with the outcome of events. The Bishop of London's anguished statement may have expressed his true feelings, but it is doubtful whether most of the citizens were favourers of heresy or even anticlerical in sentiment. The Church was well rooted in society, as was shown by the continuing flow of gifts to parish guilds and churches, and its courts were popular and well respected. Once the episcopal bench had made plain that it had no wish to encroach upon the King's rights it could be sure of Henry's support. It is significant that the Criminous Clerks Act was never, in fact, renewed, and although Standish went free and eventually became Bishop of St Asaph's, promotion to a minor Welsh see was hardly a resounding triumph.

Wolsey and the royal administration

In December 1515 William Warham, Archbishop of Canterbury, resigned as Lord Chancellor and Henry VIII appointed Wolsey in his place. The Lord Chancellor had many of the powers of a modern prime minister, and as long as he retained the King's favour nothing short of a successful revolution could dislodge him. Wolsey's predecessors, Warham and Morton, both had degrees in law, but Wolsey did not allow his lack of professional qualifications to inhibit him from doing justice. As Chancellor he presided over the Court of Chancery, in which the formalism and rigidity of the common law were softened by principles derived mainly from common sense. Wolsey was determined to enforce the law against those who assumed they were beyond its reach, but he also used Chancery to pursue private vendettas. This typical mix of altruism and self-aggrandisement resulted in arbitrary decisions that alienated many common lawyers (whom he treated with a marked lack of respect) and undermined their confidence in Chancery as a court.

As the King's chief minister, Wolsey was closely associated with the royal Council. This remained, as it had done under Henry VII, a large and amorphous body. During Wolsey's ascendancy the total membership was about 120, but the largest recorded attendance at any meeting was 54 and the average was anything between 11 and 25. The King himself was rarely present, since he left Wolsey in charge of the routine work of government.

The Council would have been more efficient if had been smaller in size and limited to ministers and officials. Wolsey realised this, and in the Eltham Ordinances of 1526 he set out the ground plan of just such a body. But this project, like so many others associated with him, never progressed far beyond the drawing board.

Wolsey made so many policy decisions himself – though always in concert with the King – that the Council was left with little to discuss. It therefore devoted much of its time to judicial questions, and as a consequence the Council sitting to do justice in a room known as the Star Chamber developed into a formal institution – the Court of Star Chamber. As far as membership was concerned, Council and Star Chamber were identical, but whereas the Council met throughout the year, Star Chamber functioned only during the law terms. Wolsey took a prominent part in Star Chamber proceedings, and Cavendish describes how, after sitting in Chancery 'until eleven of the clock, hearing suitors and determining of divers matters, [he] would divers times go into the Star Chamber, as occasion did serve, where he spared neither high nor low, but judged every estate according to their merits and deserts'.

Wolsey made many enemies by the firmness with which he enforced what he called the 'new law of the Star Chamber' – which was not, in fact, a new law but a new vigour in the application of existing laws. He liked to pose as the champion of the poor and helpless against their social superiors, and in many ways he was. But he also relished the opportunity to humble offending magnates and gentlemen who, unlike him, had acquired a privileged status simply through birth. The poet John Skelton gave voice to their sense of outrage:

'He plucks them by the hood,
And shakes them by the ear,
And brings them in such fear ...
Their wits, he saith, are dull;
He saith they have no brain
Their estate to maintain;
And maketh them to bow their knee
Before his majesty.'

Although Star Chamber would sometimes take the initiative in bringing prosecutions, particularly against powerful offenders, most of the cases that came before it were the result of complaints from private individuals. It was a long-established principle that all subjects who believed they had suffered injustice should have the right to appeal to the King, and Wolsey encouraged them to do so. But this simply led to a repetition of what had happened in Henry VII's reign, when the Council was overwhelmed by property disputes thinly disguised as cases of riot or corruption. Wolsey tried to lessen the burden on Star Chamber by transferring much of this business to conciliar committees, but the court still had more cases than it could handle and it remained too open to suits that could and should have been dealt with by the common-law courts.

Star Chamber was not confined to judicial business, since no clear distinction was made between judicial and administrative matters. Sheriffs were often called before the court to account for their actions, and Justices of the Peace were encouraged to attend upon certain formal occasions, when the Lord Chancellor would harangue them about the need to be conscientious in carrying out their duties. In 1526 Wolsey also asked them to provide him with information about how the law was being administered in their localities – a typical example of the way in which he sought for information as a prelude to remedial action. In Kent, and no doubt in other counties, he increased the number of gentry who were appointed to the Commission of the Peace and strengthened the ties that linked them to the central government.

One of the conciliar committees established by Wolsey in an attempt to relieve pressure on Star Chamber acquired a life of its own. By 1521 the Councillors appointed to give special consideration to the petitions of poor men were meeting regularly during term time at Whitehall and had become established as an autonomous Court of Requests. Wolsey also created a council in the north, under the nominal presidency of Henry's bastard son, the Duke of Richmond, to protect the poor against the effects of enclosure and rack-renting. This was given a criminal and civil jurisdiction similar to that of Star Chamber, but it could not control magnates as powerful as the Earl of Northumberland and Lord Dacre, and its work was therefore confined mainly to Yorkshire.

Wolsey's position as the King's principal adviser was facilitated by the fact that York Place, the London house of the archbishops of York, was only a short walk from the royal palace of Westminster. This was Henry's nominal residence, but after the private apartments were destroyed by fire early in his reign he moved downriver to Greenwich, some five miles south-east of the capital, and established his court there. Shortly afterwards, Wolsey started building his own palace at Hampton Court, south-west of the city, where he accommodated his household, which rivalled the King's in size and exceeded it in political importance. Skelton, once again, made the appropriate commentary:

'*Why come ye not to court?*
To which court?
To the King's court
Or to Hampton Court? ...
The King's court
Should have the excellence,
But Hampton Court
Hath the pre-eminence.'

By the time he moved to Greenwich Henry had emancipated himself from the tutelage of the older advisers inherited from his father, and as Wolsey took over responsibility for government the King could enjoy the company of a younger circle of boon companions, known as the King's 'minions'. They had little or no political significance, and their status was ill defined until 1518, when Francis I, King of France, despatched a large and imposing delegation to London to sign the treaty of universal peace that marked the apogee of Wolsey's diplomacy. The delegation included a number of Francis's closest friends, who bore the title of 'Gentlemen of the Chamber', and Henry, out of politeness and in order to maintain formal parity between guests and hosts, allowed his minions to be called 'Gentlemen of the King's Privy Chamber'. When a reciprocal English delegation was sent to Paris later in 1518, Henry insisted that a number of his minions should be included.

Wolsey resented the favour shown to these young men, whom he regarded as a potential threat to his monopoly of power, and it is more than likely that he was involved in the coup that led to their dismissal from the King's Privy Chamber in May 1519. The nominal excuse was that they had picked up the worst French fashions and brought them back to London. One chronicler described how 'when these young gentlemen came again into England, they were all French in eating, drinking and apparel – yea, and in French vices and brags ... so that nothing by them was praised but if it were after the French turn'. The expelled minions were replaced by older and more experienced men, whom Wolsey could rely on to support his policy of peace and reconciliation with the major European powers. The problem with this arrangement, from Henry's point of view, was that as the Privy Chamber became more institutionalised it no longer provided him with the companionship of young friends with whom he could relax. He solved the problem by bringing back the minions, but this meant that the Privy Chamber remained uneasily poised between formality and informality, a place where policies were discussed and formulated but also a retreat where the King could enjoy himself in a care-free fashion.

As long as Henry was content to leave governing to Wolsey, the Privy Chamber was sufficient for his purposes, but from 1519 onwards he started taking more of an interest in the affairs of his kingdom and complained about the lack of Councillors at court. One of the aims behind Wolsey's Eltham Ordinances was to provide a Council attendant, and although this never materialised, the proposal showed awareness of the fact that the Privy Chamber was an institution in its own right and could not act also as the King's private Council. The situation remained confused, however, until Wolsey's downfall, when Hampton Court ceased to be an alternative power centre, and the undivided Council was truly the King's.

Wolsey and Parliament

Wolsey's passion was for administration and he had little time for a talking shop like Parliament. As long as Henry VIII could live off the funds his father had so painstakingly accumulated there was no need to request assistance from his subjects, but he could not possibly assert his claim to the French throne out of his own resources. Henry therefore summoned Parliament in 1512 and called on it to vote supply. Wolsey took the opportunity to rationalise the traditional method of raising taxes. Henry VII had initiated various experiments designed to break out of the restraints imposed on him by the ossified fifteenths and tenths, but it was Wolsey who laid down clear guidelines for a new system of taxation. In future, centrally appointed commissioners would oversee the work of local assessors, whose task would be to work out how much each taxpayer was worth and therefore how much he should contribute. The subsidy, as the new tax came to be known, was highly successful in its first applications, and the total amount raised in the period 1513–15 was about £300,000. This was a large sum, but it represented less than 20 per cent of what Henry needed. Whether or not his subjects approved of his display of traditional martial virtues, they would clearly have to contribute increasingly to its costs.

Peace with France was concluded in 1514, but by 1522 war was once again imminent, and Wolsey therefore ordered a detailed survey to be carried out, on a county basis, of the military and financial resources of the kingdom. He planned to use the knowledge so gained to reform the militia system, but that had to be postponed while he concentrated on the more immediate business of raising money for Henry's campaigns. The survey provided him with an accurate estimate of what was available, and on this basis he levied forced loans amounting to £260,000. In theory these were to be repaid, but they never were. Henry was pleased with the result, but his richer subjects felt aggrieved about being compelled to part with their money. This coloured their attitude when a new Parliament assembled in 1523. Wolsey tried to overawe the Commons by informing them that he had been 'from the King's own person sent hither unto you for the preservation of yourselves and all the realm'. He then demanded a subsidy of four shillings in the pound, which would have yielded £800,000. No doubt this was meant as an opening bid, but although Wolsey insisted that the Commons should give him 'a reasonable answer,' all he received by way of reply was 'a marvellous obstinate silence'.

For several weeks there was deadlock, since the Commons – in tune with their constituents – were complaining about the burden of taxation they had endured since 1512, while Wolsey was refusing to compromise. Only towards the end of an exceptionally long session was an agreement brokered by the Speaker, Sir Thomas More, one of Wolsey's protégés. He persuaded the Commons to vote a subsidy, spread over two years, with additional – though much smaller – sums to be collected in years three and four. There was considerable taxpayer resistance, and the money came in slowly – too slowly for Henry VIII, who wanted to take advantage of the situation created in February 1525, when the French army was crushed at the Battle of Pavia (see p. 42). Under pressure from Henry, Wolsey sent out commissioners in the spring of 1525 to collect what he called an 'Amicable Grant' but what was, to all intents and purposes, a benevolence. This new demand, coming while the supply voted by Parliament two years earlier was still being collected, sparked off hostile demonstrations all over the country. In East Anglia there was open revolt, and the Dukes of Norfolk and Suffolk had to be sent in, with armed men, to restore order. According to one chronicler, 'all people cursed the cardinal and his coadherents as subversor of the laws and liberties of England. For, they said, if men should give their goods by a commission, then were it worse than the taxes in France, and so England should be bond and not free'.

Henry – who claimed, with whatever justification, that he had known nothing of Wolsey's initiative – had to step in, cancel the 'Amicable Grant,' and pardon all those who had openly opposed it. This was Wolsey's first real check. It showed that the English 'political nation' – that section of the population which counted politically – was not prepared to pay for

Henry's wars and blamed Wolsey for attempting to finance them. It also showed that Henry's ear was tuned to public opinion more finely than Wolsey's, and that he was prepared to sacrifice unpopular measures (even if not, as yet, their proponent) in order to preserve the stability of his regime.

Foreign policy

The opening phase of Henry's personal foreign policy, which involved making war on France, came to an end with the peace agreement of 1514 and a marriage between Louis XII and Henry's sister, Mary. Not long after the marriage, however, Louis died, and on the first day of 1515 the throne of France passed to his nephew, the twenty-one-year-old Francis I. Francis embodied the ideal of a Renaissance prince – handsome, charming, a lover of the arts, a great builder, and a devotee of his own glory. It seemed inevitable that his accession would mark a further stage in the rivalry between France and Spain for control of the Italian peninsula, but the Pope was anxious to preserve peace among the major European states. He wanted them to combine against the Ottoman Turks – who, as Moslems, were enemies of the catholic Church – and check their advance into the eastern Mediterranean. In order to obtain Henry's support for this crusade the Pope sent Cardinal Campeggio to England as his legate, but Wolsey kept Campeggio cooling his heels at Calais while he took over the papal initiative and turned it into one of his major diplomatic triumphs. He began with a treaty between England and France, which included the restoration of Tournai in return for increased pension payments to Henry, and in 1518 persuaded Maximilian I, the Holy Roman Emperor, and Charles I, the new King of Spain, to add their names to it. The Treaty of London, as it was now called, had a system of collective security built in to deter any of the signatories from resorting to war to settle their disputes with other members. Wolsey and his royal master were now acknowledged as the peacemakers of Christendom and basked in the acclaim that this novel role brought them.

Wolsey, who had some claim to be a Christian humanist, may genuinely have hoped to preserve peace, particularly in view of the high costs of war and the difficulty, from his point of view, of funding it. Unfortunately for the ambitions of both Wolsey and Henry, England could not maintain peace unaided. In the last resort everything depended on the balance of power in Europe, and this was radically altered by the death of the Emperor Maximilian in January 1519, for the German prince-electors nominated as his successor his grandson Charles, who was already King of Spain and Duke of Burgundy. To Francis I it seemed as though France was now encircled by imperial power, since Charles was ruler of The Netherlands on her northern frontier, of Luxemburg and Franche Comté in the east, and of Spain to the south. Only by securing French control of Italy could he hope to break out of this stranglehold.

Both Francis and Charles were eager to secure the support of England in the forthcoming struggle, but Wolsey – as always, with Henry's approval – preferred to keep on good terms with both rulers. In 1520 Henry took his courtiers over to Calais to meet Francis and the French courtiers amid scenes of unparalleled splendour on the Field of Cloth of Gold, but this was followed by an equally important, though unpublicised, meeting between Henry and the new Emperor. By the following year Charles and Francis were at war, and Wolsey assumed that the Emperor was certain of victory because of the enormous resources at his disposal. If Henry was to profit from this situation he would have to commit himself to Charles V, and in August 1521, therefore, Wolsey went over to Bruges and concluded an agreement with the Emperor, which was ratified when he made a state visit to England in 1522. Charles promised to marry Henry's daughter Mary, when she came of age. Henry, in return, agreed to declare war on France the following year. It was to enable Henry to fulfil this obligation that he and Wolsey decided to summon Parliament in 1523 and ask for supply of £800,000.

Wolsey's primary motive in these complex negotiations was to derive the maximum advantage for his royal master. It may be that he also favoured an imperial alliance because Charles had promised to support his candidature for the papacy, but if that was the case it is surprising that he made so little effort to build up a following in the papal court. His name came forward for consideration in late 1521, following the death of Leo X, and again in 1523, when Leo's successor died, but he was not a serious contender for the papal throne. In fact the pressure on him to put his name forward may have come from Henry, who would have enjoyed basking in the reflected glory of an English Pope.

Henry's ambitions extended beyond his own dominions. He seems genuinely to have believed that France was rightfully his, and he also made it known that he would be willing to accept the crown of the Holy Roman Empire if it was offered him. In the early sixteenth century there was only one Emperor in Europe, but Henry was already giving indications that he regarded his authority over England and its dependencies as 'imperial', since he acknowledged no superior except God. When Cuthbert Tunstall told him in 1517 that 'the crown of England is an empire of itself', he was merely confirming what the King already believed.

Despite the refusal of the 1523 Parliament to make a positive response to Wolsey's demands for supply, Henry despatched an expedition to France in the autumn of 1523, as did the Emperor. They hoped to profit from the treason of one of Francis I's greatest subjects, the Duke of Bourbon, who had come out in revolt against him, and for a moment it looked as though Henry's commander, the Duke of Suffolk, might capture Paris. But lack of co-ordination between the various forces, as well as the onset of winter, compelled Suffolk to return to England, and although there was talk of further campaigning in 1524 the necessary funds were simply not available. Wolsey now made peace overtures to France, but unfortunately for him this drifting away from the imperial alliance was ill timed. In February 1525 the French army was shattered at the Battle of Pavia, in Italy, and Francis I was taken prisoner by the Emperor. When Henry heard the news he immediately sent envoys to Charles to congratulate him upon his victory and press him to restore English sovereignty over France. But Charles saw no need for gratitude to the English, who had been on the verge of deserting him. Not only did he reject Henry's demand for the crown of France; he also announced that he would marry a Portuguese princess instead of waiting for Henry's daughter, Mary.

Faced with this rebuff, Wolsey had little alternative but to adopt an openly anti-imperial policy, and he spent 1526 knitting together the League of Cognac with France and the papacy. The aim of this league was to expel imperial forces from Italy, or at least compel Charles to negotiate. It was agreed that England would take no immediate part in hostilities, but would gradually commit herself if Charles remained intransigent. Charles responded to the league by calling for help from the German princes, and they provided an army that moved into Italy and advanced south. It was this army, paid for by Charles and acting in his name, that captured Rome in May 1527. The unpaid, mutinous soldiers, many of them Lutheran, indulged in an orgy of rape and pillage and sacked the eternal city. Clement VII was obliged to seek safety in the castle of San Angelo, where he remained a virtual prisoner of the Emperor.

In the following year France and England formally declared war on Charles, but in June 1529 the French army was routed at Landriano, north of Pavia, leaving Charles the undisputed master of Italy. The Pope accepted the inevitable and announced that he had decided 'to become an imperialist and to live and die as such'. The accord between Clement and the Emperor was sealed by the Treaty of Barcelona in June 1529, and this was followed, a month later, by the Peace of Cambrai which brought to a halt the long struggle between France and Spain for supremacy in Italy. It was high time, for the Ottoman Turks were at the gates of Vienna, and in Germany the unity of Christendom was being eroded by the rapid spread of Lutheranism.

Henry VIII's 'great matter'

Wolsey was conspicuous by his absence from this feast of peacemaking, for England had abandoned Charles too soon to profit from his victory. What was worse from the cardinal's point of view was that he had made an enemy of the Emperor at the very moment when he most needed his support, for shortly before the Battle of Landriano a remarkable scene took place at Blackfriars, where Henry and his wife, Queen Catherine, appeared before Wolsey and his fellow legate, Cardinal Campeggio, to answer charges that their marriage was invalid and that they were therefore living in sin.

There had been difficulties about the marriage from the beginning, for according to *Leviticus* 20:21 if a man marries his deceased brother's widow 'it is an unclean thing. He hath uncovered his brother's nakedness. They shall be childless'. A papal dispensation had been necessary in order for Prince Henry, as he then was, to marry Catherine, the widow of his brother, Arthur, but there was some doubt whether the Pope had the right to dispense with canon law when it had the unequivocal sanction of scripture behind it. Although the dispensation had been issued in late 1504 the marriage did not take place immediately – mainly because the dowry had not been fully paid – and in June 1505 Henry, who was not quite fourteen at the time, made a formal protest against the validity of the proposed union. He was no doubt prompted by his father, who was having second thoughts about the advisability of a Spanish alliance, but it meant that the marriage was further postponed. Indeed, it was eventually celebrated only in June 1509, by which time Henry VII was in his grave.

The marriage seems to have been reasonably happy, but unfortunately for Catherine her children died at birth or soon after. The only exception was a girl, Mary, born in 1516. By 1525 Catherine was forty, all hope of a male heir had gone, and Henry was in a quandary. As a conventionally devout man he was afraid that his failure to produce a son was a sign of God's anger. Moreover, a male heir seemed essential if the Tudor dynasty was to survive, for it was not certain whether a woman had the right to inherit the throne. The last female ruler of England had been Matilda, the designated successor of Henry I (d.1135), but her nominal reign had been marred by civil war and she was never able to assert her authority. More recent civil wars, brought about by the struggle between York and Lancaster for possession of the crown, had left their scars, and Henry was conscious that he was only the second Tudor and that a number of his subjects had a better hereditary claim to the throne than he did. For this reason he had Edmund Stafford, Duke of Buckingham, executed in 1521, and he also considered making his bastard son, the Duke of Richmond, his legitimate heir.

Henry was moving hesitantly and was unclear about his destination, but at this crucial moment he fell in love with Anne Boleyn, whose sister was already his mistress. Henry's love letters to Anne show how deeply the King's passion had been aroused, but Anne refused to become merely another of his mistresses. She wanted to be Henry's wife, and this was an aim shared by the King, since the son he hoped to have by her could not inherit the throne unless his parents had been formally married. Concubinage might have satisfied Henry's physical needs, but not his political imperatives.

By early 1527 Henry had come to the conclusion that his union with Catherine was contrary to scripture and must be ended. Julius II had issued the dispensation making the first marriage possible, so Henry now looked to Julius's successor, Clement VII, to declare it invalid. He saw no reason to anticipate difficulties. Popes usually gave a sympathetic hearing to princely petitioners, and Henry was an ardent supporter of the papacy. Indeed, he had been rewarded with the title of *Fidei Defensor* for defending the catholic faith against Luther. There was no question at this stage of breaking away from Rome, since papal co-operation was taken for granted. Henry even went so far as to ask Clement VII for a dispensation permitting him to marry Anne, whose sister had been his mistress. The canonical impediment to such a match was precisely the same as that which, Henry claimed, invalidated his union with Catherine of Aragon: if a man may not marry his brother's widow, neither may he marry his mistress's sister. Yet while the King denied papal competence in the former case he was quite prepared to acknowledge it in the latter. This suggests that Henry's overriding objective was to marry Anne Boleyn, and that all other considerations, however sincerely held, were secondary.

Wolsey can hardly have relished the prospect of having Anne as Queen, since she was the niece of the Duke of Norfolk – Wolsey's collaborator in government but rival for power – and was also suspected of Lutheran leanings. However, as he later told Campeggio, Wolsey felt that Henry should be allowed to have his way, since otherwise the Church would be at risk. Campeggio – who was titular Bishop of Salisbury – had been sent back to England by Clement VII to join Wolsey in judging 'the King's great matter', but the Pope was not anxious to arrive at a quick verdict. He did not wish to offend Henry, but he was even more anxious not to offend Charles V – who, as well as being Holy Roman Emperor and master of Italy, was also Catherine of Aragon's nephew – at a time when he was relying on him to oppose the dual threat posed to catholicism by the German Lutherans and the Ottoman Turks. Henry wanted a brief examination of his case and a swift and favourable judgement. Charles would have preferred the case not to be tried at all, and was bound to be deeply upset and angry if the Pope decided that his aunt's marriage was invalid.

Clement's tactics were dictated in large part by the military situation in Italy. When French forces were in the ascendent he sent Campeggio a decretal commission empowering him to pronounce final judgement. But Campeggio, who was old and tired, took a long time over his journey to England, and meanwhile the imperial fortunes in Italy were beginning to revive. Clement therefore told him that after showing his commission to Henry and Wolsey as proof of the Pope's good faith, he should destroy it. Furthermore, he ordered Campeggio not to pronounce judgement without first obtaining papal approval, for 'if so great an injury be done to the Emperor [by a decision in Henry's favour] all hope is lost of universal peace and the Church cannot escape utter ruin, as it is entirely in the power of the Emperor's servants ... Delay as much as possible'.

Campeggio did not approve of this double-dealing. 'I do not see', he told the papal secretary, 'supposing the King cannot be got from his opinion, how without scandal we can delay what, by our own commission, we have to proceed with and try. It will easily seem to them that I have been sent to gull them, and they may be furious about it'. When Campeggio eventually arrived in England, in October 1528, he joined Wolsey in trying to persuade Catherine to resolve the problem by acknowledging that her marriage was invalid. Catherine, however, refused to compromise, and a public trial of 'the King's great matter' could not be avoided. Henry now seemed to be having doubts about the outcome, for he sent Stephen Gardiner, one of Wolsey's bright young men, to Rome with a warning that unless a quick decision in his favour was given by the two legates he would renounce his allegiance to the papacy.

The legatine court opened at Blackfriars in May 1529, and on 24 June both the King and Queen were present. Catherine threw herself at Henry's feet and begged him to remember how good a wife she had been to him and how dishonourable it would be, not only to her but to the King and his people, if judgement was given against her. Henry was moved to tears and publicly affirmed that 'she hath been to me as true, obedient and as conformable a wife as I could in my fancy wish or desire,' but when he declared his willingness to accept an impartial verdict on the validity of their marriage, she called for the matter to be decided at Rome.

The court went into recess while the legates considered their verdict, but when it reassembled in July 1529 Henry was still confident that it would give judgement in his favour. Unfortunately for him, Campeggio was playing for time while he waited for instructions from Rome, and announced that no final decision could be arrived at until after the three-month summer vacation. The court never, in fact, re-assembled, and Henry's feelings were expressed by his brother-in-law, the Duke of Suffolk, who, as a contemporary account records, stepped forward and 'spake these words with a stout and hault countenance: "It was never merry in England whilst we had cardinals among us". Which words were set forth with such a vehement countenance that all men marvelled what he intended.'

Wolsey's fall from power

Henry's anger was translated swiftly into action. The King had no further use for Wolsey, who had failed to procure the annulment of his marriage, and he summoned Parliament in order that an act of attainder should be passed against the cardinal. The act was not needed, however, for Wolsey had also been commanded to appear before the common-law judges and answer the charge that by publishing his bulls of appointment as papal legate he had infringed the Statute of Praemunire (*see* p. 22). Despite the fact that he derived his legatine authority from the Pope, to whom he could have appealed for support, Wolsey made no effort to defend himself but simply acknowledged his guilt. No man knew better than he did that the real source of his power was Henry, and now that Henry had decided to dispense with him he had to go. His palaces and collegiate foundations were declared confiscate to the crown as a punishment for his offence of praemunire, and he was ordered to make his way to York, to visit for the first time the province of which he had been archbishop for the past fifteen years.

Unfortunately for Wolsey, he could not accept that his fall from power was permanent. Henry, he thought, might be persuaded to change his mind, particularly if his fellow sovereigns urged him to do so. Wolsey therefore began secret negotiations with Francis I and the Emperor, in the hope of securing their support. He also continued his lavish lifestyle, and planned a magnificent ceremony in York Minster at which he would be enthroned as archbishop. His servant, Thomas Cromwell, wrote to warn him that he needed to allay suspicion rather than arouse it. 'Some allege you keep too great a house[hold] and are continually building ... I think you happy you are now at liberty to serve God and banish all vain desires of the world.' But the vain desires of the world still dazzled Wolsey, and reports of his activities aroused the King's suspicions. He ordered the cardinal's arrest on a charge of high treason, and Wolsey was sent southwards, under guard, towards London. He got no further than Leicester Abbey where, on 29 November 1530, he died, lamenting that 'if I had served God as diligently as I have done the King, He would not have given me over in my grey hairs'.

Wolsey was a prince of the Church, in a tradition so alien to modern assumptions that it is difficult to comprehend him. He promoted education and made his household a place where men of intelligence and ability learned how to serve the state. He was also tolerant in matters of religion, preferring to burn heretical books rather than the heretics themselves. He rose to power by royal favour and became rich in the King's service, yet he served Henry unstintingly and gave good value for money. He was often arrogant and mean-minded, yet he knew how to win men's hearts when he wanted to. As Shakespeare put it, Wolsey was:

'*Lofty and sour to them that loved him not,*
But to those men that sought him, sweet as summer.'

King Henry VIII; iv,ii.

CHAPTER THREE

The break with Rome

The Reformation Parliament

The Parliament which met in November 1529 had been summoned to deal with Wolsey, but now that Wolsey had capitulated without a struggle there was no obvious work for it to do. Henry was determined to end his marriage to Catherine of Aragon, and he was aware that Denmark, Sweden and much of north Germany had already repudiated papal supremacy. He did not see the need to follow suit at this stage, since he was confident that Rome would in due course declare his marriage invalid, but he was not averse to putting pressure on Clement VII, and one obvious way of doing this was through Parliament. The Commons and many of the temporal lords were still demanding an end to abuses in the Church, and by giving them their head Henry would not only increase his popularity but also strengthen his claim to be a godly monarch. At the same time he would be indicating to the Pope that a head of steam had built up against certain practices which the Church had failed to reform and that only he, Henry, could keep it within bounds.

The Commons went ahead and passed bills limiting the fees to be charged for probate of wills, restricting rights of sanctuary, and forbidding pluralism and non-residence. The spiritual lords did not accept these measures with equanimity. Although they had been unable, or unwilling, to initiate reform themselves, they resented action by the laity, and the bill to limit probate fees provoked Bishop Fisher to an angry outburst: 'Now with the Commons is nothing but "Down with the Church!" And all this, me seemeth, is for lack of faith only.' It was probably during this opening session of Parliament in late 1529 that the Commons started drawing up the list of grievances against the Church which was to take shape in 1532 as the *Supplication against the Ordinaries*.

Henry's next step was prompted by a chance meeting, during the summer of 1529, between Thomas Cranmer, fellow of Jesus College, Cambridge, and Stephen Gardiner and Edward Foxe. Gardiner, one of Wolsey's protégés, had recently been appointed Henry's secretary, while Foxe held the same position in Wolsey's household. Cranmer was already known to Wolsey, who had employed him on a diplomatic mission to Spain, and also to the King, but his principal occupation was that of lecturer in theology. During discussions between the three men about 'the King's great matter', Cranmer proposed that the leading European theologians should be asked whether the interdiction on a man marrying his brother's widow was based on canon law, which could be set aside by the Pope, or on God's law, which was irrevocable. The idea appealed to Henry, who summoned Cranmer to London, where he became a member of the household of Thomas Boleyn, father of Anne.

Cranmer's suggestion led to the mounting of a major campaign in 1530 to marshal informed European opinion behind the King. Libraries were searched for supportive evidence and money was distributed on a lavish scale to all those scholars who professed to see merit in Henry's case. As a result of this activity eight universities, including the prestigious Paris and Bologna, came down on the King's side, and their opinions were made known to a wider audience by the publication in November 1531 of *The Determination of the most famous and most excellent Universities of Italy and France, that it is unlawful for a man to marry his brother's wife; that the Pope hath no power to dispense therewith*. Cranmer had played a major part in drawing up the final version of this treatise, which included an appeal to the English bishops 'to withstand the Pope openly to his face' if he did not accept the justice of Henry's cause.

The *Determination* was the joint work of a number of scholars committed to providing a theoretical foundation for the King's position. Another of their productions, though it remained unpublished, was the *Collectanea Satis Copiosa* ['The sufficiently abundant Collections']. This was made up of extracts designed to show that the Kings of England had originally been supreme over all their subjects, clerical as well as lay, even though this supremacy had been subsequently obscured by an unjustified extension of papal power. Henry read the draft of this work and was highly pleased with its conclusions, which supplied exactly the sort of historical justification that he needed. The *Collectanea* also provided a basis for the claim later made explicit in the Act of Appeals of 1533 that England was an empire under the supreme headship of the King. Henry, who traced his descent (via King Arthur) from Constantine, the first Christian

Emperor, had long been convinced that he wielded an imperial authority. He may have derived this belief in part from his father, for Henry VII had christened his eldest son Arthur and also, in 1489, issued a new coin on which he was portrayed wearing an imperial crown, closed over the head with loops, rather than the traditional open circlet. It is perhaps significant that Henry VIII, who built up the royal navy, chose the name *The Henry Imperial* for one of his new ships, and some years later, when he defended the papacy against Luther by writing the *Assertio Septem Sacramentorum*, he insisted that the duty of obedience to the Pope did not extend to temporal matters.

A great deal depended, of course, upon the definition of 'temporal', but 1531 witnessed an important development in this respect. Henry's forays into France had left him desperately short of money, and he looked to the Church to subsidise him. Early in 1531 the Attorney-General, acting on Henry's behalf, indicted a number of clergy before the Court of King's Bench on the grounds that by acknowledging Wolsey's legatine authority, which was derived from papal grant, they had infringed the Statute of Praemunire. The indictment was subsequently extended to all the clergy of the province of Canterbury, who were faced with the prospect of having their possessions confiscated. Henry now called upon Convocation to grant him a subsidy of £100,000 and offered, in return, to pardon the clergy's 'offence'. Convocation agreed to make the required grant, but rejected Henry's draft wording, which styled him 'sole protector and supreme head of the English Church and clergy'. The King's spokesmen had to fight hard to persuade them to accept a compromise version in which they acknowledged Henry as 'their singular protector, only and supreme lord, and, as far as the law of Christ allows, even supreme head'.

Convocation, in fact, had given little away, for a royal supremacy so hedged about with qualifications was virtually unenforceable. But Henry was satisfied that he had achieved his immediate aim of opening up the way, if it proved necessary, to an 'English' solution of his marital problems. He therefore assented to an act of 1531 giving the clergy formal pardon for their offence in exercising independent spiritual jurisdiction. However, the Commons feared that by appearing before Church courts and accepting their judgments, they had been unwitting accessories of the clergy. Their fears were allayed by a second act in which the King pardoned his lay subjects, this time free of charge.

As long as Henry emphasised his role as a godly prince, putting into effect the Erasmian reform programme which the Church under Wolsey had so conspicuously failed to adopt, he could count on the support of informed public opinion. But he had to tread warily, for in 1517 Martin Luther had made his celebrated challenge to the papacy, thereby setting off a new and more aggressive reform movement that threatened to split Christendom into warring fragments. Henry did not approve of Luther and regarded many of his beliefs as heretical. Yet Lutheran ideas were already spreading in England, and there was a very real possibility that Henry, by undermining the authority of the ecclesiastical hierarchy, might hamstring the Church at a time when it needed all its strength to meet the Lutheran challenge. Henry therefore had to consider his next moves carefully, but he may well have been uncertain what options to take. If this was the case, however, his period of uncertainty was short, for he found in the person of Thomas Cromwell not only a brilliant executant of royal policy but a man with ideas of his own about the lines along which Henry should proceed.

Thomas Cromwell

Cromwell, the son of a clothworker and alehouse-keeper, was born at Putney, south-west of London, at about the time that the Battle of Bosworth was fought. He became a roving soldier in Italy, entered the service of the Frescobaldi, a famous banking family, and then went on to The Netherlands, where he made his living as a business consultant. This early experience was invaluable to him, since through it he acquired first-hand knowledge of the trading networks that linked the north Italian city states with Antwerp and London.

During his stay in Rome, Cromwell got to know Cardinal Bainbridge, Henry's ambassador to the papal court, and following Bainbridge's sudden death in 1514 he returned to England with the cardinal's entourage. He spent some time studying the common law and then entered Wolsey's household, that nursery of statesmen and administrators. When Wolsey decided to suppress twenty-nine monasteries and use their wealth to endow his new colleges at Oxford and Ipswich he chose Cromwell as his agent. From his vantage point in Wolsey's household Cromwell had a close-up view of the lifestyle of the ecclesiastical hierarchy. He knew that corruption had crept into the Church, yet he was not obviously anticlerical, nor was he without faith. In the will which he drew up in 1529 he left £20 to poor householders to pray for his soul and £5 to the orders of friars. He also instructed his executors to arrange for masses to be said for him for seven years by 'an honest and continent priest'. The adjectives are significant.

When Wolsey fell it looked as though Cromwell would fall with him, so closely had he been identified with the cardinal's policies, but he told George Cavendish, Wolsey's biographer, that he would go to court, where he would, to use his favourite phrase, 'either make or mar ere I come again'. Cromwell had already sat in Parliament, in 1523, and once he was informed that the King had no objection to his standing for election again, he secured a seat at Taunton in Somerset. In the following year, 1530, he entered royal service and shortly afterwards was made a Councillor. By the end of 1531 he was acknowledged in the Commons as one of Henry's principal spokesmen, and he was entering the inner ring of the King's advisers.

The third session of the Reformation Parliament opened in January 1532 and the Commons immediately reverted to the question of clerical abuses. The outcome of their debates was a list of grievances which Cromwell probably helped draw up, called *The Supplication against the Ordinaries* [i.e. the judges in ecclesiastical courts]. This called into question the Church's right to make its own laws, and Henry therefore passed it on to Convocation and invited their response. The bishops were in no mood to welcome such a document, for they were at last engaged in putting their house in order. New canons were being drafted, dealing with non-residency, simony (the sale of ecclesiastical office) and other abuses, and this entire reform programme would be put at risk if the Church's legislative power was undermined. Warham had already taken a stand by formally dissociating himself from any parliamentary statutes that derogated from the authority of the Pope or the liberties of the Church, and it was with his encouragement that Stephen Gardiner drew up a reply to the *Supplication* affirming that the Church's right to make its own laws was 'grounded upon the scripture of God and determination of Holy Church, which must also be a rule and square to try the justice of all laws, as well spiritual as temporal'.

Gardiner was known to be in the King's favour and had only recently been appointed Bishop of Winchester. He would hardly have committed himself to such an uncompromising defence of the Church's position unless he felt confident the King would support him. However, Gardiner and his fellow bishops had miscalculated, for by putting so much emphasis on the Church's independence and autonomy they appeared to be challenging the King's belief that he wielded an imperial authority. When Henry received the clergy's reply to the *Supplication*, in April 1532, he passed it on to the Commons with a broad hint about his own opinion: 'We think their answer will smally please you, for it seemeth to us very slender. You be a great sort of wise men. I doubt not but you will look cir-cumspectly on the matter, and we will be indifferent between you.'

This indication of royal dissatisfaction set debate going again in Convocation, and Henry now insisted that the Church should abandon its claim to make laws without royal permission. Moreover, it should submit existing canons to a mixed commission of clergy and laymen that would decide whether or not they were valid. This demand was no more accept-able to the bishops than the *Supplication* had been, but there were those among them who urged Convocation to take a softer line. They were alarmed by the increasing assertiveness of the Commons and aware that only the King could hold it in check. If, in order to assure themselves of his support, they had to part with some of their cherished rights, so be it; they had no other choice.

There were many bishops, of course, who regarded the idea of conces-sions as a betrayal of their episcopal responsibility, but they salved their consciences by staying away from the assembly. The handful who con-tinued to attend signed the *Submission of the Clergy* in which they accepted Henry's demands. It had seemed for a brief moment that Archbishop Warham might rally the hard-line defenders of the Church, for he had talked of following Becket's example. In the end, however, he gave way. He was now an old man, over eighty, enfeebled and in poor health. He died only a few months after setting his hand to the *Submission*. In the event, it was a layman who took up the challenge thrown down by the King and Commons. On the day the *Submission* was presented to Henry, Sir Thomas More, whom the King had chosen to succeed Wolsey as Lord Chancellor, resigned from office.

While the English clergy were being brought to heel, the Pope was being threatened with a cut in his revenues. For many centuries, annates – the payments by newly-appointed bishops of their first year's income to the Pope – had been a cause of complaint in England. Now, in 1532, came the Act in Conditional Restraint of Annates, which forbade the payment of these dues to Rome but left it to the King to decide when the prohibition should be put into effect. The act also provided that if the Pope refused to issue the bulls required to consecrate a bishop, the consecration should take place all the same. Furthermore, if the Pope reacted by excommuni-cating those who had taken part in the ceremony, the excommunication should be of no effect.

Care was taken in the act to present this action as the removal, by an orthodox and devout monarch, of a long-standing abuse, and this emphasis upon renovation rather than innovation helps explain the lack of concerted opposition from the bishops and informed laymen. They could not see at what point and on what grounds to take a stand, and having accepted the early measures they found themselves unwittingly committed to all that followed. They may have had reservations about certain of Henry's actions, but they felt bound by the biblical commandment to fear God and honour the King, particularly since, in this case, the King had publicly defended the catholic Church and papacy against the attacks of Luther. Henry's support of orthodoxy was demonstrated in the early 1530s, when at least half a dozen heretics were burnt at the stake, and in March 1532, at the very moment when Convocation was considering its reply to the *Supplication*, the King warned Hugh Latimer, a celebrated preacher who had been accused of heresy, that 'I will not take upon me now to be a suitor to the bishops for you unless you promise to do penance as ye have deserved, and never to preach any such things again. Ye shall else only get from me a faggot to burn you.' William Warham was one of the few bishops who saw that the key issue was that of papal sovereignty over the Church, but he died in August 1532 and the King chose as his successor Thomas Cranmer.

Thomas Cranmer

Cranmer spent most of 1530 abroad, helping to collect opinions on 'the King's great matter' from Italian universities. After lengthy spells in both Rome and Bologna, he returned to England at the end of the year, and during the course of 1531 he made a number of contacts with prominent European reformers who were visiting London. These included Martin Bucer, who had carried the process of reform at Strasburg well beyond the relatively moderate Lutheran position and closer to the evangelical model set up by Ulrich Zwingli at Zurich. Such contacts began to affect Cranmer's own approach to religion, but for the time being he was fully occupied in the King's business. In 1532 he was despatched as ambassador to the Emperor Charles V and thereby had the opportunity to study the Lutheran reformation at first hand in the city of Nuremberg. It impressed him in more ways than one, for he fell in love with the niece of a prominent Lutheran pastor and married her. Cranmer had already been married once before, and had had to renounce his fellowship at Jesus as a consequence. Readmitted to the fellowship after his wife's death, he had now taken a step which openly challenged the ban on clerical marriage. Moreover, he had done so just before his life was changed for ever by receipt of a letter from Henry VIII informing him that, consequent upon the death of Warham, he was now Archbishop of Canterbury. Years later, Cranmer recalled his reaction to this unwelcome news: 'he feeling in himself a great inability to such a promotion, and very sorry to leave his study ... devised an excuse to the King of matter of great importance' which would prevent his immediate return home. He did so in the hope that the impatient Henry 'would have bestowed it [i.e. the archbishopric] upon some other'.

Cranmer's wish to return to the relative obscurity of his scholar's life at Cambridge might well have been granted had it not been for the influence of the Boleyn family. He was already on close terms with Sir Thomas Boleyn, recently created Earl of Wiltshire, and he had also won the approval of Sir Thomas's daughter, Anne, who was deeply committed to the cause of reform of the Church and acted as the patron of many of those who would in due course carry it through. Anne and Henry had by now gone through a secret marriage ceremony, and by the time Cranmer returned to England she was pregnant. Henry never doubted that the child would turn out to be the longed-for male heir, and in order to secure the boy's inheritance it was essential that Henry's marriage to Anne should be publicly and authentically confirmed. Cranmer would play a key role in this procedure, and it was therefore important that nothing should be lacking in the details of his appointment. The Pope issued the necessary bulls without difficulty. He did not know much about Cranmer, and was pleased to be able to gratify Henry at a time when relations between the English King and the papacy were at a low ebb. He was also aware that Henry had not yet made permanent the restraint of annates and that a conciliatory gesture on his part might persuade the King to delay such action indefinitely.

At the end of March 1533 Cranmer was formally consecrated archbishop, but after taking the oath of loyalty to the papacy he made a solemn protestation that this would not in any way impede the 'reformation of the Christian religion, the government of the English Church, or the pre rogative of the crown'. One of the first acts of the new archbishop was to preside over a meeting of Convocation that discussed the question of Henry's marital status. John Fisher insisted that Henry's marriage to Catherine was lawful, since it was based upon a valid papal dispensation, but he could not carry the majority with him. Whatever their private convictions, the bishops did not think it expedient to oppose the King, and their fears about what would happen if they did were confirmed a few days later, when Henry ordered Fisher's arrest. Meanwhile, Parliament had passed the Act in Restraint of Appeals which ruled out any possibility of settling the question at Rome. The way was now legally open for the

Church in England to give the final verdict on 'the King's great matter', and Cranmer presided over the formal trial that opened at Dunstable on 10 May 1533.

Catherine, who did not acknowledge the court's competence, refused to appear before it, and two weeks later Cranmer pronounced judgment that Henry's so-called marriage to the Queen had never been valid and that he must immediately stop cohabiting with this woman who was not his wife – a provision that Henry found easy to fulfil since he had been living apart from Catherine ever since the divorce proceedings began. Cranmer subsequently declared that Henry's marriage with Anne Boleyn was lawful, and on Whit Sunday 1533 he crowned Anne as Queen in a magnificent ceremony in Westminster Abbey. A few months later, on 7 September, Anne gave birth to her child. Unfortunately for her, and disappointingly for Henry, it was a daughter, whom they named Elizabeth.

The royal supremacy revealed

In English law Cranmer's verdict on Henry's marital status was final, since the Act of Appeals laid down that all 'causes of matrimony and divorces ... coming in contention, debate or question within this realm ... shall be from henceforth ... finally and definitely adjudged and determined within the King's jurisdiction and authority, and not elsewhere'. The justification for this order was given in the preamble to the act, which clearly owed much to the arguments first assembled in the *Collectanea Satis Copiosa*: 'By divers sundry old authentic histories and chronicles it is manifestly declared and expressed that this realm of England is an empire, and so hath been accepted in the world, governed by one supreme head and King having the dignity and royal estate of the imperial crown of the same, unto whom a body politic, compact of all sorts and degrees of people divided in terms and by names of spirityalty and temporalty be bounden and owe to bear next to God a natural and humble obedience.'

Despite the fact that his authority had been openly defied, the Pope was slow to take retaliatory action, hoping that even at this late stage the breach could be healed. Not until July 1533 did he quash Cranmer's verdict and excommunicate him. Henry was given until September to take back Catherine, failing which he also would be excommunicated. Henry riposted by issuing letters patent confirming the (hitherto temporary) restraint of annates. His principal adviser, Thomas Cromwell, also launched a propaganda campaign against the papacy, and *The Articles devised by the whole consent of the King's most honourable Council,* issued in December 1533, referred to 'the Bishop of Rome, by some men called the Pope'. This was not mere word play. It was an assertion that the Pope's authority was confined to his own diocese, as was the case with all other bishops, and that his claim to spiritual overlordship of Christendom was spurious.

The denial of papal supremacy left the English Church without a clearly defined head, and made further legislation necessary in 1534. First came the Act in Absolute Restraint of Annates, which confirmed Henry's letters patent cutting off this source of papal revenue. It also laid down that in future bishops were to be elected by cathedral chapters only after the King had issued a *congé d'élire* ['licence to elect'] containing the name of the person he had chosen. If the chapter failed to elect the royal nominee its members would be liable to the penalties prescribed in the Statute of Praemunire. Another act of 1534, asserting that the realm had been impoverished by 'intolerable exactions of great sums of money', forbade the payment to Rome of Peter's Pence – an annual tribute regularly made since the Norman Conquest – and prohibited the sale of papal dispensations in England. Any remaining hope of reconciliation with Rome ended in March 1534 when Clement VII finally gave judgment in Catherine's favour. In November of that year Parliament put the coping-stone upon the new structure of the English Church by passing the Act of Supremacy. This did not grant a parliamentary title to Henry; it simply made formal acknowledgment of the fact that 'the King's majesty justly and rightfully is … the supreme head of the Church of England'.

It was one thing to enunciate Henry's supremacy; it was another to put it into effect. In the early years of the reign the King had relied on Wolsey to govern both the Church and the state, but now that papal power had been removed there was no one invested with legatine authority who could override the bishops and make the English Church truly 'Henrician'. In January 1535, therefore, the King appointed Thomas Cromwell as his Viceregent or Vicar-General for ecclesiastical affairs, with the right to carry out visitations and take whatever steps he deemed appropriate to enforce the supremacy. Cromwell did not exercise his new powers immediately, since he was engaged in mounting a propaganda campaign to swing public opinion behind the King, but his quasi-legatine authority was ready to be employed whenever he thought fit.

The formal enunciation of the royal supremacy was followed almost immediately by the Treason Act, making it an offence to attempt by any means, including writing and speaking, to deprive the King and his heirs of their titles or accuse them of heresy or tyranny. The heirs in question were named in the Succession Act of March 1534 as the children of the Boleyn marriage, and all the King's subjects were ordered to take an oath accepting these provisions. The oath as administered included the statement that no 'faith, truth and obedience' should be given to any 'foreign authority or potentate'. This wording was unacceptable to Sir Thomas More and Bishop John Fisher, even though they were prepared to acknowledge the succession as laid down by statute. Henry regarded their refusal to take the entire oath as open defiance of his rule, and he ordered the imprisonment of both men.

More, when pressed to comply, insisted that he was 'not bound to change my conscience and conform it to the counsel of one realm against the general counsel of Christendom'. His appeal from the law of the state to 'the law of God and His holy Church' worried Sir Thomas Audley, More's successor as Lord Chancellor, who was presiding at his trial, and he asked Lord Chief Justice Fitzjames for his opinion. Fitzjames replied that if 'the act of Parliament be not unlawful, then is not the indictment in my conscience insufficient'. This reply went to the heart of the matter. More was executed because he denied the sovereignty of statute, upon which Henry and Cromwell were building the Tudor state. His idealism and his appeal to conscience, as well as his courage and humanity, make More's execution seem a flagrant example of tyrannical injustice. Yet his opponents were also, in their different way, idealists, except that they saw the path of salvation, in this world as well as the next, leading through the secular state which acknowledged no superior on earth.

The assumption of Henry and Cromwell that anyone who refused wholeheartedly to accept the royal supremacy was a potential traitor, found some confirmation in Fisher's case, for the reports of the imperial ambassador over the previous two years had quoted 'that excellent and holy man, the Bishop of Rochester', as calling for the Emperor to take prompt action against Henry. In May 1535 the Pope created Fisher a cardinal. Henry took this as a personal affront and swore that by the time the red hat arrived Fisher would no longer have a head to put it on. The following month Fisher, found guilty of treason, was executed, appropriately enough on the eve of the feast of St Thomas Becket.

More and Fisher were the most important victims of the 'Terror', the stage common to every revolution when the leaders or possible leaders of a conservative reaction are struck down. The Henrician terror was a small-scale affair, but Henry made it clear that he would not tolerate open opposition to his will. Elizabeth Barton, 'the Nun of Kent', a visionary whose 'revelations' had given her a great reputation, was executed in 1534, along with her accomplices, for prophesying the King's death. The following year, while Fisher and More were awaiting judgment, a number of monks from the London Charterhouse were hanged, drawn and quartered for denying the royal supremacy. This show of force apparently sufficed, for no leader emerged to mount a major, let alone a successful, challenge to Henry or his policies.

The theoretical foundations of the royal supremacy

By the middle of 1535 Henry and Cromwell had accomplished the first stage of their revolution by destroying papal authority in England and firmly establishing the royal supremacy in statute law. There were theoretical as well as legal foundations to this supremacy. Most obvious was the justification of expediency: intervention by the King was necessary because the Church, under the feeble and corrupt leadership of the papacy, had failed to curb abuses. The only power that could effectively challenge papal pretensions and set reform on foot without causing chaos was that of the lay ruler. For this reason early reformers, including Luther, appealed to them for support. The right of princes to intervene in ecclesiastical affairs was not based solely on expediency. The Bible showed the Jewish kings of the Old Testament exercising authority over the Church, while in the New Testament St Paul had written 'There is no power but of God. The powers-that-be are ordained of God. Whosoever therefore resisteth the power resisteth the ordinance of God, and they that resist shall receive to themselves damnation' (*Romans* 13: 1,2).

The evidence of scripture was reinforced by the appeal to history. In the ancient world the Emperor Constantine's authority had been accepted by the early Christian Church, and the reformers claimed that his position, and therefore his powers, had been inherited by the rulers of the European states. Until Becket, it was argued, English kings, while acknowledging the spiritual headship of the Pope, had not tolerated any papal interference in the day-to-day running of the Church. It was Becket who gave voice to the full Hildebrandine claim that the Church was a monarchy ruled over by the Pope, with the European princes as his vassals. King John, facing a baronial revolt, had formally surrendered his kingdom to the Pope and received it back as a papal fief, but Henry VIII told the imperial ambassador in March 1533 that he would put John's action into reverse by asserting his and his kingdom's freedom from papal suzerainty. Moreover, he intended to reunite to his imperial crown 'the goods which churchmen held of it, which his predecessors could not alienate to his prejudice'. Since the encroachment upon royal rights, as Henry saw it, had begun with Becket, he ordered the destruction of St Thomas's shrine at Canterbury in 1538 and forbade the celebration of his feast day on the grounds that 'there appeareth nothing in his life and exterior or conversation whereby he should be called a saint, but rather a rebel and traitor to his prince'.

The advocates of reform drew a distinction between *Potestas Jurisdictionis*, or the right to exercise jurisdiction over the Church, and the *Potestas Ordinis*, the right to exercise spiritual powers – although in practice this distinction was nothing like so clear-cut as it was in theory. Henry VIII, in particular, had highly idiosyncratic views about the nature of his position and acknowledged few, if any, limits to his authority. The Henrician Reformation was portrayed as the transfer to the crown of the *Potestas Jurisdictionis*, with the *Potestas Ordinis* remaining in the hands of the bishops. The appeal to history and the distinction between the two types of authority account for the tone of the statutes that brought about the destruction of papal power in England. History and the Bible, it was claimed, showed that the *Potestas Jurisdictionis* belonged to the lay ruler. All that remained, therefore, was to sweep away papal encroachments and restore to the King his rightful authority. The argument was a strong one and it carried many waverers with it.

Conservatives and radicals both looked to the King for support. The conservatives were afraid that without royal protection the Church would fall victim to the radicals' onslaught: better a state Church with catholic doctrine than the heresies of Luther and Zwingli. The radicals, on the other hand, hoped that by destroying papal supremacy the King would open the door to a Church reformed in doctrine as well as government. Stephen Gardiner, who was a prominent conservative, wrote that 'the King – yea, though he be an infidel – representeth the image of God upon earth'. William Tyndale, translator of the Bible, who stood at the opposite extreme to Gardiner and was eventually burnt as a heretic, agreed with him on this point. 'He that judgeth the King', he wrote, 'judgeth God, and he that resisteth the King resisteth God'. For those whose consciences were less scrupulous than Sir Thomas More's – that is to say, the vast majority – obedience to the prince was sufficient in itself and largely replaced dependence upon relics, indulgences and outward observances which had previously given hope of salvation to men well aware of their wicked ways but unable to abandon them. Now they could take refuge with Shakespeare's soldier in *Henry V*: 'We know enough if we know we are the King's subjects. If his cause be wrong, our obedience to the King wipes the crime of it out of us.' It is left in the play to the disguised Henry

V to make the rejoinder of the later reformers: 'Every subject's duty is the King's. But every subject's soul is his own.' [*King Henry V*; iv, i].

Obedience to the sovereign became a religious duty not only because the sovereign was head of the Church but also because society as a whole, organised under the King, was assumed to have a spiritual function. It was this belief which explains the otherwise paradoxical combination of worldliness and deep religious feeling that characterised so many people in early Tudor England. Their worldliness, as shown in their hunger for money, lands, honours, titles and glory, led to the adulation of the monarch from whom such assets flowed. Yet at the same time their awareness of God and sin and judgment suffused secular society with a spiritual purpose. This was true not only of England but of other Christian countries, whether they were communities like Calvin's Geneva, where the state was conceived to be an aspect of the Church; Lutheran Germany, where the Church was subordinate to the lay magistrate; or catholic France, where the King and the Pope operated a dual headship. In all these countries the state, whether it was a city, principality or kingdom, became the unit in which and around which matters spiritual were organised.

In England the new society was mapped out by writers like Thomas Starkey, who were the direct heirs of the early sixteenth-century humanists. These men were products of the Renaissance. They had studied the learning of the ancient world and wanted to apply their knowledge to the benefit of the Church and the state. Cardinal College was a humanist centre, and Thomas Starkey was among those students already at Oxford whom Wolsey persuaded to transfer to his new foundation. In the years after Wolsey's fall many of the scholars who had been at Cardinal College, and would normally have gone on from there to be trained in Wolsey's household, found a new patron in Reginald Pole.

Pole was a member of a distinguished family connected by blood to the throne, and was renowned for his learning. His household at Padua (where his studies were paid for by Henry VIII) was a centre for English scholars like Starkey and Thomas Lupset – one of the leading figures in the academic world, a friend of Erasmus and lecturer in Greek at Oxford. But the smooth development of English humanist studies was broken up by the divorce question. Pole was too big a name for the King to ignore, and Henry put pressure on him to give a favourable opinion. Pole was at first far from clear about what he thought of 'the King's great matter', but Starkey saw in the rise of Thomas Cromwell an opportunity to reform society along humanist lines, and in 1534 he left Pole at Padua and returned to England. Starkey assumed that Pole would eventually take the

King's part and that English humanists would remain united in the tradition of service to the state which Wolsey had fostered. But in 1536 Pole published his *Pro Ecclesiasticae Defensione* which came out clearly against the King. Henry thereafter regarded Pole as his enemy.

Starkey, meanwhile, was working for Cromwell. His most famous work, *A Dialogue between Pole and Lupset*, was not published until the nineteenth century, but his *Exhortation to Unity and Obedience*, which grew out of his discussions with Cromwell and reflects the views of both men, was produced in 1536 by the King's printer. For Starkey the state was a means to a better life: 'Good policy is nothing else but the order and rule of a multitude of men, as it were conspiring together to live in all virtue and honesty'. The contrast between the humanism of Starkey and that of More is nowhere more striking than in their attitude towards the state. Starkey revered it. More despised it and described it as 'nothing but a conspiracy of rich men procuring their own commodities under the name and title of a commonwealth'.

For Starkey the Bible was the sole source of authority. What it commanded was, by definition, good. What it condemned was bad. But on those topics about which it was silent – for instance, papal power – society should decide for itself. These topics were the *adiaphora*, 'matters indifferent', which were not essential to salvation and belonged by right, as well as expediency, to the sphere of authority of the lay ruler. Where reformation of the Church was concerned, Starkey recommended a middle course between the extremes of total preservation and total rejection, maintaining, for instance, that ceremonies and traditions, being *adiaphora*, should be permitted in so far as they were 'things convenient to maintain unity' and as long as they were not repugnant to 'God's word nor to good civility'. In this he was sketching out the position that the anglican Church was eventually to make its own.

The Henrician Reformation

Henry VIII repudiated papal authority because he saw no other way by which to free himself from his marriage to Catherine of Aragon. If only the Pope had granted him a divorce there is every reason to assume that he and his kingdom would have remained within the papal fold. Henry's actions, however, came at a time when the Catholic Church throughout Europe was under attack. In a sense, the Christian humanists had prepared the ground for this. By exposing the weaknesses of the Church which they loved they had put weapons into the hands of those who hated it. In 1516, for example, Erasmus had published an edition of the New Testament in which the Greek text appeared side by side with the Latin version. Had Erasmus been born half a century earlier, his edition would have been disseminated only gradually, by means of more or less imperfect handwritten transcripts, but the invention of printing changed all that. His New Testament, produced in multiple copies, each one an exact replica of the other, was quickly bought up by literate laymen as well as clerics throughout Christendom and provided them with a source of authority to which they could appeal even against the traditions of the Church and the decrees of the Popes. With one fell blow the Church's exclusive ownership of sacred texts had been overthrown and religion ceased to be a mystery which only a handful of initiates could fully comprehend. In this way, as Stephen Gardiner later observed, Erasmus laid the egg that Luther hatched.

The printing press played a key role once again in the propagation of Luther's ideas, for in the 1520s he wrote a number of powerfully-argued tracts that circulated widely throughout Europe and made him a household name. In these he elaborated the doctrine that human beings were born into sin and so corrupted by it that they could not lift a finger to save themselves. Only the direct intervention of God could raise them out of the mire and lead them towards salvation. 'Good works', in the accepted sense of pious observances, acts of charity, pilgrimages, etc., made not the slightest difference. Without faith in God they were of no value. With faith they were superfluous. The Catholic Church, with its elaborate hierarchy, its shrines, pilgrimages, relics and indulgences, was totally irrelevant to the human condition.

Luther's ideas found a responsive audience in some quarters in England. The White Horse tavern at Cambridge provided a meeting place for those who welcomed Luther's initiative, yet to describe the White Horse group simply as 'Lutheran' misrepresents the situation. For one thing, there was considerable variation in attitudes and beliefs between different individuals; and, for another, their views were constantly evolving. Luther was only one of the influences on them. Among the others were the Swiss reformers Ulrich Zwingli and Martin Bucer, who differed fundamentally from Luther on the nature of the sacrament.

The English 'Lutherans' were men of independent minds who developed their own opinions. Thomas Bilney's close study of Erasmus's New Testament led him to accept Luther's insistence that justification – the freeing from sin, which opens the way to salvation – comes solely through faith, and that rites and ceremonies are of no effect. Yet he remained traditional in his acceptance of 'transubstantiation,' the catholic belief that in the mass the bread and wine change their substance, or essential nature, at the moment of consecration and become the veritable body and blood of Christ, who therefore has a 'real presence' and not merely a symbolic one. Bilney was the first English 'Lutheran' to suffer death at the stake, in 1531. He was followed by John Frith, one of a number of young Cambridge dons whom Wolsey invited to transfer to Cardinal College and who took their unorthodox views with them. Frith eventually adopted a more radical position than Bilney, rejecting transubstantiation and denying the existence of purgatory. This brought him up against Sir Thomas More, the Lord Chancellor, but it was the Bishop of London who sent him to the stake in July 1533.

Among those who came into contact with Bilney and was strongly influenced by him was Robert Barnes, another Augustinian friar. He was accused of heresy in 1526 and narrowly escaped burning, so he took refuge in Germany, where he became a companion of Luther and wrote a treatise in defence of his doctrines. This came to the attention of Thomas Cromwell, who was now the King's chief minister. Cromwell was probably close to Barnes in his religious opinions, but he also saw the need to recruit not simply Erasmian humanists but also radical reformers to engage in polemics on Henry's behalf. At Cromwell's invitation Barnes returned to England, where he worked for the King and was employed on a number of diplomatic missions to German Lutheran princes. Yet his defence of the royal supremacy and his relatively moderate position on disputed points in religion – he was deeply opposed, for instance, to the 'sacramentarians', who denied that there was any trace of the real presence in the sacraments – could not save him from the conservative reaction which set in after Cromwell's fall, and he was burnt at the stake in 1540.

One incident in Barnes's life symbolised the fusion of old and new heretical movements, for in 1527 he had a meeting with two Lollards from Essex. The Lollards' rejection of orthodox catholic doctrines went much further than anything that Luther proposed, and the Church had persecuted them ever since their first appearance in the fourteenth century. The two Lollards who met Barnes went up to London specially to see him. They told him how they had begun to convert their vicar to Wycliffe's doctrines. They also showed him some manuscript copies of parts of the Lollard Bible. Barnes displayed a tolerant contempt for this old-fashioned version of the scriptures and before parting with his visitors he sold them a copy of Tyndale's recent translation of the New Testament.

William Tyndale was among the leading figures of the early

Reformation in England. He spent his undergraduate years at Oxford and then transferred to Cambridge, where he became a close friend of John Frith, who assisted him in preparing an English version of the New Testament. Tyndale was appalled by the way in which the externals of religion were accepted without any real understanding of their inner significance. He described how 'thousands, while the priest pattereth St John's gospel in Latin over their heads ... cross so much as their heels and the very soles of their feet, and they believe that if it be done in the time that he readeth the gospel (and else not) that there shall no mischance happen to them that day'. Tyndale felt that the only hope of bringing back the masses to a true understanding of the fundamentals of religion lay in giving them a vernacular Bible, and he asked permission from the Bishop of London to undertake the task of translation. When this was refused, he went into voluntary exile in Germany, where by 1524 he had completed work on the New Testament. Copies were soon circulating in England and were among the 'Lutheran books' that were burned in public bonfires, such as that at St Paul's which took place in Wolsey's presence in 1526.

In 1528 Tyndale, who was by then in The Netherlands, published *The Obedience of a Christian Man*, in which he declared that even the rule of a bad king was preferable to anarchy, for 'it is better to suffer one tyrant than many'. For obvious reasons this argument appealed to Henry VIII, and in 1531 he made repeated attempts to persuade Tyndale to return to England and work for him, despite the fact that he did not approve of his theological views. When Cromwell sent an agent to Antwerp to urge Tyndale to come out openly in support of the King, Tyndale demanded that Henry should first agree to promote the cause of reform in England by licensing a version of the Bible in the vernacular. Henry was not at that time prepared to accept such a condition, and angrily broke off negotiations. A few years later Tyndale's hiding-place was betrayed and he was burned at Antwerp as a heretic. He died praying God to open the King of England's eyes.

Tyndale had taken holy orders early in his career, but unlike so many of the other leading reformers, both in England and elsewhere, he had never been a monk or friar. The very fact that the most assertive proponents of reform came from within the Church shows that it was far from dormant. It was the failure on the part of the ecclesiastical hierarchy to harness this critical spirit and use it to bring about fundamental change that drove advocates of reform into more radical and unorthodox positions. Not all these advocates were clerics. Lawyers were also prominent – as Sir Thomas More had demonstrated, though he subordinated his genuine commitment to reform to the need to preserve and defend the Church once he perceived it to be in danger. Simon Fish was another of the lawyer-reformers. At Oxford, and subsequently at Gray's Inn, he formed part of a circle of young men who denounced the wealth and corruption of the Church. Fearing that Wolsey might take action against him, Fish fled to The Netherlands, where he made the acquaintance of Tyndale. Indeed, after his return to London he acted as an agent for the sale of Tyndale's New Testament. This brought him to the attention of the authorities and he thought it best to take refuge once again in The Netherlands. There, in 1528, he composed *A Supplication for the Beggars*, a rumbustious and hard-hitting attack upon clerical wealth and vices. Fish's beggars complain that their livelihood is being taken away from them by 'strong, puissant and counterfeit holy and idle beggars' and point out to the King, to whom the *Supplication* is addressed, that the bishops and clergy who make up these 'ravenous wolves ... have gotten into their hands more than the third part of your realm'. Henry saw a copy of the *Supplication*, possibly recommended to him by Anne Boleyn, and apparently found it amusing. Fish's suggestion that Henry should reform the Church by statute may also have made some impression.

Another prominent reformer–lawyer was Christopher St German, who had studied at Oxford and the Inner Temple. In 1532 he published his *Treatise concerning the division between the spiritualty and the temporalty*, which had the distinction of eliciting two rebuttals from Sir Thomas More. St German's language was measured, quite unlike Simon Fish's, but his knowledge of history and the law made his criticism of the Church highly effective. He was not content merely to attack abuses such as benefit of clergy. He denied that the clergy had any right to rule themselves or make their own laws. Like Cromwell, he believed that clergy and laity, since they were all the King's subjects, should be united under the crown and subject to statute and the common law.

Cromwell's sympathetic attitude towards the advocates of reform in the Church, taken in conjunction with the King's willingness to use them for his own purposes even if he did not always approve of their theological opinions, made the Henrician Reformation more radical than it appeared to be on the surface and drove it beyond a mere transfer of the *Potestas Jurisdictionis*. In 1535, to take one example, royal Injunctions were issued to the universities abolishing courses and degrees in canon law. They also laid down that all divinity lectures should be 'according to the true sense of the scriptures' and that all students should study the Bible for themselves. In July 1536 a meeting of Convocation, presided over by Cromwell as the King's Vicegerent, produced the *Ten Articles*, defining the doctrinal position of the Church of England. On the sacraments of the altar, baptism and penance the *Articles* were relatively orthodox, but no mention was made of the other four sacraments – confirmation, ordination, matrimony and extreme unction. The real presence was affirmed, and in general the *Ten Articles* were moderate in tone, but they showed clear signs of Lutheran influence. This was an indication of the way in which the Henrician Church was being driven towards doctrinal reform, even though the King himself was reluctant to go down this path.

Reformers of all shades of opinion agreed on the need for an English version of the Bible. There was nothing particularly revolutionary about such a demand. In many other countries the scriptures had been translated into the vernacular with the blessing of the ecclesiastical hierarchy, but in England, because of the Lollards, the bishops associated vernacular Bibles with heresy, and the emergence of a new heresy in the shape of Lutheranism hardened their attitude. As late as 1530 they were still taking a stand against authorising any translation of the scriptures. This was short-sighted since it meant that the work was undertaken by men of more radical persuasion. Among the earliest complete versions of the Bible in English to be published in Henry VIII's reign was that by Miles Coverdale – a friend of Robert Barnes, whom he had come to know when they were both Augustinian friars, and also of Thomas Cromwell. When Coverdale's Bible was printed, in October 1535, Cromwell showed a copy to the King, who passed it on to Gardiner and other bishops to examine. When they reluctantly conceded that there appeared to be no heresies in it, Henry declared 'Then in God's name let it go abroad among our people.' His will was transformed into law by Cromwell's Injunctions, issued in October 1538, which required 'one book of the whole Bible of the largest volume in English' to be set up in a convenient place in every parish church, where the people might go and read it.

Although all parish priests were now obliged to provide their flock with an English Bible, no authorised version had been produced, because of the opposition of the bishops. Cromwell therefore ordered Coverdale to provide a truly authentic English translation of the scriptures. This, the *Great Bible*, was eventually published in 1539, and a royal proclamation of May 1541 ordered that it should be made available in accordance with the Injunctions of 1538, unless another version had already been purchased. Cranmer wrote the preface to Coverdale's new edition, and it is often referred to, somewhat unfairly, as 'Cranmer's Bible', but the archbishop's enthusiasm was not shared by many of his episcopal colleagues.

The language of the *Great Bible* was too radical for their tastes, and they opposed its further distribution. As a consequence, no more copies were printed in Henry's reign after 1541. Not until the radicals came to power with Edward VI did it once again become available.

The Dissolution of the monasteries I: The smaller houses

The heyday of the religious orders in England had been during the thirteenth and fourteenth centuries, when their studies in divinity and canon law made the monks the intellectual leaders of Christendom. But the fifteenth century saw the spread of the new learning, with its emphasis on classics and philosophy, and although this did not affect England until the reign of Henry VII, English education had meanwhile shifted its emphasis towards the study of common and civil law. Assumptions about the nature of the Christian life were also changing. The place of the Church was held to be in the world, though not of it, and there was no longer widespread and instinctive sympathy for the monastic ideal. This was shown by the falling number of novices and the drying-up of benefactions. Colet, for instance, who inherited a fortune from his father, used it, like a good humanist, to found St Paul's School rather than endow a monastery. Indeed, the declining appeal of the monastic life is indicated by the fact that both Colet and More, who in an earlier period might well have entered the cloister, preferred to live their godly life in the secular world.

Humanist condemnation of the monks was given expression by Erasmus, himself a former Augustinian canon. In his *Enchiridion* of 1504 he asked: 'Do we not see members of the most austere monastic orders maintaining that the essence of perfection lies in ceremonies or in a fixed quantity of psalmody or in manual labour? And if you come to close quarters with these men and question them on spiritual matters you will scarcely find one who does not walk according to the flesh.' Simon Fish, who was far less temperate in his language, included abbots and priors among his 'ravenous wolves' and singled out for condemnation 'the infinite number of begging friars'. All these 'sturdy loobies', he declared, should be turned 'abroad in the world, to ... get their living with their labour in the sweat of their faces'. Fish's *Supplication*, written as it was in a racy, Rabelaisian style, became a popular hit. Sir Thomas More was so alarmed by its impact that he tried to counter it with a *Supplication of Souls*, reminding his readers that the prayers of the monks shortened the time which the souls of the dead had to spend in purgatory as penance for the sins committed during their life on earth. But by now the doctrine of purgatory was itself coming under attack. Luther rejected it out of hand, and although English reformers were divided on the issue, opinion gradually moved in the same direction.

The monasteries in early Tudor England had still not recovered from the Black Death (1348), which had halved the number of inmates and wiped out some communities altogether. Monastic revenues were now so large, relative to the number of monks, that they encouraged worldliness, and the reports of episcopal inspectors or 'visitors' in the century preceding the Dissolution show how standards were declining. In many places, though not all, feasting had replaced fasting, dress was extravagant, and divine service was neglected. Sometimes there were more serious faults. In 1514, to take one example, the Prior of Walsingham was a notoriously dissolute and evil liver, who dressed flamboyantly, kept his own jester, and paid for his luxurious lifestyle by appropriating the priory's plate and jewels. Visitations could be an effective way of maintaining standards, but much depended on the quality of the visitor, and even when these were conscientious the punishments they prescribed were either inadequate or not enforced. In 1491 a deacon of Langley Priory cut off another monk's hand in a violent brawl. He was sentenced by the visitor to imprisonment in another house, but six years later he was back at Langley, this time as sub-prior.

Richard Redman, abbot of the Premonstratensian house at Shap, in Westmorland, from 1458 to 1505 is an example of a conscientious visitor. He toured the twenty-nine abbeys under his care at regular intervals of three or four years, taking about three months for each circuit, and did not hesitate to reprove and punish those monks whose manner of living was not consonant with their calling. Another outstanding figure was Marmaduke Huby, abbot of the magnificent Cistercian house at Fountains in Yorkshire from 1494 until 1526. Huby is remembered, among other things, as the builder of the great tower at Fountains, and this serves as a reminder that during what turned out to be the last decades of their existence the monasteries were actively engaged in construction. Building took place even throughout the turbulent years of the late fifteenth century and continued right up to the eve of the Dissolution. Peterborough's fan vaulting dates from the period immediately preceding Wolsey's fall, and the last prior of Bath had not yet brought to completion the splendid work set in train by his predecessors when the royal commissioners arrived to close down his house.

Some monasteries ran a school for the poor children of the neighbour-hood, at the same time as they trained the sons of the rich in the abbot's household. The education of the monks themselves, however, was fre-quently neglected, particularly the obligation to send them to university. This had serious consequences at a time when the number of learned laymen was increasing, for it left the monks unprepared for the intellectual challenges presented by the Renaissance. Many monasteries possessed fine libraries, but they had not been kept up to date, and although one of the traditional tasks of monks had been to copy manuscripts, this particular activity was increasingly irrelevant in the age of the printed book. A high standard of musical performance was maintained in some big houses where the numbers permitted it. Robert Fayrfax was director of music at the abbey of St Albans during the first twenty years of the sixteenth century; and at Waltham Abbey, in the years immediately preceding the dissolution, the organist and choirmaster was Thomas Tallis. But these examples were not typical. In the majority of houses there were either too few monks to provide trained choirs, or a lack of enthusiasm for choral activities.

If standards of music were generally declining, the same is true of other monastic functions such as charity and hospitality. Almsgiving may have averaged the stipulated one-tenth of monastic income, but it was indis-criminate and did little to relieve the problem of poverty in the outside world. Hospitality was still offered on a generous scale, particularly in the north of England where inns were rare, but this had the effect of disrupting the rhythm of monastic life by bringing lay people into the cloister – unless, as at Glastonbury and St Albans, separate guest houses were constructed for the reception of visitors.

On the eve of the Dissolution there were some eight hundred and fifty monastic houses in England and Wales, including friaries, but they varied enormously in size and wealth. Westminster and Glastonbury had rev-enues approaching £4,000 a year, but some of the smaller houses were heavily in debt. The total annual income of all the houses was about £165,000, derived mainly from their property, which amounted to a quarter of all the cultivated land in the kingdom. Much of this money was spent on estate maintenance and the provision of divine service, but it still seems an excessive amount for the eleven thousand monks and nuns – all of them dedicated to poverty – who benefited from it. In fact the wealth of the monasteries was a weakness, for it opened them to criticism from moralists and reformers at the same time as it promoted envy from those with more worldly motives.

The leaders of the Church saw the need for reform. In 1528 Wolsey secured a papal bull authorising him to close houses with fewer than a dozen monks and transfer their inmates to larger establishments, which were in general better run. A year later he was given power to use monastic wealth and property for the creation of a number of new dioceses, in order to align the secular Church more closely with the distribution of population, which had changed markedly over the centuries. Indeed, had Wolsey not fallen from power at this juncture the English Church might well have taken the wind out of its critics' sails by putting into effect a major programme of reform and renewal.

Wolsey's departure from the scene did not mean that the idea of reform was abandoned. The power vacuum was filled to some extent by magnates such as the Dukes of Norfolk and Suffolk, who had resented the way in which Wolsey and his fellow bishops lorded it over them, and were determined to cut the Church down to size. This group was behind a petition presented to Parliament in 1529, calling for the King to be authorised to reform ecclesiastical abuses, and for the Church to be partially disendowed. At about the same time, Henry showed his sympathy with such an approach by telling the imperial ambassador that there was much with which he agreed in Luther's criticisms and that in his view the clergy had no authority other than that which came from their power to absolve the laity from their sins. While Henry probably shared the anti-prelatical attitude of the great magnates, he was also influenced by Anne Boleyn's support for the evangelicals, who wanted to put the Bible, rather than papal pronouncements, canon law, and the traditions of the Church, at the heart of the Christian message.

Nothing came of the 1529 petition, but in 1534 a similar but more detailed plan was drawn up which, if it had been carried into effect, would have transferred most of the Church's wealth to the crown. Bishops and abbots were to be paid a fixed stipend, and the surplus funds were to be used for defence purposes and the maintenance of the King's government. This was doubtless a genuine reform proposal, but its timing was determined by Henry's parlous financial situation. He had consumed his inheritance in war, and by breaking with Rome he had opened himself up to possible military intervention by major catholic powers such as France and Spain. The primacy of financial considerations at this juncture is indicated by the fact that when Parliament not only voted the King a subsidy but also gave him the right to collect First Fruits, i.e., annates – or the first year's income of newly-appointed bishops – and also to levy an annual tax of 10 per cent on clerical incomes, the more radical reform proposals were dropped. Nevertheless, as money remained in short supply the need to find additional sources of revenue became acute, and Cromwell's attention therefore turned to the monasteries. It had long been acknowledged that the smaller houses were the weakest links in the system, and by proposing to dissolve them Cromwell could hope to be seen as a reformer at the same time as he secured additional resources for his royal master.

There were a number of precedents for dissolution. Edward III and Henry V had suppressed alien priories as well as one or two English houses, but the first systematic dissolution was carried out by Wolsey. Between the cardinal's fall and the final dissolution, no major suppressions took place, but in 1532 the Augustinian canons at Aldgate in London declared themselves bankrupt and handed over their house and remaining possessions to the King. This was the first instance in which monastic property was secularised, rather than being used for religious or charitable purposes.

Thomas Cromwell had been Wolsey's agent in dissolving the twenty-nine monasteries which were suppressed in order to fund the building of Cardinal College and the smaller institution at Ipswich. He was therefore well fitted for the task that now confronted him. The commissioners whom he sent round the country to collect the oaths prescribed by the Acts of Succession and Supremacy met little opposition, and by the end of 1535 all except a handful of monks had rejected the Pope and accepted that the King was head of the English Church. Only the Observant Franciscans – the favourite order of Henry VII – held out until the King suppressed their seven houses in 1534, while the Bridgettines of Syon only gave in after their head, Richard Reynolds, had been executed. Opposition also came from members of the London Charterhouse, following the example set by their prior, John Houghton. He and two other Carthusian priests refused to take the oath of supremacy and were therefore executed. Altogether, eighteen Carthusians suffered death before the London Charterhouse was effectively subdued.

In 1535 Cromwell ordered an assessment to be made of the wealth of the Church. This was a remarkable administrative feat. Commissioners were appointed for each diocese to record all sources of ecclesiastical revenue, and their returns were incorporated into the *Valor Ecclesiasticus*, Cromwell's Domesday Book of the Tudor Church. The same year also saw a general visitation of the monasteries by Cromwell's agents. Four of these – Richard Layton, Thomas Legh, John Tregonwell and John London – had been trained in civil law, while the fifth, John ap Rice, was a common lawyer. The main purpose of their enquiries was to gather as many examples as they could of superstitious practices and immoral conduct. Where mild measures were of no avail they resorted to threats, and ap Rice described Legh at work: 'At Burton he behaved very insolently ... At Bradstock and elsewhere he made no less ruffling with the heads than he did at Burton ... Wherever he comes he handles the fathers very roughly.'

The Cromwellian visitors travelled at great speed. When Legh and Layton were working in northern England they inspected some 120 monasteries in a mere two months, covering more than a thousand miles in the process. Although their reports were not entirely condemnatory, and the gossip they retailed was already common knowledge, they were hardly dispassionate observers. Yet even if they had wished to make a careful and thorough enquiry into the true state of the houses they visited they did not have the time to do so, in spite of the fact that some areas, including the whole of Lincolnshire, appear to have been left out of their visitation.

Cromwell, who probably believed that purgatory did not exist, could see little purpose in monasteries. As for Henry, he resented the fact that many monasteries were daughter houses of one or other of the continental orders, and therefore not within his direct control. Moreover, the highest level of opposition to his policy had come from some of the regular clergy and might well continue to do so unless they were forcibly silenced. The reports from Cromwell's visitors, though incomplete, had given the minister sufficient lurid evidence to shock the Commons, and even those members who wanted the monastic life to continue may have reasoned that if the King was allowed to take the smaller houses he would leave the remainder alone. In 1536, therefore, Parliament passed the Act for the Dissolution of the Smaller Monasteries, authorising the suppression of all houses whose incomes fell below the level of £200 a year, on the grounds that 'manifest sin, vicious, carnal and abominable living' was 'daily used and committed' by their inmates. These conditions were contrasted with those said to prevail in the 'great solemn monasteries of this realm, wherein, thanks be to God, religion is right well kept and observed'.

The act affected some four hundred monastic houses. To enforce it, new commissions were appointed in each county, consisting of a mixture of local gentry and officials. Their reports make a revealing contrast to those of Layton, Legh and their colleagues, for they show that there was no ill feeling towards the religious and their houses on the part of the local population and that many of the charges made by Cromwell's agents were either unfounded or based upon (deliberate?) misunderstanding.

Some indication of the extent to which the monks and nuns were committed to the enclosed life is given by comparing the number of those who, when they were offered the opportunity, left the cloister, with those who opted for transfer to one of the larger houses. The figures do not give the whole picture, since some of the regulars abandoned their houses after the initial visit of Cromwell's agents, without waiting for the dissolution commissioners to arrive. In eight Norfolk monasteries, for example, numbers had dropped during this period from sixty-nine to thirty-two. But Cromwell can hardly have believed that the vast majority of religious were itching to quit the cloister, since he made provision for about a quarter of the smaller houses to remain open in order to contain the monks and nuns who wished to continue the cloistered life but could not immediately be transferred.

The proportion of those opting to leave varied from county to county, but for England and Wales as a whole the figure was 40 per cent for men and 10 per cent for women. This striking difference between the sexes does not necessarily mean that nuns were more committed to the monastic life than their male counterparts. It has to be remembered that ex-nuns would not fit in easily to the secular world. There was no question of allowing either monks or nuns to marry, even though they were no longer enclosed, for the vow of chastity which they had taken was regarded as permanently binding, but whereas former monks could hope to find employment as secular priests, former nuns had little chance of gainful employment. In the world outside the cloister walls, women were expected to marry and bear children. There was no obvious place in it for ex-nuns, lacking means and vowed to chastity.

Henry VIII was not as yet committed to the dissolution of all religious houses. He actually refounded the priory at Bisham, in Berkshire, which had voluntarily surrendered to the royal commissioners, renaming it 'King Henry's new monastery of the Holy Trinity', and he also placed some Premonstratensian canonesses in the buildings of the Cistercian priory at Stixwould in Lincolnshire to pray for the good estate of himself and his third wife, Jane Seymour, who died in October 1537 after giving birth to a son. It seems highly likely that these 'new' foundations were Henry's formal acknowledgement of God's blessing in granting him the male heir he had been longing for.

The Dissolution of the monasteries II: The Pilgrimage of Grace and the larger houses

Because the dissolution of the monasteries could be seen as part of a reform process which went back to Wolsey and beyond, it aroused little opposition, certainly in southern England. Things were different in the north, where the monasteries were valued, among other things, for the hospitality they provided in bleak upland areas. In 1536 three commissions were at work in Lincolnshire. One was occupied with closing down the smaller monasteries in the county, another with assessing and collecting the parliamentary subsidy voted in 1534, and the third with enquiring into the state of life of the parish clergy. The rumour spread that this third commission was preparing the way for the confiscation of all Church plate, and that in future no man's property would be safe. A popular rising broke out at Louth, where the magnificent spire, erected some twenty years earlier, attested the commitment of the townsfolk to their parish church. Soon the whole of Lincolnshire was up in arms, and the gentry promptly asserted their control over the movement, which might otherwise have got dangerously out of hand. The rising lasted little more than a week, for when the news came that the Earl of Shrewsbury was advancing towards the county with a royal army, the gentry preferred to capitulate rather than fight. The common people felt betrayed, but having entrusted their cause to their social superiors, they had no choice but to go along with them.

While an uneasy calm was settling on Lincolnshire a far more serious revolt broke out in Yorkshire, which acquired the name of 'The Pilgrimage of Grace'. It was led by Robert Aske, a lawyer and an idealist who gave to the movement most of its spiritual quality, yet it was essentially an uprising of the common people protesting against economic and social changes, many of them imposed by a remote government based in London, which were adversely affecting their lives. What gave the disparate elements some sense of cohesion was their demand that the traditional Church should be restored and maintained. They took as their symbol the five wounds of Christ, and as they marched they sang:

'Christ crucified
For thy wounds wide
Us commons guide
Which pilgrims be.'

Aske confirmed the religious priorities of the rebels when he addressed them at York in October 1536. They had embarked on their pilgrimage, he told them, 'for the preservation of Christ's Church, of this realm of England, the King our sovereign lord [and] the nobility and commons of the same' from the evil men who spoke on Henry's behalf. Aske wanted the monasteries to be restored and preserved, especially in northern

England, where they 'gave great alms to poor men and laudably served God', and although the uprising lasted only a few months the Pilgrims secured the reopening of sixteen of the fifty-five houses suppressed by Henry's commissioners in the north.

The ordinary people who joined in the Pilgrimage of Grace did so largely as a protest against agrarian changes, such as higher entry fines and enclosures, which were threatening their livelihood. But they shared with gentlemen and clerics the fear that increasing governmental activity in the north would erode the autonomy of the region and subvert the established order. Any change was bound to be for the worse, from their point of view. In general, the aristocracy took no part in the rising. The Earl of Northumberland, who was head of the powerful Percy family, held ostentatiously aloof, although in practice he did nothing to obstruct the rebels. His brothers became Pilgrims – in part, no doubt, because the earl had made known his intention to bequeath his vast wealth and estates not to them but to Henry – as did a number of Percy tenants, but this did not turn the Pilgrimage into a 'feudal' revolt against the King. The Earl of Westmorland and Lord Dacre, who were the other major figures in the north, kept a low profile. As for the Earl of Derby, the leading landowner in Lancashire, he came out firmly on the King's side.

Two nobles who were caught up in the rebellion were Lord Darcy and Lord Hussey. They were careful to give the impression that they had been dragged into it against their will, but in fact both men had good reasons for opposing Henry's policies. They were conservatives in religion as well as their social attitude; they despised and distrusted upstarts such as Cromwell; and they were part of the loose-knit 'Aragonese faction' which supported Queen Catherine and her daughter Mary. A year or so before the Pilgrimage, Darcy had discussed with the imperial ambassador the possibility of organising a popular rising to force Henry to change course, and there is evidence to suggest that a number of simultaneous disturbances had been planned for 1536. Aske was taken aback when he heard that Lincolnshire had erupted prematurely, and although he went ahead and the revolt spread to Westmorland, Cumberland and Lancashire it never became the general rising that he and his associates had hoped and planned for.

The Pilgrimage was not an attempted revolution, for there was never any suggestion that the King should be deposed and a new government established. It was more in the tradition of the protest of 1525 which had persuaded Henry to abandon the Amicable Grant. The Pilgrims probably assumed that the King shared many of their aims and only needed assurance of their support to free himself from the evil counsellors who were using him for their own sinister purposes. Unfortunately for the Pilgrims this was a misreading of Henry's attitude. Moreover, their success in attracting widespread support confronted him with a challenge to his authority that he would not tolerate.

Henry began his counter measures by summoning the Duke of Norfolk (formerly the Earl of Surrey) out of the sulky semi-retirement into which Cromwell's rise to power had driven him. Norfolk was the King's best soldier, and the Pilgrims could hardly complain about his 'villein blood', nor accuse his colleague, the Earl of Shrewsbury, of low birth. Norfolk assembled a large army, but his men were not all reliable and he was short of money. He therefore made offers to the Pilgrims that amounted to free pardon, but he showed his true mind when he asked the King 'to take in good part whatsoever promise I shall make to the rebels ... for surely I shall observe no part thereof'.

At a meeting with Darcy and other leaders of the rising, held at Doncaster in late October 1536, Norfolk agreed that two gentlemen should be sent to Windsor, to carry the rebels' demands to Henry personally, and that in the meantime there should be a truce. Henry returned an uncompromising reply, complaining that he found the aims of the Pilgrims 'general, dark and obscure', but Norfolk persuaded him to buy time by allowing further negotiations to take place. In preparation for these the Pilgrims held an assembly at Pontefract in early December at which they drew up a list of articles that covered the entire spectrum of discontent. Religious demands included the suppression of heretical books, especially those written by Luther, Wycliffe, Bucer, Tyndale and Barnes; the acknowledgement of the spiritual headship of the Pope; the restoration of the suppressed monasteries; and the statutory confirmation of the traditional rights of the Church, including sanctuary and benefit of clergy.

A number of articles dealt with economic complaints and called for limits to be placed on entry fines and for the enforcement of existing laws against enclosure. Gentry grievances were reflected in the demand that the Statute of Uses (*see* pp. 95–6) should be repealed, and there were also articles which dealt with political issues – among them the legitimation of Princess Mary and the infliction of 'condign punishment' upon 'the Lord Cromwell, the Lord Chancellor and Sir Richard Rich ... as the subverters of the good laws of the realm'. Sir Thomas Audley, the Lord Chancellor, and Sir Richard Rich, Chancellor of the newly established Court of Augmentations which managed the income from dissolved monasteries, were both protégés of Cromwell, and he was obviously the man the

Pilgrims most wanted to get rid of. One article which more than any other showed the deep unease felt, not only in the north, about the apparent arbitrariness of the King's government, demanded that 'the common laws may have place, as was used in the beginning of your grace's reign'.

When Aske and his fellow leaders presented these articles to Norfolk at Doncaster during the first week of December 1536 the Duke offered them, on the King's behalf, a general pardon if they laid down their arms, and promised them that a Parliament would be called at York to consider their grievances. Aske was prepared to accept this offer. He was convinced of the King's fundamental integrity and goodwill: indeed, the whole rationale of the Pilgrimage was based upon this assumption. When he made his report to the thousands of Pilgrims assembled at Pontefract, Aske met with a hostile response, but he urged them to disperse peacefully and rely upon the King to do what was right. He then returned to Doncaster with other gentry leaders of the rising, and there, in the presence of the Duke of Norfolk, they solemnly tore off the token of the five wounds of Christ which they had adopted as the symbol of the Pilgrimage and declared that in future they would 'wear no badge nor sign but the badge of our sovereign lord'.

The Pilgrims had won a significant victory, but many of the rank and file felt they had been betrayed, and further revolts erupted in the north. Whether or not these were prompted by the King, they gave him the excuse to order savage reprisals. In the opening weeks of 1537 Norfolk was busy carrying out the King's orders to 'cause such dreadful execution upon a good number of the inhabitants, hanging them on trees, quartering them, and setting the quarters in every town, as shall be a fearful warning'. Pilgrims who had taken no part in the post-December uprisings were in general exempt from these proceedings, but some hundred and fifty of the common people who continued their revolt were put to death. When the fifty or so Lincolnshire rebels who were also executed are added to the number, the total comes to about two hundred. Among the handful of Pilgrims who were called to account, even though they had laid down their arms after the December agreement, was Aske. He was arrested, sent to London, tried in May 1537 on charges of treason, and returned to York to be executed in June.

Although the Pilgrimage and the associated revolts had been crushed, the rebels achieved some of their aims. The apparent drift away from catholic orthodoxy was brought to an abrupt halt by the Act of Six Articles of 1539, and a year later Thomas Cromwell, the rebels' *bête noire*, was dismissed from office and sent to the block. But if the rebels had hoped to put an end to the dissolution of the monasteries, they in fact achieved quite the opposite. While the great Yorkshire abbeys had stood aloof from the Pilgrimage, the Cistercians in Cumberland and Lancashire had given it their support. The dispossessed monks of Sawley, for instance, had returned to their house, not far from Clitheroe, which they turned into a propaganda centre for the Pilgrims. Henry showed his anger by directing that the 'abbot and certain of the chief of the monks' should be 'hanged upon long pieces of timber, or otherwise, out of the steeple', and it was clear that the suppressed houses would not be restored. The greater monasteries continued in existence, but subject to increasing pressure. As early as April 1537 the abbey of Furness, in Lancashire, gave itself into the King's hands, and in the winter of that year Cromwell sent out commissioners to encourage similar surrenders. They reinforced the lesson of the Pilgrimage by striking hard at any sign of resistance. Robert Hobbes, Abbot of Woburn in Bedfordshire, was charged with treason for denying the royal supremacy, condemned, and hanged outside his own monastery. The heads of three other large houses, at Colchester, Reading and Glastonbury, were also executed.

The process of 'voluntary' surrender accelerated during 1538, particularly after June, when the Emperor and the King of France held a meeting at Nice to discuss joint action against the heretic King of England, prompting Henry to embark upon another round of expensive defence works. The end came in April 1540 when the last surviving monastery, the abbey of Waltham, in Essex, surrendered to the commissioners. With the respect for legal forms that characterised the Henrician Reformation, a second Dissolution Act was passed in 1539, confirming all the surrenders that had taken place or were forthcoming, and formally vesting the surrendered property in the crown.

With the great abbeys fell the friaries, though these houses were so poor that they yielded little in the way of moveable property. The increasing radicalism of the government was shown by the concurrent attack upon the famous English shrines. Early in 1538 the tomb of St Edmund at Bury was dismantled. It was followed by the Precious Blood of Hailes, in Norfolk, and finally the magnificent shrine of St Thomas at Canterbury, the focus for pilgrimages from Chaucer's day and beyond, was destroyed. No matter the source, the treatment of confiscated property was the same. Moveables such as plate and jewels were sent up to the royal treasury. What was left was sold on the spot, including the lead from the roofs which was stripped off and melted down. In some places, such as Lewes, in Sussex, and Chertsey, in Surrey, the buildings were razed to the ground, while elsewhere they were left to casual plunder. The work of destruction was done so efficiently at Sempringham Priory, in Lincolnshire – the mother house of the Gilbertines, the only native English order – that the conventual buildings, with their great tower and twin cloisters, completely disappeared and even the site was lost to memory until rediscovered by archaeologists in the mid-twentieth century. Part of the wall of the priory church of Our Lady of Walsingham, in Norfolk, survives, but is only a faint reminder of what had been one of the most famous pilgrimage places in England, visited by Henry III and Edward I, who richly endowed it, as well as by Henry VIII, in his younger and more orthodox days. An Elizabethan poet gave voice to the sense of loss and pain that the destruction of the religious houses caused to many of Henry's subjects:

'*Level, level with the ground*
The towers do lie,
Which with their golden glittering tops
Pierced once to the sky
Where were gates no gates are now,
The ways unknown
Where the press of peers did pass
While her fame far was blown …
Sin is where Our Lady sat,
Heaven turnèd is to hell.
Satan sits where our Lord did sway.
Walsingham, O, farewell.'

Where a monastic site was sold, the new owner was in theory bound to dismantle the church and community buildings, but this was an expensive business and the non-habitable parts were often pillaged for re-usable material, as at Fountains, then left to picturesque decay. A few were adapted for other purposes, as at Malmesbury, where a rich clothier set up a factory in the former abbey. In other cases, such as Bolton, Pershore and Worcester, the local parish bought the monastic church to use as its own. A significant number of private houses were created out of the monasteries. The palatial home of the Duke of Bedford is appropriately named Woburn Abbey, while Syon Park, on the western outskirts of London, which belongs to the Duke of Northumberland, incorporates the cloister of the Bridgettine nunnery that formerly stood there. Many smaller houses bear the name of abbey, priory or grange, which denotes their monastic origin and bears witness to one of the greatest land redistributions in English history.

A handful of monasteries, the lucky ones, survived intact as cathedral churches, either for established sees, such as Canterbury, Durham and Winchester, or for the six new ones – Westminster, Gloucester, Peterborough, Chester, Oxford and Bristol – that Henry created. In these cases many of the personnel were retained along with their houses: at Winchester all except four of the monks became secular canons of the cathedral, while at Durham about half the community stayed on. The six new sees were tokens of a much greater reorganisation of the English Church that was envisaged but never put into effect. Many of the existing dioceses were too big, and Henry had himself sketched out a plan for thirteen new ones, making use of monastic buildings and land. Indeed, it was the assumption that the wealth of the monasteries would be used for more relevant purposes that had persuaded opponents of Henry's policies reluctantly to go along with them. In the event, however, plans for major reform were watered down. Fear of invasion and heavy expenditure on defence works meant that financial considerations overrode all others.

The dispossessed monks and nuns were provided for by the government. Heads of houses were well treated, particularly if they fully co-operated with the dissolution commissioners and did not attempt to sell off moveable property or parcels of land in private deals. About thirty ex-abbots became bishops in the years immediately following the Dissolution, and the rest received pensions which were at worst adequate and at best generous. Some abbots and priors retired to country homes, perhaps near their former house or even on part of its property, and not a few married – at the risk of being called to account later on for breaking their vow of chastity – and added their names to the roll of county families.

The monks also were given pensions, except for those who had abandoned the cloister before the surrender of the larger houses began. These pensions, averaging £5. 10s [£5.5] per annum, were enough to exist on in 1539, but they took no account of inflation. By 1550 £5 was the wage of an unskilled labourer, and monks who had no resources other than their pension must have been in dire straits. They did not, in any case, receive the full amount. In most years the King called on the clergy to pay a tenth of their income by way of taxation, and this was deducted from pensions as well. A further fourpence [1.67p] was payable to the Court of Augmentations, to cover administrative costs. Overall, pensioners lost between 10 and 12 per cent of their nominal income, and this was particularly hard on nuns, whose pensions were far smaller than those of their male colleagues. A list of 1573 shows a number of aged nuns who were living together losing four shillings [20p] out of their meagre individual pensions of £2 6s 8d [£2.33]. Pensions were apparently paid regularly down to the death of the last claimant, early in the seventeenth century, except for brief periods, as in 1552–3, when the government was virtually bankrupt.

If Henry had held on to all the monastic property seized by the crown, he would have had no more financial problems, but his commitment to war made land sales inevitable, and by the time he died well over half the former monastic estates had been alienated. Nevertheless, he was now, as Cromwell had promised, the richest King England had ever known, and had good reason to be satisfied with the results of the Dissolution. So did those many subjects who bought monastic properties from the crown, for they had enlarged their estates and enhanced their prestige. Only the eleven thousand former monks and nuns had cause to be dissatisfied with the lightning bolt that had flung them out of the cloister into a harsh and indifferent world.

CHAPTER FOUR

Henry VIII's government

Court, Council and Chamber

Because the government of England was monarchical, the royal court was normally the centre of power. This ceased to be the case during the twenty years of Wolsey's predominance, when policy was made – or at least initiated – at Hampton Court rather than Greenwich Palace. In 1529, however, Henry dismissed the cardinal from office and took over the direction of affairs himself. He signalled the new dispensation by seizing York Place, Wolsey's London residence, and transforming it into the royal palace of Whitehall. From now on this was the seat of government, and never again did Henry have cause to complain that he was ill attended. In the immediate post-Wolsey period he sought advice initially from older men such as the Dukes of Norfolk and Suffolk, who wanted to see the magnates return to their traditional role as the King's principal counsellors. But Henry was determined to preserve his independence, and he could do this more easily if he worked through an efficient administrator who was totally dependent upon him. Such a man was Thomas Cromwell, and his rapid rise to power put an end to the magnates' hopes of turning the clock back.

Cromwell, like his old master, Wolsey, was committed to administrative reform, and in June 1534 he jotted down a note 'To remember the King for the establishment of the Council.' However, he had little time for such projects, since he was fully occupied in enforcing the royal supremacy and dissolving the smaller monasteries. These tasks took him well into 1536, the year when the Henrician regime was threatened by its most serious revolt, the Pilgrimage of Grace. Cromwell and his associates, who were denounced by the Pilgrims as upstarts and heretics, moved out of the limelight, leaving vacant a space that was filled by their conservative rivals.

It was these men, still under the leadership of Norfolk and Suffolk, who formed a smaller, more select body to deal with the revolt. During the autumn of 1536 a Privy Council of nineteen nobles and office-holders came into existence and operated as the channel through which the King's will was transmitted both to the Pilgrims and to his field commanders. After the defeat of the rebellion Cromwell moved back centre stage, but only briefly, for in June 1540 he fell from power. The Privy Council now resumed control and acquired its own clerk and minute book. As for those former members of the Council – the majority – who did not form part of the new body, they were allowed to retain the title of 'Councillor' as long as they lived, but they played no further part in central government.

The Privy Council was dominated by nobles – old ones such as Norfolk, the eighth duke, and John de Vere, sixteenth Earl of Oxford, as well as newly created peers, like Suffolk, whom Henry made a duke in 1514, and Sir John Russell, another of the King's favourites, who became a baron in 1539. The clerical group, headed by Archbishop Cranmer, included Cuthbert Tunstall and Richard Sampson, bishops respectively of Durham and Chichester. The royal household was represented by its treasurer, Sir William Fitzwilliam, its controller, Sir William Paulet, and its vice-chamberlain, Sir William Kingston. The Privy Council, unlike its amorphous predecessor, was a tight-knit body whose members were expected to reside at court, ready at all times to give their advice to the King. Their closeness to the sovereign was indicated by the fact that the Council chamber, which had hitherto been on the periphery of the private apartments, now moved into them. At Whitehall it opened off the gallery that led to the King's bedchamber.

Although the Privy Council consisted of Henry's principal advisers, he was rarely if ever present at its meetings. When Cromwell was at the height of his power he and the King decided matters of policy between them, leaving the Council to deal with routine administration. The Council was delicately balanced between autonomy and dependence. It could act on its own initiative, but it was immediately responsive to the King's will. This dual personality was demonstrated towards the end of the reign, when the conservatives among the Councillors tried to topple Cranmer. Henry allowed them to go ahead, but he warned the archbishop what was afoot and instructed him to 'appeal ... to our person and give to them this ring ... which ring they well know that I use it to none other purpose but to call matters from the Council unto mine own hands'.

While the Privy Council served the King politically, the Privy Chamber served him personally. The grooms of the Privy Chamber had originally carried out menial functions, but Wolsey's refashioning of this department in 1519 led to a rise in the status of its personnel. They tended to be men of good family, often wealthy in their own right, and as their numbers expanded a hierarchical structure developed. By 1526 the staff of the Privy Chamber, headed by the Groom of the Stool, amounted to nearly thirty persons, but Wolsey's Eltham Ordinances cut this figure by half. Within a few years, however, many of those expelled by Wolsey had made their way back, and as 'the King's great matter' rendered the cardinal's position increasingly unstable various factions emerged within the Privy Chamber. Wolsey's supporters constituted one group. Another revolved around George Boleyn, Viscount Rochester, and used its influence in favour of his sister, Anne Boleyn. Because Anne was known to favour the evangelicals, who were committed to significant reform of the Church, the Boleyn faction was opposed by religious conservatives, known as the 'Aragonese', since they upheld the position of the Queen, Catherine of Aragon. However, factions were not clearly defined groups with a stable identity and a coherent programme. They could unite for short-term tactical purposes – as the Boleyn and Aragonese factions did to get rid of Wolsey – but would then pull apart.

The Privy Chamber was not a self-contained body, nor was it immune to outside influences. About half a dozen of its members were also Privy Councillors or held some other office in the royal administration, and the entire body was an integral part of the larger world known as the court. Factionalism was a court phenomenon after Wolsey's fall and was not confined to the Privy Chamber. Thomas Cromwell made use of it for his own ends, and although not a member of the Privy Chamber himself, he used the former followers of Wolsey to buttress his position there. He also cooperated with the Boleyn faction, because his evangelical approach to religion was close to that of Anne, who was now Queen. This alliance worked well as long as Anne retained her hold on the King's affections, but the marriage quickly turned sour, and by the end of 1535 Henry was falling under the spell of Jane Seymour, one of Anne's ladies-in-waiting.

This development did not pose an immediate threat to Anne, who was pregnant, but the emotional stress it caused may have contributed to her miscarriage in January 1536. Anne's failure to produce a male heir confirmed Henry in his suspicion that his marriage was not acceptable to God, and the Aragonese faction now saw their opportunity to stage a comeback. Cromwell was determined that Anne's downfall should not be accompanied by his own. He therefore threw in his lot with the Aragonese and master-minded the strategy which led not only to Anne's destruction but also to that of her close associates and relatives. However, once Anne had been removed from the scene Cromwell turned the tables on the Aragonese faction by accusing its leaders of treasonable involvement in the Pilgrimage of Grace. This was a charge they could not easily deny, since there was a good deal of evidence to support it, and a number of them were sent to the block. The removal of the Aragonese from the Privy Chamber, following on as it did from the expulsion of the Boleyn faction, left that department half empty, and Cromwell took the opportunity to fill it with young men who shared his twin commitments to evangelical reform in the Church and administrative efficiency in the state. They remained there even after his abrupt removal from the scene in June 1540 and spent the remainder of Henry's reign trying to restrict the growing influence of the conservatives.

The secretaryship

The increasing political importance of the King's secretary was a phenomenon common to all the major states of sixteenth-century Europe, for this was the age of kings, and as they extended their power by cutting down or taking over feudal, ecclesiastical and corporate franchises their servants became figures of public significance. In the late Yorkist and early Tudor period the King's secretary, as his name implies, looked after the monarch's correspondence, had custody of the seal known as the signet, and was frequently employed on diplomatic missions. The development of the King's secretary into a Secretary of State came under Thomas Cromwell, for he was quick to spot the advantages of an office that had an indeterminate range of authority and therefore indefinite possibilities of expansion. Cromwell replaced Stephen Gardiner as Henry's secretary in April 1534, and from then on he dealt with every aspect of the King's government.

The increasing prestige of the secretaryship was shown by its change of status. The Eltham Ordinances of 1526 placed the secretary, for purposes of precedence, in the fourth group of officials, but by 1539 he came immediately after the great officers of state. Cromwell gave up the secretaryship in 1540 and it was then shared between two of his protégés, Ralph Sadler and Thomas Wriothesley. Division of the office was made necessary by the continuing importance of the household element in Tudor government. Sadler was a gentleman of the Privy Chamber, which meant that he had easy access to the King and could smooth out any difficulties or misunderstandings that might impede communications between Henry and Cromwell. Wriothesley acted as Cromwell's secretary, but also kept in close touch with Sadler, in order to facilitate the business of government. In other words, although the secretaryship had blossomed under Cromwell into a major department, it had not become bureaucratised or 'moved out of court' in the way that older offices such as Chancery and the Exchequer had done. Furthermore, while Cromwell gave up the secretaryship he retained many of its most important functions. This was because there were no fixed boundaries between offices that were located within the royal household. In the last resort everything depended upon personalities and personal relations, and also, of course, upon the volatile temperament of the linchpin of the whole system – namely, Henry himself.

Financial administration

Under Henry VII the royal Chamber had become a national treasury, eclipsing the Exchequer. This increased the prestige and importance of the Treasurer of the Chamber but left him little time to carry out his original function of keeping control over the King's private finances. His role was filled by the Groom of the Stool, and after the young Henry VIII appointed his friend and jousting companion, William Compton, to this post the Privy Chamber handled increasing amounts of money, which were paid to it direct, by-passing the Chamber. Wolsey, who distrusted Compton, put an end to this practice, but the Chamber now had to make provision for the very large sums that Henry demanded for his own use. In 1514 it paid Compton £17,500 and in 1515 £18,000. Thereafter the amounts varied between £2,000 and £7,000. This meant that by the time of Wolsey's fall the Chamber was dealing with routine expenditure, while the Groom of the Stool, who was *ipso facto* keeper of the King's privy purse, was responsible for running Henry's household and also meeting the cost of implementing his policies at home and abroad. Regular Chamber payments to the Groom continued until 1529, but thereafter a reversal of roles took place, since it was the privy purse which now began funding the Chamber. One of the main sources of revenue for the privy purse was the French pension, which brought in over £20,000 a year, but it also drew money from the privy coffers or private treasuries that Henry VII had set up and Henry VIII maintained – particularly the one which was located in Whitehall Palace. These reserves were swelled by the seizure of Wolsey's extensive properties and cash resources, but they were not boundless. In fact, the crown was living off its capital and thereby seriously undermining its financial health.

The privy purse might have followed the example of the Chamber by developing into a national treasury, had it not been for the rise of Cromwell. In April 1532 he was appointed Master of the Jewels, a relatively minor post but one which allowed him to gain control over the privy coffers. The Privy Chamber now reverted to its primary function of supervising the King's private expenditure, while Cromwell assumed the task of managing the national finances. He did this with his customary efficiency, but he came up against the problem that the royal revenue was inadequate. Henry's total annual income may have been as little as £80–90,000, well below that of his father. The crown needed re-financing, and it was Cromwell who identified the way in which to do this – by dissolving the monasteries and transferring their property and goods to the King. By the late 1530s the financial crisis was over and Henry was richer than he had ever been.

In 1536 a new financial institution, 'The Court of the Augmentations of the Revenues of the King's Crown', was established by statute to deal with all aspects of the transfer of monastic estates, including sales and collection of rents. However, there was no reversion to overall Exchequer control. Financial administration remained a household activity, so much so that a quarter to a half of all revenues were stashed away in the King's private treasuries. Henry kept some of the money for his immediate purposes in the secret jewel house at Whitehall, while the rest was handed over to Sir Anthony Denny, the Chief Gentleman of the Privy Chamber – in effect, deputy Groom of the Stool. Between 1542 and 1546 Denny received close on a quarter of a million pounds, including more than £120,000 paid in a single year. Henry's obsession with money was not that of a miser. His main objective was still what it had been at the beginning of his reign – to emulate Henry V by leading his army into France and asserting his claim to the French throne. The various revenue departments were allowed to spend what they needed for their own purposes on an annual basis. The surplus was then transferred to the King's coffers, to be used as a war chest.

The Court of Augmentations did not handle the ecclesiastical revenues, since these came under the purview of the Court of First Fruits and Tenths, set up by act of Parliament in 1540, after the fall of Cromwell. Another act, which Cromwell had sponsored, created the Court of Wards. Henry VII, determined to enforce his feudal right to guardianship of minors' estates, had appointed a Master of Wards in 1503, who quickly built up an organisation covering the whole country, but not until 1540 was it given a formal structure. Cromwell's strategy of placing the principal financial departments on a statutory basis may have been intended to give the system greater coherence, but if this was his aim he fell from power before it was fully achieved. In the event, the new courts were swallowed up by the revived Exchequer early in the reign of Mary I, and only Wards and the Duchy of Lancaster preserved their independence.

Better administration, as well as the confiscation of monastic property, sent the King's revenues soaring. Monastic lands brought in £140,000 a year from rents and sales, while First Fruits and clerical subsidies added a further £70,000. In effect, the King's income had been trebled, and although expenditure increased – the cost of the royal household, for instance, rose from £25,000 to £45,000 a year, while the Pilgrimage of Grace cost £50,000 to put down – Henry was living well within his resources. The royal revenue was now adequate for everything except prolonged war.

The government of the localities

The key figures in every shire were the Justices of the Peace, drawn from leading gentry families. In their judicial capacity they dealt with the entire gamut of crime, passing serious cases on to the assize judges but punishing lesser offenders themselves, either at Quarter Sessions or the increasingly frequent smaller meetings that were eventually to be formalised as Petty Sessions. In addition to acting as judges, Justices had a wide range of administrative duties, for it was their task to ensure that the infrastructure of the shire was adequately maintained and that inferior officers – such as constables and bailiffs – carried out their duties properly.

While the importance of Justices of the Peace had increased in the two centuries preceding Henry VIII's accession, that of the sheriff had declined. The sheriff had originally been the crown's principal officer within the shire, but now his duties were confined to serving writs, empanelling juries, and carrying out sentences. He was also responsible for organising parliamentary elections and for raising forces within his county when disorder threatened. Sheriffs were appointed by the crown, as were Justices of the Peace, who were named in the annual 'commission of the peace'. But these formal links between the central government and the localities were supplemented by broader and in some ways more significant informal ones. Ever since Richard II's reign the crown had been concerned to build up its own local affinities, and Henry VIII continued this policy. A wide range of offices, both at court and in the countryside, was at the King's disposal, and he used these to single men out for distinction, thereby giving them a sense of obligation which strengthened their commitment to the crown. Many a local landowner who gloried in the title of knight or esquire of the body made only occasional appearances at court – if, indeed, he went there at all – but he was nevertheless the King's special servant. Conversely, Privy Councillors and Gentlemen of the Privy Chamber were nominated as Justices of the Peace. They rarely if ever took their place on the bench, but the presence of their names in the commission of the peace symbolised the close links between the court and the country.

In an age of poor communications, the effectiveness of central government diminished with distance. The northern and Welsh borderlands were two areas where its authority needed reinforcement, and an embryonic conciliar structure already existed. As soon as the Pilgrimage of Grace had been suppressed, Cromwell established a new council for northern England. Unlike its predecessors it was not responsible for managing the royal estates in the region; it was concerned exclusively with administration and justice. The head of the council was the Lord President – the first being Cuthbert Tunstall, Bishop of Durham – and his colleagues included three or four peers, half a dozen knights and a similar number of common and civil lawyers. The council had full jurisdiction in civil and criminal matters within the area north of the river Humber, which gave it greater authority in this respect than the Privy Council. Cromwell's reconstruction of 1537 marks the formal establishment of the Council of the North, and from that date until its abolition a century later it had an unbroken existence. Throughout the Tudor and early Stuart period it was the principal instrument by which the crown enforced order in this remote part of the realm. It did its work well, but the north remained a potential tinderbox, as was shown in Elizabeth's reign, when revolt broke out there.

The Council in the Marches of Wales was a direct descendant of the body that had administered Edward IV's marcher lands. Wolsey revived and reconstituted this council in 1525, but it was not very effective in putting down disorder. Cromwell therefore set up a formal council similar to that later developed in the north, and he had his friend, Rowland Lee, Bishop of Coventry, appointed its first president. One of the problems confronting the King's government in this region was the existence of marcher lordships outside the boundaries of the Principality of Wales. Cromwell dealt with this in 1536 by the so-called Act of Union that divided the whole of Wales into twelve shires, each with its own body of Justices of the Peace and also with the right to elect a member to the House of Commons. This reorganisation did not, however, eliminate the need for a prerogative court, and the Council of Wales, now established at Ludlow, supervised the administration of justice throughout the border region. However, difficulties arose as the union began to take effect, for the common-law jurisdiction of the Council of Wales came up against that of the four Courts of Great Session created by statute in 1543, and quarrels between them undermined the authority of the council and blunted its effectiveness.

A third, short-lived, council was set up in the west of England in the 1530s. Henry had earlier relied on Henry Courtenay, Earl of Devon, to watch over this distant part of his dominions. But Courtenay, whom he created Marquis of Exeter in 1525, was Edward IV's grandson and therefore a potential claimant to the throne. His descent made him suspect, particularly in the aftermath of the Pilgrimage of Grace, and he was accused of treason, tried and executed in December 1538. This left the west country leaderless, at a time when it was threatened by a French invasion. Henry therefore transferred the substantial properties of the dissolved abbey of Tavistock to his close companion, Sir John Russell, whom he made a baron. He also appointed him president of the newly-established Council of the West. In other words, Henry was applying two distinct remedies to the problems of the west country – one quasi-feudal, the other bureaucratic. In the event it was the quasi-feudal solution which proved durable. The Council of the West lacked direction, especially after Russell's appointment to the demanding post of Lord Admiral in 1540. It also cost a great deal of money for which the King could find better use, and soon after it had been established it lost its greatest patron when Cromwell fell from power. Its shadowy existence was therefore terminated and Henry relied on Russell, with his network of informal contacts, to govern the west country.

Parliament

The sixteenth century is often regarded as a golden age for Parliament, the period when it established itself beyond challenge as an integral part of the English political system. Yet in some respects this is an illusion, for Tudor monarchs summoned Parliament less frequently than had been the case in the period 1327–1485. During that stretch of 158 years there had only been 42 without a Parliament. However, in the 94 years from 1509 to 1593 there were 43 in which no parliamentary session took place. Moreover, there were gaps of up to eight years between meetings both prior to 1529 and after 1558. Henry VIII's reign after the fall of Wolsey, and those of Edward VI and Mary I, were exceptions, in that Parliament met virtually every year. As a consequence of this concentrated activity the nature of Parliament changed, along with that of statute. Sir Thomas Smith, writing in 1565, declared that 'the most high and absolute power of the realm of England consisteth in the Parliament'. This body 'abrogateth old laws, maketh new, giveth orders for things past and for things here-after to be followed'. Its supreme authority derived from the fact that 'every Englishman is intended to be there present, either in person or by procuration ... and the consent of the Parliament is taken to be every man's consent'.

The transformation of Parliament's position could hardly have been foreseen prior to 1529, for under Wolsey relations between it and the gov-ernment reached their nadir. The Commons, in particular, resented being called on to pay for wars of which they did not approve, and adopted what Wolsey obviously regarded as a negative attitude. Had he stayed longer in office it is likely that Parliament would have met less and less frequently. Cromwell's accession to power changed this situation, for it was he who persuaded Henry that the break with Rome could not be carried out solely by exercise of the royal prerogative. On the contrary, the King's policies would be easier to implement if he gained the co-operation of his subjects and demonstrated to the world that he had done so. He would also need to give his actions the sanction of law. For both these purposes Parliament was the most effective instrument, as Cromwell realised. He was the first English statesman to exploit the enormous potentiality of statute, and the number of acts of Parliament passed during his period in office shows the use he made of it. The twenty-two years from Henry VII's death to Cromwell's accession to power had seen the passing of almost one-hundred and fifty public acts, but in the brief eight years of Cromwell's ascendancy there were two hundred. The corresponding figure for Elizabeth I's long reign of forty-five years was under eighty.

When Henry VIII came to the throne the House of Lords consisted, in almost equal proportions, of temporal and spiritual peers, but the Dissolution of the Monasteries removed some thirty abbots, and although Henry created five new bishoprics, this still left the spiritual lords in a per-manent minority. The House of Commons had less than three hundred members at the outset of the Tudor period, but a significant expansion took place after 1529. The enfranchisement of Cheshire and Wales accounted for the greater part of this increase, but Henry also created four-teen new parliamentary boroughs – a practice that was extended by his successors.

From 1529 onwards Parliament had such an important part to play in the implementation of Henry's policies that the government exerted all the influence it could bring to bear on both Houses. The Lords presented few problems, for the spiritual peers had long been among the crown's most loyal servants, while many of the lay ones were Tudor creations or were conscious of the need to retain the King's goodwill. As far as the Commons were concerned, some boroughs were effectively in the crown's gift, and approved men could simply be nominated as their members. Others were under the influence of landed families which were usually amenable to royal pressure. Shire elections were more difficult to influence, but the outcome of these was generally determined by local interests rather than national issues. In Henry VIII's reign as in Henry VII's more and more of the King's Councillors were securing seats in the Commons. Indeed, the Pilgrims complained in 1536 that 'the old custom was that none of the King's servants should be of the Commons House, yet most of the [present] House were the King's servants'.

Cromwell paid particular attention to elections. In 1534 he was busy revising the list of members of the Commons so that he could get a clear picture of what changes had taken place and decide who to recommend as candidates at by-elections. Two years later he intervened directly at Canterbury, putting forward the names of two men for election as burgesses. The mayor replied that the election had already taken place by the time the minister's letter arrived, but Cromwell wrote back immediately, ordering him to 'proceed to a new [election] and elect those other, according to the tenor of the former letters to you directed for that purpose, without failing to do so, as the King's trust and expectation is in you, and as ye intend to avoid his highness's displeasure, at your peril'. The two government-sponsored candidates were duly elected.

There are no other examples of forceful intervention on the Canterbury pattern, and it may be that Cromwell was reacting to a particular situation in which sectional interests were trying to rig the election. In 1539, however, he was once again very active and informed the King that 'I and other of your grace's Council here do study and employ ourselves daily . . . to bring all those things so to pass that your majesty had never more tractable Parliament.' Cromwell was not concerned to build up his own group within the Commons – indeed, it was this very Parliament that passed an act of attainder against him – but to use all the means at his disposal to ensure that the Lower House would co-operate with the King at a time when the complications of foreign and religious policy made the situation extremely delicate. In this aim he was entirely successful.

Cromwell's active interest was not confined to elections. Even before Parliament met he would be busy jotting down memoranda and drawing up draft bills, and he had a staff of expert advisers, including the judges, working for him. His frequent corrections and insertions in the draft bills show his infinite capacity for taking pains, and it was this laborious attention to detail that normally produced a smooth passage for legislation.

The House of Commons was not just a rubber stamp for validating government measures. Members had a right, which they cherished, to discuss the proposals that were put before them, and at the beginning of every session the Speaker made a formal claim for freedom of speech, though its limits were not clearly defined. In 1523 Sir Thomas More, in his petition as Speaker, requested that members should have 'licence and pardon freely, without doubt of your dreadful displeasure, every man to discharge his conscience, and boldly, in everything incident among, declare his advice'. On the face of it, More was asking that there should be no limits to the Commons' freedom of discussion, but his speech, which is the first of its type to be recorded, was probably no more than a variation on a standard theme. More, like all those he spoke for, took it for granted that the initiation of policy belonged to the King. What he wanted Henry to grant was permission for members to speak their minds freely on the issues he and his ministers presented to them. Henry's reply is not recorded, but since he had nothing to fear from the Commons there is no reason to assume it was other than conventional.

Henry was remarkably tolerant of those members who declined to toe the line. The Commons' proceedings were not publicly reported, and there are no private journals surviving from this period – quite possibly because none were written. As long as the outcome of a debate was satisfactory the discussion which preceded it had little significance, and Henry could therefore make light of isolated protests. In 1529, for example, John Petite, one of the London members, objected to a bill cancelling the King's debts on the grounds that while he was content to accept this himself he could not speak for his neighbours, who might suffer from it. Henry took no offence, but it was reported that he used occasionally to 'ask in Parliament time, in his weighty affairs, if Petite were of his side?' Similarly, when Sir George Throckmorton opposed the Act of Appeals, the King merely sent for him, made him a speech justifying royal policy, and allowed him to return to the Commons.

Henry enjoyed posing as 'bluff King Hal', but members of both Houses of Parliament knew that his joviality could swiftly turn to anger and that he would not tolerate any fundamental dissent from the policies to which he was, at any given moment, committed. There were a number of occasions, however, on which members displayed a stubborn independence of judgement. In 1532 the Bill in Conditional Restraint of Annates ran into a barrage of criticism in the Lords, despite the fact that Henry himself was sometimes present. Although the bill was eventually passed, the bishops came out unanimously against it. There was opposition, too, in the Commons, and the bill only completed its passage after the Speaker had taken the unusual step of ordering a division.

In 1533 the Commons insisted on amending the Act in Restraint of Appeals before allowing it to pass, and in the following year they refused to accept the original version of the act making spoken words treason. One of the most striking examples of Parliament asserting its own judgement is the rough ride given to the Proclamations Act of 1539. It may be that the first draft of this would have authorised the enforcement of royal proclamations in common-law courts, and that amendments by the Lords removed this provision and substituted a special tribunal. Both Houses of Parliament consisted primarily of landholders and lawyers who were determined that the protection which the common law provided for them should not be diminished or undermined. This attitude presumably accounts for the insertion of a clause in the act forbidding proclamations to interfere with the life or property of the King's subjects. The same concern for property doubtless prompted the Lords, in 1534, to make drastic alterations to a Cromwellian measure designed to put a brake on enclosing (see p. 142) by restricting the right of landlords to buy up farms. Two years later Cromwell's comprehensive scheme of poor relief was given such a savage mauling by the Commons that he had to withdraw it and substitute a far milder measure.

There was one issue, however, on which the government would not yield, and this concerned 'uses'. In theory, land held from the crown *in capite* (i.e. 'in chief', on a feudal tenure) could not be freely bequeathed. On the death of the landholder it reverted to the King, who regranted it to the heir only after the appropriate feudal incidents – relief, wardship, marriage, livery – had been applied. To avoid these exactions many tenants-in-chief made over all or part of their land to a third person to hold in trust for their heir. This meant that the nominal owner of the land was not in fact its user, and since this device, the 'use', could be repeated indefinitely, a large amount of land was passing out of the King's suzerainty. Henry was determined to halt this development, which was diminishing his feudal revenue, and in 1529 he persuaded the Lords that the 'use' should apply only to part of a tenant's estate, while the remainder would be liable to the customary incidents. However, a bill along these lines was thrown out by the Commons in 1532, presumably because members, whose estates were usually smaller than those of the Lords, hoped to continue evading feudal dues altogether. Henry did not conceal his anger. He told a delegation from the Commons that 'I have sent you a bill concerning wards and primer seisin, in the which things I am greatly wronged. Wherefore I have offered you reason as I think – yea, and so thinketh all the lords, for they have set their hands to the book . . . I assure you, if you will not take some reasonable end now when it is offered, I will search out the extremity of the law, and then will I not offer you so much again.'

Henry was as good as his word. At this stage he might have been prepared to accept feudal dues on only half or even a third of the land held *in capite* and allow the rest to pass to the heir without any obligation. But once the Commons blocked the way to compromise, he brought a case at law and secured a verdict from the judges that land held on a feudal tenure could not be legitimately bequeathed. The Commons realised that their stand had led to the opposite effect from what they intended, but their repentance came too late. The Statute of Uses, which passed both Houses in 1536, acknowledged the legality of 'uses' but laid down that the user of the land was to be treated as if he was the owner. In other words, while a 'use' could be set up, it would not free the estate in question from its liability to feudal incidents.

The Statute of Uses is important in many ways. It showed how vigorously the King's will could be opposed in Parliament, particularly when it came up against property-rights. It also demonstrated the power of the King, since he could, in the last resort, compel landholders to accept a measure from which they stood to lose. But head-on confrontations of this sort were rare, for both the King and the landholders understood the need for agreement if the social system from which they all benefited was not to be undermined. The explosion over the Amicable Grant in 1525 had shown the King how dangerous it was to press his demands beyond a certain point, and he learnt a similar lesson from the fact that the Statute of Uses contributed to gentry dissatisfaction which found expression in the Pilgrimage of Grace. After the suppression of the Pilgrimage the crown significantly modified its position over 'uses'. In 1540 the Statute of Wills confirmed the legal right of all those who held *in capite* – an increasing number because of the creation of new feudal tenures on former monastic properties – to bequeath two-thirds of their land. Feudal obligations were to be enforced only on the remaining portion.

Because he had no reason to fear any increase in the Commons' power, Henry encouraged the Lower House to assert its privileges. As a result of

Strode's case in 1512 it was enacted that members of Parliament, being judges of the highest court in the land, should not be subject to suits in lesser courts while Parliament was sitting. Until Henry's reign, if a member of the Commons was arrested during a session the Speaker applied to the Lord Chancellor for a writ ordering his release, but as the Commons became more self-confident they began flexing their muscles. In 1542, following the arrest for debt of George Ferrers, member for Plymouth, the House sent its Sergeant-at-Arms to fetch him from the London jail where he was lodged. The jailer and the sheriffs of London refused to recognise this unprecedented demand, and when the Sergeant tried to free Ferrers a brawl ensued in which his mace was broken.

The Commons promptly complained to the Lords, who declared that the City authorities were guilty of contempt. The Lord Chancellor offered to issue a writ for the immediate release of Ferrers, but the Commons were 'in a clear opinion that all commandments and other act of proceeding from the nether House were to be done and executed by their Sergeant without writ, only by show of his mace, which was his warrant'. The sheriffs of London were by this time aware that they had behaved imprudently – albeit legally – and when the Sergeant appeared before them again they handed Ferrers over. The Commons made this precedent doubly binding by ordering the imprisonment of the sheriffs and other officers who had initially defied their authority.

When Henry heard of these proceedings he consulted the judges before summoning a delegation of the Commons to present themselves before him. Once they were assembled, he commended the way in which the Lower House had asserted its privileges. However, there is room for doubt about whether he totally approved of their behaviour, for shortly afterwards he took the unusual step of knighting the sheriff who had been principally involved. He also dissolved Parliament before it passed a bill giving statutory confirmation to the Commons' privileges. In public, however, Henry expressed his satisfaction and developed his favourite theme that he and his people formed an organic unity. This had not always been the case, even in theory, for the fifteenth-century assumption was that the King was outside Parliament, separate from the three estates of lords spiritual, lords temporal and Commons who represented his subjects. Henry's view, however, was quite different, as he made plain: 'We be informed by our judges that we at no time stand so highly in our estate royal as in the time of Parliament, wherein we as head and you as members are conjoined and knit together into one body politic, so as whatsoever offence or injury during that time is offered to the meanest member of the

House is to be judged as done against our person and the whole court of Parliament.'

The increasing importance of Parliament under Henry VIII is shown by the greater length of sessions. In the twenty-four years of Henry VII's reign there were seven Parliaments, which met for a total of some twenty-five weeks, but the last eighteen years of Henry VIII's reign saw five Parliaments, whose sessions occupied one hundred and thirty six weeks. Longer sessions were accompanied by an extension of Parliament's competence, for it demonstrated during the period after 1529 that there was nothing, not even matters spiritual, which fell outside its range.

Cromwell's fall and the closing years of Henry VIII's reign

In January 1536 Catherine of Aragon died, and in the following May Anne Boleyn was executed. Henry was now free to make an unchallengeable marriage, and as his affections had long been focused on Jane Seymour, she soon became his third wife. Jane fulfilled the King's hopes by giving him a boy prince, Edward, in October 1537, but she died shortly afterwards. Now that Henry had a legitimate male heir and was no longer saddled with a doubtful marriage the original reasons for breaking with Rome had disappeared. But the links with the papacy, so swiftly cut, could not be swiftly reforged, and in any case Henry had no desire to reforge them . He had long insisted that his imperial authority freed him from any overlord, and he was genuinely convinced that he bore the sole responsibility for the wellbeing of his subjects in the spiritual as well as the secular sphere.

The relative ease with which Henry had broken away from Rome owed much to the weakness of the papacy at that time. Wolsey's fall was a demonstration of this weakness, for although he embodied the authority of the Pope, Clement VII never lifted a finger to save him. Moreover, in the following years, when the Church in England was under attack, it received no help or even guidance from Rome. Given these circumstances it is hardly surprising that many committed churchmen saw Henry as their saviour and willingly accepted the royal supremacy. However, in the mid-1530s the decline of the papacy was halted and the slow process of reform began.

The turning-point came in 1534 with the election as Pope of Paul III, for he appointed a commission to consider what was wrong with the Church and to suggest measures to restore it to health. Among the commissioners was the Englishman Reginald Pole, whose household in Italy was a centre of opposition to Henry's policies. Pole maintained close links with his homeland, where a conservative reaction was slowly gathering way. It was given added strength by the infiltration into England of 'sacramentarian' beliefs propagated by radical reformers such as the Zwinglians and anabaptists who, although they differed sharply among themselves, agreed in denying the existence of a real presence in the consecrated sacraments. In 1538 Pole was busy touring the major states of Europe as the Pope's representative, trying to persuade their rulers to sink their differences and combine against Henry. A clear lead was given in the closing months of that year by Paul III, when he formally excommunicated Henry VIII and declared him deposed. Henry reacted by imprisoning and executing most of Pole's relatives, including his aged mother, the Countess of Salisbury. He also increased the size of the royal navy, ordered the shire levies to be mustered, and began building artillery forts along the south coast. All these measures entailed heavy expenditure and could not have been carried through without the transfer of monastic goods and property to the crown.

It was Cromwell, of course, who had initiated this transfer and carried it through to completion, and his position seemed more secure than ever. Yet the religious conservatives remained unreconciled, and their hopes began to rise when, in September 1538, one of their leaders, Stephen Gardiner, Bishop of Winchester, returned to England from a three-year spell as ambassador to France. Another indication that the situation was becoming more favourable to them was Henry's decision to break off contact with the German Lutherans, who had been trying to form an alliance with England. The King decided the negotiations were getting nowhere, and as the international situation became more and more threatening he needed to secure the support of the conservatives at home in order to demonstrate his orthodoxy abroad. Despite the break with Rome, Henry remained committed to the catholic faith, even though his interpretation of it was highly idiosyncratic, and on Good Friday 1539 he observed the traditional ceremony of 'creeping to the cross', which evangelicals regarded as gross superstition.

Henry was drawing closer to the Duke of Norfolk, who was Gardiner's principal secular ally, and authorised him, in May 1539, to put a number of propositions before the House of Lords. These became the nucleus of the Act of Six Articles which defined the doctrines of the autonomous Church of England in an unambiguously catholic manner. The first article dealt with transubstantiation and declared 'that in the most blessed sacrament of the altar, by the strength and efficacy of Christ's mighty word, it being spoken by the priest, is present really, under the form of bread and wine, the natural body and blood of our Saviour, Jesus Christ'. The second denied the necessity of communion in two kinds, since both body and blood were present in each sacrament. The third and fourth insisted on clerical celibacy and the binding nature of vows of chastity, while the last two articles affirmed the validity of private masses and auricular confession. The act, in effect, announced the end of the reform movement in England. Diversity in opinions, which Henry found so distasteful, was now outlawed, and anyone denying the articles risked being burnt as a heretic.

Henry was present in the House of Lords on at least a couple of occasions to ensure the acceptance of the proposed legislation, and by June 1539 the Act of Six Articles had completed its passage through Parliament. Its significance was all too obvious. The French ambassador summed up the general opinion when he said that Henry had 'taken up again all the old opinions and constitutions, excepting only papal obedience and destruction of abbeys and churches of which he has taken the revenue'. While the clause on transubstantiation attracted much attention, both at home and abroad, it was broadly acceptable to a wide range of reformist opinion. A mere two years before, Cranmer had told one of the leading continental reformers that he had no desire 'to weaken or undermine a doctrine so well rooted', and both he and Cromwell denounced the sacramentarians on the grounds that they denied transubstantiation. The reformers were more worried by the other articles, but what gave them most concern was the fact that Henry had clearly thrown in his lot with the conservatives.

Cromwell's position, while undoubtedly weakened, was far from desperate. He still hoped to forge an alliance between Henry and the German Lutherans, and was negotiating for a marriage between Henry and Anne, the sister of the German Duke of Cleves. The duke himself was catholic, but his brother-in-law was the Elector of Saxony, one of the greatest of Lutheran princes. In October 1539 agreement was reached upon the articles of marriage, and in the following January Anne of Cleves became the King's fourth wife. This was a triumph for Cromwell's diplomacy but it had dangerous implications, for it tied the King to a particular course in foreign policy at a time when he needed to keep his options open. Even worse, it bound Henry to a woman he found physically repugnant.

However, there were no outward signs that Henry was dissatisfied with his principal minister. On the contrary, the King appointed him to the prestigious office of Lord Great Chamberlain and subsequently, in April

1540, created him Earl of Essex. But Henry was falling under the spell of Catherine Howard, and this posed a threat to Cromwell, for she was a niece of the Duke of Norfolk and therefore closely linked to the conservative faction. The conservatives, as distinct from the catholic reactionaries, were content to accept the royal supremacy, either because they believed in it or because they thought it imprudent to challenge Henry on so sensitive an issue. Nevertheless, they opposed any further drift away from traditional catholic positions, and they hated Cromwell, whom they regarded, correctly, as a proponent of continuing religious reform.

The conservatives' best chance of eliminating Cromwell lay in persuading Henry that the minister was a sacramentarian, out to destroy the entire structure of the English Church. Henry was by nature suspicious, and age had not mellowed him. Furthermore, his aversion to Anne of Cleves and his passion for Catherine Howard made him more inclined to believe what the conservatives were telling him. He made up his mind in a typically abrupt manner and on 10 June 1540 ordered Cromwell's arrest. A bill of attainder was pushed through Parliament, condemning the fallen minister as a heretic and traitor. The charges were flimsy but Cromwell could make no effective rebuttal, for, as he told Henry in one of a number of letters in which he pleaded for mercy, 'I have meddled in so many matters under your highness that I am not able to answer them all.' He was kept alive for six weeks so that he could give evidence in the divorce action which Henry brought against Anne of Cleves, and then, on 28 July, was led to the scaffold.

Henry did not appoint another chief minister to replace Cromwell. Gardiner and Norfolk were his principal advisers, but the King took most of the major decisions himself, while routine work was dealt with, as always, by the Privy Council. Cromwell's fall left the conservatives exultant, but the situation remained extremely volatile, as was shown only two days after Cromwell's execution when Robert Barnes and two other so-called 'sacramentaries' were burned as heretics, while three 'papists' were hanged as traitors. Along with Cromwell, Henry rid himself of the Cleves marriage. It was declared invalid in July 1540, and on the day Cromwell was executed the King celebrated his wedding to Catherine Howard. Henry now seemed to have attained happiness, but in late 1541 Cranmer wrote him a letter giving details of accusations of sexual misconduct made against the Queen. Henry appointed a commission to enquire into these charges, and when this declared them to be well founded his anger overflowed. All those accused of complicity with Catherine were executed in late 1541, and in February of the following year the Queen herself was condemned by act of attainder and shortly afterwards beheaded. Not until July 1543 did Henry remarry. He chose as his sixth and last wife Catherine Parr, a good-natured widow of reformist inclinations in religion, who succeeded where so many others had failed in maintaining her hold on the King's affections until his death.

The closing years of the reign were marked by the struggle between reformist and conservative factions at court and in the country at large. Henry's main concern was, as always, to hold in check the bitter controversies over religion that threatened the peace of his realm. In 1537 he had authorised Cromwell, acting as his Vicegerent, to summon a synod for the purpose of defining the Church of England's position on matters of faith. The discussions were heated and exhausting, and Hugh Latimer – at that time Bishop of Worcester and a prominent advocate of reform – recorded his opinion that 'it is a troublous thing to agree upon a doctrine in things of such controversy, with judgements of such diversity, every man (I trust) meaning well, and yet not all meaning one way'. The outcome was *The Institution of a Christian Man*, a relatively moderate document which Henry licensed for three years. However, he would not give it his explicit approval, and it was therefore called *The Bishops' Book*. This remained in force until 1543, when a revision was undertaken. The conservatives were now in a stronger position and their influence was reflected in the new statement drawn up by Convocation, known initially as *The Necessary Doctrine and Erudition of any Christian Man*. This was not without Lutheran traces, but on the key issues of predestination and justification by faith alone it took an orthodox position very close to Henry's own. For this reason it came to be known as *The King's Book*.

A further triumph for the conservatives followed shortly afterwards, in May 1543, when Parliament passed an act condemning all unauthorised translations of the Bible and forbidding persons below the status of gentleman to study it at home, even in the approved version. This was a reversal of one of the major achievements of Cromwell and Cranmer, but the archbishop made no protest. His silence may have been prompted in part by prudence, for the conservative tide was still running strongly, as was shown in June, when a number of Windsor men who had fallen foul of the Act of Six Articles were executed for heresy. In the following month Henry chose Stephen Gardiner to officiate at the wedding between himself and Catherine Parr. Cranmer was not even invited to the ceremony.

The conservatives were already preparing their campaign to topple the archbishop and had warned the King that he was not sound on religion. But Cranmer's quiet acceptance of the reverses suffered by the reformers

helped persuade Henry that the charges against him were without substance. One evening in September, when the King was enjoying a boat trip
on the Thames, with accompanying music, he met Cranmer near the archbishop's palace at Lambeth and greeted him with the announcement that
'I know now who is the greatest heretic in Kent!' Cranmer had been
accused of tolerating heresy within his diocese, but the King left him free
to hold his own enquiry, and this exonerated him. Later that year, probably in November 1543, the conservatives on the Privy Council asked the
King's permission to present heresy charges against the archbishop. Henry
assented, but warned Cranmer what was afoot and told him not to assume
he would get a fair hearing: 'Do you not think that if they have you once
in prison, three or four false knaves will be soon procured to witness
against you and to condemn you, which else now being at your liberty dare
not once open their lips or appear before your face?' Cranmer's enemies
were confident of victory, but their hopes were dashed when the archbishop insisted that the matter should be referred to the King, and showed
them Henry's ring as his warrant (*see* p. 84). The whole episode bore out
Cromwell's earlier comment to his friend that 'you were born in a happy
hour, I suppose . . . for do or say what you will, the King will always well
take it at your hand. And I must needs confess that in some things I have
complained of you unto his majesty, but all in vain, for he will never give
credit against you, whatsoever is laid to your charge'.

Cranmer had not only survived the attacks directed against him; he had
also strengthened his position and his influence with the King. One of the
first consequences of this was the publication of an English *Litany* in May
1544. This work can be regarded as the fulfilment of Erasmus's programme for encouraging vernacular worship, but it went beyond Erasmus,
in the direction of the radical reformers, by suppressing prayers to the
saints.

Religion was not Henry's only, or even major, preoccupation during
1544, for that year saw a renewal of the war against France which had
been on hold ever since the downfall of Wolsey. It may be that Henry's
assault on France was determined in part by his concern for the succession.
A year earlier he had concluded the Treaty of Greenwich with James V of
Scotland, whereby James's only child, Mary, would in due course marry
Henry's son, Prince Edward, thereby uniting the two kingdoms. The
French, who were the traditional allies of Scotland, stood to lose by this
development, and in December 1543 they persuaded the Scots to annul the
treaty. Henry showed his anger by sending his brother-in-law, Edward
Seymour, Earl of Hertford, on a marauding expedition across the border

in spring 1544, and his decision to invade France in the summer of that year could well have been part of the same reaction. But it is also possible that, with old age drawing on and the wealth of the monasteries in his coffers, Henry was simply determined to accomplish now what he had been unable to do in his salad days. Whatever the motivation, the King crossed over to France in July 1544 and assumed command of an army of nearly 50,000 men – the largest force at that date ever to have left English shores. The King's principal objective was Boulogne, to which he laid siege, and by September the town was his. The war dragged on in a desultory fashion for another two years, but in June 1546 Francis I agreed that Boulogne should remain in English hands until 1554 and that if the French then wanted it back they would have to pay for it.

The campaign in France and the big expansion in the navy that accompanied it were enormously expensive. The total cost came to some two million pounds – a scale of expenditure which was beyond the resources of an English King, even one as rich as Henry. In fact, Henry had already called on his people for assistance, and in the period 1541–47 the yield from parliamentary taxation was over £800,000. When forced loans and benevolences are included, this already high figure swells to more than £1,150,000. It appears that this vast sum was collected without overt resistance, which is in itself evidence of the popularity of the King and his policies, but it could not fill the gap in the crown's finances. In August 1545 Lord Chancellor Wriothesley wrote despairingly to the Council: 'This year and last year the King has spent about £1,300,000. His subsidy and benevolence ministering scant £300,000, and the lands being consumed and the plate of the realm molten and coined, I lament the danger of the time to come . . . And yet you write to me still "Pay! Pay! Prepare for this and that!" '

Crown lands were sold to meet the deficit, and before his death Henry had parted with well over half the monastic estates. The currency was debased, outstanding debts were gathered in, and there was even a plan to unload accumulated reserves of lead – mainly from melted-down monastic roofs – on to the European market. In spite of all these expedients, however, the royal finances remained in a parlous state, and Henry left his son an empty treasury and a diminishing revenue. The annexation of monastic property had completed the work begun by Edward IV and Henry VII of making land revenues the financial underpinning of royal government and had thereby restored to the crown the freedom of manoeuvre that late-medieval rulers had lost. However, the end of Henry VIII's reign saw the process reversed. As land was sold off and income declined it became necessary to tap other sources, and this immediately raised questions about precedents and consent. Despotic rule – if indeed it had ever been more than a pipedream – was no longer even a remote possibility after the 1540s.

During the last years of his life Henry continued to grapple with the problem of maintaining the unity of his realm and thereby ensuring a peaceful succession for his son. He valued unity above all things and in a speech to his last Parliament in November 1545 he pleaded for an end to discord. 'Behold then what love and charity is amongst you, when the one calleth the other "heretic" and "anabaptist", and he calleth him again "papist", "hypocrite" and "pharisee". Be these tokens of charity amongst you? Are these signs of fraternal love between you?' He had not, said Henry, given his subjects an English Bible in order to provoke discord among them. 'I am very sorry to know and hear how unreverently that most precious jewel, the Word of God, is disputed, rhymed, sung and jangled in every alehouse and tavern, contrary to the true meaning and doctrine of the same. And yet I am even as much sorry that the readers of the same follow it, in doing, so faintly and coldly: for of this I am sure, that charity was never so faint among you ... Love, dread and serve God (to the which I, as your supreme head and sovereign lord, require you) and then I doubt not but that love and league that I spoke of in the beginning shall never be dissolved or broken between us.'

Henry's concern for harmony in the body politic, and his fear of a possible catholic reaction after his death, drove him closer to the reformers. The ablest man in his Council, and one who would probably have the greatest influence upon Henry's heir, was the Prince's uncle, Edward Seymour, Earl of Hertford, who was known to favour the reformers. Hertford could count on the support of Sir William Paget, the King's secretary and one of his closest advisers, and also on Sir Anthony Denny, a leading member of the Privy Chamber, who was appointed Groom of the Stool in October 1546. The main aim of the trio was to drive the conservatives from power, but in fact they hardly needed to do so because of their opponents' blunders. The first of these was made by Stephen Gardiner, Bishop of Winchester, who rejected Henry's demand for an exchange of lands. Gardiner's principled defence of the Church's property was no doubt admirable but it merely served to infuriate Henry at a time when the conservatives desperately needed his support. The second, and far more serious, miscalculation was made by Norfolk's son, the Earl of Surrey – a fine poet but an impetuous and arrogant young noble. It was revealed that Surrey had begun quartering the royal arms with his own, and although his intention may have been to proclaim the antiquity of his lineage when compared to that of 'upstarts' such as Hertford, his action could be held to imply a claim to the throne.

Henry was by now a sick man, so huge with dropsy that he had to be carried upstairs, bloated, suspicious (as he always had been) and in constant pain. He was determined to strike down anybody who stood in the way of his son's inheritance, and he ordered the arrest of both Surrey and his father on charges of treason. When Parliament reassembled in January 1547 acts of attainder were passed against the two Howards. Surrey was executed on 19 January, and Norfolk was due to meet the same fate on the 28th. But the duke was saved by the luckiest of chances, for on that very day, early in the morning, Henry died.

The King had been reluctant to face up to the fact that his end was fast approaching, but Denny, who was in constant attendance, persuaded him to turn his mind to spiritual matters, and the King ordered Cranmer to be sent for. By the time the archbishop arrived Henry was incapable of speech, but Cranmer, 'exhorting him to put his trust in Christ and to call upon His mercy, desired him, though he could not speak, yet to give some token with his eyes or with his hand that he trusted in the Lord. Then the King, holding him with his hand, did wring his hand in his as hard as he could'.

CHAPTER FIVE

Edward VI and Mary I

Protector Somerset

Parliament had conferred on Henry VIII the authority to determine the order of succession to the throne, and in his will he made Edward his heir, with Mary and Elizabeth next in line – a tacit acknowledgment of their legitimacy. He also appointed a Regency Council from which Gardiner and Norfolk were excluded. The leadership of the conservatives therefore rested with Thomas, Lord Wriothesley, appointed Lord Chancellor in 1544, and Cuthbert Tunstall, Bishop of Durham, neither of them heavyweights. Against them were ranged the reformers, led by Edward's uncle, Edward Seymour, Earl of Hertford, and his friend, Archbishop Cranmer. Henry's will had not in fact been signed by him. In his closing years he had delegated the task of authorising official documents to his close advisers, principal among them William Paget, his secretary, and Sir Anthony Denny, Groom of the Stool. These were given the responsibility for affixing a facsimile of Henry's signature known as the 'dry stamp' and inking it in. Paget and Denny worked hand in glove with Hertford and Lisle, and it may well be that Henry's will was altered in such a way as to ensure the triumph of the reformers. The Regency Council was given unlimited power to rule as it thought fit, and an 'unfulfilled gifts' clause was either inserted or reworded which allowed it to make whatever gifts and promotions the late King had intended – a usefully elastic terminology.

The reformers, then, were well prepared. Indeed, Paget was later to remind Hertford of the plotting that had taken place 'in the gallery at Westminster before the breath was out of the body of the King that dead is'. Hertford quickly rode to Hatfield, where the nine-year-old Edward was staying, and escorted the new King to London. When the Regency Council assembled for its first meeting it appointed Hertford 'Protector of all the realms and dominions of the King's majesty that now is, and . . . governor of his most royal person.' The new Protector immediately paid his debts to those who had made his bid for power successful. Paget announced that Henry had drawn up an honours list before his death and that this, under the terms of the 'unfulfilled gifts' clause, would now be implemented. Hertford himself became Duke of Somerset, while his principal associate, John Dudley, Lord Lisle, was made Earl of Warwick. Among the other promotions was that of Lord Chancellor Wriothesley to the earldom of Southampton, but that did not prevent him from being dismissed from office a few weeks later.

For the next three years Protector Somerset was in control of the destinies of England. He carefully cultivated the image of himself as the patron of all those who wanted further reformation in the Church and state, and he appointed a leading English humanist, Sir Thomas Smith, as one of his secretaries. Yet Somerset's humanism was far removed from that of Erasmus and More. It derived rather from the enormously influential *Il Cortegiano* ['The Courtier'], the work of the Italian Baldassare Castiglione, who had spent twelve years in the ducal court of Urbino. *Il Cortegiano* inspired a number of English imitations, of which the most successful was Sir Thomas Elyot's *The Boke named the Governour*, published in 1531. This new humanism – as was to be expected, given its source – put the emphasis upon the role of the ruler rather than the rights of the ruled, and was based upon the assumption that the state was a divinely sanctioned way of organising human society.

Somerset took an essentially pragmatic approach to political problems and confined his idealism largely to rhetoric. As he told the imperial ambassador, his aim was to give the people of England 'a little more reasonable liberty without in any way releasing them from the restraints of proper order and obedience'. For this reason, gestures like the repeal of the heresy laws, the treason legislation of Henry VIII, and the Statute of Proclamations cannot be taken entirely at face value. It might be thought, for example, that the repeal of the Proclamations Act would have left the government dependent solely upon statute for the enforcement of its will. In fact, proclamations reverted to their earlier prerogative basis, and Somerset used them on an unprecedented scale.

Somerset was an arrogant man, and he displayed a love of money and of outward magnificence that were typical of the age in which he lived. The most obvious example of this was the great palace he built for himself by the side of the Thames, not far from Whitehall, and christened Somerset

House. Although he had been named in Henry's will simply as one member of the Regency Council among others, he secured letters patent in King Edward's name giving him quasi-monarchical authority, including the right to appoint whom he wished to the Privy Council. Like Henry VIII he left routine matters to this body while reserving all major decisions to himself. Consequently, during the first year of Somerset's protectorate his own secretaries, Sir Thomas Smith and William Cecil, were more important than the King's Secretaries of State. Somerset obviously enjoyed power, but in the process of distancing himself from the Council he turned into a remote and isolated ruler, lonely as a king but without the quasi-mystical aura of royalty that gave monarchs a better chance of survival than ordinary mortals.

The First Prayer Book

Although the reformers came to power with Edward VI they were split between moderates and radicals. The moderates thought it best to move by gradual steps, taking the people with them. The radicals, by contrast, saw no reason to procrastinate. They wanted to use all the powers of the state to bring into being in England a radically reformed Church along the lines of those established in various Swiss cities by Ulrich Zwingli, Martin Bucer and Jean Calvin – even though these were not cut to the same pattern. Somerset's religious views were probably close to the radicals', but his attitude was affected by other considerations, above all the problem of Scotland. He intended to solve this by annexing that kingdom to England, and he realised that his chances of doing so would be significantly lessened if England were to be plunged into anarchy through precipitate action on the part of the radicals. Somerset also had to take into account the attitude of the Emperor Charles V, for the Scots were bound to call upon France for assistance, and if the Emperor joined in as well, Edward VI's regime would be in grave danger. However, if the pace of religious change in England was kept moderate, and if Princess Mary – who had never wavered in her commitment to the Roman Catholic faith – was allowed freedom of private worship, the probability was that the Emperor would remain neutral.

Somerset began by putting into effect a plan drawn up in the closing years of Henry VIII's reign for dissolving all chantries and transferring their endowments to the crown. This was justified in the Dissolution Act of 1547 on the grounds that chantries, which existed to provide prayers for the dead, served no valid purpose now that belief in the existence of purgatory had been abandoned. In fact the dissolution of the chantries, like that of the monasteries before them, owed as much to financial as to doctrinal considerations, but the radicals hailed the move as a first step along their preferred path. They were in an optimistic mood, for the removal of Henry VIII's restraining hand had left the printing presses free to produce quantities of religious literature, much of it violently anti-catholic and anti-clerical in tone. It was now that the works of the major continental reformers appeared in English translations, and the effect of this spate of publications was to build up popular pressure in favour of further reform.

The doctrine of the Church of England was still, in law and in theory, that set out in the *King's Book* of 1543, but this was no longer acceptable even to moderate reformers. Somerset looked to Cranmer to produce a new formulary, and the archbishop was already at work on this. He had taken advantage of the change of climate created by Henry's death to invite a number of distinguished European reformers to England. He did so partly because he wanted their advice and guidance while he was drawing up his statement of faith and doctrine, but also because he recognised the need to raise the level of theological learning at the universities and among the clergy in general. In late 1547 Peter Martyr Vermigli, Bucer's friend, arrived in England and was subsequently appointed Professor of Divinity at Oxford. Bucer himself remained at Strasburg until the Emperor Charles V defeated the German protestants and imposed the conservative religious settlement of Augsburg.

Rather than accept the Augsburg settlement, Bucer left for England, where he arrived in April 1549 and was warmly greeted, not only by Cranmer but also by Edward VI, an ardent supporter of religious reform. Cranmer and Bucer had long been in contact by way of letters, and formed a close friendship. Bucer's arrival came at a key moment in Cranmer's development, for the archbishop's views on the nature of the sacrament were changing. During Henry VIII's reign Cranmer had clung to the belief that Christ was bodily present in the mass, but in the last year of Henry's life he was moving away from it. In late 1547 he sent a letter to Bucer asking for his opinion, and Bucer replied that 'the bread and wine do not change in their nature, but ... they become signs ... We do not consider that Christ descends from heaven, nor that he is joined with the symbols, nor that he is included in them'. This statement of belief was close to Cranmer's own thinking and helped confirm his rejection of the concept of the real presence.

Cranmer had invited Philip Melancthon, Luther's right-hand man and one of the leading protestant theologians, to take refuge in England, but he was unwilling to leave Germany at a time when the future of the Reformation was at stake, following the death of Luther in early 1546. Cranmer had hoped that Melancthon's presence in England, along with that of Bucer and other leaders of the continental Reformation, would make possible the construction of a pan-European reform movement, better equipped to confront the challenge from the revived Roman Catholic Church and the Holy Roman Emperor, but Melancthon's refusal to come to England left his project in limbo.

Cranmer therefore concentrated on the lesser but more pressing task of advancing the cause of reform at home. In conjunction with Somerset he set on foot a formal visitation of the Church that focused on the removal and destruction of images, which the archbishop believed were impediments to true belief, since all too frequently they were valued in their own right and not as symbols of something more profound. It was the same desire to remove superstitious practices that led him in 1548 to forbid the use of candles at Candlemas, of ashes on Ash Wednesday, and of palms on Palm Sunday. Cranmer was by now clear in his own mind that 'good works', in the sense of pilgrimages and offerings to the saints, were of no effect. Salvation, or 'justification', came through faith alone, as he made plain in his contribution to the book of homilies published in 1547. His old adversary Stephen Gardiner, Bishop of Winchester, rejected this assertion and was promptly imprisoned. Another blow to the conservatives came in March 1548 when a royal proclamation ordered the enforcement of a parliamentary statute requiring communion to be administered in two kinds. The laity, in other words, were to be given both the bread and the wine, in contrast to the catholic practice which reserved the wine for the officiating priest.

During the course of 1548 Cranmer was busy drawing up an official definition of faith. If there had been no restraints upon him it would have been considerably more radical than was in fact the case. But Somerset and the Privy Council, aware of the potential instability that accompanied the accession of a minor, were anxious to appeal to as wide a range of opinion as possible, and Cranmer went along with them. He would have liked to eliminate from the communion service any wording which could be held to imply the real presence, but in the event the rubrics referred to the 'sacrament of the body' and the 'sacrament of the blood' and instructed the priest to say, as he administered them, 'the body (blood) of our Lord Jesus Christ which was given (shed) for thee preserve thy body and soul unto everlasting life'. There was no question of elevating the host, which could imply adoration of the sacraments, and Cranmer probably thought this omission would signal that the bread and the wine were symbols rather than transformed substances. However, many radicals were disappointed with what they regarded as Cranmer's failure to carry his reforming impulses into full effect. John Hooper, who was shortly to be made Bishop of Gloucester, declared that he was 'so much offended with that book that if it be not corrected I neither can nor will communicate with the Church in the administration of the [Lord's] supper'.

Under Henry VIII statements of faith had been issued on the authority of the King, but the First Prayer Book of Edward VI was authorised by Parliament. The Act of Uniformity of January 1549 ordered its use in all English churches from the following Whit Sunday and prescribed penalties for any clergyman refusing to comply. While the Book was too conservative for the radicals and too radical for the conservatives, its author regarded it as essentially an interim statement. Bucer, after his first meeting with Cranmer, reported back to Strasburg that 'some concessions have been made both to a respect for antiquity and to the infirmity of the present age . . . They affirm that there is no superstition in these things and that they are only to be retained for a time, lest the people, not yet thoroughly instructed in Christ, should by too extensive innovations be frightened away from Christ's religion'.

While the First Prayer Book was in some ways a moderate document, this was not true of the Edwardian Reformation as a whole, even in its opening stages. The destruction of the chantries was a clear break with the past and a rejection of purgatory. It may well have affected ordinary people more than the dissolution of the monasteries, for chantries were to be found in many parish churches, and guilds to maintain them were highly popular. Another obvious change took place in the status of the clergy. No longer were they singled-out as celibate miracle-workers who changed bread and wine into the body and blood of Christ. They were not only permitted but encouraged to marry, just like the laity around them, and although they were still allowed to hear confessions, these were now optional instead of obligatory. The clergy conducted the new forms of worship just as they had done the old, but since the Prayer Book prescribed services in English they were no longer privileged by their knowledge of Latin (however fragmentary that may have been).

The Western Rising and Kett's rebellion

Cranmer's Prayer Book may have been too moderate for many radicals, but it offended many conservatives, particularly those who lived far away from the hothouse atmosphere of London. Trouble had been brewing in Cornwall ever since commissioners arrived to take inventories of the chantries prior to dissolving them, for rumours soon began to circulate – just as they had done in Lincolnshire on the eve of the Pilgrimage of Grace – that the treasures of parish churches, the gifts of generations of local people, were also to be confiscated. When another group of officials, headed by the Archdeacon of Cornwall, appeared at Helston in 1548 to supervise the destruction of images, riots broke out, and in April the unfortunate archdeacon was assassinated. The final straw, so far as the Cornishmen were concerned, was the imposition of the new English Prayer Book. They claimed that it had no basis in law, for changes in doctrine could only be made by virtue of the royal supremacy, and this, in turn, could only be exercised by an adult monarch, not by a minor or those acting in his name.

While rebellion was spreading in Cornwall a spontaneous revolt had broken out in the village of Sampford Courtenay in Devon, for although the priest obeyed the law by using the Prayer Book on Whit Sunday, his infuriated parishioners forced him to revert to the traditional rite on the following day and came out in open defiance of the Protector's government. They were encouraged by the arrival of the Cornish rebels in June 1548, and the combined forces moved on to besiege Exeter. The rebellion was driven largely by religion, but it was also an expression of economic dissent. At Somerset's bidding Parliament had imposed a tax on sheep to check the enclosure of open fields and pay for the war against Scotland. Enclosures were not a problem in Devon and Cornwall, where open fields had either never existed or long since disappeared. Sheep, on the other hand, were kept by rich and poor alike, and all stood to suffer from the new measure.

The west-country rebels were drawn from the common people and did not look to local gentry for leadership, since they regarded them as betrayers of their religious and economic inheritance. The Cornishmen were reported as saying that it would be best to 'kill the gentlemen, and we will have the Six Articles up again and ceremonies as they were in King Henry VIII's time'. The articles drawn up on behalf of the rebels by local clergy were concerned almost exclusively with religious grievances and amounted to a demand that the Henrician Church, with its ceremonies and images, should be restored, along with the old forms of service. They denounced the new Prayer Book as no better than 'a Christmas game' and called for a return to 'mattins, mass, evensong and procession in Latin, not in English, as it was before'.

Somerset, in his reply to the rebels' demands, insisted that the Prayer Book was 'none other but the old: the selfsame words in English which were in Latin, saving a few things taken out'. But the insurgents were in no mood to engage in theological debate and the Protector therefore called on Lord Russell, the King's representative in the west, to suppress the rising by force. Russell moved slowly, because he found it difficult to raise levies locally for service against their fellow-countrymen, and Somerset could send him only token support. Fortunately for the government Exeter held out, and in early August 1549 Russell at last relieved the town. The besiegers retreated, but the rebellion smouldered on until the arrival of forces under the command of the Earl of Warwick. The end came in mid-August when the rebels were finally routed at Sampford Courtenay, where the Devon rising had started. The usual process of retribution was soon under way. The leaders of the rebellion were sent up to London to be hanged. Lesser men were strung up all over the west country as a warning to any who felt inclined to follow their example.

Somerset had not been able to despatch reinforcements to Russell because a major rebellion had broken out in Norfolk. This was, like the Western Rising, a conservative revolt, but the rebels in this case were protesting not against religious changes, which they welcomed, but against the less easily identifiable economic forces that were transforming their lives. The twin evils with which Tudor governments had constantly to contend were inflation and enclosure (using this term, as contemporaries did, to embrace a wide diversity of agrarian changes). Inflation, which prompted landowners to increase rents and bore heavily upon the poor, had complex causes, but it was made worse in England by the debasement of the coinage that Henry had set in train and that continued under his successor. Sir Thomas Smith urged Somerset to put an end to debasement and restore a stable currency, but the Protector was in desperate need of money to finance the war against Scotland, which was now costing some £200,000 a year. He could not bring himself to abandon a practice which, however ruinous in the long run, brought the government an immediate profit.

There were other voices, notably that of John Hales, which put the responsibility for inflation and its attendant social ills not upon anything so impersonal as the government's financial policy but on the selfishness and greed of private individuals. This was in tune with Somerset's own conventionally moralist assumptions, and it offered him an alternative to Sir Thomas Smith's austere prescription. In June 1548, therefore, he issued a proclamation against enclosure and followed the example of Wolsey by setting up commissions to tour those counties which had suffered badly from it. The only commission which really got going was that under John Hales, which was concerned with the midland area, but it came up against sustained opposition from the landowners, who effectually frustrated its efforts. Somerset, however, refused to change tack. He was convinced that his policy was correct and he was determined to force it through. 'Maugre [i.e.despite] the devil, private profit, self-love, money, and such-like the devil's instruments', he declared, 'it shall go forward'. In May 1549 he issued a second proclamation against enclosure, and in June, four days after the outbreak of the Western Rising, he announced a general pardon for all those who had taken the law into their own hands and thrown down fences.

Somerset's championship of the common people won him their acclaim. It also prompted them to demonstrations which were designed to show their support for him but which quickly developed into massive protest movements that no government could have tolerated or ignored. In June 1549 there were a number of risings in Norfolk and Suffolk which led to the setting up of camps outside Norwich, Ipswich and Bury St Edmund's. The Suffolk protest fizzled out, largely through the influence of Sir Anthony Wingfield, a member of the royal household who was also the head of an old-established and well-respected Suffolk landowning family. Norfolk, however, had been left without any dominating figure since the fall of the Howards, and the leadership of the rising was assumed by yeomen and lesser landowners who normally had little or no share in the government of their local communities. Indeed, the revolt was in part a protest by such men against the traditional gentry rulers of the region, whom they accused of caring too much for their own interests and too little for those of the people at large.

The Norfolk insurgents had assembled first at Wymondham, where they persuaded Robert Kett, a local landowner, to be their head. They then advanced on Norwich, throwing down fences as they went, and set up their camp to the north of the city, on Mousehold Heath. By the end of July they had made themselves masters of Norwich, but the bulk of the rebel forces remained in the camp, where Kett, with the help of an elected council, maintained good order and discipline. It was a remarkable demonstration of self-government and it showed the quality of the rebels. They were not a motiveless rabble but a company of small farmers and peasant cultivators, gathered together in defence of what they regarded as their traditional rights.

The main grievance of the rebels, as shown in the articles they drew up, was the excessive number of sheep being pastured by the landowners.

Much of the country was well suited to sheep farming, and the peasants, who had little land of their own, were dependent upon their right of common pasture. A few sheep could make a big difference to a family's finances, and when a landlord increased the number of animals he turned out to graze he threatened the peasants' livelihood: hence the demand 'that no lord of no manor shall common [i.e. put his sheep to pasture] upon the commons'. Inflated rents were another grievance, as was shown in the request 'that copyhold land that is unreasonably rented may go as it did in the first year of King Henry VII, and that at the death of a tenant or sale the same lands . . . be charged with an easy fine, [such] as a capon or a reasonable sum of money'.

Significantly absent from the list of grievances was any demand for a return to the old ways in religion. The rebels used the new Prayer Book for their public services, and among those who were invited to preach to the thousands assembled on Mousehold Heath was Matthew Parker, future Archbishop of Canterbury. Moreover, one of the articles in the Norfolk list pointed in a very radical direction by proposing that any priest who was 'not able to preach and set forth the word of God to his parishioners may be thereby put from his benefice, and the parishioners there to choose another, or else the patron or lord of the town'.

Kett and his followers were convinced – much as Robert Aske and the 'Pilgrims' had been twelve years earlier – that their action was not only morally justifiable but also lawful, and that they would therefore win the approval of the government. But Somerset was alarmed at the indications that public order throughout the kingdom was breaking down, and he called on the Norfolk men to abandon their protest and return peacefully to their homes. He offered them free pardon if they did so, but warned them that if they continued their insurrection he would have to resort to force. He had already sent a detachment of mercenaries to William Parr, Marquis of Northampton, but the marquis's half-hearted attempt to capture Norwich was easily beaten off. By this time, however, the Earl of Warwick had returned from the west country, after successfully crushing the rebels there, and he now prepared to repeat his performance in Norfolk. In late August 1549 he seized Norwich, after several days of fierce street fighting. He then turned on the encampment at Mousehold Heath and encircled it. Kett gave the order to move out rather than face starvation, but this merely provided Warwick with the opportunity he was looking for. He sent his cavalry in among the rebels and turned their orderly withdrawal into a rout in which many hundreds of them were slaughtered.

Kett's rebellion was now all but over. A special commission was set up to deal with the prisoners, of whom just under fifty were executed. Kett and his brother William were sent to London to be tried on treason charges. After conviction they were returned to Norfolk for the last scenes of their personal tragedy. Kett was hanged at Norwich castle. His brother was strung up from the steeple of Wymondham church. Whatever sympathy Protector Somerset may have felt for the Norfolk peasants, he behaved like every other Tudor ruler when it came to dealing with rebellion.

Although Somerset had managed to restore a semblance of order to England there were many people in the upper levels of society who blamed him for allowing things to get out of hand in the first place. The Earl of Warwick was numbered among his critics, and now that he had command of the only army in the kingdom he was in a position to dictate terms. Somerset was with the King at Hampton Court in October 1549 when he became aware that Warwick was plotting against him. He seems to have contemplated resistance, for he hurried the King away to Windsor, which was easier to defend. But Somerset had alienated many of his potential supporters by his combination of arrogance and ineffectualness, and his popularity with the common people – who called him 'the good duke' – did little to impress the landowners, on whose co-operation his government ultimately depended. As Paget brusquely informed him, the breakdown of order had been caused by 'your softness, your opinion to be good to the poor. The opinion of such as saith to your grace "O sir, there was never man that had the hearts of the poor as you have".'

Somerset was in no position to fight, so he gave himself up to Warwick, who sent him to the Tower. There he remained until the following February, when he was released. This gesture of conciliation on Warwick's part served its turn by giving him time to gain the young King's confidence and thereby establish himself more firmly in power. But Somerset was too dangerous to be left at large. He was planning a comeback, and was open about his desire for revenge. Warwick therefore decided upon a pre-emptive strike. In October 1551 Somerset was arrested and tried for treason. In January of the following year he was executed on Tower Hill, showing no sign of fear and publicly affirming that he had been 'ever glad of the furtherance and helping forward of the common wealth of this realm'.

Northumberland and the Second Prayer Book

Somerset had been associated with a policy of moderate protestantism and it seemed at first as though his fall might be the signal for a catholic reaction. Cranmer had, after all, been closely linked with Somerset, while Warwick had allied with Southampton, the leader of the conservative faction in the Council. But whatever hopes the catholics had, they were destined not to be fulfilled. Although later, on the scaffold, Warwick proclaimed his constancy to the old faith, he gave no sign of it during his brief tenure of power. The radical reformers had long counted him among their adherents. Hooper, for instance, who had such scruples about wearing vestments that, as Bishop of Gloucester, he risked open confrontation with Cranmer, called Warwick 'that most faithful and intrepid soldier of Christ'. Another admirer was the young King. Edward had developed into a committed protestant under the tutorship of Richard Cox and John Cheke, and he gave a sympathetic ear when Warwick outlined his plans for removing all remaining traces of popery from the Church of England. The earl did not proclaim himself Protector: that title had too many associations with Somerset. He preferred to bring the King forward and use him as a shield behind which he could effectively shape the course of events.

With Warwick in power, and working closely with Cranmer, the pace of religious reformation quickened. In November 1550 the Privy Council ordered that all remaining altars were to be destroyed and replaced by a simple wooden table, on the grounds that 'the use of an altar is to make sacrifice upon' while 'the use of a table is to serve for men to eat upon'. When George Day, Bishop of Chichester, refused to implement this order he was imprisoned and subsequently deprived. A similar fate lay in store for Stephen Gardiner, who had been released from prison by Protector Somerset in the vain hope that he would agree to co-operate with the new regime. Discussions were still going on when Somerset fell from power, but Gardiner remained obdurate. In December 1550 he was put on trial before royal commissioners headed by Cranmer, but far from submitting he accused the archbishop and his colleagues of promulgating 'the manifest and condemned error against the very true presence of Christ's body and blood in the sacrament of the altar'. Gardiner was sent to the Tower and deprived of his bishopric of Winchester, which was given instead to one of Cranmer's protégés. Yet the fallen bishop managed to publish a book in which he claimed that his belief in the real presence was consonant with the wording of the Prayer Book. Cranmer promptly issued a rejoinder asserting that 'Christ's body and blood be given to us indeed, yet not corporally and carnally but spiritually and effectually'.

While Cranmer may have been clear about his own position, there were many in the governing circle, including Warwick himself, who believed that a new and more uncompromising statement of faith needed to be drawn up. While he was in the north, Warwick had met and been impressed by John Knox, the radical and outspoken Scottish reformer, and he invited him to London to assist Cranmer in preparing a new Prayer Book. In fact Cranmer had almost completed work on this and resented Knox's intrusion. He was already suspicious of Warwick's motives, believing him to be more interested in self-enrichment than the good of the Church, and although he acknowledged that the First Prayer Book was no longer acceptable, he was also aware of the need for moderation in the rate of change if he was to carry popular opinion with him.

Nevertheless, the Second Prayer Book, which was authorised by Parliament in 1552, was uncompromisingly protestant. This was shown in the communion service – no longer sub-titled the mass – where Cranmer (doubtless bearing in mind Gardiner's comments about ambiguous wording) replaced terms such as 'the sacrament of the body' and 'the sacrament of the blood' with 'the bread' and 'the cup'. Moreover, in case anyone should still suppose that the elements were transubstantiated, the officiating priest was instructed to say 'Take and eat this, in remembrance that Christ died for thee, and feed on him in thy heart by faith, with thanksgiving.'

Cranmer's more cautious side was shown in the provision that communicants should still kneel to receive the sacraments. This was something Knox had strongly opposed, but the Privy Council accepted that kneeling was appropriate. However, it inserted what became known as the Black Rubric, which declared that 'it is not meant thereby that any adoration is done or ought to be done ... For as concerning the sacramental bread and wine, they remain still in their very natural substances and therefore may not be adored, for that were idolatry to be abhorred of all faithful Christians'.

The new Prayer Book was enforced by the second Act of Uniformity, which broke with precedent by making it obligatory for everyone to attend church on Sundays and take part in the Prayer-Book service. The doctrines of the Church of England were further defined by the *Forty-Two Articles* of 1553 which affirmed predestination and dismissed all belief in 'purgatory, pardons, worshipping and adoration as well of images as of relics, and also invocation of saints' as 'a fond [i.e. foolish] thing, vainly feigned and grounded upon no warrant of scripture, but rather repugnant to the word of God'.

The Prayer Book and *Forty-Two Articles* represented the positive side of the Edwardian reformation, but ordinary men and women would have been more aware of the negative. In hundreds of parish churches stained-glass windows were smashed, shrines and monuments desecrated, and statues defaced, on the grounds that they encouraged idolatry. In 1551 the confiscation of church plate was ordered, except for the minimum required for carrying out services. At the universities libraries were searched for heretical books, which were then destroyed, and the marked decline in the number of degrees awarded at Oxford in Edward's reign – an average of just over thirty a year compared with nearly one hundred and thirty in the first three decades of the sixteenth century – indicates the impact of these developments upon education. The enforcement of the Reformation varied widely from one part of the country to another. In places such as Lancashire, where the authority of the central government was weak and conservative attitudes deeply embedded, the changes were superficial. Elsewhere, and particularly in the south and east, protestantism was beginning to take root, and the pressure for change came as much from below as from above.

In October 1551 Warwick was created Duke of Northumberland. He suffered much at the time, and has done so since, by being unfavourably compared with Somerset. But Northumberland was not without his virtues. For one thing he was far less aloof than the Protector had been, and worked in close co-operation with the Privy Council. He also began the political education of Edward VI by encouraging him to attend Council meetings – though the King was still too young to do more than listen to what was said and signify his approval. Somerset had proclaimed himself the champion of the poor and oppressed, and had thereby unleashed the forces of disorder. Northumberland avoided rhetorical gestures and acquired a reputation for harshness, but in fact there was no sharp reversal of the government's social policies, and enclosure was still officially frowned upon. Northumberland's sympathies were with the landowners, yet he was determined that they should not evade their fiscal obligations, and his success in this respect was shown by the substantial rise in receipts from the Court of Wards – in sharp contrast to the decline under Somerset. Northumberland also stimulated the development of English overseas trade by revoking the privileges of the German Hanseatic League in 1552 and giving active encouragement to English explorers such as Willoughby and Chancellor (*see* p. 146).

Northumberland was not, of course, a free agent. His hold on power was uncertain and he had to buy support by allowing his adherents to enrich themselves at the state's expense. The members of the Privy Council, for example, voted themselves royal estates worth £30,000 a year, and the rule that all former Church lands sold by the crown were to be held on feudal tenure, to ensure that incidents such as wardship continued to be paid, was relaxed. The effect of this was further to diminish the King's revenue, but Northumberland now embarked on a number of policies designed to put the crown's finances on a sounder footing. He began by abandoning Somerset's military occupation of Scotland, which instead of breaking the union between the Scots and the French had made it even tighter, at the same time as it imposed an intolerable financial burden upon England. He also brought the French war to a close, in March 1550, by allowing Henri II to buy back Boulogne – which had proved to be virtually indefensible.

The end of military operations eased the strain upon the Exchequer, but by this time the government was close to bankruptcy. In 1551 its total net income amounted to a little under £170,000, but ordinary expenditure consumed the greater part of this, and the £36,500 that was left over could not possibly provide for extraordinaries, when garrisons alone cost £80,000 a year and the foreign debt amounted to £250,000. Northumberland dealt with the immediate crisis by suspending government payments – including monastic pensions – and selling crown lands to the value of £150,000. He also melted down confiscated Church plate and turned it into coin, at the same time as he raised further loans at home and abroad. Yet he was not content with these short-term palliative measures, because, unlike Somerset, he recognised that the public finances would never be soundly based until the quality of the coinage was restored. After one final orgy of debasement in May 1551, new coins of better quality were issued from the mint and the precipitous decline in the value of the English currency was slowed down and eventually halted. In a further effort to improve the royal finances Northumberland appointed commissioners in March 1552 to enquire into the system of revenue courts and make recommendations for greater efficiency in their operation. By the time the commissioners' reports were ready Northumberland's tenure of power was nearing its end, but he had laid the foundations for the financial recovery which took place in Mary's reign.

Since the 1530s there had been various proposals for stripping the Church of its wealth and turning bishops and clergy into salaried state officials. Northumberland began implementing some of these policies in the closing years of Edward VI's reign. John Ponet, who succeeded Gardiner as Bishop of Winchester in 1551, was persuaded to hand over all the endowments of his see to Northumberland in return for an annual pension equivalent to one-third of his former income. The remaining two-thirds went to the crown. John Hooper, the radical Bishop of Gloucester, came to a similar arrangement, and in March 1553 the passage through Parliament of a bill dissolving the Bishopric of Durham suggests that radical reorganisation of this vast and unwieldy see was also being planned.

It seems that most of the lands and money taken from the Church were used to improve the crown's finances, but Northumberland was so identified with the government that it is difficult to determine whether his primary concern was with public ends or his own private ones. Whatever the truth, the duke and his allies were making substantial profits at a time when the state was heading for bankruptcy, and Northumberland knew what the attitude of members of Parliament was likely to be when that body reassembled. He told William Cecil, one of his principal advisers, to be careful not 'to seem to make account to the Commons of his majesty's liberality and bountifulness in augmenting or advancing of his nobles, or of his benevolence showed to any his good servants, lest you might thereby make them wanton and give them occasion to take hold of your own arguments'.

From the point of view of the protestants the opening years of Edward VI's reign had been very successful. A decisive break had been made with the old catholic world, and new structures had been put in place that would lead – or so they hoped – to the creation of a genuinely reformed Church, drawing support from the mass of the people. Edward, not yet sixteen, was likely to rule for many years, and his commitment to the cause of reform was undoubted. Time, in short, was on their side – as long as the King lived. But in the spring of 1552 Edward contracted measles and smallpox, and although he recovered, his health remained fragile. In the winter of the following year it began to worsen markedly, for the young King had now been struck down by the fatal disease of tuberculosis. Northumberland knew that Edward's death would not only halt the protestant reformation in mid-course but also leave him dangerously exposed, for the heir to the throne was the King's half-sister, Mary, who had resisted all attempts to make her abandon catholicism. There seemed little reason to doubt that when she came to the throne she would remove her brother's protestant ministers and return England to communion with Rome. The only means of avoiding this fate was to change the order of succession. Henry had been empowered to do this by will, and Edward gladly assented to Northumberland's proposal that in order to ensure the continuance of the Reformation in England he should nominate a protestant successor.

The person chosen for this doubtful honour was the fifteen-year-old Lady Jane Grey, descended from Henry VII through the second marriage of his daughter, Mary, to Charles Brandon, Duke of Suffolk. The nearest protestant claimant was in fact Mary's half-sister, Elizabeth, but she was ruled out on the nominal grounds that she might take as her husband a foreign and papist prince. To avoid such a fate befalling Lady Jane she was ordered to marry Northumberland's fourth son, Lord Guilford Dudley. The marriage took place, much against Lady Jane's will, on 25 May 1553. At about the same time Edward drew up a 'device' in which he formally bequeathed the throne to Lady Jane and her protestant descendants. The leading figures in the administration – Councillors, judges and bishops – were called on to add their signatures. Some tried to withhold their assent. Cranmer, who was Edward's godfather, pleaded with the King not to take such a dangerous course, but Edward, as the archbishop later recalled, 'trusted that I alone would not be more repugnant to his will than the rest of the Council were'. In the end the King had his way, and when he died, on 6 July 1553, he had the comfort of knowing that he had secured a protestant succession.

In the hothouse atmosphere of London, plots could be hatched and political decisions made with relative ease, but in the country things were different. Mary was at Hunsdon House in Hertfordshire, not far from London, when she heard rumours that plans were being made to exclude her from the throne. She left immediately for Kenninghall, in Norfolk, a property which the crown had confiscated from Thomas Howard, Duke of Norfolk, after his attainder and imprisonment in the Tower. There she was joined by a number of local gentlemen, and she took these with her when she moved on to another former Howard property, Framlingham Castle in Suffolk. There she raised her standard and called on all loyal subjects to rally to her. Supporters flocked in, and it quickly became apparent to Northumberland and his accomplices that their gamble had failed. The duke had left London with a small force to bar Mary's advance, but no sooner did he depart than the Privy Council proclaimed her Queen. Northumberland, deserted by his troops, bowed to the inevitable, and by the end of July he was a prisoner in the Tower. On 3 August 1553 Mary entered London in triumph, and on the next day Bishop Gardiner and the Duke of Norfolk were released from prison. The catholic reaction had begun.

Mary I

Queen Mary was thirty-seven when the death of her half-brother brought her to the throne, and the catholics rejoiced at the prospect of a reign in which the old faith would be restored. Success seemed assured, for the Queen herself was popular. She had shown her courage by raising her standard in the face of what must have seemed formidable odds, and for years before that she had resisted all the efforts of Edward VI's ministers to persuade her to abandon her faith. When a deputation of Councillors waited on her in August 1551 and urged her to change her attitude she not only refused but also put them firmly in their place by reminding them that her father 'made the more part of you out of nothing'. Her courage and pride were typically Tudor, but Charles V's ambassador thought she was too accessible and too innocent of the arts and subterfuges of politics to make a successful ruler. 'I know the Queen to be good', he wrote, 'easily influenced, inexpert in worldly matters, and a novice all round', and the years that followed were in many ways to confirm this judgement. For Mary, politics were an aspect of religion and morality. Principle came first and she could see no virtue in compromise. The simplicity of her approach, combined with her natural stubbornness, explains why this well-intentioned woman became a symbol of intolerance and cruelty.

Mary had no experience of power, and her long exclusion from the world of politics, combined with her reclusive personality, made her initially dependent upon those friends and advisers who had been with her at Kenninghall and Framlingham. These conservative catholics formed her first Council, but as she moved towards London she added more people to it, drawn for the most part from men who had deserted Northumberland and now declared their loyalty to her. As a result her Privy Council swelled in size to above forty. Some of its members had held the same position under Edward VI or Henry VIII. These included Stephen Gardiner, restored to his bishopric of Winchester and appointed Lord Chancellor; William Paulet, Marquis of Winchester, who had been Lord Treasurer since 1550 and was confirmed in office; and William, Lord Paget, a former Secretary of State, who was later to be made Lord Privy Seal. An inner core of nineteen members came to dominate the Council, effectively excluding many of the Kenninghall–Framlingham group, but the latter remained in a dominant position at court. A major impediment to the smooth functioning of the Privy Council was the frequent disagreement between Gardiner and Paget. This was not just a matter of personalities. Paget stood for a moderate and relatively tolerant approach, particularly towards the problem of religion, while Gardiner wanted a speedy and total restoration of the authority and privileges of the Catholic Church.

Mary avoided opening her reign with a bloodbath. Northumberland was executed, along with two of his accomplices, but otherwise there were no reprisals against those who had tried to bar the Queen from her rightful inheritance. Lady Jane Grey and her husband were condemned to death for treachery, but remained alive as prisoners in the Tower. The same was true of Cranmer, who could have fled abroad rather than face the accession of a catholic monarch, but did not do so. He revered royal authority, which he believed to be divinely instituted, and since God had made the choice of ruler he felt bound to acquiesce: to quote his own words, 'to private subjects it appertaineth not to reform things, but quietly to suffer that they cannot amend'. Mary had no doubt that Cranmer was a traitor, since he had given his support, however reluctantly, to 'Queen Jane', but she regarded him as guilty of a far greater offence, namely that of heresy, and was determined to put him on trial. Until such time as formal proceedings could begin, however, she kept him in the Tower, away from the public eye.

Protestant exile and catholic reaction

The leaders of the continental reformation movements who had found refuge in England under Edward VI were now encouraged to depart. English protestants who preferred exile to life under a catholic sovereign were also free to leave the country, and many chose this course. Peter Martyr, who had returned to Strasburg to take up his chair in theology, reported from there that 'English youths have come over to us in great numbers within a few days, partly from Oxford and partly from Cambridge; whom many godly merchants are bringing up to learning, [so] that should it please God to restore religion to its former state in that kingdom they may be of some benefit to the Church.' Other groups settled at Frankfurt and elsewhere in Germany, as well as in France, Switzerland and Italy. In all, some eight hundred people, mostly from the upper levels of English society, went into voluntary exile. Mary's accession had been foreseen, of course, and no doubt many of those who left had made appropriate arrangements beforehand. But it seems unlikely that the exile as a whole was centrally planned and directed. Rather, it was a spontaneous reaction from those who put religious considerations above all others and preferred the uncertainties of life in a foreign country to acceptance of the mass and all that went with it.

Although Mary had a Privy Council composed largely of men whose loyalty to her was beyond question, she rarely attended its meetings or asked its advice. On matters that affected her personally she preferred to consult the imperial ambassador, for she was half-Spanish by birth, and ties of blood as well as religion made her desire an alliance with the Habsburgs. The Emperor Charles V welcomed this prospect and proposed a marriage between Mary and his son Philip, the future ruler of Spain. From Mary's point of view this would be the perfect match, but the intensive negotiations which preceded it held up the achievement of her principal objective, which was the return of England to communion with the Roman Church and papacy. Pope Julius III had already appointed Reginald Pole as legate to the Queen, and Mary was looking forward to his arrival so that the process of reconciliation could be set in train. Pole was the obvious choice for this mission. Not only was he the Queen's cousin and a cardinal; he was also famous throughout the catholic world for his learning and piety. Yet it was this combination of qualities that made him unacceptable to Charles V, for the Emperor feared that if Pole reached England before Philip he might advise the Queen not to commit herself to a marriage that would tie her hands and provoke opposition at home. Charles therefore put obstacles in the way of Pole's journey, and the cardinal was left kicking his heels in Europe more than a year after he should have been in London.

While Mary by herself could not bring about a reunion with Rome she could at least oversee the dismantling of the protestant Church in England. Of Edward VI's bishops, four, including Miles Coverdale, who had been appointed to Exeter, fled to the continent. Another four, among whom were Cranmer, Ridley (London) and Hooper (Gloucester), were imprisoned, and four more were deprived. Five former Henrician bishops who had been expelled from their sees after Northumberland seized power were now restored. They included Gardiner, who returned to Winchester, Cuthbert Tunstall, who went back to Durham, and Edmund Bonner, who became the new Bishop of London. These actions were carried out by virtue of the royal supremacy, even though this particular dignity was repugnant to Mary, but more fundamental changes in the nature of the Church could only be made by statute. Accordingly, in October 1553 the first Parliament of the reign was summoned to undo the work of its immediate predecessors. The First Statute of Repeal declared unlawful the reformed Liturgy, the First and Second Prayer Books, and the administration of the sacrament in both kinds. It also reimposed the ban on clerical marriage. This had an immediate effect, particularly in the south-east, where about a quarter of all parish clergy were deprived of their livings for having wives. Elsewhere the figure was much smaller. There was little logic behind the evictions, for married priests were not necessarily bad pastors to their flocks. Because there was a shortage of clergy many of those evicted found livings elsewhere. They often maintained a relationship with their former wives and were sometimes called to account for doing so. A celibate clergy was obviously desirable from a catholic viewpoint, but this particular 'reform' did little to improve spiritual conditions at the grass-roots level.

The Spanish match

The Act of Repeal had a difficult passage through Parliament, and on the final reading in the Commons just under a third of those present voted against it. This opposition did not spring from disloyalty to Mary. It was caused rather by fear that the next step would be the restoration to the Church of former monastic property, which would have been anathema to the many members of both Houses who held Church lands and had no intention of parting with them. It also sprang from a deep-seated hostility towards papal claims, and it is significant that in all the legislation of this Parliament no mention was made of the Pope.

The basic loyalty on which Mary could, in the last resort, rely was weakened by her determination to marry Philip of Spain. For her the advantage of such a match was obvious; it would give her the support of a catholic husband at the same time as it bonded her kingdom with the greatest catholic power on earth. Not surprisingly, when a deputation from the Lords and Commons pleaded with her to take an English husband she brushed them aside with the proud reply that 'Parliament was not accustomed to use such language to the Kings of England, nor was it suitable or respectful that it should do so ... She would choose according as God inspired her.'

The news of the projected Spanish marriage caused dismay. Under Henry VIII the claim that England was an empire, sufficient unto itself, had become a fact, and emerging concepts of 'Englishness' were closely linked to the idea of national independence. Mary, of course, had been opposed to the policy of cutting off England from the international Catholic Church and severing all ties with Rome. While her subjects feared subordination to a Spanish king, she looked forward to incorporating England once more into a community of catholic states under the spiritual leadership of the Pope. Since she was Queen she had her way, and the terms of marriage were agreed upon in January 1554. Philip was to be called King and was to assist Mary in the government of the country, but only the Queen, acting by herself, would make appointments to offices in the state and Church, and she would be required to choose Englishmen. There was to be no Spanish take-over of the administration.

While these terms were being drawn up, a group of conspirators was plotting to make sure they never came into effect. Sir Thomas Wyatt, son of one of the finest poets of early Tudor England, planned a revolt against Mary, with simultaneous risings throughout the country. He had assurances of support from France, and it may be that Mary's half-sister, Princess Elizabeth, was also in the secret. Although Wyatt counted a number of protestants among his supporters they were not in the majority nor was the rebellion primarily religious in its motivation. Its main cause was fear that the influence of the 'Spanish party' would become dominant in English politics, despite the provisions of the marriage treaty, thereby depriving native-born Englishmen of the places at court and in local administration to which they felt they had a prescriptive right.

The ultimate aims of the rebels were not clear, nor were they ever to become so, for news of the projected risings leaked out and the plotters had to act at once, even though their plans had not been fully worked out. Partly as a result of this the attempted risings in the west and midlands went off at half cock and were easily suppressed. The Kentish rising, under Wyatt, was the only one to achieve any success, for several thousand men rallied to his standard and this enabled him to march on London. The situation was serious and the City might have fallen to the rebels had not Mary, with her accustomed courage, ridden to the Guildhall and appealed to the citizens to remain loyal. Her bold move succeeded. The bridges were held against Wyatt and when he forced his way in from the Surrey side he found no one to support him. In the end he surrendered without fighting and was immediately sent to the Tower.

Wyatt's rebellion had turned out to be a small-scale affair and it gave no evidence of widespread opposition to Mary or, for that matter, to catholicism. Yet although it had been defeated with relative ease it had come alarmingly close to success, and no mercy was shown to the participants. Some ninety of the rank and file were sent to the gallows, forty-six of them being hanged in London in a single day. Wyatt himself was executed, and so were Lady Jane Grey and her husband, even though they had taken no part in the rising. Mary was discovering, as her father had done before her, that pretenders to the throne were too dangerous to be left alive.

The failure of Wyatt's rebellion cleared the way for the Spanish match to go ahead. Parliament accepted the proposed terms in April 1554, and in the following July Bishop Gardiner conducted the marriage ceremony in his cathedral church at Winchester. On personal grounds the marriage was a failure. Philip had little love for his wife, whom he found unattractive, and although at first Mary could blind herself to this she could not remain unaware of her husband's increasingly prolonged absences. She longed for a child, but even this was denied her. The failure of her marriage soured Mary. She who had devoted her life to the restoration of the Catholic Church in England had to accept the fact that her work would be in vain, for she would be succeeded by the protestant Elizabeth.

Persecution

In November 1554 Cardinal Pole at last arrived in England. Like Mary, he wished to see the country restored to full communion with Rome as soon as possible. This could not be done, however, until the nation had publicly expressed its desire for forgiveness. Parliament, which was held to epitomise the nation and which had shared the responsibility for schism, would have to take the initiative in formally requesting absolution. This it was willing to do, and on the last day of November 1554 a joint session of both Houses took place at which Mary and Philip, as well as Pole, were present. Gardiner, as Lord Chancellor, read aloud a petition asking for pardon and reconciliation, which Pole accepted. Then, while all present kneeled, the cardinal legate pronounced absolution and declared the kingdom of England restored to the unity of the Catholic Church.

Pole had originally assumed that the return to the status quo of the first part of Henry VIII's reign would automatically entail the handing back to the Church of all the property, including the monastic estates, of which it had been deprived, for it ran against his conscience to condone what he regarded as an act of sacrilege as well as robbery. However, the Pope, under pressure from Philip of Spain, came to the conclusion that it would be better to leave the current owners in possession of their ill-gotten gains rather than risk 'the shipwreck of this undertaking'. This made it possible for Pole to assure Parliament that his task was 'not to pull down, but to build; to reconcile, not to censure; to invite, but without compulsion. My business is not to proceed by way of retrospection or to question things already settled'. The Second Statute of Repeal confirmed this implicit bargain. It started by annulling all laws passed against Rome since the fall of Wolsey, but it also declared that the holders of monastic lands might 'without scruple of conscience enjoy them' and be free 'from all dangers of the censures of the Church'.

The Second Statute of Repeal was preceded by an act reviving the heresy laws. The annulment of the statutes against heresy had been one of the first actions of Edward VI's government, but this had given scope to religious radicals, including anabaptists, publicly to proclaim their unorthodox opinions. Cranmer was so alarmed by their increasing appeal, especially in London, that he set up a tribunal to examine them. Most were prepared to exercise voluntary restraint, but Joan Boucher, known as Joan of Kent, proved obdurate. In May 1550, therefore, the government used the crown's inherent powers over heresy to have her burnt at the stake. Mary could have used the same powers, but she preferred to put her actions beyond dispute by having their justification enshrined in statute. This turned out to be more difficult than she had anticipated, for when the bill reached the House of Lords it was thrown out. This was not because the majority of peers had protestant sympathies but because they were reluctant to increase the authority of the bishops, who were already – in their eyes – too powerful. Far from blocking the revival of the heresy laws, they gave approval to a similar bill some six months later.

The use of these laws against protestants was originally advocated by Gardiner, though the Queen gave her approval. She may have been misled by Northumberland's recantation into assuming that protestantism was only a veneer and that strong action against a handful of ringleaders would encourage the remainder to conform. Even so, there was no centralised campaign against heresy. The initiative was left to local clergy, churchwardens, Justices of the Peace and constables, or to private individuals, and the area most affected was south-eastern England, where protestantism had begun to establish itself.

Between February 1555 and November 1558 just under three hundred men and women were burnt at the stake, displaying a courage that had quite the opposite effect to what Gardiner and Mary had intended. The majority of the Marian martyrs came from the lower levels of English society and included weavers, tailors, hosiers, labourers, brewers and butchers. Some fifty women were among those who were burnt. Not all the martyrs were 'conventional' protestants. In Kent, for example, many came from areas where Lollardy was still active and they often held opinions that would have been regarded as unacceptable even in Edward VI's reign. One striking thing about the roll of martyrs is the high proportion of rural labourers recorded. It is often, and rightly, assumed that towns were the seedbed of radicalism in both religion and politics, but it is apparent that by the middle of the sixteenth century parts of the country-side had also become radicalised, particularly in the south-east. This impression is confirmed by the story of a small farmer from Cambridgeshire who in 1555 travelled to Colchester for the sole purpose of taking part in spiritual exercises. He seriously considered going on from there to Oxford, as he had doubts about Christ's divinity and wished to consult two prominent protestant divines, Nicholas Ridley and Hugh Latimer, who were in prison there, awaiting execution.

The punishment of death by burning was an appallingly cruel one, but it was not this that shocked contemporaries. In an age that knew nothing of anaesthetics a great deal of pain had to be endured by everybody at one time or another, and the taste for public executions, bear-baiting and cock-fighting suggests a callousness that blunted susceptibilities. What made the Marian persecution unpopular was the way in which it struck down small offenders while letting the big ones go free. All too often those accused of heresy would find themselves called before a man who had been an active propagator of reformed doctrines in the previous reign. When Thomas Watts, a protestant linen draper from a small Essex town, was summoned by the local Justice of the Peace to tell him 'who hath been thy school-master to teach thee this gear, or where didst thou first learn this religion?', Watts replied 'forsooth, even of you, sir. You taught it me, and none more than you. For in King Edward's days in open session you spoke against the religion now used; no preacher more'.

The persecution probably did little harm to the catholic cause in the short run, but it failed in its aim of forcing the protestants into conformity. Mary was repeating Northumberland's mistake of trying to do too much too quickly and putting the emphasis on the negative, destructive aspects of change rather than the positive. Protestant pamphleteers at home and abroad were swift to take advantage of this error, and the accession of Elizabeth was followed by the publication of John Foxe's *Book of Martyrs* which recorded in loving and gruesome detail the lives and deaths of all those who were put to death for their refusal to conform to catholicism. Foxe's *Book* came to be almost as widely read in England as the Bible. Mary had given the protestant English Church its martyrs. Foxe made sure the record of their suffering would inspire generations to come.

The Marian government hoped that the threat of an agonising death would drive protestants to recant, and one big success would have made this more likely. This is why it put so much pressure on Cranmer to make public confession of his errors. Cranmer, Ridley, Hooper and Latimer had all been imprisoned. Hooper was burnt in the early days of the persecution and Latimer and Ridley went to the flames at Oxford in October 1555. Cranmer was left alone to decide what to do. He was in a genuine dilemma since obedience to a divinely-appointed monarch was for him an article of faith, yet by accepting the commands of his sovereign lady Mary he would be going against his own conscience. Under pressure from himself as well as his interrogators he recanted, but at the last moment he changed his mind. Led out to die at Oxford in March 1556 he denounced his recantation as 'things written with my hand contrary to the truth which I thought in my heart, and written for fear of death and to save my life if it might be', and he plunged his hand into the flames so that it could never again betray him.

Cranmer's dilemma was shared by many protestants. The early reformers in England and on the continent had transferred to the King the reverence that Roman Catholics gave the Pope and had elevated royal authority because it offered the best possible security against papal power. Now, however, the royal supremacy which had been employed to destroy the Roman Church in England was being used to rebuild it, and protestants had to reconsider their attitude. The first of the Marian martyrs had shown the way when he appealed from the monarch to the word of God, unto which, he said, 'must all men – king and queen, emperor, parliament and general councils – obey. The word obeyeth no man. It cannot be changed or altered'. The Marian martyrs, by making the Bible their touchstone, helped prepare the ground for the growth of Elizabethan puritanism, as did the Marian exiles.

It is not possible to plot the religious map of Marian England with any certainty, but the fact that most of the exiles as well as most of the martyrs came from the south-east confirms the impression that this was the region where protestantism had really taken hold. The figures for married priests provide further evidence. Some Suffolk clergy had taken wives in the mid-1530s, a decade before clerical marriage was formally authorised, and by the time Mary came to the throne probably a quarter of all the clergy in East Anglia were married. In London the proportion was nearer a third. This was in marked contrast to the north of England where only one out of every ten priests, on average, had a wife. Married priests were not necessarily protestant, but they were certainly more numerous in protestant areas.

In London during Mary's reign there was an underground protestant church with a total membership of some two hundred, which varied its place of meeting in order to avoid detection. It kept in close touch with the exiles and also with the reformed churches on the continent, and it had links with another underground congregation at Colchester. This type of active defiance of the Marian regime required great courage and was relatively rare. Passive resistance, however, appears to have been widespread and took the form of refusing to build altars or attend mass.

The surviving evidence about popular attitudes towards Mary's religious policies probably gives a distorted picture, for where the restoration of catholic worship was accepted without difficulty there was nothing to report and therefore no record for posterity. In many places the opening months of Mary's reign saw the mass celebrated once again, with the appropriate ritual, even before this was made compulsory by the First Act of Repeal, passed in December. About a fifth of all churches benefited from the voluntary restoration of articles sold in Edward's reign, and where essential equipment was missing parishes often raised considerable funds to provide replacements. The first year of the reign saw high altars set up and vestments, books and crosses purchased. In 1554 this activity extended to the provision of side altars, plate, candlesticks and banners. Where funds were available, 1555–6 marked the reinstatement of roods, rood lofts and images, and increasing attention was given to the repair and maintenance of churches' fabric. The general picture is of a catholic north and west, including some places where the old faith had never died out, and a protestant south-east. Within this broad framework there was, however, considerable variation. In parts of Lancashire, which was generally speaking a catholic stronghold, the evangelising activities of young graduates of radical persuasion stimulated the emergence of protestant cells; while in parts of the south midlands, which were on the whole protestant, the commitment of a number of catholic gentry families ensured the survival of orthodox enclaves.

Although Mary's determination to make England a truly catholic country once again may have been the driving force behind the burnings, she left the constructive aspects of reform largely in the hands of Pole, who was already acting as Archbishop of Canterbury even though he could not be formally elected until after the execution of Cranmer in March 1556. It was by virtue of his legatine authority, however, that Pole summoned a national synod which met in London in December 1555 and drew up twelve decrees designed to set the Church on its new course. One of them tackled the long-standing problems of pluralism and non-residence by forbidding the holding of more than one benefice and insisting that all priests should be resident. This was a statement of intent rather than a practical proposition. Mary had returned First Fruits to the Church, and in due course she relieved the clergy of the burden of taxation, but a great deal of

Church wealth remained in lay hands and many parishes were so poorly endowed that they could not possibly maintain a priest of their own. Nevertheless, Pole scrutinised all applications for dispensation from the decrees very carefully and envisaged a redistribution of resources that would gradually eliminate the need for priests to hold more than one living.

Another decree required all clergy to carry out their obligation to preach, and Pole broke with tradition by choosing as bishops men who were trained in theology and pastoral care rather than civil law. Their commitment and integrity were demonstrated after Mary's death, when Elizabeth began turning the Church back in a protestant direction, for all except one of them preferred to give up their livings rather than abandon their principles.

Perhaps the most important of the decrees, for the long-term health of the Church, was the eleventh, which dealt with the education of the clergy. Pole hoped to see the establishment of seminaries for training priests in every diocese, but although some progress was made he came up against the obstacle that there were too few clergy of sufficient quality to staff them. To remedy this situation he needed to increase the flow of graduates from the universities, and he was able to take the initiative since both Oxford and Cambridge elected him as their chancellor. In this capacity he carried out formal visitations of the two universities and appointed catholic masters to many of the colleges. He did not undertake any new foundations himself but encouraged others to do so. In 1555 Sir Thomas Pope, a member of Mary's Privy Council who had amassed a fortune out of monastic property, made amends by founding the college 'of the Holy and Undivided Trinity' at Oxford, while his friend, Sir Thomas White, established one which he dedicated to St John the Baptist. These measures bore fruit in Elizabeth's reign when Oxford provided a significant number of the catholic priests who went on the 'English mission'.

The shortage of good priests which affected the operation of the Church at all levels and throughout the entire kingdom was not something that could be overcome in a few months or even years. By the time of Mary's death, however, the number of new priests was reaching levels unknown since Wolsey's day, and there were many indications that the revived catholic Church was establishing itself in the hearts and minds of the Queen's subjects. All that was needed was time, and Pole was working on the assumption that God would provide this. The same long-term view dictated his response to suggestions that a campaign of catholic evangelisation should be launched to eliminate heresy. The

Jesuits offered to send over members of the Society of Jesus to take the lead in this campaign, but Pole decided against such an initiative. In his view England had suffered from an excess of evangelism, and he did not wish to stir up religious controversy at a time when it seemed to be dying down. In Pole's own words, 'I think that it is better to check the preaching of the word rather than proclaim it, unless the discipline of the Church has been fully restored.'

Pole was an aristocrat by temperament as well as birth and he shied away from mass movements. He was also an autocrat who took it for granted that leadership belonged only to the chosen few and that the duty of the many was to obey. Eventual success depended, in Pole's view, upon restoring the full functioning of the Catholic Church in England so that its rituals, its ceremonies and its discipline could exert their benign spiritual influence. But many parish churches, despite the best efforts of their congregations, were still suffering from the depredations of the 1530s and '40s, and the situation could not be remedied until the nature and extent of the problem had been accurately assessed. This was one of the reasons why Pole adjourned the national synod in February 1556. He hoped that by the time it reassembled he would be able to put before it a detailed statement about the existing state of the Church that would provide the basis for a coherent programme of renovation. Meanwhile, he encouraged the revival of monasticism, to provide a reservoir of spirituality on which the Church could draw. The Observant Franciscans returned to Greenwich, the Carthusians to Sheen, the Dominicans to Smithfield, and the Benedictines to the great abbey of Westminster.

Pole, like Wolsey before him, derived his legatine authority from the Pope, and he looked to Rome as a source of inspiration. In May 1555, however, Cardinal Caraffa was elected Pope as Paul IV. Caraffa was a hard-line reactionary who suspected that all liberals – among whom he included Pole – were closet heretics. He was also violently anti-Spanish, since he wanted to free Italy from the Habsburg yoke. The Emperor Charles V had abdicated in October 1555 and the Pope's anger was directed towards his heir, Philip, who was now King of Spain and England and overlord of Italy. While Pole was addressing the synod that seemed to promise a new era for the Catholic Church in England, Paul IV was negotiating a treaty of alliance with France. Philip II, by way of riposte, sent his general, the Duke of Alva, to occupy the papal states. Paul promptly excommunicated Philip and withdrew all his representatives from the King's dominions. He also deprived Pole of his legateship and ordered him to return to Rome to answer heresy charges.

Mary, a devout daughter of the Roman Catholic Church, was in the invidious position of being married to an excommunicate husband and having as her archbishop and principal adviser a suspected heretic. The situation would have been comic if it had not been so full of tragic implications, and even had Mary lived it is conceivable that England would again have seceded from Rome. Rather than lose Pole, Mary ordered him to stay in England and petitioned the Pope to restore his legatine authority. As for Philip, her continued support for him was made clear in June 1557 when she declared war on his enemy, France. The war was a failure. Calais, the only surviving English possession on the mainland of Europe, had poor defences and an insufficient garrison, and when French troops made an unexpected mid-winter assault in January 1558 the town was forced to surrender. Calais had been a symbol, even though a hollow one, of English greatness, and its loss was one more nail in Mary's coffin. She and her Church were now identified not only with persecution and foreign domination but also with defeat.

Financial reorganisation and the closing years of Mary's reign

Mary depended for advice in financial matters upon the aged William Paulet, Marquis of Winchester, whom she confirmed in office as Lord Treasurer – a post to which he had first been appointed by Protector Somerset in 1550. Winchester began putting into effect the report of the commission on courts of revenue set up by Northumberland, and as a consequence the Court of Augmentations was dissolved, along with the Court of First Fruits and Tenths. Control over the royal finances was restored to the Exchequer, except for the Court of Wards and the Duchy of Lancaster which preserved their separate identities.

No doubt Winchester hoped that by slimming down the administration of the royal finances he would eventually cut costs, but the immediate need for money could only be met by Parliament, which was summoned in 1555. In the earlier Tudor period requests for parliamentary supply had been based on the country's defence needs and were usually related to war. In 1534, however, the emphasis was deliberately shifted to the King's outstanding services to his country, and a similar approach was made in 1545, even though at that time there was a war in progress and defence needs could have been stressed. In 1555 the country was at peace, but Winchester justified his request for a subsidy by emphasising 'the great and sundry benefits' which Philip and Mary's subjects had derived from their rule and the compelling need to deal with 'the great debts wherewith the imperial crown of this realm was charged'. There were some dissentient voices, but in the end the Commons voted a subsidy which ultimately yielded more than £180,000. Even so, the government was still short of ready cash, and in 1556 it resorted to forced loans. More of these were levied in the following year, and the crown was enriched by about £65,000.

In 1557, at Winchester's suggestion, a commission was appointed to enquire into the reasons 'why Customs and subsidies be greatly diminished and decayed'. It recommended, among other things, that the Book of Rates – which listed the official prices of commodities, upon which the amount of Customs duty was based – should be brought up to date. This was done and in May 1558 a new book was issued which took full account of inflation. As a consequence the yield from Customs increased by more than 75 per cent. The level of rents and entry fines on crown lands was also raised, and attempts were made to reduce expenditure on the royal household. If Mary could have kept her country at peace the public finances would have undergone significant improvement, but involvement in the war against France led to a deterioration. Crown lands had to be sold and the government was forced once more to raise loans on the Antwerp money market. This meant that by the time Mary died the annual deficit was running at £100,000 and the total debt which she bequeathed Elizabeth was close on £300,000.

The Commons' initial reluctance to grant a subsidy in 1555 was linked to the fact that in the same session the government had introduced a bill to restore First Fruits and Tenths to the Church. It seemed on the face of it a contradiction in terms to give away the crown's resources and then plead poverty. Also, the idea of returning to the Church the assets that had been forcibly taken from it might be an indication that Church lands should also be given back. In the end the First Fruits bill passed the House, but only at the late hour of 3 p.m., which suggests intense debate. Another measure, authorising the crown to seize the lands of those who had gone into exile on the continent, was rejected after Sir Anthony Kingston, one of the knights of the shire for Gloucestershire, locked the doors of the House and refused to open them until the Speaker put the bill to a vote. Kingston and his associates were opponents of the government on principle, but it would be wrong to talk of an organised opposition based on adherence to protestantism. Many members who were generally loyal to Mary were alarmed by the exiles bill, just as they had been by that on First Fruits, not on grounds of religion but because it implied a threat to property rights. This was always a sensitive issue and would have provoked opposition under any ruler.

Financial reorganisation and the restoration of catholicism had this in common – they both needed time for their full effect to be felt. But time was not granted to Mary any more than it had been to Edward VI. By the autumn of 1558 she was very ill and spent long periods in a coma, during which, so she told her attendants, she had good dreams and saw 'many little children like angels play before her, singing pleasing notes'. Early on the morning of 17 November she died at St James's Palace. On the other side of the river Cardinal Pole was also lying ill in his palace at Lambeth. He survived Mary by only a few hours. The catholic reaction had ended as abruptly as it began.

CHAPTER SIX

Tudor England

Population and the price rise

An increase in population and a steep rise in prices determined much of the course of English history in the Tudor and Stuart period. The hundred years preceding Henry VII's accession to the throne had seen recurrent attacks of plague which wiped out around a third of the population and produced an acute labour shortage. Land was abundant, demand was small, and prices and rents were consequently low. This situation was already changing by 1485, for growing immunity to plague had allowed the population level to stabilise at around two million. Thereafter a rapid increase took place, and by 1600 this figure had doubled, to four million.

As the population increased so did the demand for food, and this put pressure upon agricultural prices, which began rising steeply from about 1510. By the middle of the sixteenth century they were twice as high as they had been at the beginning, and by the end of the century six times. Industrial prices also went up from the 1540s, as demand increased. If population pressure had been the only cause of inflation, prices would have gone steadily upwards, but their irregular movement was a sign that other factors were at work. Increased government expenditure in the 1540s was one of these. Another was the scarcity of grain caused by a series of bad harvests in the 1590s. The most important factor, however, was the debasement of the coinage which began in 1542 and lasted until 1551. During this period the quantity of pure metal in silver coins was cut by 75 per cent and in gold coins by 25 per cent. The crown made an immediate profit, but it destroyed public confidence in the currency. Coins were no longer valued at their nominal rate but only according to the amount of pure metal they contained. Since this was less than before, more coins were demanded for goods, the value of money dropped, and inflation accelerated.

Mary Tudor put an end to debasement and Elizabeth issued a new coinage, but money continued its decline. One of the reasons for this was the influx of Spanish silver from the New World, which affected price levels throughout Europe. Until the mid-1580s this silver came into England by way of normal commercial transactions, mainly with the Spanish Netherlands. The outbreak of war with Spain disrupted this trade, but privateering expeditions, such as the one that Drake led in 1577–80 (*see* p. 147), resulted in the delivery of large quantities of bullion to the Mint, which turned it into coin. This had much the same effect as debasement, for although there was more money in circulation there was little or no increase in the amount of goods available, and inflationary pressures therefore increased.

Agriculture and enclosures

Agriculture was the main occupation of Tudor England, but its practice varied from one region to another, and there was a broad distinction between the highland zone of the north and west and the lowland zone of the south and east. The highland zone included extensive areas of mountains and moorlands, whose thin soils were best suited to pasture farming. The population of this zone tended to be dispersed in isolated farmsteads or tiny hamlets, and the communal regulation of agricultural activities, as well as manorial supervision, were difficult to enforce. The lowland zone, by contrast, had richer soils suitable for both arable and pasture. Its inhabitants were generally settled in tight-knit nuclear villages under close manorial control, and the cultivated area was divided into two or three large open fields, which were partitioned into individual strips. Around them were the commons and wastes which were for the use of the whole community.

These common lands were essential to the existence of cottagers, who constituted about a third of the rural population. The luckier ones might hold a few acres of land, but these smallholdings would not provide them with a living. They made money by selling their labour to the yeomen farmers and gentry, but they were dependent upon the commons for pasturing any sheep or cattle they might possess and upon the wastes for supplies of winter fuel. Yet the expansion of population was putting pressure on these communal lands, particularly in the midland region of England, for the most obvious way in which to provide more work as well as more food for the increasing number of inhabitants was by bringing the commons and wastes under cultivation. Even where they remained in their original state they were often so diminished in size that they could no longer serve the needs of the community, especially since the more enterprising yeomen and husbandmen (small farmers) were putting more and more sheep and cattle out to pasture in order to meet the growing demand from urban markets.

In areas suitable for mixed cultivation the open fields also were being eroded by the practice of enclosure. During the first half of the sixteenth century the cloth industry was booming and the demand for wool sent prices soaring. Landowners reacted to this by increasing the number of sheep on their estates and turning arable into pasture. It made more sense, from their point of view, to abandon the strip system and instead create enclosed fields in which their sheep and cattle could be kept apart. Even if they did not give up arable farming they still favoured enclosure, since this made it easier for them to try out new techniques and crops. Outside the midland area a great deal of enclosure, either of arable strips in the open fields or of common and waste ground, had already taken place by 1500, much of it by agreement. During the course of the sixteenth century problems arose when no agreement could be reached and landlords acted alone, evicting tenants at will and buying out freeholders. Sir Thomas More spoke of sheep devouring men, and Sir Thomas Smith, in *The Discourse of the Common Weal of this Realm of England*, written in 1549, makes the husbandmen say 'all [the land] is taken up for pastures, either for sheep or for grazing of cattle. So that I have known of late a dozen ploughs within less compass than six miles about me laid down within these seven years. And where forty persons had their livings, now one man and his shepherd hath all'.

The outcry against enclosure became intense in the mid-sixteenth century, but the actual amount which took place in Henry VIII's reign was limited and largely confined to the midland region. Even where landlords were as ruthless and covetous as the pamphleteers held them to be, they were restrained by the fact that their freehold and copyhold tenants enjoyed security of tenure. It was the cottagers and landless labourers who suffered most from enclosure. If they held a few acres they would be compensated, but the small parcel of land they received would not make up for the loss of the commons and wastes which had previously been available to them. If they had nothing but their cottage they were not eligible for compensation, nor could they find work if the estate on which they lived was turned over to pasture. They had little alternative but to take to the road, creating big problems for the local authorities, particularly in the towns, where many of the poor sought refuge and employment.

Tudor governments, which lacked any police force or standing army, were sensitive to symptoms of unrest and tried to check depopulation and enclosures in general. A statute of 1489 recited how 'great inconveniences daily doth increase by desolation and pulling down and willful waste of houses and towns within this ... realm, and laying to pasture lands which customably have been used in tilth [i.e. tillage]', but merely ordained that similar decay should not be allowed to take place in future. In 1515 Wolsey turned his attention to the matter and showed his usual clarity of vision and administrative capacity. He persuaded Parliament to pass an act requiring the restoration to tillage of all lands that had recently been con-verted to pasture, and then appointed commissioners who toured the country, gathering an enormous mass of information which they passed on to Chancery. The commissioners did their task thoroughly, but it was often difficult to prove that an enclosure was recent, within the terms of the act. A royal proclamation of 1526 therefore ordered the pulling down of any enclosures that had been made since the accession of Henry VII, but this was no more effective in practice than the statute had been. The crown was up against the difficulty that enforcement of government policy depended on the men of property in the localities who were often the worst offenders.

Following Wolsey's fall the initiative in reform passed to Thomas Cromwell. He attacked the problem from a different direction by attempting to limit the number of sheep that owners were allowed to keep, but the bill which he introduced to this effect in 1533 was so badly mauled in its passage through the Lords that it had little or no effect. However, the combination of successive harvest failures and debasement in the late 1540s revived interest in Cromwell's approach, even though he was no longer in power. In March 1549 Parliament passed an act imposing a tax upon sheep, on the assumption that farmers would be unlikely to convert their land from arable to pasture if, by so doing, they made themselves liable to taxation. This act, which caused widespread resentment among farmers and wool merchants, marked the climax of the attempt to hold back agrarian change by legislation, but it was as ineffective as its prede-cessors. Peasant unrest, which had been stimulated by the government's decision, in 1548, to appoint commissioners to enquire into agrarian griev-ances, brought down Protector Somerset, whom the peasants regarded as their champion, and opened the way to Northumberland. The change of ruler did not bring about a *volte-face* in government policy, for although

Northumberland was more sympathetic to big landowners, and quickly secured the repeal of the poll tax on sheep, an act passed in the second Parliament after he seized power made it an offence for anyone to convert to pasture land that had been under the plough since 1509, and prosecution of enclosure continued, though at a declining rate. Somerset's fall coincided with the collapse of the overseas market for English cloth, and this succeeded where government action had failed, by removing the incentive to switch from cultivation of the soil to sheep farming.

The enclosure movement did not come to a complete halt, nor did conversion from arable to pasture, though much of this was now for the fattening up of cattle to supply urban markets, particularly London. In the early years of Elizabeth's reign there was an attempt to reinvigorate the anti-enclosure legislation, and in 1565 commissioners were appointed once again to carry out detailed investigations into the situation on the ground. This was a short-lived initiative, however, for Parliament was losing interest in enclosures now that grain supplies seemed assured. In 1593 it signalled a complete change of course by repealing all legislation forbidding the conversion of arable to pasture, but this was followed by the worst harvests of the century, which caused such a shortage of grain that maintenance of arable cultivation became once more a priority. In 1597, therefore, Parliament passed an act requiring the restoration to cultivation of property converted to pasture since the beginning of Elizabeth's reign. It also ordered 'that all lands which now are used in tillage, having been tillable lands ... by the space of twelve years together at the least ... shall not be converted to any sheep-pasture or to the grazing or fatting of cattle ... but shall ... continue to be used in tillage for corn and grain'.

Harvest failure and plague

In many ways it was fortunate for England that the attempts made by successive Tudor governments to perpetuate traditional patterns of land use and occupation failed, for a growing population could only be fed by increasing the amount of land under cultivation and making the best possible use of it. Open-field farming was not necessarily inefficient, nor was it incompatible with experimentation, but enclosure gave farmers a greater degree of freedom in adapting to the demands of their markets. There were some improvements in agricultural techniques, of which the two most important were the flooding of meadows, in order to improve the quantity and quality of their grasses, and the switch to 'up-and-down husbandry', which meant ploughing up land for a number of years and then putting it down to grass for a time, to allow the soil to recover. But improved techniques by themselves would not have enabled agricultural production to expand, as the population was doing, at the rate of one per cent annually. Bigger supplies of home-produced grain and livestock could only be obtained by extending the cultivated area, and this was done so successfully that the expanding population was fed. Admittedly, the poorer elements in society lived dangerously close to the famine level, but only when there were repeated harvest failures, as in the late 1540s and 1590s, did starvation become a reality. Generally speaking, English agriculture met the challenge of a rising population, and by the end of the Tudor period it was producing more grain than was needed for home consumption in normal circumstances.

Abnormal circumstances were brought about by harvest failure. A long spell of bad weather would cut grain yields and send prices rising. Small farmers operating on narrow margins would have to choose between eating the seed corn, which they needed to keep for their next year's crop, or going hungry. One bad harvest caused suffering, but when there were several in a row the results could be catastrophic, especially for the poor. In 1549 the harvest was bad, in 1550 it was no better, and in 1551 it was worse. This terrible sequence coincided with the collapse of the Antwerp cloth market and the climax of debasement, and produced what is sometimes called 'the mid-Tudor crisis'. For the greater part of Elizabeth's reign harvests were reasonably good, with occasional years of abundance, but 1594–7 saw four successive years of crop failure which produced such an acute shortage of grain that there were food riots in many counties. The north-east was harder hit than the south, with reports that some of the poorer inhabitants were 'starving and dying in our streets and in the fields for lack of bread'. But even in the southern town of Reading, which was well sited for the delivery of grain via the river Thames, the number of deaths increased fourfold. Over the country as a whole the death rate in 1596–8 may have been as high as six per cent.

Bubonic plague was another scourge that struck without warning and caused not only suffering but acute social dislocation. Outbreaks of this dreaded disease became particularly virulent after the harvest failures of 1545 and 1550, and the death rate increased sharply. In 1563 London was struck by plague again, to be followed two years later by Bristol, and there was a further severe outbreak in the capital in 1593. Plague attacks in big cities, where large populations were huddled together in insanitary conditions, could kill off as much as 20 per cent of the population – a figure that would have been even higher had not the wealthier citizens fled into the country as soon as the symptoms of plague appeared. In 1578 the government issued the first printed book of plague orders, requiring infected households to be quarantined. This was designed to prevent the disease from spreading, but it added to the number of deaths by shutting up the healthy members of a family with the sick ones. Moreover, it took no account of the fact, unknown at the time, that plague was transmitted by rats and fleas which were undeterred by official restrictions on movement. Plague was not the only killer at large in Tudor England. Henry VII's accession coincided with the irruption of a form of influenza, known by the graphic name of 'sweating sickness', and this took a heavy toll in the crisis years 1557–59, when deaths from various causes amounted to well over 10 per cent of the entire English population.

Commerce

'It is not our conquests', said one seventeenth-century writer, 'but our commerce; it is not our swords but our sails that first spread the English name in Barbary, and thence came into Turkey, Armenia, Muscovy, Arabia, Persia, India, China, and indeed over and about the world.' During the first half of the sixteenth century, however, there was little to suggest that the English would eventually take a leading part in the phenomenal expansion of western Europe over the oceans. English commercial energies were fully engaged in the lucrative cloth trade with the Spanish Netherlands. The Company of the Staple was still exporting raw wool to its depot at Calais, but heavy taxation had made their product less competitive, and English wool went increasingly to native manufacturers. The weaving of cloth was big business in Tudor England, and a virtual monopoly over its export had been established by the Merchant Adventurers of London, who were granted a charter by Henry VII. Their overseas headquarters was Antwerp, from where English cloth found its way all over Europe, and as long as trade flourished between England and The Netherlands there was no capital to spare for voyages of exploration.

Henry VII was determined to expand English trade, since Customs duties gave him a share of the profits. By making commercial treaties with the Baltic states he hoped to break the stranglehold of the north German Hanseatic League, which had a big depot – the Steelyard – in London and enjoyed privileges even greater than those granted to native merchants. In this attempt he failed, because the Hanseatic League was well entrenched in the valuable Baltic trade, and without its goodwill the supply of timber and other shipbuilding essentials would have been interrupted. The Hanse kept their key role in English commerce until the mid-sixteenth century. Thereafter, the increase in the number of home-built ships and the growth of continental rivals to the Hanse gradually eroded the profits and the privileged position of the League. Henry VII was more successful in breaking the monopoly of Venice over Mediterranean trade, and English merchants were building up a flourishing commerce with Italy when they, like the Venetians, were checked by the westward expansion of Turkish power.

Shortage of shipping was a hindrance to the growth of English trade, and Henry attempted to remedy this at the outset of his reign by a Navigation Act forbidding merchants to use foreign ships when English ones were available. By encouraging the building of merchant ships, by creating the nucleus of a royal navy, and by claiming for his subjects a greater share of European commerce, Henry VII set an example which his successors duly followed. His prescience was also shown by his grant of letters patent to the Italian John Cabot in 1496, authorising him 'to sail to all parts, regions and coasts of the eastern, western and northern sea' in the hope of finding a new route to those oriental lands from which came the spices and precious metals that were held in such high regard. John Cabot – who may have been accompanied by his son, Sebastian – sighted Newfoundland and came back to report that the sea was covered with fish, but he was convinced that he had made landfall in Cathay – the contemporary name for China – and in 1498 he set out on a second voyage from which he never returned.

Under Henry VIII there was little exploring activity, for the cloth trade continued to flourish and the King's money and energy were spent fighting in France. By 1550, however, the quality of English cloth was declining and over-production had glutted the European market. New outlets were needed, and the initiative was taken by the Duke of Northumberland, who claimed at this late date a share for England in the great adventure of overseas exploration that had so far been left largely to Portugal and Spain. The two catholic powers controlled the southern approaches to the orient, so English attention was focused on the attempt to find a northern passage. This had the additional attraction that the cold climate of the northern regions meant there should be good prospects for the sale of woollen cloth. In 1554 Sir Hugh Willoughby and Richard Chancellor set sail to find a north-east passage to Cathay. They did not succeed, and Willoughby perished in the attempt, but Chancellor made his way into the White Sea and from there journeyed to Moscow, where he appeared at the court of Ivan the Terrible. This epic voyage inaugurated a flourishing trade between England and Russia and led, in 1555, to the foundation of the Muscovy

Company. One of the people who helped bring this into existence was Sebastian Cabot, who personified the link between the first and second generations of English explorers.

The cloth trade picked up, particularly after the recoinage carried out in 1560 at the suggestion of Sir Thomas Gresham, a prominent London merchant, but The Netherlands market remained unstable, even before the outbreak of the revolt against Spain in 1572. Elizabeth's accession took place at a time when the price rise and unemployment had so badly affected the English economy that Parliament authorised the drastic measures contained in the Statute of Artificers (*see* pp. 154–5). It also coincided with the emergence of Spain as the strongest power in the western world and the champion of Counter-Reformation catholicism. This was a threat to the protestant Queen and her subjects, and Elizabethan seamen responded by challenging the Spanish monopoly of trade with the New World.

In 1562 John Hawkins set out on the first of three voyages in which he collected slaves from the West African coast and shipped them to the Spanish colonies in America. The Spanish government resented this heretic invasion of their empire, even though it was a peaceful one, and on his third voyage Hawkins was lucky to escape from a surprise attack on his ships while he was sheltering in the harbour of San Juan de Ulloa, near Vera Cruz in Mexico. News of this event reached England at a time when Elizabeth was putting pressure on Philip II of Spain to moderate his aggressive policy in The Netherlands. In order to show him that she was not to be trifled with, she encouraged – and sometimes invested in – the many English expeditions which set out for the New World. Most famous of these was Drake's expedition of 1577. He passed through the Magellan Straits, sailed up the west coast of America, where he captured a Spanish ship laden with silver, and returned to England by way of the Indian Ocean and Cape of Good Hope. Not only did he have the glory of being the first English circumnavigator. He also gave the shareholders in his expedition a profit of nearly 5,000 per cent.

English seamen were short of bases in the New World, and the first attempts at colonisation were designed to provide these. In 1584 Sir Walter Ralegh obtained a patent for the foundation of a colony in America, and in the following year a settlement was established on Roanoke Island, in the area that Ralegh named 'Virginia' in honour of the Queen. The colony managed to survive, short of supplies, until the following year, when Drake, returning from one of his voyages, took the settlers home with him. A second attempt in 1587 was no more successful, for although English colonists were once again established on Roanoke they were then left alone for several years, since all English shipping was needed in home waters to deal with the Armada. Not until 1591 did Richard Grenville make his way to Roanoke, only to find that the settlers had disappeared without trace.

At the time of Elizabeth's death in 1603 no English colony had been firmly established in the New World, but English sailors were to be seen in all quarters of the globe. As the Hanseatic League declined, the English Eastland Company took its place in trade with the Baltic, while the Muscovy Company extended its commerce with Russia. In the Mediterranean, English fortunes revived in the last decades of the sixteenth century and Leghorn (Livorno) became one of the principal outlets for cloth. Further east the merchants of the Levant Company took over much of the trade of Venice, now in decline, and transmitted to the western world the spices and riches of the orient. They were already trying to establish direct links with India and the Spice islands, and in 1599 they took a leading part in the discussions that led to the decision 'to set forth a voyage this present year to the East Indies and other islands and countries thereabouts, and there to make trade'. On the last day of 1600 the Queen issued a royal charter to these adventurers and thereby began the official career of the East India Company.

Industry

England was not a major industrial producer at the beginning of the Tudor period, except for cloth, and even here production was concentrated on coarse white broadcloths which were shipped to Flanders and Italy to be dyed and finished. Nor was industrial activity self-contained and located in factories and urban areas as it is today. Wool, for instance, was collected from the sheep farmers by clothiers who distributed it, or 'put it out', to be spun, woven and carded in private dwellings all over England and Wales. The major areas for manufacture were East Anglia, Yorkshire, Somerset, Gloucestershire and Wiltshire, and the clothmakers included many housewives, for this was one of the few activities in which they could fully participate. Domestic industry was a valuable source of additional income in woodland and pasture regions where the population was increasing but employment opportunities were limited. Even heavy industry was located in rural areas, and although the total numbers engaged in it were large, the actual units of operation were small. If a firm consisted of twenty men it was big business.

The most important heavy industry was the manufacture of iron, especially after the 1540s, when a French engineer pioneered the casting of iron cannon in England, thereby giving it a virtual monopoly of the process. English industry gained a great deal from foreign inventions. Blast furnaces, for example, were in use on the continent long before they were brought to England in the late fifteenth century. They were worked by water power and fuelled by charcoal, so had to be located in woodland regions where water was available. The Weald of Sussex and Kent was well suited for this purpose, and of some seventy blast furnaces known to have existed by the 1570s – compared with only three before 1530 – more than fifty were located in this region.

Lead, tin and copper were the principal non-ferrous metals mined in England. The main deposits of lead were in the north and south-west parts, and once extracted the ore had to be transported long distances to the major outlets in the midlands, London and the continent. Production was hit by the Dissolution of the Monasteries, because the lead stripped from the roofs of conventual buildings glutted the market, and by the development of new German mines in the second half of the sixteenth century. Tin came principally from Cornwall, and was despatched to English and foreign destinations by sea. Copper also was to be found in Cornwall, but there were other centres of extraction in Wales and the Lake District. The biggest of all extractive operations, however, took place in the coal industry, located primarily in the Durham area, from where the coal was sent for distribution to Newcastle. Some was shipped abroad, but the greater part was consumed in London, whose ever-growing population needed this cheap fuel to keep it warm in winter. 'Sea-coals' from Newcastle were already a feature of the London scene during Elizabeth's reign, and so were the smogs which they produced.

Tudor governments were anxious to encourage industry, partly to provide employment for an expanding population, but also to bring England abreast of continental techniques and free her from dependence upon foreign manufacturers. Sir Thomas Smith and William Cecil were active promoters of new projects, and one of the devices employed to protect these in the early stages of their development was the grant of a patent of monopoly, giving the projector sole rights of manufacture for a given period. The first such patent was issued for the glass industry in 1552, and they were also used to protect the manufacture of fine cloths, known as 'New Draperies', by refugees from France and The Netherlands who settled in England during Elizabeth's reign. Monopoly patents subsequently became a bone of contention between Elizabeth and her Parliaments, for they were increasingly used as a means of raising money for the crown rather than encouraging new processes. Nevertheless they served their original purpose. The stocking frame, invented by a Nottinghamshire parson in the 1590s, was protected by a patent and was soon being produced in considerable numbers and used, on a 'putting-out' basis, to establish a new industry of stocking knitting. Elizabeth's reign also saw a big expansion in the manufacture of small but essential items such as pins and nails, and the growth of a consumer market meant that commodities that had earlier been the preserve of the rich were now becoming accessible to all but the very poor.

Towns

One of the most striking phenomena of sixteenth-century England was the capital city, London. When Henry VII came to the throne it had a population of about sixty thousand, which made it far and away the biggest town in the kingdom. By 1600, however, London and its suburbs contained some 225,000 inhabitants, and the number was steadily rising. This increase in population was entirely due to immigration, since the death rate in the city exceeded that of live births. People flooded into London for a variety of reasons. Lawyers went there because the major law courts were located at Westminster. Government servants had to be resident there, at least for part of the year, and so did an increasing number of merchants, for during the Tudor period London established itself as the principal centre of English commerce.

As cloth exports were concentrated into a single outlet at Antwerp, so London became the port from which the majority of them were despatched, and by the middle of the sixteenth century about 90 per cent of all cloth destined for overseas markets went through the capital. London was also becoming a centre for luxury trades, and set fashions that the rest of England felt compelled, however reluctantly, to adopt. Its dominance was often resented in the provinces, and one writer complained at the way in which 'no gentleman can be content to have either cap, coat, doublet, hose or shirt made in his country [i.e. locality], but they must have their gear from London'. The 'outports', such as Bristol and Southampton, were badly hit by the shrinkage of their direct trade with the continent, but their fortunes picked up in the second half of the sixteenth century, following the collapse of the Antwerp market.

The commercial predominance of London increased its appeal to all those who wanted to carve out a career for themselves in trade. Younger sons of gentry families whose rights of inheritance were limited by the custom of primogeniture, whereby the eldest son received the lion's share, often bound themselves as apprentices to London merchants and became inhabitants of the city while they remained in tutelage. They had their professional counterparts in the trainee lawyers who took up residence in one of the inns of court that were sited on the north bank of the Thames, between the City proper and Whitehall. Apprentices, law students and the like were 'betterment migrants' who went to London in order to improve their career prospects. But their numbers were tiny compared with the thousands of 'subsistence migrants', poor people from all over England who made their way to the capital in the hope of scraping a living there. They sought shelter in the burgeoning suburbs, including those on the south bank, where they lived in acute squalor.

The slum tenements of the poor were in sharp contrast to the riverside mansions which the Tudor aristocracy built for themselves to the east of the royal palace of Whitehall. The land here had formerly belonged to the Church – as had Whitehall itself, until Wolsey handed it over to Henry VIII – but the disappearance of the abbots and the diminishing wealth and importance of the bishops led to its secularisation. Mansions were to be found also within the City. In the 1560s Sir Thomas Gresham, who was a leading financier and raised loans on the Antwerp market for Edward VI, Mary and Elizabeth, built Gresham House in Bishopsgate Street as his principal London residence. Its arcaded ground floor supported by marble pillars was inspired by the buildings with which Gresham had become acquainted in Antwerp, and his house in turn served as a model for the Royal Exchange, which he erected at his own expense in 1568 and gave to the City as a place where merchants could congregate and do business.

Gresham was a member of the Mercers, and this and other livery companies, such as the Goldsmiths and Drapers, were the strongholds of the merchant oligarchs who dominated London life. It was from among their number that the Lord Mayor and aldermen, who actually governed the metropolis, were chosen, and although they were nominally inferior in rank to the aristocracy and often looked down upon by the gentry, their power and influence were considerable, as was the range of their connections. Queen Elizabeth was descended through her mother from a Lord Mayor of London, and some of the leading figures of Stuart England, like Oliver Cromwell, John Hampden and Sir Thomas Osborne, were grandchildren of London aldermen. In this as in so many other ways the City made its mark on Tudor history.

Apart from London there were about half a dozen towns which emerged as regional centres in the sixteenth century. The most important were Bristol, York, Norwich, Exeter and Newcastle, which had populations of around ten thousand – small by London standards, but significantly bigger than the 1,500–7,000 inhabitants of the hundred or so towns whose significance was confined to their own counties. Further down the scale there were some five hundred market towns with populations ranging from six hundred to a thousand.

Generally speaking, the first half of the sixteenth century was a difficult time for English towns. Industries from which they had formerly benefited were moving into the countryside, where they were free from guild restrictions and also had easier access to water power and fuel. Overseas trade was dislocated by war and increasingly confined to London. High taxation, particularly in the 1520s and 1540s, fell heavily on the urban communities, and a further blow came with the Dissolution of the Monasteries, since the abbeys had been big purchasers and large-scale employers of labour. This difficult period reached its climax in the mid-Tudor crisis, but thereafter conditions began to improve. An act of 1554 gave corporate towns a virtual monopoly over retail trade in manufactured articles. Another, in the following year, placed restrictions upon the rural textile industry, and one of 1557 reinforced urban control over the whole process of cloth manufacture. It was also during these middle years of the century that the merchant oligarchs who ruled most large and medium-sized towns bought charters of incorporation from the crown. In 1547 there were some sixty corporate boroughs in England and Wales, but this figure had more than doubled by 1600. The royal government approved of oligarchic rule in the localities, since this was preferable either to magnate domination or to the involvement of the majority of the population, with all that this implied in the way of factiousness and undesirable influences. As for the oligarchs themselves, a royal charter gave them clearly defined powers and greatly strengthened their authority.

The poor

The principal cause of poverty in the sixteenth century was the rise in population, though even before this set in, enclosures and conversion from arable to pasture were creating the problem of vagrancy. Tudor governments, with only limited powers of coercion, distrusted vagrants because they represented a threat to the social order, and as early as 1495 the Vagrancy Act ordered that beggars should be set in the stocks and then returned to their customary place of abode. These provisions were repeated in an act of 1531 which laid down that a convicted vagrant was to be 'tied to the end of a cart naked and ... beaten with whips ... till his body be bloody'. He was then to return to his native parish 'and there put himself to labour, like as a true man oweth to do'.

The 1531 act, like its predecessor, assumed that the cause of poverty was idleness, the 'mother and root of all vices', but it followed medieval precedents in distinguishing between 'aged, poor and impotent persons', who were to be licensed to beg, and 'persons being whole and mighty in body and able to labour', who should earn a living by the sweat of their brows. This act was sponsored by Thomas Cromwell, but he realised that telling the poor to find work was pointless if no work was available. Cromwell turned for advice to a circle of humanists, of whom the most influential was William Marshall, and they drew up a scheme for employing the poor on public works paid for by a graduated income tax and supervised by a specially created 'Council to avoid Vagabonds'. A bill to implement these proposals was laid before Parliament in 1536, and Cromwell persuaded Henry VIII to appear in person to demonstrate his support for the measure. But members of Parliament, who represented the established order, found the bill unpalatable, and turned it into a pale shadow of what had originally been intended. They were still thinking in terms of compulsion, and in 1547, at the height of the mid-Tudor crisis, they passed an act ordering vagabonds to be enslaved, initially for two years, to ensure that they could be put to work. However, the idea of turning Englishmen, even poor ones, into slaves was so unappealing that the act remained a dead letter until its repeal in 1550.

One of the weaknesses of Tudor paternalism was that it had little statistical information on which to base its policies. Cromwell attempted to remedy this in 1538 by requiring all parishes to record details of baptisms, marriages and deaths, but he fell from power before this scheme was fully implemented. On a smaller scale, however, urban authorities were following a similar path. At Coventry, in 1547, a census of the poor was conducted in an attempt to discover what caused poverty and how best it might be relieved. This initiative was seconded by Parliament in an act of 1552 ordering the appointment in every parish of alms collectors who were to record the number of the poor and the amounts paid out to assist them.

In London a comprehensive scheme of poor relief was created in the 1540s and 1550s. 'Idle rogues' were set to labour in a workhouse created out of the old royal palace of Bridewell, while former ecclesiastical property was used to provide and maintain a number of hospitals to care for orphans, the sick and the aged. But there remained the need to provide relief for those who were temporarily out of work, and the cost of this exceeded the sums given by way of voluntary contributions. In 1547, therefore, London instituted a compulsory poor rate, and other towns, including York, Ipswich and Norwich, adopted similar solutions. The state once again codified these local initiatives, and an act of 1563 prescribed that anyone refusing to contribute towards the relief of poverty was to be brought before the Justices of the Peace, who could, if they saw fit, levy his contribution by distraint and send him to prison to reflect upon his lack of charity.

The crisis caused in the 1590s by successive harvest failures spurred Elizabeth's government to draft comprehensive measures which codified the Tudor poor law. These were given parliamentary approval in 1598 and confirmed, with only minor changes, in 1601. Vagabonds, as before, were to be whipped and sent back to their native parishes or places of recent abode and set to work in specially erected Houses of Correction. As for 'poor impotent persons', they were to be provided by their parishes with 'convenient houses of dwelling'. The money to build and maintain these was to be raised by a compulsory poor rate collected by Overseers of the Poor, who were to be appointed by, and responsible to, the local Justices of the Peace.

The Tudor poor law was designed as a framework within which national, local and individual initiatives could be combined. By itself it would have been insufficient, for it was only enforced sporadically, but the various systems of relief set up in towns, where the problem of poverty was too self-evident to ignore, functioned regularly and were, on the whole, effective. Private charity also made a substantial contribution, especially when individuals used their wealth to endow trusts which either relieved suffering through the payment of doles in money or kind, or stimulated self help by providing the deserving poor with the tools of a trade. Although accurate figures are hard to come by, it seems that by 1600 private charity was providing two to three times as much as poor rates.

While the Tudor poor law in its final form was the product of the 1590s crisis, the earlier mid-Tudor crisis had prompted the Statute of Artificers, or Apprentices, which was passed into law in 1563. This was an ambitious attempt to resolve the interrelated problems of poverty, vagabondage, unemployment and rising prices by conscripting the entire male population below the level of gentry. All craftsmen were to serve a seven-year apprenticeship, during which time they were to be under the control of their master. Non-craftsmen between the ages of twelve and sixty were to be set to work in agriculture. Justices of the Peace were instructed to see that these provisions were put into effect, and were also authorised to regulate wage rates by annual assessments. While the act, in theory, was all-encompassing, in practice it was only partially and sporadically enforced. The coercive mechanisms available to the Tudor state were far too limited to enable the regimentation of society on such a massive scale, and as economic conditions improved in the 1570s and 1580s the act lost much of its relevance.

The structure of society

English society was a pyramid that broadened out from the crown at the top to the mass of the population in the lower layers. Immediately below the sovereign and royal family came the aristocracy. Half the noble families in existence when Henry VII came to the throne had become extinct in the male line by the time Henry VIII died, because of the natural failure of heirs, helped on by executions. However, the aristocracy was self-generating through the grant of new titles, most of which went to men who had made their mark in the royal service. The older nobility was not excluded from the administration, but if individual members were employed it was because the King wished to employ them and not because of any prescriptive right on their part. When the Duke of Norfolk in Henry VIII's reign suggested that the northern borderlands should be ruled by noblemen, the Council was quick to rebuff him. The King, they told Norfolk, would choose whom he pleased to serve him, and if he 'appoint the meanest man to rule there, is not his grace's authority sufficient?' Norfolk's son, the Earl of Surrey, subsequently gave his answer to this question on the scaffold, for he died complaining that the King 'would deny the noble blood around him and employ none but mean creatures'.

The nobles were a small group, numbering just under fifty in 1547 and a little over in 1603. Elizabeth followed the example of her grandfather, Henry VII, when it came to making peers, and there were only two totally new creations during her long reign. One of these was the barony of Burghley granted to Sir William Cecil, but it says much about Elizabeth's attitude that the most long-serving, faithful and competent of her servants should have been advanced only to the lowest rung of the peerage ladder. At the top, the execution of the Duke of Norfolk in 1572 removed the last surviving duke, and no more were created, apart from members of the royal family, until 1623.

The peers were in general large landowners and had suffered badly from the effects of inflation, for while they had to pay more for the goods and services they required, their income from rents remained static. By the late sixteenth century, however, leases were falling in, copyholds were running out, and noble landowners were able to bring rents and entry fines up to a more realistic level. As a consequence, their incomes began to rise at a rate outstripping inflation, and although there were big variations between one family and another, the economic crisis of the aristocracy was all but over by the time Elizabeth died. This did not mean that the nobles were out of debt, for indebtedness was a reflection of their lifestyle rather than of any fundamental financial weakness. They were addicted to conspicuous consumption. They built huge houses for themselves and they spent vast sums of money on entertaining, extravagant clothes, jewellery, plate, and endless lawsuits. The days of armed retainers had gone, but households were still large. In 1590, for example, the Earl of Derby had 150 men on his payroll.

Below the aristocracy, and often connected with them by blood, came the gentry. They were already well rooted in the localities and in public life at the accession of Henry VII, but the redistribution of land which followed the Dissolution of the Monasteries gave them an even bigger stake in the country. The aristocracy and gentry were distinguished by the fact that they did not have to earn their living by manual labour. This was not the case with the yeomen, who formed the next layer of rural society. In theory, yeomen were the possessors of freehold land worth at least forty shillings a year, but in practice they held their property by a variety of tenures, and what counted was the size of their estate rather than its legal status. The term 'yeoman' was applied to men who farmed fifty acres or more, and substantial yeomen were virtually indistinguishable from lesser gentry. If they had little or no rent to pay they were well placed to profit from the increase in agricultural prices, and Elizabeth's reign was a golden age for many yeomen. Their good fortune did not endear them to those who were nominally their social superiors. Thomas Wilson, author of *The State of England, 1600*, was the younger son of a gentry family, who had to make his own way in the world. He commented acerbically on the sons of well-to-do yeomen who were 'not contented with their states of their fathers to be counted yeomen and called John or Robert', but each must 'skip into his velvet breeches and silken doublet and, getting to be admitted into some inn of court or Chancery, must ever after think scorn to be called any other than gentleman'.

Not all yeomen were flourishing, of course, and at the lower end of the scale they merged with the husbandmen – peasant cultivators who farmed anything from five to fifty acres. Below them came the cottagers, who might have one or two acres, and the landless labourers who relied on wages for their livelihood. The bottom layer consisted of the poor who were without any means of subsistence and depended upon private and parish charity.

The amount of land that a family held at any time gives an indication of its status, but Tudor society was far more fluid than categorisation implies, and although prevailing trends might favour one group rather than another, much depended upon individual circumstances. Recusancy might cripple one family, extravagance another, incompetence or sheer bad luck a third. In parts of the country agriculture was profitable enough for a landowner to flourish and extend his estates, while in other parts some extra source of income – the law, perhaps, or trade, or marriage to an heiress – was needed. Much depended also upon personal character- istics. One man might make a handsome profit out of holding public office while another would merely acquire expensive habits that led him to live above his income. One man would run his estates with ruthless and prof- itable efficiency, while his neighbour would be held back by timidity, social conventions, tender-heartedness, or simply lack of interest and ability.

Education

Both before and after the Reformation the Church made provision for primary education. In 1530, for instance, Convocation ordered all incum- bents to teach the alphabet to the boys in their parishes and train them to read. Chantry priests performed a similar function, with children as young as seven or eight years of age, until the dissolution of the chantries in 1547. There was no automatic transition from reading to writing, and ninety per cent of the population of early Tudor England were unable even to write their names. Yet a gradual improvement took place during the course of the sixteenth century, stimulated by the advent of protestantism, which placed such an emphasis on the word of God as revealed in the Bible. By the 1590s the great majority of gentlemen were literate, as were some 60 per cent of yeomen and 45 per cent of persons involved in commerce. Among husbandmen, however, the figure was much lower, a mere 13 per cent, and generally speaking the social distribution of literacy mirrored the hierarchical structure of Elizabethan England.

Most children from poor families, particularly in rural areas, started work at thirteen or earlier, and so had little time for anything but the most rudimentary education. The luckier ones, who came from families higher up the social scale, would often become apprentices, and more and more boys, as well as a small number of girls, followed this route in the hundred years after 1550. Towns were expanding and served as a magnet for those in search of employment. By the end of Elizabeth's reign London was attracting between four and five thousand apprentices every year, and they were an essential ingredient in maintaining the capital's population growth. Apprenticeship covered virtually every sort of gainful activity, but its cost varied according to the status of the trade or profession. Parents of apprentice shoemakers or blacksmiths, for instance, would pay only a few pounds, but those whose sons were contracted to a successful merchant might have to find £100 or above. A small though rising proportion of apprentices came from lesser gentry families, but many more were sons of yeomen or husbandmen. Urban tradesmen and artisans also used this means of giving their children work skills and the prospect of employment.

While apprenticeships gave a technical education, grammar schools concentrated on teaching Latin, which was regarded as not only an international language but also the repository of the wisdom of the ancient world. The Church had been forced to abandon its claim to a monopoly of secondary education by a judgment given in the Court of King's Bench in 1411. This upheld the right of a layman to set up a school, and during the course of the sixteenth century more and more were founded, not only by individuals but also by boroughs, livery companies and guilds. There were some two to three hundred grammar schools in Tudor England, and the passion for education at all levels of society except the lowest meant that the number of pupils was constantly going up.

Despite the 1411 judgment the Church still had a major role in education in the early Tudor period. Monasteries sometimes established schools of their own, as at Reading, and also acted as trustees for independent foundations. The Dissolution put an end to all this, of course, and although schemes were drawn up for re-establishing schools in the new dioceses that were created, they were not all put into effect. It was left to local and individual effort to plug the gap. At Sherborne, the town bought the abbey church and used it for a school, while in London the Mercers Company acquired a monastic institution and turned it into the Mercers' School in 1542. The dissolution of the chantries was an even bigger threat to education than that of the monasteries, for many established schools had received bequests as part of a chantry foundation and now found their endowments at risk. However, Edward VI's government appreciated the value of secondary education in spreading protestant doctrines and therefore instructed the Court of Augmentations to make appropriate provision where necessary. This meant that part of the profits accruing to the crown from dissolving the chantries was used to endow, or re-endow, what were thereafter known as King Edward VI grammar schools.

Elizabeth's reign was a period of consolidation as far as secondary education was concerned. After the suppression of the religious community re-established by Mary at Westminster, Elizabeth authorised the transfer of some of its funds to what became Westminster School, but this was virtually the end of her initiative in this field. Once again the lead was taken by individuals, companies and corporations. London merchants were particularly active in setting up schools, and there were a number of instances of flourishing yeomen using their wealth for this purpose. The overall result of both public and private activity was a net gain of some 130 grammar schools in the Tudor period – a remarkable achievement in view of the setback at the time of the Dissolution.

Instruction in Latin was the principal objective of grammar schools, and learning was largely by rote and enforced by strict discipline. The first attempt to break away from this time-honoured but sterile approach came with the establishment of Magdalen College School at Oxford in 1480, for the headmaster developed methods of teaching Latin grammar based on the enlightened Italian model. A number of his pupils stayed on to train as teachers, among them William Lily, who was chosen by John Colet to be the head of the new school he set up at St Paul's (of which he was Dean) in 1510. Colet wanted St Paul's School to be a committedly humanist institution, where students would acquire not merely a knowledge of Latin but a real understanding of the works of both classical and Christian writers. There were no suitable books available, so Lily wrote them himself, with the assistance of Erasmus. His Latin grammar, published in 1513, soon established itself as the basic textbook on this subject, but the influence of St Paul's was slow to make itself felt. Humanists were relatively few in number, and teachers of the quality of Lily were thin on the ground.

The two universities, Oxford and Cambridge, underwent considerable change in the Tudor period. At the time of Henry VII's accession they were still what they had been for several centuries, centres for training clerical administrators. But humanist influences were making themselves felt, and Erasmus struck a responsive chord when he declared that clergy should not simply be men who were expert in civil or canon law but committed preachers engaged in active evangelisation. One of Erasmus's patrons was John Fisher, who became Chancellor of Cambridge University in 1503. Fisher was also chaplain to Henry VII's mother, Lady Margaret Beaufort, and it was at his suggestion that she instituted the Lady Margaret chairs in divinity at both universities and increased the educational provision for future preachers by founding first Christ's College and then St John's, both at Cambridge. Her example was followed by Richard Fox, Bishop of Winchester and Lord Privy Seal, who founded Corpus Christi College at Oxford.

Erasmus was resident for a time in Cambridge, and gave the first recorded Greek class there in 1511. Seven years later the first Reader in Greek was appointed by the university, and at the same time Greek was probably being taught in Cardinal College, Wolsey's princely new foundation at Oxford. This survived Wolsey's fall but was later suppressed by Henry VIII so that he could resurrect it as his own foundation of Christ Church. The new college was established in 1546, and in the same year Henry swept a number of small Cambridge institutions into his palatial new foundation of Trinity College. The King also established five regius professorships at both universities, in Greek, Hebrew, divinity, civil law and medicine.

The universities still regarded it as their main task to produce graduate clergy for the Church of England, and in Elizabeth's reign this function became increasingly important in view of widespread criticism of the ministry. However, laymen from the upper sections of English society were also attending the universities in larger numbers than before, especially if they were thinking of a career in public life, for the Renaissance state demanded educated men for its service. In 1535 William Cecil went up to St John's College, Cambridge, where he stayed for six years and then moved on to Gray's Inn without taking a degree. Walter Mildmay, a future Chancellor of the Exchequer, did exactly the same, except that he chose Christ's as his college. Cecil, who was to become Chancellor of Cambridge as well as Elizabeth's principal minister, always retained a deep affection for his university. Apart from anything else he had a family link with it, for he married the sister of John Cheke, the first Regius Professor of Greek at Cambridge. As for Sir Walter Mildmay, he showed his commitment by founding a new college, Emmanuel, and choosing as its first master Laurence Chaderton, another Christ's man. Chaderton was a distinguished scholar but notorious for his puritan views, which was why Mildmay chose him. The Queen was suspicious and asked her minister whether he intended to erect a puritan foundation. 'Far be it from me to countenance anything contrary to established laws', replied Mildmay, 'but I have set an acorn which, when it becomes an oak, God alone knows what will be the fruits thereof'.

There was no problem about finding students for the expanding universities, since demand for places was high, except for a slight fall-off in the 1580s. Most of the undergraduates were drawn from the upper sections of English society, and although this may have been good for the prestige of the universities it meant they were less fitted to carry out their traditional function of educating the poor as well as the rich. As for the quality of teaching, this varied from college to college, and although the humanists had succeeded in modifying the medieval scholastic curriculum, too much of its framework remained for some tastes. Francis Bacon, for example, who went up to Trinity at the age of twelve, was happy to leave it two years later, for he found Cambridge 'only strong for disputations and contentions, but barren of the production of works for the benefit of the life of man'.

Many of the young men who attended the universities went on to complete their education at one of the inns of court. The four principal ones were Lincoln's Inn, Gray's Inn, Middle Temple and Inner Temple – the last two so-called because they occupied the former property of the Knights Templar on the north bank of the Thames, between Whitehall and the City. Not all those who became members of an inn of court intended to make their career as lawyers. Tudor England was an intensely litigious society, and it therefore made sense for property owners to acquire at least a partial knowledge of the law. However, it was also the case that litigiousness increased the demand for lawyers, as well as the profits to be made out of their profession. Numbers therefore were going up, from some forty a year for the four major inns in the early sixteenth century to three hundred by the early seventeenth. The study of law at one of the inns was a very expensive process, and entry was in general confined to the sons of the well-off. Not all of them worked hard, but the contacts they made could be very useful. As for students who did well, they could look forward to a lucrative and prestigious career.

CHAPTER SEVEN

Ireland and Scotland in the Tudor period

IRELAND

Henry VII and Kildare

At the time of Henry VII's accession English rule in Ireland was confined to the Pale, a strip of land stretching northwards from Dublin for fifty miles and extending some twenty miles inland. The rest of the country, the 'Irishry', was occupied by Gaelic-speaking clans under the leadership of their hereditary chieftains. However, the most powerful families were the Anglo-Irish, descended from the Anglo-Norman invaders of the twelfth century. Principal among these were the Butlers, Earls of Ormond, and the FitzGeralds (Geraldines), Earls of Kildare. The King's representative in Ireland was the Lord Deputy. In 1485 this was the eighth Earl of Kildare, who had held the same office under Edward IV and was a Yorkist sympathiser. Henry would have liked to remove him from office, but there was no obvious replacement, and his control of Leinster as well as his connections with many of the leading Irish families made him all but indispensable.

Kildare's loyalty was tested early in the new reign when Lambert Simnel landed at Dublin in May 1487, claiming to be the Earl of Warwick, the Yorkist heir to the throne (*see* p. 1). Kildare and his

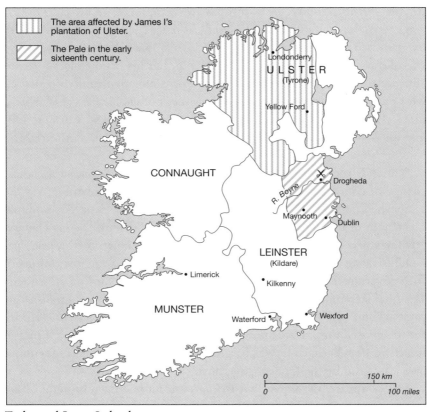

The area affected by James I's
plantation of Ulster.

The Pale in the early
sixteenth century.

Londonderry

ULSTER
(Tyrone)

Yellow Ford

CONNAUGHT

R. Boyne

Drogheda

Maynooth

Dublin

LEINSTER
(Kildare)

Limerick

Kilkenny

MUNSTER

Waterford

Wexford

0   150 km
0   100 miles

Tudor and Stuart Ireland

associates were apparently taken in by the pretender, for they allowed
Simnel to be crowned King as 'Edward VI' in Dublin Cathedral, and an
Irish contingent sailed with the Yorkist expedition to England. Simnel's
career as a pretender to the throne was ended by the battle of Stoke, and
Henry now had to decide what to do about Ireland. A total English take-
over would have been far too expensive and risky an operation to mount,
and in any case Ireland had little to offer. Its chief importance was negative, in that it afforded a potential base for enemies of the Tudor dynasty.
All that Henry required was the passive acceptance of his rule by the
Anglo-Irish lords, and he therefore sent over Sir Richard Edgecumbe with
five hundred men to impose an oath of loyalty. Kildare took the oath and
was allowed to retain the Lord Deputyship, but his main concern was to
advance the fortunes of his family, and a possible opportunity opened up
with the appearance on the scene of another pretender, Perkin Warbeck,
in 1491. It was not so much commitment to the Yorkist cause as self-
interest that persuaded Kildare to acknowledge Warbeck as the rightful
King of England.

Kildare's repeated treachery prompted Henry VII to make a radical
change of course in his policy towards Ireland. Instead of ruling via the
established families he appointed his baby son, Prince Henry, as nominal
Lieutenant of Ireland with a soldier, Sir Edward Poynings, as his Deputy.
Poynings was given instructions to appoint Englishmen to the principal
administrative positions in the Pale and to ensure that the institutions of
Irish government should never again be taken over by Yorkist pretenders.
The final step in the process of bringing Ireland under direct English rule
came when Poynings summoned the Irish Parliament in December 1496,
for this passed the statute known as 'Poynings' Law' which stated that in
future no Irish Parliament was to assemble or pass any legislation without
prior approval by the English government.

Henry apparently hoped that Ireland, once it had been brought under
effective control, could be made to pay its way, but in fact it cost him some
£7,000 a year to keep an army there and maintain direct rule. This was far
more than Henry was willing to pay, and he therefore decided to revert to
indirect rule, although he left Poynings in Ireland for fear that Warbeck
might make a reappearance. This in fact happened in 1495, when the pretender landed in Ireland and laid siege to Waterford – the second most
important town in the country, though well beyond the Pale. But
Waterford, with Poynings' aid, held out, and Warbeck was compelled to
abandon the siege and sail away to Scotland. The way was now open for
Poynings to return to England, and following his departure Henry restored

Kildare to the Deputyship. The earl remained ruler of Ireland – or, rather, of the Pale and the FitzGerald sphere of influence outside it – until his death in 1513, during which time the country enjoyed relative peace and prosperity. It seemed that from the English point of view the best policy to adopt towards Ireland was one of benign neglect.

Henry VIII and the Kingdom of Ireland

While Henry VII was content to hold Ireland at arm's length, his son, Henry VIII, was more concerned with asserting his authority there. In 1520 he appointed his best soldier, the Earl of Surrey, as Lieutenant, and had vague plans to bring the whole island under English control. He was persuaded to change his mind when Surrey reported that conquering Ireland would be a slow process requiring a force of 2,500 men. A speedier conquest would need six thousand men and involve the forcible settlement of hundreds of English immigrants. Henry was no more willing than his father to spend sums of this magnitude, and although he made frequent changes of Deputy he had no coherent programme of action in mind.

The danger that Ireland might be used as a base by the King's enemies became acute in the 1530s, when Henry affronted catholic Europe by breaking with Rome, and Thomas Cromwell drew up plans for making it an integral part of the English monarchy. There was nothing revolutionary about his proposals – which included strengthening the Dublin administration and reducing magnate power through the extension of royal authority into the Irishry – but he pushed them forward with a tenacity that was typical of him. Kildare was summoned to London, possibly in the hope that he might agree to co-operate in the implementation of the reform programme. When he arrived, in 1534, he was caught up in the factional struggle at court, where his sympathies lay with the conservatives. His presence in Ireland would clearly present an impediment to Cromwell's policy, so he was forbidden to return. Moreover, his son and heir, known as 'Silken Thomas', was ordered to come to London and join his father. Kildare warned him not to obey, and Silken Thomas instead raised a force of one thousand men and marched on Dublin, where he denounced Henry VIII. This was a protest, not a revolt, but when Silken Thomas heard that his father had been imprisoned in the Tower of London – where he died in September 1534 – he seized the greater part of the Pale as well as adjoining districts, and by committing himself to the defence of catholicism and making common cause with the Gaelic chieftains, he turned his movement into the semblance of a nationalist crusade.

The Geraldine revolt posed a real threat to the maintenance of English authority in Ireland, but Henry was saved by the fact that the Butlers remained loyal and that Dublin held out against the rebels. However, he now had no choice but to use force, and he raised an army of over two thousand men – the largest to be sent to Ireland since Richard II's reign – and gave command of it to Sir William Skeffington, a former Lord Deputy. In March 1535 Skeffington stormed Silken Thomas's castle at Maynooth and slaughtered most of the garrison. Silken Thomas kept up the struggle for a few months longer, but his followers deserted him and he eventually surrendered. He was sent to England with a promise of safety for his person, but in February 1537 he was hanged at Tyburn along with five of his uncles. The Geraldine leadership had, in effect, been wiped out.

There was little alternative now to the reimposition of direct rule, and Cromwell despatched a number of trusted officials to Dublin to take over the administration under the aegis of Skeffington, who had been reappointed Lord Deputy in May 1534. However, the presence of a large English army was an implicit threat not only to the Anglo-Irish families but to the Gaelic chieftains as well, especially since they remained faithful to the papacy and the old religion. Discontent continued to smoulder and flared up again when Lord Leonard Grey, who took over the administration after Skeffington's death in late 1535, continued the extension of English power into the Irishry. Henry VIII was now committed, or so it seemed, to the maintenance of an army in Ireland on a permanent basis, but this involved considerable expenditure. Additional resources were found by dissolving the Irish monasteries and confiscating the lands of the attainted Geraldine leaders, but Ireland was still costing Henry some £4,000 a year, which he could ill afford.

With the recall of Grey in April 1540 and the fall of Cromwell two months later the forward policy lost its champions and Henry adopted a more conciliatory approach. The change of course was signalled in June 1541 when the Irish Parliament formally recognised Henry as King of Ireland. The new Deputy, Sir Anthony St Leger, thereupon invited the chieftains of the Irishry to surrender their lands to the crown and have them regranted as fiefs. He also encouraged them to adopt a more settled and 'civilised' way of life, including the use of the English language instead of 'barbaric' Gaelic, and to recognise that the best way of preserving their dominant role in the social hierarchy was through co-operation with the crown. In 1542 a number of chieftains made their appearance at court and were graciously received by Henry, who conferred noble titles on them: the O'Neills, for example, became Earls of Tyrone and the O'Brians Earls of Thomond. This, it was hoped, was the beginning of a process that would lead Ireland to become an integral part of the Tudor state.

Elizabeth I and the Irish Rebellion

The process of surrender and regrant, which was designed to turn nomadic Irish chieftains into English-style landlords, might well have succeeded, given time. Religion was not, at first, a problem, for there was no great love for the Pope in Ireland and most of the bishops as well as the nobles and chieftains had accepted the royal supremacy. When, in 1542, Jesuit missionaries arrived in Ulster they were given such a chilly reception that they sailed on to Scotland. The doctrinal changes of Edward VI's reign, however, were less acceptable, especially since they were imposed without any pretence at consultation. The Irish Parliament was not invited to confirm the religious settlement, nor was any attempt made to produce an Irish prayer book. As a consequence, the protestant Reformation never took root, and the attitude of the clergy was epitomised by the Archbishop of Armagh, who had accepted the King as head of the Church, but declared that 'he would never be a bishop where the holy mass was abolished'.

Protector Somerset was committed to a forward policy in both Scotland and Ireland, based on the establishment of English garrisons. He therefore recalled St Leger and replaced him with a soldier, Sir Edward Bellingham, who was given substantial support in the way of money, troops and supplies. By the early part of 1549 Bellingham had extended English power well into the Irishry and encouraged settlers to occupy the land around the garrisons. The initial plantations were small-scale, but Somerset was envisaging much more extensive settlement and would have put his plans into effect had he not fallen from power. The 'Old English' – that is to say those English people, including the Anglo-Irish families, who had become resident in Ireland and thought of it as their country – objected to the whole idea of settlement or, as it was commonly called, plantation. They preferred St Leger's policy of 'civilising' the natives, and were relieved when the Duke of Northumberland, after he became Edward VI's chief minister, reappointed him as Lord Deputy. But security considerations linked to fear of a French invasion prompted a return to more aggressive methods, and although the Old English continued to insist that the best way in which to win over the native Irish was through conciliation, the Privy Council asserted that 'we win them not by their wills but by our power ... Then shall they obey because they cannot choose'.

Mary began her reign by reverting to a policy of conciliation, not least because the military option was so expensive. Once again St Leger returned to govern Ireland and promote harmony, but in May 1556 he was replaced by Sir Thomas Ratcliffe, shortly to become Earl of Sussex. Ratcliffe made the security of the Pale his main objective and built a number of forts along its border. He also encouraged English settlement in the area immediately to the west of it, hoping thereby to create a buffer zone between the Pale and the Irishry, and to accelerate the 'civilising' process by giving the native Irish alternative role models in the persons of the 'New English'. He had a substantial army at his disposal, because of the continuing threat of a French invasion, but the Irish and Old English resented being made to pay for it. Sussex's popularity slumped and he made matters worse by becoming involved in the struggles between the Irish chieftains. Mary recalled him, but he had powerful friends on the Privy Council and was soon sent back again. He retained his office until 1563.

Down to the middle years of the sixteenth century English policy towards Ireland had alternated between direct rule (very expensive) and indirect rule (cheaper but less efficient), and the Old English had been regarded as the natural governors of the country, even if their authority was in practice confined to the Pale. The Old English, generally speaking, were catholics, though prepared to accept Erasmian humanism of the sort that Henry VIII seemed to embody. They might even have been won over to protestantism if a consistent attempt had been made. But the Church in Ireland was underfunded and understaffed, and conditions were not such as to attract committed evangelicals. The Edwardian governments pre-ferred to enforce their will by diktat rather than consultation, and they thought of the Old English as impediments to change rather than possible agents.

Another factor which transformed the English attitude was the growth of interest in the idea of colonies. England had not yet embarked upon the attempt to plant colonies in the New World, but the concept of imposing Christian rule upon native populations which were in a state of primitive barbarism made a strong appeal. It was but a short distance, mentally speaking, to transfer this way of thinking to Ireland. Whereas earlier gen-erations of Tudor statesmen had thought of Ireland as a semi-detached piece of England, with the Old English as the equivalent of the country gentry, later Tudor regimes treated it as a colony, to be subjugated by force. There was no obvious role for the Old English in this scenario, and as their pleas for a more moderate policy were brushed aside they began to think of themselves as a separate community instead of as Englishmen resident in Ireland. From about 1568 they adopted the use of the term Old English to describe themselves, and they moved towards a closer identification with the native Irish chieftains.

In 1565 the Privy Council took into consideration the question of 'whether the Queen's majesty . . . be counselled to govern Ireland after the Irish manner, as it hath been accustomed, or to reduce it as near as may be to the English government?' It opted for the second of these alternatives and thereby radically altered the course of Anglo-Irish history. Ireland beyond the Pale had its own language, customs and law, but these were now to be replaced by the English language, English law, and the system of local administration based upon counties that had evolved in England over many centuries. The assumption behind the Privy Council's thinking was that what worked well in England would also work well in Ireland, but this was to ignore the big differences between the two countries, for the inhabitants of Ireland had a profound attachment to their traditional institutions and would not easily abandon them.

The new policy in Ireland was put into operation by Sir Henry Sidney, who succeeded the Earl of Sussex as Lord Deputy in 1565. His brief was, in effect, to conquer and colonise Ireland, and he had the appropriate mental approach. He could see nothing of value in the native Irish and their ways and believed that their subjugation to the English was the only means by which to raise them out of their present appalling condition. 'There was never people that lived in more misery than they do', he told Elizabeth. 'Perjury, robbery and murder [are] counted allowable . . . I cannot find that they make any conscience of sin, and I doubt whether they christen their children or no.' One of the problems confronting Sidney concerned Ulster. Sussex had been caught up in a struggle with the Irish chieftain Shane O'Neill for control of this large region covering much of northern Ireland, and the situation was unresolved at the time of his recall. Sidney only had a small army, but the Queen sent him more men, as well as £6,000, to mount a campaign against O'Neill, which he did very successfully. O'Neill fled to Antrim but met his death there in 1567.

Sidney also had to deal with unrest in Munster, where fighting had broken out between the FitzGeralds, Earls of Desmond, and the Butlers, Earls of Ormond. The two earls were summoned to court, where they made their submission to Elizabeth, but Desmond broke the terms of his submission and was subsequently arrested by Sidney and despatched to the Tower of London, where he remained prisoner for several years. The vacuum left by his absence was filled by his cousin, James FitzMaurice

FitzGerald, who led a revolt in Munster and called on catholic powers for support. Before this could arrive, however, he was defeated by Sidney and forced to flee abroad. Sidney, meanwhile, acting on the Queen's orders, had set up provincial councils in Connaught and Munster, modelled on the Council of the North in England and the Council in the Marches of Wales. These were designed not only to maintain order in their respective areas but also to set an example of 'civilised' government in the hope that the warring clans might heed it. But they lost goodwill by riding roughshod over local customs and property rights and had to be suspended.

By 1571, when he was recalled to England, Sidney had done much to pacify Ireland, but at great cost. The Privy Council was searching for a cheaper solution to the Irish problem, but could not agree on what would be the best option. Sidney was therefore sent back to resume his rule, but three years later he returned to London for good. In the interim the Old English and their supporters at court had taken the opportunity to press their view that the forward policy was not simply too expensive but also self-defeating, since it alienated those elements in Irish society whose co-operation would be needed for any permanent settlement. The Irish Lord Chancellor argued that the best strategy would be to concentrate on the Pale and gradually extend the range of the common law outside it – what he described as 'by little and little to stretch the Pale further'. Military operations ought to be confined to the maintenance of garrisons, and every effort should be made to win over the Gaelic chieftains and their followers by persuasion. This would take time but not a great deal of money, and that, so far as the government was concerned, was the strong point in its favour.

It looked as though the advocates of conciliation had won the day, but at this critical juncture, in July 1579, James FitzMaurice FitzGerald landed in the south-west at the head of an invasion force assembled with papal encouragement and money. He was joined by his cousin, the Earl of Desmond, and sparked off a rebellion in Munster and Leinster that threatened to spread into the rest of Ireland. FitzMaurice's initial success owed much to the fact that the earlier pursuit of forward policies by the English government had lost them the support of the Old English and other inhabitants who in normal circumstances would have upheld royal authority. Conciliation now went by the board and the Queen appointed Lord Grey of Wilton as Lord-Deputy, with instructions to put down the revolt. By the middle of 1580 Grey had 6,500 soldiers at his command, more than sufficient to crush the rising. He was convinced that he was confronted with a widespread catholic conspiracy threatening the entire English presence in

Ireland, and he treated rebels and their supporters – real or imagined – with the greatest severity. By 1583 he had restored order to Munster, but only after destroying cattle and crops and reducing the native Irish to destitution. Edmund Spenser, who was Grey's secretary at the time, described them 'creeping forth upon their hands, for their legs could not bear them. They looked like anatomies of death. They spake like ghosts crying out of their graves. They did eat the dead carrions, happy where they could find them'.

The suppression of the Munster rebellion meant that there was now no obstacle to the plantation of that region. Burghley and Ralegh drew up a plan, based upon Ralegh's proposals for a settlement in the New World, by which 400,000 acres of Munster were to be confiscated and distributed to English immigrants. Plantation was a slow business, as famine, disease and incompetence all took their toll, but it was extended to Connaught and gradually undermined the traditional way of life of the native Irish.

Whereas the Old English had a certain sympathy with and respect for the natives, based on long acquaintance, this was not the case with the New English settlers. They could not understand the Gaelic spoken by the Irish, and they were shocked by their uncouth dress and primitive way of life. Their attitude was very similar to that of the Spaniards towards the American Indians and they saw their mission in much the same terms, as the imposition upon a backward people of a higher civilisation. The lack of harmony between the New English, on the one hand, and the Old English and Irish on the other, was increased by the commitment of the latter to Roman Catholicism, for protestantism had never taken root outside the Pale, and the influx of catholic missionaries from the continent which began in the 1580s helped revive and maintain the old faith, particularly as it was now linked with the defence of 'Irish' values against alien rule. Many of the New English settlers were extreme protestants who saw no difference between catholic ritual and pagan superstition, and far from wishing to fuse the two cultures, which had been the aim of English policy in the 1540s, they saw it as their God-given duty to eradicate 'Irishness' in all its shapes and forms.

The Irish chieftains, who had earlier been encouraged to anglicise themselves, might have been able to bridge the gap between the natives and the immigrants. Hugh O'Neill, for instance, the second Earl of Tyrone, had spent several years at Penshurst Place in Kent as the guest of the Sidneys, and he and his sons spoke fluent English. But when men such as these were forced to choose between the English and Irish ways of life, blood ties and the sense of their own identity made them opt for the Irish.

Tyrone, who had built up a powerful position for himself in Ulster, demanded that chieftain rule should be preserved and the Irish allowed freedom of worship as Roman Catholics. When the Queen refused to accept these conditions he appealed for support to Philip II of Spain. Philip sent money and also prepared an armada that sailed in 1596. The armada was turned back by storms before it reached Ireland, but the prospect of foreign aid ignited Irish nationalism and produced a major rebellion in Ulster, where an English army suffered a crushing defeat at the battle of the Yellow Ford, north of Armagh, in August 1598. The uprising now spread to other parts of Ireland, until only the Pale and some of the coastal towns remained loyal to Elizabeth.

The Queen, who had already spent a million pounds on Ireland, was reluctant to pour more money away on a military campaign. But the threat of an independent Ireland under Spanish patronage was too real to ignore, and the Earl of Essex, appointed Lord-Lieutenant in 1599, was despatched with some seventeen thousand men – the largest army to be sent to Ireland in the Tudor period. Essex's campaign, however, was a failure. Instead of fighting Tyrone he negotiated a truce that left the Irish leader in control of Ulster, and promptly returned to England to put his case to the Queen.

Elizabeth refused to recognise the truce and replaced her tarnished favourite by Charles Blount, Lord Mountjoy. He avoided pitched battles and waged a war of attrition instead, destroying the rebels' supplies and consolidating his gains by establishing powerful garrisons. By the autumn of 1601 Munster had been pacified and Mountjoy was about to take on Tyrone in Ulster when news reached him that four thousand Spanish troops had landed on the south coast, at Kinsale. The success of Mountjoy's pacification was demonstrated by the marked lack of support given to these 'liberators', and when Tyrone marched south to link up with them he was heavily defeated. Early in 1602 the Spaniards surrendered and were allowed to return home. With them went the last hopes of the rebels, and in March 1603 Tyrone laid down his arms.

Tyrone's surrender completed the Tudor conquest of Ireland. He was treated generously and allowed to keep his lands, as were most of the other Irish lords, but they had to accept the suzerainty of the English crown. Their authority was slowly replaced by that of the English common law, supplemented by the conciliar Court of Castle Chamber in Dublin, but no change took place in religion. The Irish adherence to the catholic faith, linked so closely to the sense of their own identity, was to remain a perpetual challenge to English supremacy and a source of conflict in the future.

SCOTLAND

James IV

The principal difference between Scotland and Ireland in the sixteenth century was that Scotland had been for many years an independent country under the rule of its own kings. James IV, who came to the throne in 1488, was determined that his kingdom should play a more prominent role in European politics, and he seized on Perkin Warbeck (*see* p. 2) as an instrument for this purpose. However, the failure of his attempted invasion of England forced him to change course, and in 1499 he signed a truce with Henry VII. This was transformed into a 'perpetual peace' in 1502, and in the following year James married Henry's eldest daughter, Margaret.

Peace between the two kingdoms lasted for the rest of Henry VII's reign, but the accession of the hot-blooded and ambitious Henry VIII brought it to an end. Henry was contemptuous of the Scots and determined to renew the struggle with France, to whom the Scots were bound by the 'auld alliance'. By 1512 England and France were at war, and Henry crossed the Channel to lead his armies in person, leaving the defence of England's northern border to the Earl of Surrey. In August 1513 James IV moved south to attack the English in the rear, but Surrey had prepared his position well. The two armies met at Flodden, south-west of Berwick, early in September, and in a battle that lasted well into the night the Scots were overwhelmed. James IV himself was killed, along with the flower of the Scottish nobility and some ten thousand of his troops, and his realm now passed to his son, the infant James V.

James V

Henry VIII's sister, Queen Margaret, acted as regent for her one-year-old son, but in 1515 she was driven out of the country by the enemies of her second husband, the Earl of Angus. James's cousin, the Duke of Albany, who had recently arrived from France, took her place as regent. Henry promoted schemes for Albany's removal, since he did not want a francophile Scotland threatening him at a time when he was planning the renewal of his war against France. Throughout 1522 there was trouble along the Anglo-Scottish border, and in the following year English troops carried out a number of punitive expeditions. Albany tried to rally the

Scots lords and lead them against England, but fear of another Flodden hampered his efforts and in 1524 he returned to France. This left the way clear for Margaret and the anglophile lords who, in 1524, declared that James V was now of age and therefore capable of ruling in his own right.

Henry VIII's break with Rome and the subsequent drift away from orthodox catholicism did not have as profound an effect on Anglo-Scottish relations as it did on those between England and Ireland, because protestantism made quick inroads into Scotland. However, James V remained loyal to the old faith, not least because he had been permitted to divert certain ecclesiastical revenues to secular purposes. In January 1537 he married a French princess, and after her untimely death he took as his second wife Mary, daughter of the Duke of Guise, the head of one of the greatest catholic houses in France. Henry VIII was faced with the prospect of a francophile catholic kingdom on his northern frontier just at the moment when he was once again preparing to invade France. Since persuasion would not work he had recourse to force, and in 1542 the Duke of Norfolk led a punitive expedition into Scotland. When the Scots counterattacked in November 1542 they were defeated at Solway Moss, near Carlisle, and James, who was already ill, did not long survive the disgrace. In December he died, leaving as heir his baby daughter, Mary, only a week old, who now became Queen of Scots.

English intervention in Scotland

The death of James V brought to power the Earl of Arran, leader of the anglophile protestant party among the Scottish nobles. Henry VIII saw an opportunity of extending Tudor sovereignty to Scotland, as he had already done to Wales and Ireland, and negotiations were set on foot for a marriage between Mary and Henry's heir, Prince Edward. These were successfully concluded in 1543 and the terms were incorporated into the Treaty of Greenwich of that year. But this agreement, presaging as it did the eventual subordination of Scotland to England, was deeply resented by the Scots, and Arran came under strong pressure to renounce it, which he eventually did.

Henry demonstrated his anger at this snub by sending the Earl of Hertford at the head of an army into Scotland, with orders to devastate the country. Hertford did his job thoroughly and left Edinburgh and Leith in flames as he returned to England. The immediate effect of this vengeful policy on Henry's part was to close Scottish ranks against the aggressor, but the religious divisions in Scotland were by now too deep to be permanently healed. John Knox was the leader of the protestants, whom he had imbued with his own particular brand of Calvinist fundamentalism, and he looked to England for support. While an English fleet cruised off the Scottish coast the protestants could maintain themselves in power, but when, following Henry's death, the ships were withdrawn, the catholic party, supported by French arms, quickly triumphed. Knox was sent to the galleys and many of his followers were imprisoned.

Hertford, now transformed into Lord Protector Somerset, determined to retrieve the situation by a display of force. In September 1547 he invaded Scotland with an army of sixteen thousand men, supported by a large fleet, and routed the Scots at the Battle of Pinkie. In order to solve the Scottish problem once and for all he decided to station English garrisons in a number of key places, where they would serve – or so he hoped – as rallying points for the protestant anglophile elements among the population. At first this scheme worked well, but the cost of maintaining the garrisons was enormous. In two years Somerset spent £350,000 on military operations in Scotland, which was far more than the English Exchequer could afford. Moreover, the very success of his policy ensured its downfall by provoking French intervention. In July 1548 some ten thousand French troops landed in Scotland, occupied Edinburgh, and removed the young Queen Mary to France. The English garrisons came under increasing pressure, and eventually Somerset was compelled to withdraw them. For the next ten years Scotland remained under French control, particularly after 1554 when the Queen Mother, Mary of Guise, became regent. However, the appointment of Frenchmen to high office in Church and state created growing dissatisfaction, and many Scots came to detest the French so heartily that even the English seemed preferable.

The protestants were meanwhile increasing in number and strength, and they appealed to nationalist sentiment by demanding that 'the liberty of this our native country may remain free from the bondage and tyranny of strangers'. The principal protestant nobles came together in the 'Band of the Lords of the Congregation', and their position was strengthened by the return of John Knox in 1559. After a spell in the galleys he had managed to find his way to Geneva, where he ministered to a congregation of English Marian exiles. He was deeply impressed by the presbyterian system Calvin had set up in the Swiss city, and was determined to introduce it to Scotland.

By the time Knox returned to his native land a protestant sovereign was once again ruling in England, but Elizabeth and her chief minister, William Cecil, might have ignored the calls for help from the Scottish protestants had it not been that the political situation made English intervention imperative. Mary, Queen of Scots, had been married to the French dauphin who, in July 1559, ascended the throne as Francis II. It looked as though France and Scotland would now be united, and the threat to Elizabeth was increased by the fact that Mary was the catholic claimant to the English throne and had publicly asserted her rights.

In Scotland the Queen Regent had decided to take action against the protestants, who were challenging her rule, but her action drove the Lords of the Congregation into open rebellion. In October 1559 they occupied Edinburgh and declared Mary of Guise deposed, but the Queen Regent drove them out, with the help of French troops. Cecil persuaded Elizabeth that immediate intervention was needed, and in January 1560 an English fleet dropped anchor in the Firth of Forth, effectively severing the French lifeline. Negotiations were set on foot, and were made easier by the death of Mary of Guise in June 1560. The following month saw the signing of the Treaty of Edinburgh, by which both France and England agreed to withdraw their forces from Scotland and leave the religious question to be settled by a Scottish Parliament. This body met in August and imposed the Reformation upon Scotland. The authority of the Pope was abolished, the celebration of mass was forbidden, and a presbyterian confession of faith was made the only legal form of worship. However, the existing structure of the Scottish Church or Kirk, including bishops, was left largely untouched.

In December 1560 Francis II, King of France, died, and in the following year his widow, Mary, returned to her Scottish kingdom. Although she was a convinced catholic, Mary agreed to maintain the reformed faith, but the protestants were afraid she might marry one of her own religion, and as Knox told the Scottish Parliament 'whensoever the nobility of Scotland, professing the Lord Jesus, consents that an infidel – and all papists are infidels – shall be head to your sovereign, ye do so far as in ye lieth to banish Christ Jesus from this realm, ye bring God's vengeance upon the country, a plague upon yourself, and perchance ye shall do small comfort to your sovereign'. Elizabeth was as anxious as Knox that Mary should marry a protestant, and put forward her favourite, Robert Dudley, Earl of Leicester. Mary declared her willingness to marry Leicester if Elizabeth agreed to recognise her as heir to the English throne, but this was a condition that Elizabeth found totally unacceptable. The Queen of Scots thereupon turned her attention to Henry Stuart, Lord Darnley, who was, like her, a great-grandchild of Henry VII. When the English Privy Council heard about this it protested that a marriage between Mary and Darnley 'would be unmeet [i.e. inappropriate], unprofitable, and perilous to the amity between the queens and both realms', but once Mary was set on a course she never allowed political considerations to divert her. In July 1565 she married Darnley

The protestant lords, led by the Earl of Moray and supported by Elizabeth, rose in rebellion against Mary, but the Queen and her husband gathered their followers and chased the rebels across the border into England. The marriage, however, did not go well, for Darnley was insufferably arrogant and stupid, as Mary quickly discovered. She turned for comfort to her Italian secretary, David Rizzio, who was rumoured to be her lover. Darnley, wounded in his pride, plotted with Mary's enemies, the protestant lords, who promised that if he got rid of Rizzio and appointed them to the royal Council, they would accept him as King-consort. The first part of the plan was put into operation in March 1566 when Darnley and his associates dragged Rizzio from the Queen's presence and stabbed him to death. Shortly afterwards, Moray and the exiles returned to Scotland.

The Queen never forgave Darnley, even though she dissembled her feelings. In June 1566 she gave birth to a son, Prince James, but there was no reconciliation between her and her husband. Instead, she drew closer to one of the protestant lords, James Hepburn, fourth Earl of Bothwell, and it was at his suggestion that Darnley, who had been ill, was sent to convalesce at Kirk o'Field, near Edinburgh. In February 1567 the house was destroyed by a violent explosion, and Darnley was found dead in the grounds, having been strangled. It was generally assumed that Bothwell was behind the assassination, but Mary showed her indifference to public opinion by allowing him to abduct her. In May 1567 she and Bothwell – who had obtained a divorce from his wife – were married in a protestant ceremony at Edinburgh. By her actions Mary had forfeited the respect of her subjects and she was therefore powerless when Moray and the protestant lords rose against her for the second time. In June 1567 Mary was taken prisoner and forced to abdicate in favour of her son, James. A year later she sought refuge in England, thereby beginning the long descent that was to bring her at last to the scaffold.

James VI

With Mary out of the way, Knox and the protestants consolidated their position. The structure of the Roman Catholic Church was allowed to remain, because the crown and nobles had succeeded in diverting much of its wealth into their own pockets. But all ministers were required by 1573 to subscribe to a Calvinist confession of faith, and bishops, although still appointed by the crown, had to be approved by a panel of protestant ministers.

The mid-1570s saw the Calvinist presbyterian movement enter a more intense phase in both England and Scotland. Knox died in 1572, but two years later Andrew Melville returned from Geneva and published what became known as *The Second Book of Discipline* (the first had been promulgated in 1560). This broke with episcopacy and set up in its place a system of autonomous Church courts. These were to have the right to impose strictures on laymen as well as ministers, and even to discipline the lay ruler if he transgressed. Such a degree of authority on the part of the Church was unacceptable to James, who, even as a boy, held an exalted view of kingship and had no intention of being dictated to by puritan ministers.

In 1572 James Douglas, fourth Earl of Morton, was appointed regent. Although a Calvinist in theology and a close friend of Knox he abhorred the whole idea of a theocracy along the lines that Melville was advocating. He had no time for what he described as 'imitation of Geneva discipline and laws' but aimed to 'bring in a conformity with England in governing of the Kirk by bishops and [royal] injunctions'. Morton had an overbearing personality and James stood in awe of him, but in 1579 James's life was transformed by the arrival from the French court of a distant relative, Esmé Stuart, Seigneur d'Aubigny. The newcomer quickly became the boy King's favourite – the first of a long line – and James created him Duke of Lennox. In late 1580 the English ambassador reported that Aubigny stood 'so high in the King's favour and strong in counsel as few or none will openly withstand anything that he would have forward'.

An important part of Aubigny's mission was to detach James from the close relationship with England that Morton had established. By exploiting factionalism among the Scottish nobles, Aubigny brought about Morton's downfall. The regent was accused of involvement in Darnley's murder, put on trial and found guilty. In June 1581 he was executed. Aubigny did not have long to savour his triumph, however, for the same factionalism that had destroyed Morton now worked against him. The leaders of the Kirk blamed Aubigny for encouraging James to claim too much authority over the Church, and they linked up with dissident nobles whose motives ranged from the defence of protestantism to naked self-advancement. In August 1582, when James was hunting near Ruthven Castle, home of the Earl of Gowrie, he was persuaded to take shelter there, but no sooner was he inside than the gates were closed. It was made plain to the King that he would not be allowed to leave until he dismissed Aubigny from his service, and by the following year the duke was back in Paris, where he died in May.

For some ten months the leaders of the coup against James, who were pro-English in their orientation, ruled in his name, but James now joined in the game of factions himself, and proved to be highly adept. In June 1583 he escaped from captivity with the aid of James Stewart, Earl of Arran, who now took over the government. The Kirk, which had backed the Ruthven lords, was promptly brought under tighter control. Andrew Melville only escaped imprisonment by taking refuge in England, and in 1584 the Scottish Parliament passed what the Calvinists called the 'Black Acts'. These confirmed 'the royal power and authority over all [e]states, as well spiritual as temporal, within this realm', and forbade meetings of the General Assembly of the Kirk without prior royal permission. Government of the Church was vested in bishops appointed by the crown, and ministers were forbidden to discuss affairs of state from the pulpit.

James's long-term aim was to bring both the Kirk and the Scottish magnates under his authority, but he was not yet strong enough to do so. Continued factionalism among the nobles, fomented by English agents, led to the overthrow of Arran's regime in 1585, and James had to conciliate the Kirk by issuing a statement in which he denied any intention to constrict its power and declared that he would allow 'no bishops according to the traditions of men or inventions of the Pope, but only according to God's word'. In subsequent negotiations between the leaders of the Kirk and representatives of the royal government it was agreed that bishops, although nominated by the King, would be formally admitted to their position by the General Assembly of the Kirk. They were to be resident pastors, like any other minister, and the only additional powers they possessed were to be exercised in conjunction with a Kirk-appointed council. This meant that bishops were little more than figureheads, and their status was further reduced in 1587 when James, desperately short of money, secured an Act of Annexation transferring to the crown the secular revenues ('temporalities') of all benefices.

Following Arran's fall, James, who was approaching twenty-years-of-age, assumed direct responsibility for government, and in May 1587 he staged a 'love-feast' in which feuding nobles walked hand in hand through the streets of Edinburgh. This was little more than a gesture, but it illustrated James's view of himself as the great reconciler, above faction. It also symbolised his determination to bring the nobles to heel. He told a French agent, sent to him on behalf of his mother, Mary, that the irresponsibility of the Scottish aristocracy sprang from the fact 'that for forty years or more they had only had for governors in this kingdom women, little children, and traitorous and avaricious regents, so that during the divisions and troubles happening in that time, the nobility, by an unbridled liberty, had become so audacious in leaning on those who commanded them that now it is not possible to subdue and reduce them all at once to their duty'. Nevertheless, added James, he was resolved that 'little by little he would have them in good order'.

One of the factors limiting James's freedom of action was shortage of money, for the royal revenues barely covered the costs of government and left little over for the expanding royal household. At the time of his marriage to Anne of Denmark in 1589 one observer recorded that the King 'has neither plate nor stuff to furnish one of his little half-built houses, which are in great decay and ruin. His plate is not worth £100, he has only two or three rich jewels, [and] his saddles are of plain cloth'. Elizabeth, by comparison, was wealthy, and although she kept a tight rein upon her finances she was prepared to consider assisting James, now that the supposedly anti-English regime of Arran had been swept away. She was also anxious to ensure peace on the northern border of her kingdom at a time when war with Spain seemed increasingly likely. In 1586 a treaty was therefore concluded by which Elizabeth acknowledged James as her successor, provided he did not, by some act of ingratitude, show himself to be unworthy of such an inheritance. At the same time it was also informally agreed that she would pay James a subsidy, though no fixed sum was mentioned, nor was anything said about when payments would be made. Following the signing of the treaty, James received £4,000, but in 1587, the year of his mother's execution, no subsidy was paid. In 1589, at the height of the Spanish threat, Elizabeth made him a grant of £6,000, but this level was not reached again until 1598. In most years the figure was around £3,000, and over the whole period from 1586 to Elizabeth's death James received a total of £58,000.

These subsidies were far smaller than those Elizabeth sent to the Dutch and Henry IV of France, but they made a big difference to James's position, because they increased his income by a sixth. Much of the money was dissipated, for James was notoriously open-handed. In December 1588 Sir Francis Walsingham, Elizabeth's Secretary of State, was informed that 'he gives to everyone that asks what they desire, even to vain youths and proud fools the very lands of his crown ... Yea, what he gets from England, if it were a million they would get it from him, so careless is he of any wealth if he may enjoy his pleasure in hunting'. James was undoubtedly extravagant, yet kings were meant to be bountiful, and the distributing of largesse was a way of reinforcing natural bonds of loyalty.

After the fall of Arran, James was his own master, and he turned for advice to John Maitland of Thirlestane, whom he appointed Chancellor in 1587. Maitland came from the Scottish equivalent of a gentry background and represented the 'new men' who were making their way in Scotland, as in England, through service to the crown. Maitland had a limited power base and depended on the King to a far greater extent than earlier magnate ministers. James made him a noble, but this carried little weight with the magnates, especially the Roman Catholic ones who dominated the highlands. Principal among these was George Gordon, sixth Earl of Huntly, a man whom Maitland regarded as potentially dangerous and far more of a threat to James's authority than the leaders of the Kirk. James was reluctant to take firm action against Huntly for a variety of reasons. He felt affection for the young man, who was married to the daughter of James's first favourite, Esmé Stuart, and he was also afraid of alienating not only the Scottish catholics but also, and more importantly, the English ones, since he would need their support, or at least their acquiescence, if he was to attain his great ambition of succeeding Elizabeth I as ruler of England.

Although James ignored Maitland's advice where Huntly was concerned, he followed the suggestion that he should mend his bridges with the Kirk. In 1592 he accepted the so-called 'Golden Act' which in effect annulled the Black Acts of 1584 and confirmed 'all liberties, privileges, immunities and freedoms whatsoever given and granted ... to the true and holy Kirk established within this realm'. The Kirk was now free to summon annual meetings of the General Assembly, though the choice of time and place was left in the hands of the King, and presbyteries were given back the right to present ministers to livings and 'to put order to all matters and causes ecclesiastical within their bounds, according to the discipline of the Kirk'. No mention was made of bishops, but although episcopacy was not formally abolished it ceased to have any significance.

Presbyterians were heartened by the fact that in 1592 James raised an army and led it north into the highlands, intending to confront Huntly, who had been in touch with Philip II, soliciting a Spanish invasion. Huntly fled rather than fight, but two years later he led a rebellion which forced James to take up arms again. This time he pressed into the heartland of Huntly's territories, laying waste as he did so, and forced the rebels to surrender. Huntly went into exile, and although he later returned to Scotland he was now a loyal subject. James's policy of curbing aristocratic factionalism was

clearly beginning to work, and in 1598 he persuaded the nobles to accept
that disputes between them must in future be settled by the crown instead
of by feuding.

Huntly's surrender made James less dependent upon the support of the
presbyterians – though they were among the last to realise this – and he
had not abandoned his aim of bringing the Kirk under closer royal control.
He was already reaching out to the moderates among the ministers in a
deliberate attempt to by-pass the hard-liners. In October 1596, when the
General Assembly was in session, he invited a number of moderate
members to confer with him at Falkland Palace. Feelings were running
high because James had allowed Huntly to return to Scotland, thereby
fuelling fears that he was going soft on catholicism. Andrew Melville had
not been invited to the conference, but this very fact, combined with his
fear of increasing Roman Catholic influence at court, drove him to gate-
crash. His intervention was made in 'so zealous, powerful and irresistible
a manner that ... [he] ... bore him [i.e. James] down, and uttered the commission as from the mighty God, calling the king but "God's silly [i.e.
simple] vassal" and taking him by the sleeve says this in effect ... "Sir, as
divers times before, so now again I must tell you there is two kings and two
kingdoms in Scotland. There is Christ Jesus the king, and his kingdom the
Kirk, whose subject King James the Sixth is, and of whose kingdom not a
king, nor a lord, nor a head, but a member".'

Two months later, when James was in Edinburgh for another conference, a riot broke out that was whipped up by prominent presbyterian
preachers. They appealed to the godly nobles for support, but none was
forthcoming and the rebellion collapsed. James did not at this stage take
action against the hard-liners, but his position had been considerably
strengthened. He was still working towards the revival of episcopacy, and
in 1600 he secured the election of three bishops at a convention held in
Holyrood House. This was a major breakthrough, for it opened the way
to episcopal government of the Scottish Church at a later stage.

While James had met with success in his efforts to bridle the nobles and
curb the Kirk, he did not manage to improve his financial situation. In
January 1596 he appointed eight Exchequer commissioners, known as the
Octavians, to reform the royal finances, but although they began by trying
to reduce expenditure on the royal household, they came up against determined opposition from courtiers and nobles who were determined to
defend their existing perquisites. The Edinburgh riot of December 1596
had its roots in this disaffection, and the Octavians, despairing of accom-
plishing their task, resigned in January 1597. Thereafter James depended

largely on Sir George Home, whom he appointed Treasurer and created Earl of Dunbar. The 1597 Parliament voted more direct taxes than ever before, and Customs duties were also raised, but the government remained on the verge of bankruptcy. Fortunately for James the crisis was averted until after March 1603 when he at last received the news of Elizabeth's death and his accession to the English throne. He left Scotland without real regret, for, as he told the Hampton Court Conference in 1604, he was happy to be in 'the promised land, where religion was purely professed, where he sat among grave, learned and reverend men – not, as before, else-where, a King without state, without honour, without order, where beardless boys would brave him to his face'.

CHAPTER EIGHT

Elizabeth I and the Church of England

Elizabeth I

Elizabeth was an attractive young woman of twenty-five when she came to the throne. She was no classical beauty – her nose was too pronounced and her hair was reddish rather than golden – but she had character and intelligence as well as a commanding personality, and she knew how to charm as well as chide. She was also well educated, for her tutors, John Cheke and Roger Ascham, had given her a good grounding in the classics and divinity and also several modern languages. Yet she was no pedant. The liveliness of her wit and the sharpness of her tongue were to become famous, and her speeches are models of their kind – involved and convoluted in the manner of the day, but full of salty comments and passages of magnificent rhetoric. Like Mary she was proud and stubborn, but she had an ebullient self-assurance that the late Queen had never known, and the Spanish ambassador reported, two weeks after her accession, that 'she seems to me incomparably more feared than her sister was, and she gives her orders and has her way as absolutely as her father did'.

The Queen's advisers assumed she would quickly marry, but this was not Elizabeth's intention. One reason for this was that all the time she remained single she could use the prospect of her marriage as a trump card in the game of diplomacy, to be brought out when hostile coalitions were threatening her. Another and more powerful reason was her reluctance to share power, for as the Scottish ambassador told her 'Ye think that if ye were married ye would be but Queen of England, and now ye are King and Queen both. Ye may not suffer a commander.'

Elizabeth did, in fact, come near to marriage with Robert Dudley, son of the Duke of Northumberland and grandson of Henry VII's notorious minister. But Dudley was already married, and although this impediment was removed in September 1560 when Amy Robsart, his wife, was found dead in her house at Cumnor Place in Berkshire, the rumours of Dudley's complicity were too widespread for Elizabeth to ignore. She continued to love Dudley, and in October 1562, when she was desperately ill with smallpox and thought to be dying, she recommended his nomination as Lord Protector of the realm. Nevertheless, when she recovered she did not marry him.

Elizabeth's illness brought the question of the succession into prominence. The Queen's early death would almost certainly have been followed by a disputed succession, for the heir presumptive, Mary Stuart, had been married to the King of France, England's traditional enemy, and was also Roman Catholic. The protestants who came to power with Elizabeth would never acknowledge a catholic as heir presumptive, especially after their experience of Mary Tudor. As for Elizabeth, she had been a 'second person' herself in Mary's reign and knew how the presence of an heir could stimulate intrigues against the ruler. She was also aware of what she described as 'the inconstancy of the people of England; how they ever mislike the present government and have their eyes fixed upon that person that is next to succeed'. She preferred therefore to temporise, and gamble on living long enough for the succession problem to solve itself. The gamble paid off, but the odds were against it, for neither of Elizabeth's siblings had been long-lived, and there was no reason to suppose that she would prove an exception. Her early parliaments therefore had good reason to be concerned about the succession.

The religious settlement

It is impossible to define exactly what was the nature of Elizabeth's religious beliefs. She was certainly not a catholic, and during Mary's reign she had chosen as her household servants men and women who were committedly protestant. She had also insisted on having an English Bible for her private use, and initially the services in her chapel were conducted in the vernacular. When Mary ordered her to change these to Latin, 'according to the ancient and laudable custom of the Church', she obeyed, but she pointed out that the English Litany had been 'set forth in the King my father's days'. Left to herself she might well have favoured a settlement close to that which had obtained in the closing years of Henry VIII, and once she became Queen she shocked protestant susceptibilities by retaining a silver crucifix and candles in the chapel royal. In practice, however, her freedom to dictate the nature of the religious settlement was limited by two groups that were too influential for her to ignore. The first consisted of the Cambridge graduates, principal among them William Cecil, whom she chose as her advisers, for they were determined to establish a truly reformed Church in England on the basis of the 1552 Prayer Book. The second was made up of the former exiles who flooded back into England as soon as they heard the news of Mary's death.

The émigrés covered a wide spectrum of religious opinions, though all within a protestant framework. Some had settled at Geneva, where they came under the direct influence of Calvin, and they would have liked to see all remaining elements of popery swept away, including much of the ecclesiastical hierarchy as well as the vestments and ceremonies that the Edwardian Church had retained. Other exiles were more moderate in their approach. The Frankfurt group, for instance, had looked for guidance to Richard Cox who had assisted Cranmer in drawing up the Second Prayer Book and therefore had a personal commitment to it. Yet all the exiles, now that they had felt the impact of the continental Reformation at first hand, wished to go beyond the 1552 book. Even the 'Coxians' at Frankfurt had modified their adherence to it in certain matters that they regarded as 'indifferent'. They abandoned the wearing of surplices, for instance, and they ignored saints' days. They also took communion seated instead of kneeling, and gave up the practice of signing with the cross in baptism. No matter what her own views were, Elizabeth could not possibly discount those of the returned exiles, for these men were the cream of English protestants whose knowledge, ability and devotion to their religion would be invaluable in creating a reformed Church in England.

On the other hand Elizabeth had to take into account the attitude of the Marian bishops who were entrenched in Convocation and the House of Lords. Furthermore, she was in a weak position diplomatically, for Mary had left her a legacy of war with France and a depleted Exchequer. Elizabeth could not afford at this stage to antagonise the catholic powers, particularly Spain, whose help she might need. Not until early April 1559, when a peace treaty with France was concluded at Câteau-Cambrésis, was she free to press ahead with her plans for restoring protestant worship. The architects of the Elizabethan settlement were William Cecil, whom she appointed her principal Secretary of State, and his brother-in-law, Nicholas Bacon, who became Lord Keeper of the Great Seal (i.e. Lord Chancellor in all but name). They had to guide them the *Device for*

Alteration of Religion drawn up by protestant leaders in late 1558, and they laid before Parliament a number of proposals for restoring the royal supremacy and the Second Prayer Book. These passed the Commons but met stubborn opposition in the Upper House, particularly from the epis-copal bench. As John Jewel, recently returned from Frankfurt, bitterly observed, 'the bishops are a great hindrance to us, for being ... among the nobility and leading men in the Upper House, and having none there on our side to expose their artifices and confute their falsehoods, they ... easily overreach our little party either by their numbers or by their repu-tation for learning'. The stand taken by the Marian bishops says much for the strength of their convictions, but it closed the door on whatever chance there had been of establishing a state Church modelled on that of Henry VIII's last years. Elizabeth could do nothing unless and until the royal supremacy was restored, and since the Marian bishops would not co-operate in this process she had no alternative but to purge them and look for allies among the protestants.

When Parliament reassembled after the Easter recess England was at peace and the Queen and her advisers were thereby freed from restraint. She ordered a conference to take place in Westminster Abbey to determine what should be the basis for the settlement of religion, but the bishops again refused to make any concessions and the Privy Council thereupon sent two of them to the Tower. Separate bills of Supremacy and Uniformity were now presented to Parliament. Despite the fact that the bishops in the Upper House voted unanimously to reject the first of these, it passed with the support of the lay peers. The Uniformity Act aroused greater resistance in the Lords, but eventually passed by twenty-one votes to eighteen.

The authorised form of worship prescribed by the Act of Uniformity was based on the Second Prayer Book of 1552, but with modifications designed to bring it closer to the Lutheran position which Elizabeth prob-ably favoured and make it more acceptable to catholics. The Black Rubric, for instance, was omitted, as was the petition to be delivered 'from the Bishop of Rome and all his detestable enormities', while in the communion service the wording of the First Prayer Book, which could be held to imply the real presence, was added to the purely commemorative formula of the Second. Perhaps most important of all, for its short-term consequences, was the clause in the Act of Uniformity prescribing that 'such ornaments of the Church and of the ministers thereof shall be retained and be in use as was in the Church of England by authority of Parliament in the second year of the reign of King Edward the Sixth'.

This harmless-sounding provision – to which Elizabeth attached so much importance that without it, according to Archbishop Parker, she would not have accepted the amended Book – was a calculated blow at the Genevans. It meant that all clergy were now obliged to wear a white linen surplice for ordinary services and 'a white alb plain, with a vestment or cope' for the administration of holy communion. Elizabeth's conservatism in religious matters was further demonstrated by the Injunctions issued on her authority, for these laid down that the communion table should be placed in the chancel, where the altar had previously stood, except when it was in use, and that the bread for the administration of the sacrament should not be the workaday product made by bakers but unleavened wafers bearing a marked resemblance to those used in catholic worship.

The Act of Supremacy restored royal control over the Church, although Elizabeth was described as 'supreme governor of this realm . . . as well in all spiritual or ecclesiastical things or causes as temporal' – a sop to those who believed that the supreme headship could not be assumed by a woman. The change in wording was not the only difference between the Henrician and Elizabethan supremacies. Henry VIII's headship of the Church had merely been 'revealed' by Parliament, since it was deemed to be inherent in his kingly position. But the Act of Supremacy of 1559 restored royal control over the Church 'by the authority of this present Parliament', and the same authority was invoked in the Act of Uniformity to compel the use of the new Prayer Book. All the Queen's subjects were required to attend their parish church on Sundays and holy days and join in the prescribed services. A fine of one shilling – one-twentieth of a pound, and no small amount, especially for the poorer members of the congregation – was to be levied for every absence.

Under the terms of the Supremacy Act all office-holders were required to take an oath acknowledging Elizabeth's governorship of the Church. When this was administered to the bishops, all but one refused to take it – an indication of just how successful Mary and Pole had been in creating a catholic episcopate. Elizabeth had hoped that the Marian bishops would act as a counter to the radical protestants who were clamouring for positions in the new Church, but now she was left even more dependent upon them. However, when it came to appointing her first Archbishop of Canterbury she chose Matthew Parker, formerly her mother's chaplain, who had remained in England throughout Mary's reign. Parker, now over fifty, was a link with the early days of the Reformation, when he had been a member of the 'Little Germany' group at Cambridge, and he symbolised the Lutheran inheritance of the Church of England that was alien to the returned exiles.

The émigrés hailed the news of Elizabeth's accession since they assumed, in the words of one of their number, that now it was 'the time for the walls of Jerusalem to be built again in that kingdom, that the blood of so many martyrs, so largely shed, may not be in vain'. However, on their return to England they were disillusioned. No new Jerusalem could be built while the walls of the old city remained in place, yet there was no question – at least so far as Elizabeth was concerned – of demolishing any part of the traditional structure of the Church. Bishops, deans, archdeacons and all the ecclesiastical hierarchy continued to exist just as if the Reformation had never taken place, and their very existence constituted an impediment to fundamental change. As for the Prayer Book, this made obligatory many practices, such as the wearing of distinctive vestments, that the returned exiles found abhorrent. Yet just as Elizabeth needed the co-operation of these committed protestants for the construction of her Church, so they needed to serve in it for fear that England would otherwise remain at best half-reformed, at worst catholic. Most of the émigrés eventually decided, as Edmund Grindal, one of their number, recorded, 'not to desert our churches for the sake of a few ceremonies – and those not unlawful in themselves'. Grindal himself became Bishop of London, while other émigrés were appointed to the sees of Ely, Worcester, Winchester and Durham. Eventually the former exiles held seventeen out of the twenty-five bishoprics.

Resistance to the religious settlement among the parish clergy was limited, and out of a total of about nine thousand only some three hundred were deprived of their livings. It would be a mistake, however, to assume that all those who took the oath accepting the supremacy were whole-hearted supporters of the new regime. Passive acceptance and outward conformity were all that the government insisted upon, and many priests observed the letter of their obligations without necessarily embracing the spirit. Immediately after the passing of the two acts creating the Elizabethan settlement, commissioners were despatched from London to enforce compliance. They were for the most part convinced protestants and engaged in one last orgy of iconoclasm, destroying the ornaments and images that local congregations had provided for their churches during Mary's reign. Yet not all the relics of catholicism were swept away. Most rood lofts remained in place until at least 1561, when an order to remove them was issued, and about half of all parishes held on to their vestments, chalices, and other articles necessary for the celebration of mass for the first ten years or so of Elizabeth's reign. The restoration of catholic worship following Mary's accession had cost parishioners a great deal of money, and they did not want to incur the same expense if and when the religious affiliation of the country was once again reversed.

The Puritan challenge

Although there were a number of features of the Elizabethan religious settlement that were unpalatable from the point of view of the returned exiles – and, for that matter, of many people of similar outlook who had remained in England during Mary's reign – there was a widespread assumption that they were merely a matter of form and would not be strictly implemented. Nevertheless their continued existence was an affront to those who were to be called 'puritans' because they wanted the Church to be cleansed or purified of all traces of catholicism. When convocation met in 1563 a group of puritan ministers introduced articles designed to eliminate these undesirable features. They called for the abolition of holy days other than Sundays and the principal feasts, such as Easter, and for the removal of organs from churches. They demanded that ceremonies such as kneeling to receive communion and signing with the cross in baptism should be left to the discretion of the minister, and that compulsory vestments should be confined to the surplice, which they regarded as the least obnoxious of the prescribed garments. However, when the puritan articles were put to the lower house of Convocation, which represented the bulk of the clergy, they were defeated by fifty-nine votes to fifty-eight, and at the same time there was mounting pressure for all ministers to conform to the rules laid down in the Prayer Book and Injunctions.

This pressure came from Elizabeth, who was probably the only person in her government who envisaged the settlement not as the first stage on a journey towards an ever more reformed Church but as the final destination. Quite apart from the belief – which was of course shared by her subjects – that God had placed her on the throne so that she could guide her people into the right path in religion, she wished to end the bitter disputes about externals of worship that tended to tear protestant communities apart. As she informed Archbishop Parker, 'We will have no dissension or variety, for so the sovereign authority which we have under almighty God would be made frustrate and we might be thought to bear the sword in vain.' At her insistence Parker and four of his colleagues drew up a list of minimum requirements to which all clergy were required to assent. When the Queen refused to give official sanction to these – for she always preferred to shift the blame for unpopular measures on to someone else's shoulders – Parker issued them on his own authority, in 1565, as the *Book of Advertisements*. This made the wearing of eucharistic vestments compulsory only in cathedrals and collegiate churches, but all clergy were required to wear a surplice when they conducted services and a long black gown and square cap for everyday use.

Parker had probably assumed that these minimum requirements would be generally acceptable, but he reckoned without the puritans. Thirty-four London ministers refused to wear the prescribed vestments and were subsequently deprived of their livings. Some took refuge in more distant parts of England, where they spread the infection of non-conformity, but the majority joined the underground of unbeneficed itinerant preachers who, because they held no official position, were not amenable to episcopal discipline. In other words the *Book of Advertisements*, which had been designed to rally the clergy behind the bishops, had the contrary effect of creating a movement of radical dissent which was to develop into a major challenge to the ecclesiastical hierarchy.

The hostile reaction to the *Book of Advertisements* was not confined to the clergy. Congregations of churches whose ministers had been deprived did not sit quietly back and wait for the arrival of a conformist. Disturbances were reported in a number of London parishes, and even more alarming from the point of view of the authorities was the action of some hundred 'godly' citizens who separated from the Church altogether and held private meetings at which they used the form of service devised by Calvin for Geneva. These people were not separatists on principle but they could not accept the legitimacy of a Church that insisted on what they regarded as popish practices. As one of their spokesmen explained to Edmund Grindal, Bishop of London, 'When it came to this point, that all our preachers were displaced . . . that would not subscribe to your apparel and your law, so that we could hear none of them in any church by the space of seven or eight weeks . . . and then we were troubled and commanded to your courts from day to day for not coming to our parish churches, then we bethought us what were best to do, and we remembered that there was a congregation of us in this city in Queen Mary's days and a congregation at Geneva.'

The effect of the controversy over vestments was to change the attitude of the puritans towards episcopacy. Just as monarchical power, which the early reformers had elevated as a shield against papal sovereignty, had come to be regarded under Mary as a threat, so the authority of bishops was now called into question. 'What talk they', wrote one pamphleteer, 'of their being beyond the seas in Queen Mary's days because of the persecution, when they in Queen Elizabeth's days are come home to raise a persecution?' The reply to this was given by James Pilkington, formerly a prominent member of the exile congregation at Frankfurt and now Bishop of Durham. 'We are under authority', he said, 'and can innovate nothing without the Queen. Nor can we alter the laws. The only thing left to our choice is whether we will bear these things or break the peace of the Church'.

Pilkington was himself a puritan in so far as he would have liked to strip the Church of its remaining popish traces. So was Grindal, another émigré, and so, in fact, were most, if not all, of the bench of bishops. They differed from the radical puritans in their attitude towards the royal supremacy, for they accepted the Queen's insistence that vestments and other 'outward signs' were *adiaphora*, 'matters indifferent', to be regulated by the lay governor. They were swayed by the argument that if something was not specifically prescribed in the Bible then the ruler had the right to decide on its use or disuse. The radicals, on the other hand, claimed that nothing should be permitted in the Church for which there was not specific biblical sanction. Another difference between moderates and radicals, between conformists and potential non-conformists, was their attitude towards tradition. Radicals were not only prepared to break with the past; they gloried in so doing, since they regarded the past as a quagmire of popery and superstition. Moderates, on the other hand, derived comfort from the knowledge that they were part of an historical development, even if 'history' in this context went back only one generation. Grindal reminded the members of the London separatist congregation that 'in this severing yourselves from the society of other Christians you condemn not only us but also the whole state of the Church reformed in King Edward's days . . . There be good men and good martyrs that did wear these things [i.e. vestments] in King Edward's days. Do you condemn them?'

Cartwright and Field

When radical puritans found that the path to further reform was blocked by the Queen's intransigence they began to question the validity of the royal supremacy. Should the Church be subject to the secular ruler, or should it be self-governing? This was a question that had been asked by many continental reformers and had received widely differing answers. It was brought into the open in England by the lectures delivered at

Cambridge in 1570 by Thomas Cartwright, the Lady Margaret Professor of Divinity. Cartwright, who was in his mid-thirties, represented a new generation of Elizabethan puritans who believed that the structure of the Church of England was incompatible with scriptural precepts. The authority of archbishops and bishops had no biblical sanction and was therefore invalid. Every congregation should elect its own minister and lay 'elders' who would form a 'presbytery' which would define doctrine and enforce discipline. This was the system put into practice by Calvin at Geneva, and the radical puritans took it as their model.

Cartwright's assault upon the structure of the established Church, including the royal supremacy, deeply offended his colleagues at Cambridge. The Regius Professor of Divinity in the university was John Whitgift, Master of Trinity College, and he could count on the support in this instance of William Cecil, Cambridge's Chancellor. Between them they persuaded the heads of the colleges to act collectively and deprive Cartwright of his chair. This they did in December 1570, and the puritan spokesman left, appropriately, for Geneva.

Cartwright's condemnation of the Church of England as it existed was not simply a matter of theory. If it had been performing what he regarded as its God-given function, he would have seen no need to change it. The problem arose from the lack of consensus on what its function should be. Elizabeth and those who thought like her believed the Church should be a stabilising influence upon society, concerned above all to maintain the traditional Christian order, though one that took account of the protestant Reformation. While acknowledging that preaching played an important part in worship, they did not accord it priority. The 1559 Injunctions had prescribed a minimum of four sermons a year, with a target of one a month, and these were to be on uncontentious themes. A greater intensity of preaching would not have been possible, even if it was desirable, since the right to preach was confined to ministers who were specifically licensed to do so by their bishop. Unlicensed ministers were instructed to read printed homilies, published with government approval. Licensed preachers were thin on the ground: in 1569 there were only seventeen in the whole of Sussex, and many churches had had no sermon since Elizabeth's accession.

For Cartwright and his fellow puritans – moderates and radicals alike – this situation was not merely deplorable; it was a denial of the Church's central purpose, which was, as they saw it, to proclaim the Christian faith in a positive, evangelical manner. It affronted them that the Church in practice seemed to be content simply to operate as the government's spiritual arm, buttressing the powers-that-be and preferring harmony to confrontation. Protestantism is often described as a religion of the word, but puritans took this to mean not only the written but also, and more importantly, the spoken word. Cartwright declared that 'the bare reading of the scriptures without the preaching cannot deliver so much as one poor sheep from destruction', and his friend and fellow-puritan, Edward Dering, described a preacher as the 'mouth of God, in whose person Christ himself is either refused or received'. The conflict between Cartwright and Whitgift, therefore, was not provoked simply by differences of opinion about the way in which the Church should be structured. The two men represented fundamentally opposing views of the role of that Church in Elizabethan England.

Cartwright's expulsion did not mean an end to puritan pressure on the establishment, for he had only put into words what many people were already thinking. As far as the London puritans were concerned, they looked for inspiration to the Calvinist churches set up in the capital by foreign congregations. The French Huguenot church was particularly important in this respect since it was frequented by John Field, an unbeneficed preacher who was to become a major figure in the puritan protest movement and act as a link between the radical ministers and their supporters in Parliament. Puritan members of the Commons had missed an opportunity to press for further changes in the religious settlement during the course of the 1566 session because they were preoccupied with the question of the Queen's marriage and the succession, but by the time another Parliament met, in 1571, they had worked out their plan of campaign. One of their number, Walter Strickland, introduced a bill designed to reform the Prayer Book by eliminating from it all those features which puritans found repugnant. This was a clear invasion of the Queen's prerogative, and the Privy Councillors in the Commons advised the House to go no further. But they were up against men who would let nothing stand in the way of religious truth. Such matters, declared one member, were God's; 'the rest are all but terrene [i.e. earthly], yea trifles in comparison'. Strickland was summoned before the Council and ordered to absent himself from the House, but members raised such an outcry against what they claimed was an infringement of their privilege of free speech that he was quickly restored to them.

Field and his clerical associates could not find safety under the protection of parliamentary privilege. They were summoned before the ecclesiastical commissioners whom Elizabeth had appointed to exercise the royal supremacy, and were instructed to accept the Prayer Book in its entirety and wear the prescribed vestments. Field refused and was thereupon forbidden to preach. He now had to earn his living as a schoolmaster, but this goaded him to even greater efforts and he set to work on an *Admonition to Parliament* which was designed as an appeal to the country at large and not simply to members of the Lords and Commons. In the *Admonition* Field openly attacked the form of government of the Church of England and set out the ground-plan for a presbyterian alternative. He dismissed the authorised form of worship as 'an unperfect book, culled and picked out of that popish dunghill, the ... mass book, full of abominations'. Field was summoned before the Lord Mayor of London and sentenced to a year's imprisonment for publishing such outspoken criticism of the Church, but this did not prevent the circulation of the *Admonition* and the widespread dissemination of Field's views.

The older generation of puritans was shocked by Field's intemperance. Anthony Gilbey, for instance – a former exile who, as minister of Ashby-de-la-Zouch in Leicestershire, had become one of the most celebrated puritan divines in England – gave it as his opinion that 'openly to publish such admonitions as are abroad [i.e. in circulation] I like not, for that in some points and terms they are too broad and overshoot themselves'. John Foxe, the martyrologist, would have nothing to do with the *Admonition*, and even Théodore Beza, Calvin's successor at Geneva, thought it 'indiscreet'. Many people who might otherwise have supported Field were afraid to do so after the Northern Rising of 1569 and the publication of the papal bull deposing Elizabeth (*see* p. 213), for any weakening of the Church of England at this stage seemed likely to play into the hands of the catholics. The views of Sir Thomas Norton, MP, are particularly interesting in this respect, for although he had translated Calvin's *Institutes* into English he had no wish to see a presbyterian Church established in his native land. He believed that the existing Church should be revitalised so that it could carry on the fight against the common enemy, and far from challenging the existing authorities he preferred to co-operate with the Privy Council, most of whose members shared his moderate puritan opinions. Field spoke for the presbyterian wing of the puritan movement, which was unwilling to accept the compromises involved in maintaining the Church of England as established by law. Norton, and those who thought like him, represented the broad stream of conforming puritans who were fully conscious of the defects of the Elizabethan Church but saw their primary task as that of strengthening and defending it. Field and his associates made the most noise, but in the long run it was the silent majority of conforming puritans who gave the Church of England time to establish itself not simply in law but in the hearts of the people.

Thomas Cartwright, who returned from exile in late 1572, went to see Field in prison and demonstrated his support for the polemicist by writing and publishing *A Second Admonition*. This brought Whitgift back into the fray, and in the ensuing pamphlet war both Cartwright and Whitgift further refined their positions. Cartwright made it plain that he was not a separatist. He accepted the need for a state Church and was prepared to tolerate the royal supremacy, but he believed that the Church established by the Acts of Supremacy and Uniformity had been wrongly constructed and needed radical alteration to bring it closer to the presbyterian model set out in the scriptures. Whitgift's argument was that the Bible, while containing everything that was necessary for salvation, did not provide a blueprint for any form of ecclesiastical organisation, and that Cartwright, whatever his stated intention, was undermining the Queen's authority. This was also the view of the ecclesiastical commissioners, who summoned Cartwright to appear before them in December 1573. He only avoided imprisonment by going into exile once again.

The initiation of proceedings against Cartwright was one of a number of indications in late 1573 that the authorities were mounting a counter-attack against the radical puritans. The publication of Field's *Admonition* and the reception it received left many bishops in a state of depression. Edmund Sandys, the Archbishop of York, gave vent to their feelings when he declared that 'our estimation is little, our authority less, so that we are become contemptible in the eyes of the basest sort of people'. Elizabeth, however, never wavered. She detested puritans, whom she described as 'greater enemies to her than the papists', and she was probably responsible for a proclamation issued in October 1573 that threatened imprisonment for anyone defaming the Prayer Book. In consequence there was a period of relative calm that lasted for several years and gave an opportunity for the moderate conforming puritans to reassert themselves. Their moment of triumph came in December 1575 when, following the death of Parker, the Queen took Cecil's advice and appointed Edmund Grindal as Archbishop of Canterbury. Grindal had been a pupil of Bucer at Cambridge and it was hardly surprising therefore that when he went into exile under Mary he chose Strasburg as his place of residence. Grindal was anxious to purify the Church of England but not remodel it, and he believed, like his old master, that obnoxious features such as ceremonies and vestments would eventually disappear of their own accord. Meanwhile, they were not worth fighting over. Grindal was, in short, a moderate conforming puritan but the opponent of radicals, presbyterians and separatists – as well as catholics.

One of the major weaknesses of the Church was the low standard of education of many of its clergy, and Grindal's determination to remedy this led him to encourage the 'prophesyings' which had come into being in many parts of England. These consisted of public meetings of ministers at which a learned preacher, acting as moderator, led the way in the exposition of a scriptural text. Prophesyings were highly popular with the laity, and audiences would cover a wide cross-section of the local population. When bishops took the lead in arranging prophesyings and appointed the moderator, these meetings served to strengthen and revive the Church. However, many of the learned preachers were radical puritans whose sympathies lay with Cartwright and Field rather than the bishops. This alarmed Elizabeth, who feared that prophesyings might turn out to be the initial stage in the creation of a presbyterian Church in England. She therefore ordered Grindal to suppress them.

Grindal was appalled by this directive, for he saw in prophesyings a swift and effective way of producing a learned ministry, and he shared the view of Cartwright and puritans in general that preaching was central to the Church's mission. Elizabeth, on the other hand, regarded preaching as potentially subversive, and told Grindal that two or three preachers were enough for any shire. The archbishop could hardly believe his ears. 'I cannot marvel enough how this strange opinion should enter into your mind', he told her, 'that it should be good for the Church to have few preachers'. As for prophesyings, these were 'both profitable to increase knowledge among the ministers and tendeth to the edifying of the hearers', and therefore he could not 'with safe conscience and without the offence of the majesty of God give my assent to the suppressing of the said exercises'.

Elizabeth responded to this open defiance of her will by sending direct instructions to the bishops in May 1577 that they were to put down these 'disputations and new-devised opinions upon points of divinity far ... unmeet of vulgar people', and in the following year she took the unprecedented step of suspending the archbishop from his functions. Since Grindal refused to resign, and the Queen was, with difficulty, dissuaded from dismissing him, he remained in limbo until his death six years later. It was a tragic conclusion to a tenure of office that had opened with such high hopes. Grindal, had he continued not simply in office but in power, might well have unified the Church of England under his moderate puritan leadership. His dismissal sent out quite the opposite signal – namely that the Church could only be truly reformed by radical structural change.

Some people were already asking themselves why an individual should submit to the authority of either bishop or presbyter. Such an attitude was implicit in protestantism, which took its impetus from the revolt of individual conscience against the Roman Catholic Church, and even in the early days of the Reformation there had been groups such as the anabaptists for whom the authoritarianism of Luther and Calvin was just as repellent as that of the Pope. There were anabaptists in England but they were few in number and of little influence. The handful of separatist congregations that did emerge, mainly in London, did so in revolt against the imposition of conformity and found their inspiration in Lollard traditions and the memory of the 'privy churches' set up by protestants in Mary's reign. However, two Cambridge men, Robert Browne and Robert Harrison, came to the conclusion that separate 'gathered' congregations of the elect were the only true churches: 'the kingdom of God', in Browne's words, 'was not to be begun by whole parishes, but rather by the worthiest, were they never so few'.

Browne and Harrison began putting their belief into practice in the diocese of Norwich, but repressive action by the bishop drove the two men and their followers into exile in Holland, and it was there, in 1582, that Browne wrote his *Treatise of Reformation without Tarrying for Any*. In this he proclaimed that every congregation was self-sufficient and did not need any form of central guidance or authority. The Church of England, he declared, was hopelessly corrupt, its ministers 'turned back after babbling prayers and toying worship ... after popish attire and foolish disguising [i.e. fancy dress], after fastings, tithings, holy days and a thousand more abominations', and the presbyterians were just as bad. Browne's teaching, with its undertones of anarchy, was anathema to the government, and in 1583 two members of his sect were hanged for treason since they denied the royal supremacy. Browne himself was saved by his good connections – he was a distant relative of Cecil – and eventually abandoned his heterodox beliefs, spending the last forty years of his life as a country parson. But from his protest was to grow that tough and individual form of puritan 'independency' that reached its apogee in the mid-seventeenth century.

By the early 1580s the Elizabethan Church had come of age and was increasing in confidence. Among the bishops there was far less sympathy for puritanism after the generation of Marian exiles died out. New men, such as John Aylmer who became Bishop of London in 1577, were committed upholders of the royal supremacy and fully shared the Queen's determination to maintain the 1559 settlement. They were not necessarily hostile to Calvinism but they did not regard Geneva as being any more infallible than Rome. As Whitgift said later in the century, 'I reverence Mr Calvin as a singular man and worthy instrument in Christ's Church but I am not so wholly addicted unto him that I will condemn other men's judgements that in divers points agree not fully with him, especially in the interpretation of some places of the scripture when as, in my opinion, they come nearer to the true meaning and sense of it in those points than he doth.'

Whitgift

On the death of Grindal in 1583 John Whitgift was appointed Archbishop of Canterbury, and for the rest of Elizabeth's reign he devoted himself to defending the Church of England not simply against radical puritans and catholics but also against the laity, who had already stripped it of much of its wealth and hoped to grab more. Elizabeth was also, in theory, the defender of the Church, but in practice she continued to plunder its assets. An act passed in the first year of her reign gave the Queen the temporalities of vacant sees, as well as the right to exchange crown property for episcopal lands, and the temptation to hold up appointments so as to pocket the profits was too great to resist. The diocese of Oxford was left without a bishop for more than forty years, Ely for nineteen and Bristol for fourteen, and even when bishops were eventually appointed they were often required to exchange some of their more valuable lands for scattered royal manors or for impropriate tithes which were difficult to collect and aroused a great deal of hostility. The Queen and a small group of courtiers were the main beneficiaries from this forced transfer of Church wealth. The Earl of Oxford, for instance, had £1,000 a year out of the bishopric of Oxford, while the rich coal-bearing lands of the bishopric of Durham were leased by the Queen and her favourite, the Earl of Leicester, to Thomas Sutton, a professional soldier. Sutton paid them a high rent but made an immense fortune by developing coal-mining on his new estates, which enabled him to found a hospital and school on the site of the former Charterhouse in London.

Not surprisingly, the value of bishoprics declined. Durham, which had been worth £2,800 a year in 1535, was valued at £1,800 forty years later, while Lincoln dropped from nearly £2,000 to under £900. The bishops as individuals were still relatively rich, and lived in the appropriate style. Archbishop Parker, to take one example, had a gross income of £3,000 a year – well above the average for lay peers – and was usually attended by seventy retainers when he went on progress. Yet at the bottom of the ecclesiastical hierarchy many parish priests and curates had to eke out a living from inadequate tithes or such sums as the patron of their living condescended to pass on to them. It was hardly to be wondered at that the quality of the clergy in the early years of Elizabeth's reign was very poor, for ambitious young men, as one minister observed, 'when they look upon our contempt and beggary and vexation, turn to law, to physic, to trades, or anything rather than they will enter into this contemptible calling'.

Whitgift realised that reform was needed, but believed it should be carried out gradually, so as not to damage the structure of the Church at a time when its opponents were only too eager to dismantle it. Abuses could not be eliminated overnight, particularly since they were not without their positive side. Impropriate tithes, for example, swelled the revenues of bishops and university colleges, and pluralism did at least free the ministers of amalgamated parishes from constant money worries. The only way in which the Church could be truly reformed would be by renewing its financial underpinning, but Whitgift was sufficient of a realist to know that this was unlikely to happen. Such a renewal would require the support of the Queen and Parliament, but these represented the big property-owners, the very people who had a vested interest in maintaining the existing state of affairs since it brought them such rich dividends. It was better, in Whitgift's opinion, to focus on piecemeal improvement and jealously to guard what remained of the Church's patrimony. 'The temporalty', he declared, 'will not lose one jot of their commodity in any respect to better the livings of the Church. And therefore let us keep that we have. For better we shall not be. We may be worse, and that, I think, by many people is intended'.

Whitgift chose Convocation as his instrument for reforming the Church from within, and this body passed a number of decrees designed to improve the educational standards of the clergy and limit the impact of pluralism. Bishops were instructed to conduct regular examinations of the clergy within their sees and ensure that they had a good knowledge of the scriptures. They were also required to subject candidates for ordination to careful scrutiny in order to keep out of the ministry those who were not fitted for it. As for non-residence, which was one of the worst consequences of pluralism, the 1589 convocation decreed that all ministers holding one living should be resident in their parish while those with two should split their time between them. If any minister had good reason to be absent he should appoint a curate to carry out his duties.

Whitgift believed that if the Church was to defend itself against the acquisitive laity it needed a united and conforming clergy. In 1583, therefore, he instructed all ministers formally to subscribe to the statement that the Prayer Book 'containeth nothing in it contrary to the word of God'. This aroused a storm of protest, and pressure from Cecil among others persuaded the reluctant archbishop to allow ministers to subscribe that they accepted the Prayer Book in so far as it was compatible with the scriptures. However, even this modified affirmation was too much for the more radical puritans. Some three to four hundred ministers refused to subscribe, but in the event only a handful of them were deprived of their livings. The fact that the vast majority of the clergy did as they were told shows that they put the unity of the Church above whatever private reservations they may have had, and this same consideration persuaded Whitgift to treat the rebels leniently. Yet by taking such a firm stand on the Prayer Book issue Whitgift widened the gap between the episcopate on the one hand and the many hundreds of moderate puritan clergy on the other. In the long run the unity of the Church which he was so anxious to maintain might have been more effectively preserved by allowing a greater diversity of opinion within the ministry.

From early in her reign the Queen had appointed ecclesiastical commissioners, including laymen, to exercise the royal governorship over the Church, and these had developed into autonomous Courts of High Commission – a southern one for the province of Canterbury and a northern for the province of York. Under Whitgift the southern High Commission, which was based in London, became the principal instrument for enforcing conformity, since it could deal with all matters affecting the Church, except where property rights were involved. It could also imprison and impose fines as well as spiritual penalties such as excommunication that were the only weapons in the armoury of the ordinary Church courts. However, the enforcement of conformity by High Commission aroused protests from puritan gentry and clergy in the southern, midland and eastern counties, and in early 1584 the Privy Council summoned the archbishop to appear before it to answer his critics.

Whitgift, aware of his dignity and determined not to submit to lay interference, declined to appear, and far from relaxing his campaign for conformity he introduced the *ex officio* oath. This gave any dignitary of the Church the right 'by virtue of his office' to question a man on oath about his beliefs. The common lawyers – who tended to sympathise with the puritans and also resented the High Commission as an upstart tribunal threatening their own jurisdiction – challenged the validity of the *ex officio* oath on the grounds that a man should not be compelled to incriminate himself. They had to wait until 1591 before the issue was decided by Cawdrey's case, when the judges ruled that the authority and procedure of the courts of High Commission derived from the royal supremacy, and since this was legal, so was the oath. Meanwhile, Whitgift, undeterred, had been pressing ahead with his investigations, suspending as many as forty-five ministers in a single day in Suffolk.

The puritan sympathisers on the Privy Council kept up their criticisms of Whitgift's policy. Sir Francis Knollys, who was Treasurer of the Household and the Queen's cousin, told William Cecil, now Lord Burghley, how much it grieved him 'to see the zealous preachers of the gospel, sound in doctrine, who are the most diligent barkers against the popish wolf to save the fold and flock of Christ, to be persecuted and put to silence'. Burghley was sufficiently impressed by this complaint to write to Whitgift in similar terms, asserting that the use of the *ex officio* oath was 'too much savouring of the Romish Inquisition'.

Burghley was a good example of a firm supporter of the Church of England and upholder of the royal supremacy who was at the same time an advocate of leniency towards the puritans, even the radicals, because he saw just how much they had to contribute in the way of learning and commitment. Queen Elizabeth's favourite, the Earl of Leicester, who was also a Privy Councillor, extended his patronage to puritans and defended them when they were under attack. Whitgift, however, was not without allies, the most prominent of whom was Sir Christopher Hatton, another of Elizabeth's favourites and appointed by her to the Privy Council in 1578. The archbishop could also take comfort from the knowledge that the Queen approved of his actions. She demonstrated this in 1586 when she broke with tradition by making him a Privy Councillor. From then on Whitgift was at the heart of government and could defend himself in person.

Whitgift's suspicion of puritan activities was not without justification, for even before he became archbishop the presbyterian movement was making headway once again. In October 1582 a group of ministers from around the Essex village of Dedham decided to hold regular conferences to consider matters of religion, and to keep a record of their deliberations. These meetings, unlike the earlier prophesyings, were confined to clergy and held, with the minimum of publicity, in private houses. The Dedham group constituted what the presbyterians called a *classis*, and could be seen as the first step in setting up a presbyterian sub-structure within the established Church.

Dedham's example was not widely followed, but in many parts of south-east and central England puritan ministers were establishing closer contact and co-ordinating their activities. This tendency to self-help on the part of the puritans was given additional impetus by the failure of the 1584–5 Parliament to secure further reform of the Church. Elections for this Parliament were probably more hotly contested than for any other in the Tudor period, but although many puritan sympathisers found seats they were mainly in boroughs with small electorates, where the will of a puritan patron was likely to prevail. They failed to capture more than a handful of the prestigious county seats, even in East Anglia, where they were at their strongest. In December 1584 one of the puritan members of the Commons, Dr Peter Turner, proposed the setting up of a presbyterian system in England, but Elizabeth sent for the Speaker and ordered him to allow no debate on religious issues since these fell within her sole competence as supreme governor. If members had any complaints, they were to be directed to the bishops or to members of her Council. In the last resort appeals could be made to her directly, but she told the Speaker to inform the House that 'she will receive no motion of innovation, nor alter or change any law whereby the religion or Church of England standeth established at this day'. This inhibition made the House so angry that motions were put forward rejecting the Queen's command and censuring the Speaker for attending her without members' permission. The House as a whole did not support these proposals, but several bills on Church matters passed both the Lords and Commons, and Whitgift had to appeal to the Queen to delay or veto them.

The classical movement

By 1585 Cartwright was back in England and he and Walter Travers – another Cambridge man, who had spent several years at Geneva, where he became a close friend of Beza – drew up a *Book of Discipline* in time for a conference of puritan ministers that assembled in London to coincide with the parliamentary session of 1586. The *Book* set out the ground plan for a presbyterian organisation or 'discipline' in England. The smallest unit, the presbytery, consisted of a minister and a number of elected 'elders' or other officers. Next came the *classis*, consisting of representatives of several presbyteries. *Classes*, in turn, would send delegates to provincial synods from which would be chosen the members of the national synod, the governing body of the Church. The big advantage of the 'Discipline' was that it was well thought out and provided a uniform pattern, instead of leaving each puritan congregation to make its own arrangements. In 1587 the 'Discipline' was set up in Northamptonshire, and two delegates from each of the three *classes* came together every six weeks or so to discuss matters of common concern. The *classes* themselves met every three weeks, and at the parish level congregations elected 'elders' to keep watch over their morality and general behaviour.

The puritan leaders made elaborate preparations for the meeting of Parliament in 1586, and the increasing sophistication of their political techniques was shown by a letter which the head of the Dedham *classis* wrote to John Field: 'I hope you have not let slip this notable opportunity of furthering the cause of religion by noting out all the places of government in the land for which burgesses for the Parliament are to be chosen, and using all the best means you can possibly for ... procuring the best gentlemen of those places, by whose wisdom and zeal God's causes may be preferred.' Field had in fact already taken steps to secure the return of members sympathetic to the puritans' aims, and he had also prepared a survey of the clergy in over 2,500 parishes covering London and the surrounding counties. This survey, which other evidence suggests is reasonably accurate, reported that in Essex, for example, over half the benefices were held by ignorant and unpreaching ministers. Many of the unfavourable reports were based upon the failure of the minister to live up to the puritan ideal. One was condemned for being 'sometimes a popish priest, a gross abuser of the scriptures', but although prejudice was everywhere apparent there was sufficient truth in the survey to make it a powerful indictment of the established Church.

The 1587 Parliament contained a number of members who were committed to the establishment of a presbyterian system in England, and it was one of these, Anthony Cope, who acted as the radical puritans' spokesman in the Commons. He introduced a bill which would have abolished the Prayer Book, replaced it by the Genevan form of service, and swept away the entire ecclesiastical hierarchy. In other words it would have completed the work of protestant reform that the Acts of Supremacy and Uniformity, in the eyes of puritans, had hardly begun. When the Speaker tried to hold up discussion of this highly provocative measure, another of the puritan radicals, Peter Wentworth, came to Cope's defence by putting to the Speaker a number of questions on the Commons' privilege of free speech which he said should be immediately debated.

The skill and vigour of the obviously pre-planned puritan attack drove the Queen to stronger action than any she had yet taken. Cope, Wentworth and three other members were imprisoned and the Speaker was commanded to prevent any discussion of religious matters. In fact, the majority of the Commons were moderate rather than radical puritans, and they therefore gave a sympathetic hearing to Sir Christopher Hatton when he led a counter-attack, pointing out that a presbyterian system would mean the establishment of a theocracy that would leave no place for landowners' rights of clerical patronage. Yet there was a strong feeling in the Commons that continuing abuses in the Church should no longer be tolerated, and a committee was set up to propose measures for the better education of the clergy and the curbing of the use of the *ex officio* oath. But Elizabeth again intervened, insisting that the government of the Church fell within the sphere of the royal prerogative, and blocked any further discussion.

The puritans, frustrated in Parliament, were forced back on self-help. As Field said, 'seeing we cannot compass these things by suit nor dispute, it is the multitude and people that must bring the 'Discipline' to pass which we desire'. The *classes*, however, were divided. The radical puritans made a lot of noise but they were thin on the ground. The Dedham *classis*, for instance, had a total membership of only twenty ministers during the course of its seven-year existence, and in Northamptonshire under half of the known non-conforming clergy were active in the 'Discipline'. At this critical moment, when the puritans were uncertain how to proceed, the tide of public opinion suddenly receded and left them stranded. The defeat of the Spanish Armada in 1588 reduced the catholic threat which had made puritanism and patriotism virtually synonymous, and in the same year John Field, the organising genius of radical puritanism, and the Earl of Leicester, one of the most influential of the moderate puritans, both died. Moreover, the 1580s saw a recrudescence of the separatist, or Independent, movement under Browne's successors, Henry Barrow and John Greenwood. Many puritans now feared that if they resorted to short-term and *de facto* separation from the established Church they would thereby encourage the growth of religious pluralism and anarchy.

The radical puritans, who had scented victory in 1587, were bitter at the frustration of their hopes, and their feelings found vent in the *Marprelate Letters* that began to appear in October 1588. These were masterpieces of invective, but their unremitting abuse acted like an inoculation and induced its own reaction. Their main target – as their name implies – was the bishops, whom they described as 'right poisoned, persecuting and terrible priests ... petty anti-Christs, petty popes, proud prelates, intolerable with-standers of reformation, enemies of the gospel', while the clergy in general were dismissed as 'so many swine, dumb-dogs, non-residents ... so many lewd livers, as thieves, murderers, adulterers, drunkards, cormorants, rascals, so many ignorant and atheistical dolts'. Cartwright was appalled by the tone of the *Letters* and assured Burghley that he had 'continually upon any occasion testified both my mislike and sorrow for such kind of disorderly proceeding'.

The search for the author of the *Marprelate Letters* led to the house of a prominent Northamptonshire puritan, Sir Richard Knightley, where the printing press had been concealed. Knightley was arrested, along with many of his associates, and this led to the uncovering of the underground presbyterian organisation in the midland region. Whitgift brought the leading puritan clergy before the Court of Star Chamber, where he argued that their attempt to substitute the 'Discipline' for the Prayer Book amounted to sedition. His case was weak in law, and the Star Chamber refused to convict the ministers, but they remained in prison until 1594 and were only released after acknowledging the error of their ways and promising never to behave in like manner again.

The *Marprelate Letters* and the increasing evidence of subversive presbyterian activities within the Church of England angered and alarmed Elizabeth. When John Penry, a puritan minister suspected of being the anonymous Marprelate, took refuge in Scotland, the Queen wrote to its ruler, James VI, warning him that 'there is risen both in your realm and mine a sect of perilous consequence, such as would have no kings but a presbytery, and take our place while they enjoy our privilege'. In 1593 Penry, who had returned to England, was brought before the Court of Queen's Bench on a charge of fomenting insurrection. He was found guilty, sentenced to death, and executed in May of that year. The previous month had also witnessed the hanging at Tyburn of Barrow and Greenwood, the leaders of the Independents. If further confirmation was needed that opinion was turning against the radical puritans it came in this same year, 1593, when Parliament passed the Conventicle Act. This laid down that any person refusing to attend his parish church, or forming part of a puritan conventicle, should go into exile. If he returned to England he would be *ipso facto* guilty of felony, the punishment for which was death by hanging.

These harsh measures effectively crushed the presbyterian and separatist movements, which remained in a state of limbo for the rest of Elizabeth's reign. The last recorded provincial conference of the midland and East-Anglian puritans took place at Cambridge in September 1589. As for the Dedham *classis*, it held its eightieth and final session in June of that year, when it wrote its own epitaph: 'thus long continued through God's mercy this blessed meeting, and now it ended by the malice of Satan'.

Although radical puritanism as an organised movement had been crushed, Elizabeth had not driven all forms of puritanism out of the established Church. At the parish level many puritan ministers were firmly entrenched and neither the ecclesiastical or secular authorities could take consistent and effective action against them if – as was frequently the case – they had the support of local gentry. Many of the gentry were themselves of puritan persuasion and since they dominated local administration they could block royal initiatives of which they disapproved. Although the Queen insisted that she had sole responsibility for governing the Church, she actually increased the influence of the landowners over it, by selling off more than two thousand impropriate tithes, which usually carried with them the advowson or right of presentation to the living. This meant that the purchasers, who included a significant number of puritan sympathisers, could choose as ministers men who shared their own religious attitudes. In other words, while the Queen was asserting her control over the Church at the centre she was enfeebling it in the localities.

Puritanism was well rooted in many urban as well as rural areas. In Leeds, for instance, which was contained within a single parish, the inhabitants raised the considerable sum of £130 to purchase the advowson and promptly appointed a puritan to the living. Similarly, in 1561, the corporation of Hull invited a well-known puritan to be their vicar. He refused to wear the prescribed vestments, but this did not prevent him from retaining the living until his death thirty years later. Northampton was another town where puritanism had taken a firm hold, and when, shortly after the death of Elizabeth, an attempt was made to enforce the use of the Prayer Book, the corporation complained that this would mean adopting ceremonies that had not been current for forty years. In other words, puritan practices were the norm at Northampton: it was the advocates of conformity who appeared to be the innovators.

Hull was not content with having a puritan vicar. In 1573 the corporation decided to appoint a lecturer, or unbeneficed preacher, at a stipend of £40 per annum, and did so with the enthusiastic support of Archbishop Grindal. The first lecturer was a Cambridge man who on a number of occasions was summoned before High Commission for non-conformity, but he remained a popular and respected figure in the locality until 1598, when he died. Lectureships were established in many other towns where there was a demand for good preaching and the inhabitants were prepared to pay for it; in London, for example, almost a third of the parishes had their own lecturer by 1581. Lecturers within a given area would frequently come together in what were known as 'exercises', to distinguish them from the closely related prophesyings which Elizabeth had suppressed. 'Exercises' helped raise the level of learning among local clergy who took part, and were also aimed at evangelising the lay community. Public fasts were another means of bringing the 'godly' into contact with each other and strengthening their sense of purpose. And in the closing years of Elizabeth's reign puritan energies found a further outlet in Sabbatarianism, the insistence that Sunday should be treated like the Jewish Sabbath, a day set apart for prayer and meditation.

The Church established

During the first half of Elizabeth's reign puritan ministers were, in general, better educated than the ordinary run of parish clergy, but the disparity lessened as more graduates entered the ministry. At Cambridge two new colleges, Emmanuel and Sidney Sussex, were founded with the specific aim of preparing students to enter the Church, and by the second half of Elizabeth's reign the quality of the clergy was markedly improving. In London, for example, only 40 per cent of the clergy were graduates in 1560, but by 1595 the proportion was over 70 per cent. In the vast diocese of Lincoln more than half of all clergy were graduates at the time of Elizabeth's death and 60 per cent were licensed to preach. In other words, the Church under Whitgift was gradually moving towards the attainment of the aim which both the episcopate and the puritans shared, of creating a learned, preaching ministry. However, better-educated ministers were not necessarily better pastors, for learning could create a barrier where simple men and women were concerned. Graduate ministers, whether or not they were puritan, were sometimes accused of intellectual arrogance, contempt for popular culture, and an excessive commitment to their own order – characteristics which amounted to a form of clericalism and could easily provoke a backlash.

The creation of a graduate ministry was not an end in itself, but an important element in the campaign to create a protestant England. An even more important element was the Queen's longevity. If Elizabeth had ruled for a mere five or six years, as was the case with her half brother and sister, there is no certainty that the Reformation would have triumphed. Time was essential, as well as protestant endeavour, and fortunately for the reformers time was granted. By the 1580s England was no longer a catholic country, though whether it could be described as protestant is a moot question. The externals of the reformed faith, including the estab-lished Church, were all in position, but that did not necessarily imply a change of heart among the Queen's subjects. Elizabeth is credited with saying that she did not wish to open windows into men's souls, and this was true of her Church. It may be that this explains why Elizabethan England, unlike France, was never torn apart by wars of religion. But a price had to be paid for this immunity. All that was demanded of the Queen's subjects was that they should show outward conformity in religion. What went on in the inner recesses of their minds and souls was not the authorities' business.

The Church's critics condemned this lukewarm approach. They would have welcomed more passion and more controversy if it led to a deeper understanding of, and commitment to, the protestant religion. It is not possible even now to decide whether the Elizabethan Reformation was a success or failure, since everything depends, as it did at the time, upon the viewpoint of the observer. Elizabeth believed that in a turbulent and fallen world the established Church came as close to perfection as could be hoped or expected. She proudly informed the members of Parliament assembled in 1589 'that the estate and government of the Church of England, as it now standeth in this reformation, may justly be compared to any Church which hath been established in any Christian kingdom since the apostles' times: that both in form and doctrine it is agreeable with the scriptures, with the most ancient general councils, with the prac-tice of the primitive Church, and with the judgements of all the old and learned fathers'. Against this may be set the observation of a Kentish puritan who tested the depth of religious knowledge among his local parishioners. Only a tenth, he reported, had any knowledge of Christ or of sin and its punishment. As for the key issue of justification by faith alone, 'scarce one but did affirm that a man might be saved by his own well-doing, and that he trusted he did so live that by God's grace he should obtain everlasting life'.

By the time Elizabeth died, the Church of England, as reconstructed in 1559, had been in existence for well over forty years, which meant that a large segment of the population had grown up in it. The bishops who ruled the Church under its royal governor were no longer defensive in their atti-tudes, constantly looking over their shoulders to see where the latest puritan attack was coming from. Many puritans, and in particular the presbyterians, claimed that episcopacy was not warranted by the scrip-tures, but a small number of bishops were now swinging towards the opposite pole by claiming that their authority was *jure divino*, derived from God. Richard Bancroft, who was appointed chaplain to Archbishop Whitgift in 1592, was firmly of this opinion, and in the following year he publicly asserted that government of the Church by bishops had been ordained by God and was therefore not simply acceptable but essential.

The anti-puritan reaction also made itself felt in theological studies. At Cambridge in the 1580s the Huguenot refugee Peter Baro, who had been appointed to Cartwright's former chair as Lady Margaret Professor of Divinity, gave a series of lectures in which he submitted fundamental Calvinist doctrines to critical and often hostile scrutiny. At the same time Lancelot Andrewes, a future Bishop of Winchester, was expounding the belief – which Calvinists regarded as heretical – that divine grace and human nature, far from being in opposition, worked in harmony.

The expression of such views provoked a lively controversy, and Whitgift was called upon to define where exactly the Church of England stood. He gave qualified support to the Calvinists, and the *Lambeth Articles* he helped draw up in 1595 affirmed that God had from eternity predestined some persons to eternal salvation and reprobated others to everlasting damnation. If the *Lambeth Articles* had been officially sanctioned they would have put the Calvinist nature of the Church of England beyond dispute, but Elizabeth was determined that no such sanction should be given. She stood by the *Thirty-Nine Articles* adopted by Convocation in 1563 and confirmed by statute in 1571, and she instructed her secretary, Sir Robert Cecil, to tell Whitgift 'that she mislikes much that any allowance hath been given by your grace of any points to be disputed of predestination (being a matter tender and dangerous to weak, ignorant minds) and thereupon requireth your grace to suspend them [i.e. the *Lambeth Articles*]'.

Elizabeth has been criticised for taking too narrow a view of the Church of England and failing to recognise that minor modifications designed to make it more acceptable to puritans would in the long run have strengthened it. This may be true, but it can also be argued that after a quarter of a century of religious change, much of it violent, Elizabeth did well to impose a period of peace. The Elizabethan Church had its critics and they made a lot of noise, but it also had its defenders. The first of these was John Jewel, Bishop of Salisbury, who was encouraged by Cecil to write his *Apologia pro Ecclesia Anglicana*, which was published in 1562. It was subsequently translated into English by Cecil's sister-in law. Jewel has another claim to fame in that he paid for the university education of Richard Hooker, who became the second and greatest of the Church's champions in print. Hooker established his reputation as a theologian at Oxford, and this led to his appointment as Master of the Temple, the collegiate institution close to the Thames in London where lawyers learned their trade. Hooker preached every morning, but in the afternoon his place was taken by the puritan Walter Travers. In the words of Thomas Fuller, the historian of the Church of England, 'the pulpit spake pure Canterbury in the morning and Geneva in the afternoon'. These daily encounters persuaded Hooker of the need to draw up a justification of the Church's position, based on philosophy and history as well as theology, and he accepted a country living so that he could devote himself to this task. The first four books of his masterpiece, *The Laws of Ecclesiastical Polity*, were published in 1594. The fifth book, appropriately dedicated to Archbishop Whitgift, appeared in 1597. Hooker died in 1600 leaving behind him three more books whose publication was postponed until well into the seventeenth century.

The Laws of Ecclesiastical Polity is a work of massive learning, written in a majestic style, and it quickly took its place alongside the Bible and Foxe's *Book of Martyrs* as one of the fundamental texts of the Church of England. According to Izaak Walton, Hooker's earliest biographer, Pope Clement VIII asked to read the first books of *The Laws of Ecclesiastical Polity*, of which he had heard so much, and after perusing them gave his opinion that 'There is no learning that this man hath not searched into; nothing too hard for his understanding. This man indeed deserves the name of an author. His books will get reverence by age, for there is in them such seeds of eternity that if the rest be like this they shall last till the last fire shall consume all learning.' The story is probably apocryphal, but the judgement is sound.

CHAPTER NINE

Roman Catholics and foreign policy under Elizabeth I

Roman Catholics

England did not abruptly cease to be catholic in 1558. The degree of genuine commitment to the old faith in Mary's reign had varied from one region to another. Generally speaking it was greater in the north than in the south, but all areas had their catholic elements: among west Sussex gentry families, for instance, there were twice as many adherents of the old faith in the 1560s as there were protestants. In parts of the north such as Lancashire the priests who accepted the Elizabethan settlement did so in a half-hearted fashion and continued to hold what were in effect catholic services. Meanwhile, their brethren who had preferred to leave the Church altogether rather than take the oath of supremacy kept up an unofficial catholic ministry, relying for maintenance on contributions from the faithful.

In principle the Elizabethan government was committed to the eradication of catholicism, but in practice it was dependent on the co-operation of local gentlemen and clergy, and this was not always forthcoming. Catholicism therefore survived, but during the 1560s many catholics attended their parish churches out of a sense of social obligation. The church was, after all, the focal point of the life of the community and if gentlemen absented themselves from it they were failing to live up to the responsibilities of their position. 'Church-papists', as these conforming catholics were called, remained committed to the old faith, but they did not believe that this commitment entailed an ostentatious rejection of the state Church. In any case, the Prayer-Book services were derived from catholic models and, as the puritans pointed out with increasing bitterness, contained many 'popish' features. The administration of the sacraments was likely to cause difficulties, but communion services were held very rarely – at most four times a year – and people with scruples of conscience could usually think up a good reason for staying away.

The loyalty of English catholics to Elizabeth was demonstrated most strikingly by their refusal to support the rebellion of the northern earls in 1569 (see p. 222). In fact, catholic passivity was causing alarm at Rome, where it was feared that the old faith would die out completely unless its English adherents were pushed into a more active commitment. In 1570, therefore, Pope Pius V issued the bull *Regnans in Excelsis* in which he declared Elizabeth excommunicate and 'deprived of her pretended title to the kingdom ... And we do command and charge all and every the noblemen, subjects, people and others aforesaid that they presume not to obey her or her orders, mandates and laws'. The bull's primary purpose was to give guidance to English catholics, so that when a moment of crisis came, such as the northern rebellion, they would know how to act. In practice, however, the majority ignored its provisions and emphasised that they were, as they always had been, the Queen's faithful subjects. Nevertheless, the bull, when taken at face value, made every catholic a potential traitor, and the government felt compelled to implement appropriate counter action. A decade of relative tolerance came to an abrupt end, and events confirmed Philip II's prediction that 'this sudden and unexpected step [i.e. the issue of the bull] will make matters worse, and drive the Queen and her friends the more to oppress and persecute the few good catholics remaining in England'.

Elizabeth was far less alarmed by the catholic threat than many of her advisers. Parliament was informed in 1570 that so long as the catholics observed her laws and did not 'wilfully and manifestly break them by their open acts, her majesty's meaning is not to have any of them molested by an inquisition or examination of their consciences in causes of religion', and she vetoed a bill which would have made attendance at the communion service compulsory. Yet she could not turn back the tide of anti-catholicism that was now rising rapidly, and she felt it politic to accept another bill making it treasonable to bring in to the kingdom 'any token or tokens, thing or things, called by the name of an *Agnus Dei*, or any crosses, pictures, beads or suchlike vain and superstitious things from the Bishop or see of Rome'. This was the first in a series of acts that placed the catholic community in England under increasing pressure at a time when the arrival of the missionary priests was forcing it to re-examine the implications of its religious commitment.

During the first decade of Elizabeth's reign more than a hundred teaching members of Oxford university went into exile rather than acknowledge the newly-established protestant Church. Among them was William Allen, formerly the principal of St Mary's Hall, who in 1568, when he was in residence at the university town of Douai in the Spanish Netherlands, decided 'to establish a college in which our countrymen, who were scattered abroad in different places, might live and study together more profitably than apart'. As well as bringing the catholic exiles together, the college would also provide a reservoir of 'men of learning' who would be 'always ready outside the realm to restore religion when the proper moment should arrive, although it seemed hopeless to attempt anything while the heretics were masters there'.

Allen seemed content to wait for God to restore the catholic faith in England, but the young men who flocked to Douai felt called to play a more active role. They believed it was their duty, after they had been adequately prepared, to return to England and, as Allen put it, 'train catholics to be plainly and openly catholics; to be men who will always refuse every kind of spiritual commerce with heretics'. This changed the whole nature of the college by turning it into a seminary for missionary priests. The first of the seminarists landed in England in 1574, and during the next thirty years they were followed by some six hundred others. Although referred to both at the time and since as missionaries, their aim was not to convert protestants but to sustain the existing catholic community, and this they did. Their impact on English catholics was immediate, for the Bishop of London informed Secretary Walsingham in 1577 that 'the papists marvellously increase both in numbers and in obstinate withdrawing of themselves from the Church and service of God'.

Among the offshoots of Douai was the English College established at Rome in 1576. This was originally intended, like Douai, to be a haven and a study centre for English catholics in exile, but after a few years the Pope gave control of it to the Society of Jesus – one of the new orders to which the catholic reformation of the mid-century had given birth. The Jesuits were committed to missionary endeavour, and at Allen's suggestion they agreed to send some of their recruits from the English College to join the seminary priests in England.

The men chosen to inaugurate the Jesuit campaign were Robert Parsons and Edmund Campion, who arrived in England in the summer of

1580. More Jesuits followed them, and as the number of priests – both seminarists and Jesuits – increased, it became essential to organise them more effectively. The Jesuits, whose membership of a religious order gave them a sense of corporate identity that was lacking among the secular seminary priests, brought a greater professionalism to the English mission. They arranged for the reception and shelter of newly-arrived priests and in due course despatched them to the area in which they were to work. The mission was based on London – inevitably so, since it was not only the capital but also easily accessible from the south-east coast, which was the main point of entry for the priests – but gradually established a regional organisation.

The big problem facing the missionaries was that of travelling around the country, for the government's repressive measures were beginning to bite, and even people with catholic sympathies were often afraid to shelter priests. There were some areas – for instance, in Lancashire – where catholics were so thick on the ground that the priests could move about openly without disguise, but these were the exception. Elsewhere they were dependent upon the hospitality of catholic gentry whose mansions were big enough to conceal them. As the mission developed, networks of 'safe houses' were established and priests were passed from one to another as they went about their dangerous business. Without such networks the mission might never have got off the ground, but there was a price to be paid for this, and it consisted in the fact that the missionary priests – many of whom came from gentry families – became increasingly identified with the landowners, whose attitudes and assumptions they shared. Yet it would be wrong to assume that catholicism was confined to the upper sections of society. Of six catholic women imprisoned in York castle in 1577, three were married to butchers, two to tailors, and only one to a gentleman. In Hull, there were five gentlemen among the catholics held prisoner, but also three schoolmasters, a yeoman, a blacksmith, a saddler, a tiler, a weaver and a labourer. Catholicism had always been a popular movement in the north and west, but resident gentry were thinner on the ground in these areas than in the south and east and the missionary effort was therefore more diluted.

The Jesuits had acquired a reputation as the shock troops of the Counter-Reformation and they were deeply involved in the political as well as the religious life of catholic Europe. It was realised that their participation in the English mission might alarm Elizabeth's government and strengthen the hard-line protestants. They were therefore explicitly instructed to confine their activities to those who were already catholic, to take no part in English politics and to profess no views on political matters. The Jesuits observed these instructions carefully, but they were operating in a country in which Church and state were so closely integrated as to be virtually inseparable. Nothing in Elizabethan England could be 'purely religious' any more than it could be 'purely secular', and although the Jesuits were genuine in their protestations of political non-involvement they could not deny the fact that they were the sworn servants of the papacy at a time when that institution was committed to the overthrow of Elizabeth and had given aid to FitzMaurice in his rebellion against the Queen's rule in Ireland (*see* p. 170).

It was therefore hardly surprising that the English government intensified its repressive measures. An act of 1581 stated that anyone attempting to subvert the loyalty of the Queen's subjects or to convert them as a means to this end was to suffer death as a traitor, while catholic 'recusants' – so called from the Latin *recusare*, 'to refuse' – who declined to attend Prayer-Book services were to be fined the crippling sum of twenty pounds a month instead of a shilling (one-twentieth of a pound), as earlier. Missionary priests were hunted down, imprisoned, tortured and executed, and in 1585 an act was passed ordering 'all and every Jesuits, seminary priests and other priests' ordained by authority of the see of Rome to 'depart out of this realm of England'. Anyone flouting the order risked death as a traitor.

The first seminary priest to be executed was Cuthbert Mayne, in 1577; another met the same fate in 1578. By 1592 the total of all priests put to death was close on a hundred, and there were in addition thirty-six lay catholics executed for abetting the mission. Among the priests who met their end on the scaffold was Edmund Campion, in 1581. He maintained until his last moment that he had been condemned unjustly, because his mission was only spiritual, and that the catholics were 'as true subjects as ever the Queen had'. The Privy Council took a different view, however, and required catholic prisoners to answer the notorious 'bloody question': 'If the Pope or any other by his appointment do invade this realm, which part would you take, and which part ought a good subject to take?' One answer to this was given by Robert Parsons when he wrote a virulent tract against Elizabeth to be distributed by Spanish troops after they had landed from what he assumed would be the victorious armada.

Lay catholics, who were caught up in the struggle between the government and the missionary priests, inevitably suffered. The government insisted upon outward conformity in religion, but recusancy – the process whereby catholics detached themselves from their local church and community – was already gathering pace before the Pope issued the bull of deposition in 1570 and increased markedly thereafter. The missionary priests gave added impetus to this development, and the result was a marked decline in the number of 'Church-papists'. In this way the large and amorphous catholic community that had survived from Mary's reign was transformed into a smaller body with a core of committed adherents. Protestants believed that catholics were increasing in number and posed a growing threat. In fact there were probably not more than 35 to 40,000 at the close of the sixteenth century, a mere one per cent of the total popu-lation, although this figure does not include those people who were forced into conformity by social or economic pressures but remained catholic at heart.

These pressures could be extreme, especially after 1587, when it was provided by statute that if recusants failed to pay the monthly fine for non-attendance at church, two-thirds of their land could be seized by the Exchequer. Since a month was calculated at twenty-eight days, recusants were liable in theory to a fine of £260 a year. In fact, not more than sixteen people paid this crippling sum in Elizabeth's reign, but poorer recusants were often made to pay the shilling fine, and the need to preserve their property drove an increasing number of heads of households into occasional conformity from the 1590s onwards. The seizure of lands was not quite as harsh as the letter of the law implied, for property valuations were always low and a nominal two-thirds worked out in practice at a good deal less. The confiscated lands were leased out by the Exchequer in order to recover the amount due, but the purchasers of the leases fre-quently sold them back to the original recusant owner or to trustees acting on his behalf. In these ways the impact of confiscation was blunted, but it remained an expensive and frightening penalty.

The tension between secular and religious loyalties affected even the missionary priests. The Jesuits were firmly committed to the ideals of the Counter-Reformation and regarded England as only one of many mission fields in an operation that was world-wide. The seminarists, on the other hand, tended to think in more specifically English terms and believed that by accepting a subordinate place for catholicism and emphasising their allegiance to the Queen they would be able to persuade the government to ease up on repression. They wanted to signal a return to normality by re-establishing the traditional hierarchy. This would have the further advantage of placing control of the catholic Church in England firmly in the hands of bishops and secular clergy, thereby reducing the role of the Jesuits, whom they distrusted.

The seculars were counting on papal support for their campaign, but in 1598 the Pope, far from accepting their suggestion, appointed an Archpriest to take charge of the mission, and went out of his way to praise the work of the Jesuits. Those seculars who felt deeply on this issue made repeated appeals to the Pope to change his mind – hence their name of 'appellants' – and in 1602 he responded by instructing the Archpriest to take three of the appellants as his assistants and to report directly to Rome instead of consulting with the Jesuits as he had previously been required to do. In the following year thirteen of the appellants made a public assertion of their loyalty to the Queen and it seemed for a time as though the 'Archpriest controversy' would fatally divide the mission. This did not happen, however, for the appellants were only a small minority among the three hundred or more priests then in England. Tensions between the various elements among the missionaries remained, but the mission itself continued to flourish and expand well into the seventeenth century.

Foreign policy

At the outset of Elizabeth's reign France, with her ally, Scotland, was the main enemy of England, but in 1562 the political situation in Europe was transformed by the outbreak of the French wars of religion. During the next twenty years French influence fluctuated violently as aristocratic families identified with religious factions struggled for supremacy. In the interludes between bouts of fighting the French monarchy attempted to resume its European role, and this, as well as ingrained habits of thinking, blinded many English people to the fact that a dramatic shift in the balance of power had taken place.

With the decline of France, Philip II of Spain emerged as not only the greatest catholic prince in Europe but also the chief threat to England's independence. As if to demonstrate this, he moved an army under the Duke of Alva into the Spanish Netherlands in August 1567, to crush the revolt that was smouldering there. Elizabeth could hardly ignore this move, for a powerful army in The Netherlands was always a potential threat to England.

The situation in The Netherlands was complicated by internal divisions between the greater and lesser nobles, the aristocracy and the urban bourgeoisie, the Calvinists and the catholics. In the northern provinces the most prominent figures among the rebels were Calvinists from Zeeland and Holland who had taken up privateering against Spanish shipping and called themselves the 'Sea Beggars'. They used the ports of south-east

England as a base for their operations, but in 1572, in response to Spanish pressure, Elizabeth ordered them to leave. The unintended effect of her action was to transform the whole nature of The Netherlands' revolt, for the Sea Beggars did not simply return peaceably to Holland. Instead, they seized a number of ports, drove out the Spanish garrisons, and thereby shifted the heart of the rebellion from the southern to the northern provinces.

William of Orange, the Burgundian noble who had emerged as the champion of Netherlands' autonomy in the face of Spanish attempts to reimpose direct rule, realised that if the rebellion was to stand any chance of success it must be as broadly based as possible. He therefore gave his patronage to the Sea Beggars and in 1573 took the politically significant step of joining the Calvinist Church, even though this made him less acceptable to the nobles of the south, who were socially conservative and catholic in religion. William also appealed for help from abroad and called on Elizabeth to support the rebellion with men and money. However, Elizabeth did not approve of rebels; nor was she in favour of independence for The Netherlands. She wanted a return to the autonomy they had enjoyed before Philip II, and thought the rebels should negotiate rather than fight. She therefore rejected William's appeal, but at the same time she urged Philip to concede home rule to The Netherlands and warned him that failure to do so would make English intervention inevitable in the long run.

In 1577 Don John of Austria, whom Philip, his half brother, had appointed governor of The Netherlands, granted the inhabitants autonomy, but this was merely a tactical ploy, and before the year was out he had returned to the earlier policy of asserting Spanish rule by force of arms. This abrupt change of course so angered Elizabeth that she now offered the Dutch six thousand troops under the command of her favourite, Robert Dudley, Earl of Leicester. However, the Queen had not dispensed with her customary caution, and in June 1578 she sent her Secretary of State, Sir Francis Walsingham, to The Netherlands in the hope that he might be able to arrange a peaceful settlement. Walsingham, who shared Leicester's views on this issue, despaired at what he regarded as dangerous vacillation on Elizabeth's part. 'The only remedy left to us', he declared, 'is prayer. Where the advice of counsellors cannot prevail with a prince of her judgement it is a sign that God hath closed up her heart from seeing and executing what may be for her safety.'

Since Elizabeth had failed him, William turned to the Duke of Anjou, the brother of Henri III of France. Anjou had hopes of creating a powerful anti-Habsburg bloc under French protection and was willing to accept sovereignty over The Netherlands as the first step towards this. But he would not take the plunge until he had tested the feasibility of the second step, which consisted of bringing England into the coalition by means of a marriage with Elizabeth. Negotiations opened in 1578 and in August of that year Anjou was invited to be the Queen's guest at Greenwich. Elizabeth seems to have taken Anjou's courtship seriously. The marriage had much to be said for it on diplomatic grounds, and a number of Privy Councillors, including Lord Burghley, were in favour of it. The majority, however, were opposed, and Elizabeth gave in to them by postponing any decision. Anjou therefore returned to France, leaving open the question of his future.

The next two years saw the balance of power in Europe swing ever more strongly in favour of the Habsburgs. In 1579 the southern Netherlands gave up their struggle for autonomy and acknowledged Spain's supremacy, while in the Iberian peninsula the death of the King of Portugal in 1580 allowed Philip to take over that country and bring its colonial empire, as well as its powerful navy, under his control. The only hope of saving the northern Netherlands from Spanish domination now seemed to rest in Anjou, and Elizabeth reopened the marriage negotiations, using them this time as a means to persuade her suitor to accept William of Orange's proffer of sovereignty over the rebel provinces. In 1581 Walsingham was again sent on mission, this time to France, where he urged Henri III to give his support to the proposed marriage and also to join in a defensive league against the Habsburgs. Yet even now Elizabeth could not bring herself to give an unequivocal undertaking to marry. Whatever her feelings for Anjou she clung to her independence and was reluctant to play the last diplomatic trump card left in her hand. Walsingham had to make what he could out of conflicting instructions and confessed to Burghley that he was completely baffled. 'I wish to God her highness would resolve one way or the other touching the matter of her marriage ... When her majesty is pressed to marry, thus she seemeth to affect a league. And when a league is proposed, then she liketh better of a marriage.'

One thing that did become plain to Walsingham was that under the irresolute Henri III France could not be counted on to play a major role in Europe. If Elizabeth was to achieve her aim she would have to act on her own initiative. Events were in any case pushing her in this direction. Anjou had accepted sovereignty over The Netherlands but he was caught up in the factional strife that bedevilled the provinces and finally abandoned them to their fate. He died in June 1584, and the following month saw the assassination of William of Orange. Now, at last, Elizabeth acted. Leicester was despatched to Holland with an expeditionary force, but only after the Dutch agreed to hand over Flushing and Brill as security for the repayment of the Queen's expenses.

Leicester, who arrived in Holland in December 1585, had instructions to put an end to squabbles among the rebels but not to make any firm commitments on Elizabeth's behalf. It took him only a short time to discover that without some clearly defined position of authority he could not possibly overcome Dutch factionalism. He therefore accepted the office of Governor and Captain-General of the provinces, but this brought down Elizabeth's wrath upon him and he returned to England in November 1586. In the following year he went back to The Netherlands with additional supplies of men and money, but he found, as Anjou had done, that the factions were too strong for him. In 1588 he left The Netherlands for good, having accomplished little of significance: only the nobility of the warrior-poet Sir Philip Sidney, dying on the battlefield at Zutphen, redeemed his campaign from total oblivion. However, Elizabeth allowed the English troops and their officers to stay on, under Dutch command, and she continued payment of a subsidy that amounted to some £125,000 a year – about a third of her annual income.

Mary, Queen of Scots

Elizabeth may have been over-cautious in her approach to The Netherlands' problem, but she was all too aware of the enormous disparity between English and Spanish power. She was also increasingly preoccupied with the situation that confronted her at home after May 1568, when Queen Mary of Scotland took refuge in England. Mary was the catholic pretender to Elizabeth's throne and the Queen did not want her so near at hand, but she could hardly employ English arms to reimpose Mary's rule upon the protestant Scots. Nor could she allow the hapless queen to take refuge in the courts of France or Spain, where she would become a pawn in the international power game. There was no alternative, in the short run, to keeping the Queen of Scots in honourable captivity, and in 1569 she was sent to Tutbury castle in Staffordshire, under the guardianship of the Earl of Shrewsbury.

No sooner did Mary reach Tutbury than she became the focus of intrigue. Some English nobles of ancient lineage, prominent among them the Duke of Norfolk, resented the rule of Cecil and other 'new men' and drew up a plan by which Elizabeth should recognise Mary as her heir and give permission for Norfolk to marry her – thereby ensuring the dominance of the 'old' nobility after the Queen's death. There was nothing treasonable about this proposal, which had the support of a number of Privy Councillors, but Norfolk was also linked through his brother-in-law, the Earl of Westmorland, with a group of northern peers who felt increasingly out of sympathy with the Queen's government. The 'old' families such as the Percies, the Nevilles and the Dacres, resented the way in which their traditional dominance over northern England was being challenged by new men committed to the new religion. The Council of the North, for example, was dominated by protestants with only nominal links to the region. Moreover, Bishop Pilkington, who took over the great see of Durham in 1561, made himself and the Queen's government deeply unpopular by the insensitive manner in which he enforced his puritan brand of protestantism.

Henry Neville, Earl of Westmorland, was in touch with Thomas Percy, Earl of Northumberland, and the two men, who were both catholics, were already considering rebellion. There were tenuous links between them and Norfolk, and although he refused to commit himself and insisted upon his loyalty to Elizabeth, they assumed he would join them once the die was cast. Norfolk had left court in dudgeon in September 1569, having failed to gain approval for his marriage to Mary, and the two earls took this as a signal for their revolt to go ahead. In fact they were mistaken, for Norfolk returned to court the following month and threw himself on Elizabeth's mercy. The Queen had already received reports about the disturbed situation in the north, and summoned Westmorland and Northumberland to London, but rather than risk their freedom by obeying, they took the plunge into open rebellion.

Because they stood for the traditional liberties of the north against the encroachments of the London government, and because feudal ties in the area were still potent, the earls had little difficulty in raising an army. Announcing their intention to put an end to the 'new-found religion and heresy', they moved south and in mid-November occupied Durham, where mass was celebrated in the old manner. From Durham the rebel host advanced to Tadcaster, where they were within striking distance of Tutbury. But the Yorkshire gentry, whom the earls had expected to rally to the catholic cause, held aloof and there was no general rising. The earls hesitated, uncertain what to do next, but while they were deliberating their followers melted away. Before 1569 came to an end the rebellion was over. Westmorland fled abroad and spent the rest of his life in exile. Northumberland evaded capture until 1572, when he was caught and

executed at York. The rank and file were not spared. Elizabeth ordered
that at least one man should be hanged from every community that had
provided recruits for the rising, and although this bloodthirsty directive
was not carried out to the letter, some four hundred and fifty of the poorer
sort of rebels were put to death. In reacting to revolt, Elizabeth was very
much her father's daughter.

One of the back-stage figures behind the revolt was a Florentine
banker, Roberto Ridolfi, who was resident in England and distributed the
secret funds sent by the Pope to the English catholics. Ridolfi told the
Spanish ambassador, in March 1569, that he had been commissioned 'by
the Pope in person to arrange the restoration and re-establishment of the
catholic faith in England, working with the catholic peers of the country'.
The ambassador thereupon drew up a grandiose plan to topple Elizabeth,
and urged Philip II openly to espouse the cause of Mary, Queen of Scots.
Before any of the elements in the plan could be put into operation it was
overtaken by events, in the shape of the rebellion of the northern earls. But
this merely confirmed the ambassador in his belief that Spain should
actively intervene to remove Elizabeth from the throne and replace her by
Mary.

By this time Anglo-Spanish relations had taken a sharp turn for the
worse. In December 1568 a Spanish fleet bound for The Netherlands and
carrying a considerable quantity of bullion for the payment of Alva's army,
had been forced by bad weather to take shelter in English ports on the
south-west coast. The ambassador secured Elizabeth's authorisation for
the cargo to be unloaded and taken overland to Dover for transhipment.
However, it remained on shore, because news had just arrived that Spanish
forces in the Caribbean had attacked a merchant fleet commanded by John
Hawkins that included two of the Queen's warships. The newly arrived
and inexperienced Spanish ambassador informed Alva, quite wrongly, that
Elizabeth had confiscated the bullion, whereupon Alva ordered all English
goods in The Netherlands to be seized, and imposed an embargo on trade
between the two countries. This action so enraged Elizabeth that she seized
the bullion on the grounds that it was not the property of the King of Spain
but of the Italian bankers who had loaned it to him.

Philip II was already considering what action to take against the heretic
Queen. He instructed Alva to send money and munitions to the English
catholics and also asked for his views on a possible invasion of England.
Philip made plain his belief that he was doing what God willed, but Alva
remained sceptical. 'Even though the principal means must come from
God', he told the king, 'nevertheless since He normally works through the

resources He gives to humans, it seems necessary to examine what human resources would be needed to carry out your wishes.' Alva clearly wanted to avoid any deeper involvement in the English situation, but this was not the case with Ridolfi and De Spes, the Spanish ambassador. In March 1571 the English government uncovered details of a plot, master-minded by Ridolfi, which involved the King of Spain and the Pope, along with the Queen of Scots and the Duke of Norfolk. The duke was to lead the English catholics into rebellion against Elizabeth, who was to be taken prisoner at the same time as Mary was released from captivity. Meanwhile, a Spanish expeditionary force would be landed on the east coast of England, thereby ensuring the success of the uprising. It is highly unlikely that the plot would ever have succeeded, but Cecil discovered what was afoot and grasped the opportunity to remove Norfolk from the political scene, once and for all. The duke was arrested, put on trial for high treason, and found guilty. Six months later, after the Queen's doubts and hesitations had at last been overcome, he was executed on Tower Hill.

Relations between England and Spain were apparently moving towards breaking point, and Elizabeth told the French ambassador that as Philip 'had worked so hard to provoke and create havoc in [her kingdom] . . . she no longer held herself restrained by the consideration she had always showed him until now'. Nevertheless, neither side wanted an open break at this stage, and Elizabeth took steps to lower the tension between them by opening negotiations with Alva, who – unlike his royal master – was guided by reason rather than a sense of divine mission. These negotiations were successful, and by 1575 normal commercial relations had been restored. But there could be no long-term agreement between England and Spain while Philip persisted in his attempt to reimpose Spanish rule on the Low Countries. Elizabeth's open intervention in 1585, when she sent over Leicester and his army to aid the Dutch, made a clash with Spain inevitable, and matters were not improved by Francis Drake's privateering expedition to the West Indies, which set out in the same year. By the time he returned to England in 1586 Drake had plundered Spanish ships and cities and extorted vast sums by way of ransom. He had thereby demonstrated that Spain, despite her wealth and power, was not invulnerable, and that England's naval strength was potentially formidable.

Philip II's policies would have stood a better chance of success if Elizabeth could have been removed from the throne. Throckmorton's plot, in 1583, was designed to do just this, and the Spanish ambassador therefore gave it his blessing. But the plot was uncovered before it could come to anything, and the ambassador had to pack his bags and leave. Mary,

Queen of Scots, had also been party to the conspiracy, and the Privy Council reacted by drawing up the *Bond of Association*, which pledged its signatories, in the event of a successful attempt on Elizabeth's life, to hunt down and destroy the person on whose behalf the assassination had been carried out. Mary was not named, but she was clearly uppermost in the minds of those who flocked to sign the *Bond*, and in Parliament and the Council the prevailing opinion was that the Queen of Scots should be put to death.

Elizabeth, who knew that the stability of her own throne depended, in the last resort, upon a general reverence for monarchy, was unwilling to sanction the execution of a fellow sovereign, and she refused to accept that Mary was really complicit in the plots against her life. It was left to Sir Francis Walsingham to provide irrefutable evidence. In 1586 he got wind of a new plot to murder Elizabeth and release Mary with the help of a Spanish army, in which the go-between was a young English catholic named Anthony Babington. Walsingham tapped Babington's correspondence with the Queen of Scots, and through his agents he prompted the sending of a letter asking for Mary's explicit approval of all the details of the plot, including Elizabeth's assassination. In July 1586 came Mary's reply, giving her full assent. Even Elizabeth could not ignore this evidence, and she ordered Mary to be put on trial.

The result of the trial was a formal condemnation of the Queen of Scots, and Parliament petitioned for Mary's execution. But Elizabeth still could not steel herself to take so drastic a step, which would outrage public opinion in France and Spain and leave England ever more isolated. As always, she hoped to shift the responsibility to other shoulders and hinted that Mary's murder would not be displeasing to her. The hint was not taken, but in the end the Council acted on its own initiative and despatched the death warrant to Fotheringay Castle in Northamptonshire, where Mary was being held prisoner. On 8 February 1587 she was led out to a scaffold specially constructed in the great hall of the castle, and there executed.

Elizabeth was furious when she heard the news, refused to admit Burghley to her presence, and sent William Davison, the Secretary of State who had been entrusted with the safe-keeping of the warrant, to the Tower. Her anger was genuine, for her ministers, even though they acted in good faith, had betrayed her trust in them. Yet she was too much of a realist not to appreciate the advantages of Mary's removal from the scene. Among these was the fact that the catholic claimant to the English throne was now Philip of Spain's daughter. English catholics, who might have risen in Mary's cause, were unlikely to feel much enthusiasm for a Spanish pretender.

Spanish armadas

The removal of the Queen of Scots from the stage of European politics clarified the situation for Philip II. Although he had championed Mary's claim to the English throne he had been aware that if ever she succeeded she would almost certainly bring her realm within the orbit of Spain's enemy, France. In fact, even before the news of her execution reached him, he had decided to take direct action against Elizabeth. His plan was that a large Spanish fleet, under the command of the Duke of Medina Sidonia, would sweep the English Channel and leave it clear for the army of the Duke of Parma – the new governor of The Netherlands – to cross over into England. Throughout 1586 ships were being built and assembled along the Channel coast, and in England the Council ordered the setting up of beacons at prominent places so that news of a Spanish invasion could be quickly transmitted. The Armada was almost ready in 1587 and might have set sail that year had not Drake swooped on Cadiz and destroyed the ships and stores assembled there. In the event it did not quit port until May 1588, and even then it was short of provisions and ammunition and lacked sufficient guns.

Lord Howard of Effingham, the English commander, and Drake, the vice-admiral, wanted to attack the Armada off the Portuguese coast, but bad weather, lack of supplies, and the Queen's cautiousness kept them in home waters. By July 1588 the Armada was in the Channel, where William Camden, the antiquary, saw it 'built high like towers and castles, rallied into the form of a crescent whose horns were at least seven miles distant'. Medina Sidonia had about 130 ships carrying more than twenty thousand soldiers and sailors, and he kept them in so tight a formation that the English could not break it up. Howard had about the same number of ships at his command, but they were far more manoeuvrable than the cumbersome Spanish galleons, 'so fast and nimble', wrote the duke, 'they can do anything they like with them'. The English ships were also better armed, and their cannon inflicted heavy damage on the Spanish vessels when they came to close quarters.

Medina Sidonia's orders were to keep his fleet intact until the rendezvous with Parma, and he showed his capacity as a commander by doing just this until the night of 28 July 1588, when he ordered the Armada to anchor off Calais while he awaited news from Parma. This was the opportunity Howard had been looking for. He sent fireships sailing downwind towards the anchored ships and these caused such alarm and confusion that the Spaniards cut their cables and stood out to sea. By the time daylight came the great fleet was scattered over the waters, and the English darted in and around it, doing great damage. They could have done more if they had not run out of ammunition.

In effect the battle was over, for the Spanish ships were short of supplies, and many of them had been so badly damaged by English fire that they could fight no more. Since Howard blocked the southern route back to Spain, Medina Sidonia ordered his leaky ships to sail north, round the coasts of Scotland and Ireland, where rough winds and high seas took a heavy toll. Only half of the great fleet that had set out to humble the protestant Queen eventually returned to harbour, and the enemies of the Catholic Church all over Europe hailed this defeat as a sign of God's blessing on their cause. Elizabeth, too, saw the manifestation of the divine will in the success of her arms, for the commemorative medal that she ordered to be struck recorded not the skill of her sailors but the favour of almighty providence. *Afflavit Deus et dissipati sunt*, it declared with laconic directness: 'God blew and they were scattered.'

The defeat of the Armada did not mean the end of the Anglo-Spanish war. The problem for the English was how best to exploit their victory, and opinions were divided. Hawkins wanted to bankrupt Spain by blockading her coast and cutting her lifeline with the New World, while Drake was in favour of attacking Lisbon and sparking off a nationalist revolt that would lead to the Portuguese regaining their independence. In the end Drake's plan was adopted, and in April 1589 a fleet carrying twenty thousand men set sail for Portugal. But the expedition was a total failure. Land and sea operations were not co-ordinated, and more damage was done to the English forces by incompetence, drunkenness and sickness than by the Spanish defenders. Vigo was sacked, but apart from that nothing was accomplished. American bullion continued to flow into Spain, Portugal remained part of Philip II's empire, and the half of the Armada that had returned to port was left to refit in safety.

In 1595 another expedition was sent out, under the command of Drake and Hawkins. It was intended to revive the glories of former years by attacking the Caribbean area known as the Spanish Main, but the Spaniards had by now built up their defences in the New World and they beat off an assault on Puerto Rico. The English ships had to return ingloriously home, bringing with them the disheartening news that both Hawkins and Drake had died during the voyage.

English privateering went on, but was now left largely to individuals and small groups. The only other major expedition to be mounted in Elizabeth's reign was that to Cadiz. This set sail in 1596, under the command of Howard of Effingham and the young Earl of Essex, Leicester's stepson and his successor in the Queen's favour. The expedition marked the adoption of Hawkins's policy of setting up a permanent blockade of the Spanish coast, and the capture of Cadiz gave it a brilliant start. However, it soon became apparent that the English had neither the will nor the resources to hold the great port indefinitely, and after sacking the town they returned home. While they had wounded Spanish pride they had not established English supremacy at sea. This was shown by the fact that before the year was out Philip II despatched a second Armada towards England. Fortunately for Elizabeth it was turned back by strong winds and high seas, and the same fate befell it when it made another attempt in 1597.

Part of the blame for the limited success of English naval activities after 1588 must be attributed to the peculiar nature of the expeditions, for they were financed by a number of shareholders, of whom the Queen was only one, and their main objective was to make money. The Queen could not possibly have met the entire cost of these ventures out of her own resources, for her finances were under heavy and increasing strain. Following the assassination of Henri III in July 1589 the protestant Henry of Navarre became titular King of France as Henri IV. He was opposed, however, by the Catholic League and called upon Elizabeth to support him. She responded by sending money and some four thousand men, but this merely provoked the League to appeal to Philip II. Spanish troops now moved into France and threatened to occupy the Breton coast, where they would be well placed to launch an invasion of England. To counter this threat Elizabeth sent over more troops in 1594, and she continued her assistance to Henri IV until 1598, when peace was finally concluded between France and Spain. Her support for Henri involved a total of some twenty thousand English soldiers, of whom about half were killed, as well as thousands of pounds in money. At the same time Elizabeth was maintaining a force of four thousand men in Dutch service and a large army in Ireland. Little wonder, then, that she could not afford to finance naval operations on an adequate scale.

CHAPTER TEN

Government, Parliament, and the royal finances under Elizabeth I

The Privy Council

Elizabeth I was twenty-five years old when she came to the throne and had no experience of governing. She left the day-to-day administration of her realm in the hands of the Privy Council, and rarely attended its meetings. Mary's Council, which had had some thirty active members, was too large for efficient functioning. Elizabeth reduced the number to just under twenty and during the course of her reign its size fluctuated between twelve and eighteen. Magnates played a significant role in the Elizabethan Council. The older nobility were represented by Lords Arundel and Clinton, along with the Earls of Shrewsbury and Derby who occasionally attended meetings but were primarily concerned with their local power bases. Office holders formed another key element in the Council. Some of the major ones were peers: Clinton, for instance, was Lord Admiral, and the Marquis of Winchester continued as Lord Treasurer until his death in 1572. The holders of offices in the royal household, on the other hand, tended to be drawn from a gentry background and had made their way in the world through ability rather than birth.

One of these 'new men' was William Cecil, now thirty-eight, whom the Queen appointed her principal secretary. The Cecils were not numbered among the great families of medieval England, but they had established themselves as country gentlemen at Stamford in Lincolnshire and were moving into the upper levels of English society. William Cecil, according to his own account, entered Parliament in 1542, when he was in his early twenties, and was sufficiently well known by the time Henry VIII died to be chosen by Protector Somerset as his private secretary. At Somerset's fall he was imprisoned for a time, but he transferred his allegiance to Northumberland and received his reward in the shape of a knighthood, large grants of crown lands, and formal appointment as one of the two Secretaries of State. He might well have gone down with Northumberland, but Cecil was a born survivor, and although he gave up public office and lay low during Mary's reign, he kept in touch with Princess Elizabeth. When she came to the throne and appointed him her secretary she told him: 'This judgement I have of you, that you will not be corrupted by any manner of gift, and that you will be faithful to the state, and that without respect of my private will you will give me the counsel which you think best.' Cecil lived up to Elizabeth's expectations, and although he could not take her confidence for granted, particularly in the first decade of the reign, he gradually established a close relationship with her that lasted until his death.

If ability had been the sole criterion for influence and office, Cecil would have had little to fear, but there were also the Queen's emotional attachments to take into consideration. She fell in love early in her reign with Robert Dudley (*see* p. 185), and although she never married him she continued to love him and to give him signal marks of her favour. She made him her Master of the Horse and bestowed on him the coveted order of the Garter; she appointed him to the Privy Council; she presented him with a valuable parcel of royal lands, including the castle of Kenilworth in Warwickshire; finally, in 1564, she created him Earl of Leicester.

Cecil had viewed the emergence of a royal favourite with apprehension, since he was not a magnate, had no power base of his own, and was entirely dependent on Elizabeth's support. Although by nature cautious he was trying to persuade the equally cautious Queen of the need to intervene immediately in Scotland, where the protestant lords had risen in revolt against the Queen Regent, Mary of Guise. Elizabeth reluctantly agreed, but it was clear that if anything went wrong the blame would light upon Cecil. Fortunately for him the ensuing naval and military operations were so successful that the French agreed to withdraw their forces from the kingdom as long as the English did likewise. The Scots were now free to decide their own fate, but the establishment of a Calvinist Church in Scotland made them far better disposed towards protestant England than to catholic France. The successful resolution of the Scottish problem added to Cecil's reputation as a policy maker, and the Queen showed her approval by appointing him Master of the Wards in January 1561. This was a major office and a highly lucrative one. Cecil's financial as well as his political future had now been assured. However, he always had to take Leicester into account, for Dudley was not only the royal favourite; he was also a man of intelligence and ability, with decided views on religious and foreign policy, which he put forward in Council.

Cecil and Leicester were not faction leaders. Neither of them could get his way without the support of other Councillors, who were powerful and independent men, not easily persuaded. Moreover, they were not at odds on every issue. They agreed on the need to uphold the protestant religious settlement in England and to defend the realm against its catholic enemies. Where they parted company was over the choice of strategy by which to accomplish these aims. Leicester was an activist. In religion he inclined towards the puritans and he shared their belief that the true (protestant) faith should be proclaimed from every pulpit and instilled into the hearts and minds of all the Queen's subjects. He took a similarly positive approach to foreign affairs, calling for intervention on behalf of the Huguenots – the French protestants – and, later, the Dutch Calvinist rebels against Spanish rule. Cecil was also moderately puritan in his approach to religion, but he put the maintenance of order and social cohesion first. He believed that outward conformity would, in God's good time, produce a truly protestant nation, and that any attempt to speed up the process would do more harm than good. Similarly, in foreign affairs, he was a non-interventionist – apart from Scotland. This was not simply a question of temperament. Leicester took little account of logistics, but Cecil, who was the archetypal civil servant, realised that the financial and military resources available to Elizabeth were limited, and that as a general rule she would always gain more by negotiation than war.

Much of the political discussion in the Council during the first decade of Elizabeth's reign revolved around the question of the succession. Cecil hoped the Queen would clarify matters by marrying the Archduke Charles of Austria, but Leicester – although reluctant to rule out the prospect of one day marrying Elizabeth himself – felt that Mary Stuart, the Queen of Scotland, should be openly acknowledged as Elizabeth's successor. The situation was transformed in May 1568 when Mary took refuge in England (see p. 221) and became, in effect, a prisoner of Elizabeth, though one who was treated with all outward signs of respect. Leicester was among those who hoped that Mary could be persuaded to marry a protestant Englishman, and he supported the Duke of Norfolk's campaign to win the Scottish queen's hand. Mary indicated her willingness to accept

Norfolk, but it seems that Elizabeth was not kept fully informed about the situation. As for Cecil, he was opposed to the whole idea of acknowledging Mary as heir presumptive, whether or not she was married to Norfolk, because he feared that as Queen of England she would pursue the same policies as her namesake, Mary Tudor. If this situation ever arose, it was doubtful whether English protestantism – or, indeed, English independence – would survive.

The divisions within the Privy Council were only resolved when Elizabeth made a decisive intervention. In December 1569 she ordered Norfolk to give up any attempt to marry Mary Stuart. Norfolk reacted by leaving court in a sulk and retiring to his house at Kenninghall. Although he subsequently made his peace, his involvement in the Ridolfi plot led to his execution in 1572. The removal of Norfolk from the political scene left Cecil in a much stronger position. Leicester managed to avoid involvement in the duke's downfall, mainly because of the Queen's continuing affection for him, but his relative strength had diminished. Cecil's ascendancy was dramatically demonstrated in February 1571 when Elizabeth created him a baron, with the title of Lord Burghley. The following year, after death had removed the long-serving Marquis of Winchester from office, the Queen appointed him Lord Treasurer.

Although Burghley was now Elizabeth's chief minister he still had to take account of Leicester, who continued to advocate a more interventionist policy abroad and was open in his support for the puritans at home. Yet there was no great rift between the two men, especially as relations with Spain deteriorated and war drew ever closer. The Council was now united in its determination to keep Mary Stuart from the throne, and not only organised the trial which brought her to the block but also ordered her execution without waiting for the vacillating Elizabeth to give her approval. The Queen vented her anger against those she held responsible for this 'betrayal' – including Burghley – but she had been forced to learn the art of accommodating her feelings to political realities, and in the end she accepted the inevitable.

Although the Council was from time to time confronted with major problems of high politics, its regular concerns were more mundane. In 1566, to take just one example, it drew up a proclamation 'that no person should print or cause to be printed ... any book against the force and meaning of any ordinance, prohibition or commandment contained ... in any the statutes or laws of this realm', and authorised the Stationers' Company to take all appropriate action to ensure that the censorship was effective. The Council did not confine itself to matters of public policy; it also responded to petitions from many private individuals who were involved in lawsuits. It never gave a formal hearing to these, as the Court of Star Chamber did, but would either issue an administrative order to resolve the points at issue, or, more usually, refer the matter to the appropriate court. The petitioners probably expected no more, but they valued the Council's intervention since it had the effect of speeding up the judicial process. Another category of Council business concerned internal security. Whenever it was warned of suspected treason the Council took all necessary steps to investigate the accusation and arrest those who were suspected, so that they could be brought to trial.

The wide range of the Privy Council's activities stemmed from the fact that it was the heart and centre of Elizabethan government. Making policy – or, rather, advising the Queen on how best to make it – was only one aspect of the Council's work, and not necessarily the most important. Its main function was to link the centre with the localities, making sure the Queen's will was transmitted to the furthest corners of her realm. It also supervised the entire range of administration, including justice, and took whatever measures were necessary to improve its functioning. While Elizabeth was the Queen, whose will always prevailed in the end, the Council was 'the crown', the formal embodiment of the government of the state that went on all the time with only occasional reference to the sovereign.

Parliament

Elizabeth summoned ten Parliaments in the course of a reign that lasted nearly forty-five years and they took up, in total, a mere three years. There were thirteen sessions in all, and the average length of each session was less than ten weeks. Meetings took place at approximately three-year intervals, which meant that for most of the time Parliament was not in session. Yet although Parliament was an intermittent assembly its prestige was high and there was intense competition for seats in the Commons. The Queen was pressed to create additional parliamentary boroughs, and in the first thirty years of her reign she added sixty-two members to the Lower House by so doing. The majority of these new members were not, however, townsmen, for more and more boroughs were choosing neighbouring gentlemen or lawyers rather than residents to represent them. In Elizabeth's first Parliament just under a quarter of the burgesses were true townsmen, but by 1601 this figure had dropped to 14 per cent. There is no evidence that Parliament attracted the upwardly mobile, except perhaps for lawyers, whose membership of the Commons increased from 16 to 27 per cent during the course of the reign.

Parliamentary seats were not necessarily contested. In the case of elections for knights of the shire, the leading families would often decide between themselves who was to be put forward, while in the boroughs much depended on the patron. Candidates for election had to spend a great deal of money on wooing the electorate, yet despite all the effort they put in to securing a seat in the Commons, fewer than half the members were regular attenders at debates. One reason for this was that they were more interested in local than national issues, and only turned up when a piece of legislation which they had promoted, or in which they or their constituency had a particular interest, was due to be considered. Conversely, when the House was debating matters that did not directly affect them, they often stayed away. Yet there was no hard and fast line between local and national issues. Members might well discover during the course of informal discussions that the problems facing their constituents were similar to those elsewhere, and that a public rather than a private bill would be the most appropriate remedy. The most famous example of this interconnection is the Statute of Artificers, which was based on proposals put forward by the representatives of York, Exeter and possibly other cities.

Under Henry VIII the number of private bills per session had averaged just over eight; the corresponding figure for Elizabeth's reign was more than thirteen. Private bills clogged up the parliamentary machine, and matters were made worse by the fact that there was never enough time to consider all the bills put before one or other of the Houses. Under Edward VI and Mary some 68 bills were considered in each session. In the first half of Elizabeth's reign the average was 126, falling to 95 in the second half. Yet despite the increasing pressure of legislative business, Elizabeth kept sessions short. The shortest of all was that of 1576, which lasted only thirty-one days, but during that time the Commons had more than a hundred bills under discussion. Traditionally, the House sat only in the mornings, the afternoons being reserved for committee meetings. However, the pressure of business under Elizabeth meant that debates were sometimes extended into the afternoon, but even so the Commons could still not meet the demands made upon them, and about half the bills introduced into the Lower House failed to complete their passage. The Lords were more efficiently organised, and had the judges present to assist them on legal matters. They also had a lighter work load. In the period 1584–1601, 105 bills began their life in the Upper House, compared with

468 in the Lower. Interest groups which hoped to secure legislation for themselves would often introduce a draft bill into the Lords simply because this gave it a better chance of becoming law.

The practice of sending bills to a committee for detailed consideration was gradually developed during the Tudor period, but was still relatively rare at the time of Elizabeth's accession. By 1601, however, it was standard practice. The assumption was that committees, which were informal gatherings free from the limitations on debate applied in sessions of the whole House, could examine a draft bill closely and propose amendments. Quite a number of bills never emerged from committees, but those that did were usually given a third reading by the House. The bill – assuming it had begun life in the Commons – was then despatched to the Lords, and once it completed all its stages there it was presented for signature to the Queen. This was by no means a formality, since Elizabeth exercised her right to veto legislation of which she disapproved. In the 1597 Parliament alone she vetoed twelve bills, and the total for her entire reign was seventy-two. She rejected public as well as private bills, usually acting on Burghley's advice, presumably because they were not sufficiently well thought out or too partisan.

The use of the veto, particularly against public bills, reflected badly on the management of both Houses, since it meant that a great deal of time had been spent to no purpose. Proceedings in the Commons were guided by the Speaker. He was invariably a lawyer in Elizabeth's reign, and the Queen paid him £100 per session. She relied on the Speaker to transmit messages from her to the House, to make sure that her prerogative rights were upheld, to consult with her and her advisers when controversial topics were under discussion, and to take delaying action where necessary in order to inhibit debate.

The Speaker looked for guidance and support to those members of the Privy Council who had been elected to the Commons, and, by virtue of their office, occupied seats close to his chair. In theory non-noble Councillors could attend the Upper House, though they could not take part in debates there. In practice, however, they preferred to stand for election to the Commons, where they played an invaluable role in keeping debates within the bounds laid down by the Queen. Councillors were looked up to because of their office and their closeness to the sovereign, and many members were content to follow where they led. But there were some matters – the principal being religion – that were so contentious that the Councillors had to fight hard to retain control. Cecil was, of course, the crown's leading spokesman in the Commons, but after his elevation to the peerage in 1571 he could no longer sit there, and new arrangements had to be made. The Council had already begun the practice of liaising with certain members of the Commons who were known for their commitment to the Queen's service, and encouraging them to speak in favour of its policies. Following Cecil's metamorphosis into Lord Burghley, these 'men of business' – prominent among them Thomas Norton and William Fleetwood – became of increasing importance to the Council, because they were not identified with the government and commanded the respect given to persons of independent judgement. Yet as Norton declared, 'all that I have done I did by commandment of the House, and specially of the Queen's Council there, and my chiefest care was in all things to be directed by the Council'.

Norton and Fleetwood were both lawyers, but they seem to have been content to work behind the scenes and to serve the Queen and her ministers without looking for advancement. Men of business played a key role in the management of the Commons during the 1570s and early 1580s, but death and retirement decreased their numbers and they were not replaced. In the last two decades of Elizabeth's reign the Council turned once again to lawyers, but this time to men who were actively seeking office and in many cases obtained it. These acted in effect as surrogate Councillors and without them the system of management might well have broken down, for in the 1590s the Privy Council became smaller and more aristocratic, with the consequence that there were only five Councillors left in the Commons. Yet the lawyer-spokesmen were too obviously identified with government policies to carry conviction as truly independent members, as had been the case with the men of business. This meant that the Council was more detached from the House by the end of Elizabeth's reign than it had been earlier on.

Because Parliament had too much to do, and too little time available, the Elizabethan Commons made increasing use of committees to take an overall view of legislation and work out a strategy for dealing with it. The Lords did the same, and there is every reason to think that Councillors welcomed this development since it made for greater efficiency. They were automatically appointed to committees, for their expertise was invaluable, and they guided discussions in them just as they did in the House itself. Yet the problem of absenteeism affected committees as it did the Commons as a whole. Moreover, procedure in committees was not always a model of efficiency. In 1584 William Fleetwood described a committee meeting at which 'twenty at once did speak, and there we sat talking and did nothing until night'.

Committees functioned best when they were small, but during the last decade of Elizabeth's reign there was an increasing tendency in both Houses to set up large committees. In fact, some of the Commons' ones were so large that they resembled what came to be known in 1606–07 as the Committee of the Whole House. One of these was the committee elected in 1593 to take into consideration the laws relating to poor relief. This included all the Councillors and leading lawyers in the Commons as well as sixty other members, but when it reported to the House it confessed that it 'could come to no conclusion, but rather to a mere confusion upon the points of the matter'. It has been suggested that large committees were devised in order to evade the Speaker's control, since he was never a member of them, but this seems unlikely. If the Commons felt dissatisfied with the Speaker's actions they could always call him to account, though they rarely did so, and in any case the automatic selection of Councillors to sit on committees meant that a government presence was maintained there, as in formal sessions of the House. The Tudor period, where Parliament was concerned, was one of experimentation, and larger committees may simply have been another stage in the attempt to organise business efficiently.

The Commons' privilege of free speech

The Commons had a number of privileges, of which the most highly valued was freedom of speech, but this was not at all clearly defined. Elizabeth was faced in her early years with a difficult situation abroad that needed tactful handling and she was also involved in arguments at home about the succession and the religious settlement. She claimed that these matters, since they affected her so closely, were not for public consideration, but many members of the Commons were of the opinion that it was their duty as well as their right to discuss them. In the opening speech to the first Parliament of her reign the Queen responded to the Speaker's request for confirmation of the Commons' privileges by granting them without any specific restrictions. However, when the House later petitioned her to marry she responded that it was a 'very great presumption, being unfitting and altogether unmeet for you to require them that may command'. Despite this rebuke the Commons revived their petition in 1566 and were not silenced by a message assuring them that the Queen was minded to marry. Elizabeth thereupon commanded the House, via her Councillors, to cease debating the issue, but this brought Paul Wentworth to his feet to ask whether such a commandment 'be a breach of the liberty of the free speech of the House?' By shifting the focus of discussion in this way he rallied the Commons behind him, and a petition was drawn up which described the privilege of free speech as 'an ancient laudable custom, always from the beginning necessarily annexed to our assembly'. The petition was never presented to the Queen, for she withdrew her commandment, but in her closing speech she told members that while she had no intention of infringing their lawful liberties, neither did she wish their liberty to make her bondage.

Perhaps as a result of this tussle, the Queen gave a more precise definition of freedom of speech when Parliament again assembled, in 1571. The Lord Keeper, speaking on her behalf, told members of the Commons that they would 'do well to meddle with no matters of state but such as should be propounded to them, and to occupy themselves in other matters concerning the commonwealth'. He did not define what he meant by 'matters of state' but the practice of Elizabeth's reign showed that she included in this category anything that directly affected herself or her prerogative – among them the question of her marriage, the succession, and the royal supremacy over the Church. Elizabeth's restrictions went far beyond anything that her father or grandfather had attempted to impose. Complaints about clerical abuses had been discussed in Parliament under the first two Tudors, and as for royal marriages and the question of the succession, Henry VIII had invited Parliament to consider these matters and resolve them by statute. Henry Yelverton was not simply indulging in rhetoric when he told the Commons in 1571 that prior to Elizabeth 'all matters not treason or too much to the derogation of the imperial crown was tolerable there [i.e. in Parliament], where all things came to be considered of, and where there was such fullness of power as even the right of the crown was to be determined'.

The limitations on free speech, as indicated by the Queen at the opening of the 1571 Parliament, did not inhibit the Commons from debating religious matters, for it was in this session that Strickland introduced his bill for reforming the Prayer Book (*see* p. 194). He was summoned before the Council and told to stay away from the House, but this only led to further, and more heated, discussion. Yelverton shifted the issue to the Commons' privileges, and said that while it was proper for princes to have their prerogatives, these should 'be straitened within reasonable limits'. At moments like this Elizabeth's cause would have been lost without her Councillors. On this occasion as on many others they 'whispered together. And thereupon the Speaker made this motion, that the House should stay of any further consultation hereupon'. Next morning Strickland was back in his place. The Queen had given way in this instance but had not abandoned the general principle that she had the right to restrict discussion on matters that directly concerned her.

The 1571 session saw the maiden speech of Paul Wentworth's brother, Peter, who was to become the champion of freedom of speech in the Commons. His finest moment came in the 1576 Parliament, when he delivered a discourse he had been brooding on for several years. His theme was freedom of expression, and when he considered the forces which endangered this liberty he put 'rumours and messages' first. The House, he complained, was full of rumours such as 'Take heed what you do. The Queen's majesty liketh not of such a matter. Whosoever preferreth it, she will be much offended with him.' Then there were messages 'either of commanding or inhibiting, very injurious unto the freedom of speech and consultation. I would to God, Mr Speaker, that these two [i.e. rumours and messages] were buried in hell'. Developing his argument, he went on to claim that 'free speech and conscience in this place was granted by a special law, as that without which the prince and state cannot be preserved or maintained'.

Wentworth was in no way a typical member of the Commons, and the House was so shocked by his outspokenness that it sent him to the Tower. There he stayed for a month until the Queen ordered his release, and one of the Councillors used the occasion to remind members that liberty did not mean licence. 'Freedom of speech', he acknowledged, 'hath always been used in this great council of the Parliament and is a thing most necessary to be preserved among us, yet the same was never, nor ought to be, extended so far as though a man in this House may speak what and of whom he list.'

Elizabeth could never afford to relax in the struggle to keep her wealthy, independent-minded Commons under control, and from 1571 onwards her reply to the Speaker's petition for confirmation of the House's privileges emphasised that freedom of speech did not extend to matters of state. She never entered the House of Commons, let alone listened to a debate, but from her palaces at Whitehall, Richmond, Nonsuch and Greenwich she kept a constant watch over parliamentary business and initiated those 'rumours and messages' of which Wentworth complained. She was fortunate in having Councillors who were not only loyal to her but men of considerable stature in their own right. After Cecil left for the Lords in 1571 leadership of the Commons passed to Sir Christopher Hatton, who was ably supported by Sir Francis Knollys, Sir Francis Walsingham and Walter Mildmay, all of them widely respected.

Elizabeth's attitude was never merely negative. In the 1589 session, for example, financial grievances came to the fore and two bills were introduced to check abuses concerning the Exchequer and the practice of purveyance. The Queen informed the Commons that since these matters affected her closely she would take action herself, and she asked that four members of Parliament should be chosen to confer with a group of Privy Councillors and household officials about the best ways in which to remedy the grievances. By so doing she preserved her prerogative while at the same time satisfying the Commons' desire to deal with abuses.

In 1593, when Parliament again assembled, Hatton, Mildmay and Walsingham were all dead and a new generation of members had emerged which did not unquestioningly accept traditional restraints. Perhaps for this reason the Lord Keeper's reply to the Speaker's customary petition defined the privilege of freedom of speech more precisely than ever before. 'For liberty of speech,' he said, 'her majesty commandeth me to tell you that to say "Yea" or "No" to bills, God forbid that any man should be restrained or afraid to answer according to his best liking, with some short declaration of his reason therein, and therein to have a free voice – which is the very true liberty of the House: not, as some suppose, to speak there of all causes as him listeth and to frame a form of religion or a state of government as to their idle brains shall seem meetest. She saith no King fit for his state will suffer such absurdities.'

Elizabeth was far less tolerant of breaches of her instructions in this session. She sent Peter Wentworth to prison for publishing a tract on the succession, excluded from the House two members who had dared to attack the High Commission, and reminded the Speaker that she had the right not only to summon and dissolve Parliament but also to decide what it could and could not discuss. By 1593 she was sixty years old and had been ruling England before many of the members were even born. She regarded a number of them as young hotheads who needed to be disciplined, and she particularly resented 'such irreverence [as] was showed towards Privy Councillors'. Yet even young hotheads had their way to make in the world and were aware that a speech in opposition to the Queen's policies could end their chances of promotion. When the Earl of Essex tried to obtain an office for a friend who sat in the Commons, he failed because, as he told the unfortunate man, the Queen 'startles at your name, chargeth you with popularity, and hath every particular of your speeches in Parliament . . . She stands much upon the bitter speech against Sir Robert Cecil [Burghley's political heir and by that time the Queen's principal adviser]'.

Parliament and the royal finances

When Elizabeth ascended the throne the ordinary revenue of the crown amounted to some £200,000 a year, to which parliamentary subsidies added on average £50,000. By the 1590s the ordinary revenue had increased to £300,000 and parliamentary subsidies were now worth £135,000, giving Elizabeth a total annual income of close on £450,000. Yet her expenditure had gone up faster than her income, particularly after her involvement in war with Spain in the 1580s, and the gap could only be filled by selling off crown lands. In the first part of the reign, down to 1574, lands worth well over £250,000 were sold, but the corresponding figure for 1589–1601 was more than £600,000. The crown was, in effect, disendowing itself.

Burghley, who became Lord Treasurer in 1572, pursued a policy of retrenchment at home and restraint abroad. Where public finances were concerned, he was a conservative, who believed in making the best of the existing system, despite its inadequacies. As a consequence, the royal revenue did not keep pace with inflation. Customs duties, for instance, which had brought in about £90,000 a year in the early part of the reign, dipped to £60,000 in the 1570s and only regained their previous level in the 1590s. In other words, Elizabeth was receiving the same amount of money from Customs in 1600 that she had done in 1560, yet during that time prices had risen by at least 75 per cent. Burghley would have been well advised to follow the example set in Mary I's reign by issuing a new Book of Rates, but he preferred not to risk provoking opposition.

Burghley's conservatism was also to be seen in the Court of Wards, of which he was appointed master in 1561, for the annual revenue from wardship declined from £24,000 to £13,000 during his tenure of office. When Robert Cecil took over from his father in 1598 he quickly doubled the yield, but this still meant that in real terms the Queen was receiving less from wardship at the end of her reign than at the beginning. The same lack of expansion was apparent in the land revenues. Crown estates were not exploited to anything like the extent that private estates were – partly because they were used as much for patronage as for revenue, and also because the crown felt morally obliged to set an example of restraint – and although the nominal yield increased during the Queen's reign from under £70,000 a year to close on £90,000, this concealed a diminishing return when inflation is taken into account.

Elizabeth could hardly have avoided bankruptcy had it not been for the subsidies voted by Parliament. She was the first Tudor to ask for a grant

from her first Parliament, and only one Parliament – that of 1572 – passed
without a request for supply. She followed the precedents set in her father's
reign by asking for assistance in peacetime, but the preambles of the supply
bills always referred to military and defence needs, although the emphasis
was on the Queen's good government. Elizabeth's spokesmen also called
attention to her modest lifestyle. In 1571 Sir Walter Mildmay reminded the
Commons that she 'lived in most temperate manner, without excess either
in building or other superfluous things of pleasure', and a similar message
was conveyed in 1593: 'in buildings she hath consumed little or nothing;
in her pleasure not much. As for her apparel, it is royal and prince-like,
beseeming her calling, but not superfluous or excessive. The charges of her
house[hold] small – yea, never less in any King's time'.

Parliamentary spokesmen in this case were telling no more than the
truth. Whereas Henry VIII had spent a fortune on building, Elizabeth
restricted herself to care and maintenance. She even disposed of seven
palaces superfluous to her requirements. Although she made generous land
grants to her favourites she gave little money away. Salaries to government
officials were held at a pre-inflation level, and economies were enforced at
court. As for her wardrobe, Elizabeth's costumes were indeed 'royal and
prince-like', but careful examination of the many pictures made of her
reveals that her dresses were cut up and reassembled. This was majesty on
the cheap.

Until 1589 it had been customary for Parliament to vote one subsidy by
way of supply, but in that post-Armada year two were granted. The continuing pressure of war on the royal finances made further demands
inevitable, and in 1593 the Lords persuaded a reluctant Commons to
increase their supply to three subsidies. The next Parliament, in 1597, saw
another grant of three subsidies, and in 1601 the last Parliament of the
reign took the unprecedented step of voting four. Members expressed
doubts about whether the country could bear so heavy a tax burden, yet
the fact that they supported the crown in this apparently generous manner
is a sign that the policies which Elizabeth was pursuing met with general
approval.

However, there was an element of hypocrisy in the Commons' attitude,
for although they were voting more subsidies their yield was steadily
diminishing. At the beginning of the Queen's reign a subsidy had been
worth some £140,000 but by the end the figure had dropped to about
£80,000. This was because the commissioners who drew up the assessment
in every county were local nobles and gentry, and they were concerned to
reduce the rate at which they and their fellows were taxed. A

Cambridgeshire peer told Burghley in 1589 that 'there is no man assessed before me but is known to be worth at least in goods ten times as much as he is set at, and six times more in land'. This can hardly have come as a surprise to the Lord Treasurer, since although he had an income of some £4,000 a year he was assessed at just over £133. There was general awareness of the disparity between actual and assessed wealth, and Sir Walter Ralegh was only telling members of the Commons what they already knew when he reminded them in 1601 that 'our estates [which] are £30 or £40 in the Queen's books are not the hundredth part of our wealth'. The obvious solution would have been for the government to replace the subsidy with a newly assessed tax, but neither Burghley nor Elizabeth would consider such a proposal. One of her household officers informed the Commons in 1593 that he had heard the Queen declare 'that she loved not such fineness of device and novel inventions, but liked rather to have the ancient usages offered'.

Although Elizabeth was more dependent than her predecessors on parliamentary subsidies there is little or no evidence to suggest that the Commons took advantage of this to secure redress of their grievances, nor that the Queen, once the subsidy had been granted, brought the session quickly to an end. The subsidy bill always took priority over other business, but it rarely caused problems. Until 1576 the initiative in proposing a grant was taken by a private member selected by the Council, but thereafter this fig leaf was removed and the Chancellor of the Exchequer set out the need for supply and formally proposed it. The House then set up a committee to consider its response, but the Councillors nearly always had a draft bill prepared and there was usually little discussion. 1593 was an exception, for the government's use of the Lords to pressurise the Commons into increasing their grant caused tempers to rise, but even so the extra subsidy was voted. There are some indications also of increasing debate in committees in the last decade of the reign. This may reflect inadequate preparation on the part of the Councillors. It was also, no doubt, prompted by awareness of the heavy and increasing burden of taxation. From the opening of the reign until 1571 parliamentary subsidies brought in £690,000. The corresponding figure for 1576–87 was £660,000, while that for 1589–1601 was £1.1 million. This gives a total of close on £2,500,000 for the entire reign, of which nearly half was concentrated in the last decade. The clergy were also taxed, with their contributions rising to an annual figure of £35,000. This meant that in her closing years Elizabeth was receiving an average of £115,500 per annum from lay and clerical taxation.

Patronage and corruption

Resentment against the crown was fuelled by the fact that many of the patentees and projectors who battened on the Queen's subjects and grew rich by fleecing them were clients of courtiers and royal servants. The English monarchy had traditionally depended for administration on ecclesiastics who could be rewarded by advancement in the Church, but the anticlericalism released and generated by the protestant Reformation changed this. Bishops remained men of substance, even after their estates had been pillaged by the crown, but their political importance declined dramatically. They had played a major role in Council during the early Tudor period, but there was not a single bishop on Elizabeth's Privy Council until the appointment of Archbishop Whitgift in 1586. Government was now the preserve of laymen who could not, in the nature of things, be rewarded for their services by clerical benefices, yet Elizabeth was in no position to pay them a realistic salary.

Expenditure on the royal household had risen to a peak in the early years of the reign of Mary, as the government accepted its obligation to increase stipends in line with inflation, but thereafter economy became the order of the day. Elizabeth, by the end of her reign, was actually spending less on her household than Henry VIII, whereas, to take account of inflation, she should have been spending two or three times as much. Since office-holders could not live on their official salaries they had to supplement them with fees and perquisites from those who needed their services. They were also engaged in a perpetual struggle to obtain some grant from the crown that would bring in money either directly or indirectly.

Elizabeth, like her father, had the disposal of some 1200 offices appropriate to gentlemen. There were about two hundred positions in the royal household traditionally reserved for the leading families, and other offices were available in the central administration – the Treasury, the Secretariat, and the Court of Wards. The judiciary also provided many profitable appointments, though these were confined to men trained in the law, and so did the armed forces, whose commanders disposed of temptingly large sums of money. The Queen appointed to many offices in the Church as well, and she alone could confirm a man's local standing by making him Lord Lieutenant or Justice of the Peace, or by giving him the titular stewardship of a royal park or manor. Tudor England was a hierarchical society and a man's place in it at any given moment depended upon the titles, offices and perquisites with which he was endowed. Unfortunately, since Henry VIII's day the number of gentry had expanded, with a consequent increase in the demand for patronage, which far exceeded the supply.

A high level of unsatisfied demand led to corruption, as suitors offered incentives to courtiers and others to secure them some mark of the Queen's favour. Although a statute of 1552 forbade the buying or selling of offices it was a dead letter. Burghley saw the evil that flowed from allowing a market in offices, yet one of his correspondents observed that 'the same fault, it is said, is winked at, and the mart kept within the court'. It was well known that Sir Thomas Heneage, Chancellor of the Duchy of Lancaster, was open to bribery – indeed, would not exert himself in any matter unless he was sure of a handsome recompense. Another official, Sir Thomas Shirley, the Treasurer at War, was accused in 1593 of diverting funds provided for military assistance to the Dutch into his own coffers and bribing Burghley's clerk in order to cover his tracks. His official salary was under £400 a year, but his income was ten times as much and at one stage rose to £16,000. Robert Cecil, Burghley's second son but political heir, was another minister whose income far exceeded his salary, and he seems to have been less scrupulous than his father when it came to making deals.

Only a thin line separated gifts from bribes, and there is some evidence that the distinction was becoming more blurred in the closing years of Elizabeth's reign. Burghley was noted for his integrity, but his profits from the Court of Wards were not entered in the official records but on a paper marked 'To be burned'. He frequently complained about the meagre rewards of royal service, declaring that 'my fees of my Treasurership do not answer to my charge of my stable – I mean not my table!' But this did not take into account the unofficial income to which high office opened the door. If Burghley really was impoverishing himself by acting as the Queen's principal minister, how was it that he became one of the richest landowners in England, built two enormous palaces at Stamford (Lincolnshire) and Theobalds (Hertfordshire), left plate worth £15,000 and established his family so securely in the upper echelons of English society that it remains there to this day?

Burghley owed his barony to Elizabeth, but he was one of the very few to be so honoured. Generally speaking, the Queen was extremely reluctant to create new titles, even though this cost her nothing, and at her death the peerage was smaller than it had been at her accession. The same was true of the knightage. In 1560 there had been some six hundred knights, but by 1580 the figure was down to three hundred. It rose thereafter to about five hundred and fifty, but this was largely the work of military commanders who had the right to confer knighthoods on the battlefield. The Earl of Essex alone created some one hundred and fifty knights, displaying an open-handedness that was typical of him but not of his royal mistress.

The Queen was somewhat more generous when it came to gifts and pensions, leases of crown lands, and monopolies. Direct grants from the Queen were usually confined to a handful of favourites, but they had far more than a token value: Leicester, for instance, was awarded an annual pension of £1,000, while Christopher Hatton was granted £400 a year in 1576. Leases of royal estates could be almost as lucrative, since crown lands were usually under-exploited. A typical example was Uttoxeter Moors in Staffordshire which the Earl of Essex leased from the crown for £23 a year but sublet for £167. The Queen could also occasionally be persuaded to exchange some of the scattered manors of the crown for a more consolidated block belonging to a subject. The new owner could make a handsome profit by selling some of the manors to cover his purchase price and increasing the rents on those he retained.

Monopolies were another sought-after gift at the Queen's disposal. These were patents granted by the Queen to a favoured courtier or sold to a businessman, and they gave the holder the sole right to manufacture or trade in a given commodity. Monopoly patents were highly profitable and could become a significant element in a courtier's finances. This was the case with Elizabeth's favourite, Leicester, to whom she gave the monopoly of sweet wines, and after his death she presented it to her new favourite, Essex. The system of monopolies was justified on the grounds that it protected new inventions, but in fact it was used by the crown primarily for patronage. The consumer suffered as prices inevitably rose, and the discontent thereby created reflected upon the Queen and led to some sharp criticism in the last parliaments of her reign.

The demand for patronage was insatiable and as the Queen could not deal with it all herself she looked for advice to those around her. Persons who were well placed to channel the flow of royal favour became some of the most influential figures in Elizabethan England, and constellations of suppliants clustered around them. Burghley received between sixty and a hundred letters a day from clients and would-be clients, and much the same was true of Leicester, for as one contemporary remarked 'advancement in all worlds be obtained by mediation and remembrance of noble friends'.

One of the key posts where patronage was concerned was the Mastership of the Wards. In theory the Master's task was the straightforward one of selling the guardianship of tenants-in-chief who were minors, but in practice he acted as the nerve centre of a complex system of financial deals, often of dubious morality, in which nearly all the upper section of English society was involved. To take only one example: Sir Edward Coke, the distinguished lawyer, bought a wardship from the Court of Wards, for which he paid £300. This was a substantial sum, but it was little compared with the £1,000 he gave the Master as a token of his gratitude. Nor did he lose on the transaction, for no sooner had his grant of the wardship gone through than he sold it for £4,000. The Queen was lucky if she received as much as a fifth of the profits of wardship during Burghley's period as Master from 1561 to 1598. After Robert Cecil took over from his father he increased the official price of wardships and brought the Queen's share up to about a third.

The last decade of Elizabeth's reign

The death of William Cecil, Lord Burghley, in August 1598 marked the break-up of the Elizabethan regime. The Queen was still there, of course, but she was an old lady, increasingly out of touch with the younger generation at court and in the country. Instead of bringing new blood into the Privy Council she allowed its numbers to decline. By the end of 1601 there were a mere thirteen Councillors, of whom one, Archbishop Whitgift, was a cleric and five were peers. Of the non-nobles, Sir Thomas Egerton was Lord Keeper of the Great Seal and therefore presided over the House of Lords, while another, Sir John Popham, was Lord Chief Justice. This left only five Councillors eligible for election to the Commons, at a time when discontent in Parliament was mounting.

The major cause of dissension between Elizabeth and the Commons was monopolies. In 1597 the Queen responded to mounting criticism by ordering her Councillors to examine all monopolies, so that she could suppress any that were against the public interest, and the grateful Commons turned their petition of complaint into a thanksgiving address. The Queen, in her reply, reminded her 'dutiful and loving subjects' that they must not entrench on her prerogative, which was 'the chiefest flower in her garland and the principal and head pearl in her crown and diadem'.

Although Elizabeth did in fact cancel some of the more obnoxious monopolies her desperate need for money to meet the costs of war and of the Irish rebellion led her to grant at least thirty new patents on items that included currants, iron, bottles, vinegar, brushes, pots, salt, lead and oil. In these circumstances it was hardly surprising that the 1601 Parliament, the last of her reign, took up the issue again. One member called monopolists 'bloodsuckers of the commonwealth' because they brought 'the general profit into a private hand'. 'The end of all', he declared, 'is beggary and bondage to the subject'. Francis Bacon, although not yet an office-holder, tried to persuade the House not to take direct action itself but to ask the Queen to do so: 'The use hath ever been by petition to humble ourselves unto her majesty and by petition desire to have our grievances redressed, especially when the remedy toucheth so nigh in point of prerogative.' But members were in an angry mood, disillusioned by the Queen's failure to take decisive action after their earlier petition. When the Speaker tried to switch the debate to discussion of the subsidy he was shouted down, and several members were unable to make themselves heard in the general confusion. Robert Cecil, after reminding the Commons that he had been a member of six or seven parliaments, said he had never seen the House in so great a confusion: 'This is more fit for a grammar school than a court of Parliament', he declared.

The Queen realised her prerogative would be endangered if she clung to monopolies, for they were a real grievance and opposition to them was widespread – Cecil reported that while he was in his coach he heard someone say 'God prosper those that further the overthrow of these monopolists! God send the prerogative touch not our liberty!' Proclamations were therefore issued cancelling the principal monopolies complained of and authorising anyone with a grievance to seek for redress in the courts of common law.

Fears about the prerogative and its effect upon traditional liberties were not confined to anti-monopolist demonstrators. Educated Englishmen were aware that absolutist regimes were increasingly common in mainland Europe, and they kept up to date with the controversies sparked off by the French Wars of Religion about the rights of rulers and the limits, if any, on their power. Whereas earlier generations had been brought up on Cicero, as a model of oratory to be used in public debate, attention was now turning increasingly towards Seneca and Tacitus who wrote at a time when the institutions of the Roman republic were becoming little more than facades concealing the reality of the emperors' power. England had its 'imperialists', who argued that the sovereign was the source of all law and that the royal prerogative could not be restrained. Their views seemed to be echoed by the judges in Cawdrey's Case, 1591, when they declared that 'this kingdom of England is an absolute empire and monarchy', whose kingly head is 'furnished with plenary and entire power, prerogative and jurisdiction'. Given these circumstances it is hardly surprising that the suspicion grew among some at least of Elizabeth's subjects that a narrowly based court and Council were leading England towards what the poet Fulke Greville called a 'precipitate absolutism'.

While the study of Tacitus raised fears of despotism at home it also taught the lesson that traditional liberties had to be stoutly defended if they were not to be irrecoverably lost. This concern overlapped with the defence of protestantism abroad against a catholic Church and rulers who were regarded as innately absolutist. One of the champions of English involvement in the wider protestant cause had been Leicester, despite the fact that he was Elizabeth's favourite. His circle included the poet Sir Philip Sidney, who met his death fighting for the Dutch, and Sir Walter Ralegh, whose complaint that Elizabeth 'did all by halves' was widely echoed. Leicester's death in 1588 came at a time when the Queen seemed to have embraced his policies, but the defeat of the Armada was followed by a return to a more cautious approach, partly dictated by shortage of money. Leicester's mantle fell on his stepson, Robert Devereux, second Earl of Essex, who became in turn the Queen's favourite. Sidney had earlier made the symbolic gesture of bequeathing Essex his sword, and the earl sealed the pact by marrying Sidney's widow.

Essex, even more than Leicester, believed that England should be actively involved in defence of the protestant cause wherever it was threatened. He preferred decisive action to negotiated compromises, and had the impatience of a soldier as well as the arrogance of an aristocrat. Yet he was well read in the classics, and a confirmed Tacitean. Essex's personal secretary, Henry Cuffe, was Professor of Greek at Oxford, and his clients included Henry Savile, another distinguished Oxford scholar and the Queen's tutor in Greek, who in 1591 published the first translation into English of some of Tacitus's works – with a preface probably written by Essex. Part of Tacitus's *History* dealt with the civil war that erupted in the Roman Empire under Nero, but Savile, in his commentary, praised the rebels for their commitment to good government and condemned Nero for his misrule. Essex took this judgement to heart and applied it to England.

Essex had been a ward of Burghley as a boy and held him in respect. Burghley likewise had a high regard for his protégé and acted as one of his patrons at court after Leicester's death. Burghley realised that the generation of Elizabethan statesmen with which he had been identified was coming to the end of its existence and he was anxious to transfer some measure of political responsibility to younger men such as Essex and his own son, Robert Cecil. He presumably hoped that they would preserve harmony within the body politic by arriving at a *modus vivendi* similar to that which he had established with Leicester. Unfortunately, such an arrangement was unattainable without mutual regard, and this was conspicuous by its absence. Robert Cecil was far less open than his father, and less trustworthy. As for Essex, he was not interested in sharing power with a man he loathed, but wanted to be the Queen's principal counsellor. Burghley, against his will, was forced to make a choice, and naturally he chose his son. As the old statesman's life entered its final phase he and Robert set about creating 'Cecil's Commonwealth' – a Cecilian monopoly at the heart of government. This did not go unnoticed. The poet Edmund Spenser, an adherent of Essex, recorded his grief:

'To see that virtue should despised be
O him [i.e. Burghley] that first was raised for virtuous parts,
And now, broad spreading like an agèd tree,
Lets none shoot up that nigh him planted be.'

Essex was determined to wrest power from his rival before it was too late. In 1596, when he was not yet thirty, he enrolled as one of the commanders of the expedition against Cadiz, fought brilliantly, and became the idol of the soldiers. He hoped to be rewarded on his return with the vacant Mastership of the Wards, which would have strengthened his fragile finances, but Elizabeth, although she had great affection for him, distrusted his desire for 'popularity' – always a sin in her eyes – and also resented the imperious manner in which he claimed advancement. She left the Mastership vacant but instead offered Essex command of the army that had been assembled to put down rebellion in Ireland. Essex accepted, no doubt counting on a string of victories to confirm the reputation he had established at Cadiz and make him so popular that even his rivals would have to come to terms with him. But he knew that his Irish venture was a gamble, for he told a friend that 'I am not ignorant what are the disadvantages of absence – the opportunities of practising enemies when they are neither encountered nor overlooked; the construction of princes, under whom *magna fama* [great fame] is more dangerous than *mala* [evil], and *successus minus quam nullus* [success less than nothing] ... All these things which I am like to see I do foresee.'

Essex's forebodings were justified. The Council, either by accident or design, was slow to send supplies, and he saw himself committed to a long and possibly unsuccessful campaign that would keep him far from the Queen – the ultimate source of all power. His rivals had already taken advantage of his absence – Robert Cecil, for example, had secured the coveted Mastership of the Wards – and the longer he stayed away the weaker his influence would become. In defiance of the Queen's explicit orders, therefore, Essex abandoned his command in Ireland, even though the rebellion was far from subdued, returned to England in September 1599, and rode post-haste to Elizabeth at Nonsuch. The Queen was at first glad to see him, but as she reflected on his disregard of her wishes her anger mounted. 'By God's son', she burst out to one of her gentlemen, 'I am no Queen! That man is above me. Who gave him commandment to come here so soon?' Essex's valuable monopoly of sweet wines was taken away from him and he was kept prisoner until June 1600, when a special tribunal stripped him of his offices.

Out of his anger against those who, he was convinced, had ousted him from Elizabeth's favour, Essex hatched a plot for an armed rising, to take over the government and force the Queen to accept new advisers. It looked as though the struggle between the Essex faction and 'Cecil's Commonwealth' might lead to civil war, and Essex House became a centre where groups of discontented nobles and clients – including Shakespeare's patron, the Earl of Southampton – drew up plans for a rising. The Council was alarmed, especially when Shakespeare's company staged *Richard II* at the Globe Theatre – the story of an English monarch who had been deposed because he listened to evil counsellors – and summoned Essex to appear before it. This sparked off the revolt, and on 8 February 1600 the earl rode into the City at the head of two hundred armed men, crying out 'For the Queen! For the Queen!' Nobody joined him, and troops blocked his way forward. The rebellion was over before it had even begun.

The Essex rising showed how factional conflict, which Elizabeth had avoided for the greater part of her reign, was now dangerously out of control. Not for nothing did Edward Coke, who led the prosecution against Essex, hark back to the Wars of the Roses, when he prayed that 'this Robert might be the last of his name, Earl of Essex, who affected to be Robert the first of that name, King of England'. Essex was sent to the block, but his removal did not solve the problem of an ageing Queen and an empty treasury, even though, by confirming Robert Cecil in power, it restored at least a semblance of the harmony that Burghley had established.

Cecil's supremacy apparently depended on the Queen's life, for James VI of Scotland, her likely successor, had been a friend and supporter of Essex. In the last years of Elizabeth's reign Robert Cecil spent £25,000 on buying land, presumably to cushion his anticipated fall from power, but at the same time he was working hard to make sure that such a fall did not take place. The real barrier to James's nomination as successor was

Elizabeth's refusal to discuss the subject, but Cecil now took the considerable risk of opening secret negotiations with James and assuring him of his goodwill. James's attitude changed rapidly from suspicion to warm friendship, and when Cecil sent him the draft proclamation for announcing his succession, James made no corrections. This music, he said, 'sounded so sweetly in his ears that he could alter no note in so agreeable a harmony'.

By March 1603 the Queen was obviously dying and sat for long periods in her grandfather's palace at Richmond, saying nothing. When, however, Cecil and the other officers of state asked her to name her successor she was said to have given a sign that she acknowledged James. After that she prayed with Archbishop Whitgift until she fell into a stupor. Early on the morning of 24 March she died, and a few hours later, while a messenger rode north as fast as relays of horses could carry him, James VI of Scotland was proclaimed James I of England.

CHAPTER ELEVEN

James I: Finance and Religion

The new king

The accession of James VI of Scotland to the English throne was carried through in such a peaceful manner that it concealed what was in fact a major change. James was the first male ruler of England for half a century. He was also a foreigner, who had never been to England and had little direct knowledge of its people and customs. Moreover he came from a country that had adopted Roman law, with its emphasis on the authority of the ruler, whereas the English prided themselves on their common law, which, they believed, preserved and protected the rights won for them by their ancestors.

James had been a monarch for virtually the whole of his life and had thought deeply about his role. In *The Trew Law of Free Monarchies*, written about 1598, he argued that kings were appointed directly by God and were responsible to him alone, not to their people. Belief in the divine right of rulers was commonplace, and Elizabeth, not to mention her father, took it for granted. However, James was aware that his emphasis on the rights of the ruler might alarm his new English subjects, and possibly for this reason he issued an authorised version of his second major work, the *Basilicon Doron*, which was published in London shortly before his arrival in the capital. This was a manual on ruling addressed to his eldest son, Prince Henry, and consisted in large part of bland statements about the need for kings to uphold the law and subordinate their own desires to the common good.

Whatever doubts the English had about their new ruler were swept aside by their relief that the change of dynasty had taken place so smoothly. James, who was thirty-six when Elizabeth died, had two sons, which meant that the succession was assured. He left Edinburgh in April 1603 and so many Englishmen flocked north to greet him that his journey turned into a triumphal progress. Robert Cecil's half-brother Thomas, who was President of the Council of the North, welcomed James at York and was very impressed by him: 'He has won the hearts of all men that come to him with such familiarity and gracious courtesy as he possesses all men's hearts with hope of as gracious a prince as ever England had.' James was equally delighted with his reception. As he later recalled, 'The people of all sorts rid and ran, nay rather flew to meet me, their eyes flaming nothing but sparkles of affection, their mouths and tongues uttering nothing but sounds of joy.' The King showed his pleasure by creating over three hundred knights on his way south, and he revelled in the entertainments provided for him at the great country houses where he stayed. The journey took him a month, and it was May before he eventually entered London and established his court at Whitehall.

The rapturous reception accorded James was in part a reflection of the discontent that had been mounting in the closing decade of Elizabeth's reign. As the members of James's first Parliament were to record, they had put up with a number of abuses 'in regard of her sex and age, which we had great cause to tender, and much more upon care to avoid all the trouble which by wicked practice might have been drawn to impeach the quiet of your majesty's right in the succession'. Now they were confident that with 'freer access to your highness of renowned grace and justice', these abuses would be remedied. Their expectations, unfortunately, were not fulfilled, for corruption, which was one of the principal abuses, remained endemic in public life, and James's good intentions were frustrated by the financial problems which confronted him, and which he made worse by his own extravagance.

James I and the royal finances

Elizabeth bequeathed James a debt of £300,000, but this was not as bad as it seemed, for the subsidies voted by her last Parliament had not yet been collected in full, and by the time they were all paid in to the Exchequer the net debt was a mere £100,000. Elizabeth had reigned during a period of acute inflation, the effects of which were exacerbated by war, and it is a tribute to her skill in managing her finances that she left James a smaller debt than she herself had inherited. Yet in some ways her success was self-defeating, for she thereby encouraged her subjects to believe that the royal finances were fundamentally sound – which was far from the case – and she also misled James into assuming that he could give up all attempts to curb his natural generosity now that he had left impoverished Scotland behind him. As James himself said, he felt like 'a poor man wandering about forty years in a wilderness and barren soil, and now arrived at the land of promise'.

Even if James had been as thrifty as Elizabeth he would have found it hard to make ends meet, for unlike his unmarried predecessor he had three households to maintain – his own, his wife's, and his eldest son's. He was also expected to uphold the dignity of the crown in an age when expenditure on courts throughout Europe was rising dramatically; to reward his loyal servants, both Scottish and English; and to signal an end to the stringency of Elizabeth's closing years. Unfortunately for James the crown's resources were no longer adequate for these purposes. The land revenue had been one of the major pillars of the royal finances in the reign of Henry VII, but half a century of property sales meant that this was no longer the case. As for Customs, the other major pillar, their value depended upon the Book of Rates, which had not been revised since Mary's reign. James's first Lord Treasurer, the Earl of Dorset, used the opportunity provided by the accession of the new King to issue a revised Book of Rates in 1604, and he also abandoned the practice of direct collection of the Customs, which had led to widespread corruption. This task was now transferred to a syndicate of wealthy merchants and financiers, known as the Customs farmers. They paid a fixed rent for the privilege and pocketed any profits. As a consequence of these measures the income from Customs increased by 50 per cent during James's reign.

The Customs duties, under the name of Tonnage and Poundage, were voted to James for life by the first Parliament of his reign and therefore had a statutory basis. This was not the case with Impositions, which were also levied on trade but by virtue of the royal prerogative. Impositions had originated in Mary's reign but had been continued under Elizabeth, though only on a small scale. They were resented by the merchant community, and in 1606 John Bate, a member of the Levant Company, refused to pay the duty on currants imposed under Elizabeth. James could have insisted on his prerogative in this matter, but as a stranger to English law he allowed the case to go before the judges, who upheld his right to levy the duty. This opened the way to a substantial increase in both the number and range of Impositions, and by the time James died they were bringing in about £70,000 – the equivalent of a parliamentary subsidy every year.

Despite the increase in his income, James could not make ends meet. By 1608 he was in debt to the tune of a million pounds and running an annual deficit of £140,000. This alarming situation could only be remedied by Parliament, but many members were critical of what they regarded as James's excessive generosity, particularly towards the Scots. By 1610 he had given away some £90,000 in gifts to his Scottish followers and more than £10,000 a year in pensions. Moreover, James's new subjects were longing for an end to the heavy taxation which had been a feature of the second half of Elizabeth's reign. They were, in Robert Cecil's words, worn out 'with great and heavy burdens, which they endured the better in hope of the change of your blessed government, which in matter of payment continues yet not a little burdenous to those that expected ease in contributions'.

Elizabeth's last Parliament had voted her four subsidies and eight-fifteenths, which brought in more than half a million pounds, but there was a widespread feeling that the limits of taxation had been reached. In the public perception it was the number of subsidies that counted, not the yield, and members of the Commons clearly regarded a grant of two subsidies as generous. In 1606 they voted three, as well as six fifteenths, but they did so in the aftermath of the Gunpowder Plot, to show their relief and thankfulness for their delivery from destruction. However, James seems to have regarded this as a sign that his days of stringency were over, and he celebrated by giving £44,000 to three Gentlemen of his Bedchamber – two of them Scots – to pay off their debts. Such behaviour helped create the impression that James's financial problems were self-generated, and that any aid he was given would be wasted. As one of Secretary Winwood's correspondents observed in 1610, 'I conceive by the common discourse that the Parliament could be content to replenish the royal cistern (as they call it) of his majesty's treasury were they assured that his majesty's largesse to the Scots' prodigality would not cause a continual and remedy-less leak therein'.

The King's chief minister, Robert Cecil, later Earl of Salisbury, who succeeded Dorset as Lord Treasurer in 1608, reminded James that though his liberality was a virtue it was not appropriate for England, which, by comparison with other kingdoms, was far from opulent. 'It is not possible,' he insisted, 'for a King of England ... to be rich or safe but by frugality'. James acknowledged the validity of Cecil's implied criticism, and promised, in 1607, to observe 'as strait a diet [as] ye can in honour and reason prescribe unto me'. He accepted Cecil's suggestion of a 'Book of Bounty', requiring all those who sought grants from the King to make their case to a commission of ministers. He also agreed to an entail on the remaining crown lands, even though this would limit his right to dispose of them. James genuinely wished to be free from the constant press of suitors, but he found it difficult to adopt the degree of restraint that Salisbury regarded as essential. James shared the view of his fellow monarchs that the task of treasurers was to find sufficient sources to fund the royal lifestyle, and this was one reason why he succumbed to the blandishment of 'projectors' who put forward ideas for enriching the crown at the same time as they made money for themselves. But projects alone could not solve the King's financial problems, and James eventually accepted Salisbury's suggestion that Parliament should be offered inducements to re-endow the crown.

Kings of England possessed a number of prerogative rights that were too valuable for them to abandon without compensation but were deeply resented by their subjects. One of these was purveyance, which enabled the royal household to commandeer provisions and services at below the market price. In the 1606 session of James's first Parliament Salisbury pressed the Commons to buy out purveyance, but members were angered by the fact that, despite the existence of close on forty statutes designed to restrict the activities of purveyors, the system and all its accompanying abuses had continued unchecked. They preferred to strengthen existing laws rather than purchase their freedom from what they regarded as an unjustified and in many respects illegal operation.

The Commons' reluctance to co-operate was a setback for Salisbury, but in 1610 he put forward proposals for a 'Great Contract' which, if it had been carried through, would have re-endowed the crown and set English history on a different course. His plan was that Parliament should vote the King 'supply' of £600,000, to eliminate the accumulated debt and provide a reserve fund for emergencies. It should also grant 'support' by way of a permanent tax of £200,000 a year. In return for this funding, the crown would surrender many of its feudal prerogatives, abolish purveyance, and reform the Court of Wards.

The sums involved in the Great Contract were so large as to be, in effect, outside the Commons' comprehension, and the House never gave more than cursory consideration to the demand for 'supply'. Members concentrated their attention on 'support' but made it plain that they were not interested in the relatively minor concessions that Salisbury had offered. Abolition of purveyance would be welcome, but what they wanted more than anything else was the end of wardship, which imposed arbitrary penalties upon landowners' estates whenever they passed into the hands of minors. James was persuaded to agree to this, though he did so reluctantly, and Salisbury and the Commons then spent several months haggling over the amount of compensation. Eventually, in the summer of 1610, the House gave a formal commitment to provide £200,000 a year in perpetuity in return for the abolition of purveyance and wardship.

This was a triumph for Salisbury, but it was short-lived. When the Commons reassembled after the summer recess it became clear that opinion had swung against the Contract. This was, no doubt, because members had consulted their constituents and found there was widespread opposition to the proposed new tax, equivalent to some three subsidies every year. There was also justifiable scepticism about the King's ability to restrain his generosity so as to keep within the limits of his expanded income. And even if the principle of 'support' had been accepted, there was no agreement on how the money would be raised. James insisted that it should be by a land tax, since this was certain and invariable, but there was a body of opinion in the Commons which wanted to base the tax on trade. This was because members had never accepted the legality of Impositions, despite the judgment in Bate's Case, and now saw a way of eliminating them by subsuming Impositions in the new tax – thereby, of course, diminishing its net worth.

James was by no means inflexible on the issue of Impositions. He offered to accept a bill outlawing them for the future. He even offered to abandon existing ones provided the Commons made up the shortfall in his income. What he could not afford was to give up Impositions without compensation. If he were to surrender purveyance, wardship and Impositions in return for an annual grant of £200,000 he would in fact be worse off than he was already. Impositions, therefore, although they never constituted a formal part of the Great Contract, cast their shadow over the negotiations and helped create the tide of ill will and suspicion in which it eventually foundered. When it became clear that the Commons would not implement their commitment to 'support' the crown, let alone consider the question of 'supply', James cut his losses and dissolved Parliament.

Now that a parliamentary solution to James's financial problems had been ruled out – at least for the present – the King was left with no choice but (as Salisbury put it) 'to stand upon your own foundation, fixed only upon the firm and lasting pillars of your ancient powers and profits ... It is not now a work to repair some small defects, but to raise a new building'. Salisbury began the task of reconstructing the royal finances on a prerogative basis, but he died in 1612. James replaced him with a commission, on which the key figures were Henry Howard, whom the King had created Earl of Northampton; Henry's nephew, Thomas Howard, Earl of Suffolk; and Sir Julius Caesar, the Chancellor of the Exchequer. James instructed them to examine his estate and advise how he 'might abridge his expenses or improve his revenues or increase the same by new projects'. Northampton set on foot an inquiry into the state of the naval administration, which was notoriously corrupt. He also called on the services of a London merchant, Lionel Cranfield, to advise him on how to increase the revenue from trade.

Meanwhile, Caesar, a hard-working bureaucrat, was examining numerous projects, but he came to the conclusion that they would never eliminate the debt – even though it had been reduced, by land sales and other measures, to £500,000 – or even the annual deficit, which had risen to £160,000. He advocated another appeal to Parliament, but James had no wish to engage once more in the sordid business of bargaining away the prerogative. He was hopeful of raising money by marrying his eldest son, Prince Henry, to a French princess, and even though Henry died in November 1612 he continued negotiations, this time on behalf of his surviving son, Charles. The French were talking in terms of a dowry worth close on £250,000, which seemed like manna from heaven to James, but just as the treaty was close to conclusion a revolt by the princes of the blood led to civil unrest in France. James therefore accepted the inevitable and agreed to summon Parliament in 1614. He had been assured that this time the Commons would prove more tractable, but in the event they refused to vote supply until James abandoned Impositions and he thereupon dissolved this 'Addled' Parliament.

Soon after the dissolution Northampton died, but James confirmed the supremacy of the Howards by appointing Northampton's nephew, Thomas Howard, Earl of Suffolk, as Lord Treasurer. Suffolk drew up a reform programme on the now traditional lines, balancing retrenchment by the King with an expansion of the revenue through projects, but he lacked Northampton's ruthlessness and determination. His principal achievement consisted in making so much money for himself that he built a great palace at Audley End in Essex. Meanwhile, James was living from hand to mouth, hoping, like Mr Micawber, that something would turn up. Resort to a benevolence provoked protests but produced £65,000, not far short of a parliamentary subsidy. James also committed himself to a scheme to increase the Customs revenue put forward by a plausible projector, Sir William Cockayne (*see* p. 388), which left the royal finances in a weaker state than they had been before. As the accumulated debt mounted again the pressure to summon another Parliament increased, but the King declared that he would 'rather suffer any extremity than have another meeting with his people and take an affront'. In 1616 he accepted an offer by the Dutch to buy back the 'cautionary towns' – transferred to Elizabeth as a guarantee that her expenses in assisting the Dutch struggle against Spain would be repaid – for £250,000, even though this was only half the sum nominally owing. And in the following year he despatched John Digby to Madrid to open negotiations for a marriage between Prince Charles and a Spanish Infanta (princess). The ambassador was instructed to demand a dowry of £600,000.

While James was searching for a way out of his financial predicament through political means, he made matters worse by setting out on a state visit to Scotland in 1617. Suffolk was unable to cope with the demands made upon him, but he remained Treasurer because of his friendship with James and also with the royal favourite Robert Carr, Earl of Somerset, who had married Suffolk's daughter. However, Somerset's hold on the King's favour was threatened by the emergence of a rival favourite, George Villiers, the future Duke of Buckingham (see p. 287), and as early as 1615 Villiers had established friendly relations with Cranfield, whose continuing investigation into the royal administration was daily revealing more evidence of Suffolk's laxness. In 1617 one observer reported that 'the King is now preparing an exact examination and censure of the abuses in the Exchequer, which in all men's opinions are likely to prove very foul', and it became clear that Suffolk's days as Lord Treasurer were numbered. In July 1618 the King dismissed him from office, and he was subsequently brought to trial before the Court of Star Chamber on charges of malversation.

Just as he had done after Salisbury's death, the King left the office of Lord Treasurer vacant and relied on commissioners to carry out its functions. Cranfield was appointed to the Treasury commission in 1619 and under his guidance expenditure was further reduced, especially in the Navy and Ordnance departments, while the yield from Customs and Impositions was increased. Another source of revenue, monopolies, was also tapped, even though these were known to be unpopular. From 1603 until 1617 the average number of patents of monopoly granted by the King was four a year, but in 1618 there were nineteen grants and in 1619 twenty-four. The activities of the patentees and projectors were authorised by royal proclamations, which swelled in number and provoked fears that they were undermining the common law.

The Treasury commissioners risked offending public opinion because their measures were beginning to pay off. By 1620 they were close to eliminating the annual deficit, which was a major achievement, but they could do nothing about the debt, which now stood at £900,000. Meanwhile, the foreign situation was causing alarm, for the Thirty Years War had broken out on the continent and money was needed for diplomatic missions and defence preparations. These considerations were behind the decision to summon the Parliament that met in January 1621. This voted two subsidies, but only after the Commons had launched a bitter attack on monopolies and toppled Lord Chancellor Bacon, who was accused of corrupt practices. They also called into question the activities of Buckingham, now Lord Admiral, who continued to support the reform programme but was engaged in constructing his own power base and demanded that exceptions should be made for himself, his family and clients.

The £160,000 brought in by the subsidies provided the King with short-term relief but offered no solution to the basic problem of under-endowment. James continued to rely upon Cranfield, whom he appointed Lord Treasurer in late 1621 and subsequently created Earl of Middlesex. These marks of favour signalled James's commitment to the policies of restraint and retrenchment with which Cranfield had identified himself. The former merchant did not pull his punches when it came to advising his sovereign to be less open-handed. 'Being left to yourself you may take care of yourself', Cranfield told him, 'and not, by pitying and relieving other men's necessities, bring yourself into extremity'. James took this lesson to heart, and expenditure on the royal household gradually fell to Elizabethan levels.

Cranfield needed time for his reform programme to take full effect. He also needed peace, and was appalled at the prospect of a renewal of war against Spain in the 1620s. His spirits rose when, in 1623, Prince Charles made an unannounced and incognito journey to Madrid, accompanied by Buckingham, in the hope of finally concluding the marriage negotiations that had been dragging on for years. Had he been successful the royal Exchequer would have benefited from a dowry of half a million pounds, and costly war preparations would have been unnecessary. But Charles returned from Spain without the Infanta and it soon became clear that he and Buckingham were determined on war. The Treasurer did everything he could to prevent this, even going so far as to promote an alternative favourite, but all he achieved was his own downfall. No sooner did Buckingham return from Spain in late 1623 than he set about Cranfield's overthrow. James, who knew the true worth of his gritty and rough-spoken Treasurer, did his best to shield him, but when the last Parliament of James's reign assembled in 1624 the leaders of the Commons were only too willing to second Buckingham's efforts. Cranfield was impeached on charges of 'bribery, oppression, wrong and deceit', found guilty, and sentenced by the Lords to be dismissed from office, imprisoned, and heavily fined.

The charges against Cranfield were not spurious, for like other early Stuart statesmen and administrators he had pursued his own enrichment as well as the King's, and had not been over-scrupulous about the methods he employed. Apart from James, he had few friends in high places, for his policy of retrenchment had threatened all those who benefited, or were hoping to benefit, from the King's bounty. James made the most perceptive, albeit cynical, comment on Cranfield's fate when he told the Lords 'he cannot, you know, but have many enemies, for a Treasurer must have hatred if he love his master's profits'.

The 1624 Parliament offered James three subsidies and fifteenths, which was described in the act as 'the greatest aid which ever was granted in Parliament, to be levied in so short a time'. James had originally asked for six subsidies and twelve-fifteenths – which, even if they had been granted him, would not have covered the costs of war – but the Commons dismissed this demand as totally unrealistic. Their attitude was summed up by Sir Edward Coke, when he declared that 'all England hath not so much'.

It remained the case, as Salisbury had argued, that long-term reconstruction of the royal finances could only be carried out through Parliament. However, with Impositions bringing in the equivalent of a parliamentary subsidy every year, and capable of indefinite expansion, it was possible for the crown to survive in the short and medium term by exploiting all available sources of prerogative revenue. The Commons feared that such a development would remove the need for Parliament's existence, but they were unable, as well as unwilling, to make the positive gestures that might have opened the way to a harmonious resolution of the crown's financial difficulties.

James I and the Church of England

The accession of a new sovereign had been, for the previous three reigns, the occasion for a redefinition of religious policy, and in 1603 the puritans were hoping that James, whose Scottish background was presbyterian, would show sympathy with their demands for modification of the Elizabethan Settlement. They struck early, by presenting him with the Millenary Petition while he was on his way south from Scotland. This document – which takes its name from the claim that it had been signed by a thousand ministers 'desiring reformation of certain ceremonies and abuses of the Church [of England]' – was the work of conforming puritans who described themselves as neither 'fractious men affecting a popular parity in the Church', nor 'schismatics aiming at the dissolution of the state ecclesiastical', but 'faithful servants of Christ, and loyal subjects to your majesty'. What they wanted was what their Elizabethan predecessors had vainly tried to extract from the Queen – namely, an end to pluralism and non-residence, the establishment of a preaching ministry, and the abolition of such remaining 'popish' ceremonies as signing with the cross in baptism, using the ring in marriage, and wearing the clerical cap and surplice.

James was himself anxious to eliminate pluralism and improve the quality of the clergy, and in July 1603 he had given an earnest of his intentions by writing to the Vice-Chancellors of Oxford and Cambridge, informing them that he intended to devote the proceeds of all impropriations in royal hands to increasing the value of poorer livings, so that they would be able to attract and maintain learned ministers. He also invited representatives of the puritans to meet him and the bishops at Hampton Court, early in 1604, to consider what other changes were needed. The puritans were delighted by this response and in Northamptonshire and a number of other counties they began drawing up reform petitions and organising public opinion. They seem to have envisaged a repetition of the 1586–7 campaign, including a survey of the clergy and the sending of delegates to London to act as informal advisers to their representatives at Hampton Court.

This flurry of puritan activity alarmed the bishops, who feared that their new sovereign might not be so stout in defence of the established Church as his predecessor. Yet in fact they had little to fear, for James's experience in Scotland had convinced him that presbyterianism and monarchy were incompatible. It is not clear who chose the four ministers who eventually presented the puritan case at Hampton Court, but they were all moderates and often had more in common with the bishops than with their radical brethren. When they argued the case for a learned preaching ministry they were pushing at an open door, for this was everybody's aim; the only differences of opinion were over the best way to achieve it. However, when they urged that the disciplinary powers of bishops should be modified, in practice, by requiring them to consult with representatives of the lesser clergy – whom the principal puritan representative incautiously referred to as a 'presbytery' – they provoked James into forthright opposition. A Scottish presbytery, he declared, 'as well agreeth with monarchy as God and the devil. Then Jack and Tom and Will shall meet and at their pleasures censure me and my Council and all our proceedings ... Stay, I pray you, for one seven years before you demand that of me, and if you then find me pursy [i.e. short-winded] and fat and my wind-pipes stuffed, I will perhaps hearken unto you'.

James's anger, as so often, was short-lived, and discussion continued on ceremonies. James took the view that these should be retained unless it could be clearly shown that 'they had either the word of God against them, or good authority'. When he applied this test to the ceremonies objected to by the puritans he found their arguments invalid. This was a disappointment to the puritans, but they could take comfort from the fact that James warmly welcomed their suggestion that a new translation of the Bible into English should be undertaken.

After the final meeting of the Hampton Court Conference, on 18 January 1604, a declaration was issued summarising its conclusions. There were to be minor changes in the descriptions of certain services in the Prayer Book, an expansion of the articles of religion, and a slight reduction in the powers of the Court of High Commission. The conference also committed itself to the objectives of providing a learned ministry, encouraging preaching, and limiting pluralism. The amendments to the Prayer Book were authorised by a proclamation issued in March, but its tone indicated James's basic conservatism in religious matters, for it announced that he had found 'no cause why any change should have been made at all in that which was most impugned, the Book of Common Prayer ... neither in the doctrines, which appeared to be sincere, nor in the rites and form, which were justified out of the practice of the primitive Church'.

Not surprisingly, the radical puritans, particularly those who had gone to London to act as a pressure group, blamed the feebleness of their representatives at the conference, as well as the intransigence of the bishops, for what they regarded as its failure. Now that the King had dismissed their case they were determined to appeal to Parliament, where they were likely to find a more sympathetic audience. Meanwhile, James instructed the bishops to set on foot a codification of Church law, which had been in limbo ever since Henry VIII severed all links with the papacy.

A month after the ending of the conference John Whitgift died. He was succeeded by his former chaplain, Richard Bancroft, Bishop of London, who had been one of the Church's principal spokesmen at Hampton Court and took the lead in codifying Church law. The *Canons*, published by royal authority in September 1604, defined the doctrines and structure of the Church of England, and included, among many other clauses, the demand that every candidate for holy orders should subscribe to three articles modelled on those drawn up by Whitgift in 1583. The most contentious of these affirmed that 'the Book of Common Prayer . . . containeth in it nothing contrary to the word of God . . . and that he himself will use the form in the said Book prescribed in public prayer and administration of the sacraments, and none other'.

Although the article applied only to prospective clergy it was also used as a test for those already in the ministry. Bancroft, spurred on by James, set about enforcing conformity, and as a consequence some eighty ministers were deprived of their livings. Although they constituted less than one per cent of all clergy they were often men of considerable talent as well as integrity, and the action taken against them led to protests in Parliament and a revival of the petitioning campaign. The climax of this came with the presentation to James of a petition from the gentlemen of Northamptonshire calling on him to prevent the deprivation of 'many faithful preachers who . . . out of the tenderness of their consciences and fear to offend the King of Heaven . . . make scruple to use the ceremonies and yield to the subscription enjoined'. James was furious and ordered the framers of the petition to be deprived of their official positions in the county administration, yet his essential moderation quickly re-asserted itself and there was a marked slackening in the campaign against puritan nonconformists.

As far as theology was concerned James had no quarrel with the puritans, nor had most of his bishops. There was general agreement on the doctrine of predestination and the commemorative nature of the communion service. Indeed, in many parish churches the communion table had long since been removed from the chancel, where it looked too much like an altar, and placed in the nave, where it was often treated with scant respect. James was not in favour of this practice. He preferred to see the chancel screened off to provide an area dedicated to prayer, and in the new or rebuilt churches of his reign the altar was normally placed in the centre of the chancel with seats arranged around it, so that communicants could fully participate in the service. However, they were required to kneel when receiving the sacraments. James abhorred the presbyterian practice of taking these seated, on the grounds that communicants were then placed 'Jack-fellow-like with Christ at the Lord's table, as [if they were] his brethren and comrades.' The 1604 *Canons* laid down that pulpits should be provided in every church and 'set in a convenient place', so that the congregation could hear the sermon. They also made it obligatory for the minister to have a seat from which to conduct the service, which included readings from the scriptures. This triple function of conducting, preaching and reading was symbolised by the three-decker pulpits, of which the oldest surviving English example dates from 1610.

James discharged his duties as supreme governor of the Church with great conscientiousness. Elizabeth had taken her time over filling vacancies in the episcopate, and she often made it a condition that the incoming bishop should exchange some of his most valuable properties for scattered royal manors of lesser worth or a handful of impropriate tithes that made for bad relations with the laity. James put an end to such practices. He promoted a statute in his first Parliament that forbade the alienation of episcopal property, and he rarely allowed sees to be vacant for more than a few months. The bishops whom he appointed were often known to him personally, since they had been royal chaplains. All but one were doctors of divinity, and many had acquired useful administrative experience as heads of colleges. Nearly all the bishops spent the greater part of their time in their dioceses, carrying out regular visitations of their clergy and also reviving the practice of confirmation, which proved to be highly popular. They were for the most part committed preachers, much to James's satisfaction, and although there were, inevitably a few time-servers in the episcopate they did not significantly detract from its reputation for godly living and spiritual leadership.

A small number of clergy were coming to believe that the English Church had moved too far in a Calvinist direction, but they were of limited influence during the greater part of James's reign. A similar group had emerged in the United Provinces, under the stimulus of the Dutch theologian, Jacob Arminius, and the English high-Churchmen came to be called Arminians even though they had arrived at their opinions independently. James was critical of the Dutch Arminians, not so much on theological grounds as because they had created disunity within the United Provinces at a time when the Dutch were about to renew their struggle for independence from Spain. When, in 1619, he sent representatives to the conference called at Dort (Dordrecht) to settle the dispute between the Arminians and their opponents, he instructed them to support the anti-Arminians but also exert a moderating influence.

James took his stand on the *Thirty-Nine Articles* and saw no need for public debate on abstruse theological matters. As he told one of his bishops, 'it appeared to him a very bold attempt for men to dispute ... about such questions of God's predestination, and so peremptorily to decide matters as if they had been in heaven and had assisted at the divine Council-board'. He showed by his appointments to the episcopal bench that he was determined to make the Church of England representative of a broad spectrum of protestant belief, including the high-Churchmen. Lancelot Andrewes, one of the most distinguished of the English Arminians, was given the bishopric of Chichester in 1605 and subsequently translated to Winchester. John Overall, who had strongly criticised the *Lambeth Articles* (*see* p. 210), held the sees successively of Coventry and Norwich, while Richard Neile, a determined opponent of the hard-line Calvinists, was appointed to Lincoln in 1614 and later promo ted to Durham. Neile picked as his chaplain William Laud, who represented the younger generation of high-Churchmen, and it was partly as a result of Neile's advocacy that Laud became bishop of the Welsh see of St David's in 1621.

However, the key positions in the Jacobean Church went to committed Calvinists. In 1607 James chose as Archbishop of York Toby Matthew, an assiduous preacher who took a tolerant line towards the puritans, prefer ring to focus his attention upon the catholics. As for the province of Canterbury, this remained under the rule of Bancroft until his death in 1610. Many people assumed that James would replace him with Lancelot Andrewes, but he chose instead George Abbot, a conforming puritan. Abbot, rather surprisingly, was Bancroft's preferred choice, but he had come to James's attention as chaplain to the King's principal Scottish adviser, the Earl of Dunbar. In 1608 he had accompanied Dunbar to a general assembly of the Kirk, and had won high praise for the way in which he reconciled conflicting factions within it and promoted the revival of episcopacy north of the border.

Under the leadership of Abbot and Matthew the Jacobean Church kept within its fold the great majority of puritans, but there were some who found conformity too high a price to pay, and the early decades of the seventeenth century saw a proliferation of congregations which either cut themselves off altogether from the established Church or else adopted a semi-separatist position by remaining within it but forming what were in effect detached cells. Sometimes congregations would include both separatists and semi-separatists. This was the case with the group that gathered around Henry Jacob, a former Brownist, at Southwark in 1616.

Formal separation from the established Church was a crime, and conventicles, where they were discovered, were broken up. But in practice the Church of England permitted a degree of diversity that satisfied the consciences of most of its members. If the minister in one parish was a non-preaching 'dumb dog', the more zealous among his parishioners could always take themselves off to a neighbouring church or go to the nearest market town to hear the 'combination lectures' which the diocesan authorities provided from a panel of local ministers. Moreover, James's reign saw a continuing improvement in the qualifications of candidates for ordination. By the time he died the aim of providing a learned preaching ministry for the Church seemed to be close to fulfilment.

Any initial doubts about James's identification with the protestant faith had been swept aside by the Gunpowder Plot of November 1605, and for the rest of his reign James drew on the spiritual capital this gave him. Because he was a peace-lover by nature, and was appalled at the idea of Christians fighting each other, he longed to preserve the uneasy equilibrium between protestants and catholics that had been established on the continent in the opening years of the seventeenth century. He reinforced his links with German protestants by marrying his daughter, Elizabeth, to the Calvinist Frederick, Elector of the Palatinate, but he wanted to balance this by marrying his son – first Henry, then Charles – to a daughter of the King of Spain, the greatest catholic ruler in Europe. The idea caused consternation among his subjects, who regarded Spain as the agent of the Pope, whom they identified with Antichrist.

The outbreak of the Thirty Years War in 1618 marked the end of James's hopes of preserving peace in Europe, but he struggled to contain the rising tide of anti-catholicism at home. In 1622 he issued *Directions to Preachers*, ordering all clergy to avoid 'bitter invectives and indecent railing speeches against the persons of either papists or puritans'. Instead, they were 'modestly and gravely' to uphold the doctrine and discipline of the Church of England. Such admonitions were in vain, because religious passions were getting out of control. Arminians, stung by the charge of being papists in disguise, riposted by denouncing their opponents as puritans who aimed to destroy the established Church and replace it with a Genevan presbytery. In 1624 an Essex minister, Richard Montagu, wrote a tract called *A New Gag for an Old Goose*, in which he defended the catholic inheritance of the anglican Church and downplayed the Calvinist elements within it. In a letter to an Arminian friend he also referred to the anti-Arminians as 'riff raff rascals' who, by the violence of their criticisms, encouraged catholics to assume that the 'frantic fits and froth of every puritan paroxysm' were in fact 'the received doctrine of our Church'.

When Parliament met in 1624 the Commons condemned Montagu's views and called on Archbishop Abbot to take appropriate action. Abbot was only too willing, and ordered Montagu to write another tract 'revising' his opinions. But the archbishop could no longer count on the

King's backing, for James was grateful to the Arminians for supporting the 'Spanish match', and was increasingly resentful of puritans and their sympathisers who condemned it. In this context it is significant that Montagu entitled his second tract *Appello Caesarem* ['I Appeal to the King'] and in it expressed his unorthodox views more forcefully than before.

James's apparent approval of Montagu's opinions puzzled many of his subjects. Sir John Eliot, speaking in the House of Commons, said 'it seemed strange to some that King James should so affect him, his doctrines being opposed to the decisions made at Dort, and that synod being so honoured by the King, of which he assumed the patronage and so much gloried in it'. It may be that James was moving away from the Calvinist beliefs he had hitherto upheld, but it is more likely that the puritans' criticism of his foreign policy had revived his old fears that the presbyterians among them were out to destroy the monarchy. The Arminians, by contrast, were emphatic in their professions of loyalty, not least because they had no one but the King to protect them against their enemies in Parliament and the country at large.

The Roman Catholics

Roman Catholics, like puritans, hoped that the accession of James I would open a new and happier chapter in their history. They had good reason to be optimistic, for James did not believe in persecution. In a letter written on the day of Elizabeth's death he assured one of their number, Henry Howard, that 'as for the catholics, I will neither persecute any that will be quiet and give but an outward obedience to the law. Neither will I spare to advance any of them that will by good service worthily deserve it'. This relatively relaxed attitude did not mean that James was in favour of toleration. Like all protestants he was convinced that the Church of Rome had strayed far from the path of true Christianity, and although he had called upon the Pope to summon a general council of the Church and declared his willingness to abide by its conclusions there was no question, in practice, of his returning to the Roman Catholic fold. By offering an olive branch to English catholics, he hoped to persuade them to accept outward conformity to the established Church, in the hope that over the course of time they would become genuinely attached to it. James's attitude towards the catholics, in fact, was very similar to his attitude towards the puritans. In both cases he aimed to split the moderate majority from the minority of hard-liners.

James blamed the obduracy of a section of the catholic community upon the Jesuits and seminary priests who kept the old faith alive, and no sooner did he become King of England than he issued a proclamation ordering all missionary priests to leave his realms. At the same time, in order to encourage the moderates among lay catholics, he reduced the rate at which recusancy fines – for non-attendance at Prayer-Book services – were levied. This won him no friends in Parliament, whose members were alarmed at the way in which catholics, who had hitherto kept a low profile, were coming into the open. One contemporary reported that it was 'hardly credible in what jollity they now live. They make no question to obtain at least a toleration, if not an alteration of religion; in hope whereof many who before did dutifully frequent the Church are of late become recusants'. James was shocked by such reports, not least because they made it more difficult for him to establish good relations with Parliament, which he summoned in 1604. He let it be known that he was totally opposed to toleration for catholics, and informed the Privy Council that if either of his sons was in favour of it 'he could wish the kingdom translated to his daughter'. He also ordered the penal laws to be put into full operation once again.

The catholics – like the puritans after the Hampton Court Conference – felt bitter at the betrayal of their hopes, particularly since the signing of peace with Spain in 1604 meant they could no longer look to that country for support. It was now apparent that, under James as under Elizabeth, they would remain an isolated minority in a hostile protestant community, and that time was running against them. The situation seemed so desperate that a number of young catholic gentlemen devised a plan to blow up the Houses of Parliament on 5 November 1605, at the very moment when James was formally opening the new session. Fortunately for the King the Gunpowder Plot was discovered before it could be carried out, and Guy Fawkes and his fellow conspirators were captured, tried and executed. When Parliament at last reassembled, in 1606, it passed an act imposing further restrictions upon English catholics, but laying the principal blame on the 'wicked and devilish counsel of Jesuits, seminaries and other like persons dangerous to the Church and state'. The head of the Jesuit mission in England, Father Henry Garnett, had already been tried and condemned on a charge of complicity in the Plot. The evidence against him was largely circumstantial, but the government was determined to tar all the missionary priests with the brush of sedition in the hope that by doing so it would deprive them of support from the lay catholic community.

Under the terms of the 1606 act, catholics were barred from living in or near London, from practising the law, and from holding public office. They were also required to take the new oath of allegiance that James had drawn up. His aim was to distinguish between loyal and disloyal catholics, but while all except a few fanatics were prepared to vow that they would 'bear faith and true allegiance to his majesty, his heirs and successors', many moderates had reservations about the section of the oath which required them to swear that 'I do from my heart abhor, detest and abjure as impious and heretical this damnable doctrine ... that princes which be excommunicate or deprived by the Pope may be deposed.' In other words, while perfectly happy to accept James as King, even in the event of his being excommunicated, English catholics would have preferred not to become involved in controversy about the limits on papal power. In the event, most catholics, clerical as well as lay, took the oath, but it never led to reconciliation between them and the protestants, which had been James's intention.

Although the King had ordered the missionary priests to quit his realms, they continued their dangerous work of keeping catholicism alive in England. He therefore issued another proclamation in the summer of 1616, warning them that if they did not leave they would face death. Nineteen Jesuits and missionary priests were executed during James's reign, and although this was a far cry from the 124 put to death under Elizabeth it still ran counter to James's wishes. He had issued the 1616 proclamation 'with no other purpose but to avoid the effusion of blood, and by banishing them ... to remove all cause of such severity as we shall otherwise be constrained to use'. James was opposed to persecution since it could not change men's hearts. He told the judges in 1616 that he was 'loth to hang a priest only for religion sake and saying mass, but if he refuse the oath of allegiance ... I leave them to the law. It is no persecution, but good justice'.

Lay catholics put themselves in danger only if they gave priests shelter or otherwise assisted them, but they were always subject to the penal laws. From time to time James relaxed the enforcement of these, but by so doing he risked confrontation with the Commons. He also weakened his already precarious financial position, since recusancy fines were bringing in some £8,000 a year by1614. James's lack of enthusiasm for persecuting catholics was most unwelcome to his subjects, and especially to their representatives in Parliament. Even worse from their point of view was that he tolerated and even encouraged the presence of catholics and crypto-catholics at court. In the early years of his reign the most notorious of these was Henry Howard, whom he created Earl of Northampton, while in the closing years there were a number of prominent catholic converts in the circle of his favourite, the Duke of Buckingham. These included Buckingham's mother and sister. His wife had given up her catholic faith in order to marry him, but it was widely (and correctly) assumed that in her heart she remained loyal to the old religion.

The execution of Henry Garnett did not put an end to the English mission. Jesuit numbers grew rapidly, from under twenty at the end of Elizabeth's reign to over a hundred by the end of James's. The Benedictine mission was also increasing in size and eventually numbered about half that of the Jesuits, but the largest group still remained the seculars, headed by the Archpriest. Many of the seculars had a degree of commitment equal to that of the regulars, but in general they were poorly organised, and resentful of what they felt to be their inferior status. Unlike the Jesuits, they hoped, even if they did not believe, that England would in due course resume its obedience to the see of Rome, and they saw no reason why the ecclesiastical organisation in their country should be different from that in other catholic states. Above all, they wanted the episcopal hierarchy restored, for if a bishop was appointed he would automatically take charge of all the priests on the English mission, regular as well as secular, thereby cutting the Jesuits down to size. He would also be well placed to insist that the substantial financial contributions from English catholics should go initially to him and be used for the general good of the mission.

The papacy was reluctant to restore the hierarchy in England for fear of offending James, but in 1623 the aptly named William Bishop was appointed Bishop of Chalcedon, with jurisdiction over all English and Scottish catholics. He died early in 1624, but was succeeded by Richard Smith. The seculars were delighted at the way in which Smith set about asserting his authority over the catholic gentry, but the gentlemen concerned were just as anticlerical as their protestant neighbours and took umbrage. The seculars' triumph, in short, was achieved only at the cost of alienating the very people upon whose support the mission was dependent and of strengthening, rather than weakening, the bonds between the gentry and the regulars.

One of the major influences upon James's attitude towards the English catholics was his desire for the Spanish match. Since both Prince Charles and the Infanta Maria were still little more than children, negotiations went ahead at a snail's pace, but it became clear that one of the terms the Spaniards would insist upon was the abrogation of the legal penalties against catholics. Whenever negotiations appeared to be moving forward, James would relax the enforcement of the penal laws; but he had to take into account the negative reaction this caused in Parliament. The situation changed dramatically after the outbreak of the Thirty Years War in 1618, for James was convinced that the Spanish match offered the best chance of restoring peace before Christendom was torn apart. In 1623 he gave his blessing to the unannounced visit that his son, Prince Charles, and his favourite, the Marquis (soon to be Duke) of Buckingham, made to Madrid. It was widely assumed that this would lead to a swift conclusion of the marriage treaty, and James gave a solemn assurance to the Spanish envoys in England that he would suspend the operation of the penal laws and do all in his power to persuade Parliament to repeal them. He was as good as his word, for a London letter-writer reported in July 1623 that 'the judges, before they went on circuit, were admonished by the King to deal favourably with the papists, except they found them turbulent and seditious'. He also noted that 'the priests and Jesuits swarm here extraordinarily'.

When news of James's concession leaked out it was not well received. Archbishop Abbot was known to have reservations about the wisdom of James's policy, and a letter appeared under his name warning the King of the danger 'lest by this toleration and discountenancing of the true profession of the gospel ... your majesty do not draw upon the kingdom in general and yourself in particular God's heavy wrath and indignation'. Abbot denied authorship of the letter, but it accurately reflected his feelings and those of the vast majority of his fellow countrymen.

As it happened, both the protestants' despair and the catholics' rejoicing were premature, for Charles and Buckingham returned from Spain without the Infanta and bent on war with Philip IV. Parliament was summoned in 1624, to provide the necessary funds, and the Commons formally requested the reimposition of the penal laws. They also demanded that in any future negotiations with catholic states the King should never agree to relax them. This was a delicate matter for James, since Charles was now determined to marry Henrietta Maria, sister of Louis XIII of France, and it was common knowledge that the Pope would not issue the necessary dispensation without assurances of better treatment for James's catholic subjects. Charles tried to lower the temperature by announcing in the House of Lords that if he married a catholic princess she should only have liberty of worship for herself and her entourage, and that there would be 'no advantage to the recusants at home'. The entire marriage project could well have foundered on this rock, and it was only rescued when James agreed to give a written promise to free his catholic subjects from persecution. He salved his conscience by insisting that this should not form an integral part of the marriage treaty but be merely a private understanding between himself and the King of France.

Although James's concession was theoretically secret, the substance of it became obvious when he instructed the judges to stop implementing the penal laws. One of his old Scottish friends noted that this order 'makes men believe that the same course goes on now with the French that was concluded with the Spaniard'. He added that Parliament, when it reassembled, was likely to take up the matter. It was fortunate for James that he died before the two Houses reconvened. It was left to Charles to reconcile the inconsistencies of royal policy, if such a task was possible.

CHAPTER TWELVE

James I: The law and Parliament

James I and the common law

James was a stranger to common law, for in Scotland the civil law – derived from that of imperial Rome – had gained acceptance during the sixteenth century. Civil or Roman law was assumed to be more concerned with the rights of the ruler than the liberties of the subject, and it was indeed the case that James, in his published writings, put a great deal of emphasis on his royal authority. He did so because he was defending his Scottish throne against the twin threats from presbyterianism, which he regarded as innately republican, and the papacy, which claimed jurisdiction over all lay rulers. Yet statements which resonated in one way in Scotland struck a different note in an English context. James's new subjects were likely to be apprehensive about the assertion made by him in *The Trew Law of Free Monarchies* that 'the King is above the law, as both the author and giver of strength thereto'. James qualified this by saying that a good King would 'frame all his actions to be according to the law', but as a philosopher and political theorist he felt impelled to add that the ruler 'is not bound thereto but of his good will and for good example-giving to his subjects'.

In one way James was saying nothing new. English kings had always been above the law to the extent that there was no prescribed legal way in which they could be called to account for their actions. Judges were appointed by the King, writs ran in his name, and although the creation of new law was a function of Parliament the statutes it made had no validity until the King had signified his assent to them. What now worried many Englishmen, especially the broad cross-section of the political nation that was familiar with the common law and held it in high regard, was that

James might make law independently of Parliament. The King had an acknowledged right to issue proclamations having the force of law, and James made frequent use of these in the early years of his reign. This created problems of overlapping, and the decision was therefore taken to publish all extant proclamations in book form, so that their exact text would be available.

The book was published in 1609, and when Parliament reassembled in the following year it immediately took up the matter. The Commons drew up a petition complaining that the printing of proclamations 'in such form as acts of Parliament formerly have been and still are ... seemeth to imply a purpose to give them more reputation and more establishment than heretofore they have had'. In addition, the Commons argued, the extensive use of proclamations had spread a general apprehension that they would 'by degrees grow up and increase to the strength and nature of laws [and] in process of time bring a new form of arbitrary government upon the realm'.

James gave a conciliatory reply, acknowledging that proclamations were inferior to common and statute law but defending their use as a temporary measure in cases where no statutory remedy existed. James also consulted the judges about the limitations upon his authority where proclamations were concerned, and Sir Edward Coke later recorded how he gave his opinion 'that the King by his proclamation cannot create any offence which was not an offence before'. This bald statement failed to reflect the careful phrasing of the judges' response, for in fact they agreed that in cases of necessity the King *could* create an offence and provide for its punishment in the prerogative court of Star Chamber. But although James continued to issue proclamations far more frequently than Elizabeth had done, he never gave any indication that he wanted to extend them into a system of arbitrary government. James may have been inclined to absolutism in theory, but in practice he remained a strictly constitutional sovereign. As he told Salisbury in 1610, although he was King by hereditary right and not dependent in any way upon public approval, yet 'the law did set the crown upon his head, and he is a King by the common law of the land'. It was dangerous, James added, to try and define the authority of a King, but he 'did acknowledge that he had no power to make laws of himself or to exact any subsidies *de jure* without the assent of his three estates [i.e. Parliament]'.

James's explicit statement that he had no right to tax at will arose out of the problems associated with Impositions and, in particular, the judgment given in Bate's Case in 1606 (*see* p. 255). As a newcomer to the English throne, and one who was unfamiliar with English law, James remitted Bate's case to the Court of the Exchequer, which dealt with financial disputes. The Earl of Dorset, as Lord Treasurer, was nominal head of this court – whose judges were referred to as barons – and he made known to the Chief Baron, Sir Thomas Fleming, his hope for a favourable verdict that would establish 'an assured foundation for the King's Impositions for ever'. Whether or not Dorset's intervention influenced Fleming is a matter for conjecture, but in the event he and his fellow judges found in favour of the crown.

When Fleming delivered the judgment he clearly intended to resolve the legitimacy of Impositions once and for all, since he enlarged on a distinction between the ordinary and absolute prerogative that he had first made in the Case of Monopolies in 1601. In his view the ordinary prerogative was sanctioned and limited by the common law and could not be altered or enlarged except through Parliament. The absolute prerogative, on the other hand, concerned matters of policy and government, and was therefore not 'guided by the rules which direct only at the common law'. Fleming included in this category 'all commerce and affairs with foreigners, all wars and peace, all acceptance and admitting for current foreign coin . . . No exportation or importation can be but at the King's ports. They are the gates of the King, and he hath absolute power by them to include or exclude whom he shall please'. Fleming acknowledged that the King's right to levy Impositions at will might appear limitless, but this, he insisted, was to be 'referred to the wisdom of the King', for 'many things are left to his wisdom for the ordering of his power, rather than his power shall be restrained'.

Fleming's judgment did not mean that the King was free to act as he liked, for the judges had the sole authority to determine where the dividing line ran between the ordinary and the absolute prerogative. Nevertheless, members of the Commons were alarmed at the prospect of the King levying taxes without their consent, for if this were the case he would have no need of Parliament. In the debate on Impositions that took place in the 1610 session, several speakers came within striking distance of the concept of sovereignty – of an authority within the state that was superior to all others. James Whitelocke, for instance, argued that the King's power was twofold. He could act alone and he could act through Parliament. 'And if, of these two powers in the King, one is greater than the other and can direct and control the other, that is *suprema potestas*, the sovereign power, and the other is *subordinata*. It will then be easily proved that the power of the King in Parliament is greater than his power out of Parliament and doth rule and control it.'

To modern ears this sounds like an unqualified assertion of parliamentary sovereignty, but in 1610 few people were thinking in such terms. The current assumption was that England was a 'mixed monarchy', or, to use the term coined by the famous fifteenth-century jurist Sir John Fortescue, a *dominium politicum et regale*, in which the monarch was not absolute but limited by law. As a system of government it was no doubt lacking in clarity, but it had the big advantage that it seemed to work. James and his people were in agreement that it was unwise to subject this time-honoured system to too close or too critical an analysis, for as Sir Thomas Wentworth was later to say, 'he … which ravels forth into questions the right of a King and of a people shall never be able to wrap them up again into the comeliness and order [in which] he found them'.

As it happened, Dr John Cowell, Professor of Civil Law at Cambridge, had recently been engaged in just such a 'ravelling forth'. He believed that the civil law and the common law had much to learn from each other but that mutual ignorance barred the way to fruitful intercourse. In order to remedy this situation he published, in 1607, a legal dictionary called *The Interpreter*. This consisted mainly of uncontroversial definitions, but when he came to what might be called 'constitutional' concepts Cowell's attempt to translate these into civil-law language caused uproar in Parliament. Under the heading 'King', Cowell wrote that 'though at his coronation he take an oath not to alter the laws of the land, yet this oath notwithstanding, he may alter or suspend any particular law that seemeth hurtful to the public estate'. As for 'Prerogative', this was the 'especial power, preeminence or privilege that the King hath in any kind over and above other persons and above the ordinary course of the common law'. Parliament, according to Cowell, was the highest of all courts, but it was subordinate to the King, and although he was well advised to use it for the making of laws, such laws could not possibly bind him.

Cowell's offence did not consist simply in opening up topics that were best left obscure. As a civil lawyer he had failed to comprehend the complexity of some of the issues he dealt with. His definition of the King's prerogative, for instance, applied only to the absolute prerogative. He made no mention, and may even have been unaware, of the ordinary prerogative, which operated within a far wider area and was specifically sanctioned by the common law. James had good reason to be angry with Cowell for adding to the difficulties he was already experiencing with Parliament. In order to defuse a situation that looked as though it was becoming explosive, the King issued a proclamation suppressing *The Interpreter*. He also went down to Parliament to assure members of his commitment to the common law, drawing a distinction between primitive states, in which the ruler's will was law, and states 'settled in civility and policy', where the King ruled according to law. 'Therefore all kings that are not tyrants or perjured will be glad to bound themselves within the limits of their laws, and . . . for my part, I thank God I have ever given good proof that I never had intention to the contrary.'

James regarded it as an essential part of his kingly function to watch over the administration of law in his dominions and resolve disputes where they arose. This brought him into conflict with Sir Edward Coke, one of the most formidable common lawyers of his day. During the sixteenth century the appearance of new courts such as the Councils of Wales and the North, as well as the expanding jurisdiction of courts of equity like Chancery and Requests, had led to overlapping and confusion. Matters were made worse by the fact that cases concerning the Church were handled by its own courts or by the prerogative courts of High Commission. Unscrupulous litigants could inflict damage on innocent defenders by constantly switching courts, and there was an obvious need for clear lines of demarcation to be drawn between them.

During the closing decade of Elizabeth's reign the central courts at Westminster had made increasing use of 'prohibitions' to prevent inferior courts from adjudicating matters that were outside their sphere of competence, but the number and range of prohibitions increased dramatically after the appointment of Coke as Chief Justice of Common Pleas in 1606. The Church courts, in particular, found their proceedings inhibited, especially in tithe cases, which straddled the hazy border between religion and property. Archbishop Bancroft regarded Coke's use of prohibitions as part of a general assault upon episcopal authority and appealed to James for support. James assumed that as head of state and supreme governor of the Church it was his responsibility to sort out this clash of jurisdictions, but Coke would not agree. For him the common law was a craft or 'mystery', knowledge of which could only be acquired by arduous study over many years. He admitted that the King was gifted with 'excellent science and great endowments of nature', but he was not learned in the law. He should therefore leave all legal matters to the judges, since only by so doing would he enable the law to act as 'the golden metwand and measure' holding in due balance the rights of the subject and the authority of the ruler.

Coke's vision of the law as an impartial arbiter between government and the governed was a noble one, but not entirely in accordance with the facts either of history or of the age in which he lived. James's approach made better sense, and he had the backing of lawyers like Francis Bacon, the Attorney-General, and Lord Ellesmere, the Lord Chancellor, who were just as learned as Coke and no less distinguished. Yet James – despite, or perhaps because of, the suspicion that he was only a lukewarm upholder of the common law – did not choose to exert his authority by forbidding or regulating the use of prohibitions. These were, after all, well-established and useful means of resolving disputes between courts, and he did no more than urge the judges to employ them in a responsible manner.

Coke remained the odd man out in the judiciary, immensely learned but cantankerous and wilful. In 1616 he launched an assault on the right of Chancery to redress unfair judgments given in common-law courts, and created a great deal of bad blood before he was eventually forced to concede. He then adopted an even more extreme stance by asserting that the King had no right to ask the judges to hold up consideration of a case in which the royal prerogative was involved until they had been fully appraised of the details. This was the final straw so far as James was concerned. He did not want the judges to be mere yes-men, but neither did he think it right for them to be wilfully obstructionist. He shared Bacon's view that the judges should be 'as the twelve lions under Solomon's throne. They must be lions, but yet lions under the throne. They must show their stoutness in elevating and building up the throne'. In 1616, therefore, James took the unprecedented step of dismissing Coke from the judicial bench. He replaced him with Sir Henry Montagu, who signalled a reversion to normality by announcing that he would not be 'a heady judge ... busy in stirring questions, especially of jurisdictions'.

James I and Parliament: 1604–14

As King of Scotland James had had to defend his authority against the twin assaults of the catholics and presbyterians, and had done so by asserting the divine origin of kingly authority. He carried this belief with him to England, and in 1610 he informed members of Parliament that 'kings are justly called gods, for that they exercise a manner or resemblance of divine power upon earth ... They make and unmake their subjects. They have power of raising and casting down, of life and death, judges over all their subjects and yet accountable to none but God only'.

There was nothing new in James's belief that kings were appointed by God and ruled in His name. Elizabeth took it for granted that her office was of divine origin, and the *Homily on Obedience* issued in the aftermath of the Northern Rising of 1569 stated that God had 'ordained and set earthly princes over particular kingdoms and dominions in earth', and that these princes, 'in authority, power, wisdom, providence and right-eousness in government ... should resemble His heavenly governance'. Any challenge to the ruler's authority was an affront to God, and even bad rulers had to be obeyed, because God had sent them to chastise a wicked people. 'A rebel', according to the *Homily*, 'is worse than the worst prince, and rebellion worse than the worst government of the worst prince'. Belief in the divine right of monarchs was a commonplace assumption at all levels of society, and even those who criticised some of James's policies never contested the source of his authority. John Pym, for example, told James in 1621 that 'the image of God's power is expressed in your royal dignity'.

James was a philosopher King, but his philosophy and his kingship were not always compatible. As a good King he had every intention of ruling according to law, but as a philosopher he felt impelled to point out that all laws derived from royal grant. Kings, he explained, existed 'before any parliaments were holden or laws made ... And so it follows of necessity that the kings were the authors and makers of the laws, and not the laws of the King'. The same was true of the subjects' liberties, and, in particular, the privileges of the House of Commons. He told his first Parliament that 'he had no purpose to impeach their privilege, but since they derived all matters of privilege from him, and by his grant, he expected they should not be turned against him'.

The Commons refused to accept that their privileges were dependent upon the King's grant, for what one King gave another could take away. They made their position plain in *The Form of Apology and Satisfaction* drawn up in June 1604, which, although it was never formally adopted by the House, probably represented the opinion of most of its members. 'Our privileges and liberties', they declared in the *Apology* 'are our right and due inheritance, no less than our very lands and goods' and 'cannot be withheld from us, denied or impaired, but with apparent wrong to the whole state of the realm'. They acknowledged that under James they had little or nothing to fear, but reminded him that good kings were not immortal and that 'the same God who in his great mercy hath given us a wise King and religious doth also sometimes permit hypocrites and tyrants in his displeasure'.

The Commons were so apprehensive about threats to traditional liber-ties that they sometimes saw danger where none existed, but their fears were increased by James's project of creating a statutory union between his two kingdoms. This project was very dear to James's heart, and when he opened his first Parliament in March 1604 he reminded members that although he was both a Lancastrian and Yorkist by descent 'the union of these two princely houses is nothing comparable to the union of two ancient and famous kingdoms'. James did not mean by union simply 'one worship to God, one kingdom entirely governed, [and] one uniformity in laws'. He also wanted the separate names and identities of England and Scotland to be subsumed in the new, all-embracing one of Great Britain.

This was in many ways a noble aim, but James's attempts to achieve it provoked opposition in the Commons, for members feared that any change would lead to the loss of those rights which Englishmen had won by their own endeavours over the course of their history. James was baffled by the Commons' intransigence, for he saw no reason to doubt that English and Scottish liberties would be as firmly entrenched in the new political entity of Great Britain as they already were in its constituent parts. Since the Commons refused to accept his assurances he turned to the judges for confirmation, but in late April 1604 they gave their opinion 'that the first hour wherein the Parliament gives the King the name of Great Britain, there followeth necessarily ... an utter extinction of all the laws now in force'.

The judges' verdict strengthened the hand of the many opponents of union in the Commons, but not all of them were motivated by constitutional considerations. There was a great deal of chauvinism and anti-Scots prejudice in the House, and it emerged in the debates. One member of the Commons, Sir Christopher Pigott, speaking in the second session, informed the House that the Scots were beggars, rebels and traitors, who had murdered all their kings. It was as reasonable to unite England and Scotland as it would be to place a judge on an equal footing with a prisoner at the bar. James was highly indignant when Pigott's remarks were reported to him and insisted that the Commons should take appropriate action. The House duly expelled Pigott and sent him to the Tower, but it is significant that they did so only after pressure had been exerted on them. There is little doubt that many members, probably the majority, shared Pigott's sentiments, even though they were too discreet to express them in so forthright a manner.

It is hardly surprising that James, who was not only a Scot but proud of his native land, was deeply wounded by the evidence of English contempt for his fellow-countrymen. Following the judges' decision on the effects of uniting the two kingdoms, he sent a letter to the Speaker in which he accused members of displaying 'jealousy and distrust either of me, the propounder, or of the matter by me propounded. If of me, then do ye both me and yourselves an infinite wrong, my conscience bearing me record that I ever deserved the contrary at your hands'. The Commons resented this criticism, not least because it was well founded, but they vented their anger on the Bishop of Bristol who in May 1604 published *A Discourse plainly proving the evident Utility and urgent Necessity of the desired happy Union of England and Scotland*. This tract, they claimed, had brought their proceedings into disrepute, and although the bishop apologised for any offence he had inadvertently caused, the House refused to be mollified. Their sense of grievance and their simmering resentment contributed to *The Form of Apology*, drawn up the following month, and although James was never formally presented with this he was aware of its contents, for when he prorogued Parliament in July 1604 he told members that 'the best apology-maker of you all ... cannot make all good'. He drew a contrast between his rule in Scotland, where he was 'heard not only as a King, but, suppose I say it, as a counsellor' and in England, where there was 'nothing but curiosity from morning to evening to find faults with my propositions. There, all things warranted that come from me. Here, all things suspected'.

The union issue did more than anything else to sour relations between James and the Commons at the outset of his reign. The two Houses had accepted James's invitation to nominate commissioners to negotiate the terms of union with their Scottish counterparts, but they did not authorise them to consider the question of the royal title. James cut the Gordian knot by issuing a proclamation announcing that 'we have thought good to discontinue the divided names of England and Scotland out of our regal style, and do intend and resolve to take and assume unto us ... the name and style of King of Great Britain'. Proclamations, unlike statutes, did not affect the common law, and James was still hoping for parliamentary confirmation of his new title, but his action led to fears that whenever he failed to obtain what he wanted from Parliament he would have recourse to prerogative action.

The commissioners for drawing up the terms of the union proposed, in their draft document, that all laws reflecting the former hostility between the two kingdoms should be abolished, that there should be free trade between England and Scotland, and that Scots born before James's accession to the English throne – who were referred to as *pre-nati* – should be given dual nationality. The Commons accepted the first proposal, did nothing about the second, but were adamantly opposed to the third. Far from agreeing to naturalise the *pre-nati* they argued that dual nationality should be denied even to the *post-nati*, born after James became ruler of both kingdoms. James turned once again to the judges, and on this occasion they found in his favour. Their decision was not only a rebuff to the Commons. It was also a reminder that the common law, which they held in veneration, might not be as effective in safeguarding their concept of English liberties as they had hitherto assumed. In their eyes the *post-nati* ruling confirmed the unfavourable impression given by the judgment in Bate's case (*see* p. 277), and added to their fears and apprehensions.

James has often been criticised for his inept handling of Parliament, yet in fact he went out of his way to try to establish a harmonious relationship with the Commons. At the very beginning of the 1604 session a dispute arose over which of two contestants had been lawfully returned for the county of Buckinghamshire, and this resurrected the issue – which had been raised but never settled in Elizabeth's reign – of whether problems over membership of the Commons should be settled by the House, or, as hitherto, by the crown. The dispute held up discussion on other topics, particularly the union, and there appeared to be no way of resolving it until James took the initiative by calling a conference at which the judges and Privy Councillors were present, as well as the Commons. At James's suggestion it was decided to annul the Buckinghamshire election and hold another – a solution that preserved the Commons' self-esteem, especially since the King publicly acknowledged that they were a court of record and had a valid, though not an exclusive, competence in electoral matters. The Commons showed their pleasure by appointing a committee to wait on the King and express their thanks.

Although, on this occasion, James and the Commons were at one, the King frequently lost patience with the way in which proposals became bogged down during the course of prolonged discussion. This was in sharp contrast with the Scottish Parliament, which was remarkably efficient; in 1584, for instance, it passed forty-nine acts in a session lasting a mere two days. Business was transacted speedily in Scotland because it was prepared in advance by a body called the committee of the articles, to which James appointed his officers of state and principal Councillors. The English House of Commons, with 475 members, was many times bigger than its Scottish counterpart and far less amenable to royal influence, even when this came via the Speaker and Privy Councillors. Members were passionate in asserting their independence and regarded freedom of debate as essential to it. Yet the Commons' time-honoured procedures were not conducive to efficiency, for only about a third of the bills introduced into the House completed all their stages. Shortage of time was one reason. Lack of numbers was another, for absenteeism was a recurring problem and many, if not most, debates, took place with only half the members present.

James did not abandon his cherished project of uniting his two kingdoms, despite the lack of progress during the first session of Parliament. In 1607 he told the members that when he first proposed it 'I thought there could have been no more question of it than of your declaration and acknowledgment of my right unto this crown, and that as two twins they would have grown up together.' But he hastened to assure them that he blamed himself for the lack of progress. 'The error was my mistaking. I knew mine own end, but not others' fears.' He tried to remove these fears by emphasising 'the truth and sincerity of my meaning, which in seeking union is only to advance the greatness of your empire seated here in England', but the Commons were still unconvinced. They did not doubt James's sincerity, but they doubted whether he fully appreciated the risks involved in the proposed union. As Sir Edwin Sandys told the first session of Parliament 'the King cannot preserve the fundamental laws by uniting, no more than a goldsmith two crowns . . . We shall alter all laws, customs, privileges, by uniting'.

The failure to bring about the union soured the atmosphere of James's first Parliament, and when to this was added criticism of the King's generosity to his Scots' favourites, opposition to his ecclesiastical policy, the attack on Impositions, and the ultimate refusal to implement the Great Contract, it is hardly surprising that by the time he dissolved it in 1610 James had had his fill of parliaments. Four years later, however, shortage of money drove him to summon another. Before he did so he was offered conflicting advice on how to ensure its success. One former member suggested – no doubt with an eye to his own advancement – that James should give office to men who were respected by the Commons and would therefore be well placed to 'undertake' the handling of the crown's business there. Francis Bacon, on the other hand, who was at this time Attorney-General, urged James to 'manage' the Commons by co-operating with the 'courtiers and the King's servants' who were members of it, and at the same time trying to intimidate or win over potential critics.

In the event James did nothing until the last moment and then tried a mixture of 'undertaking' and 'management' that had little practical effect other than to alarm the Commons and increase their suspicions. The King could no longer rely on Salisbury for advice, since he had died in 1612, but given that his first Parliament had ended in failure he may well have thought that he could do without such assistance. Indeed, he was to tell a later session that when he arrived in England 'I knew not the laws and customs of this land. I was led by the old counsellors that I found, which the old Queen had left, and it may be there was a misleading and misunderstanding between us which bred an abruption.' Yet in 1614 the new Parliament was even less co-operative than the old one, for the Commons quickly succumbed to the influence of 'fiery spirits' who led them in a bitter attack on both Impositions and the Scots. James could have done with more and better-briefed Councillors in the Lower House, for his chief representative was Sir Ralph Winwood, who had only been appointed Secretary of State shortly before the opening of the session and had no parliamentary experience. Winwood urged the Commons to win the King's goodwill by voting supply, but members preferred to discuss their grievances, and, when, after two months, it became clear that nothing constructive would be accomplished, James dissolved what came to be known as the 'Addled Parliament'.

The King demonstrated his anger with the Commons by sending four of its members to the Tower. They included Thomas Wentworth – son of Peter, who had been such a thorn in the side of Elizabeth – and John Hoskyns. Wentworth had outraged James by declaring that the levying of Impositions by French kings had led them to die 'like calves upon the butcher's knife'. Hoskyns' offence consisted in attacking the Scottish favourites and making a pointed reference to the Sicilian Vespers. This notorious massacre of the French had taken place in the thirteenth century, but Hoskyns seemed to imply that something similar might occur in Jacobean England. The intemperance of such language went well beyond the bounds of what was permissible, yet the House was reluctant to take action against the members involved. This merely confirmed James in his dislike of Parliament as an institution. The Commons, he told the Spanish ambassador, 'is a body without a head. The members give their opinions in a disorderly manner. At their meetings nothing is heard but cries, shouts and confusion'. His view was widely shared. John Chamberlain, a London citizen and writer of newsletters, said that the 1614 session had been marred by too many 'bold and petulant speeches', and that the Commons was 'many times more like a cockpit than a grave council, and many sat there that were more fit to have been among roaring boys than in that assembly'. James could not abolish parliaments, but he determined to rule without them, at least for the immediate future.

James I and Parliament: 1621–4

The Addled Parliament had done nothing to solve James's financial problems, and the only way in which to deal with these seemed to be a renewed programme of reform and retrenchment. Among the Councillors who urged this most strongly were Lord Chancellor Ellesmere, Archbishop Abbot, Secretary Winwood, and the Lord Chamberlain, the Earl of Pembroke. This group was sometimes referred to as the 'protestant interest' because it was strongly opposed to Roman Catholicism, with its pro-Spanish orientation. The members of the 'protestant interest' knew that James, desperate to find a way out of his financial difficulties and egged on by the Howards, was hoping to conclude the Spanish match, since the Infanta Maria would bring with her a dowry of half a million pounds. They also knew that their alternative policy of retrenchment would take time to make its effects felt and that the King might well lose patience.

Rather than allow the Howards to increase their hold on James, the 'protestant interest' took the dangerous step of promoting a rival favourite. James had already met George Villiers, the handsome twenty-two-year-old son of a Leicestershire knight, whose charms he found most appealing. Archbishop Abbot now urged the King to ignore the protests of the Earl of Somerset, the current favourite, and choose Villiers as one of the Gentlemen of his Bedchamber. James agreed, and in 1616 Villiers was appointed to this position, which placed him in close attendance on the King. He was also knighted, given the prestigious post of Master of the Horse, and awarded a pension. Later that same year he was elevated to the dignity of Viscount Villiers, and James presented him with a landed estate to maintain his newly-acquired status. In 1617 Villiers was created Earl of Buckingham, in the following year he became a marquis, and by 1623 he was Duke of Buckingham and the most important subject in the kingdom.

Buckingham's rise, even though it led to the fall of the Howards, did not alter the course of English foreign policy, because this was determined by James himself. The Spanish match was designed as a counterpoise to the earlier, protestant marriage between James's daughter, Elizabeth, and the Elector Frederick, the protestant ruler of the Palatinate. James hoped that by linking himself in this way to the two main religious groupings in Europe he would be well placed to restrain religious passions and preserve peace. But in fact Elizabeth's marriage contributed indirectly to the outbreak of the war which James was so anxious to avert, for in 1618 the protestant nobles of Bohemia renounced the allegiance they had sworn to the Archduke Ferdinand, heir to the Holy Roman Emperor, and offered the Bohemian throne to the Elector Frederick. They reckoned that with James and the whole of protestant Europe behind him, Frederick would be able to preserve Bohemia's independence along with its protestant faith. Frederick asked James's advice before accepting this tempting offer, but did not wait for the answer. James was against the whole idea, since he saw its dangers, but by the time his message reached Frederick, the Elector was on his way to Prague. He took with him the hopes of James's subjects, for the English thought in black-and-white terms when it came to foreign policy and believed that the best way to cope with the threat from international catholicism was by fighting it.

James had no wish to fight, but public opinion was flowing strongly in favour of war. He was even under pressure from members of his own household, for Charles and Buckingham were urging him to take the sword in his hand. War fever mounted after Frederick was defeated at the battle of the White Mountain in November 1620 and driven out of the kingdom of Bohemia in which he had spent only one brief winter. From now on the 'Winter King' and his English wife, the 'Winter Queen', were refugees. They could not even return to the Palatinate, since this had been overrun by imperial and Spanish troops. In such circumstances it obviously made sense for James to look to his defences, but he could not possibly do so without the support of Parliament. In any case it was always advisable, in moments of crisis, for the King to summon the representatives of his people to Westminster, to demonstrate the unity of purpose between them. Yet in many ways the circumstances were unpropitious. England was in the throes of an economic depression, and even if members of Parliament had been willing to vote the large sums of money that were needed, they had to take into account their constituents' straitened circumstances.

During the eleven years that had elapsed since the last effective Parliament, the pressure had increased for an end to what were widely perceived as abuses. Principal among these were monopolies, which were blamed for worsening the depression even if they had not caused it. Much of the public anger was focused upon Buckingham, for the King had showered money, lands and honours on the new favourite, as well as his relations, friends and clients, at the very moment when he was pleading poverty. Buckingham was no more scrupulous than Somerset had been where money was concerned, and the line between legitimate perquisites and bribery, which had never been easy to determine, virtually disappeared during the years of his ascendancy. Everything was for sale – crown lands,

offices in the King's gift, even titles of honour. James had already cheap-
ened the prestige of knighthood by the lavish grants he made in the
opening years of his reign, and it was common knowledge that the dignity
was for sale. Indeed, Ben Jonson, the playwright, was briefly imprisoned
for making one of his characters say – in a broad Scottish accent, not
unlike the King's – 'I ken the man weel. He's one of my £30 knights.'

As the prestige of knighthood declined the need arose for a more
respectable title, and the dignity of baronet was created in 1611, open to
anyone willing to pay £1,000 towards the maintenance of the army in
Ireland. However, by 1622 baronetcies were being sold for £250 apiece,
and their prestige declined with their price. The same was true of peerages.
In the last thirty years of her reign Elizabeth had created only one new
peerage, and the pent-up demand caused by social change led to pressure
on James to be more generous. At first he was relatively restrained in his
grants, but after Buckingham's rise to power peerages were sold for cash
and the number of peers increased from just over eighty in 1615 to almost
one hundred and thirty by 1628.

James summoned the 1621 Parliament mainly in order to get supply,
and the members duly voted him two subsidies: they did not add the customary fifteenths, the surviving relic of the medieval system of taxation,
since these were held to press too heavily upon the poor. The two subsidies
eventually brought in £145,000, but the sum bore no relation to the
amount James would need if he was to engage in hostilities. He had set up
a Council of War to advise him on what measures he should take, and this
recommended the creation of a force of thirty thousand men to help defend
what was left of Frederick's possessions in the Palatinate. It estimated that
raising such a force would cost £250,000, while close on a million a year
would be needed to maintain it. Clearly a grant of two subsidies, however
generous it might seem in the eyes of members of Parliament, would go
nowhere meeting commitments of this sort, and it may be that James was
secretly relieved and his pacific inclinations strengthened by this latest evidence that his subjects' bellicosity would not be translated into cash grants.
Since he could not afford to go to war, James resorted to the more congenial alternative of negotiation, and despatched envoys to the major
European capitals.

From James's point of view Parliament had served its purpose by voting
supply. For members, on the other hand, the principal function of
Parliament was to remedy the abuses of which their constituents complained. This meant striking at the monopolists, and the Commons began
with one of their own number, Sir Giles Mompesson, who was a kinsman of

Buckingham. Mompesson was involved, along with the favourite's half-brother, in the monopoly patent for the manufacture of gold-and-silver thread, which had aroused opposition from a number of London artificers and led to a clash between the patentees and the City authorities. Mompesson also held a patent for licensing inns that many members of the Commons found offensive, not simply because of the corrupt way in which he used it to make money but also because it undermined the authority of Justices of the Peace who normally issued such licences. Feelings in the House were running high, but it was not clear whether the Commons had any jurisdiction in such matters. After searching the records for precedents they decided to act in concert with the Lords, thereby making Parliament in practice what it already was in theory, namely the highest court in the land.

James did not try to oppose this revival of parliamentary judicature. He was no lover of monopolies, as he had shown at the very beginning of his reign by issuing a proclamation against them. Moreover, he recognised the right of the Commons to take action over undoubted grievances: in his own words 'the Commons best know the state of the country and are to inform the King of the disorders so that he may show himself a just King'. James showed his feelings by cancelling the patents of inns and gold-and-silver thread which Mompesson had brought into discredit, and during the parliamentary recess he issued a proclamation annulling virtually all those monopolies of which the Commons had complained.

In the course of their enquiries into monopolies the Commons had come across evidence that Francis Bacon, Viscount St Alban and Lord Chancellor, had been taking bribes. They presented this evidence to the Lords, who carried out their own investigations and prepared to bring Bacon to trial. Not since the fifteenth century had a great officer of the crown been overthrown in Parliament, and Bacon no doubt assumed he could count on James's protection, particularly since he was on good terms with Buckingham. James, however, told the Lords that while they should proceed with all due care they should not scruple to pass judgment where they found good cause. Bacon knew what this implied, and rather than trying to defend himself without the King's support he acknowledged his guilt. The Lords thereupon sentenced him to be fined and imprisoned and never again to hold public office. By refusing to shield his Chancellor James had identified himself with the parliamentary campaign against abuses and thereby retained the initiative. When the Commons, flushed with success, turned their fire on the Lord Treasurer, Viscount Mandeville, James restrained them by making plain that they 'should not be so careful for his honour as to destroy his service'.

In June 1621 James prorogued Parliament, but before the Commons went into recess they returned briefly to foreign affairs and passed a motion declaring that if the King's efforts to achieve a peaceful resolution of the problem of the Palatinate should meet with no success, they would be ready 'to the utmost of their powers, both with their lives and fortunes, to assist him'. As the international situation grew ever more alarming, James summoned the two Houses to reassemble in November to hear a report from John Digby, now a peer, who had just returned from an embassy to the imperial court at Vienna. Digby called for firm action by England, but although the Commons agreed with this in principle they were uncertain how to proceed in practice. Foreign policy was, after all, a prerogative matter, and they were reluctant to discuss it without guidance. They were given the green light – or so, at least, they assumed – by Sir George Goring, one of their members who was a hunting companion of the King and known to be in Buckingham's confidence. Goring told the House about a letter which James had written to the King of Spain, calling for his assistance in securing the restoration of the Palatinate to Frederick. He then suggested that they should petition James to make it clear that unless he received a satisfactory reply he would be prepared to declare war. The Commons drew up a petition along these lines, but they went considerably beyond the limits that Goring had laid down by requesting that 'our most noble Prince may be timely and happily married to one of our own religion'. Not only did this offend Charles as well as his father. By striking at the Spanish match it also threatened to block the diplomatic option the King was most anxious to keep open.

James showed his anger by ordering the House not to 'presume henceforth to meddle with anything concerning our government or deep matters of state, and namely not to deal with our dearest son's match with the daughter of Spain'. The Commons, convinced that they had only followed the path that James, via Goring, had indicated, were taken aback by this message. Although, in their reply, they protested that they never meant 'to encroach or intrude upon the sacred bounds of your royal authority, to whom and to whom only we acknowledge it doth belong to resolve peace and war and of the marriage of the most noble Prince, your son', they added that they had an 'ancient and undoubted right' to freedom of speech.

James responded to this by pointing out that the privileges of the Commons 'were delivered from the grace and permission of our ancestors and us', though he gave his word that he would uphold them 'as long as you contain yourselves within the limits of your duty'. Such an assertion awakened all the Commons' latent fears about the expansion of prerogative power and the contraction of their own and the subjects' liberties. They therefore drew up a *Protestation* that was formally entered in their journal. In this they deliberately echoed the writ of summons to Parliament by declaring that "arduous and urgent affairs concerning the King, state, and defence of the realm and of the Church of England . . . are proper subjects and matter of counsel and debate in Parliament; and that in the handling and proceeding of those businesses every member of the House of Parliament hath, and of right ought to have, freedom of speech to propound, treat, reason and bring to conclusion the same'. It was a high-sounding declaration, but James showed what he thought of it by sending for the Commons' journal and tearing out the *Declaration*. Subsequently he dissolved Parliament.

James now placed all his hopes on the Spanish marriage, especially since Digby, who was now Earl of Bristol and principal ambassador at Madrid, reported favourably on his negotiations. It was well known, however, that the Spaniards were adept at spinning matters out, and no-one could be sure they were negotiating in good faith. It was probably in order to test their sincerity that in February 1623 Prince Charles and Buckingham slipped away from the English court disguised and unheralded, crossed the Channel into France, and then rode hard until they reached the Spanish capital. Had their journey been announced beforehand the Spaniards would almost certainly have blocked it. As it was, the first they knew about it was when the Prince and his companion arrived, weary and travel-stained, at Bristol's residence.

Charles and Buckingham had assumed that within a few weeks of their arrival they would be sailing back to England with the Infanta. In fact they had to spend many months in the Spanish capital, and during the course of their negotiations Buckingham became convinced that the Spaniards were playing a double game. By keeping James's hopes alive they were staving off England's entry into the war at the same time as they consolidated their position in the Palatinate. Buckingham – whom James created a duke – also became aware of the scope of Spanish ambitions and of the danger that the Habsburg family might re-establish its preponderance in Europe. When he and the Prince at last left Spain, in September 1623, the marriage articles had been signed and agreement reached that the Infanta would be sent over to England in the following spring. But the duke, at any rate, was determined that the Spanish marriage would never take place. The tortuous course of the negotiations at Madrid had convinced him that the anti-Habsburg powers in Europe should join together for their common safety. He had taken the first step by making informal approaches to the government of Louis XIII, and suggesting both a marriage alliance and a military pact.

Although James was delighted to have his son and his favourite restored to him, he had no intention of abandoning his pacific foreign policy. And although a significant proportion of the Privy Council was in favour of war with Spain, many members found it difficult to believe that Buckingham, who had for so long been the King's mouthpiece, had genuinely changed course. Buckingham, with the invaluable support of the Prince, now concentrated on the task of convincing the King that Parliament should be summoned, hoping he would be able to persuade the Commons to vote the necessary supply. James eventually agreed, and in February 1624 the two Houses assembled at Westminster.

Buckingham had prepared the ground well by winning over many of the crown's former critics in the Commons, but there was a fundamental divergence between his aims and those of most members of Parliament. They wanted a war of religion against the catholic enemy, a revival of what they mistakenly conceived to have been the Elizabethan strategy of fighting Spain at sea and leaving the continent to look after itself. Apart from any other considerations, this would be the least costly option, for a naval war could in theory pay for itself through the capture of enemy vessels. As Sir John Eliot put it, 'Spain is rich. Let her be our Indies, our storehouse of treasure.' Buckingham, on the other hand, knew that James would never willingly become involved in a war of religion. He also believed that such a war would not be in the best interests of England, since both the immediate aim of recovering the Palatinate and the long-term one of checking the expansion of Habsburg power required a secular approach, in order to unite France, a major catholic state, with protestant countries like Denmark, Sweden and the United Provinces.

The King had asked Parliament for six subsidies and twelve fifteenths – about £800,000 – for the proposed war. This was, if anything, too little, but the Commons were appalled by such a demand. After much debate they voted three subsidies, accompanied by fifteenths, but only on condition that these were used solely 'for the maintenance of that war which may hereupon ensue, and more particularly for the defence of this your realm of England, the securing of your kingdom of Ireland, the assistance of your neighbours the ... United Provinces and other your majesty's friends and allies, and for the setting forth of your navy royal'.

James was reluctant to make such a concession, but under pressure from Buckingham he agreed that the moneys raised by taxation should be handed over to treasurers named and appointed by Parliament. They would make payments only on instructions from the Council of War, whose members were also named, and both groups would be 'answerable and accountable for their doings or proceedings herein to the Commons in Parliament'. James made a further concession by promising that he would not enter into any peace negotiations 'without first acquainting you with it and hearing your advice, and therein go the proper way of Parliament in conferring and consulting with you in such great and weighty affairs'.

While Parliament was in session, negotiations were taking place for a French marriage and military alliance, and by the end of 1624 these had both been concluded. The first fruits of the alliance were to consist of an expedition under an experienced mercenary commander, Count von Mansfeld, that would attempt to recapture the Palatinate. Mansfeld's force was to be made up of twelve thousand English infantry, who were to be shipped to France, where they would be joined by three thousand French cavalry. But difficulties arose before the troops had even embarked, for James – who was still hoping to keep out of war with Spain, and had not abandoned his innate suspicion of French motives – insisted that Mansfeld's force should not pass through any territories belonging to Spain or her allies. Since it was virtually impossible to get from France into the Palatinate without infringing this embargo, Louis XIII declared that he would not allow Mansfeld's men to land in his country. At the last moment, therefore, and in the depths of winter, the English soldiers – recruited from the dregs of the population, ill equipped and barely trained – had to be sent to Holland, where nothing had been prepared for them. What disease and desertion failed to accomplish was completed by starvation, and Mansfeld's force melted away before it had accomplished anything. Buckingham had been hoping for a victorious inauguration of the as-yet undeclared war against Spain. Instead he had to take the blame for an ignominious failure.

CHAPTER THIRTEEN

Charles I: Parliament and religion

Charles I

James I died in March 1625 and was succeeded by his only surviving son who, at the age of twenty-four, became King Charles I. For the first twelve years of his life Charles had lived in the shadow cast by his self-assured and charismatic elder brother, and even after Henry's death in 1612 he remained introverted and reserved. He had a slight impediment in his speech, and told his first Parliament how grateful he was that the business in hand required so little explanation, 'for I am neither able to do it, nor doth it stand with my nature to spend much time in words'. This brevity was not, at first, unwelcome to his subjects. Sir John Eliot, for instance, observed that 'both the sense and the shortness of this expression were well liked, as meeting with the inclination of the time, which wearied with the long orations of King James that did but inherit the wind'.

There was a marked change of tone at court, for as the puritan Mrs Hutchinson was later to recall, 'King Charles was temperate, chaste and serious, so that the fools and bawds, mimics and catamites of the former court [i.e. James's] grew out of fashion, and the nobility and courtiers who did not quite abandon their debaucheries yet so reverenced the King as to retire into corners to practise them. Men of learning and ingenuity in all arts were in esteem and received encouragement from the King, who was a most excellent judge and a great lover of painting, carvings, [en]gravings, and many other ingenuities less offensive than the bawdry and profane abusive wit which was the only exercise of the other court.'

Charles I and Parliament: 1625–9

Charles's gravity and depth of religious commitment were qualities that his subjects rated highly. He therefore had good reason to expect a harmonious meeting with Parliament, especially since he had co-operated with the leaders of both Houses in 1624 by bringing pressure to bear on his father to break off negotiations with Spain. Now that James had been removed from the scene, war against Spain seemed inevitable, and Charles reminded the members of his first Parliament, which assembled in June 1625, that although he 'came into this business willingly, freely, like a young man ... it was by your entreaties, your engagements'. He called on them now to honour their promises, and to remember 'that this being my first action, and begun by your advice, and entreaty, what a great dishonour it were, both to you and me, if this action, so begun, should fail for that assistance you are able to give me'.

Charles and Buckingham were apparently relying upon mutual goodwill and shared objectives to carry the Houses along with them, for they made no attempt to brief Councillors or to guide business. This was a major error, for the Commons, after voting two subsidies for the impending war, were left to their own devices, and promptly took up the question of religion. They had been shocked by the arrival of the new Queen, Henrietta Maria, since she brought with her a train of catholic priests who wandered around London in their outlandish garb, causing outrage and revulsion among the citizens. Charles's accession coincided with one of the worst outbreaks of bubonic plague that England had so far experienced, and there were many people who took this as a sign of God's displeasure. Another sign was the failure of Mansfeld's expedition. In their opinion the remedy lay in strict enforcement of the penal laws, yet such action would run counter to the spirit, if not the letter, of the marriage treaty and alienate the French at a time when Charles and Buckingham were trying to implement the military alliance.

At the beginning of a new reign it had long been the practice for Parliament to vote the sovereign the Customs duties – Tonnage and Poundage – for life. These duties formed a substantial part of the royal revenue and would be essential now that war was imminent. But Tonnage and Poundage were not the only levies on trade. There were also Impositions, which the Commons continued to regard as illegal despite the judgment in Bate's case. If they simply voted Charles Tonnage and Poundage without raising the question of Impositions they might give the impression of tacitly sanctioning these prerogative levies. Moreover, since

Charles was such a young man, a lifetime grant of the Customs would leave the issue of Impositions unresolved for so long that the crown would establish a prescriptive right to them. Tonnage and Poundage, in short, were too valuable a bargaining counter for the Commons to grant them unconditionally.

There were some members of the Commons, principal among them John Pym, who believed that the dispute over Impositions could not be resolved without taking into account the whole question of the royal finances. The crown needed re-endowing, so that it could meet the ordinary costs of government without having to call on Parliament for support. Re-endowment, however, would be a complex business requiring time to resolve, but members were anxious to make the session as brief as possible, so that they could escape from plague-ridden London. The Commons therefore granted Tonnage and Poundage for one year only. Their intention was that the crown should enjoy its traditional revenue, while Parliament would be given the opportunity to reconsider the problem of the royal finances at a subsequent meeting when it would not be under such pressure.

The Commons' action might have been acceptable had it been concerted with the Upper House, but the Lords were affronted by the breach of precedent implied in a one-year grant and threw out the Commons' bill. As a consequence, Charles was deprived of a vital part of his revenue just as he was about to spend great sums of money on a war that Parliament, in 1621 and 1624, had passionately advocated. Faced with this situation Charles decided to collect Tonnage and Poundage on grounds of necessity. He made it clear that he would do so only until Parliament made him a lifetime grant, but this meant that, for the immediate future, the Customs duties would be based on the same prerogative authority as the hated Impositions. In other words, the Commons' determination to get rid of what they regarded as an illegal levy had only resulted in expanding the scope of prerogative taxation. This increased members' fears that Parliament, to which English rulers had traditionally turned when they needed supply, would lose its *raison d'être* and cease to play a significant political role.

When Charles and Buckingham realised their mistake in not giving the Commons more information about the King's needs, they instructed Sir John Coke – one of the duke's most trusted servants, and also a member of the Lower House – to explain that the sums voted in 1624 had all been spent on the four purposes listed in the subsidy act and that a further £150,000 was urgently needed. Sir John also revealed that Charles had promised to pay his uncle, the King of Denmark, £30,000 a month, and Count Mansfeld £20,000, in order to keep their armies in the field. Moreover, substantial additional funding would be needed to set out what Coke described as the 'invincible navy'. He gave no overall figure for the amount of money the King needed. His main aim was to prompt the Commons into voting additional supply. But the rapidly diminishing number of members at Westminster were not prepared to take such an unusual step. They did not trust Buckingham, they did not believe the financial situation was as bad as Coke had painted it, and they were anxious to get away from London. Charles therefore adjourned the session in July but announced his intention to reconvene it on the first day of August at Oxford, which the plague had not yet reached.

At Oxford, the members of Parliament were well briefed, first of all by Sir Edward Conway, Secretary of State, and then, once again, by Sir John Coke. The Privy Councillors in the Commons urged the voting of additional supply – a grant of two subsidies was proposed – but the Commons refused to follow their lead. Many members gave their opinion that the country could not afford more taxes at a time of plague and economic recession: as Sir Thomas Wentworth put it, 'We fear the granting thereof will be esteemed by [the King's] subjects no fair acquittal of our duties towards them or return of their trusts reposed in us.' The House was also swayed by increasing doubts about Buckingham's suitability as the King's chief adviser. If the crown was poor, was this not because so much of its wealth had been diverted into his hands? And if more money was provided, what guarantee was there that it would not be thrown away on expeditions as futile as Mansfeld's? Despite a long speech from Buckingham to both Houses, in which he defended his policies, assured members of his commitment to the war, including a naval assault upon Spain, and gave them details of the King's financial obligations, the Commons refused to vote additional supply. Charles thereupon dissolved Parliament.

Since earlier parliaments had clamoured for a sea war against Spain, Buckingham provided just this in the shape of an expedition to Cadiz. Money was raised by holding back the payment of wages, pledging the crown's credit, and using the £120,000 paid by France for Henrietta Maria's dowry. The counties were ordered to raise troops and equipment at their own expense, and ten thousand men – mostly jailbirds and vagabonds – were assembled for the expedition. The lack of organisation, of adequate supplies, and of any clear strategy did not promise much hope of success, yet the blame for these deficiencies should not be attributed solely to Buckingham. Combined expeditions were notoriously difficult to mount, as the Elizabethans had found to their cost and Cromwell was to discover thirty years later. England had neither a professional navy nor a standing army, and the surprising thing is that in this instance the troops were actually embarked and transported to the Spanish coast. After landing, they captured a fort and marched on the town of Cadiz, but the lack of food and the abundance of local wine which they found *en route* turned them into a drunken rabble. An assault on Cadiz was out of the question. The troops – or as many of them as were in a fit state – were re-embarked, and the ships sailed back to England with their cargo of sick, starving and dying men. One observer reported that those who eventually landed at Plymouth 'stink as they go, and the poor rags they have are rotten and ready to fall off if they be touched'.

The King was so short of money that he had no option but to summon another Parliament, and this met in February 1626. In line with his belief that the failure of his first Parliament had been due to a handful of malcontents, the King excluded those he regarded as the principal offenders by pricking them as sheriffs and thereby obliging them to remain in their counties. Familiar figures such as Sir Edward Coke, Sir Robert Phelips and Sir Thomas Wentworth were conspicuous by their absence from the Commons, but their exclusion had the opposite effect to what the King intended, for it left a vacuum that was filled by populists who were even less restrained in their criticism of royal policies. Chief among these was Sir John Eliot, formerly one of Buckingham's clients but now numbered among his bitterest enemies. No sooner did debate open in the Commons than Eliot launched a savage attack upon those he held responsible for the Cadiz fiasco. 'Our honour is ruined,' he thundered, 'our ships are sunk, our men perished, not by the sword, not by an enemy, not by chance, but . . . by those we trust'. Eliot had no doubt that the responsibility rested on Buckingham, and at his suggestion the Commons refused to consider the King's request for subsidies until their grievances, including the greatest grievance of all, were redressed.

Charles regarded the Commons' criticism of the duke as unfair, but he also believed that the ultimate target was himself. He warned the House not to call to account 'such as are of eminent place and near unto me', and made it plain that Buckingham had done nothing 'but by special directions and appointment, and as my servant'. When the Commons ignored this warning and pressed ahead with their investigation into the duke's conduct, Charles summoned both Houses to Whitehall and reminded them that it was with their encouragement and assurances that he had broken with his father's policy and moved towards war with Spain. 'Now that you have all things according to your wishes', he added, 'and that I am so far engaged that you think there is no retreat, now you begin to set the dice and make your own game. But I pray you be not deceived. It is not a parliamentary way, nor is it not a way to deal with a King'. Charles declared his willingness to redress the Commons' grievances on condition that they acted responsibly by voting supply, without which the war could not be waged. If not, he warned them 'that Parliaments are altogether in my power for their calling, sitting and dissolution. Therefore, as I find the fruits of them good or evil they are to continue, or not, to be'.

The Commons' reply took the form of a remonstrance, drawn up at Eliot's suggestion. This affirmed 'that it hath been the ancient, constant and undoubted right and usage of parliaments to question and complain of all persons, of what degree soever, found grievous to the commonwealth in abusing the power and trust committed to them by their sovereign'. By way of demonstrating this right they went ahead with a formal impeachment of the Duke of Buckingham.

Throughout these proceedings Eliot insisted on the Commons' loyalty to the King. None of their actions, he declared, were intended 'to reflect the least ill odour on his majesty or his most blessed father'. On the contrary, the Commons were concerned to enhance the King's dignity by removing all those who threatened to eclipse his glory. Buckingham was the principal villain in this respect. 'His profuse expenses, his superfluous feasts, his magnificent buildings, his riots, his excesses – what are they but . . . a chronicle of the immensity of his waste of the revenues of the crown? No wonder then our King is now in want, this man abounding so. And as long as he abounds, the King must still be wanting.' Eliot, carried away by his feelings, as was often the case, went on to compare Buckingham with Sejanus, the notorious favourite of the tyrannical Roman emperor, Tiberius. When Charles was told of Eliot's comment he observed that 'if the duke is Sejanus, I must be Tiberius'.

The King kept Parliament in session for a little longer, in the hope that it would eventually vote supply, but although the Commons had decided in principle on a grant of three subsidies and fifteenths, they would not complete the passage of the subsidy bill until their grievances had been redressed. Charles found this attitude offensive. The proposed grant would go nowhere near making him 'safe at home and feared abroad', which the Commons had declared to be their objective. And as for its conditional nature, this was, in the King's words, 'very dishonourable and full of distrust'. In June 1626, therefore, Charles dissolved his second Parliament. In a proclamation which he issued to justify his action, he stated that the Commons' remonstrance against the Duke had a more sinister purpose, for 'through the sides of a peer of this realm they wound the honour of the sovereign'. It was still Charles's belief that the Commons had been misled by a handful of malcontents, but he was now moving towards the opinion that Parliament as an institution was inimical to his monarchy. When, later in 1626, the Privy Council suggested summoning another Parliament, the King is reported to have said that 'he did abominate that name'.

Charles's sense of betrayal became even more acute when the news reached England, in September 1626, that his uncle and ally, the King of Denmark, had been defeated at the battle of Lutter. Charles put part of the blame on himself, for having been unable to fulfil his promise of financial assistance to Christian IV, and under his guidance the Privy Council now decided to levy a forced loan from all those who would normally have contributed to parliamentary subsidies. In financial terms this was a success, for it brought in almost £270,000, which by this date was the equivalent of five subsidies. But it aroused widespread resentment, which was compounded by the demand that coastal towns should provide ships at their own expense for the crown's service, while the counties arranged free billeting for the troops being raised for another expedition Buckingham was preparing.

This time the English attack was directed against France, for relations between the two countries had deteriorated as the result of an uprising by the French protestants, the Huguenots. Cardinal Richelieu was by now Louis XIII's chief minister, and it was fear of his intransigent catholicism that prompted the Huguenots to rebel. Richelieu held it as axiomatic that France could not engage in foreign ventures while torn by internal dissent. He therefore moved away from co-operation with England and mended his bridges with Spain. This change of course confirmed all Buckingham's latent suspicions, and he decided to intervene on the Huguenots' behalf in the hope that they would help either to topple Richelieu or force him to revert to his former policy. In fact Buckingham had little choice, for Charles I, like his father, had promised to uphold the Huguenots' freedom of worship, and public opinion in England was firmly behind them.

La Rochelle was the main centre of Huguenot resistance, and Buckingham planned to boost it by seizing the nearby island of Ré. Since he had been blamed for the failure of the Cadiz expedition even though he took no part in it, he decided to lead the attack on Ré in person. Shortage of money was, as always, a major problem, but by the end of June 1627 the expeditionary force, consisting of some seven thousand men and close on a hundred ships, was at sea. Two weeks later the army landed on Ré. A counter-attack by the French was beaten off, but the defenders subsequently took refuge in the citadel of St Martin, from which it proved impossible to dislodge them. In November, after a vain attempt to take the citadel by storm, Buckingham ordered a retreat to the ships. Many men were lost in the process, and when the news of this latest defeat reached England it provoked an angry reaction. Sir Thomas Wentworth – one of those who had been imprisoned for refusing to contribute to the forced loan – declared that 'since England was England it received not so dishonourable a blow', and balladmongers pinned the blame on Buckingham, whom they accused of 'treachery, neglect and cowardice'. Only Charles, who had failed to supply the duke with the much-needed supplies he had promised to send, struck a different note. 'With whatsoever success ye shall come to me,' he told him, 'ye shall be ever welcome.'

The plight of La Rochelle was now desperate, for Richelieu had invested it from both land and sea and was determined to starve its inhabitants into surrender. Only England could prevent the collapse of Huguenot resistance, but if another expedition was to be mounted money would somehow have to be found. Buckingham and other Councillors argued that the only solution lay in Parliament, and Charles reluctantly agreed. Before Parliament actually met, the seventy or so gentlemen who had been imprisoned for refusing to contribute to the forced loan were freed. They included five knights who had tried to obtain bail by bringing an action for *habeas corpus* before the Court of King's Bench. They intended thereby to raise the fundamental question of whether forced loans were legal, but the crown circumvented the issue by certifying that the knights had been imprisoned 'by special command of the King'.

English rulers had long had the power to arrest persons suspected of treason and hold them incommunicado, so the judges had little choice but to deny the prisoners bail. But they were clearly unhappy about sanctioning such a procedure in a case that did not involve state security and they therefore declined to give specific approval to the King's action. However, the Attorney-General, as the chief legal officer of the crown, took it upon himself to tamper with the official record in order to imply that judgment had been given in the King's favour. Meanwhile, Parliament had assembled, in March 1628, and it was not long before one of the lawyer members of the Commons revealed what had happened. The House was shocked and alarmed. Bate's case had shown that the common law could not be relied on to defend Englishmen from arbitrary taxation. Now the Five Knights' case had demonstrated its inability to secure them from arbitrary arrest. If English liberties were to be preserved, Parliament would have to clarify and strengthen the law.

While this might be the principal concern of the Commons, it was not the reason why Charles had summoned his third Parliament. 'The only intention of calling this assembly', he informed the members in his opening speech, 'is for present supply; and this way of Parliament is the most ancient way and the way I like best. Wherein, if you do use such speedy resolution as the business requireth . . . I shall be glad to take occasion thereby to call you oftener together.' It was widely known that the King had become disillusioned with Parliament as an institution, but his speech opened the way to reconciliation. Sir Benjamin Rudyerd, speaking later in the Commons, urged the House to make a positive response. 'This is the crisis of parliaments' he declared. 'By this we shall know whether parliaments will live or die.'

The King was followed by Sir John Coke, now Secretary of State, who gave details of what needed to be done to sustain the anti-Habsburg coalition. He reminded the Commons that this was not merely a question of 'the King's interest or pleasure' but of 'the defence of us all. Every day we run into more danger'. When the debate began, members stressed the danger to their liberties at home, rather than that from abroad, but Sir John Coke had proffered them an olive branch by admitting that 'illegal courses have been taken'. Clearly some sort of bargain was on offer, and the Commons responded by agreeing in principle to a grant of five subsidies. However, this was dependent upon the safeguarding of their liberties, and Coke had already assured them that they could do this 'by way of bill or otherwise'. Sir Thomas Wentworth proposed that the House should concentrate upon four specific issues, of which the two most important were arbitrary imprisonment and arbitrary taxation. Sir Edward Coke supported him. 'Let a bill be drawn [up] to supply defects of the law', he urged. 'The prerogative is like a river without which men cannot live, but if it swell too high it may lose its own channel.' A committee was thereupon appointed to draw up a bill of liberties, a kind of seventeenth-century *Magna Carta*, but the King made it known that while he was willing to confirm existing statutes that enshrined his subjects' rights he was not prepared to accept any new ones. It was at this point that Sir Edward Coke proposed that the House should proceed by a legal device known as a petition of right.

Coke's proposal was quickly adopted, and after numerous conferences with the Lords the *Petition of Right* was formally presented to the King. It requested that non-parliamentary taxation, imprisonment without cause shown, the billeting of troops and the imposition of martial law should be declared illegal. Charles, in his reply, affirmed his willingness to see 'that right be done according to the laws and customs of the realm, and that the statutes be put in due execution', but this did not satisfy the Commons. They wanted the King to make the traditional response to petitions of right, for only this, they were persuaded, would give their petition the force of law. The King therefore summoned the two Houses before him once again and instructed the clerk to pronounce the customary formula: *Soit droit fait comme est désiré* ('Let right be done as is requested.'). The assembled members threw their hats in the air, and as the news spread beyond Westminster there were similar rejoicings in towns and villages throughout the land.

The Commons blamed Buckingham for the hitches in the approval of the *Petition* and drew up a remonstrance against him, at the same time as they passed the subsidy bill and sent it to the Lords, who completed the process. Charles might well have dissolved Parliament at this stage, but he was hoping that the Commons, in the new atmosphere of reconciliation, would at last make him a grant of Tonnage and Poundage. The House had, in fact, begun preparing a bill on this topic, but complained that there was too little time left to complete it. Members contented themselves, therefore, with asking the King to refrain from levying the duties, on the grounds that 'the receiving of Tonnage and Poundage and other impositions not granted by Parliament is a breach of the fundamental liberties of this kingdom and contrary to your majesty's royal answer to the ... *Petition of Right*'. Charles did not wait for the Commons' remonstrances to be presented. On 26 June he summoned the two Houses before him once again, declared that depriving him of Tonnage and Poundage – 'one of the chief maintenances of the crown' – would be highly prejudicial, and brought the session to an immediate close.

A month later the King was at Portsmouth to speed the departure of Buckingham, who had organised another expedition for the relief of La Rochelle. It was while he was at prayers that news was brought him that the duke had been murdered. The assassin was John Felton, an army officer who had fought in the Ré campaign and held a grudge against Buckingham for failing to promote him. Under questioning, Felton made it plain that he had been prompted to this act of violence by 'reading the remonstrance of the House of Parliament' against the favourite, for this had persuaded him that 'by killing the duke he should do his country great service'. Charles concealed his emotions at the loss of his closest friend, but there is little doubt that he regarded the leaders of the Commons as accessories to Buckingham's murder.

Although the assassination of the duke was a personal blow to Charles it ought to have opened the way to more harmonious relations between him and Parliament. One observer summarised informed opinion by commenting that 'the stone of offence being now removed by the hand of God, it is to be hoped that the King and his people will come to a perfect unity'. The very fact that the King summoned the two Houses to reassemble in January 1629 was an indication of his continuing commitment to 'the parliamentary way', for he accepted that there was little prospect of additional supply being voted. In order to remove one of the outstanding bones of contention between him and the Commons, he ordered Sir John Coke to put before the House a draft bill on Tonnage and Poundage, with the request that members would give it priority.

However, the Commons were more concerned with the growth of Arminianism, particularly since it had political implications. Roger Mainwaring, for example – whose high-Church inclinations led him to be regarded as an Arminian, whether or not he was – declared in a sermon preached before Charles I at the height of the controversy over the forced loan that resistance to royal authority was sinful and that kings had a right to take their subjects' property if they needed it for 'the supply of their further necessities'. When the 1628 Parliament came into session, the Commons drew up articles of impeachment against Mainwaring and presented them to the Lords, who sentenced him to be fined and imprisoned. But Charles directed a pardon to be drawn up for him and appointed him to a living recently vacated by Richard Montagu, another of the Commons' Arminian bugbears, whom Charles appointed Bishop of Chichester in July 1628.

The Commons regarded this as a provocative action, and in the 1629 session religion became for the first time a major cause of controversy. One of the reasons for this was uncertainty about the exact nature of the established Church, particularly since the Arminians insisted that they were the true guardians of its traditions. In 1626 Charles had followed his father's example by issuing a proclamation forbidding public discussion of disputed topics and requiring preachers to base their sermons on 'the sound and orthodoxal grounds of the true religion sincerely professed and happily established in the Church of England'. But what were these 'sound and orthodoxal grounds?' In 1626 a conference had taken place between the Arminians and their critics at York House, Buckingham's London residence, but no clear conclusions were reached. Before the opening of the 1629 session of Parliament, therefore, Charles issued another proclamation, affirming that the *Thirty-Nine Articles* were the foundation of the

Church's doctrine and once again forbidding public debate on controversial issues. This did not satisfy the Commons, however, for it was the interpretation of the *Articles* that concerned them. No sooner did the session start than they passed a resolution confirming the *Thirty-Nine Articles* only as these had been expounded by 'the public acts of the Church of England' and rejecting 'the sense of the Jesuits, Arminians and all other wherein they differ from it'.

When the Commons at last turned their attention to Tonnage and Poundage they demonstrated that they were in no mood to be conciliatory. One reason for this was the absence of moderate and constructive leaders. Sir Edward Coke, now approaching eighty, had decided to stay at home on the grounds that he was suffering from a mortal illness known as old age, while Sir Thomas Wentworth had at last achieved his ambition of holding office under the crown – as President of the Council of the North – and was now a viscount and member of the Upper House. This left the Commons under the influence of hotheads such as Sir John Eliot, Denzil Holles and Benjamin Valentine. It was Eliot who took the lead in attacking the Customs officers who had seized the goods of those merchants who refused to pay Tonnage and Poundage. He insisted that they had acted on their own authority, and therefore unlawfully, since Parliament had never granted the duties. Sir John Coke rebutted him by informing the House, on behalf of the King, 'that what those men have done they have done by his command' and that 'he will not have us proceed against them, for that he conceiveth it doth highly concern him in point of government'.

The Commons decided to draw up a remonstrance against the continued collection of Tonnage and Poundage, as well as one against Arminianism. Charles realised there was no point in continuing with the session, and in March 1629 he announced an adjournment, widely (and correctly) seen as a prelude to dissolution. The House of Lords immediately adjourned, but when the Speaker of the Commons stood up to close proceedings Holles and Valentine forced him back into his chair, while one of their associates locked the doors of the chamber. Eliot then delivered a passionate attack on popish influences at court and called on the House to pass three resolutions. These affirmed that anyone advising the King to collect Tonnage and Poundage, or paying this levy before Parliament had made a grant, or propounding innovations in religion, should be reputed 'a betrayer of the liberties of England and an enemy to the same'. With Black Rod, the King's official messenger, knocking at the door, and the House in indescribable confusion, the Commons at last adjourned themselves.

Charles never recalled this Parliament. As for the men who had led the Commons in this violent act of disobedience, Eliot, Valentine and Holles were tried in King's Bench and sentenced to be imprisoned until such time as they acknowledged their fault. Valentine remained a prisoner until January 1640, Eliot until his death in 1632. Holles alone managed to escape abroad. For the next eleven years Charles ruled England without a Parliament. There is no reason to suppose that he never intended to summon it again, but he wanted time to show how beneficial royal rule could be when it was given a chance to operate unhindered.

The Church of England during the personal rule

The closing years of James's reign had seen the Arminians strengthen their position, largely because they supported the King's attempts to preserve peace in Europe while their opponents, whom they lumped together as puritans, were clamouring for war. 'Arminian,' like 'puritan,' was a term of abuse, and it should not be assumed that all those who were so designated shared the same views on, for instance, predestination or the sacraments. What most of them had in common was a rejection of the Calvinist insistence on the primacy of preaching – the religion of the word – and a desire to reinstate the older and more traditional concept of the Church as the body of God on earth, preserving in its liturgy and ceremonies a visual representation of fundamental spiritual realities.

One of the leading figures among the Arminians by the 1620s was William Laud. He had already earned a reputation as a formidable controversialist, and this prompted the King to call on his services in 1622. The Countess of Buckingham, mother of the favourite, had fallen under the spell of a Jesuit priest – one of a number who circulated under cover in court circles – and was on the verge of converting to Rome. James chose Laud to engage in debate with the Jesuit in the Countess's presence, and so well did he argue his case that the Countess stayed within the Church of England – for the time being. Buckingham was impressed with Laud's performance and extended his patronage to him, but while James was alive Laud never rose higher in the Church than the Welsh see of St David's. James acknowledged Laud's skill in debate, but complained that 'he hath a restless spirit and cannot see when matters are well, but loves to toss and change and bring things to a pitch of reformation floating in his own brain'. Laud's prospects improved dramatically after the accession of Charles I, who was looking for someone just like him to take the Church in hand after the lax rule of Archbishop Abbot. In 1627 Laud was appointed to the Privy Council; in 1628 he became Bishop of London; and in 1633, following the death of Abbot, he was elevated to the Archbishopric of Canterbury.

Laud worked so closely with the King that it is difficult, if not impossible, to distinguish between their respective contributions to decision-making. This was the case with one of the policies with which Laud became identified, namely the shifting of altars to the east end of churches, where they were to be railed in. The very term 'altar' was anathema to many churchgoers, since it had catholic overtones of sacrifice and transubstantiation, but for Laud the altar was 'the greatest place of God's residence upon earth. I say the greatest. Yea, greater than the pulpit, for there 'tis *Hoc est corpus meum*, "This is my body," but in the pulpit 'tis at most but *Hoc est verbum meum*, "This is my word."' The Elizabethan Injunctions of 1559 had laid down that the communion table should be 'set in the place where the altar stood,' except at communion services, when it could be moved into the chancel, to facilitate the administration of the sacraments. However, during the Queen's reign it became the practice in many churches to move the holy table into the body of the church and leave it there. Puritans in particular were so anxious to avoid any suggestion of venerating the sacraments that they would use the table as a hatstand, and Laud complained that ' 'tis superstition nowadays for any man to come with more reverence into a church than a tinker and his bitch come into an alehouse'.

After Laud became Dean of Gloucester in 1616 he ordered the removal of the communion table to the east end of the cathedral, but he never attempted to impose this practice on parish churches within the diocese. When, in 1634, he was preparing for a formal visitation of the province of Canterbury his instructions made no mention of how the holy table should be placed or whether it should be railed in. It was the King who added the provision that it should be placed in a north-south position – like the former altar – at the east end of the church and protected by rails 'one yard in height and so thick with pillars that dogs cannot get in'. Charles also made it obligatory for communicants to come to the rails to receive the sacraments. Laud shared Charles's desire to enhance the dignity of the communion service, which was at the heart of the Church's worship, but despite his reputation for intransigence he took a less rigid line on enforcement. He instructed his officials to rely on 'fair persuasions' rather than compulsion, and to take the sacraments down into the chancel if communicants refused to come up to the rails. The railing-in of altars only became the rule in his diocese of Canterbury after 1637, and even then he allowed individual parishes considerable latitude.

Among the parishes which resisted the requirement to move the holy table to the east end of the church was St Gregory's, which stood in the shadow of St Paul's Cathedral in London. The order to do so was given, in this instance, by the chapter and Dean of St Paul's – a Calvinist with alleged puritan inclinations – who had already re-sited the altar in the cathedral. The dispute came before the Privy Council in November 1633, and the King, who was present, resolved that the placing of the communion table was not 'to be left to the discretion of the parish, much less to the fancy of any humorous person', but was to be determined by the practice of the 'cathedral mother church, by which all other churches depending thereon ought to be guided'. This left the decision in such matters in the hands of the bishops, who had differing views on the subject, but shortly afterwards the King curtailed their autonomy by recommending that the table should at all times stand in the chancel.

Laud and Charles were at one in their belief that places of worship should be worthy of their high function, and in October 1629 the King issued a proclamation – the first of its kind – for 'preventing the decays of churches and chapels'. Bishops were now required to carry out surveys of the physical state of all such buildings in their respective dioceses, and were warned 'not to rely on the churchwardens' presentments, who, to save themselves and their neighbours from charge will easily omit to make known the decays of their churches and their own defaults'. Among the places of worship which had been allowed to decay was St Paul's Cathedral, brought into its tumbledown condition, according to a report drawn up in 1631, through 'the neglect and sufferance of the dean and chapter in times past'. It may have been at Laud's prompting that Charles made an official visit to St Paul's and set on foot a campaign for its restoration. The King paid the entire cost of a new portico, designed, in classical fashion, by Inigo Jones, and Laud set up a commission, including himself and representatives of the City of London, to raise funds. This initiative did not meet with universal approbation. Some critics argued 'that it was more agreeable to the rules of piety to demolish such old monuments of superstition and idolatry than to keep them standing', but by late 1634 nearly £30,000 had been raised, and further sums continued to come in right up to the Civil War.

Arminian bishops and clergy were prominent in another campaign, this time to improve the internal appearance of churches by removing unsightly pews. These were a feature of many churches, and reflected the social standing, or at least the aspirations, of the families concerned, but they often blocked the view of members of the congregation or towered over the pulpit or altar in a manner that suggested secular rather than spiritual considerations. When he visited Worcester, Charles personally ordered the removal of chairs at the west end of the cathedral, where the mayor and aldermen usually sat, and he took similar action at Durham, when he stayed there *en route* to Scotland in 1633. Disputes between clergy and laity over seating arrangements were not new, but they acquired a sharper edge during the Personal Rule. Some bishops, like Matthew Wren, were uncompromising in their attitude, but others treated the issue as a minor one. Richard Neile, a leading Arminian, told a fellow bishop in January 1635 that 'to remove any from the place where they and their ancestors have time out of mind accustomed to sit will beget more brabbles, suits in law and prohibitions than either you or I would be content to be troubled with'.

Laud encouraged the clergy to assert themselves, for he hoped, as Matthew Wren put it, 'to live to see the day when a minister should be as good a man as any Jack Gentleman in England'. By securing the appointment of parish clergy as Justices of the Peace and upholding ministers in their frequent disputes with local gentry, he did much to improve their morale. Many gentlemen, of course, resented this threat to their status, particularly since the Arminian bishops were often of non-gentry stock. Wren was the son of a mercer (a dealer in fabrics), Richard Neile of a tallow-chandler (a dealer in candles), and Laud himself of a Reading clothier. Puritan militants, such as the lawyer and pamphleteer William Prynne, took great delight in emphasising the bishops' lowly origins and condemning them as 'tyrannising lordly prelates raised from the dunghill'. One of the reasons why Laud was so sensitive to these attacks and punished them severely was that they struck at his whole concept of the clergy as a spiritual élite.

Laud used the prerogative court of Star Chamber to punish the authors of such attacks, and in so doing he gave it a reputation for savage sentences that still endures. In fact it usually imposed fines, which were far from crushing and rarely collected in full. Corporal punishment was reserved for those who, by slandering great men, had brought the Church or royal government into disrepute. This explains the harsh treatment of the lawyer William Prynne, the clergyman Henry Burton and the physician John Bastwick in 1637. All three had originally accepted episcopacy as a valid way of governing the Church, but the increasing number and influence of Arminian bishops, whom they regarded as neo-papists, turned them into opponents. Burton accused the bishops of bringing in popish symbols such as altars and crucifixes, while Prynne attacked Wren in particular and claimed that he was preparing the ground for the reintroduction of Roman Catholicism. Bastwick, meanwhile, had published *The Litany*, a scathing condemnation of episcopacy in the tradition of the *Marprelate Letters*, in which he declared that 'such a multitude of trumperies and grollish cere-monies are brought in by the prelates as all the substance of religion is thrust out'.

Star Chamber found the defendants guilty and sentenced them to stand in the pillory, have their ears cropped and spend the rest of their lives in prison. Such harshness had the opposite effect from what Laud intended. The three men became popular heroes, and the political nation was more impressed by Prynne's words than by his fate. 'You see,' he announced from the pillory, 'they [i.e. the bishops] spare none of what society or calling soever. None are exempted that cross their own ends. Gentlemen, look to yourselves. You know not whose turn may be next'.

Laud's aim of restoring the clergy to a prominent role in English life and government was in some ways reactionary, for it had echoes of Wolsey and pre-Reformation days. Charles, who fully supported Laud in this objective, also looked back to an England where the lords and gentry lived in their country houses, dispensing hospitality and maintaining order in their localities. In Charles's opinion such persons had no valid reason for spending time in London, and he issued a number of proclamations ordering them to leave the capital and return to their rightful sphere.

Charles did not share the puritan distrust of popular sports and enter-tainments, nor the belief that Sunday should be treated like the Jewish Sabbath, devoted exclusively to worship and Bible-reading. Although he was a devout Christian and regular churchgoer, the King was content to spend the rest of his time on Sundays in work and pleasure. Indeed, in the latter part of his reign, Sunday was frequently chosen for meetings of the Privy Council. Laud, like his master, was no sabbatarian, and he was angered to learn not only that the magistrates of Somerset had suppressed the customary 'wakes' or revels in their county but that their action had been approved by Sir Thomas Richardson, the Chief Justice. Richardson was summoned before the Council, where Laud spoke so vehemently against him that he complained of being 'choked with the archbishop's lawn sleeves'.

It was probably the action of the Somerset magistrates that prompted Charles to reissue the *Declaration of Sports* first put out by his father in 1618. James had found 'that his subjects were debarred from lawful recre-ations upon Sundays after evening prayers ended ... and he prudently considered that if these times were taken from them, the meaner sort, who labour hard all the week, should have no recreations at all to refresh their spirits'. He therefore ordered that 'after the end of divine service, our good people be not disturbed ... or discouraged from any lawful recreation'. By reissuing the *Declaration of Sports* Charles caused great offence to the puritan-inclined 'middling sort' who occupied many of the lesser offices in local communities and were preoccupied with the problem of maintaining social discipline. In their eyes Sunday sports and other revels were simply an occasion for drunkenness and sexual licence, and undermined traditional hierarchies. Some Arminians, with Wren in the forefront, enforced the *Book of Sports* to the letter, but this was not the case with Laud. For him it was probably a peripheral issue, but the anger it generated contributed to the increasing feeling among all sections of English society that royal policy, under Arminian influence (or so it was assumed), was misconceived and potentially dangerous.

Laud, like his royal master, believed that the anglican Church should be directed by the bishops and parish clergy, and he was deeply distrustful of freelance preachers, or 'lecturers', who were, in effect, laws unto themselves. As Bishop of London, Laud had persuaded Charles to issue instructions that lecturers, who tended to be puritan and non-conformist, should wear a surplice and hood and read the prescribed Prayer-Book service before delivering their sermons. It was also laid down that in future no lecturer should be appointed by any municipality unless he accepted a benefice and thereby brought himself under episcopal supervision. Four years later Laud took action against the Feoffees for Impropriations, whom he described as 'the main instruments for the puritan faction to undo the Church'. The Feoffees solicited funds from their supporters to buy up impropriations, and used the income to improve the stipend of 'godly' ministers and lecturers. These were the very people who, in Laud's eyes, were undermining the authority of both bishops and the Prayer Book. He therefore had the Feoffees summoned before the Court of the Exchequer, where they were found guilty of acting as a corporation although they had never been legally constituted as one. The court ordered their suppression, and their endowments were transferred to the King, who used them to augment the income of orthodox ministers.

Laud accepted the authority of the Bible in questions of faith, but insisted on his right to regulate *adiaphora* – matters on which the scriptures were silent. 'Unity cannot long continue in the Church', he said, 'when uniformity is shut out at the church door. No external action in the world can be uniform without some ceremonies ... Ceremonies are the hedge that fences the substance of religion from all the indignities which profaneness and sacrilege too commonly put upon it'. Laud rarely, if ever, went beyond the limits laid down in the *Canons* of 1604. It was these which prescribed that 'when in time of divine service the lord Jesus shall be mentioned, due and lowly reverence shall be done by all persons present'; that ministers, when they were conducting services, should wear surplices and, if graduates, hoods; and that holy communion should be administered at least three times a year.

Laud's unpopularity derived in part from the fact that under his predecessor the 1604 *Canons* had not been systematically enforced. He regarded Abbot's tenure of the archbishopric as twenty years of neglect, and he was all too aware that, as he told Wentworth, 'The Church . . . is so bound up in the forms of the common law that it is not possible for me or for any man to do that good which he would.' In the year when he was appointed archbishop Laud also became sixty, which in the seventeenth century was the entry to old age. This explains his impatience to reimpose the discipline of Whitgift's days, and his rough treatment of those who stood in his way. Laud was an old man in a hurry, but John Selden, the distinguished lawyer and member of Parliament, judged that he and his fellow bishops 'were too hasty. Else, with a discreet slowness, they might have had what they aimed at'.

Charles I and the Roman Catholics

Critics of Laudian 'innovations', who looked on themselves as the true custodians of the Church of England, were incensed at the contrast between the way in which they were persecuted while papists, the real enemy of the Church, were treated with kid gloves. Yet in some respects the impression of mildness was misleading, for it was largely confined to court, where the influence of Henrietta Maria made catholicism fashionable and led to a number of prominent conversions. Among the King's ministers, Richard Weston, the Lord Treasurer, had a catholic wife and was known to favour the idea of reunion with Rome. Secretary Windebancke shared these sentiments, and so did Francis Cottington, the Chancellor of the Exchequer, who was widely assumed to be a covert catholic. The greatest advocate of reunion was Charles I himself, and he held long and frequent discussions on the subject with a papal agent, George Con, who was officially in attendance upon the Queen, but became, in practice, the papal representative at court.

Laud's enemies accused him of being a catholic at heart, and the Pope went so far as to offer him a cardinal's hat if he changed his religious allegiance, but the archbishop was totally committed to the Church of England. Indeed, one of the reasons for his advocacy of greater ceremonial in anglican services was his desire to counter the attraction of catholicism and check the flow of conversions to Rome. Laud was no friend of the Queen and her circle. It was at his insistence that Charles, in 1637, issued a number of proclamations forbidding proselytising by catholics, whether priests or lay persons, and threatening severe punishment for all those who attended services in the Queen's chapel, which was theoretically reserved for Henrietta Maria and members of her household. These measures had little or no effect, but they demonstrated Laud's awareness of the dangers of court catholicism and his desire to curb it.

Outside the circle of the court there was no weakening in the official attitude towards recusants. In 1625, under pressure from his first Parliament and in contravention of the assurances given to the French, Charles ordered the penal laws to be put into operation, and a special department was set up within the Exchequer to handle the revenue from recusancy fines, which were bringing in more than £20,000 a year in the mid-1630s, compared with £6,000 a decade earlier. Yet in one respect catholics were better off than before, since Charles encouraged them to compound for their recusancy by agreeing to pay a regular annual sum. In return, they were freed from harassment by informers and generally left alone.

The alliance between the catholic gentry and the religious orders, especially the Jesuits, was cemented in Charles's reign. Bishop Richard Smith made himself so unpopular by trying to impose his authority that he sparked off an anticlerical reaction among the catholic laity, similar to that which Laud was provoking among their protestant counterparts. In late 1628 Smith was denounced to the Privy Council, which ordered his arrest. He took refuge in the French embassy, hoping the Pope would intervene on his behalf, but the papacy came to the conclusion that the restoration of the hierarchy had been a mistake, and it encouraged Smith to return to France, where he spent the rest of his life.

The secular priests, who had welcomed the bishop as the guarantor of their supremacy over the regulars, were now without a head, and in effect there were two catholic missions, only loosely connected. The seculars' numbers continued to increase, and by 1640 there were well over four hundred of them, twice as many as at the beginning of the century. Meanwhile, the regulars had achieved a fourfold expansion. In 1640 there were nearly two hundred Jesuits on mission in England, as well as a hundred Benedictines. This was a scale of provision for the catholic community not matched until the nineteenth century, but the regulars' concentration on the catholic gentry confirmed the pattern already emerging in Elizabeth's reign. The south and midlands had more priests than they really needed, while traditionally catholic areas in the north and west were poorly provided for. The mission certainly kept English catholicism alive, but only at the cost of narrowing its geographical range and accepting its sectarian, minority status.

CHAPTER FOURTEEN

Charles I: The breakdown of prerogative rule

Financial expedients

No minister after 1628 ever monopolised royal favour in the way that Buckingham had done. Power was distributed rather than concentrated, but among the most important members of Charles's government was Sir Richard Weston, appointed Lord Treasurer in 1628 and created Earl of Portland in 1633. Portland was not an original or creative thinker. He worked within the existing system, much as Burghley had done, and his critics gave him the nickname of 'Lady Mora', from the Latin for 'delay'. Yet in his own unspectacular way Weston was an efficient Treasurer, pursuing the inevitable policies of pruning the expenses of the royal household and the administrative departments at the same time as he exploited all means of increasing the royal revenue.

Weston, like Cranfield before him, was an advocate of peace, since Charles could clearly not afford to engage in war, and he wholeheartedly approved of the treaties that put an end to the state of hostilities first with France, in 1629, and the following year with Spain. Peace meant an increase in the Customs duties, which were leased out for anything from one to five years. In 1633 Weston instituted three-year leases at an average rent of £150,000, but in 1638 – by which time William Juxon was Treasurer – the existing Customs farmers lost out to a new syndicate which offered £172,500. There were some voices calling for the Customs to be directly administered, but the advantage of leasing their collection was that the farmers could be prevailed upon to make substantial loans to the crown. These took the form of advance payments of part of the following year's rent, and produced some £30,000 annually. In 1633, however, the farmers extended their anticipations to two years ahead, which doubled the figure to £60,000.

The main source of extraordinary revenue remained Parliament, and the Commons' grant of five subsidies in 1628 was worth some £275,000. But the violent ending of the 1629 session, coming as it did on top of the Commons' refusal to make a formal grant of Tonnage and Poundage, left Charles dependent on his own resources. New taxes were out of the question, for the English were notoriously resistant to taxation at the best of times, and in the absence of Parliament Charles had to make sure he kept within the bounds of law. That is why his advisers resurrected old measures that had at least a tincture of legality rather than adopting new ones.

The first device was Distraint of Knighthood. All men with land worth £40 a year were under a legal obligation to take up knighthood, but rapid inflation during the sixteenth century pushed many people into this category who were below the social level of knights and had no desire to take up an honour which might well oblige them to perform functions in their local communities for which they were not fitted by birth, education or status. The summons to take up knighthood became a mere formality and was confined to occasions such as coronations. Elizabeth made no use of it, but the summons was issued at the time of James I's coronation, though never apparently enforced. Following the dissolution of Parliament in 1629, the need for money persuaded Charles to agree to the appointment of commissioners to collect fines from more than nine thousand people who, while possessing the minimum qualification for knighthood, had not taken it up. The total sum raised was close on £175,000, but it was obtained only at the cost of alienating the affections of a significant section of the King's subjects. Clarendon later observed that 'though it had a foundation in right, yet in the circumstances of proceeding [Distraint] was very grievous and no less unjust', and it is hardly surprising that the Long Parliament abolished it.

The revival of Distraint of Knighthood had been the work of Sir Julius Caesar, a distinguished civil lawyer who held the office of Master of the Rolls. The revival of the forest laws was initiated by a common lawyer, William Noy, who was Charles I's Attorney-General. Forests were, in effect, huge game reserves, subject to a special law, but over the centuries their bounds had shrunk and in many places it was not clear whether land was or was not 'forest'. Since the crown wished to exploit its rights over the royal forests it needed to establish their exact limits, and Noy revived the medieval practice of holding forest 'eyres' or hearings which the local inhabitants were required to attend, so that they could be questioned on the nature of their tenure. There was nothing wrong with Noy's scheme, and Charles may have approved of it because forests were an integral part of that traditional England which he wished to recreate. They were also a reserve of timber for the navy which he was constructing.

Noy died in 1634, and his successor, Sir John Finch – another lawyer, who had been the Speaker held down in his chair on 2 March 1629 – was primarily concerned with making a profit for the crown. On the basis of old documents he professed to have discovered, Finch enlarged the forest boundaries to their maximum extent in the Middle Ages. Entire counties, such as Essex and Northamptonshire, were now declared subject to the forest law, and hundreds of people were prosecuted for breaches of the law who did not even know they were subject to it. After being fined they were frequently given the option of buying themselves out of the 'forest', but this made it even more clear that the principal motivation of the crown was financial. The fines levied amounted to more than £80,000, but many of them were still unpaid by 1641, when the Long Parliament restored the forest boundaries to what they had been in James I's reign. While Distraint of Knighthood had alienated the middle section of society, the manipulation of the forest boundaries affected what Clarendon described as 'persons of quality and honour, who thought themselves above ordinary oppressions and [were] therefore like to remember it with more sharpness'.

The most notorious of all the financial devices of the Personal Rule was Ship Money. It had long been accepted that, in times of emergency, the ports and coastal regions should provide ships for the defence of the kingdom – or, if they had no ships available, money in lieu. Shortly before Elizabeth's death the Privy Council had been planning to call for contributions from the whole country, and early in 1628 Charles I adopted a similar stance by announcing his intention to charge all counties a proportion of the cost of setting out the fleet. In the event he did not do so, but in 1634 he sent out Ship Money writs to the seaports, and in the following year he extended these to inland counties as well, on the grounds that 'that charge of defence which concerneth all men ought to be supported by all'. The levy proved so successful in financial terms that Ship Money was thereafter demanded every year. While remaining strictly within the letter of the law the King had circumvented the convention that taxation should only be levied with parliamentary consent.

Technically speaking, Ship Money was not a tax but a rate, and it was presumably in order to emphasise this crucial distinction that the Privy

Council devised a new way of administering it. Instead of leaving the assessment to local gentlemen, as was the case with subsidies, it fixed the total sum it intended to raise from the whole kingdom and then apportioned this among the counties. Furthermore, it made the sheriff of each county its local agent, not the subsidy commissioners or Justices of the Peace. During the first three years of its operation Ship Money brought in about £190,000 a year, and over the entire period 1634–40 the Treasurer of the Navy received close on £800,000, which was twice as much as all the subsidies granted by Charles's first three parliaments. Only in and after 1638 did refusals to pay make a major impact. It should be added that Charles was not being totally cynical when he demanded Ship Money. The seas were infested by privateers from Dunkirk and the dreaded Barbary corsairs from the coast of North Africa, who in 1631 sacked Baltimore. The money raised was paid direct to the Treasurer of the Navy and was used solely for the construction of a fleet. But this did not alter the basic objection to Ship Money – namely, that it was a non-parliamentary tax – and while the majority of people paid up, however grudgingly, there were a number who refused to do so on principle.

These included the leading members of a company which had been set up to establish a puritan colony on Providence Island (Providencia) in the Spanish West Indies. Among the shareholders were some of the men who were to mastermind the opposition to Charles I. They included Lord Saye, well known for his puritan views, and John Hampden, a Buckinghamshire gentleman of considerable wealth. Saye refused to pay Ship Money and sued the constable who distrained his goods. The crown carefully avoided taking up this challenge by calling for legal advice from the judges, who gave their considered opinion that Ship Money was legal. It was left to Hampden to provoke the crown into action, for by stubbornly refusing to pay he achieved what he had been aiming at, namely a formal trial in which he intended to raise the basic issue of whether a regular tax could be levied without parliamentary consent. The case aroused widespread interest, and the speech made by Hampden's counsel, Oliver St John – who was also solicitor to the Providence Island Company – centred on the argument that if the King could force his subjects to contribute taxes at his pleasure, their property rights would be violated.

The judges, as in the Five Knights' Case, were not well placed to consider the broader implications of the crown's actions. The King had stated that an emergency existed and that by virtue of his absolute prerogative he was empowered to levy contributions from his subjects without waiting for their consent in a parliamentary manner. Sir Robert Berkeley, Chief

Justice of the King's Bench, upheld this contention and declared 'that it is a dangerous tenet, a kind of judaizing opinion, to hold that the weal public must be exposed to peril of utter ruin and subversion rather than such a charge as this, which may secure the commonwealth, may be imposed by the King upon the subject without common consent in Parliament'. Berkeley was careful to add that the King's absolute prerogative applied only in cases of emergency, and that in the normal course of affairs he would raise money solely through Parliament. But who was to decide whether and when an emergency existed? The common law was not fitted to give guidance on such a subject, and Berkeley could only insist that the King could be relied on never to abuse his trust. Not all his colleagues were so confident of this, however, and five out of the twelve judges gave their verdict in Hampden's favour.

Charles had hoped that a unanimous verdict in his support would stifle opposition to Ship Money, but as it turned out the views of the dissenting judges carried more weight with public opinion than those of the supportive majority. This was made plain by the sheriff of Cheshire, who told the Council in 1638 that he had been unable to collect the full quota for his county because 'the general bruit of the late arguments of those judges who concluded against Ship Money is so plausibly received by those who were too refractory, and countenanced by some of rank, that I have found more difficulty than in all the rest'.

In terms of their effect on public opinion the financial expedients of the Personal Rule were disastrous, but they did at least expand the royal revenue. Every source of income was exploited. Monopolies were revived, taking advantage of loopholes in the Monopolies Act of 1624, and became a major element in crown finances, yielding about £100,000 by 1640. By the same date wardship, which had been worth some £40,000 a year at the end of James I's reign, was yielding £84,000. Duties on trade, including both Customs and the hated Impositions, were bringing in more than £350,000, and by the time the Personal Rule came to an end the annual royal revenue was approaching a million pounds. This was a striking demonstration of the inherent financial strength of the monarchy – and, by implication, of the financial irrelevance of Parliament – but what the crown gained in money it lost in goodwill. Charles was dependent for the maintenance of his rule upon the active co-operation of the political nation and the passive acquiescence of the underprivileged majority, yet by seeming to exploit his subjects the King strained their loyalty, in some cases to breaking point.

Yet throughout the greater part of the Personal Rule the property-owners did co-operate, if only because they dreaded the breakdown of order. The period following the dissolution of the 1629 Parliament coincided with bad harvests that caused severe distress and sparked off riots in several parts of England. In January 1631, therefore, the Council issued the *Book of Orders*, giving detailed instructions about the duties of Justices of the Peace, particularly in relation to the enforcement of the poor law and vagrancy regulations. They were also required to hold monthly meetings and make quarterly reports to the sheriff about the conditions prevailing in their area. The sheriff, in turn, was charged with the task of drawing up a composite statement on the whole county, to be presented to the assize judges on their bi-annual visitations and passed on by them to the Privy Council.

A copy of the *Book of Orders* was sent to every county and corporate town, and this evidence of government vitality has often been taken as indicative of the efficiency of the Personal Rule, in contrast to the laxness of earlier periods. In fact, the government was only following the path laid down by its predecessors. It had long been established practice, in times of emergency such as plague and famine, for the Council to issue precise instructions to magistrates and to supervise their work. The 1631 *Book* was the brainchild of the Earl of Manchester, who had first sketched it out at an earlier period of distress in the middle years of James I's reign, basing it upon his knowledge of what was being done in his native county of Northamptonshire. Magistrates in general complied with the *Book of Orders*, since it served their own interests as well as the King's, but they resented the demand for regular reports and rarely made these after 1632, when the immediate crisis had passed. Nor did the Council continue to press for them, since it was turning its attention increasingly to revenue-raising devices, which entailed much greater and more consistent pressure upon the localities.

The destruction of prerogative monarchy

James I had found the formality and dignity of Church of England services increasingly in tune with his own preferences, and he hoped to move the Scottish Kirk closer to this pattern, with the ultimate aim of uniting the two churches. In 1616, as a step forward along this path, he requested members of the General Assembly of the Kirk to draw up 'a common form of ordinary service to be used in all time hereafter'. The Scottish bishops took a leading role in framing the new Liturgy, which would have been published in 1619 but for the fact that James was caught up in the controversy over the Five Articles (*see* p. 489). The Liturgy remained in limbo for a decade, until it was taken to London and shown to Charles I and Laud. They would have preferred the Kirk to adopt the English Book of Common Prayer, but they recognised that Scottish susceptibilities had to be taken into account, and they accordingly instructed the Scottish bishops to produce an acceptable version of the English Book. However, the role of episcopacy in the Kirk had long been a matter of controversy, and the very fact that bishops had produced the Scottish Prayer Book made it unacceptable to many Scots. Their antipathy to the project was intensified by its English origins and, in particular, its links with Laud, whose high-Church views made him deeply unpopular north of the border. They also distrusted Charles, who had little understanding of or sympathy with Calvinism, and showed no affection for his native land.

In July 1637 the Scottish Prayer Book was used for the first time in St Giles's Cathedral, Edinburgh, and provoked a riot. 'The mass is entered among us!' shouted one woman; another flung her stool at the preacher, and soon the whole cathedral was in uproar. The revolt spread quickly, and early in 1638 a *National Covenant* was drawn up, pledging its signatories to defend the existing system of worship and uphold the role of the Scottish Parliament and General Assembly in deciding what changes, if any, were to be made. Charles was urged to withdraw the Book, but although he sent his cousin, the Scottish Duke of Hamilton, to Edinburgh as his representative, he told him he was 'resolved to suffer my life rather than to suffer authority to be contemned' and would use force if necessary to bring his rebellious subjects to heel. When Hamilton reached Scotland he quickly realised that the King had little support there, but even though he returned to London to explain the situation, Charles remained adamant that his authority must be upheld. Otherwise he would 'have no more power in Scotland than as a Duke [i.e. Doge] of Venice, which I will rather die than suffer'.

Charles did give Hamilton permission to summon a General Assembly, but when this met, in November 1638, it denounced not only episcopacy but the Five Articles as well. Hamilton tried to pursue James I's strategy of driving a wedge between the hard-liners and the moderates, but Charles's refusal to contemplate concessions made his task impossible. The King was not simply being obtuse. Covenanter tracts, written for an English readership, were already circulating widely. The *Information to All Good Christians within the Kingdom of England*, which made its appearance in February 1639, maintained that English and Scottish bishops were pursuing the same objective, of reconciliation with Rome, and Charles knew that if he allowed episcopacy to be weakened in Scotland he would be

undermining the foundations of the Caroline Church in England. He therefore recalled Hamilton and set on foot plans to raise an army of thirty
thousand men and send it across the border.

Years of peace had left England unprepared for war, and one observer
reported that 'the King's magazines are totally unfurnished of arms and all
sorts of ammunition, and commanders we have none, either for advice or
execution'. He added that 'the people through[out] all England are generally so discontented . . . I think there is reason to fear that a great part of
them will be readier to join with the Scots than to draw their swords in the
King's service'. In March 1639 Charles went north, to York, to join his
army, but it quickly became obvious, even to him, that the ragged collection of poorly trained conscripts arrayed under his banner was no match
for the Scots, who were led by men who had made their career as professional soldiers in foreign armies. In June 1639, therefore, he agreed to
the Pacification of Berwick, whereby both armies were to be disbanded
while a Scottish Parliament and the General Assembly of the Kirk deliber-
ated on how to restore peaceful relations between the King and his
rebellious subjects.

Charles now needed a strong man at his side, and he sent for
Wentworth. 'Come when you will', he wrote, 'ye shall be welcome to your
assured friend Charles R'. Wentworth, created a viscount in 1628 and
appointed first to govern the north of England and subsequently Ireland,
was a self-confident, overbearing man who longed to use his considerable
talents to their maximum advantage. He had established a close friendship
with Laud, and in their correspondence the two men coined the term
'Thorough' to describe the sort of policies they believed Charles should
adopt. 'Thorough' meant cutting through red tape and administrative
delays, which they identified with Lord Treasurer Portland, 'Lady Mora',
and making sure the King's rights were fully enforced. Wentworth had
been sent to Ireland, as Lord Deputy, in 1632, and it was widely assumed
that his rule there was a try-out for 'Thorough'. He took the initiative in
recovering for the crown and Church many of the lands that had been
alienated during the previous half-century of disturbance. When this
brought him up against the common lawyers he secured letters patent from
Charles giving the prerogative Court of Castle Chamber the ultimate authority in such matters. Royal power was, of course, less restrained in Ireland
than in England, since there was no strongly-entrenched gentry group to
take into consideration, but English property-owners feared that in due
course they also would be called upon to surrender former Church and
crown lands, and that the common law would show itself, once again,

powerless to protect them. They feared and hated Wentworth because he was the only man in the King's service who had the will and capacity to turn Charles's personal rule into absolutism – or so at least they believed.

Wentworth was now Charles's principal adviser, and the King demonstrated his trust in him by creating Wentworth Earl of Strafford. The earl, who had earlier been a member of the House of Commons, advised the King to summon parliaments in England and Ireland as well as Scotland, arguing that the traditional enmity between England and its northern neighbour would help unite public opinion behind the crown. In the Scottish Parliament and the General Assembly members demanded the abolition of episcopacy as their price for co-operation, but the Irish Parliament, well managed by Wentworth, set a better example by voting over £150,000 for the King's needs. Wentworth may have assumed, or at least been hoping, that the English Parliament would be as amenable as the Irish one, but he was swiftly disillusioned.

The King did not summon the English Parliament in order to ask for its advice on whether or not to resume his campaign against the Scots, for he had already decided on that course. When he opened the session in April 1640 he called on members to 'lay aside all other debates', so that they could 'pass an act for such and so many subsidies as you ... shall think fit and convenient for so great an action'. The Lords were prepared to accept this request, but the Commons insisted that the major grievance of prerogative taxation should be dealt with first. Sir Henry Vane, the newly appointed Secretary of State, therefore made it known that if the House granted twelve subsidies the King 'would be graciously pleased to part with Ship Money'. It looked as though the shape of a bargain was emerging, but the buying-out of Ship Money raised the same difficulty for the Commons as Impositions had earlier done. They regarded both levies as illegal, despite the fact that they had been sanctioned by the judges, and were reluctant to pay for the removal of what should never have been there in the first place. If they set a precedent by 'rewarding' the King for illegal taxation, they might encourage him to collect more prerogative levies, albeit under a different guise.

A deal might have been worked out over Ship Money and prerogative taxation, but religion proved to be a more intractable issue. John Pym, the bull-necked west-countryman who was establishing a reputation as one of the Commons' best speakers, had long been apprehensive about the growth of Arminianism and focused his fire on 'the introduction of popish ceremonies', such as 'the setting-up of altars, bowing to them and the like', as well as 'bowing at the name of Jesus'. Pym, who was in touch with the

Covenanter leaders, believed that the Scots were right to resist innovations in religion, and he was at work on a petition which would urge Charles not to fight the rebels but to come to terms with them. The King feared being caught in a trap, whereby he would be compelled to make concessions in order to receive supply. Wentworth and other Councillors urged him to allow discussions to continue, in the hope of achieving a positive result, but Charles's experience of Parliament in the opening years of his reign gave him little cause for optimism. In his eyes the malcontents were fast gaining the upper hand and the only way in which to check them was by removing the forum from which they made their subversive appeals to his subjects. On 5 May 1640 he therefore dissolved the Short Parliament after a session that had lasted only three weeks.

Although Charles had put an end to Parliament he ordered Convocation to continue sitting. This clerical assembly voted £20,000 a year for the support of its royal governor and also approved a number of canons defining the doctrines of the anglican Church. Canon VI gave particular offence, since it required all clergy to swear that they would never give their consent 'to alter the government of this Church by archbishops, bishops, deans and archdeacons, etc. as it now stands established'. No one could be certain exactly what fell within the scope of the enigmatic abbreviation, and the 'Etcetera Oath', as it came to be called, inflamed controversy rather than putting an end to it.

The King was determined to renew military operations against the Covenanters before they took complete control of Scotland. He assembled an army of some twenty thousand men, but their sympathies were with the rebels rather than the King, for as they marched north they burnt 'Laudian' altar rails and lynched a couple of officers accused of popery. In June 1640 their nominal commander, the Earl of Northumberland, declared that things could not 'long continue in the condition they are now in. So general a defection in this kingdom hath not been known in the memory of any'. Lack of money hindered operations, and the attacks on prerogative taxation that were a feature of the Short Parliament made the King's subjects even more reluctant to pay the sums demanded of them. The English forces took up their position at Newburn, on the Tyne, but the Scots, who were better prepared, put them to flight and then advanced into England, occupying the two northernmost English counties.

The King, in desperation, decided to summon a great council of peers to meet him at York, but when this assembled all it could propose was the conclusion of a truce with the Scots, to last until such time as another Parliament could settle the affairs of the kingdom. Writs were accordingly sent out, and on 3 November 1640 members of both Houses assembled at Westminster for what was to be the last Parliament of Charles's reign. The King could not, this time, resort to an early dissolution, for the commissioners appointed by the great council to negotiate with the Scots reported their demand for £850 a day to cover their occupation costs while they remained in possession of Northumberland and Durham. Only the City of London could advance the large sums of money needed to meet this obligation, and it would not do so unless repayment was guaranteed by Parliament.

The King may have been hoping that even at this late stage Parliament would rally to his support against the Scots, but the 'Bishops' Wars', as they were called, had been deeply unpopular and there was no question of renewing them. Parliament eventually voted the King six subsidies – only worth, by this time, some £50,000 each – but its priorities were set not by the Privy Councillors, whose influence had sharply diminished, but by an informal 'Junto' of 'godly' lords and commoners. The Earls of Bedford, Essex and Warwick, along with Viscount Saye, were the key members of the group in the Upper House. In the Lower, there were Bedford's client, John Pym, Saye's son, Nathaniel Fiennes, Denzil Holles, son of the Earl of Clare, Oliver St John and John Hampden. Pym was more than ever convinced that the troubles of the King and kingdom had been caused by the machinations of papists and their Arminian sympathisers. He told the Commons in his first major speech of the session that 'There is a design to alter law and religion. The party that affects this are papists, who are obliged by a maxim in their doctrine that they are not only to maintain their religion but also to extirpate others.' Strafford, the King's principal adviser, was a long way from being a papist, but as far as Pym was concerned he was part of the popish conspiracy. He was a close friend of Archbishop Laud, he had raised a catholic army in Ireland for possible use against the Scots, and, at the King's orders, he had been trying to secure a loan from Spain, the greatest and most feared of all catholic powers.

Strafford missed the opening of Parliament, for he was with the King's troops in the north, and by the time he reached London the Commons were ready to impeach him. The earl had few friends in Parliament, and when the Lords received formal notice of impeachment from the Commons, they ordered him to be sequestered from their House and held in custody until he was brought to trial. Two weeks later the Commons presented their articles against Strafford. These included the assertion that he had 'traitorously abused the power and authority of his government to the increasing, countenancing and encouraging of papists, so that he might settle a mutual dependence and confidence betwixt himself and that party, and by their help prosecute and accomplish his malicious and tyrannical designs'.

The writing was clearly on the wall for those members of Charles's administration who were identified with Arminianism or suspected of popery. Archbishop Laud was impeached and sent to the Tower, where he remained until his execution in January 1645. Secretary Windebancke only avoided a similar fate by fleeing to France. The Commons also attacked those ministers who had been linked with the extension of prerogative rule. Lord Keeper Finch, accused of bringing pressure to bear upon the judges in the Ship Money Case, was a leading candidate for impeachment, but after making a robust defence of his actions before the Commons he followed Windebancke's example and escaped overseas. Meanwhile, the release had been ordered of all those who had suffered at the hands of the bishops, and in November 1640 Prynne and Burton made a triumphal return to London. They were followed a week later by Bastwick.

Strafford's trial before the Lords opened in Westminster Hall on 22 March 1641. He was charged with nine general and twenty-eight specific offences that the Commons claimed were treasonable. This was difficult to demonstrate in so far as treason, under the terms of the 1352 act, was defined as directed against the King, whereas Strafford had been the King's agent, acting on his authority. Pym therefore developed the novel argument that while Strafford's actions might not be treasonable in themselves, when taken together they amounted to an attempt to change the constitutional framework which, if it had succeeded, would have made the King odious to his people. As Pym put it, 'Other treasons are against the rule of the law. This is against the being of the law. It is the law that unites the King and his people, and the author of this treason hath endeavoured to dissolve that union, even to break the mutual, irreversible, indissoluble band of protection and allegiance whereby they are, and I hope ever will be, bound together.'

Strafford, who defended himself with great skill and courage, denied that he had extended the prerogative beyond its proper range or attempted to bring in arbitrary government. On the contrary, he had always insisted that 'the happiness of a kingdom consists in [the] just poise of the King's prerogative and the subject's liberty, and that things should never be well till these went hand in hand together'. As for Pym's doctrine of constructive treason, 'how can that be treason in the whole which is not in any of the parts?' If the Lords accepted such a novel argument they would be undermining the rule of law and opening the way to their own destruction:

'Let me be a Pharos [i.e. lighthouse] to keep you from shipwreck, and do not put such rocks in your own way.'

The Lords were impressed by Strafford's defence, and there was a distinct possibility that they would acquit him. Pym still wanted to press ahead with the impeachment, but he was overruled by other members of the Junto, who insisted that they should abandon it and proceed by attainder instead. The bill of attainder simply recited the offences of which Strafford had been accused and declared that, without any further process, he should be 'adjudged and attainted of high treason' and put to death. The bill passed the Commons by a majority of 204 votes to 59, but these figures show that only half the total number of members were present. Many of those who absented themselves presumably did so because their desire to get rid of Strafford would not lead them to countenance injustice. Even at this early stage, then, the Commons were divided between those who believed that the law must guide, and if necessary curb, their actions, and those who, in pursuit of their political aims, would bend, alter or ignore it.

It is possible that the Junto, when they originally launched the impeachment, would have been content with Strafford's removal from power. What changed their attitude was the King's refusal to condemn, let alone abandon, the fallen minister. Strafford had become a symbol of arbitrary rule, and Charles's reluctance to send him into limbo, in contrast to his abandonment of Laud, suggested he was still hankering for non-parliamentary solutions to the problems confronting him. The Junto hoped to counter such tendencies by becoming involved in the administration themselves, and they were heartened by the King's declaration in mid-January 1641 that he wished to 'reduce all matters of religion and government to what they were in the purest times of Queen Elizabeth's days'. He also promised 'that what parts of my revenue ... shall be found illegal or grievous to the public I shall willingly lay down'.

Bedford and Pym, the leading members of the Junto, had already drawn up plans for refinancing the King's government by putting into effect the principles adumbrated in 1610 by Robert Cecil, Earl of Salisbury, when he proposed the Great Contract (*see* p. 257). They would also increase the Customs revenue by publishing a new Book of Rates, and introduce an excise tax on internal trade. For immediate purposes a supply of cash would be raised by selling off lands belonging to cathedral deans and chapters. Bedford was a key figure in the Junto, since Charles knew and respected him. An indication that the strategy was working came with the appointment of Oliver St John as Solicitor-General in January 1641, and rumour had it that Bedford would shortly be made Lord Treasurer, while Pym would be offered the position of Chancellor of the Exchequer which he had long coveted.

In February Bedford was made a Privy Councillor, as were Essex and Saye, but the anticipated major appointments never took place. Strafford was the principal stumbling block. Charles accepted that the earl's political career was over, but he was determined, if he possibly could, to save Strafford's life. Bedford and Pym might have been prepared to compromise on this issue, but any softening of their stance would have lost them much of their support, for opinion in both Houses, reflecting that in the country at large, was deeply hostile towards the man identified with prerogative rule. Essex stated bluntly that 'stone dead hath no fellow', while St John observed that 'it was never accounted either cruelty or foul play to knock foxes or wolves on the head . . . because they be beasts of prey'. The unofficial leaders of both Houses were so dependent upon majority opinion that the range of options open to them was limited. What they regarded as constructive dialogue might well seem to their followers like the betrayal of principles in return for office, and their support would diminish or even disappear.

Since both the King and his critics were circumscribed in their freedom of action the plan for bridge appointments never had much chance of succeeding, and the last faint hope disappeared in May 1641 when Bedford was struck down by smallpox and died. There had been some measure of trust between Bedford and the King, but none at all between Charles and Pym. Charles believed that Pym was planning to overthrow his monarchy. Pym, for his part, suspected Charles of being lukewarm in his commitment to protestantism and absolutist by temperament. He was particularly concerned at the King's refusal to disband the army Strafford had raised in Ireland, since he suspected Charles of planning to use it closer to home. He was also aware that he and his fellow Junto members had laid themselves open to a charge of treason through their close contacts with the King's enemies, the Scottish Covenanters, and that Charles would show no mercy towards them if the situation changed and he was able to recover his power and authority.

While the Lords debated the attainder bill, mobs of people – their presence encouraged, if not organised, by the Junto – swarmed outside the House and in the adjoining streets. Many lords preferred discretion to valour and stayed away. Of those who were present in early May, when the debate concluded, twenty-six supported the bill while nineteen opposed it. Charles had promised Wentworth, at that time in Ireland, that if he came back to England he would not be harmed. But now, from the Tower, Strafford wrote to Charles releasing him from his engagement. 'To set your majesty's conscience at liberty, I do most humbly beseech your majesty (for prevention of evils which may happen by your refusal) to pass this bill.'

The King had to weigh the life of his minister, and the value of his own word, against the danger to himself and the crown, and it was only after long and agonising deliberation that he gave his consent. 'My lord of Strafford's condition', he sadly observed, 'is happier than mine'. Strafford went to the block on 11 May 1641, looking up at Laud's window as he walked towards it so that he could receive the archbishop's blessing. A huge crowd had gathered on Tower Hill to witness the end of 'Black Tom' and one observer described how 'many that came up to town on purpose to see the execution rode in triumph back, waving their hats and with all expressions of joy through every town they went crying 'His head is off! His head is off!'' Laud was one of the few people who genuinely mourned Strafford's death, and he permitted himself a rare criticism of the King who had brought this about. Strafford, he wrote, 'served a mild and gracious prince who knew not how to be, or be made, great'.

While Strafford's fate had been the major obstacle in the road to a negotiated settlement between the King and the Junto, episcopacy was another. In December 1641 a petition said to represent the views of hundreds of London citizens, and calling for the abolition of episcopacy 'with all its dependencies, roots and branches', was presented to the Commons. This threatened to fragment the unity of the House, for although members had been as one in their detestation of prerogative taxation, they were divided on the question of Church reform. Some members had been so alarmed by the developing Arminian influence on the episcopal bench during the Personal Rule that they thought the safest course of action was to get rid of bishops altogether. But others – and they were a substantial number – valued the presence of bishops in the Church as long as they remained within the Elizabethan parameters, and rejected any suggestion that episcopacy should be abolished.

Pym managed to defer consideration of the Root and Branch Petition, but it came before the Commons again in early February, 1641, and the subsequent debate revealed just how deeply the House was split on this issue. Pym and the Junto were anxious to lower the political temperature, but the Scottish commissioners who had been sent to London to deal with matters of common concern to the two kingdoms sponsored a pamphlet that advocated the abolition of episcopacy as well as Strafford's execution.

This paper was called to the House's attention by a moderate lawyer member, Edward Hyde, and it sparked off another heated debate which demonstrated that even the group centred around Pym was divided between those who welcomed the Scots' intervention and those – including Pym himself – who thought the best course was to say nothing. What the debate also revealed was the existence of a significant body of opinion within the House which was in favour of episcopacy. Charles could capitalise on this to try and win back some of the ground he had lost to the Junto. Moreover, he now had a link with these more moderate members via Hyde, whose action in challenging the Scottish commissioners' intervention drew him closer to the King.

The Root and Branch Petition overlapped with another measure the Commons were considering, aimed at depriving the bishops of their votes in the House of Lords. This would have weakened Charles's position there, since the bishops were among his most committed supporters, and in January 1641 he had summoned the two Houses before him and warned them not to go along this route. 'In all the times of my predecessors, since the Conquest and before', Charles told the members, the bishops had enjoyed the privilege of voting in the Upper House, 'and I am bound to maintain them in it as one of the fundamental constitutions of this kingdom'. The Commons reacted to the King's speech by pushing ahead with a bill that banned clergy from holding secular offices and excluded bishops from the Lords. The Upper House was deeply offended by this unwarranted tampering with its membership and threw out the measure. Once again it seemed that the radicals in the Commons, by pressing ahead too fast, had given credence to the King's claim to be the guardian of the constitution.

Unfortunately Charles, on this as on a number of occasions, was pursuing two contradictory strategies. In April 1641 the King was involved in plans to infiltrate loyal officers into the Tower of London, who would work with discontented elements in the army to engineer Strafford's escape. Nothing came of this scheme, but the alarm it generated did much to undo the work of Hyde and others in portraying the King as a ruler who would only act according to law. Members of Parliament feared that Charles would refuse to sign the attainder bill against Strafford and then order the two Houses to dissolve. The King had already accepted a Triennial Act, making it illegal for more than three years to pass without a Parliament. He was now confronted with a new bill forbidding any dissolution of the existing Parliament without the consent of both Houses. This deprived him of one of his most important prerogative rights, but it was presented to him at the same time as the bill for Strafford's attainder, and he signed both for the same reason – namely, that he had no alternative. Further legislation which he accepted removed the last relics of prerogative monarchy. The Courts of Star Chamber and High Commission were abolished, as was the Council of the North. Ship Money and Distraint of Knighthood were outlawed, and the bounds of the royal forests were restored to what they had been in James I's reign. Another act made a temporary grant of Tonnage and Poundage to the King, but laid down that the imposition of any duties on trade without parliamentary consent was illegal.

In the panic atmosphere created by revelations about the Army Plot, Pym persuaded members to endorse the *Protestation*, to be taken on a nationwide basis, binding all subscribers to defend 'the true reformed protestant religion expressed in the doctrine of the Church of England against all popery and popish innovation within this realm'. In June 1641 both Houses went further by accepting the *Ten Propositions*, which called on the King 'to remove such evil counsellors against whom there shall be just exceptions' and to commit 'his own business and the affairs of the kingdom to such counsellors and officers as the Parliament may have cause to confide in'.

The *Ten Propositions* were designed, among other things, to persuade Charles to give up a plan he had formulated to make a journey to Scotland, or at least to delay his departure until 'some of the business of importance concerning the peace of the kingdom, depending in Parliament, may be despatched'. Charles, however, was not to be persuaded. London was no place in which to pass the summer months, especially with the mobs still roaming the streets. Although he had a handful of guards they could not be relied on to protect him and his family against an explosion of popular violence, and he no doubt recalled how similar circumstances had opened the way to the assassination of Buckingham. A further consideration was the positive advantages that might accrue from his stay in Scotland. Negotiations for peace between his two kingdoms were far advanced, and Charles had agreed to many of the Scots' demands. He could therefore count on a reasonably friendly reception and on personal encounters which might enable him to rebuild a 'King's party' in Scotland and weaken the links between the Covenanters and their sympathisers in England. There was the further consideration that on his way north he would visit his troops still stationed near the border and sound out the loyalty of their officers. He needed to move quickly, for Parliament had passed a Poll Tax bill designed to raise money for disbanding the army, and suspicions of

Charles's intentions had been increased by the revelation in June 1641 of a second Army Plot. Brushing aside all objections, therefore, Charles set out for Scotland in August 1641.

The Grand Remonstrance and the five members

The King was not the only person preparing to leave London in the late summer of 1641. Many members of Parliament were exhausted after their long session and anxious to return home, particularly since the plague was making an unwelcome reappearance. The parliamentary recess began in early September, but absenteeism had become increasingly marked well before then. Pym did not leave town, for he had been appointed secretary of the committee appointed by both Houses to deal with any emergencies that might arise in the period before they reassembled in October. They had instructed it, among other issues, 'to take into consideration what power will be fit to be placed, and in what persons, for commanding of the trained bands'. This was an implicit challenge to the King's right to appoint the Lord Lieutenants who controlled the county militias, and he would almost certainly reject any such measure. However, a way out of this dilemma had been opened by another bill that Parliament had passed, naming commissioners to keep an eye on Charles while he was in Scotland. This required the royal assent to become law, but the King was out of easy reach, on his way north. Rather than wait for the normal procedures to be completed, both Houses accepted the assurances of an antiquarian member of the Commons, Sir Symonds D'Ewes, that they had the right to issue ordinances on their own authority which would be as binding as statutes. The first parliamentary ordinance was issued in late August, and more rapidly followed. The Commons and Lords, as long as they acted together, now had a means of legislating without the King's involvement. They were also, via the recess committee, learning how to govern, for the orders it issued were accepted by the royal officials who were responsible for day-to-day administration. These orders bore Pym's signature, of course, and as he was performing a quasi-royal function he acquired the nickname of 'King Pym'.

Pym was one of only a small band of members of Parliament who acknowledged that the public finances needed to be reconstructed. At his suggestion, Parliament had already granted the King six subsidies, and now it had sanctioned a poll tax to enable the army to be dissolved. All these measures were strictly necessary in financial terms, but they were deeply unpopular. As one Yorkshire housewife put it, 'I am in such a great rage with Parliament as nothing will pacify me. For they promised us all should be well if my Lord Strafford's head were off, and since then there is nothing better, but I think we shall be undone with taxes.'

While Parliament was losing much of the goodwill that had attended its opening, the King's appeal was increasing. One reason for this was his apparent change of course over Arminianism. Despite his approval of all that Laud had done, he made no attempt to prevent his impeachment or to assist him in any other way. Moreover, during his stay in Edinburgh he appointed Laud's old enemy, John Williams, as Archbishop of York, and named five new bishops, none of whom was an Arminian. He also wrote to the Lords, assuring them 'that I am constant to the discipline and doctrine of the Church of England established by Queen Elizabeth and my father, and that I resolve, by the grace of God, to die in the maintenance of it'.

The implications of this development were not lost on the property-holders who were strongly represented in Parliament. Since Charles had abandoned Arminianism and consented to the abolition of prerogative monarchy they saw no need for any further measures. 'Innovation', in the sense of changes to accepted practices and conventions in Church and state, was anathema to them. Pym and the Junto, however, distrusted Charles and believed that new limitations must be placed upon him for fear that otherwise he would return to his old ways. It was in order to swing public and parliamentary opinion behind the Junto that Pym began work on a remonstrance listing all the reforms that had so far been achieved. Yet even this might have failed to give the Junto the majority they needed in Parliament had it not been for a totally unexpected event that took place in Charles's third kingdom, Ireland.

In early November 1641 the news reached London that the Irish catholics had risen in revolt against the protestant English settlers and were massacring them. Pym could have asked for no more graphic proof of his belief in the existence of a popish conspiracy, for as one member of the Commons declared, 'all these plots in Ireland are but one plot against England, for it is England that is the fine sweet bit which they so long for and their cruel teeth so much water at'. What was even more alarming was the rebels' assertion that they were acting under a royal commission. If this really was the case then it gave far greater credibility to Pym's argument that the King must be deprived of his right to appoint the Lord Lieutenants, who controlled such military forces as existed in England. An army would obviously have to be raised and sent over to Ireland to suppress the rebellion, but there could be no question, at least in Pym's mind, of allowing the King to exercise his traditional prerogative of choosing its commander.

The need to win over a majority of members of Parliament prompted Pym to transform his remonstrance into the *Grand Remonstrance*, a document of more than two hundred clauses listing all the grievances under which the country had groaned during the Personal Rule and calling for further action to make sure they should never recur. Pym was careful to focus blame not upon the King, who still had many supporters in Parliament, but on those who had misled him. These included 'the Jesuited papists' and 'the bishops and the corrupt part of the clergy'. The aim of all these evil advisers, or so the *Grand Remonstrance* declared, was to subvert 'the fundamental laws and principles of government upon which the religion and justice of this kingdom are firmly established'. In order to frustrate their 'malignant and pernicious design' it was necessary for the King to dismiss these men from his service and to rely in future on 'such persons . . . as your Parliament may have cause to confide in'. Charles was also asked to agree that bishops should be deprived of their votes in the Upper House; that tender consciences in religion should be salved 'by removing some oppressive and unnecessary ceremonies'; and that there should be 'a general synod of the most grave, pious, learned and judicious divines . . . who may consider of all things necessary for the peace and good government of the Church'.

The *Grand Remonstrance* was bound to split the Commons, as the moderates were organising themselves under the leadership of Edward Hyde. But Pym was not prepared to make concessions, since the outbreak of the Irish Rebellion had convinced him of the need for the 'godly' to act swiftly, before their enemies could recover lost ground. He therefore pressed ahead with the *Grand Remonstrance*. The final debate on this document opened at noon on 22 November 1641 and went on until past midnight. The House eventually divided and the vote was taken by candlelight. With 159 members voting in favour of the *Remonstrance*, and 148 voting against, a majority of eleven was achieved. The moderates immediately claimed the right to enter a protest, and members sprang to their feet, reaching for their swords. 'I thought we had all sat in the valley of the shadow of death', wrote one of them, 'for we, like Joab's and Abner's young men, had catched at each other's locks and sheathed our swords in each other's bowels, had not the sagacity and great calmness of Mr Hampden, by a short speech, prevented it.'

The *Grand Remonstrance* was regarded at the time and later as a turning point. The member for Cambridge, Oliver Cromwell, told Lord

Falkland, one of the moderate leaders, that if it had not been passed 'he would have sold all he had the next morning and never seen England more, and he knew there were many other honest men of the same resolution'. Hyde now despaired of winning the Commons over to moderation and offered his services to the King, hoping thereby to prevent Charles from making mistakes that would widen the gulf between him and Parliament.

While the Commons were debating the *Grand Remonstrance* Charles was on the last stage of his return journey to London. His visit to Scotland had been successful in so far as he had come to terms with the Earl of Argyll (whom he created a marquis), a leading nobleman who had embraced the Covenanting cause. He was also encouraged by the evidence of the continuing popularity of the monarchy in the villages and towns through which he passed on his way to and from Scotland, for crowds of people flocked into the streets to cheer him. Even London gave him a warm reception when he made his state entry on 25 November, and Charles showed his pleasure by knighting the Lord Mayor. But appearances were deceptive, for although the City elite, made up principally of the directors of the East India and Levant Companies, looked to the crown as the guarantor of their trading privileges, the many merchants and businessmen who were outside the charmed circle pinned their hopes on Parliament. In the elections for the Common Council which took place in December 1641 the radicals won control, and from then on the City was to be numbered among the King's most committed opponents.

Charles, at Hyde's suggestion, set out to win over the moderate members of Parliament by making the sort of bridge appointments that Bedford had earlier advocated. He even went so far as to offer Pym the Chancellorship of the Exchequer, and when Pym declined he gave it instead to Sir John Colepeper, one of Hyde's associates. Another of the moderates, Viscount Falkland, renowned for his integrity and love of peace, was persuaded by Hyde, who was his close friend, to accept office as Secretary of State.

However, at the same time as Charles was making these gestures of reconciliation he was preparing a *coup d'état* against the militants, for he shared Pym's belief in the existence of a conspiracy, though he was convinced that the principal conspirators were to be found in the House of Commons, not the court or Privy Council, and that they were aiming at nothing less than the destruction of his monarchy. On 3 January 1642 the Attorney-General, acting on the King's instructions, appeared before the House of Lords, where he impeached one peer, Lord Mandeville, and five members of the Commons – John Pym, John Hampden, Arthur Hazelrig,

Denzil Holles and William Strode – of high treason. They were accused of subverting the fundamental laws by attempting to deprive the King of his rightful prerogatives, alienating the affections of his subjects from him, and conspiring with the Scottish rebels.

Charles assumed that the Lords would order the arrest of the impeached members, as they had done with Strafford, but in fact they thought his initiative ill-conceived, and refused to take any action. On the following day, therefore, Charles made his way to Westminster, accompanied by a bodyguard, and entered the Commons. 'By your leave, Mr Speaker,' he said, 'I must borrow your chair a little', and stepping on to the dais he scanned the rows of faces to see if the Five Members were among them. When he realised they were not present he turned to the Speaker and demanded to know where they had gone. William Lenthall, in an uncharacteristic moment of greatness, fell on his knees and answered 'May it please your majesty, I have neither eyes to see nor tongue to speak in this place but as the House is pleased to direct me, whose servant I am here.' Charles knew that his *coup* had failed. 'Well', he replied, 'since I see all the birds are flown I do expect from you that you shall send them unto me as soon as they return hither', and he made his way out of the House amid a clamour of voices and shouts of 'Privilege! Privilege!'

The Five Members, who had been warned of Charles's plan by friends at court, had taken refuge with puritan radicals in the City. Charles drove in to the City and called on the Common Council to hand over the fugitives so that they might stand trial, but the citizens would not abandon their heroes, and angry crowds surged round the King's carriage as he went back, empty-handed, to Whitehall. London was becoming too dangerous a place for Charles and his family to stay in, and on 10 January 1642 he left for Hampton Court. The next day the Five Members returned in triumph to Westminster.

The drift towards war

By abandoning London the King had given a trump card to his opponents, for the capital was the seat of government. As reports reached the two Houses of armed men gathering in various parts of the country they ordered that the counties should 'put themselves in a posture of defence', which meant calling out the trained bands. Technically speaking such commands were invalid, since only the King had the right to issue them, but the very name of Parliament carried authority and the governors of the localities had no way of knowing whether, in any particular instance,

'Parliament' meant the two Houses acting alone or that nebulous but all-powerful entity known as the 'King-in-Parliament'. The general fear of catholic conspiracy made it essential that the trained bands, the county militias, should be in the hands of men who were committed both to protestantism and parliamentary rule. Charles, who was trying to restore his own credibility after the Five Members' incident, agreed in principle that Parliament should nominate the Lord Lieutenants as long as their commissions ran in his name and could be revoked when he saw fit. He also accepted the Bishops' Exclusion bill which the Lords, in the panic atmosphere created by the King's failed *coup*, had finally passed. But Pym and the majority in the Commons were determined not to compromise on the vital question of who should control the trained bands, and the two Houses therefore issued their bill as the Militia Ordinance, to which they demanded obedience from all the King's subjects.

Parliament, by issuing the Militia Ordinance, had stepped over the invisible line that divided constitutional action from innovation, and Charles, under Hyde's guidance, accused it of breaking the fundamental laws which he was committed to protect. By June 1642 the royal propaganda campaign was in full flood, and in the following month Charles published an open letter to the judges who were about to set out on their assizes. In it he asserted his determination to maintain the protestant Church of England and to rule according to law. In many places his words fell on receptive ears. Yet events were moving at such a pace that the King could not wait for a gradual change in public perceptions to take effect. In February 1642 he had sent his wife over to Holland, carrying with her the crown jewels, which she was to pawn in order to raise money for the purchase of arms and ammunition, for Charles was determined to fight rather than make further concessions. 'What would you have?' he asked a parliamentary delegation that waited on him at Newmarket in March. 'Have I violated your laws? Have I denied to pass one bill for the ease and security of my subjects? I do not ask you what you have done for me. God so deal with me and mine as all my thoughts and intentions are upright for the maintenance of the true protestant profession and for the observation and preservation of the laws of this land.' The Earl of Pembroke, who was one of the delegates, urged him to give up his right of appointing Lord Lieutenants, even if only for a limited period, but Charles would have none of it. 'By God, not for an hour!' he told Pembroke. 'You have asked that of me in this was never asked of a King.'

While Charles was ready to fight to preserve his rights, it became clear, as he made his way north to York, that his subjects wanted a peaceful resolution of the differences between him and the two Houses. He had already called on them to state their terms, and they eventually did so in the *Nineteen Propositions* sent to him in June 1642. These contained demands that Parliament should control appointments to the principal military and civil offices; that 'no public act ... may be esteemed of any validity, as proceeding from royal authority, unless it be done by the advice and consent of the major part of your Council, attested under their hands'; and that 'such a reformation be made of the Church government and liturgy as both Houses of Parliament shall advise'.

These were terms that, as the parliamentary leaders knew full well, Charles would never accept. In fact, he regarded the *Nineteen Propositions* as clear proof that they were not interested in a negotiated settlement. Since they had taken over control of the Lieutenancy through the Militia Ordinance – which he denounced as illegal – he reverted to the pre-Lieutenancy device of issuing Commissions of Array. These were directed to named individuals in every county and major city, and instructed them to raise forces on the King's behalf. The commissions were sent out in June 1642; in July the King's recruiting campaign got under way; and on 22 August Charles raised the royal standard at Nottingham. It was a call to arms, for civil war was now inevitable.

CHAPTER FIFTEEN

The Civil War

Roundheads and Cavaliers

In June 1642 the Commons felt certain the King would have to accept their demands because he would find no-one to fight for him, yet four months later Charles was advancing on London with an army of some ten thousand men. From that time until the present day the problem of who fought for whom, and why, has engaged the attention of historians, but it still defies any clear-cut and all-embracing solution. As far as the ordinary soldier was concerned, pay and the chance of plunder, as well as traditional loyalties, seem to have been the main incentives. But the political nation, which had been united in opposition to prerogative taxation and Arminianism in 1640, split apart for a variety of reasons, of which the most important was religion. The Civil War was fought between those who wanted to preserve the episcopal Church of England, especially now that it had been cleansed of its Laudian accretions, and those who wanted either an alternative, non-episcopal Church or total liberty for all men and women to worship as they wished – provided, of course, that they were not catholics or anglicans.

In many, if not most, counties the immediate reaction to the outbreak of fighting was a determination to hold aloof from the struggle. Where a county community was divided in its opinions, 'neutralism' reflected the desire to maintain harmony, for the gentry were fully aware that divisions between them would endanger the social order, which was already under strain from economic depression. Yet commitment to the county community might well be at odds with commitment to the religious community, whether of the 'godly,' the conformists or the papists. In Herefordshire, for example, where the gentry were overwhelmingly royalist, the puritan Sir Robert Harley and his wife, despite their ties of blood and friendship with their neighbours, felt compelled to side with Parliament.

Elsewhere the converse was true, for although the 'godly' professed their desire to maintain the social order it seemed to many of their compatriots that they were unleashing forces which threatened it far more than the King had ever done. Moderates were appalled by reports from many parts of the country that common men and even women were mounting into pulpits and preaching what they claimed to be the word of God as it had been directly revealed to them. Sir Edward Dering – a Kentish gentleman who, in an unguarded moment, had agreed to introduce the Root-and-Branch bill into the Commons – told the House in November 1641 how shocked he had been when a 'bold mechanic [i.e. artisan]' had said to him 'I hope your worship is too wise to believe that which you call your creed.' Dering's comment that 'one absurdity leads in a thousand, and when you are down the hill of error there is no bottom but in hell', must have struck home. It was echoed in an outburst by a former Lord Mayor of London about the general lack of respect for rank and dignity. 'Before God,' he exclaimed, 'I have no more authority in the City than a porter ... If to be governed by people whose authority we know not, and by rules which nobody ever heard of or can know, be a sign of arbitrary power, we have as much of it as heart can wish.'

The King knew that one of his main strengths came from his identification with the traditional social order. In his reply to the *Nineteen Propositions*, which was drafted by Falkland and Colepeper, Charles warned that Parliament was opening the way for the common people to 'set up for themselves, call parity and independence liberty [and] destroy all rights and proprieties, all distinctions of families and merit'. By such means, he declared, 'this splendid and excellently distinguished form of government' would collapse in chaos and confusion, 'and the long line of our many noble ancestors [would end] in a Jack Cade or a Wat Tyler'. Charles extended the same analysis into the religious sphere when he told his troops in September 1642 that they would 'meet with no enemies but traitors, most of them Brownists, anabaptists and atheists, such who desire to destroy both Church and state'.

Not everybody was convinced by the King's arguments. His opponents included many of the gentry and 'middling sort' who were equally concerned to see the social order preserved, along with a truly protestant Church, but believed that only Parliament could be trusted to ensure this. In fact, both King and Parliament claimed to be fighting for the same causes, which made it difficult for ordinary people to choose between them. The adherence of a community to one side or the other was often determined by a committed minority, and it is therefore mistaken to assume that certain regions were wholeheartedly parliamentarian while others were wholeheartedly royalist. Almost the only area of which this is true was Wales, which never wavered in its loyalty to the King. Elsewhere the pattern was a complex one of varied and shifting allegiances. Essex, for instance, was one of the first counties to put the Militia Ordinance into effect and took the lead in providing troops for the parliamentary armies, yet there was a significant body of opinion within the county that favoured a compromise with the King.

The Civil War

By the autumn of 1642 Charles had an army of some six thousand foot and 3,500 horse and was ready to strike at London, the nerve-centre of his enemies. In mid-October he left Shrewsbury and moved south-east towards the capital, taking with him his twenty-three-year-old nephew Rupert, one of the sons of the Winter Queen, who had come to England to fight for him. The Earl of Essex, who had been appointed by the two Houses to command the parliamentary forces, marched out to meet the King, and the two armies clashed at Edgehill, north of Banbury in Oxfordshire. In this first engagement of the war the pattern was set for many of the later encounters. Rupert's cavalry, on one wing, charged right through their opponents and disappeared into the distance. But the round-head cavalry on the other wing broke the royalist line and captured the King's standard. It was left to the infantry to decide the outcome, but by the time night fell neither side had won a decisive advantage. The King was ready to give battle again the next morning, but Essex drew off his men and left the road to London open.

Rupert was all for a swift advance upon the capital, but Charles, shocked by the slaughter he had witnessed and understanding for the first time what war entailed, let Essex march round him and enter London first. However, Charles followed up the earl, and by early November his army had reached Brentford, on the western outskirts of the city. There his advance stopped, for winter was drawing in and the approaches to London were so heavily defended that savage fighting would have been needed to break through them. Charles therefore pulled back his troops and established his headquarters at Oxford. Meanwhile, discontent was mounting in the capital. Royalist forces in control of Newcastle had cut the supply of coal to London, where a little over half the Commons and about a fifth of the Lords exercised power in the name of King and Parliament. Theatres were closed, food was dear, fuel prohibitively expensive, and the failure to obtain the swift victory that Pym had predicted revived the peace party in Parliament. Early in 1643 parliamentary commissioners arrived at Oxford to try to negotiate a settlement, but on the fundamental questions of Church reform and the accountability of royal ministers the gap between the two sides was too great to bridge. There was not even agreement on a temporary cessation of hostilities. Charles, elated by the news that his forces in Cornwall had been victorious at Braddock Down (halfway between Bodmin and Plymouth), was coming to realise, as Parliament was later to do, that armies raised to strengthen his negotiating position might open the way to total victory, after which no concessions would be needed.

The Commons were divided over the question of what to do next. Holles – who, as one of the Five Members, had no reason to love Charles – was in favour of peace at almost any price, but at the other extreme there were men like Henry Marten who was prepared to fight until the King was destroyed. Between these two wings came the mass of members, and Pym had to move skilfully to avoid antagonising them, in order to secure the passing of measures needed to finance the war. He persuaded the House to order the confiscation of all property belonging to royalists in areas controlled by Parliament and to impose a regular weekly assessment throughout the kingdom. He could count on the support of London's governors after the election of his ally, Isaac Pennington, as Lord Mayor in 1642, but below that level there was no unanimity. The richer merchants wanted peace and gave a sympathetic ear to royalist propaganda. But there was also a radical group that set up its own committee and took as its hero Sir William Waller, the parliamentary commander in the west, rather than Essex, whom it accused of not wanting outright victory.

Both sides used the winter of 1642–3 to improve their organisation. The King ordered the sequestration of the estates of parliamentary sympathisers and also imposed a regular assessment on the counties he controlled. He was not desperately short of money. His richer supporters made generous gifts to the royal coffers and also raised men at their own expense, while Oxford and Cambridge colleges sent the King much of their silver plate to be melted down. But the defection of the fleet – which, under the Earl of Warwick, had declared for Parliament – was a serious blow, since it meant that the King could not collect Customs duties from ships entering London and other major ports. For arms he depended on the capture of local arsenals and supplies from abroad. Hull, on the north-east coast, would have been a valuable acquisition, not only as a port but also for its well-stocked magazine, but it stood firm for Parliament. However, there were many smaller places from which royalists could operate, and the King managed to keep his supply routes open.

Charles had established his court at Oxford, which was well placed to serve as a rendezvous for the forces being raised on his behalf in the west and midlands. The King intended to launch widespread attacks on his enemies when the campaigning season opened in 1643, and at first all went according to plan. In June, the Earl of Newcastle, commander of the royalist army in the north, brought Sir Thomas Fairfax to battle at Adwalton Moor, near Bradford, and heavily defeated him. Yorkshire was now effectively under the King's control, and siege was laid to Hull. In the following month the parliamentary forces under Sir William Waller were virtually wiped out at the battle of Roundway Down, to the north of Devizes in Wiltshire, and by September Sir Ralph Hopton, who commanded the King's troops in the west, had pushed as far east as Arundel in Sussex. But the most resounding victory was won by Rupert, who had been sent to besiege Bristol, the second largest port in the kingdom and far too dangerous and powerful to be left in the rear of the advancing cavalier armies. In July 1643 Rupert took the city by storm, and the news sent royalist spirits soaring.

These defeats intensified the jockeying for power in Parliament. Three main groups had now emerged, though each could count on only thirty or so adherents, and their total numbers amounted to less than half the active membership of the Commons. The peace party were desperately anxious for a settlement, and were prepared to trust the King if he agreed to maintain the constitutional, non-prerogative monarchy re-established by the legislation of 1641. The war party, on the other hand, wanted outright victory, leading to a dictated settlement that would go well beyond that of 1641. They were determined to reconstruct the Church of England along puritan lines and to limit the King's powers to such an extent that he would never be able to go back on the concessions he had been forced to make. Between these two extremes tacked a middle group, of which Pym was the most prominent member. Its adherents agreed with the peace party in being prepared to accept the 1641 legislation as a basis for settlement, but they also insisted on a puritan reshaping of the established Church.

Following the defeat of the parliamentary forces in the summer of 1643 the peace party put forward its proposals, which were only narrowly rejected. Now the initiative passed to the war party, which with the support of its radical allies in London campaigned for the vigorous prosecution of the war through the appointment of a more committed commander-in-chief than Essex. Pym may have had reservations about

Essex's military capacity, but the earl was too valuable a political ally for him to dispense with. He therefore persuaded the Commons to give Essex command of an army to be raised largely from the London trained bands, which would march north-west to block the King's advance. He also secured their acceptance of his proposal to approach the Scots, who felt threatened by the King's successes, and invite them to intervene once again in English affairs. Parliamentary commissioners were nominated – of whom the most influential was Sir Henry Vane the younger, son of Charles's former Secretary of State – and sent to Edinburgh to negotiate an alliance.

Pym was by now a dying man, but he managed to complete his reorganisation of the financial system by getting the Commons to approve the levy of an excise on a wide range of goods being traded within the country. He lived long enough to know that his faith in Essex had been justified. In September 1643 the earl caught up with Charles's army at Newbury in Berkshire, and mauled it so badly that the King drew back his forces. There was no more question now of his advancing on London. The parliamentary army returned home in triumph, yet the overall situation was one of stalemate, and both sides were looking for a way out. The King was hoping for reinforcements from Ireland, where his commander, the Earl of Ormond, had signed a truce with the rebels in September 1643. Charles was also, on Hyde's advice, preparing to appeal to all moderate men by summoning a Parliament to Oxford. This body, which assembled early in 1644, consisted of about thirty peers and over a hundred members of the Commons, and Hyde hoped it would serve as both a symbol and a guarantee that the King had abandoned all thought of prerogative rule.

The Westminster Parliament also had extended its appeal by setting up an Assembly of Divines to reconcile differing opinions in religion and make recommendations for a settlement of the Church. There was no question of episcopacy being retained, since the Scots had demanded, as the price for their military intervention, that the Church should be remodelled along presbyterian lines. Parliament apparently committed itself to this by adopting the *Solemn League and Covenant*, whereby members swore to make a religious settlement 'according to the word of God and the example of the best reformed Churches'. The Scots believed that their own Church was one of the 'best reformed' and assumed that Parliament had now pledged itself to establish presbyterianism as it was already practised north of the border. But not all puritans were presbyterians. Vane, for instance, was deeply opposed to this form of religion and had accepted the approved wording because it satisfied the Scots but left the English uncommitted – at least in his opinion. In this respect it is significant that when a Committee of Both Kingdoms was set up in January 1644 to co-ordinate the direction of the war, its twenty-one members included only six presbyterians.

In 1644 the tide of war began to turn against the King. The Scots crossed the border in January with an army of twenty thousand men and drove the Marquis (formerly Earl) of Newcastle back towards York. In the same month Sir Thomas Fairfax, in a westward swoop from Yorkshire, fell on the troops who had just landed from Ireland and captured most of them at Nantwich, south of Manchester. A further setback for the King came in March, when Waller defeated his western army at Cheriton, just outside Winchester. It was now a matter of urgency to save the northern army, which was bottled up in York. Charles therefore instructed Rupert that 'all new enterprises laid aside, you immediately march . . . with all your force to the relief of York'.

Rupert had about fifteen thousand men, but was outnumbered by his opponents, for the Scots had been joined by the army of the Eastern Association under the Earl of Manchester, and also by Fairfax and his vic-torious soldiers. As the Prince advanced, the investing forces drew off and marched to intercept him, but in a brilliant manoeuvre Rupert swung round them and entered the city that Newcastle had so gallantly defended. Newcastle wanted to rest his tired men, but Rupert, conscious of the King's orders, insisted on an immediate engagement.

The two armies drew up on Marston Moor, outside York, on 2 July 1644. Oliver Cromwell – who had transformed himself from a member of the Commons into a brilliant soldier – was on one wing of the parliamen-tary army, commanding the cavalry of the Eastern Association. Fairfax and the northern cavalry were on the other wing, while the Scottish infantry were concentrated in the centre. In the royalist army Rupert com-manded the cavalry opposite Cromwell, Lord Goring was in charge of the other wing, while the centre was composed of Newcastle's infantry, raised at his own expense. The day was drawing to a close and Rupert, deciding there would be no fighting until morning, allowed his troops to break ranks. Cromwell saw his opportunity, charged, and drove Rupert's cavalry from the field. As he did so, Goring's horse advanced to the attack and broke right through Fairfax's cavalry. Everything now depended upon the speed with which either side could exploit its victory, and here the advan-tage went to Cromwell, who had trained his men not to scatter in pursuit of the fleeing enemy but to rein in their horses and wait for further orders. Newcastle's infantry were gradually overcoming their Scottish opponents when Cromwell brought back his cavalry, swept away the remains of Goring's horse, and attacked Newcastle's men from the flank.

The Yorkshire infantry refused to give way and were cut down where they stood. With them died the King's hopes of holding the north. York, which Charles regarded as one of the brightest jewels in his crown, surrendered to Fairfax, and the Marquis of Newcastle fled to the continent. Cromwell, meanwhile, wrote to inform the Commons that 'truly England and the Church of God hath had a great favour from the Lord in this great victory given to us, such as the like never was since this war began ... God made them as stubble to our swords'.

Parliament could have won the war after Marston Moor if its armies had been unified and commanded by men determined on victory. But Essex was entangled with the King's forces in Cornwall, while Manchester was playing for time. He had been an opponent of the King from his early days, and in January 1642, when he was still Lord Mandeville, had been accused of treachery, along with the Five Members. Yet Manchester, like Pym, wanted a negotiated settlement, and feared that outright victory would play into the hands of the radicals in the war party and open the way to religious anarchy.

Parliament was far from united on the religious issue. The majority of members of both Houses probably wanted to preserve a national Church. Some were in favour of episcopacy on the 'primitive' or Elizabethan model, but since the *Solemn League and Covenant* ruled out bishops they were prepared to accept what one disgusted Scottish commissioner subsequently described as 'a lame, erastian presbytery'. Others would have welcomed the setting up of an autonomous Scots-style presbyterian Church in England. There was also a small but influential minority of Independents, who believed that every congregation should be self-sufficient. Some of them were willing to accept a loose federation of congregations as a bulwark against anarchy, but not the rigidly centralised structure of provincial and national synods inherent in presbyterianism.

In the Westminster Parliament the majority of episcopalians adhered to the peace party, and had opposed the *Solemn League and Covenant*, yet they now realised that the Scots shared their hostility towards the Independents and their desire for a peace deal with the King. The peace party and the Scots therefore joined forces to persuade Parliament to open negotiations. These began at Uxbridge – roughly halfway between London and Oxford – in early 1645, but they got nowhere. The parliamentary delegates insisted that the King should commit himself to the abolition of episcopacy, the setting-up of a presbyterian Church, and parliamentary control of the militia. Charles offered compromises – which may or may not have been genuine – on all these issues, but the lack of trust in him that had done so much to bring about the war now blocked the path to peace.

Meanwhile, the war party, with strong support from the Independents, had been pressing ahead with a plan to reshape the parliamentary armies as a prelude to victory. They were determined to get rid of the aristocratic commanders who, they believed, were holding up the war effort, but they did not want to antagonise the House of Lords. They therefore framed a Self-Denying Ordinance by which all members of Parliament would lay down their military commands. The Lords held this up while they awaited the outcome of the Uxbridge negotiations, but by mid-February 1645, when it became plain that these were getting nowhere, they passed not only the Self-Denying Ordinance but also one creating a New Model army. Sir Thomas Fairfax was appointed to command this force, and he gave charge of the cavalry to Oliver Cromwell, who was temporarily exempted from the provisions of the Ordinance.

The New Model was a national army, as distinct from the various associations of county forces that had hitherto fought the war, but its military significance should not be exaggerated. It had been in existence only a few months when the King was finally defeated at Naseby, north of Oxford, and in that engagement it was the steadiness of Cromwell's cavalry – mostly drawn from the eastern counties and renowned for their discipline long before the New Model was thought of – that won the day. In the battle, which was fought on 14 July 1645, Rupert again succeeded in driving his opponents from the field, but Cromwell, on the other flank, broke the royalist cavalry opposite him and then turned to attack the infantry. When Rupert returned with his exhausted horsemen he could only look on as Charles's last army was destroyed. After Naseby it was simply a matter of time before the King surrendered. Charles still hoped that more troops might arrive from Ireland, or that Montrose's astonishing successes in Scotland (*see* p. 493) would eventually save him, but by the spring of 1646 he could fight no more. In May he rode into the Scottish camp outside Newark in Nottinghamshire and gave himself up.

The problems of the post-war settlement

Now that the war was over the problems of peace came to the fore, and amongst these the most intractable was the religious settlement. The Westminster Assembly of divines, set up by parliamentary ordinance in July 1643, included both presbyterians and Independents. Its remit was to decide how 'such a government shall be settled in the Church as may be agreeable to God's holy word', and by the beginning of 1645 it had drawn up a *Directory of Worship* to replace the Prayer Book. In the summer of that year it at last submitted to Parliament its plan for setting up a presbyterian Church in England, in accordance with the promise apparently made in the *Solemn League and Covenant*. But members of Parliament were unwilling to accept the proposal that authority to excommunicate should be left in the hands of the ministers of the Church, for they had not destroyed Laudian clericalism merely to submit themselves to a presbyterian version of it. Sir John Holland probably reflected the prevailing mood when he declared that he would as readily 'live under the tyranny of the Turk as the tyranny of the clergy', and in these circumstances it was hardly surprising that Parliament insisted on having the final say in matters ecclesiastical. Once this principle had been accepted, it published the *Directory of Worship* in late 1645 and also prescribed a presbyterian structure for the Church.

Parliamentary action came too late, however, for while the ensuing three years saw the emergence of presbyterian *classes* in London and eleven shires, principally in the south-east and north-west, the majority of counties held aloof. Moreover, with the breakdown of ecclesiastical discipline from 1640 onwards, many congregations had come into existence that acknowledged no external authority. There were thirty-six in London alone, and others had sprung up in the provinces, often linked with army garrisons. If Parliament had been all-powerful it could have imposed presbyterian uniformity, but it had to take into account the strongly sectarian sympathies of the army it had called into being. Cromwell acted as the army's spokesman, for he was convinced that its triumph in the Civil War had signalled God's approval of the way in which religious differences had been subordinated to the common aim. 'Presbyterians, Independents, all have here [i.e. in the army] the same spirit of faith and prayer,' he told Parliament in September 1645. 'They agree here, have no names of difference. Pity it is it should be otherwise anywhere . . . For brethren in things of the mind we look for no compulsion but that of light and reason.'

The ending of the war did not put an end to divisions within Parliament, for the minority groups continued in existence, albeit under different names. The adherents of the former war party were now known as the 'Independents', since they drew their main strength from the religious Independents in the two Houses and their sympathisers among the army officers. The peace party, by contrast, became known as the 'Presbyterians', though not all its members were of that religious persuasion. The middle group survived under its own name and pursued Pym's aim of a settlement based on the legislation of 1641 but with additional safeguards in the shape of parliamentary control of the militia and appointments to high office.

These minority groups were engaged in a constant struggle to win over the uncommitted majority. The 'Presbyterians', under the leadership of Denzil Holles, had the most influence, but the middle group – of which Oliver St John and Lord Saye were the most prominent members – feared that the 'Presbyterians'' overriding aim of returning the country to normality might lead them to sell out to the King. In order to prevent this they allied with the 'Independents'. As a consequence, the propositions presented to Charles at Newcastle in the summer of 1646 were uncompromising. Not only was the King to accept the establishment of presbyterianism on a permanent basis; he was also to give up control of the armed forces for at least twenty years. As Hyde commented, 'whoever understands [the propositions] cannot imagine that, being once consented unto, there are any seeds left for monarchy to spring out of'.

The King's rejection of the *Newcastle Propositions* left the Scots in an awkward position. They could not stay in England indefinitely, but they had no desire to take Charles with them to Scotland, where he might become a focus for dissension. All that kept them south of the border was shortage of money, for their occupation costs had not been fully paid. In September 1646, however, Parliament took steps to raise the required amount by formally abolishing episcopacy and putting the bishops' lands up for sale. By the end of January 1647 the first instalment of money had been paid to the Scots, who were now ready to leave. Before doing so they handed over the King to parliamentary commissioners who, in February, escorted him to honourable captivity at Holdenby House, north-west of Northampton.

Holles and his allies hoped that with the King in their custody they could quickly arrive at a settlement, but they were not prepared to await the outcome of negotiations before disbanding the army, which they regarded as a hotbed of religious and political radicalism. Military rule was unpopular in the localities, for although the county committees that organised the parliamentary war effort had been remarkably efficient, they were frequently dominated by relative newcomers to local government, lacking the social standing that made the élite of upper gentry the natural rulers of the shires. Furthermore, the army cost a great deal to maintain. Kent, to take one example, was paying more by way of the assessment every month than Ship Money had cost it in an entire year.

Holles and the moderates in the Commons knew that if they could make a substantial reduction in the size of the army and return the country to rule by traditional élites they would confirm their hold on power. They therefore decided to send part of the army to restore order in Ireland. The rest was to be disbanded, but if this was to be accomplished peacefully the soldiers would have to be given their arrears of pay. Had this been done, the regiments due for disbanding would probably have gone quietly, but Parliament had committed all available resources to paying off the Scots and it did not dare levy further taxes for fear of provoking popular risings.

Holles and the 'Presbyterians', who were in effective control of the Commons, went some way towards meeting the soldiers' demands. In May 1647 funds were voted for the part payment of their arrears and a comprehensive Indemnity Ordinance was approved. This was very important from the soldiers' point of view, for many of the actions that the exigencies of war had driven them to commit – commandeering horses, for instance – had created widespread resentment among the civilian population, and if they returned home without legal indemnity they would be liable to prosecution. However, the goodwill created by these gestures was offset by Parliament's failure to recognise the army's sense of its own identity and the *esprit de corps* it had developed. By refusing to accept an army petition setting out the case for better treatment it provoked mutinies in several regiments. The mutineers elected representatives – known as 'agitators' because they acted on behalf of their fellows – and these were probably the initiators of the scheme to remove Charles from Parliament's control. In early June 1647 William Joyce, who held the junior rank of Cornet of Horse, appeared at Holdenby House and ordered the King to go with him to Hampton Court. When Charles demanded to see his warrant, Joyce pointed to the line of musketeers outside the main entrance.

The King was now the prisoner of the army, and while he was on his way south the regiments were coming together at Newmarket in Cambridgeshire, where they decided to set up an Army Council representative of both officers and men. The assembled soldiers also took the 'Engagement', by which they swore not to disband until their grievances had been met. Later that month the Army Council drew up a declaration asserting that 'we are not a mere mercenary army, hired to serve any arbitrary power of a state, but called forth ... by ... Parliament to the defence of their own and the people's just rights and liberties'.

Holles and his 'Presbyterian' supporters, now thoroughly alarmed, were attempting to build up a counter-force to the army from among the

London militia and the many ex-soldiers looking for employment. It was this threat that drove the army, for the first time, to take direct action against Parliament. Marching towards London, it established itself at St Albans and called for the impeachment of Holles and ten of his associates in the Commons. When Parliament ignored this demand it moved closer in, to Uxbridge, whereupon the eleven accused members – following the example set by the Five Members in January 1642 – withdrew to the safety of the City. The agitators on the Army Council wanted the advance on London to continue, thereby enabling the 'Independent' minority within Parliament to work out a settlement for Church and state more in accord with the army's preferences. They were restrained by Cromwell, who – as both an army officer and member of the Commons – wished to preserve an element of co-operation between the two institutions rather than impose the army's will. However, his hand was forced by the action of the City apprentices and other supporters of the 'Presbyterians' who invaded the House of Commons in late July 1647 and held down the Speaker while they called for the upholding of the *Covenant* and the return of the Eleven Members. Faced with the threat of continuing violence, the Speaker and some sixty members – including middle-group adherents as well as 'Independents' – sought refuge with the army. At their request the army moved into London in early August and took possession of the capital.

The future pattern of English government now depended on the army, and it presented the King with the *Heads of the Proposals*, summarising its demands. These were, in many respects, more moderate than the *Newcastle Propositions*. As far as the Church was concerned, the way was left open for the restoration of episcopacy, on condition that the bishops should be without any coercive powers and that no set form of service should be made compulsory. In secular matters, Parliament was to have control over the militia and appointment to major offices for at least ten years. But the most remarkable provision was that which called for biennial Parliaments, elected on a franchise that would accurately reflect the distribution of property and wealth throughout the kingdom. This embodied the army's view that parliamentary despotism was no more acceptable than royal tyranny, and that the Commons must respond to the will of the people rather than impose their own.

At this stage another group entered the debate by publishing its demands. The Levellers had emerged from among the radical religious sects in London, but their insistence on freedom of worship brought them up against established authorities and turned them into a political movement. They found supporters among the small traders, craftsmen and shopkeepers in London who had been brought to an exceptional degree of political awareness during the hothouse years of the 1640s, but they also appealed to the thousands of people throughout the country who were disillusioned with Parliament and wanted to see a profound transformation of existing religious and political structures. Their leaders included John Lilburne, Richard Overton and William Walwyn, and they called for freedom of religion, the extension of the franchise, the use of English rather than Latin in law courts, the curbing of trading monopolies, and an end to press censorship.

The Levellers found many sympathisers among the soldiers quartered in and around London, and their shared views were presented in *The Case of the Army Truly Stated*, published in October 1647. *The Case of the Army* put the strictly military demands of the soldiers into the broader Leveller context and posed a direct challenge to the army's high command. This responded by calling the general council of the army into session at Putney, on the western edge of London, where they were joined by Leveller representatives. The object of the meeting, which took place in Putney church, was to discuss the draft Leveller constitution that had just been set out in *The Agreement of the People*, and a series of remarkable debates took place. One of the officers, Colonel Rainsborough, proclaimed his conviction that 'the poorest he that is in England hath a life to live as the greatest he', and went on to argue that men should only live under forms of government to which they had given their assent. This was far too radical for Henry Ireton, who was not simply the formulator of the *Heads of the Proposals* but also Cromwell's son-in-law. 'I think we ought to keep that constitution that we have,' he argued, 'because it is the most fundamental we have, and because there is so much reason, justice and prudence in it.' He was supported by Cromwell, who reminded the Levellers that if they insisted on a new form of government there was nothing to stop other innovators insisting on theirs: 'while we are disputing these things, another company of men shall gather together and put out a paper as plausible perhaps as this'. Such a plethora of proposals, he warned them, would lead only to anarchy.

The Putney debates broke up without agreement, but Cromwell and Ireton had been made aware of the widespread sympathy for Leveller ideals within the army and the need to take an innovative approach to the problem of post-war reconstruction. Outside the army, however, conservative opinion was appalled by the Leveller demands and feared that any concessions would open the way to the destruction of society as it was constituted. Reports reaching the King at Hampton Court painted the radical threat in lurid colours, and in November Charles made his escape to Carisbrooke Castle in the Isle of Wight. From there he opened negotiations with Parliament and the Scots.

Except for a tiny handful of anti-monarchists, both Lords and Commons accepted that there could be no permanent settlement without the King. Disagreement came over the terms to be offered him. The 'Independents' and their middle-group allies were adamant that Charles must accept certain preconditions, such as parliamentary control of the militia, before negotiations started. But the King was pinning his hopes on the Scots and therefore rejected Parliament's conditions. This confirmed the 'Independents' in their suspicion of Charles's good faith, and they concurred with Cromwell's judgement that he was 'so great a dissembler and so false a man that he was not to be trusted'.

The two Houses responded to the King's rejection of their preconditions by passing a vote of No Addresses in January 1648, thereby putting an end to all negotiations. The middle group played a major part in bringing this about, yet by doing so it cut the ground from under its own feet, for it was still committed to the principle of a negotiated settlement. Members of Parliament were not, of course, operating in a political vacuum. They had to take note of the opinions of their constituents, who were crying out for a return to normality. People were tired of having unpaid troops quartered on them, of being threatened by unemployed disbanded men, and, above all, of being harried by the hated excise collectors. The latter were frequently attacked and beaten up, but this only added to the fear that order was breaking down – a fear that was compounded by the harvest failures of 1647–8 that led to a sharp rise in food prices. Popular resentment found an outlet in the 'Clubmen' revolts, and the declaration of the Sussex Clubmen was typical in its condemnation of 'the insufferable, insolent, arbitrary power that hath been used amongst us, contrary to all our ancient known laws ... by imprisoning our persons, imposing of sums of money ... and exacting of loans by some particular persons stepped into authority who have delegated their power to men of sordid condition whose wills have been laws and commands over our persons and estates, by which they have overthrown all our English liberties'. These sentiments were echoed in the petitions sent to Parliament in early 1648, urging the disbandment of the army, the reduction of taxation, and a return to the rule of law.

These petitions came particularly from counties in the south and east that had been parliamentary strongholds during the Civil War, and they demonstrated the extent to which the local communities had become alienated from their present governors. The revolt of the localities was an integral element in the uprisings that broke out in the spring of 1648 and are usually known as the Second Civil War. If the Scots had been ready to move, the risings might have developed into a major challenge to the parliamentary regime, but Fairfax had time to subdue those in Essex and Kent, while Cromwell put down the Welsh revolt before going north to deal with the Scots.

The pressure of public opinion and the need to restore order forced Parliament to reconsider its ban on negotiations with the King. The 'Independents' were adamant in their opposition to any discussions with Charles, but the middle group was prepared to switch its support to the 'Presbyterians' in order to obtain a negotiated settlement. In May 1648, therefore, Parliament rescinded its vote of No Addresses, and in the following September commissioners were dispatched to Newport in the Isle of Wight to open discussions with the King. The new pattern of alliances was symbolised by the fact that the commissioners included not only Holles, the leader of the 'Presbyterians', but also Lord Saye and a substantial middle-group contingent.

By the time the commissioners reached Newport events were moving strongly in favour of the army and their 'Independent' allies. During the early part of 1648, when Parliament was holding aloof from the King, Charles had reached an agreement with the Scots by accepting the temporary establishment of presbyterianism in return for the restoration to him of all the royal prerogatives, including control of the militia. In May, while members of Parliament were agonising over whether or not to rescind their vote of No Addresses, the Scots were arming, and early in July they moved south across the border once again. This second invasion, however, met with a very different response from the first, for the English army was now highly trained and commanded by seasoned officers. As the Scots pushed down through Lancashire, Cromwell caught up with them at Preston in August and, in a hard-fought battle, drove them from the field.

In reporting his victory to Parliament, Cromwell called on it to recognise that 'this is nothing but the hand of God' and to 'take courage to do the work of the Lord in ... seeking the peace and welfare of this land'. Such sentiments might seem unexceptional, but Cromwell's views on the nature of a just settlement and those of the 'Presbyterian'-middle-group allies in Parliament were now poles apart. Cromwell had been with his brother officers at Windsor in the spring of 1648 when the Second Civil

War broke out, and had taken part in a prayer meeting at which they came to 'a very clear and joint resolution ... that it was our duty ... to call Charles Stuart, that man of blood, to an account for the blood he had shed and mischief he had done ... against the Lord's cause and people in these poor nations'. In other words, the settlement to which the army was now committed had no place in it for the King.

Pride's purge and the trial of Charles I

As the army put down rebellion in England and drove the Scots back across the border it became clear to members of Parliament that if they did not reach a swift settlement with the King the army would impose its own. Charles had already agreed to give up control of the militia for twenty years, but he would only consent to the establishment of presbyterianism for a three-year period. These concessions fell short of what the 'Presbyterians' and their middle-group associates had been hoping for, but the circumstances were such that they felt compelled to accept them. On 5 December 1648, therefore, Parliament resolved that the King's answer was 'a ground ... to proceed upon for the settlement of the peace of the kingdom'.

Unfortunately for the members who voted in favour of this resolution, events were no longer under their control. Following the break-up of the alliance between the 'Independents' and the middle group, the more radical 'Independents' had concluded that the only way of achieving their aims was by allying with the army. Ireton wanted a forcible dissolution of Parliament, but the radical 'Independents' persuaded him to ensconce them in power by excluding their enemies. On 6 December, therefore, as members of the Commons arrived to take their seats, they found their way blocked by Colonel Pride, holding a list of names in his hand. Some forty members were arrested, others were turned away, and only a rump of a hundred or so was allowed into the House.

Pride's Purge was a *coup* carried out by the radical wing of the 'Independents' against moderates of all persuasions. This explains why the Rump included a number of 'Presbyterians' while moderate 'Independents' were among those excluded. Yet the radicalism of the men who conceived and executed Pride's Purge was more apparent in the religious than the political sphere. They had no love for established Churches, whether anglican or presbyterian, but they cherished the established social order – indeed, they had been driven to act as they did from fear that the reactionary nature of the settlement reached between the King and the

'Presbyterian'-middle-group alliance might cause an explosion that would tear the social fabric to tatters.

The radical 'Independents' realised that having seized power they would have to make at least a gesture towards popular radicalism. The most obvious gesture, and one to which both the Rump and the army were committed, was the bringing to trial of the King. Parliament, under pressure from the army, set up a high court, under the presidency of a lawyer named John Bradshaw, and it opened its sessions in Westminster Hall on 20 January 1649. Charles had been brought to London as a prisoner of the army, and was now summoned before the high court to answer the charge that 'being admitted King of England, and therein trusted with a limited power to govern by and according to the laws of the land', he had wickedly designed to erect 'an unlimited and tyrannical power to rule according to his will, and to overthrow the rights and liberties of the people'.

Charles never showed to better advantage than at this, the supreme moment of his life. Throughout the proceedings he conducted himself with a calm dignity that impressed even his opponents, and he steadfastly refused to acknowledge the jurisdiction of the court. He took his stand on the known laws. If, he said, the army could set up a court and invent new laws for it to apply, 'I do not know what subject . . . can be sure of his life or anything that he calls his own . . . I do plead for the liberties of the people of England.'

Bradshaw, of course, would not accept that the court over which he presided had no validity, and since the King remained contumacious he proceeded to pronounce judgment that 'the said Charles Stuart, as a tyrant, traitor, murderer and public enemy to the good people of this nation, shall be put to death by severing of his head from his body'. Fifty-nine judges were persuaded to sign the death warrant, and by their authority a scaffold was erected outside the Banqueting House in Whitehall. An enormous crowd gathered there on the afternoon of 30 January 1649, when the King was led out to execution, but only those near the scaffold heard Charles proclaim that he died in the cause of law and the Church. 'For the people,' he said, 'truly I desire their liberty and freedom as much as anybody whomsoever, but I must tell you that their liberty and freedom consist in having of government – those laws by which their life and their goods may be most their own. It is not for having a share in government. Sirs, that is nothing pertaining to them. A subject and a sovereign are clean different things.' As for the Church, Charles declared that 'I die a Christian according to the profession of the Church of England as I found it left me by my father.'

On this occasion there was none of the jubilation that had attended Strafford's execution. The vast crowd was silent until they saw the axe swing in the air, 'at the instant whereof', according to one eye-witness, 'there was such a groan by the thousands then present as I never heard before and desire I may never hear again'. By the manner of his death Charles went far towards wiping out the memory of his eleven years' prerogative rule. For the anglicans he was a saint, for the royalists a martyr who had sacrificed his life to protect the traditional constitution from the abuse of arbitrary power. Cromwell may have been right in believing that the execution of the King was a political necessity, but in carrying it out he created a spectre that was to haunt his own regime and frustrate his efforts to build a stable and godly society out of the ruins of Charles I's England.

CHAPTER SIXTEEN

Commonwealth and Protectorate

The rule of the Rump

The Rump, having got rid of the King, went on to abolish the monarchy, on the grounds that it was 'unnecessary, burdensome and dangerous to the liberty, safety and public interest of the people'. Experience had also shown that 'the House of Lords is useless and dangerous to the people of England', so that was abolished as well. England was now declared to be a 'Commonwealth and Free State' under the rule of a unicameral Parliament, and the government was entrusted to a Council of State under the provisional chairmanship of Cromwell.

Radicals of all sorts welcomed these moves, for they seemed to presage even more fundamental changes. Yet the revolution, in effect, was over, for the Rump, despite its public commitment to early elections, gave no indication of any willingness to dissolve, and it clearly intended that political reform should strengthen, not transform, the existing structure of society. The Levellers were bitterly disappointed. In January 1649 they had persuaded the Army Council to adopt much of their programme, as set out in *The Agreement of the People*, but the Rump was not prepared to consider this document, nor was Cromwell. In the spring of 1649 the Levellers published a number of pamphlets in which they poured scorn upon the unholy alliance of the army and the Rump. One of them declared that the most favourable opportunity for establishing true freedom since the Norman Conquest had been thrown away, and that the conservatives who dominated the Rump had ensured that such changes as were made should be 'only notional, nominal, circumstantial, whilst the real burdens, grievances and bondages be continued, even when the monarchy is changed into a republic'.

Cromwell was particularly alarmed by the revival of Leveller agitation in the army, which prompted sporadic mutinies, and had come to the conclusion that 'there is more cause of danger from disunion amongst ourselves than by anything from our enemies'. He and Fairfax pursued the mutineers into Oxfordshire and caught up with them at Burford, where they suppressed the revolt and executed three of its ringleaders. When Cromwell returned to London he summoned John Lilburne, 'Free-Born John', the principal spokesman for the Levellers, before the Council of State, where that irrepressible champion of popular liberties heard him thumping his fist 'upon the Council table until it rang again, and saying, "I tell you, Sir, you have no other way to deal with these men but to break them in pieces . . . If you do not break them, they will break you."'

From August 1649 until the spring of the following year Cromwell was in Ireland, restoring order to that unfortunate country and forcing it to accept the authority of the new rulers of England. He returned in time to deal with the Scots, who had been angered by the high-handed way in which the English Parliament had dealt with Charles I – who was, after all, *their* King – despite having promised in the *Solemn League and Covenant* 'to preserve and defend the King's majesty's person and authority'. In February 1649 they proclaimed Charles's eldest son King of Scotland and began raising an army to restore him to the English throne.

Fairfax, who had never reconciled himself to the execution of Charles I, resigned his command rather than fight Charles II, so it was left to Cromwell to meet the challenge from the Scots. This he did in what was now becoming his familiar manner. In September 1650 he routed the Scottish army at Dunbar and went on to occupy Edinburgh. His further advance was only halted by illness, which brought him close to death and kept him off the battlefield until the following summer. The Scots took advantage of this opportunity to re-form their army, and in August 1651 they crossed into England, taking with them their new sovereign. Cromwell caught up with them at Worcester on 3 September and won a victory that put an end to royalist hopes. It was, in his own words, 'a crowning mercy'. The young Charles II had to make his way, disguised, to the south coast, where he managed to find a ship to take him to France.

While Cromwell and his fellow officers were away fighting, the Rump ruled England. Despite being regarded as a temporary expedient it was in power for four years, but it never solved any of the major problems with which it was confronted. Initially it bought peace in the army by selling off crown lands and using the money to pay the soldiers their arrears, but at the same time, in order to placate the population at large, it lowered the assessment from £90,000 a month to £60,000. This was insufficient to meet the costs of the military establishment, and the soldiers started complaining once again of lack of pay.

The Rump did little about law reform. The Levellers had called for the creation of county courts and the end of imprisonment for debt, and Parliament duly appointed a committee to take these matters into consideration. In 1652 it also set up an extra-parliamentary commission under Sir Matthew Hale, a distinguished jurist, to survey the whole problem of law reform. The Hale commission adopted many of the Leveller proposals, though with modifications to make them more generally acceptable, but in the event the Rump took no action on its recommendations. One of the reasons for this was the large number of lawyers in Parliament, who constituted nearly a third of its active membership. They were not opposed to the principle of reform of the legal system, but their idea of what constituted significant change was far removed from that of the Levellers.

The religious divisions within the Rump prevented it from resolving the problem of what sort of ecclesiastical organisation would be appropriate for the new republic. In August 1641 a motion to establish presbyterianism had been defeated by the Speaker's casting vote, but no consensus emerged on any alternative. Presbyterians, Independents and sectaries were adept at blocking moves of which they disapproved but lacked the power to impose their own orthodoxies. In the absence of any agreement on how to remunerate incumbents, tithes were retained, even though they were deeply unpopular. There were some minor achievements to the credit of the Rump. The sum of £20,000 was provided to augment clerical stipends where these were inadequate, and a commission was established to redraw parochial boundaries, with the aim of eliminating the grosser inequalities. Not only presbyterians but well over a hundred Independents were appointed to parishes, and the Elizabethan ideal of uniformity gave way to diversity – though Prayer-Book and Roman Catholic services were still officially proscribed. The Rump repealed the statutes making attendance at Sunday services compulsory, but in 1650 it passed an ordinance for the due observance of the Sabbath. Sunday games were firmly suppressed, and other ordinances outlawed adultery, fornication, swearing and blasphemy. Such measures pleased the godly, but they were of limited effect.

Although the Rump was unpopular it was efficient, and its reform of government administration provided a ground plan for the sweeping changes of the later Stuart period. It also enhanced the prestige of Britain abroad by asserting itself with vigour and success. No sooner did it come into existence than it set on foot the construction of a large fleet, mainly to deal with the threat posed by Charles II, who had found refuge in Holland. But the existence of this fleet opened new vistas, especially for the influential nucleus of Rump members who had links with trading companies and regarded the United Provinces as a major commercial rival. The Dutch republic was linked with the Stuart monarchy, since in May 1641 Charles I, anxious to demonstrate his protestant commitment, had married his daughter, Mary, to William of Orange, who was *Stadholder* – a cross between president and prince – of the Netherlands. The execution of Charles I had outraged public opinion in Holland, where it was attributed to the Independents, whom the presbyterian Dutch regarded as little better than sectaries.

When the Rump sent envoys to the United Provinces to propose a union between the two republics, they were deliberately insulted, and the reaction in the Rump enabled the commercial interests represented there to win support for a trade war. This began soon after the passing of the Navigation Act of 1651 which restricted English trade to English vessels. The Rump navy, led by Robert Blake – the son of a Bristol merchant, and the greatest English sailor since Drake – inflicted a series of defeats on the Dutch and blockaded them so effectively that their trade, and with it their livelihood, began to dry up. When the Dutch admiral, Van Tromp, tried to break out of the stranglehold in July 1653, his ships were routed and he himself killed.

The war did nothing to solve the Rump's financial problems, for the fleet was very expensive to maintain. Moreover, armies despatched to Ireland and Scotland were consuming well over a million pounds a year. In order to avoid bankruptcy the government increased the monthly assessment to its highest-ever level of £120,000 in November 1650. It also sold off the confiscated estates of some 750 leading royalists. But these measures failed to put the public finances on a sound footing and they caused intense resentment in the localities, which were having to cope with a continuing economic depression. Lilburne, now a prisoner in the Tower, was expressive of general opinion when he told one of his visitors 'I had rather choose to live seven years under old King Charles's government (notwithstanding their beheading him as a tyrant for it) when it was at the worst, before this Parliament, than live one year under their present government that now rule. Nay, let me tell you, if they go on with that tyranny they are in they will make Prince Charles have friends enough not only to cry him up but also really to fight for him, to bring him to his father's throne.'

Throughout its existence the Rump was a prisoner of the circumstances that had brought it into being. It never had the support of more than a tiny fraction of the English population, as was indicated by the runaway success of *Eikon Basilike*. This book, which purported to have been written by Charles I himself (though it was in fact the work of John Gauden) portrayed the King as a saintly figure concerned only for the spiritual well-being of his subjects. It appeared on the streets shortly after Charles's execution and went through thirty-five editions in one year. The Council of State was so alarmed by the *Eikon Basilike* phenomenon that it commissioned John Milton to write a refutation, but demand for this proved so limited that it never even went into a second edition.

The main weakness of the Rump was its unrepresentative nature. Despite the fact that many of the members excluded by Colonel Pride returned to the House during the course of 1649, it could never convincingly claim to represent the people of England. Only sixty to seventy members took a regular part in debates, and this group included thirty-four who also sat in the Council of State, which was responsible for day-to-day administration. In other words, the government of the Commonwealth was in the hands of a self-appointed oligarchy which, however well intentioned, had no popular mandate. Yet the Rump was in no haste to dissolve itself and order new elections. Members enjoyed the fruits of office, but they were also aware that if free elections were held they would probably produce a royalist Parliament – or at least an anti-army one. Such a result would be unacceptable to both the army and the Commonwealthsmen, yet if elections were ruled out, what other solution was there to the problem of legitimacy? The Rump had no answer to this question. It was playing for time, in the hope that it would eventually be seen as a guarantor of stability and accepted as such by the political nation.

If the Rump had committed itself to a programme of godly reformation the army officers might have been content to keep it in place, but they found the combination of timid pragmatism and immobility unacceptable. Once they had suppressed the rebellions at home and brought Ireland and Scotland to heel they called on the Rump to dissolve itself. In February 1653 the Parliament at last agreed to terminate its existence, but only in November of the following year. The exact nature of its plans remains unclear, but the Rump seems to have decided that it should be replaced by a single chamber of four hundred members elected from among persons of 'known integrity, fearing God, and not scandalous in their conversation'. Since these qualities were not easily assessable, the Rump reserved to itself the right to scrutinise the list of those elected to the new assembly and weed out any of whom it disapproved.

The draft bill was condemned by the army officers, and Cromwell called a meeting between them and some twenty members of the Rump to discuss alternative plans. He thought he had secured agreement that the Rump should hand over power to a much smaller body, nominated by itself, which would carry out the reform programme it had so conspicuously failed to implement. When, on the following day, 20 April 1653, he heard that the majority of members of Parliament had rejected this solution and were pressing ahead with the draft bill, he strode off to the House, calling on his guards to follow him. Once inside, he listened to the debate for a while, his anger mounting until he could sit still no longer. Rising to his feet he shouted at the assembled members 'Come, come! I will put an end to your prating. You are no Parliament! I say you are no Parliament! I will put an end to your sitting.' As the members looked on, stupefied, Cromwell called in his troops and told them to clear the House. Speaker Lenthall was hustled from his chair so quickly that he left the mace, the symbol of civil authority, behind him. When Cromwell caught sight of it he told one of his soldiers to 'take away this bauble', but as Lenthall proudly informed him 'you are mistaken to think that the Parliament is dissolved, for no power under heaven can dissolve them but themselves. Therefore, take you notice of that'.

Oliver Cromwell and the Parliament of Saints

Oliver Cromwell was descended from Henry VIII's minister, Thomas Cromwell, through a nephew who had done well out of the Dissolution of the Monasteries and demonstrated his gratitude by taking his uncle's name. Oliver was born in 1599 to a branch of the family that had settled in Huntingdonshire, and he grew up imbued with nostalgia for the great days of Queen Elizabeth that he had just missed. He was first elected to the Commons in 1628, but he only emerged from obscurity in the Long Parliament. In that assembly he represented Cambridge, and a fellow member described him wearing 'a plain cloth suit which seemed to have been made by an ill country tailor ... His countenance [was] swollen and reddish, his voice sharp and untunable, and his eloquence full of fervour'.

The war showed Cromwell to be a natural leader of men, and it also brought out the radical streak in him. He was a conservative in so far as he wanted to preserve as much as possible of the old social order, but he also recognised that talent took no account of birth or wealth. At times he could use Leveller language, as when he told the Earl of Manchester that he hoped to live to see the day when there was not a nobleman left in England, but he subsequently informed the first Protectorate Parliament that the hierarchy of 'a nobleman, a gentleman, a yeoman' was 'a good interest of the nation, and a great one'. Cromwell had no intention of shaking the foundations of English society, particularly at a time of acute instability. He was uncertain what to do after impulsively expelling the Rump, but was impressed by the suggestion of a fellow officer, Major-General Harrison, that he should call on the assistance of the puritan 'saints' who had set up their Independent and sectarian congregations throughout England and Wales.

Harrison belonged to the Fifth Monarchists, who condemned existing institutions as the work of sin and called for their destruction, and his radical proposal was challenged by the more cautious Lambert, who proposed that the officers should choose a small executive council to prepare the way for new elections. In the event the two schemes were fused. The officers nominated a new assembly, which included members from Scotland and Ireland as well as a substantial number of 'saints'. For this reason the 'Nominated Assembly' soon became known as 'The Parliament of Saints'. It was also called the 'Barebones Parliament' after one of its most prominent members, Praise-God Barbon or Barebones, a London leather-seller and Independent minister.

Not all the 144 members of the Nominated Assembly were 'saints'. The majority were property-owners, men of substance in the traditional mould, and the Speaker was Francis Routh, Pym's half-brother. But there were many more lesser gentry in this Parliament than in former ones, as well as a dozen or so Fifth Monarchists. At its opening session in July 1653 Cromwell told the Assembly that he expected it to sit for a year only, and then appoint another body to 'take care for a succession in government'. However, Harrison and the hard core of 'saints' were determined to seize the opportunity to push through a radical reform programme, and they claimed all the authority that previous parliaments had exercised. They persuaded the Assembly to make a symbolic gesture by choosing the former House of Commons as its meeting place and sending for the mace that Cromwell had treated with such scorn. In the event, the Parliament of Saints had only five months of existence, but during that time it passed over thirty acts.

The Parliament followed in the steps of the Rump by appointing a committee to consider law reform, but there the resemblance stopped, because the committee had no lawyers on it. Perhaps for this reason it made far-reaching recommendations, including the abolition of the Court of Chancery (notorious for its interminable delays) and the simplification and codification of the law, especially concerning the treatment of debtors. These measures alarmed the conservative majority in the Assembly, which regarded the law as one of the last surviving bulwarks of property, but they were outmanoeuvred by the radical minority.

The Assembly managed to maintain a semblance of harmony until it turned to the question of Church reform. Most members wanted to retain tithes as a means of paying ministers, and property-owners, in particular, wanted to hold on to their income from impropriate tithes. The sectarians, however, were firm supporters of the principle that every congregation should maintain its own minister, and when the question was debated, in December 1653, their views prevailed, albeit by a narrow majority. The way now seemed open for a radical reconstruction of the Church.

Cromwell was not happy with this development. In his opinion the proposed legislation would 'fly at liberty and property ... Who could have said that anything was their own if they had gone on?' Even worse, from his point of view, was the radicals' populist campaign to get rid of the excise and reduce the monthly assessment. Such measures would doubtless gain them support in the country at large, but they were likely to drive the army into revolt. It was doubtless with Cromwell's tacit consent, therefore, that on 12 December 1653 the moderate majority in the Parliament arrived at the House before the radicals, who were attending a prayer meeting, and made speeches accusing them of undermining the Church, the army, property and the law. They then processed to Whitehall, where they formally resigned their authority into Cromwell's hands. When the radicals eventually made their way to the empty House they decided on a sit-in. Cromwell sent troops to remove them, and when the colonel in charge asked the recalcitrant members what they were doing there, they replied 'We are seeking the Lord.' 'Then you may go elsewhere,' said the Colonel, 'for to my certain knowledge He has not been here these twelve years.'

The Protectorate

The failure of the Parliament of Saints confirmed what Rumpers had instinctively known, that 'godly rule' was incompatible with the existing framework of society. Cromwell would never accept this. Not long before his death he declared that 'if anyone whatsoever think the interest of Christians and the interest of the nation inconsistent or two different things, I wish my soul may never enter into their secrets'. However, his brief honeymoon with the sects was over, and he now turned to Lambert and accepted his draft constitution, entitled *The Instrument of Government*. The Rump and the Parliament of Saints had both demonstrated the need for a powerful executive to hold the legislature in check. The *Instrument* therefore provided that 'the supreme legislative authority ... shall be and reside in one person and the people assembled in Parliament, the style of which person shall be "The Lord Protector of the Commonwealth of England, Scotland and Ireland."'

Lambert did not intend the *Instrument* to be a constitutional fig leaf, covering the nakedness of military dictatorship. The authority of the Protector was balanced by that of Parliament and also the Council of State, nominated in the *Instrument*. Cromwell praised the constitution specifically because 'it limited me and bound my hands to act nothing to the prejudice of the nations without consent of a council [and] Parliament'. As Lord Protector he would be responsible, in conjunction with the Council of State, for administration and foreign affairs, but although he was provided with a permanent revenue to maintain his household and the armed forces, he was dependent upon Parliament for any extra supply. Parliament was to be summoned at least once every three years and was not to be dissolved without its own consent until it had sat for a minimum of five months. The Protector could hold up bills for twenty days, after which time they were to become law with or without his consent, unless they were clearly contrary to the provisions of the *Instrument*.

The unicameral Parliament was to consist of four hundred members for England and Wales and thirty each for Scotland and Ireland. Some places not previously represented, such as Halifax, Leeds and Manchester, were given seats, while many rotten boroughs were disfranchised. The right to vote was confined to those who held property or goods worth £200, and the number of county members was increased at the expense of the boroughs. In the Long Parliament there had been ninety representatives of the counties in a Lower House numbering more than five hundred members. Now, in a smaller House, there were two hundred and sixty-four. Cromwell liked the idea of a Parliament dominated by the country gentry, from which group he had sprung, but their independence of spirit made them difficult partners in the business of government.

The Instrument of Government was in many respects a conservative document. It signalled the end of a decade of innovation and the return to something more like the traditional pattern of English government. Only in the religious sphere did it break away from earlier assumptions, for

Cromwell and his fellow officers were adamant that while the state should give its formal approval and support to the Church it should not impose uniformity. Cromwell believed that religious liberty had been the greatest gain from the Civil War. 'Religion was not the thing at first contended for,' he said, 'but God brought it to that issue at last, and ... it proved that which was most dear to us. And wherein consisted this more than in obtaining that liberty from the tyranny of the bishops to all species of protestants to worship according to their own light and consciences?' It was in accordance with this belief that the *Instrument* provided 'that such as profess faith in God by Jesus Christ (though differing in judgement from the doctrine, worship or discipline publicly held forth) shall not be restrained from, but shall be protected in, the profession of the faith and exercise of their religion'.

This liberty was not, in theory, extended to anglicans or Roman Catholics, but in practice they were allowed a great deal of latitude. In London and many country areas anglicans were able to attend Prayer-Book services, and as for catholics, the abrogation of the penal laws and the abolition of High Commission and the Church courts left them freer than at any time since the Reformation. Nor was the principle of religious liberty applied only to Christians, for in 1656 Cromwell persuaded the Council of State to agree to the readmission of Jews to England, thereby reversing the expulsion carried out by Edward I in 1290. As far as the parochial organisation of the Church was concerned, Cromwell built on the foundations laid by the Parliament of Saints. Livings were left in the gift of patrons, but in 1654 'Triers' were appointed to examine candidates for the ministry and make sure they met minimum standards of learning and godliness. The majority of the Triers were Independents, but presbyterians and baptists were also included. Furthermore, in order to prevent the re-emergence of clericalism, a third of all Triers were laymen. At the county level the Triers were complemented by lay 'Ejectors' (with clerical advisers) who were authorised to expel ministers and schoolmasters found guilty of 'scandalous living'.

The first Protectorate Parliament, on which Cromwell was pinning his hopes for a permanent settlement, did not meet until September 1654. In the interim he persuaded the Council of State to cut the monthly assessment from £120,000 to £90,000. He also joined with Councillors in drawing up and promulgating more than eighty ordinances, as provided for in the *Instrument*. These dealt mainly with security and legal matters. In the first category came the ban on race meetings, cock-fights, and similar public assemblies which could provide a cover for seditious activities, while the second category included an ordinance regulating, but not abolishing, the Court of Chancery. The ordinances were essentially pragmatic and did not add up to a coherent reform programme, although it was hoped they would be generally acceptable to the gentry who were about to assemble in Parliament.

The parliaments of the Protectorate were strictly speaking new institutions, depending for their existence upon *The Instrument of Government*, yet their members were drawn from the same gentry background as in former parliaments, and they quickly made it plain that they regarded themselves as inheritors of the parliamentary tradition. They chose William Lenthall, who had presided over the Commons in 1629 and from 1640, to be their Speaker, and they ordered the mace to be brought in by the Long Parliament's Sergeant-at-Arms. More than a hundred former members of the Long Parliament were elected to the first Protectorate Parliament. Although the majority were moderates there were a number of Commonwealthsmen, committed republicans who regarded Cromwell as the betrayer of 'the good old cause' and were determined to cripple his rule even if they could not bring it to an end.

The Lord Protector had supporters in the House – Councillors of State, officials of his household, members of his family – but he made no attempt to organise them and direct them, as Elizabeth had done. Failing a lead from the government, the republicans seized the initiative and immediately challenged the validity of the *Instrument*. Cromwell responded by surrounding the House with soldiers and calling on members to accept the fundamental principle of rule by a single person and Parliament. The republicans withdrew from the assembly rather than acknowledge the Protectorate, but this did not mean that Parliament now consisted solely of yes-men. Many members were highly critical of the army and wanted to reduce its numbers (and influence) by creating a militia that would take over many of its duties. Cromwell was deeply unhappy about this proposal, which would be unacceptable to the army. He was also offended by attacks upon his policy of religious toleration. The growth of sects such as the baptists and quakers, whose adherents openly displayed their contempt for established social hierarchies, alarmed the gentry who dominated the House and prompted them to support measures against blasphemy and heresy and for the enforcement of attendance at church. But Cromwell regarded religious toleration as one of the most precious achievements of the previous decade, and rather than put it at risk he dissolved Parliament in January 1655. 'Is there not yet upon the spirits of man a strange itch?' he angrily demanded. 'Nothing will satisfy them unless they can put their finger upon their brethren's consciences, to pinch them there ... What greater hypocrisy than for those who were oppressed by the bishops to become the greatest oppressors themselves as soon as their yoke was removed?'

Although Cromwell would not abandon the principle of religious toleration he recognised the need to rein in the sects, and during the absence of Parliament he issued a proclamation making it an offence to disrupt Church services. He also reduced the size of the army from close on sixty thousand to forty thousand, and was thereby able to cut the monthly assessment to £60,000. No doubt he would have been happy to see the influence of the army further diminished, so that he could base his rule firmly on consent, but there was little public enthusiasm for his regime and many royalists remained unreconciled. A group of malcontents under the leadership of John Penruddock organised a rising in Wiltshire in March 1655. It was easily suppressed, but the mere fact of its occurrence suggested that the Justices of the Peace and other local governors had been lax in the performance of their duties.

Cromwell therefore took the drastic step of imposing direct military rule in the localities. England was broken up into ten (later eleven) districts, each under the control of a major-general. These officers were responsible for maintaining security, administering poor relief, regulating the economy, upholding public morality, and enforcing godliness. They were also instructed to raise a new militia from among local supporters of the regime, and pay for it by levying a ten per cent decimation tax on delinquent royalists. Further measures forbade clergy who had been ejected from their livings since 1642 to serve as private chaplains or schoolteachers, and imposed heavier penalties on anyone found using the anglican Prayer Book. It seemed as though Cromwell, for the time being at least, had abandoned his aim of creating a consensus that would facilitate a return to civilian rule.

The major-generals varied in effectiveness. In Lincolnshire, Edward Whalley made himself thoroughly unpopular by hounding the magistrates to put down alehouses and suppress many of the entertainments to which the gentry were addicted. Elsewhere the new rulers of the localities were given grudging acceptance and a measure of co-operation. Indeed, without some assistance from local office-holders they would have been unable to carry out their prescribed duties. Yet however efficient and well-intentioned their rule, the presence of the major-generals was an affront to the local elites, who were beginning to return to public life now that the radical Commonwealth had been replaced by the more moderate

Protectorate. Even Cromwell was forced to acknowledge that if he wished to base his regime on consent rather than force he would have to recall his satraps. As he told the army officers, 'it is time to come to a settlement and lay aside arbitrary proceedings, so unacceptable to the nation'.

Cromwell's failure to find a satisfactory constitutional basis for his rule at home contrasted with his success in establishing his reputation abroad. He began by putting an end to the war with the United Provinces that the Rump had begun, and tried, unavailingly, to bring about a union between the two protestant states. He subsequently concluded a treaty with Denmark, reopening the Baltic to English shipping, and another with Portugal, which secured English merchants access to the Portuguese colonies. He also decided on war with Spain, to revive the glories of Elizabeth's reign and wipe out the humiliation of the 1625 expedition to Cadiz. In the spring of 1655 a force was despatched to the West Indies to capture Hispaniola, which Cromwell thought of as another Providence Island from which the Spanish hold on the area could be challenged. He was confident of success since, as he told the commanders, 'the Lord Himself hath a controversy with your enemies – even with that Romish Babylon', but in the event it seemed that the Lord had turned His head away. The raw British levies could not overcome the resistance of the seasoned Spanish defenders, and Hispaniola remained uncaptured. The subsequent seizure of Jamaica was insufficient compensation in Cromwell's eyes.

During the Protectorate the navy became a full-time regular service with a ladder of promotion and standard rates of pay. Robert Blake commanded the fleet, which carried out an arduous but successful blockade of the Spanish coast all through the winter of 1657 and in April of the following year destroyed a Spanish treasure fleet in the bay of Santa Cruz. Blake died on the journey back to Plymouth, but he had made Britain a more significant maritime power than at any time since Elizabeth's reign. Yet even the Protectorate navy could not safeguard British shipping against the attacks of the Dunkirk privateers. Losses mounted throughout 1656, and the problem was not resolved until two years later, when Cromwell allied with Spain's most powerful enemy, France. British troops fought alongside the French at the Battle of the Dunes in June 1658 and took part in the subsequent capture of Dunkirk. The privateer base was then handed over to Cromwell as his reward.

The outbreak of war with Spain in 1656 made another Parliament necessary, since the government was heavily in debt. Cromwell, like the Stuarts before him, had already been driven into punishing those who challenged his right to tax. In November 1654 George Cony, a silk merchant, refused to pay a levy on Spanish wine on the grounds that it had been imposed by ordinance of the Protector instead of by Parliament. The Protector's right to issue ordinances was clearly set out in *The Instrument of Government*, but this document had never been ratified by Parliament, despite Cromwell's pressure on members to do so. Cromwell was not prepared to have the validity of the *Instrument* tested in the courts, and he therefore ordered Cony and his legal counsel to be imprisoned until such time as they agreed to drop their case. Two judges had earlier been dismissed for questioning the authority of the *Instrument*. Now one of the chief justices resigned rather than be party to the high-handed treatment of Cony, which savoured too much of the Personal Rule of Charles I.

The second Protectorate Parliament assembled in September 1656. The Council of State excluded nearly a hundred members whom it regarded as troublemakers, whereupon another sixty refused to take any further part in proceedings. As for the two hundred or so members who remained, many were deeply critical of Cromwell's tolerant approach in religion, particularly where quakers were concerned. The quakers were one of the most successful of the sects, and their numbers had risen to about thirty thousand by the late 1650s. Their refusal to doff their hats to social superiors, or to swear an oath, or to make any signs of outward conformity, outraged the traditional rulers of the localities, who treated them harshly. Parliament followed suit by imposing savage punishment upon James Nayler, a prominent quaker, who had re-enacted in Bristol Christ's entry into Jerusalem, with himself in the leading role. The House found him guilty of 'horrid blasphemy' and sentenced him to be branded and flogged and have a hole bored through his tongue. Parliament claimed the right to act in this judicial capacity by virtue of its descent from 'the High Court of Parliament'. This assumption was technically incorrect, but although Cromwell called on the House to explain by what right it had taken action against Nayler he was not willing to risk an open breach now that war with Spain had broken out. Nevertheless, the episode rankled with him, especially since it had shown up the weakness of the existing constitution. Members of Parliament, he told his officers, 'by their judicial authority ... fall upon life and limb; and doth the Instrument in being enable me to control it? ... The case of James Nayler might happen to be your own case'.

Cromwell realised that the *Instrument* needed to be modified or replaced, and he was listening to a range of opinion, including that of the former royalist, Lord Broghill, who urged him to break with the military and establish his regime on a civilian basis. A test of strength between the military element in Parliament and its civilian opponents was inadvertently provoked by Major-General Desborough just before Christmas 1656, when he proposed that the decimation tax should be formally sanctioned by the House. Broghill attacked this suggestion, and in January 1657 Parliament rejected it. Members followed up the defeat of the military interest by voting the generous provision of £400,000 for the war against Spain, thereby showing Cromwell that there could be a civilian solution to the problems confronting him.

The moderates in Parliament, encouraged by their initial success, took the lead in drawing up a constitution based on a limited monarchy of the sort that Pym and the Junto had tried to construct in 1640–1. *The Humble Petition and Advice*, which was the outcome of their deliberations, was presented to Cromwell in March 1657. It called on him to assume the title of King and appoint members to a newly created Upper House of Parliament. Cromwell took time to consider this offer. As King, he would wield an authority which would be not merely traditional but demonstrably civilian, yet for this reason the army was likely to oppose the change. Some of the generals, such as John Lambert, had ambitions of their own and did not want to be barred from succeeding Cromwell by the establishment of a hereditary succession. Among the junior officers there were many who felt that the Civil War had been fought to overthrow monarchy, and that any return to kingship would be a betrayal of their ideals. It would also be an affront to God, who had shown by granting victory to the army that He was no lover of kings. What seems to have weighed most with Cromwell himself was the thought that many honest men, 'men that will not be beaten down with a carnal or worldly spirit', would not welcome the advent of King Oliver. In a confused speech that reflected the conflict in his mind, Cromwell declined the crown and asked 'that there may be no hard thing put upon me – things, I mean, hard to them [i.e. men of goodwill], that they cannot swallow'.

Apart from the offer of the crown, Cromwell accepted the *Humble Petition and Advice*, which now became law. It was the first of the constitutional experiments of the Interregnum to have a measure of popular support, for it originated from Parliament, the people's representative, and not from the army. It also provided for the continuance of the Protectorate by granting Cromwell authority 'to appoint and declare the person who shall, immediately after your death, succeed you in the government'. The *Humble Petition* took account of the financial weakness of the protectoral regime by providing 'a yearly revenue of £1,300,000, whereof £1,000,000 for the navy and army, and £300,000 for the support of the government'. But it also created a barrier against the sort of action to which Cromwell and the Council of State had previously resorted by stipulating that 'those persons who are legally chosen by a free election of the people to serve in Parliament may not be excluded from sitting in Parliament to do their duties but by judgement and consent of that House whereof they are members'.

The religious clauses of the *Humble Petition* followed the principles laid down in *The Instrument of Government* by providing that 'the true protestant Christian religion, as it is contained in the Holy Scriptures of the Old and New Testament, and no other, be held forth and asserted for the public profession of these nations', but they went further, and into a more contentious area, by requiring that 'a Confession of Faith, to be agreed by your highness and the Parliament', should be 'recommended to the people of these nations'. The idea that the government should commit itself to a statement of doctrine was unwelcome to Independents and sectarians, for although the *Humble Petition* added the rider that no one should be compelled to accept the official formulary, the religious minorities feared that at some future stage they would be faced with the reimposition of uniformity.

Cromwell's hopes that the *Humble Petition* would inaugurate a period of political harmony were soon dashed. The last of his Parliaments assembled in January 1658, but the Lower House contained a hard core of republicans who had no time for a quasi-monarchical Lord Protector, while the government was weakened by the elevation of some thirty of its most effective speakers to the second chamber. No sooner did Parliament open than members began to question the authority of the 'other House' and to pour scorn on the newly-created titles of nobility. As the political temperature rose once again, a petition was circulated in the City calling for the abolition of the Protectorate and the restoration of a sovereign unicameral Parliament. Cromwell was alarmed by the threat to order implied in this campaign, particularly since shortage of money meant that army pay was in arrears once again and the soldiers were restless. Fearful of an alliance between his opponents in the Lower House and the malcontents in the army, Cromwell ignored the constitutional provisions of the *Humble Petition* and dissolved Parliament after a session that had lasted little more than two weeks. When members protested against this abrupt termination of their proceedings, Cromwell appealed, like Charles I before him, to divine sanction. 'Let God judge between you and me', he said; to which some of the republican members replied 'Amen'.

The Restoration

In 1658 the quaker leader, George Fox, went to visit the Lord Protector at Hampton Court, one of his official residences, and recorded how 'I saw and felt a waft of death go forth against him, and when I came to him he looked like a dead man.' Cromwell died on 3 September 1658, the anniversary of the Battle of Worcester, and was succeeded by his eldest son, Richard. The public reaction to Cromwell's death seems to have been one of indifference, but Richard's accession was widely welcomed. The very fact that he had never been an army officer made him acceptable to all those who were tired of military rule, and the peaceful way in which the transfer of power took place gave promise of a period of political stability.

Richard made a promising start by raising the army's pay, but this was little more than a gesture, given the chronic state of indebtedness he inherited from his father. The new Protector summoned Parliament and called on it to provide the necessary funding, but members of the Lower House were as deaf to his request as their predecessors had been to Charles I's. Instead of tackling the problem of the soldiers' arrears of pay, now totalling close on a million pounds, they discussed the possibility of raising a militia under their immediate control. When the Council of Officers made plain its opposition to such a move, they resolved that the Council should in future only meet with Parliament's permission, and that every officer should take an oath renouncing the use of force against the representative of the people. The generals reacted by calling on Richard to dissolve Parliament. He stood out against this, hoping the rank and file of the army would stand by him. In the event, however, they followed their commanders, leaving Richard with no choice but to comply. In April 1659 he dissolved Parliament. A month later he abdicated and retired into private life.

The Council of Officers was now ruling Britain, but its members were anxious to re-establish some form of constitutional rule and had been impressed by assurances given them by former Rumpers. They therefore invited Speaker Lenthall to reassemble the surviving members of the Rump. Some sixty-five out of a total of seventy-eight duly made their appearance, but the revived Rump suffered from the paralysis demonstrated in its first incarnation, for it could not agree on how to deal with any of the major problems confronting it. The Rump proved to be effective only in the localities, where it weeded out supporters of the protectoral regime and replaced them by its own men. These, however, were frequently radicals and sectarians of the sort who alarmed the traditional élites. The presbyterians feared that the ideal of a national Church would be called in question, and they therefore made overtures to the royalists, who were equally apprehensive. Plans were drawn up for concerted risings against the Rump, but the only one to take effect was that in Cheshire, led by the presbyterian Sir George Booth. This was crushed by Lambert's forces in August 1659.

The army had once again demonstrated its indispensability, and now it called on Parliament to treat it as an equal, by agreeing that no officer should be dismissed except by a court martial. The Rump showed what it thought of this demand by promptly dismissing Lambert, but the general's men remained loyal to him and once again used force to put an end to Parliament's sitting. Fleetwood was now named commander-in-chief by his brother officers, with Lambert as his deputy. Desborough was appointed to command the horse, while the infantry came under the nominal control of George Monck, who was in charge of the army stationed in Scotland. A Committee of Safety made up of the leading officers and their civilian associates took over responsibility for governing the country, but there was increasing resistance to its directives in the localities and ominous signs that order was beginning to break down.

Monck, who had a highly trained and disciplined army, was a presbyterian and favoured a national Church. He was alarmed by the increasing radicalism of Lambert, who had strong support among the sects, and came out openly against the Committee of Safety. At the same time he took the precaution of remodelling his army and dismissing officers who were not prepared to back him. Meanwhile, in the south, the navy had rebelled against the military regime and established a blockade of the Thames. Fleetwood and his fellow generals accepted that they could no longer maintain even a pretence of rule, and shortly before Christmas 1659 they dissolved the Committee of Safety and handed power back to the Rump, which had reassembled with the connivance of soldiers in the capital who saw it as their best chance of securing payment of their long-overdue arrears.

The newly restored Rump was dominated by moderate republicans who proclaimed their commitment to a national non-episcopal Church supported by tithes, along with freedom of worship for the Independents and sectarians. This might have been an acceptable solution a few months earlier, but the tide of public opinion was flowing so strongly in favour of a 'free' Parliament – meaning one that included the two hundred or so former members 'purged' by Colonel Pride in December 1648 – that the Rump's power was circumscribed, especially in the localities.

Everything now depended upon Monck, who had led his army into England, sweeping aside Lambert's small force at Newcastle in December 1659. The Rump now instructed him to bring his men to London, and when he did so it ordered him to restore order in the city, where demonstrations against its authority were a daily occurrence. Monck seemed inclined at first to comply, but in early February 1660 he asserted his independence by inviting the survivors of Pride's Purge to return to the House. The Long Parliament was soon in full session again, and in response to pressure from Monck it ordered the setting up of a national presbyterian Church, with toleration for all those who preferred to stay outside it. Monck himself was appointed commander-in-chief of the state's armed forces, and control of county militias was returned to the traditional local élites. Having completed its task to Monck's satisfaction, the Long Parliament dissolved itself on 16 March 1660. Elections then took place for what was called a Convention, since no legal authority existed to summon it.

If Monck had chosen to make himself another Cromwell, no one could have stopped him, but although a soldier by profession he believed in civilian rule and had already established contact with Charles II, in exile in Holland. Monck insisted that a restoration of the monarchy would only take place if the soldiers were guaranteed payment of their arrears and indemnity for all actions committed during the previous twenty years. Meanwhile, elections to the Convention had confirmed the widespread rejection of republicanism and the desire for a return to normality on the old pattern. The King's willingness to respond to this mood was demonstrated in the declaration that Charles II, at Monck's suggestion and with the help of his Chancellor, Edward Hyde, issued from Breda. In it he expressed his desire that 'those wounds which have so many years together been kept bleeding may be bound up', and promised to issue a general pardon to all those who rallied to him. He also gave an assurance that 'no man shall be disquieted or called in question for differences of opinion in matters of religion'. All other issues would be dealt with 'in a free Parliament, by which, upon the word of a King, we will be advised'.

After formally accepting the Declaration of Breda, the Convention decided to request Charles to return to his kingdom. In May 1660 he arrived in London, where that staunch anglican, the diarist John Evelyn, described how 'the ways were strewed with flowers, the bells ringing, the streets hung with tapestry, fountains running with wine'. 'I stood in the Strand,' he added, 'and beheld it and blessed God. And all this was done without one drop of blood shed, and by that very army which rebelled against him.' The irony of the situation was not lost upon the restored monarch, who commented that since his subjects were obviously delighted to have him back it was doubtless his fault that he had been away so long.

CHAPTER SEVENTEEN

Early Stuart England

The government of the localities

In the early modern period the administration of every English county was in the hands of a comparatively small group of families who owed their position to birth and land. These nobles and gentry were mostly of recent origin, even though they might invent pedigrees that took them back to the Norman Conquest. There were few families in England that had dominated their localities for more than 150 years. The majority had climbed to power during the Reformation by taking over land that had formerly belonged to the Church. Yet however recent their establishment, the local rulers were key figures in the social and political life of every county, and were often linked by marriage as well as friendship. Many of them had been educated at the universities and Inns of Court, and the more important ones were elected to Parliament. But although every county had a variety of links with London, its society was largely self-contained. Sir Henry Hyde, Clarendon's father, did not go back to London after attending Queen Elizabeth's funeral, even though he had thirty years of life ahead of him, and his wife never set foot in the capital. They were in some ways untypical, for most gentlemen had to pay the occasional visit, especially if they were involved in litigation – as was frequently the case – or were members of Parliament, or needed the advice or assistance of a minister or courtier. They often went alone, but they were under increasing pressure to take their wives and families, who were less averse to travelling now that they could go in a coach instead of on horseback, and welcomed the chance to catch up with the latest fashions.

Very few gentlemen were resident in London for more than part of the year. Most of their time was spent at home in the country, where they indulged in the pleasures of the chase and reciprocal hospitality. Their presence in their localities was highly desirable from the crown's point of view, for they played a vital part in local government. The upper gentry provided the Deputy-Lieutenants and most of the Justices of the Peace, who were the rulers of their shires. Below them came a large group of middling gentry, from whom the other Justices were drawn. Below these again were the lesser or parish gentry, who served, if at all, in the lower ranks of local administration, as coroners, for example, or high constables.

The Justices of the Peace, who held their office by annual appointment to the Commission of the Peace, were the linchpins of local government (*see* p. 89). In addition to being judges they were also administrators, having had, in the words of one contemporary, 'not loads but stacks of statutes ... laid upon them'. They were responsible for supervising poor relief, keeping roads and bridges in repair, licensing and controlling alehouses, regulating wages according to the Statute of Artificers, and deciding who should be responsible for looking after illegitimate children. In their judicial capacity they were advised and assisted by the Clerk of the Peace, a full-time official, usually a professional lawyer, who kept the records of Quarter Sessions and had a small clerical staff under him. In their administrative duties they were dependent upon the unpaid services of local constables, churchwardens, and Overseers of the Poor.

The sixteenth century saw a growth in the number of gentry, partly as a consequence of the land distribution consequent upon the Dissolution of the Monasteries, and this was reflected in an enlarged Commission of the Peace in every shire. In the early Tudor period there were about ten Justices of the Peace per county, but by the end of Elizabeth's reign the average was closer to fifty. Not all Justices were active members of the Commission. Some were impeded by age or illness. Others were content to enjoy the prestige of their office without worrying overmuch about the performance of its duties. There were frequent complaints in the Privy Council that Justices were failing to carry out their principal task of law enforcement, especially in the 'penal' sphere of social and economic regulations – so called because the relevant statutes laid down that a financial penalty should be imposed in case of infringement. In 1576 the Lord Keeper gave a warning that if such negligence persisted the Queen would be driven 'to appoint and assign private men for profit and gain's sake to see her penal laws to be executed'. In fact this was already being done, for the majority of prosecutions for breaches of penal statutes were initiated by private informers. If they were successful they were rewarded with a share of the penalty, but many cases never came to trial because the accused preferred to compound with them rather than face the cost and hazards of a legal action.

Common informers, not surprisingly, were generally loathed, but the crown was reluctant to dispense with their activities, particularly since it made a profit from them. Under James I an increasing number of functions, such as the licensing of alehouses, were transferred from Justices of the Peace to groups of individuals who were authorised to act by a royal patent. All too often, however, the patentees were men of the stamp of Sir Giles Mompesson (*see* pp. 289–90), more concerned with their private profit than the public good, and their activities, like those of the common informers, were blamed on the crown, which was tainted with their corruption. The government was going beyond the bounds of the acceptable, for as a Norfolk man complained in 1593, 'the good subjects, specially of the meaner sort, are preyed upon as kites prey upon carrion, and not to her majesty's use, nor for defence of the realm, but by others (commonly the worst of all others) by patents, penal laws and many other practices to make themselves rich and all the realm poor'.

The great outcry against patentees came in the 1621 Parliament, but tension between the government and the localities had been mounting since the 1590s, under the twin pressures of war and inflation. A statute of Mary's reign required every county to form its adult male population into a militia for defence purposes, and to see that at least the core of this part-time army was given regular training and provided with modern arms and equipment. By the 1580s the cost of maintaining these trained bands was about £400 per shire, but since they were confined to home duties other troops had to be raised when overseas operations were planned. The latter, usually drawn from the dregs of the people, had first to be clothed and then conducted, under escort, to the place of rendezvous. In theory the expenditure of this 'coat-and-conduct money' was defrayed by the government, but in practice it was a further drain upon limited local resources. Northamptonshire had to find £1,000 for coat-and-conduct money in 1588, the year of the Armada, and Norfolk spent four times that amount on defence preparations. When expenditure on this scale is taken into account it becomes less surprising that local gentlemen were unwilling to increase the rate of assessment for parliamentary subsidies.

Justices of the Peace were not well suited to organise the militia, for there were too many of them and they were too amenable to pressure from their neighbours. The Council therefore placed increasing reliance on the men it appointed as Lord Lieutenants. This office had been created under Henry VIII, to maintain order during the period when disputes over religion threatened a breakdown. It was revived from time to time in subsequent reigns during periods of emergency. When Spanish invasion threatened during the 1580s, Elizabeth's government nominated Lord Lieutenants and made them responsible for co-ordinating defence preparations. These officers were usually peers and Privy Councillors and often had more than one county under their jurisdiction, so they selected members of the upper gentry to act as Deputy-Lieutenants. This meant, in effect, that the government was by-passing the Commission of the Peace and enforcing its will in the localities via an élite of some ten to twelve persons. The system was reasonably efficient, but it tended to polarise the county into the minority who were in the government's confidence and the majority who were not.

Both Queen Elizabeth and the war against Spain were popular, but the demands made by the government were a cause of mounting friction. When, in 1596, the ports were called on to provide ships for the Cadiz expedition and the counties were instructed to give them financial assistance, there was an outcry. Resentment at this breach of precedent was focused on the Deputy-Lieutenants, and many Justices of the Peace in Norfolk and Suffolk refused to obey what they regarded as unconstitutional orders. Matters were far worse in the 1620s, because Buckingham's wars against Spain and France were deeply unpopular. In 1626, when there was an invasion scare, the Privy Council followed the Elizabethan example by instructing the maritime counties to aid the hard-pressed ports in supplying ships. Again there was opposition, and the Dorset Justices protested that they could not 'find any precedent for being charged in a service of this nature'. The infuriated Council made the terse, but ominous, reply 'that state occasions and the defence of a kingdom in times of extraordinary danger do not guide themselves by ordinary precedents'.

The sheriff had originally been the crown's principal officer in the shires, but his powers had been gradually eroded since the fourteenth century and his functions were now limited to arranging parliamentary elections, empanelling juries, and carrying out sentences imposed by the courts. Sheriffs served for a year only and were not allowed to leave their shire during their term of office – as Charles I remembered in 1625 when he 'pricked' a number of his critics as sheriffs in order to keep them out of the next Parliament. The office of sheriff was not popular, for it cost the holder more than he made through fees and it entailed a great deal of work. This was especially the case after 1635, since the sheriff was charged with the task of apportioning and collecting Ship Money and was held personally responsible for any sums outstanding.

The government was not entirely dependent upon residents for local administration. Twice a year the judges of the common-law courts set out on circuits that covered virtually the whole of England. The principal object of their assizes was to try offenders accused of serious crimes, but from the 1590s onwards they were addressed by the Lord Chancellor or Keeper shortly before their departure and given a 'charge' which they were to pass on to the local magistrates. Their duties were outlined by James I in 1616, when he instructed them to 'remember that when you go your circuits you go not only to pursue and prevent offences, but you are to take care for the good government in general of the parts where you travel . . . You have charges to give to Justices of Peace, that they do their duties when you are absent as well as present. Take an account of them and report their service to me at your return'. The involvement of the judges in county administration reached a peak in the 1630s, when they were required to supervise the enforcement of the *Book of Orders* (*see* p. 321) and collect the regular reports which the Justices of the Peace were supposed to submit.

The common law, of which the judges were the guardians and interpreters, was the ancient and customary law of England. It had never been fully written down or codified but had been defined and given an element of coherence by judicial decisions over the course of several centuries. Criminal proceedings at common law were usually initiated by the Justices of the Peace, who submitted a bill of indictment to a grand jury consisting of the more substantial inhabitants of their locality. Only if the grand jury found that the bill was 'true' – in other words, that the accusation was well founded – did the case go to trial. If an individual wished to begin an action before King's (or Queen's) Bench or Common Pleas, the two main courts of common law, he had first to purchase a writ. These were theoretically limited in scope, and it was partly for this reason that the two courts had been losing business during the early sixteenth century. Plaintiffs preferred to take their complaints to Star Chamber (a prerogative court) or to Chancery (a court of equity), where they stood a better chance of obtaining a swift decision with the minimum of technicalities.

The common-law courts responded to this challenge by developing more flexible procedures and enlarging their competence. For instance, they began dealing with questions of copyhold, which had previously been left to Chancery. As a consequence, they were doing six times as much business at the end of Elizabeth's reign as they had done at the accession of Henry VII. Yet the struggle for survival had left its mark, for King's Bench and Common Pleas were competing for business with the many other courts that were functioning in Tudor and early Stuart England. When the common-law judges issued prohibitions to Church courts, forbidding them to proceed in certain cases, they were acting in defence of their own jurisdiction rather than, as James I and the bishops assumed, challenging the royal supremacy.

In some respects, such as the continued use of Norman French for formal proceedings, the common law was wilfully archaic, but the fact that the courts were attracting more and more business showed that it was successfully adapting itself to the needs of a changing society. The law had its critics, of course, not least among lawyers, and there were suggestions that it could be improved by adopting certain features of other systems of jurisprudence. Yet the common law was not as self-contained as it appeared to be. Even Sir Edward Coke, its most outspoken champion, had the major works of Roman, or civil, law in his library. Civil law was still studied in England, its practitioners were active in the Court of Admiralty and the ecclesiastical courts, and they were often on close terms with their common-law brethren. In short, while the common law appeared to be rigid and insular, in practice it was remarkably flexible and responsive.

Lawyers could be tenacious in their defence of individual or corporate rights, and were frequently to be found among the leading critics of government policy in the House of Commons. James I did not disguise his feelings towards 'wrangling lawyers' and was eventually goaded into dismissing Coke from his post as Lord Chief Justice. But the common law provided ministers for the crown as well as critics. The offices of Solicitor-General and Attorney-General were invariably filled by lawyers, and in the post-Reformation period the Lord Chancellor or Keeper was almost always a member of the legal profession.

While the law was available to all citizens, there was considerable reluctance on the part of neighbours to use it against each other. One reason for this was that many offences – particularly theft, which was the commonest crime – carried the death penalty, and even the angriest of complainants would think twice before exposing an offender to such a fate. Most communities, whether they were medium-sized towns or small villages, exercised a degree of toleration of petty crime as long as it did not seriously threaten the general well-being, and local officials were more concerned with settling disagreements between neighbours than with imposing a rigid discipline.

This tolerance was severely weakened, however, by the pressure of social and economic change. As Elizabeth's reign drew to a close the gap between rich and poor was widening, and in both urban and rural areas there was an increasing number of poor people for whom the community had no obvious place. This alarmed the 'middling sort' of yeomen farmers, substantial tradesmen and minor gentry who formed an élite in many parishes – particularly in the nuclear villages of the lowland zone – for the poor rate which they paid was an ever-growing burden. They were also afraid that the social order might break down, for they were coming to regard the poorer members of their communities as feckless, irresponsible and immoral. They thought of themselves as the 'better sort' and adopted a condescending and at times hostile attitude towards the 'poorer sort'.

Not surprisingly, the 'middling' or 'better' sort were often puritan in their religious outlook, for the assumption that they had a right, as an élite minority, to lead and direct the unregenerate majority could be justified if set in the Calvinist context of the rule of the 'elect', whom God had fore-ordained to salvation. Where the local minister was himself of puritan persuasion, the middling sort could prove an irresistible combination and would impose upon the community a discipline that was simultaneously secular and religious. Immoral behaviour, for example, was punished because it was ungodly but also because it might result in the birth of ille-gitimate children who would have to be maintained at the parish's expense. Alehouses were suppressed on the grounds that they encouraged drunkenness and debauchery, but they also provided a seductive counter-attraction to Church services.

The emergence of parish élites, at or below the level at which political participation in early Stuart England usually stopped, should have made the government's task of maintaining order easier. But James I and Charles I were opposed to the domination of Calvinist minorities, which they saw as a challenge to their rule rather than a strengthening of it. They also rejected the divisiveness of the Calvinist attitude, for as kings they held themselves responsible for the well-being of all their subjects, not just the godly. They interpreted their role in the conventional sense of maintaining minimum standards of conformity in the Church and obedience in the state, rather than actively rooting out idleness and sin. James I made clear his response to puritan demands for stricter enforcement of the Sabbath by issuing his *Declaration of Sports* in 1618. This was reissued by Charles I in 1633 and laid down that the King's 'good people', after they had attended church on Sundays, should not be 'disturbed, letted or discouraged from any lawful recreation, such as dancing – either men or women – archery for men, leaping, vaulting, or any other such harmless recreation, nor from having of May-games, Whitsun-ales and Morris dances, and the setting up of maypoles – so as the same be had in due and convenient time, without impediment or neglect of divine service'.

The *Declaration of Sports* struck at the foundations of puritan discipline, for the godly minority, who approved of strong government in the localities so long as they were the governors, now found that they were disowned by the royal administration. Indeed, the Laudians, whom Charles favoured, were so determined to demonstrate their rejection of puritan ideals that they ignored or overrode the 'middling sort', who had established their authority in villages and towns throughout the kingdom. In these circumstances it was hardly surprising that the puritan élites, like their social superiors among the godly gentry and aristocracy, found it increasingly difficult to reconcile their loyalty to the King with their commitment to God. There was no obvious way out of this dilemma while Charles I remained in power, but with the overthrow of the monarchy and the Laudian Church they came into their own. It was during the Interregnum that the godly campaign to impose moral and religious discipline upon the entire nation – this time with the blessing of the government – reached its peak. By an irony of history it thereby created a reaction that not only blocked its chances of success but opened the way to the restoration of the old order it had been so determined to transform.

The poor

The problem of poverty became even more acute in early Stuart England than it had been under Elizabeth. The 1620s were especially bad, with poor harvests and outbreaks of plague combining with the collapse of the cloth trade to increase distress. The 1630s were marginally better, though they began badly, but the later 1640s witnessed a series of harvest failures, and the numbers of the poor rose from about three per cent of the population in 1600 to five per cent in 1651.

There was no significant change in attitudes towards the poor. Parishes were still the basic units of relief, and because their resources were limited and could cope only with native inhabitants, it remained official policy that vagrants should be returned to their birthplace. In many cases this was just not possible, for local magistrates were too few and too burdened with other duties to be able to enforce all the provisions of the poor law. In July 1616 James I issued a proclamation 'for punishing of vagabonds, rogues and idle persons', which authorised the appointment in London and the home counties of Provost Marshals, whose function would be to carry out 'diligent search ... as well in the fields as in the highways and streets' for all 'idle vagrant men and masterless men'. Those they apprehended were to be sent to houses of correction, which a statute of 1610 had ordered to be erected in every shire for 'the keeping, correcting and setting to work of rogues, vagabonds, sturdy beggars and other idle and disorderly persons'. During the 1620s and 1630s the use of Provost Marshals became widespread, though never universal. They were far more effective than local constables in rounding up social outcasts, but their average annual salary of £20 was too much for some shires, which refused to appoint them.

The problem of the poor was a matter of concern for the puritan élites who by the end of the sixteenth century had established their presence in East Anglia, and, in the early seventeenth century, controlled a number of municipalities in the south and south-west. One of these was Dorchester, where the puritan governors, under the leadership of John White, adopted an integrated approach to the subject. They built a workhouse, to keep the poor employed, and established a grain store to deal with the specific difficulties created by harvest failures. They also set up a municipal brewhouse, not only to regulate the drinking habits of the poorer sort but also to generate profits which could offset the charges involved in relieving poverty. Their activity was driven by a strong moral as well as religious ideology, for they aimed to reform the behaviour of their fellow citizens and imbue them with a sense of responsibility both to themselves and the community. It was no coincidence that over half the several hundred offenders brought before the Dorchester magistrates every year were accused of failing to attend church, using profane language, and drinking too much.

A puritan impulse may also be discerned behind the establishment of the Corporation of the Poor in London in 1647–9. The idea was that this body would administer poor relief throughout the city, without being constricted by parish boundaries. It was authorised to levy a poor rate on a graduated basis, and it used the money so raised to set to work up to a thousand poor at the same time as it provided education for their children. This was in many ways an enlightened approach, but, like the Dorchester scheme, it proved too expensive. Because of the continuing economic depression there was only a limited market for the products of the workhouses, and instead of the schemes being self-financing they were subsidised by ever-rising poor rates. It was easier, and marginally less costly, to distribute outdoor relief to the 'deserving' poor and punish the undeserving. Begging was technically illegal, except for those who possessed a magistrates' licence, but it went on nonetheless. Private alms-giving helped soften the impact of poverty, as did the charitable trusts, which continued to flourish. By 1650 they were providing about

£100,000 annually, which was roughly equivalent to the total amount raised by poor rates.

The system of poor relief in early Stuart England, both public and private, was prompted as much by self-interest as by the charitable impulse, for the poor formed a potential powder-keg, and it made sense, in the interests of preserving the social order, to ameliorate their suffering. They remained at the very bottom of society and were treated with scant consideration, but after the 1620s they no longer risked total destitution and starvation. Parishes accepted a considerable burden of taxation in order to fund poor relief, but the money was well spent in so far as it provided a safety net for those who were reduced to poverty either permanently or for a time. The poor were no doubt discontented with their lot, but they were not driven by despair into rebellion.

Trade and finance

English cloth exports took some time to recover from the slump of the mid-sixteenth century, but by the time James VI became James I they were in a flourishing condition. The end of this boom period was marked by Alderman Cockayne's project of 1614. Cockayne pointed out that the Merchant Adventurers exported mainly unfinished or 'white' cloth, which was dyed and dressed in Germany and the Low Countries. If, he argued, this work was done at home, unemployment would be reduced and profits would rise. His observations were well received by James I, and in 1614 the privileges of the Merchant Adventurers were suspended. In their place a new company, 'The King's Merchant Adventurers', was set up to handle the anticipated trade in finished cloth to the continent.

The government was hoping to encourage English exports, but Cockayne's motives were less worthy. He had made no preparations for marketing the finished cloth, and it soon became apparent that he and his associates were far more interested in breaking the monopoly of the Merchant Adventurers and transferring it to themselves than in changing the pattern of the English cloth industry. The whole project was based upon the assumption that England held an unchallengeable predominance in the continental market, but this was not the case. Foreign countries reacted by forbidding the import of dressed cloth from England, and the only result of the scheme was to disrupt the English cloth industry and give its rivals an advantage they never lost. The King cancelled Cockayne's concession in December 1615 and restored the Merchant Adventurers to their former privileged position, but by that time the damage had been done.

For many years after 1614 the cloth industry, and with it English commerce as a whole, remained in recession. Exports to Germany and the Low Countries fell, and by 1622 the amount of cloth shipped from English ports was only 40 per cent of what it had been in 1614. The causes of the 1620s slump were not located solely in England. Currency depreciation in Germany and eastern European countries, following the outbreak of the Thirty Years War in 1618, made a major contribution to the crisis. English merchants could not afford to accept at their face value coins which in England and western Europe would have been worth far less, and they therefore put up their prices. This gave local manufacturers an enormous advantage, and for several years, until recoinage became effective, English cloth was priced out of the German market.

Although the trade in broadcloths steadily declined, there was a big expansion in the production of so-called 'New Draperies'. These were lighter cloths, more suitable for warmer climates, and they sold well in Mediterranean countries. Spain was an important market for New Draperies, particularly after the signing of the Anglo-Spanish peace treaty in 1604. Italy was another, with the free port of Leghorn (Livorno) serving as the distribution centre. The wars against Spain and France in 1625–30 disrupted the trade in New Draperies and brought unemployment to East Anglia, which was one of the main centres of production. It seems likely that too much cloth was being produced, for even after the restoration of peace the East Anglian industry remained depressed, and discontent was intensified by the poor harvests of 1630-31 with the consequent increase in grain prices. Depression continued throughout the 1630s, and unemployment and poverty combined with puritanism to spread disaffection in the eastern counties. The emigrants who left Essex and Suffolk for Holland and the New World were frequently motivated by their hatred of Laudianism, but years of slump also played their part in persuading men to abandon their native land and seek a better life elsewhere.

At the time the Civil War broke out in 1642 the export of New Draperies equalled in value that of broadcloths, and this reflected an important extension of the range of English trade. Broadcloths were associated with the European market, but New Draperies were sent to America, the Levant, Africa and India – in other words all over the world. This expansion was not a uniquely English phenomenon. In the new markets as in the old, English merchants were up against competition from the Dutch who, because they had few natural resources of their own, specialised in carrying the goods of other nations. In the struggle for trade, diplomacy often came to the aid of the merchants. In 1648, for example, the Dutch persuaded the King of Denmark to sell them the right for their ships to pass through the Sound without paying tolls, and six years later the waterway was closed to English shipping. Dutch and English merchants were rivals also in the East Indies, where they were struggling to take control of the empire that Portugal was too weak to hold. In 1623 seven English merchants were tortured and executed at Amboyna, and when the news of this 'massacre' reached England it caused a public outcry and created a demand for revenge that was not satisfied until the first Dutch war of 1652.

The Dutch were held responsible for the slow expansion of English overseas trade. James I and Charles I both made belligerent gestures towards them, but nothing effective was done until the passing of the Navigation Act in 1651. This measure was designed to eliminate the Dutch from the carrying trade with England by requiring that all goods coming into the British Isles should be carried in British or colonial ships or in ships belonging to the country in which the goods originated. The act could not be rigidly enforced since there was not enough English merchant shipping available, and it was only a contributory cause of the Dutch war which broke out the following year, but it demonstrates the willingness of the Commonwealth government to use political means for commercial ends.

There was nothing new about close links between the mercantile interest and early Stuart governments. Under James I, for instance, a leading City merchant and financier, Lionel Cranfield, had been ennobled and appointed Lord Treasurer. But the merchants were not a homogeneous group. The interlopers, who resented the power of the chartered companies and were determined to break into the American and West Indian trades, wanted war against Spain and attacks upon Spanish settlements in the New World. They were opposed, however, by the directors of the East India, Levant and other major companies, who preferred peaceful co-existence and shared Thomas Wentworth's belief that war tended 'to the decay of trade and losing entrance to the enlargement thereof that hath of many years been open to us'.

The merchant magnates were linked to the crown by mutual need. They wanted the privileges, including monopoly rights, that only the King could give them, while the King needed the large loans that only they could provide. James I and Charles I borrowed substantial sums of money from both individuals and privileged groups, which included the livery companies and the City Corporation. Repayment was a slow business that dragged on for many years, long after the dates originally fixed. In 1628 the crown's debt to the City was so great that it handed over land worth £350,000 in return for a further cash advance of £100,000.

Delays in repayment undermined the crown's creditworthiness, and both bribery and threats had to be used to persuade potential lenders to part with their money. Sir Baptist Hicks, for example, who was made a viscount in 1628, paid little or nothing for his title because he had already lent so much to the crown. By contrast, companies which denied the King's request for financial assistance might have their charters confiscated and their privileges transferred to rival organisations. Private individuals who failed to make a positive response could find themselves treated, as one courtier put it, like nuts that 'must be cracked before one can have any good of them, and then too at first they appear dry and choky, but bring them to the press, they yield a great deal of fat oil'.

One of the most lucrative privileges in the gift of the crown was the grant of the farm of the Customs duties. Early in the reign of James I it was decided that Customs should no longer be collected by royal officials but by a private company paying a fixed rent for the privilege. The crown gained from having a regular revenue, while the Customs farmers were allowed to keep the profits they made over and above their rent. As trade expanded and profits increased, the government adjusted the rent upwards, but even so the Customs farmers did well out of the bargain – so well, in fact, that they became one of the main sources of loans to the crown. In the crisis year of 1640 they advanced more than £100,000 to Charles I, and they were to be found, not unnaturally, among the supporters of the crown as the dispute between the King and Parliament became ever more bitter.

CHAPTER EIGHTEEN

Charles II

Charles II and the constitutional settlement

Charles II – 'a long, dark man, above two yards high', as the roundheads had described him after the battle of Worcester – arrived in London on his thirtieth birthday. He had been in exile since 1646, when he was sixteen, apart from his brief excursion to Scotland in 1651. The experience of poverty, humiliation and danger had taught him to take a cynical view of human behaviour and to value every man only for what he could get out of him. Where Charles I had been formal and reserved, Charles II was affable and easy. He charmed all who came into contact with him until they discovered, in the words of his contemporary, Bishop Burnet, 'how little they could depend on good looks, kind words and fair promises, in which he was liberal to excess, because he intended nothing by them but to get rid of importunities and to silence all farther pressing upon him'.

Charles returned to an England that was anxious to erase the memory of the previous three decades and return to the harmonious balance of the 'ancient constitution', but he was lacking in respect for this particular inheritance that had so conspicuously failed to preserve the monarchy. Sir Edward Hyde, whom Charles made Earl of Clarendon and Lord Chancellor, observed in his great *History of the Rebellion and Civil Wars in England* that the restored monarch 'had in his nature so little reverence or esteem for antiquity, and did in truth so much contemn old orders, forms and institutions'. Charles's cynical attitude was shared by a number of his associates. The Earl of Peterborough, for instance, was of the opinion that 'these old notions of mixed governments, privileges and conditions have by several accidents of state been put out of the essence of things, and they are not to be practised any longer'. Yet this rejection of nostalgia was out of tune with the conservative instincts of many of

Charles's subjects. They wanted to go backwards, while he looked ahead and felt at home in a world that was very different from the one his father had known. In other words, the euphoria of the Restoration served to conceal a gulf between the King and his people that was to widen as the reign continued.

Charles had no experience of government and was content to rely on Clarendon, who was twenty years his senior and belonged by temperament to an older generation. As Edward Hyde he had been born into a gentry family and chose the law as his profession. He opposed autocratic government and Arminianism, but he was committed to the monarchy and offered his services to Charles I at the same time as he marshalled the moderates in the Long Parliament. After the collapse of the royalist cause he joined the young Charles II in exile and became his principal adviser. Following the Restoration it fell to him to work out the shape of the political settlement, and in this he was guided by his belief that the 'ancient constitution' or 'mixed monarchy' should be reinstated. It was in this spirit that he called on members of the Convention to return 'the whole nation to its primitive temper and integrity, to its old good manners, its old good humour and its old good nature'.

For Clarendon the Personal Rule of Charles I had been as much of an aberration as the republican governments that followed it, and for this reason he opposed any restoration of the prerogative monarchy. Most of the acts to which Charles I had given his assent in the opening months of the Long Parliament remained in force, and Star Chamber, High Commission and the Council of the North were consigned to oblivion. However, the Triennial Act, which Charles I had also accepted, was considered unworthy of the restored monarchy, since it required Parliament to assemble every three years without waiting for a royal summons. Nothing was done about this initially, but in 1664 Parliament approved another Triennial Act, stating 'that hereafter the sitting and holding of Parliaments shall not be intermitted or discontinued above three years at the most'. It was left to the King to implement the terms of the new act, on the assumption – which time was to show to be unfounded – that relations between him and Parliament would be so harmonious that he would have no wish to rule without it.

Charles was very conscious of the fact that he had returned to a deeply divided country, and he began by making his government as broad based as possible. The first Privy Council he appointed contained nine advisers who had been with him during his exile, six royalists who had stayed in England, four Cromwellians – including General Monck, shortly to become Duke of Albemarle, and Edward Montagu, commander of Cromwell's fleet – and eight former supporters of Parliament during the Civil War. A similar inclusiveness was apparent when it came to the appointment of the principal officers of state. But no amount of juggling of offices would have succeeded in restoring stability while the army was in existence. This problem was dealt with by the Convention, which voted enough money to pay off the troops, thereby easing their passage into civilian life. Charles broke with tradition by retaining some 3,500 men for his private guard. This made sense at a time when the country was still disturbed and rumours of republican plots were rife, but it meant that the King, in contrast to his predecessors, now had a small standing army at his disposal.

The financial settlement

One of the basic assumptions of the 'ancient constitution' was that the King should 'live of his own', but although crown lands which had been alienated during the Interregnum were restored to Charles II they brought in only £100,000 a year – a stark reminder of the extent to which inflation and war had reduced the King's 'own' during the century that had elapsed since the Dissolution of the Monasteries. A committee was set up by the Convention to decide what the crown needed and how this should be provided. The committee fixed on the sum of £1,200,000 a year, which was somewhat more than Charles I had been receiving at the end of his reign but less than Cromwell had enjoyed, since the restored monarchy, unlike the Protectorate, would not have to maintain an army of sixty thousand men. It was thought that Customs duties would bring in £400,000. The rest was to be provided by an excise on alcoholic liquor, which it was hoped would produce a similar amount, and a number of minor duties. Half the excise was voted to the crown in perpetuity, in return for the surrender of feudal dues. The Court of Wards had not been abolished until 1646 and could in theory have been revived, but Charles and Clarendon knew how much bitterness had been created by feudal tenures, and were content to abandon them in return for a permanent parliamentary grant. This meant that Salisbury's 'Great Contract' was at last accepted, fifty years after its initial presentation in 1610. It was a good bargain for the landowners who sat in Parliament, for they had exchanged what was in effect a land tax for a levy which had to be paid by everyone who enjoyed a drink.

Although the Convention was genuine in its desire to provide an adequate revenue for the restored monarchy, its accounting techniques did not match its aspirations. In the opening years of Charles II's reign the excise yielded less than half the estimated £400,000, and although Parliament showed its good intentions by granting the crown a tax on hearths in 1662 this did not fully plug the hole in the royal finances. During the 1660s ministers had to make frequent appeals to Parliament for additional supply, and although this was usually forthcoming it limited the independence of the crown and ran counter to the principle that the King's income should be sufficient for the ordinary needs of government. As the first flush of enthusiasm for the restored monarchy faded it was only too easy for members of the Commons to slip into the assumption that extravagance was the cause of the King's financial difficulties. They were not entirely wrong, since Charles was indeed extravagant, especially when it came to making gifts to his mistresses, but royal extravagance, as under James I, merely made a bad situation worse. It was not the root cause of the problem.

It was not long before members of Parliament realised the advantages that this unintended imbalance in the constitution brought them, for as one of their number observed in 1677, ' 'tis money that makes a Parliament considerable, and nothing else'. There was, however, another side to this picture, for consciousness of his dependence upon Parliament made the King increasingly disenchanted with this aspect of the Restoration settlement. As long as he was short of money he could do little to redress the situation, but by the late 1670s, as trade expanded and the yield from Customs and the excise significantly increased, he became aware of new possibilities, which included reducing or even eliminating the role of Parliament.

The land question

The Convention restored to the crown and Church all the lands that had been taken from them during the Interregnum. As for private individuals, they had to fend for themselves. So much land had changed hands in the previous two decades that the Convention despaired of unravelling the legal intricacies and arriving at a just solution. It resolved that land which had been confiscated should be restored to the original owners, but failed to pass a general act enforcing this. Royalists wishing to reclaim their property had either to make some arrangement with the existing occupier or sue for possession. Lawsuits, however, were expensive, and the plaintiff could not always be sure that judgment would be given in his favour. Noblemen were in a stronger position, since they could more easily obtain private acts of Parliament and they had the powerful backing of the House of Lords, which issued direct orders to sheriffs, commanding them to see that confiscated lands were restored to their noble owners.

The settlement was not as unfair as appears at first glance. Many cavaliers who had been forced to sell their lands, or had allowed them to be confiscated and sold by the state, had managed to buy them back again before the Restoration took place, while others found that the new owners were content to become rent-paying tenants rather than risk expropriation. Most royalists got their land back before or after the Restoration, though the cost of recovery sometimes led to collapse in subsequent decades. For families which had been in financial difficulties prior to 1640 the Civil War was in many instances the final blow, but they would probably have succumbed sooner or later in any case. Generally speaking, the permanent changes in the pattern of landholding that took place as a consequence of the Civil War and Interregnum were no greater than would have been the case in any twenty-year period.

Royalists who had suffered from plundering, or had sold land to pay composition fines, had no legal grounds for redress. Few of them were actually ruined, but they felt bitter at the contrast between their continuing impoverishment and the relative affluence of those who remained in possession of their former estates. It became an accepted maxim among this group that the Act of Indemnity and Oblivion passed by the Convention meant indemnity for the King's enemies and oblivion for his friends. Yet in fact this was far from the case. Charles II went out of his way to reward those who had remained loyal to him, whether they joined him in exile or stayed in England. Sir George Booth, for instance, who had led the unsuccessful rising in Cheshire in 1659, was elevated to the peerage as Lord Delamere. Royalists received the greater part of the baronetcies and knighthoods granted by the newly restored monarch, and also benefited from pensions, which Charles granted on such a lavish scale that his Lord Treasurer had to urge him to desist.

As for the King's enemies, most of those who had been closely associated with the Commonwealth or Protectorate suffered as a consequence. Of the twenty-six regicides, nine who remained in England were executed, along with four other men who had been involved in Charles I's death even though they had not signed the warrant. Other prominent republicans had to choose between exile or imprisonment, and even those who escaped punishment altogether were sooner or later forced out of public life. In general, only those figures who had come to terms with Charles II before the Restoration survived the change of regime unscathed.

The restored Church

During the twenty years that elapsed between the meeting of the Long Parliament and the Restoration many ministers lost their livings, but about half the original incumbents stayed in place by agreeing not to use the Prayer Book or to preach against the new regime. Some of the expelled ministers took refuge in the households of royalist families, where they kept anglicanism alive while they waited for happier days. They included men like Gilbert Sheldon, who was to become Archbishop of Canterbury in 1664. Others went into exile, along with a number of laymen, rather than come to terms with the triumphant puritans. A century earlier the Marian exiles – upholders of a protestant Church that had barely established itself – had fallen under the influence of continental reformers and brought radical alternatives back with them to England. The Caroline émigrés, by contrast, were unimpressed by the varieties of religious practice, Roman Catholic or protestant, that they encountered on the continent. They returned home more firmly committed to the Church of England than they had been when they left.

The anglicans in exile derived great comfort from the unswerving support of Edward Hyde, the King's principal adviser, who was strongly in sympathy with the principles of royal supremacy, hierarchy, and uniformity of religious practice that characterised post-Laudian anglicanism. He was prepared to make concessions to the puritans if this was the price that had to be paid for restoring the Church and monarchy, but as he told John Cosin – a former associate and admirer of Laud – he would do so in order that 'the Church will be preserved in a tolerable condition, and by degrees recover what cannot be had at once'. Hyde's attitude was not shared by the King. Charles II wanted to re-establish the Church of England on the broadest possible basis and was determined to avoid his father's mistake of giving support to an unrepresentative minority. Of his new appointments to the episcopal bench, only three had been closely connected with Laud. Cosin, who went to Durham, was one. Another was the aged William Juxon, who had attended Charles I on the scaffold and now became Archbishop of Canterbury. Matthew Wren, however, was passed over, as were a number of other prominent Laudians, and in his use of patronage at a lower level Charles showed the same commitment to a broadly-based Church.

As the Restoration turned from a dream into reality in the early months of 1660, Hyde was working towards an accommodation with the puritans, who appeared to be in the majority in England. It was in order to assuage them that when Charles issued the *Declaration of Breda* in April he promised 'a liberty to tender consciences, and that no man shall be disquieted or called in question for differences of opinion in matter of religion which do not disturb the peace of the kingdom'. At the same time informal discussions were taking place between anglican and presbyterian representatives, who came surprisingly close to agreement. The presbyterians acknowledged the right of expelled ministers to regain their livings. The anglicans, in return, accepted that puritan incumbents who had never been ordained by a bishop should not be required to undergo this ceremony.

Puritan distrust of bishops was of long standing, but Charles took a significant step towards reconciliation by publishing the *Worcester House Declaration* in October 1660, in which he ordered that every bishop should be assisted in ordination and excommunication by the 'most learned and pious presbyters of the diocese' and that no one should be persecuted for refusing to use the Prayer Book. The presbyterians were delighted by this evidence of royal goodwill, and their representatives, led by the irrepressible William Prynne, urged that the *Worcester House Declaration* should be given statutory confirmation. However, they came up against opposition not only from the minority of committed anglicans but also from many Independents, who feared that a partnership between the King and the presbyterians would restrict religious freedom and force them once more into the strait-jacket of a national Church. It was this temporary alliance between anglicans and Independents that ensured, by a narrow majority, the rejection of the presbyterians' proposal, and from that moment their cause was lost.

Hyde was not displeased at the rejection of the *Worcester House Declaration*. In his closing speech to the Convention he described the Church of England as 'the best and the best reformed in the Christian world', and declared that 'God would not so miraculously have snatched this Church as a brand from the fire, would not have raised it from the grave after He had suffered it to be buried so many years ... to expose it again to the same rapine, reproach and impiety'. Nevertheless, he held out an olive branch to the presbyterians by offering bishoprics to three of their leaders, Richard Baxter, Edmund Calamy and Edward Reynolds. Only Reynolds accepted. Baxter was far less prepared to compromise, and his intransigent attitude largely accounted for the failure of the Savoy Conference, which opened in April 1661. Baxter assumed that the presbyterians, by virtue of their numbers and influence, had the trump cards and could afford to hold out for what they wanted. What he did not realise until too late was that all over the country anglican ministers were resuming possession of their livings and that the re-establishment of the Church of England was a *fait accompli*. Moreover, the elections that took place in the spring of 1661 produced a Parliament that was dominated by anglican royalists. While Charles and, to a lesser extent, Hyde were still thinking in terms of a compromise settlement based on toleration, the 'Cavalier Parliament' which assembled in May 1661 was determined to re-establish uncompromising and intolerant anglicanism.

At the same time as negotiations were taking place between anglican and presbyterian representatives, the bishops were at work on a revised version of the Prayer Book. They made a number of alterations designed to conciliate the puritans, but Baxter declared that the new Book was even worse than the old. However, his condemnation of it carried no weight with the Cavalier Parliament, and this was the body which now had responsibility for shaping the religious settlement. The two Houses incorporated the new Prayer Book into the Act of Uniformity of 1662, which required all ministers not only to use it before the following St Bartholomew's Day but also to make a public declaration of their 'unfeigned assent and consent to all and every thing contained and prescribed in and by the Book'. They were also instructed to commit themselves publicly to the proposition 'that it is not lawful, upon any pretence whatsoever, to take arms against the King' and to renounce *The Solemn League and Covenant* as 'an unlawful oath ... imposed upon the subjects of this realm against the known laws and liberties of this kingdom'. Clarendon persuaded the House of Lords to accept an amendment authorising the King to permit clergy of presbyterian persuasion to dispense with those parts of the Book they found unacceptable, but the Commons rejected this out of hand. St Bartholomew's Day was awaited with some trepidation, but it came and went quietly enough and Samuel Pepys recorded in his *Diary* that the presbyterian clergy had 'gone out very peaceably, and the people not so much concerned therein as was expected'.

Just under a thousand ministers were deprived of their livings for refusing to make the prescribed declarations. This was evidence of a far greater degree of resistance to the reimposition of anglicanism than the bishops had anticipated, and they were hard put to it to find suitable replacements. The impact varied from one part of the country to another. London lost over a third of its ministers, and some of the southern counties about a quarter. When earlier expulsions are taken into account the effect becomes even more dramatic. In Cheshire and Lancashire, for instance, some three-quarters of parish clergy were replaced in the years 1660–3. Those clergy who retained their livings were not always whole-heartedly committed to the new settlement. As with the sixteenth-century Reformation it took time for changes ordained from above to percolate down to the parish level. The use of a surplice had been made compulsory, but in the Essex village of East Colne the minister, Ralph Josselin, managed to avoid wearing one until 1680, and even by the time Charles II died, five years later, many parishes were without a surplice for the min-ister, a chalice for the administration of holy communion, or even, in a number of instances, a copy of the Prayer Book.

The Cavalier Parliament confirmed the victory of intolerant angli-canism by passing a series of acts known collectively as the Clarendon Code – although Clarendon was not responsible for them. The Corporation Act of 1661 empowered commissions of local gentlemen to administer oaths of loyalty to the governing bodies of corporate towns within their jurisdiction and remove aldermen and councillors who refused to swear them. It also prescribed that in future nobody should be eligible for appointment to a corporation unless he had 'taken the sacrament of the Lord's Supper according to the rites of the Church of England'. The Conventicle Act made it an offence to attend a service other than that set forth in the Prayer Book and gave Justices of the Peace authority to break into private houses if they suspected that conventicles – illegal religious meetings – were being held there. In spite of this legislation nonconformists did come together to worship, and their services were often conducted by ministers who had been ejected from their livings. The Five Mile Act was aimed at such men, since it forbade them to go within five miles of any cor-porate town.

The Cavalier Parliament's policy of imposing strict conformity was at variance with the attitude of Charles II. In December 1662 he issued a dec-laration reminding members of Parliament of the promise of toleration he had given in the *Declaration of Breda* and requesting them 'to concur with us in the making some such act for that purpose as may enable us to exer-cise with a more universal satisfaction that power of dispensing which we conceive to be inherent in us'. The plea fell on deaf ears, yet after a brief flurry of persecution following the passing of the Conventicle Act the local authorities in both urban and rural areas adopted an attitude of benign neglect. This was to be the case with subsequent campaigns against non-conformists initiated by the central government. As the memory of the puritan excesses of the Interregnum faded and it became apparent that the restored Church and monarchy were built upon secure foundations, persecution was in general confined to those such as quakers, baptists and Fifth Monarchists, who went out of their way to confront prevailing orthodoxies.

The Clarendon Code, by its explicit acknowledgement of the existence of dissent, marks the *de facto* abandonment of the ideal of comprehension, of a single Church to which all English protestants automatically belonged. Comprehension was not formally renounced until the Toleration Act of 1689, and attempts at reconciliation continued on and off until that date, but the Church could never again claim to speak for all the English people. It became increasingly the Church of the gentry and lost touch with labouring men and their families. It also lost its dominant position in politics, and after 1664, when Juxon's successor, Archbishop Gilbert Sheldon, accepted Clarendon's suggestion that the clergy should no longer tax themselves but should assume the same obligations as the laity, Convocation did not meet for a quarter of a century. The bishops remained important as individuals in the House of Lords, and they set a high standard of learning and piety. Many ministers also gave faithful and devoted service to their parishioners. But the Church had lost its independence. Church courts continued to function, but they were confined to spiritual penalties, which were of limited effectiveness. High Commission was never restored, and the exercise of ecclesiastical discipline was left, in practice, to country gentlemen, acting as Justices of the Peace, and to Parliament. In its rituals, ceremonies and hierarchy the Restoration Church was Laudian, but it had gained acceptance by the political nation only through abandoning the claim to secular authority that Laud had championed.

Clarendon

Clarendon's administration consisted of old cavaliers, like himself, Ormond and Southampton; former parliamentarians, like the Earl of Manchester, now Lord Chamberlain; soldiers, of whom the most distinguished was George Monck, created Duke of Albemarle and appointed Captain-General for life; and republicans such as Ashley Cooper, who became Chancellor of the Exchequer in 1661. Clarendon, the Lord Chancellor, was no figurehead. Because he had the ear of the King he was the chief minister and dominated the Privy Council, to which decisions on a whole host of matters, major and petty, were referred.

Clarendon's conservatism led him into problems with Parliament. At the beginning of the reign he 'had every day conference with some select persons of the House of Commons' to consult together 'in what method to proceed in disposing the House'. Yet although he kept a close watch on parliamentary proceedings and intervened when necessary, he had no intention of building up a 'King's party' in the Commons, nor did he believe that Parliament should take more than an occasional part in the government of the country. He had been out of England during the years when the Long Parliament had been forced to master the arts of adminis-tration, and he was unwilling, or perhaps unable, to accept that the divided society revealed in 1642 was to be a permanent feature of political life. In 1660 there was a superficial appearance of unity, but the fissures between anglicans and dissenters, protestants and catholics, diehard monarchists and opponents of 'absolutism,' ran too deep to be healed.

Clarendon had many enemies. Ardent cavaliers blamed him for making a constitutional settlement that left the King with too little power, while dissenters accused him of restoring a narrow and intolerant Church rather than a comprehensive one. Jealousy also played a part in moulding atti-tudes towards the Chancellor. In October 1660 it became obvious that his daughter, Anne Hyde, was pregnant, and she revealed not only that the King's brother, James, was the father of her child but that they had been secretly married. Charles was initially shocked, but accepted the situation. James now formally acknowledged Anne as Duchess of York, and Charles offered her father – at this stage Baron Hyde – a dukedom. Hyde declined so great an honour but accepted the earldom of Clarendon instead. His discretion had little effect on his rivals and critics, nor on the courtiers, who commented with acid tongues on the means by which a man who began his career as a country lawyer had wormed his way into a title and kinship with the heir to the throne. Clarendon was blamed for allowing France to purchase Dunkirk, captured for England under Cromwell, even though it cost far more to keep up than it brought into the Exchequer. Public hostility was demonstrated when mobs rioted outside the great house which Clarendon was building for himself in Piccadilly and broke its windows.

Clarendon, though pompous and self-satisfied, was a finer character than many of his critics, but they were more in tune with the amoral and cynical tone of the Restoration court and society. Even the King, while acknowledging Clarendon's wisdom and loyalty, preferred the company of younger men and women – particularly women. He was prepared to keep Clarendon in office as long as the government ran smoothly, but when the second Dutch war revealed appalling corruption and ineffi-ciency, he quickly got rid of him.

War was forced on Clarendon by men like Henry Bennett, who were ambitious for office and had built up a following in the Commons. But they also had support from the court. Prince Rupert, who made his home in England after the Restoration, was active in setting up the Royal Africa Company, which had James, Duke of York, as its president and included the King, as well as many courtiers, among its shareholders. When the company attempted to do business in West Africa it found the Dutch were already ensconced there, but it dealt with this challenge by setting out a warship and giving its commander a free hand to attack Dutch settlements and shipping. The success of this enterprise led the shareholders to form another company, the Corporation of the Royal Fishery, to challenge the Dutch dominance of North Sea fishing. Meanwhile, the English government decided to eradicate the Dutch colony of New Amsterdam which was placed astride the north American possessions of the crown. In the summer of 1664 New Amsterdam was captured and renamed New York, in honour of the King's brother.

News of this success was rapturously received in London, where pressure was mounting for war. Although the Dutch were fellow protestants they were regarded as commercial rivals whose trading empire and control of the European carrying trade stood in the way of an expansion of the British economy. War against Holland offered the possibility of rich prizes, and royalists also hoped to demonstrate that the restored monarchy could acquit itself just as honourably as the Commonwealth when it came to fighting. Clarendon, in this matter as in so many others, was out of tune with popular sentiment. So initially was the King, who recalled that his father's Parliaments had encouraged him to make war but denied him the means to fight. However, things now seemed to be different, for in December 1664 the Commons voted the enormous sum of £2,500,000 for war against the Dutch, and in March 1665 it was formally declared.

At first all went well, as the Lord Admiral, James, Duke of York, won a resounding victory over the Dutch fleet in the battle of Lowestoft, in which the Dutch admiral, Opdam, lost his life. However, this victory was not followed up, and the Dutch made such a good recovery that a year later they pounced on a fleet commanded by Albemarle and gave it a severe battering. After three days of heavy fighting he was close to defeat, but was saved on the fourth day by the arrival of Prince Rupert with a squadron of ships that had earlier been sent off to keep an eye on the French, who had joined in the war on the side of their Dutch allies. The Four Days battle ended in a draw, but the English lost twice as many ships and men as the Dutch.

While the hostile navies grappled in the Channel and North Sea, two natural disasters fell upon England. In May 1665 the first signs were observed of bubonic plague, which spread with frightening rapidity through the narrow, smelly streets and rat-infested houses of London. In the heat of the summer thousands of people died every month, and all who could afford to do so fled from the polluted city. Houses where the plague struck were closed up, with a red cross painted on their doors and the inscription 'Lord have mercy upon us', while at night carts rumbled through the deserted streets gathering up the dead and tumbling them into pits for common burial.

In September 1665 the plague claimed over thirty thousand victims, but after that it began slowly to decline as the survivors developed immunity. But hardly had life returned to normal in the City than the great fire broke out. It started in September 1666 in a baker's shop in Pudding Lane, not far from the place where The Monument now stands, and for three days and nights it burned its way westwards, fanned by a strong breeze. The diarist Samuel Pepys described the 'poor people staying in their houses as long as till the very fire touched them, and then running into boats or clambering from one pair of stairs by the waterside to another'. As darkness fell he saw the fire spread 'in corners and upon steeples and between churches and houses, as far as we could see up the hill of the City, in a most horrid, malicious, bloody flame ... The churches, houses and all on fire and flaming at once, and a horrid noise the flames made and the cracking of houses at their ruin'.

Charles went down to the City and supervised the blowing up of houses to make a fire break. Little could be done, however, until the wind dropped and the fire burned itself out. By that time the old City of London had been destroyed, and St Paul's Cathedral, which Charles I and Laud had struggled to restore, was a hollow shell. Over thirteen thousand homes and nearly ninety churches were ruined by the fire, and the homeless citizens camped out in the fields that stretched towards the villages of Highgate and Hampstead. After the first shock was over, various plans were drawn up for rebuilding the City in a more rational and dignified manner. The most famous of these came from the hand of Sir Christopher Wren, who was commissioned to construct a new St Paul's as well as many parish churches, but in the end little was done to alter the medieval ground plan of the City. However, minor changes of some significance were made. The height of houses was regulated and a minimum width was laid down for the principal streets. Charles also ordered that the new City should be built of brick and stone and not, as before, of inflammable wood.

Those who believed that plague and fire had been sent by God to punish a wicked and blasphemous people sought for a scapegoat. The honeymoon years which followed Charles's restoration were now over, and in the country as well as in Parliament there was open criticism of the profligate court and of Clarendon's administration. If the war with Holland had ended in triumph, public opinion might have swung round again in Charles's favour, but there was no chance of success since the King had insufficient money to set out the fleet in 1667. He could not blame Parliament for this, since after their unprecedentedly generous grant in 1664 the Commons had voted a further £1.5 million in 1665 and £1.8 million in 1666. The King's difficulties arose from the fact that these grants took so long to materialise. Unlike the Dutch, the English had no coherent system of public borrowing. The King could call for loans from the City of London as well as individual financiers, but he could not regularly anticipate revenue by borrowing. This only became possible after the creation of the Bank of England in 1694. Members of Parliament congratulated themselves on their generosity, but the Treasurer of the Navy had to wait for their grants to be turned into cash, and this was a slow business. By Easter 1667 he had received only a third of the total amount voted by Parliament, and the Navy Board declared that it needed an immediate £500,000 to make the fleet ready.

There was no possibility of finding such a sum, particularly as the plague and fire, not to mention Dutch attacks on British merchant ships, had led to a sharp decline in commercial activity, with corresponding effects on the income from Customs and the excise. In the early part of 1667 peace negotiations with the Dutch were opened at Breda, and the decision was taken to lay up the British fleet in the river Medway. It was there that the Dutch found it in June 1667 when, with magnificent effrontery, they broke through the defensive booms, burnt three English ships and towed away two others, including the *Royal Charles*, the flagship of the fleet. The *Royal Charles*, originally christened the *Naseby*, had been renamed by the King when it brought him back from his long exile. Its humiliating loss pointed the contrast between the efficiency and warlike strength of republican Britain and the maladministration and weakness that seemed to be the hallmarks of the Stuart monarchy.

Charles realised he would have to provide a scapegoat, for the tide of criticism was washing around the throne: Pepys, for example, recorded a rumour that 'the night the Dutch burned our ships the King did sup with my lady Castlemaine [one of his mistresses] and there they were all mad in hunting of a poor moth'. Clarendon was the obvious victim. Not only was he the head of an administration that had been responsible for England's humiliating defeat; he was also blamed for marrying the King to a Portuguese princess, Catherine of Braganza, who had failed to produce an heir. She had brought with her as dowry the ports of Bombay and Tangier, but the last of these was so expensive to maintain that Clarendon was thinking of abandoning it. Pepys describes how, when the news of the Medway disaster reached London, a crowd of 'rude people' demonstrated outside the Chancellor's new house and painted a gibbet on his gate, with 'these words writ: "Three sights to be seen – Dunkirk, Tangier and a barren queen."'

Charles could hardly part with Clarendon before peace was concluded with the United Provinces, but this was accomplished in July 1667 when the Treaty of Breda restored the status quo. The only exception was in America, where the English were confirmed in their possession of New York. Clarendon's dismissal followed shortly after. This did not satisfy his younger rivals in the Commons, who launched impeachment proceedings against him to ensure that he would be removed from the political scene once and for all. They could count on the presbyterians and their sympathisers in the Lower House, who held Clarendon responsible for the unequal treatment and sporadic persecution to which they were subjected, and also the independent country gentlemen who saw in the Chancellor the embodiment of court corruption and intrigue. Clarendon was willing to face his accusers, confident in the knowledge that he had done nothing illegal, but when it became clear that the King would not support him he fled to France. Charles allowed him to keep his titles and the income from his estates, but Parliament passed an act of perpetual banishment against him. The man who had been the architect of the Restoration settlement spent the seven remaining years of his life in exile, recalling the turbulent events through which he had lived and recording them for posterity in the *History of the Rebellion and Civil Wars in England*, which remains to this day one of the finest pieces of historical writing in the English language.

Arlington and the Cabal

The politics of the post-Clarendon period have been traditionally associated with the Cabal, so-called because of the initial letter of the names or titles of its supposed members – Sir Thomas Clifford, appointed Treasurer of the Household; Anthony Ashley Cooper, Baron Ashley, who kept his post as Chancellor of the Exchequer; the Duke of Buckingham, son of Charles I's favourite; Henry Bennet, Lord Arlington, one of the Secretaries of State; and John Maitland, Earl of Lauderdale, who ruled Scotland for the King. In this ill-assorted group Arlington and Lauderdale were the oldest, at around fifty, while the others were in their late thirties or forties, some twenty years younger than Clarendon and representative of a new political generation. In spite of its name, the Cabal was never a tight-knit body and its members had little in common. They were united initially only in their determination to get rid of Clarendon and take his place. They disliked the cumbersome Privy Council and preferred less formal and more intimate consultations. They also had little affection for the Church of England. Arlington and Clifford were Roman Catholic sympathisers, Lauderdale was a former presbyterian, Ashley had close links with the dissenters, and Buckingham had married the daughter of Sir Thomas Fairfax, the puritan commander of the New Model army during the Civil War. There was no question of the Cabal meeting regularly to advise the King on policy. Charles listened now to one minister, now to another, and played on personal rivalries so as to leave himself free to pursue his own tortuous policies. Nevertheless, he needed somebody to supervise the routine business of government and to act as his executive agent, and in practice this was Arlington.

Foreign policy was now becoming a major issue in English politics, because of the threatened domination of Europe by Louis XIV's France. Louis' immediate aim in the late 1660s was to take over the Spanish Netherlands, thereby putting at risk the independence of the United Provinces. Had Charles been a free agent he would probably have allied with Louis, for he was half French by birth and his years of exile in France had given him considerable affection for that country. However, the endemic shortage of money from which he suffered compelled him to take into account the attitude of Parliament, where informed opinion was becoming increasingly hostile to France, as the champion of absolute monarchy and uncompromising catholicism. Charles therefore, while keeping in secret touch with Louis, authorised Arlington to open negotiations with the Dutch, who were alarmed by the advance of French troops into the Spanish Netherlands. These resulted in a set of peace terms which were to be put to Louis, with the implied threat that if he did not accept them the English and Dutch would force him to do so. Further weight was given to this pact when Sweden joined what now became known as the Triple Alliance. It was successful in its aims, since Louis made peace at Aix-la-Chapelle in April 1668.

It seemed on the surface as though Charles had committed himself to a protestant foreign policy designed to contain Louis XIV, but the King always kept his options open. England was too weak to fight France on her own, and even if she did so in conjunction with her allies Charles would need a great deal of money, and the Dutch war had shown that while Parliament might make generous grants they were unlikely to be turned into cash at the necessary speed or in the requisite quantity. Charles's adhesion to the Triple Alliance had a beneficial side-effect in that it meant he could demand a higher price for coming to terms with Louis, and in early 1669 he made a secret approach to the French king to find out what terms might be on offer. This followed an extraordinary meeting between Charles, his brother James, Arlington and Clifford, at which the King – if James's later account is to be believed – told them, with tears in his eyes, that he wished to restore his country to the catholic faith. It was agreed that this could only be done with French help, and negotiations to this end were soon under way.

The outcome was the Secret Treaty of Dover, signed in May 1670. Under its terms, Charles agreed to supply sixty ships to join with half that number of French ones in an attack upon the Dutch republic, as well as four thousand infantry. Louis, in return, would provide Charles with an annual subsidy of some £230,000. But the key clause of the treaty was the second, which stated that 'The King of England, being convinced of the truth of the Roman Catholic religion, is resolved to declare it and to reconcile himself with the Church of Rome as soon as the state of his country's affairs will permit. He ... will avail himself of the assistance of the King of France who ... promises to pay to the King of England the sum of two million *livres tournois* [about £160,000], the first half payable three months after ratification of the present treaty, the other half three months later. In addition, the King of France undertakes to provide, at his own expense, six thousand troops for the execution of this design if they should be required. The time for the declaration of catholicism is left entirely to the discretion of the King of England.'

The significance of the Secret Treaty of Dover has remained a matter of controversy ever since it was signed. Charles, who died in the catholic faith, told the French ambassador in 1663 that 'no other creed matches so well with the absolute dignity of kings'. Yet during his exile he remained firmly committed to the anglican Church for which his father had died, and after his restoration he never attempted to restore links with the papacy, nor did he advance catholics to key positions in his government. It may be that Charles feared the French would come to terms with the Dutch, and made his dramatic offer in order to secure Louis' alliance. It may also be that he needed the money. Prior to 1665 his regular annual income had been around £800,000, a mere two-thirds of what the Convention had thought appropriate in 1660, but in the second half of the decade this figure slumped to under £650,000. Louis' lump-sum payment of £160,000, in addition to the £230,000 which Charles received in both 1672 and 1673, increased the King's ordinary revenue by nearly 50 per cent.

From the financial point of view, therefore, the Secret Treaty of Dover was a good bargain. Yet against this has to be set the fact that Charles had given a hostage to fortune by providing Louis with a written statement of his intention not only to announce his conversion but to return his kingdoms to the Roman obedience. Were this ever to become public knowledge, his throne would be at stake. As it happened, the exact provisions of the Secret Treaty of Dover were not revealed until long after Charles's death, but suspicion that the court was unsound on religion soon became widespread and poisoned the relationship between the King and the political nation as it was represented in the House of Commons.

Apart from Arlington and Clifford, the King's ministers knew nothing of the Secret Treaty. They were fobbed off with the open Treaty of London, concluded in December 1670, which only contained the clauses providing for joint action against the Dutch. Parliament was not informed about either treaty, since foreign relations came within the scope of the royal prerogative. When the two Houses reassembled in October 1670 they assumed that the protestant league created by the Triple Alliance was still the cornerstone of Charles's policy and they showed their approval of it by voting subsidies estimated to bring in £800,000 as well as an additional excise, to enable the fleet to be set out. The success of the government was partly due to the skilful way in which Clifford, acting on Arlington's behalf, had organised the 'King's men' in the Lower House. The lesson was not lost on one of Buckingham's protégés, Sir Thomas Osborne, nor on the King himself, who observed some time later that in this session the majority of the Commons 'were tied to his interests either by offices or by pensions'.

From April 1671 until February 1673 Parliament was prorogued, while the King made his preparations to put the Treaty of London into effect. The parliamentary grant enabled him to get the fleet ready for action but did nothing to reduce the backlog of accumulated debt with which he was burdened. Much of his annual revenue was mortgaged in advance to his creditors, but with the approach of war Charles needed all the money he could lay his hands on. In January 1672, therefore, he followed Clifford's advice by imposing 'the Stop of the Exchequer', which put an end to repayment of loans made to the King. His creditors were offered interest on the amounts outstanding, but Charles no longer acknowledged any obligation to repay the principal. In a sense this anticipated the concept of a national debt, but that only became acceptable later in the century, when the principal was guaranteed by Parliament, working through the Bank of England. The 'stop' merely served to undermine the confidence of merchants and financiers in the crown's trustworthiness, thereby making it more difficult for the King to raise future loans.

The Stop of the Exchequer was followed, in March 1672, by the *Declaration of Indulgence*, suspending the laws which penalised both Roman Catholics and dissenters. Roman Catholics were now free to worship in private; dissenters could worship publicly as long as they obtained an official licence. The initiative in issuing the *Declaration* did not come from Charles. He had been scarred by the failure of his earlier attempts to 'secure a liberty to tender consciences', and was not convinced that he had the right to suspend acts of Parliament. In the end, however, he yielded to his advisers, who had their own reasons for wanting the measure. Ashley and Buckingham had links with the dissenters and approved of toleration on principle. James and Clifford had the catholic interest at heart, while Arlington and Lauderdale wanted to elevate the royal authority and also pacify the nonconformists on the eve of a war against the Dutch that they might otherwise oppose.

The *Declaration* was an appeal to all those who recognised the futility of persecution, for, in its own words, 'the sad experience of twelve years [has shown] that there is very little fruit of all those forcible courses'. Public opinion, at least among the politically articulate, was gradually moving towards this position, but there was widespread opposition to Charles's *Declaration*. Property owners were alarmed by the King's assertion of his right to suspend the operation of statute law, but a more general fear – linked to rumours about the court's religious orientation – was that the real purpose of the *Declaration* was not to relieve protestant dissenters but to prepare the way for the re-establishment of Roman Catholicism. The long period of relatively harmonious relations between King and Parliament was now coming to an end, for more and more members were convinced that elements at court – though not, as yet, the King himself – were aiming to overthrow the existing order in both Church and state. This was to bring about a marked rise in the political temperature.

The future pattern of English politics depended to a great extent upon the outcome of the war against the Dutch which the King declared two days after issuing the *Declaration of Indulgence*. In order to win support for his plans Charles distributed honours. Lauderdale was made a duke, Arlington an earl and Clifford a baron, while Ashley was created Earl of Shaftesbury. Arlington and Lauderdale were further distinguished by being appointed to the Order of the Garter. It was at this date also that Sir Thomas Osborne, who had shown his financial ability as Treasurer of the Navy, was made a member of the Privy Council. Although Arlington continued to play a major role in government, his supremacy was threatened by the rise of Clifford and Shaftesbury, who had a deep interest in commercial matters, regarded the Dutch as dangerous rivals, and supported the policy of religious toleration inaugurated by the *Declaration of Indulgence*. In November 1672 Shaftesbury became Lord Chancellor, while Clifford was given the white staff of the Lord Treasurer.

The joint strategy worked out by England and France was that French troops, with a small English contingent, would be responsible for land operations, while the English fleet, aided by a French squadron, would attack the Dutch at sea. James and the Earl of Sandwich commanded Charles's fleet, but were caught unawares when they were attacked by the Dutch while they were revictualling in Southwold Bay on the Suffolk coast. The English ships were badly mauled, and Sandwich lost his life. On land, however, the French invasion met with success – hardly surprising, given the fact that Louis' army was nine times larger than his opponents'. The Dutch sued for peace, but the terms offered by Louis were so humiliating that they decided to fight on. William of Orange, who had been pushed into the background by the republican leaders, was recalled to power. He ordered the dykes to be cut, and the French advance slowed to a halt in a slough of mud.

Charles could not fight the war without the aid of Parliament, and the two Houses assembled in February 1673. Shaftesbury made his famous *Delenda est Carthago* speech, in which he declared that 'the States of Holland are England's eternal enemy both by interest and inclination', and the Commons responded by an offer of generous supply, but only on condition that the King abandoned the *Declaration of Indulgence*. In an address to Charles they asserted that 'penal statutes in matters ecclesiastical cannot be suspended but by act of Parliament', and when the King assured them in reply that he did not 'pretend to the right of suspending any laws wherein the properties, rights or liberties of any of his subjects are concerned', they told him his answer was 'not sufficient to clear the apprehensions that may justly remain in the minds of your people'. Charles was confronted with a clear choice between giving way on this issue or losing the parliamentary grant, and he chose to give way. Parliament thereupon voted more than a million pounds for the war, but at the same time it passed the Test Act, banning from office all those who refused to take the sacrament according to the rites of the Church of England and to make a public condemnation of the doctrine of transubstantiation. The aim of the act was to put an end to rumours of papists in high places, but when it became law these were given unexpected confirmation, for James resigned office as Lord Admiral while Clifford gave up the Treasury. This marked the point at which confidence in the court was destroyed and fear of popery developed into a paranoia that made the normal conduct of politics increasingly difficult.

Danby

Charles's priority at this stage was to restore public confidence in his rule. Rumours about secret commitments to France were in general circulation, and William of Orange was so alarmed by the pro-French drift of his uncle's policy that he sent an agent to England. It was this agent who, in March 1673, published *England's Appeal from the Private Cabal at Whitehall to the Great Council of the Nation*, in which he claimed that the alliance with France was the key element in a policy aimed at overthrowing the protestant religion in England and destroying the country's constitutional liberties. Charles replied to this challenge by choosing as Clifford's replacement Sir Thomas Osborne, a staunch anglican who believed that England should take a stand against France rather than ally with her. Osborne wanted to strengthen the monarchy by linking it more firmly with those elements of the political nation from which it had originally drawn its strength. He shared the views of one of his advisers who told him in 1676 that 'If . . . there can be any way contrived that the cavalier party may be convinced that the King loves them more than any sort of men . . . it will be a day more advantageous to the King than if he had an alliance with the most powerful prince alive.'

Osborne's long-term aim was to win the co-operation of the Commons by persuading Charles to embrace policies of which they approved. Meanwhile, he cut down on salaries and pensions and made economy and efficiency his watchwords. He had already demonstrated his financial acumen as Treasurer of the Navy, and after he was appointed Lord Treasurer in July 1673 he extended his grasp over the administration. Shaftesbury was dismissed from the Lord Chancellorship in November 1673 – 'It is only laying down my gown and putting on my sword', he commented – and Heneage Finch, a lawyer and ally of Osborne, became Lord

Keeper in his place. Arlington stayed in office long enough to negotiate the Treaty of Westminster, which brought about a separate peace between England and the United Provinces in February 1674, but resigned his Secretaryship later that year. Osborne was gradually attaining a primacy in the King's counsels unparalleled since the fall of Clarendon, and with the help of a good harvest and a trade boom he managed to raise the royal revenue to £1.5 million, which exceeded the King's expenditure. Charles showed his gratitude by creating Osborne Earl of Danby in June 1674.

At first Danby was inclined to rely upon the appeal of his policies to win support in the Commons, but in this he reckoned without Louis XIV. The French king's ambition to dominate Europe would be more difficult to achieve if England was actively engaged in a coalition against him, and he therefore authorised his ambassador to distribute money among members of the Commons and encourage them to frustrate the new chief minister. In fact the potential opposition in Parliament had sufficient stimuli to action without French gold. Following the death of Anne Hyde, the heir to the throne, James, Duke of York, had chosen a Roman Catholic princess, Mary of Modena, as his wife. This intensified fears about popery at court, and although Charles tried to stifle these by ordering that the penal laws should be strictly enforced he could not dispel the cloud of mistrust that was gathering around him. Suspicion of Charles spread over on to Danby, for how could members of Parliament be sure that the King and his chief minister were not plotting to deceive them once again by demanding supply for the navy when in fact the money would be used to create a French-style absolutism in England?

If Charles had stood firmly behind Danby, harmony between King and Parliament might eventually have been restored. Charles was certainly inclined to follow Danby's advice, but he did not want to be caught in the same trap as his father by following a policy calculated to appeal to Parliament, only to find that members were not prepared to finance it. He was always reluctant to commit himself to a course of action without preparing a way out. He therefore kept up his secret links with Louis as an insurance in case Danby did not succeed. Unfortunately by so doing he created an atmosphere of suspicion that ensured Danby's failure.

Throughout 1675 Danby tried to reach agreement with the two Houses, and as a means to this end he began organising the King's men in the Commons as Clifford had done before him. Pensions and offices were distributed to potential supporters and the nucleus of a royalist 'party' was created. However, by demonstrating that certain members were *in* the golden circle of court patronage, Danby drove the *outs* to come together. The hard core of the Commons remained, as always, the independent country gentlemen, but on either wing there were now organised groups, not strong enough to command a majority but constantly struggling to bring one into existence by winning over a sufficient number of the uncommitted members.

Although Parliament had voted supply in the autumn session of 1675, it did so only on a small scale and for strictly defined purposes. The main concern of members of the Commons was to secure the recall of British troops fighting alongside the French. They disapproved of such open support of Louis XIV and they feared that a standing army employed in the service of French absolutism might subsequently be used to establish an English version. Their apprehensions were given forceful expression in the *Letter from a Person of Quality to his Friend in the Country*, which appeared in November 1675. This pamphlet, which was probably the work of Shaftesbury, argued that ever since the Restoration there had been plans afoot to create an absolute monarchy in England and that these were now coming to fruition. Parliament's functions would be restricted to the granting of money, and any opposition would be put down by the standing army.

These assertions were, of course, exaggerated, but there was sufficient truth in them to carry conviction, and even Danby had to accept that in such a hothouse atmosphere his hopes of achieving harmonious co-operation between the King and Parliament could not be fulfilled. What was needed was a long period of political inactivity to let passions die down and reason prevail. Charles therefore prorogued Parliament in November 1675 and announced that it would not meet again for fifteen months. Louis XIV, who had feared that parliamentary pressures might force Charles into war against him, showed his relief by paying the King £100,000.

When the Cavalier Parliament met for its fifteenth session in February 1677 the King, in his opening speech, assured members that he had no aspiration to arbitrary rule. This was well received, and the Commons – where the court party, under Danby's control, was in the ascendant – responded by voting £600,000 for the navy as well as renewing the additional excise originally granted in 1671. This was a triumph for Danby, and the King showed his appreciation by making him a Knight of the Garter. The initial harmony of the session might have continued but for the fact that in March Louis XIV launched a massive assault on the Spanish Netherlands. The Commons petitioned Charles to make a firm alliance against France, and although the King rejected the petition as an invasion of his prerogative, Danby was urging him along the same path. Charles was not unwilling to enter into an anti-French alliance, but he insisted that the Commons must first grant him appropriate supply. The Commons, who were by now deeply suspicious of Charles's true intentions, demanded that the King should commit himself first. Their attitude was summed up by a member who was obviously well versed in Tudor history, for he recalled 'that example of Harry the Seventh, who got aids for the war and presently struck up a peace'.

This was the testing moment for Danby's strategy, and he came very close to success. But the King would not take the decisive step until he was certain the necessary funding would be forthcoming, and consequently the session petered out in acrimonious exchanges, with the King declaring that 'should I suffer this fundamental power of making peace and war to be so far invaded, though but once, as to have the manner and circumstances of leagues prescribed to me by Parliament, it is plain that no prince or state would any longer believe that the sovereignty of England rests in the crown'.

Political deadlock and the frustration it engendered sent the political temperature rising once again, and old fears were given new expression by the poet and Member of Parliament, Andrew Marvell, whose pamphlet *The Growth of Popery and Arbitrary Government in England* appeared in late 1677. In this he developed the theme that 'there had now for divers years a design been carried on to change the lawful government of England into downright popery'. Parliament alone had the capacity to block this design, but the majority of its members, or so Marvell claimed, were on the government's payroll and cared nothing about principles so long as they were in receipt of their pensions. This he denounced as a dereliction of duty, and he called on them to remember that 'there is no Englishman that hath a soul, a body or an estate to save, that loves either God, his King or his country, but is by all these tenures bound to the best of his power and knowledge to maintain the established protestant religion'.

If Marvell had been correct in asserting that most members of Parliament were the King's pensioners, Charles would have had little to worry about. The reality was very different, for the King was losing hope of reaching any agreement with Parliament, and was therefore willing to accept a French offer of financial assistance in return for a further prorogation. Danby encouraged Charles to pitch his demands high. Perhaps he hoped that Louis, in disgust, would withdraw his offer. At the very least there would have to be lengthy negotiations, and these would give Danby time, which he badly needed. The Treasurer had not abandoned hope of building bridges between the court and the Commons. On the contrary, he persuaded Charles to bid for the support of Parliament by agreeing to a marriage between the protestant champion, William of Orange, and James's daughter, Mary. The marriage took place in November 1677, and in the following January England and the United Provinces bound themselves by treaty to impose peace terms on Louis, if necessary by force. In other words, Charles was reverting to the policy advocated by Arlington ten years earlier, when he brought into being the Triple Alliance.

When Parliament reassembled early in 1678 Charles informed it that he had entered into an anti-French alliance, as the members had urged him to do, and that he now expected them to provide the funds for ninety war-ships and a force of thirty thousand soldiers. The Commons were distinctly lukewarm in their response. No doubt some members still suspected Charles's motives, but personal animosities – such as that of Arlington for Danby – also played a part, as did the large sums of money distributed by the French ambassador. Danby called the Commons' bluff by going ahead with war preparations, and the House thereupon voted a poll tax which eventually brought in £300,000. This was less than half what Danby had already spent, and a long way short of the £2.5 million which full-scale war would cost. Danby's belief that he could solve Charles's financial problems through co-operation with Parliament was looking increasingly chimerical. Lack of trust between the Commons and the King created too great a gulf to bridge, and the House rejected Danby's suggestion that it should at last fulfil the intention behind the Restoration settlement by bringing the ordinary revenue up to £1,200,000 a year. One member summed up the Commons' attitude by saying 'I am for keeping the revenue from being too big, for then you'll need Parliament.'

Louis was so alarmed by the direction in which Danby was moving, apparently with Charles's consent, that he authorised his ambassador to distribute whatever sums were appropriate to encourage the ministers' opponents. Most of Danby's critics in Parliament, including the well-known republican Algernon Sidney, were on the French payroll, for they believed that Louis was less of a threat than Charles and that the army raised to fight France would be used to suppress English liberties. Their fears increased after Louis and the Dutch came to terms, for although peace was concluded at Nimeguen in August 1678 Charles declined to disband his forces. The international situation was still volatile, and there were good reasons for keeping the army in being, but to the opposition this seemed proof that the King's aims – or at least those of his chief minister –

were sinister. The Commons insisted that the army should be disbanded and made it clear there was no possibility of further supply. Even Danby seems to have despaired, at this stage, of winning them over, and at the King's command he therefore wrote to Ralph Montagu, the ambassador in Paris, ordering him to speed up negotiations for a French subsidy. It was at this point, in September 1678, that Titus Oates – a turncoat Jesuit and a liar of the first quality – made his alarming revelations about a Popish Plot.

The Popish Plot and Exclusion Crisis

The catholic community in England had lived quietly and unobtrusively in the years following the Restoration. Its numbers were stable or declining, and much the same applied to the English mission. In the 1670s it included about 230 seculars – little more than half the 1640 figure – and some 260 regulars, of whom just under half were Jesuits. *De facto* acceptance of catholics as individuals and at local level co-existed with acute suspicion and fear of 'popery', by which was meant the operations of international catholicism aimed at destroying the English protestant state and all its hard-won liberties. This explains why Oates was instantly believed when he 'revealed' that the Pope had ordered the Jesuits to kill Charles and place his catholic brother on the throne. When he added that French troops were to be used to carry out this design and that it was to be accompanied by a general massacre of protestants, whatever lingering doubts there might have been about his veracity were instantly dispelled. Consciously or unconsciously Oates had used the sort of apocalyptic language that was exactly tuned to English anti-popish paranoia. He had also timed his revelations well, for Charles, by his simultaneous pursuit of mutually incompatible policies, had created such uncertainty about his real motives that anything seemed possible. By the time Parliament came together again in October 1678 the Plot was a major topic of discussion. Among the people whom Oates had accused of being implicated in it was Edward Coleman, a Roman Catholic in the service of James, Duke of York. When Coleman's papers were seized it was discovered that he had told his foreign correspondents of the 'mighty work' which lay ahead, involving the subduing of 'a pestilent heresy which has domineered over part of this northern world a long time'.

Before the end of 1678 Shaftesbury had taken up Oates and made himself the champion of the Plot. Shaftesbury was an ambitious and ruthless politician, but not unprincipled. Among his close friends he counted the philosopher John Locke, who was already at work on the *Two Treatises of Government*, which provided a theoretical basis for Shaftesbury's belief that there was an implied contract between the property-owners and the ruler that was automatically invalidated if he pursued absolutist policies. Shaftesbury was not a republican. He advocated limited monarchy on the traditional pattern, and twenty years earlier had been prominent among those who urged Cromwell to take the crown. He saw in James a threat to everything he believed in, for, in the words of a fellow member of Parliament, 'the protestant religion is so intermixed with the civil liberties of the nation that it is not possible to preserve them if a popish successor comes'. Shaftesbury's aim was to use the anti-popish paranoia whipped up by Oates to force Charles to accept a bill excluding James from the succession. In order to achieve this he built up a following in Parliament, linked with the Green Ribbon Club in London – which had close on thirty radical clubs by this date – and similar bodies in provincial centres. Pamphlets were published, processions organised and public opinion marshalled in such a manner that the opposition in Parliament became for a few years a party in the modern sense, with a political programme and national network.

The opposition won their first victory when Montagu, now a member of the Commons, revealed to a shocked House the details of Danby's negotiations for a French subsidy. This seemed to confirm that Danby, while pretending to be a supporter of the protestant interest, had all along been working to undermine it, and the Commons voted his impeachment. Rather than risk further disclosures which might reveal his own involvement, the King prorogued Parliament, and in January 1679 he dissolved it. The Cavalier Parliament – also known as the Pension Parliament and the Long Parliament of the Restoration – had been in existence for nearly eighteen years, during which time the crown had built up its influence to such an extent that long parliaments seemed to be as threatening to the liberty of the subject as no parliaments at all.

The following election was, as always, fought over local rather than national issues, but when the new Commons assembled in March 1679 it quickly became apparent that the majority of members were strongly exclusionist. They immediately revived Danby's impeachment, and the fact that the King had given him a pardon under the great seal only added to their indignation. By now the Treasurer was obviously more of a liability than an asset to the King, and he therefore resigned from office. Charles showed his gratitude by awarding Danby a huge pension, but in the following month the fallen minister submitted to the House of Lords, who committed him to the Tower to await trial.

Charles was doing his utmost to defuse the situation. In the closing months of 1678 he had ordered the rigorous enforcement of the laws against popish recusants and Jesuits, and he also accepted a second Test Act, excluding catholics from Parliament, but only after bringing intense pressure upon both Houses to provide that 'nothing in this act contained shall extend to his royal highness, the Duke of York'. However, James's presence at court was clearly an embarrassment to the King, and in February 1679 Charles persuaded his brother to go into temporary exile at The Hague. He also made a bid for broader support by enlarging the Privy Council and restoring much of its influence. The post-Restoration period had seen the emergence of a smaller body, sometimes called the Cabinet Council, which in Charles's opinion was more fitted for 'the secrecy and dispatch that are necessary in many great affairs'. Now, however, he made Shaftesbury Lord President of a Privy Council that included not only courtiers and officials – like Robert Spencer, Earl of Sunderland, newly appointed Secretary of State – but also critics of Charles such as George Savile, Earl of Halifax, and Arthur Capel, Earl of Essex. By doing this Charles hoped to divide the opposition leaders from their followers, and also to demonstrate that he was not under the influence of evil counsellors.

When the Commons turned to business they began with the old demand that the troops raised for the projected campaign against France should be disbanded, and voted £200,000 for this purpose. But their main concern was the question of whether or not James, Duke of York, should inherit the throne. Charles offered to accept limitations on the powers of a catholic successor, but the Commons were not to be bought off. John Hampden's grandson introduced a bill to exclude James from the throne, which should revert to the next in line, as though James were dead. Meanwhile, Shaftesbury was busy whipping up anger against the duke, whom he described as a man 'heady, violent and bloody, [whose] ... interest and designs are to introduce a military and arbitrary government'. These sentiments were widely shared, and the exclusion bill passed the Commons. Charles riposted by proroguing Parliament at the end of May 1679, telling his courtiers that he 'would rather submit to anything than endure the gentlemen of the Commons any longer'. In the following July he dissolved it. The session had proved sterile except for the Habeas Corpus Act which gave statutory backing to the common-law right of freedom from arbitrary arrest and imprisonment.

Elections for a new Parliament, the third of Charles's reign, were to be held in the autumn of 1679, but in August the King collapsed with a high fever, and for several days his life was in danger. The triumvirate of Sunderland, Halifax and Essex feared that Charles's illegitimate son, the Duke of Monmouth, who had won applause by putting down a revolt in Scotland, might use the occasion to assert his claim to the throne. They therefore urged James to return from exile, which he did in early September. By this time Charles was much better and he resolved the problem of the bad relationship between his son and his brother by persuading Monmouth to go into exile while James was sent north to rule Scotland. Shaftesbury challenged this decision, but Charles refused to change his mind and dismissed the earl from the presidency of the Council. The triumvirate was divided in its attitude, especially when the King delayed the meeting of Parliament without consulting them. Only Sunderland professed his loyalty, and he was rewarded by remaining in power as a member of a new triumvirate which replaced the old one. Its other members were Laurence Hyde, Clarendon's second son, and Sidney Godolphin, who was relatively unknown. Because of their comparative youth – Goldolphin was in his mid-thirties – they were familiarly known as the Chits.

Monmouth's exile was a blow to Shaftesbury, who considered him the most promising candidate for the succession if James was excluded, but in the absence of Parliament he had no platform from which to expound his views. He therefore organised a petitioning campaign, and during December the King was brought under increasing pressure to summon Parliament. He showed his anger by postponing its recall for a further ten months. Shaftesbury kept passions alive by formally indicting James before the grand jury of Middlesex in June 1680, on the grounds that he was a popish recusant. Only the judge's intervention, prompted by the King, prevented the jury from returning a true bill and thereby opening the way to James's prosecution. Nevertheless, Shaftesbury had won a propaganda victory, and he kept up the petitioning campaign. The exclusionists were nicknamed 'Whigs' – a shortened form of the pejorative label 'Whiggamores,' used to describe the Scottish rebels of 1679 (*see* p. 497). The loyalists acquired the sobriquet of 'Tories', the name given to dispossessed Irish catholics who turned to banditry in order to survive.

Shaftesbury assumed Charles would give way under pressure, for the King had never been renowned for his adhesion to principle. But over the issue of exclusion Charles stood firm. He recognised his brother's faults, but he had a genuine affection for him and was, in any case, determined to maintain the fundamental principle of hereditary succession which had brought him to the throne. Charles was also consistent in his attitude to the law, for he let it take its course even though this led to injustice. During the period 1678–81 English catholics were subject to their last period of intense persecution. The missionary priests suffered worst, for about a hundred were arrested, of whom seventeen were executed and another twenty or so died in prison. The Jesuits were particularly hard hit, for nearly half their number were imprisoned and the Provincial of their order was among those executed. Roman Catholic peers were not exempt from legal proceedings. Many went into exile and waited for the storm to blow over, but eleven who remained behind were arrested on treason charges, of whom one was executed and one died in the Tower. Catholic gentry fared better, though some four hundred of them were imprisoned, but catholic tradesmen came under strong attack in London, where about twenty of them were executed or died in custody.

In October 1680 Charles at last allowed the new Parliament to meet. In his opening speech he called upon members to unite the nation and not to tamper with the succession, but their only response was to bring in another exclusion bill. Charles made plain his opposition to it, telling one Tory member that "I will stick by you and my old friends, for if I do not I shall have nobody to stick by me.' The bill passed the Commons without difficulty, but the decisive debate came in the Lords. Charles was present throughout, having his meals sent in to him and standing with his back to the fireplace, noting the points put forward by various speakers and now and again making an effective intervention. He was aided by the Earl of Halifax, who argued that limitations, of the sort Charles had earlier proposed, were an acceptable alternative to exclusion. During the course of the heated debate Halifax rose to speak sixteen times, and his pleading, combined with Charles's presence, was decisive. The Lords rejected the exclusion bill by sixty-three votes to thirty.

In January 1681 Charles dissolved his third Parliament and summoned a fourth to meet at Oxford. No doubt he remembered the way in which the Long Parliament had drawn strength from the City of London when it confronted his father and was determined not to let the same thing happen again. In the elections the Whigs proved themselves masterly tacticians. They focused on national rather than local issues, and drew up draft instructions to candidates committing them to support exclusion. The Tories also organised themselves, adopting many of the techniques pioneered by the Whigs, and this in itself was a sign that the tide was no longer flowing so strongly in the Whigs' favour. So was the fact that in the new

House of Commons their strength was slightly reduced. Nevertheless, they could be sure of a big majority for exclusion. They were not interested in the alternative of limitations, for James as King would be able to use his prerogative authority to suspend any statutes constraining his power. Or he could simply ignore them and rely on his standing army to suppress any protests.

Shaftesbury was counting on Charles's need for parliamentary subsidies to secure the acceptance of exclusion. He was probably aware that English trade was expanding but did not realise that the increased yield of customs and excise duties was bringing the King's revenue up to and even beyond the target figure of £1,200,000. Nor did he know that Louis XIV had promised Charles an annual payment of some £130,000 for the next three years.

In his opening speech to the Oxford Parliament Charles emphasised that he had taken his stand on law, and that if the rules governing succession were changed no man's property would be safe. He reiterated that he would never agree to exclusion, but that he was prepared to accept statutory limitations on his successor's authority. Whether he was genuine in his offer of limitations was never put to the test, for Shaftesbury insisted on exclusion. 'If you are restrained only by law and justice', he told Charles in the Lords, 'rely on us and leave us to act. We will make laws which will give legality to a measure so necessary for the quiet of the nation.' 'Let there be no delusion', replied the King. 'I will not yield, nor will I be bullied. Men usually become timid as they become older. It is the opposite with me, and for what may remain of my life I am determined that nothing will tarnish my reputation. I have law and reason and all right-thinking men on my side. I have the Church' – here he pointed to the bishops – "and nothing will ever separate us.'

The Commons ignored the King's speech and pressed ahead with exclusion. On 28 March, therefore, Charles went to the Lords as usual but then sprang a surprise by appearing robed and crowned and commanding members of both Houses to attend him. The Whigs were confident of victory, but when Charles spoke it was only to announce his decision to dissolve Parliament. Had his enemies been warned they might have planned counter-action, and had they been in London they might have seized the initiative. Charles, however, had made his preparations with great care. Six hundred infantry were present to guard him at Oxford, while a strong force of cavalry kept open the road back to London, which was itself garrisoned by several thousand men. Charles, in short, was ready to fight to preserve the rights of the crown. His enemies were not. Some of the Whigs talked violence, but in the end they dispersed peacefully while the King rode back at full speed to his capital.

The Exclusion Crisis had ended in victory for Charles, but at a price. It was now clear not only to him but to the whole of Europe that his attempts to establish a working relationship with Parliament had failed. Eight years earlier, when suspicions about popery at court were beginning to sour the atmosphere, an English diplomat had observed that 'a King of England at the head of his Parliament and people, and in their hearts and interests, can never fail of making what figure he pleases in the world', but the converse was also true, that a King at loggerheads with his Parliament and people had no significant role to play on the European scene. Charles accepted this situation because he had no choice, but he thereby confirmed the view that the Stuart kings were invariably associated with political impotence.

Royalist reaction

Charles exploited his victory over the Whigs by issuing a declaration explaining why he had dissolved Parliament. This document, which he ordered to be read from pulpits throughout the land, portrayed the King as the saviour of his country, the man who had prevented another civil war. It also reminded the listening congregations that 'Religion, liberty and property were all lost and gone when the monarchy was shaken off, and could never be revived till that was restored.' The same themes were emphasised in the government propaganda campaign directed by the journalist Roger L'Estrange through his newspaper *The Observator*. The high point of the royalist counter-attack came in November 1681 with the publication of John Dryden's brilliant satire *Absalom and Achitophel*, in which Shaftesbury and his adherents are depicted as unscrupulous adventurers while Charles is compared to the biblical King David, the guardian of his people.

Shaftesbury himself was arrested on a charge of high treason, sent to the Tower, and subsequently indicted before a grand jury in London. However, the Whig sheriffs, elected at the time when exclusionist sentiment was still strong, chose a jury of their own persuasion which threw out the indictment. Shaftesbury was a free man once again, but this was only a temporary reprieve, for London was not immune from the royalist fervour that was sweeping through England, and in July 1682 two Tory sheriffs were elected. Shaftesbury immediately went into hiding and later fled to Holland, where he died the following year. The remaining Whig leaders were now contemplating armed resistance against the triumphant

King, and a number of them were implicated in a plot to assassinate Charles and his brother on their way back from the races at Newmarket at the Rye House, near Hoddesdon in Hertfordshire. The Earl of Essex committed suicide after his arrest. William, Lord Russell, and Algernon Sidney were tried on treason charges, found guilty and executed.

Charles remodelled the judicial bench to make sure it would not oppose his will. For the first eight years of his reign he had appointed judges *Quamdiu se bene gesserint* ('during good behaviour'), which gave them virtual security of tenure, but thereafter he changed this to *Durante beneplacito* ('during good pleasure'), which meant he could dismiss them as and when he thought fit. Charles I had been accused of eroding the impartiality of the bench by dismissing one judge and suspending another in a reign that lasted twenty-four years, but his son went far beyond this. By the end of 1683 he had removed eleven judges in eight years, and he appointed as Chief Justice the notorious time-server George Jeffreys. With the judges firmly behind him Charles could act as autocratically as his father had done through the prerogative courts, and he now moved to ensure his control over the localities.

The Corporation Act of 1661 had authorised the King to appoint commissioners to reshape the governing bodies of corporate towns, but this had only been a temporary measure. During the Exclusion Crisis the corporations had become Whig strongholds, but now the Tories were gaining places and they looked to the crown to ensure their victory. Charles therefore instructed his judges to undertake *Quo Warranto* investigations, to determine 'by what warrant' the corporations exercised their functions. Many boroughs derived their privileges from royal charters, but over the course of time they had assumed powers for which there was no specific authorisation. Now they were called to account and often made a voluntary surrender of their charters rather than meet the costs of a judicial inquiry. Those which held out were subjected to the full force of the law. Even London, the greatest corporation of all, was punished for its initial refusal to indict Shaftesbury by being brought before the Court of King's Bench. Judgment was given against it and an order was made 'that the franchise and liberty of London be taken into the King's hands'. Charles was pleased to restore all the traditional rights of his capital city, but only on condition that no official should be elected in future without his approval. The same stipulation was imposed on fifty or so other municipalities. This gave the King virtual control over a significant number of borough seats in the House of Commons and opened up the unusual but pleasing prospect of a co-operative, if not a subservient, Parliament, should he decide to summon one.

The closing years of Charles II's reign were the Indian summer of the Stuarts. Tories replaced Whigs in county administration as well as the boroughs, and pulpits resounded with sermons on the sinfulness of resisting the will of a divinely appointed monarch. Dissent was not tolerated, and baptists, presbyterians and quakers had to endure harsh persecution. During the course of Charles's reign some 450 quakers died in prison and at the time of his death the number confined amounted to almost 1,500. Catholics were treated more mildly as long as they kept a low profile, but Charles made no attempt to improve their legal status. The Exclusion Crisis had taught him that the maintenance of his authority depended on identifying himself with the law and the Church. As he told one of his courtiers, he would 'stick to that that is law, and maintain the Church as it is now established ... I will not be for the lessening of it, and if I do I know I less[en] my crown, for we must march together'.

The King, having entered calm waters at last, had no intention of stirring up passions by summoning another Parliament. Under the terms of the 1664 Triennial Act the two Houses were due to meet in 1684, but Charles never summoned them. Halifax protested at this open flouting of statute law, but there was no general outcry. Halifax's influence had been increasing up to this point, but now the Chits reasserted their dominance of the King's counsels. Sunderland stayed in office as Secretary of State, while Godolphin and Laurence Hyde, whom Charles had created Earl of Rochester, ran the Treasury, which had been put into commission after Danby's fall from power. Danby had abandoned the farming of the Customs in 1671 with beneficial consequences, and the new Treasury commissioners followed suit by instituting direct collection of the excise and hearth tax. The result was a substantial increase in the yield from both sources, but Rochester went further than Danby had ever dared by persuading Charles to restrain his natural extravagance and live within, or even below, his income. This was not all that much of a hardship, for by the end of Charles's reign the ordinary revenue was close on £1,400,000 a year and French subsidies brought it well above that figure.

In the last year of his life Charles came ever closer to his brother James. In February 1685, when Charles suffered a stroke and was clearly dying, it was James who sent for a Roman Catholic priest to administer the last rites. At this late stage, therefore, the King fulfilled the promise he had made fifteen years before in the Secret Treaty of Dover by declaring himself a catholic.

CHAPTER NINETEEN

James II, The Glorious Revolution, and the reign of William III

James II

'If it had not been for his popery he would have been, if not a great, yet a good prince.' In these words Bishop Burnet pithily and accurately summed up James II. The new King had much to be said for him. He was honest and hard working, and he wanted to see his country become once again a major power in Europe – not for him the dependence upon France that had come to characterise Charles II. He had, it is true, an exalted view of kingship that would sooner or later have brought him into conflict with Parliament, but he shared so many of the attitudes of the Tory squires who dominated the Commons that he could probably have arrived at a *modus vivendi* with them. Yet he threw away all his advantages because of his determination to secure toleration for his fellow catholics. He did so on the assumption that he would be succeeded by his two daughters, both of whom were protestant. When that happened, the catholics would be forced back into a shadowy existence once again, unless he could ensure that during his reign they were so firmly established in Parliament and public life that any future ruler would have to come to terms with them. This could not be done, however, until the laws which discriminated against them had been repealed.

James and the Anglicans

James hoped to secure the repeal of the penal laws through co-operation with the anglican Tories, and in order to dispel any doubts about his motives he assured the Privy Council that he would 'preserve this government both in Church and state as it is now by law established. I know the principles of the Church of England are for monarchy, and the members of it have showed themselves good and loyal subjects. Therefore I shall always take care to defend and support it'. The composition of James's first ministry showed that he meant what he said, for Laurence Hyde, Earl of Rochester, was appointed Lord Treasurer while Henry Hyde, second Earl of Clarendon, became Lord Privy Seal. These two brothers, James's relations by marriage, were pillars of the anglican Church, and so were Godolphin, now Chamberlain to the Queen, and Halifax, who retained his post as Lord President of the Council. Only Sunderland, who continued in office as Secretary of State, was lacking in any real enthusiasm for the established Church.

Sunderland prepared for the election of James's first Parliament with great care, sending letters to Lord Lieutenants and influential noblemen asking them to make sure that only 'well affected' candidates were returned. He was helped by the fact that the remodelling of the municipal corporations had brought them under much closer royal control, and when Parliament met it turned out to be the most loyal that any Stuart ever encountered. Even James reckoned that there were only about forty members of the Commons whose devotion to him was questionable. This was just as well, because James had no intention of bargaining with Parliament. He disapproved of Charles II's readiness to make concessions in order to improve relations with the Commons, and he regarded attempts at 'managing' the House through the distribution of the crown's patronage as a derogation of monarchical authority

The Commons could have taken offence at the way in which James had collected the customs and excise duties from the beginning of his reign, without waiting for a formal grant, but they preferred to overlook this slight and gave him the same financial settlement as that provided for his brother. This did not satisfy James, who demanded extraordinary supply to help him pay off Charles II's debts and build up the strength of the navy. The Commons met his wishes by voting extra duties for an eight-year period. The expansion of trade had brought the ordinary revenue up to £1,600,000 a year, and with the temporary grant James was in receipt of well over two million pounds. Even though he used the extra duties for the purposes for which they had been granted, he still had enough money to cover his expenditure, including the maintenance of an enlarged standing army.

Although Parliament had demonstrated its loyalty, there were plenty of disaffected elements in the political nation, particularly among those who had gone into exile because of their involvement in the Rye House Plot and other conspiracies. It was this group which planned a double rising against James. The Marquis of Argyll would land in Scotland, while the Duke of Monmouth would raise his standard in England. Argyll sailed first, in May 1685, but had been defeated and captured by the time Monmouth landed in the west country in June. Monmouth called on the people to join him in a protestant uprising, but his appeal evoked no response from property-owners. Only men of little substance, who had nothing to hope for from the existing order and may also genuinely have believed that their religion was in danger, threw in their lot with Monmouth. His youthful but untrained force, amounting to some three or four thousand men, succeeded in capturing Taunton, but it was no match for the regular army, commanded by John Churchill, which overwhelmed them in a battle fought in the marshes of Sedgemoor. Monmouth himself was captured, sent to London to be tried, and subsequently executed.

Monmouth's rebellion had been little more than a flash in the pan, but James was shocked by the fact that it had taken place at all, and scented treachery everywhere. His anger was shown by his instructions to Judge Jeffreys, who was sent down to do justice on the defeated rebels, to show them no mercy. Some three hundred men were sentenced to death and another eight hundred transported as serfs to the West Indies. By this savage repression James made sure that the west country would not support any further challenge to his rule.

Members of Parliament, who reassembled in November 1685 for the winter session, were shocked by the violence of James's revenge and alarmed by the contempt Jeffreys showed for legal safeguards. Their concern was heightened by the flood of protestant refugees pouring in from France in the days preceding the revocation of the Edict of Nantes – a guarantee of limited freedom of worship for French protestants – in October 1685. In the same month Halifax was dismissed from office and the Privy Council, and the hated Jeffreys was appointed Lord Keeper. The Commons were not, therefore, in so loyal a frame of mind when James demanded more money in order to increase the size of the standing army. The failure of Taunton to defend itself had shown the ineffectiveness of the militia, and James argued that he needed a larger army to protect him in the event of further rebellions. This claim had something to be said for it, but James turned opinion against him by announcing that the Roman Catholic officers he had (illegally) recruited were the only ones he could truly rely on and that he intended to retain them in his service despite the provisions of the Test Act. The Commons eventually voted James taxes estimated to bring in £700,000, but the King rejected this amount as inadequate and informed members that he 'had reason to hope that the reputation God has blessed me with would have created and confirmed a greater confidence in me'. The Commons refused to increase the proposed grant. One member went so far as to say 'We are all Englishmen, and not to be frightened out of our duty by a few high words.' There could have been no clearer indication of the extent to which James had dissipated the goodwill that greeted his accession. Rather than face a prolonged struggle, the King cut his losses and prorogued Parliament. It never met again.

James was not yet ready for an open break with the Tories. Rochester stayed on as Lord Treasurer, but Clarendon was sent into honourable exile as Lord Lieutenant of Ireland, and his place as Lord Privy Seal was taken by Sunderland, who retained his Secretaryship. Sunderland was now the King's chief minister, and the 'cabinets' which met in his house were more important in the making of policy than the Privy Council. These cabinets had no formal standing and no fixed membership. They could therefore include catholics, and Father Petre, James's Jesuit confessor, was a frequent attender.

Until such time as James could persuade Parliament to repeal the penal laws he used his prerogative powers to relieve his catholic subjects. There was some doubt, however, whether the King had the constitutional right to set aside statute law. The matter was brought to a head through a test case, Godden v. Hales, in which Edward Hales, a Roman Catholic officer whom James had appointed even though he refused to take the oaths prescribed in the Test Act, defended himself on the grounds that he had a royal dispensation. James had earlier called on the judges to acknowledge his dispensing power and dismissed two who refused to do so. In April 1685, shortly before Hales's trial began, he dismissed four more. This pressure was reflected in the verdict given in Godden v. Hales, for eleven of the twelve judges maintained that the dispensation was valid. Chief Justice Herbert went so far as to say 'that the laws of England are the King's laws; that therefore 'tis an inseparable prerogative in the Kings of England to dispense with penal laws in particular cases and upon particular necessary reasons ... [and] that this is not a trust invested in or granted to the King by the people, but the ancient remains of the sovereign power and the prerogative of the Kings of England, which never yet was taken from them, nor can be'.

This momentous judgment, with its insistence on the inalienable prerogative, meant that there was now no legal barrier preventing James from carrying out his policy of infiltrating catholics into public life. This prospect alarmed the leaders of the established Church, a number of whom made critical references to the King's policy in their sermons. James responded by issuing 'Directions to Preachers', forbidding this practice, and in July 1686 he set up an Ecclesiastical Commission to enforce them. The new body was not a court, neither did it have jurisdiction over laymen, but it bore too close a resemblance to the hated Court of High Commission abolished by the Long Parliament, to be acceptable. Among the first persons to be censured by the Ecclesiastical Commission was Henry Compton, Bishop of London, who had refused to discipline one of his clergy for preaching an anti-catholic sermon. For this offence Compton was suspended from his functions – a clear warning to any other bishop contemplating resistance.

James and the dissenters

James dismissed Clarendon and Rochester from office in January 1687. This signalled his abandonment of co-operation with the anglican Tories and the beginning of a *rapprochement* with the Whigs and dissenters. James first made overtures to William Penn, the leader of the quakers, who helped draft the *Declaration of Indulgence* which was promulgated in April 1687. This condemned the whole idea of compulsion in religion, on the grounds that 'it has ever been directly contrary to ... the interest of government, which it destroys by spoiling trade, depopulating countries and discouraging strangers', and that 'it never obtained the end for which it was employed'. The *Declaration* emphasised the King's intention to 'protect and maintain our archbishops, bishops and clergy, and all other our subjects of the Church of England in the free exercise of their religion as by law established, and in the quiet and full enjoyment of their possessions', but this was a long way removed in both tone and content from Charles II's *Declaration of Indulgence*, which gave an unequivocal commitment 'that the Church of England [shall] be preserved and remain entire in its doctrine, discipline and government', and that it would continue to be 'the basis, rule and standard of the general and public worship of God'. James was inhibited from giving such a guarantee to the established Church because of his conviction, which had been one of the main causes of his conversion to Rome, that it was not in fact a true Church but schismatic and heretical.

Another difference between the two *Declarations* was that Charles's granted only conditional freedom of worship, whereas James's subjects were now free 'to meet and serve God after their own way and manner, be it in private houses or places purposely hired or built for that use'. Moreover, the King expressed his desire 'to have the benefit of the service of all our loving subjects', and therefore announced that none of them were for the future to 'be under any discouragement or disability ... by reason of some oaths or tests that have been usually administered on such occasions'. Generally speaking, the quakers and baptists welcomed the *Declaration* as evidence of the King's commitment to the principle of religious toleration. The presbyterians were more cautious and accepted Halifax's warning, in his *Letter to a Dissenter*, that 'you are therefore to be hugged now, only that you may be the better squeezed at another time'.

In the *Declaration* James had acknowledged that 'we cannot but heartily wish, as it will easily be believed, that all the people of our dominions were members of the Catholic Church', and now that the penalties on catholics had been removed he confidently awaited a flood of conversions: as he told the French ambassador, 'the possibility of holding offices and employments will make more catholics than permission to say mass publicly'. James had already appointed a number of Roman Catholics to the Privy Council, and he now extended this practice to the Commission of the Peace. Of 455 new Justices of the Peace appointed in early 1687, more than 60 per cent were adherents of the old faith.

One of the biggest problems facing James was the need to increase the supply of catholic priests. He was also aware that there were insufficient catholic laymen with the experience and ability to fill the positions in public life which were now open to them. This was hardly surprising in view of the fact that the anglicans had a monopoly over the universities, which existed to train young men for the ministry and state service, and therefore, in the spring of 1687, James began putting pressure on Oxford and Cambridge to admit papists. When Cambridge refused to give a degree to a Benedictine monk, the Ecclesiastical Commission deprived the vice-chancellor of his office. At Oxford, the fellows of Magdalen College refused to elect a Roman Catholic as their head, so the King imposed the Bishop of Oxford, an anglican but a loyalist. The fellows rejected him as well and insisted on their legal right to make their own choice. Thereupon the Ecclesiastical Commission deprived them of their livings.

Magdalen was now all set to become a seminary for training the future clergy and lay administrators of catholic England.

Although James had suspended the penal laws he could not have them repealed without the co-operation of Parliament. In July 1687, therefore, he dissolved his first Parliament, which he had prorogued in November 1685, and ordered Sunderland to set the electoral process in train. He had already made his own preparations by personally interviewing peers, members of the Commons and office-holders in an attempt to persuade them to support repeal. Their lukewarm response confirmed him in his belief that the anglican Tories would never give him what he wanted. He therefore exerted maximum pressure on the constituencies in order to ensure victory for the Whigs and dissenters. The climax of his campaign came in October 1687, when Lord Lieutenants were ordered to put three questions to Justices of the Peace in their respective counties. Would they live in friendship with their neighbours of all religious persuasions? If elected to Parliament, would they vote to repeal penal legislation? Or, if they were not candidates themselves, would they encourage the election of those who were committed to repeal? About a quarter of the magistrates gave a positive answer to these questions, but they included the recently appointed catholic Justices. Only 16 per cent of the protestant ones were as forthcoming. Twice as many were opposed to repeal, as were most, if not all, of those who gave conditional acceptances or no reply.

The Three Questions were followed by a massive purge of local governors. By 1688 Roman Catholics, despite being a tiny proportion of the population, held fifteen Lord Lieutenantcies. Thirty per cent of the Deputy-Lieutenants were catholics and nearly twenty per cent of the magistrates who had survived the purge. Since catholics were thin on the ground, James had to cast his net wide in order to find enough Justices of the Peace to replace those he had dismissed. One Yorkshire squire, who had given loyal service to both Charles II and James II, wrote of his astonishment at the quality of the new magistrates for his county. 'The first', he declared, 'can neither write nor read. The second is a bailiff . . . And neither of them have one foot of freehold land in England.'

The appointment of catholics to offices in central and local government coincided with the active encouragement of catholic evangelisation. For this purpose the country was divided into four districts, each under the direction of a Vicar-Apostolic, who was a bishop in all but name. James opened a catholic chapel in Whitehall, and other places of worship for catholics sprang up in London and provincial towns. There were also a few catholic schools, including two run by the Jesuits in London. Missionaries could now operate freely, but there was no mass movement of conversion. Among those who did embrace the Roman Catholic faith, however, were prominent figures such as the poet laureate, John Dryden, and Secretary Sunderland, and it is hardly surprising that the anglican political nation felt the ground slipping under its feet.

Although the selection of catholics as Justices of the Peace aroused most comment, more significant from the point of view of the forthcoming election was the appointment of a much larger number of dissenters, for they could be relied on to work for a Whig victory. The same process was apparent in the urban corporations. Charles II had remodelled some fifty boroughs in order to entrench the Tories in power. James used the same method but for the opposite purpose. Some one hundred and twenty boroughs were given new or rewritten charters which made it possible for them to eject the Tories and replace them by a Whig-dissenter combination. James hoped he would thereby secure a Whig majority in the House of Commons which could be relied on to repeal the penal laws.

James's anglican subjects were increasingly alarmed by his policies, since they pointed towards the creation of a catholic England. Yet they stood little chance of persuading James to change course. For one thing he was notoriously stubborn, and, for another, he had an army of twenty thousand men at his disposal which he would use to crush any opposition. The only hope for the anglicans lay in foreign intervention, and a number of them made contact with the agents whom William of Orange had sent over to report on the situation. William had so far been concerned to retain James's friendship; at the time of the Monmouth rising, for instance, he had sent back the British troops in his service for use against the rebels. But as James continued on his headlong course, William began to fear that he might provoke a violent reaction among his subjects, and turn to France for protection. William had devoted his life to checking the ambitions of Louis XIV and was not prepared to stand by if England seemed likely once again to become a French satellite. In April 1688, therefore, he let it be known that if he was invited by 'some men of the best interest . . . to come and rescue the nation and the religion' he would do so.

April also saw James make a further bid for the support of the dissenters in the imminent election by re-issuing his *Declaration of Indulgence* and ordering it to be read on two successive Sundays in every church in the land. Archbishop Sancroft and six of his fellow bishops sent a petition to James, asking him to cancel his order. They were not, they emphasised, lacking in obedience to the royal will, nor were they opposed to some measure of toleration for dissenters, but they called in question the validity of 'such a dispensing power as hath been often declared illegal in Parliament'. James met this challenge to his prerogative by ordering the arrest of the seven bishops on the grounds that their petition was a seditious libel. Excitement rapidly mounted in London, and the bishops became, perhaps for the first time, popular heroes. But just as the trial was about to start, an event took place which transformed the entire situation. In June 1688 James's wife, Mary of Modena, whose earlier hopes of providing an heir to the throne had been frustrated by miscarriages, gave birth to a son.

The Glorious Revolution

The birth of a male heir meant that James would be succeeded not by the protestant Mary but by another catholic King. Many protestants refused to accept that James Edward was in truth the King's son and claimed that somebody else's baby had been smuggled into the Queen's bed in a warming-pan. This gave them the justification for disregarding the principle of non-resistance to a divinely-appointed monarch which they had so fervently embraced. They were now free to take action against James in order to preserve the rights of the 'true' heir, namely the King's eldest daughter, Mary. On 30 June the seven bishops were acquitted by a London jury, and while the bonfires were being lit to celebrate this unexpected outcome to their trial Admiral Herbert slipped quietly away on the first stage of his journey to the Dutch republic. He took with him an invitation to William of Orange to invade England and defend its people, who would otherwise be 'every day in a worse condition than we already are, and less able to defend ourselves'.

The seven signatories comprised two former Roman Catholics, the Earl of Shrewsbury and Lord Lumley; two anglican Tories, Danby and Henry Compton, Bishop of London; and three Whigs, the Earl of Devonshire, Edward Russell and Henry Sidney – the last two being respectively the cousin and brother of their namesakes executed in 1683 for their involvement in the Rye House plot. These men spoke for the upper section of English society which knew from recent experience that rebellion could well lead to the destruction of the social order upon which their property and liberties depended. But the establishment of an autocratic catholic monarchy was in their eyes an even greater threat and one they felt impelled to oppose. There was virtually no chance of a successful rebellion without outside help, for James had distributed his army in garrisons throughout the country, to deal with any uprisings. The army was officered mainly by Tory country gentlemen, but their sense of *esprit de corps* was strong and they might well put their loyalty to the King above other considerations. Moreover, there were reports that James intended to increase the number of Roman Catholic officers, on whose devotion he could rely. A revolt against royal authority when it was so strongly entrenched could only succeed if a countervailing force was introduced. Hence the appeal to the Prince of Orange.

This was, in effect, the second invitation that William had received to intervene in English affairs, for at the time of the Exclusion Crisis he had been urged to throw his weight into the scales against James. On that occasion he had opted for neutrality, but the subsequent course of events convinced him he had misjudged the situation. He was determined not to make the same mistake again. All he now demanded was an assurance that his intervention would be well received, and this was contained in the invitation, which stated that 'there are nineteen parts of twenty of the people throughout the kingdom who are desirous of a change and who, we believe, would willingly contribute to it if they had such a protection to countenance their rising as would secure them from being destroyed'.

James was aware that naval and military preparations were being made in Dutch ports, but he was not inclined to take rumours of an invasion seriously. He had lavished money on the navy, which was now one of the finest in Europe, and he had a well-trained army to defend him. Moreover, he thought it extremely unlikely that William would risk leaving the Dutch republic denuded of troops at the very moment when Louis XIV was poised to strike against it. He decided to let events take their course, and in August 1688 issued writs for the general election. By October, however, James had become convinced that the danger of invasion was real, and he reacted by postponing the election and making a number of conciliatory gestures. He dissolved the Ecclesiastical Commission and restored charters to boroughs which had forfeited them. He also appointed new, protestant Lord Lieutenants and restored former Justices of the Peace who had been dismissed for giving unsatisfactory replies to the Three Questions. However, these measures were interpreted as panic reactions by James's opponents, and the credit for them was given to William.

There was no widespread movement of revolt against James. Danby planned to set off a rising in Yorkshire once he received news of William's landing, which he assumed would take place somewhere on the north-east coast, and other conspirators had made similar preparations. The prevailing mood was one of hesitancy, however, and everything depended on William's arrival. After one false start he eventually set sail on 1 November with a fleet, including transports, four times as large as the Spanish Armada of 1588. He was blown down the Channel by the 'protestant wind' which prevented the English fleet from coming out to attack him, and on 5 November, the anniversary of an earlier English deliverance from a catholic threat, he landed at Torbay (Devon) with an army of over twenty thousand men.

The west country had learned its lesson after the brutal suppression of Monmouth's rebellion, and there was no general rising in William's favour. The Prince complained of English timidity, but set about securing his base. James left London to join his soldiers, but while he was *en route* he received news of a revolt in Cheshire, and during the week he spent in Salisbury the Earl of Devonshire seized Nottingham and Danby took control of Yorkshire. If James had given a firm lead his army would probably have rallied to him, but he seemed paralysed by doubt and decided to return to London. His officers responded by deserting to William in increasing numbers. Among the first to go was John Churchill, the King's friend and commander of the royal army. His wife had stayed in London, where she organised the flight of James's younger daughter, Anne, to the rebels at Nottingham.

On the last day of November James issued a proclamation in which he announced a general pardon, gave assurances of security for the Church of England, and summoned Parliament to meet in the following January. On the face of it, William had achieved all his objectives, and indeed there were some leading figures among the nobility who suggested that he should now return to Holland. But William had no intention of going home until the concessions announced by James had been put into effect. He therefore continued his advance towards London, and James fled from the city. After an abortive first attempt he managed to find a boat to take him across the Channel, and on Christmas Day 1688 he landed in France.

The Revolution settlement

James had ordered his army to disband, but without requiring it first of all to be disarmed. He had also thrown the great seal into the Thames. No doubt he hoped that the ensuing chaos would lead to a demand for his recall, but although there were popular disturbances – particularly in London, where catholic chapels were sacked – it was William who gained from them since only he could guarantee stability. He had ordered all English soldiers in or near London to leave the area, which meant that his Dutch army was now in sole control of the capital. An *ad hoc* assembly of peers, former members of Parliament and representatives of the City of London, which William convened in late December, requested him to take over the administration and arrange for the deferred election to go ahead. Since William was not King, the body which he summoned was not a legitimate Parliament, but a precedent had been established in 1660 for the election of a Convention, and this was now followed. It was the Convention, therefore, which assembled at Westminster on 22 January 1689.

In the Convention the members who remained loyal to James were initially in the majority, but the general fear of offending William limited their influence and gave the initiative to the Whigs, who were in an ebullient mood. They welcomed James's flight, since by 'excluding' himself he had enabled them to attain the objective for which they had struggled vainly in 1679–81. The Tories, by contrast, were unsure of themselves and divided in their opinions. Their commitment to the principle of hereditary succession was such that they would have liked to maintain James's nominal right to the throne by appointing William and Mary as regents. However, they failed to carry the Convention with them. The Lords, in which the Tories had a stronger presence, proposed acknowledging Mary as Queen regnant, but failed to win the Commons' support for this motion. Even had they done so it would have made no difference, for Mary rejected the suggestion and told Danby that 'she would take it extreme unkindly if any, under a pretence of their care of her, would set up a divided interest between her and the Prince'. As for William, he made it known that he would never consent to be his wife's 'gentleman-usher'. Either he must be offered the throne or he would shake the dust of England off his feet and leave its ungrateful inhabitants to defend themselves as best they could.

The leaders of the rebellion against James had intended to restore constitutional rule, not to change their monarch. Danby's son later affirmed that he could 'take God to witness I had not a thought when I engaged in it, and I am sure my father neither, that the Prince of Orange's landing would end in deposing the King'. However, James's flight and William's overwhelming military presence limited the options available, and the Convention acted accordingly. The Commons resolved 'that King James II, having endeavoured to subvert the constitution of the kingdom by breaking the original contract between King and people, and by the advice of Jesuits and other wicked persons having violated the fundamental laws, and having withdrawn himself out of his kingdom, has abdicated the government, and that the throne is thereby vacant'. The House of Lords, in which the Tories were in a majority, refused to accept that the monarchy was contractual, but William's ultimatum left them no further time for struggling with their consciences, particularly since James's flight had left England without a lawful government. Both Houses therefore agreed that the crown should be offered jointly to William and Mary, and on 13 February 1689, in a ceremony at the Banqueting House in Whitehall – from which Charles I had stepped on to the scaffold forty years earlier – the Prince of Orange and his wife were formally proclaimed King and Queen of England.

Before leaving Holland, William had issued a Declaration in which he asserted that 'this our expedition is intended for no other design but to have a free and lawful Parliament assembled as soon as is possible . . . and that the members of Parliament . . . shall meet and sit in full freedom, that so the two Houses may concur in the preparing of such laws as they, upon full and free debate, shall judge necessary and convenient'. Only by these means could he 'prevent all those miseries which must needs follow upon the nation's being kept under arbitrary government and slavery, and that all the violences and disorders, which may have overturned the whole constitution of the English government, may be fully redressed'. William, in other words, had committed himself to restore England's traditional liberties, and it was with his entire approval that the formal offer of the crown was preceded by the presentation to him and Mary of a *Declaration of Rights*. This was subsequently embodied in statutory law as the *Bill of Rights*.

The Commons' committee responsible for drafting the *Declaration of Rights* had divided its recommendations into those which simply restated existing liberties and those which contained novel elements and would therefore require legislation. In the event, however, the *Declaration* was confined to the first category, for insistence on the second was likely to prolong debate and was certain to be unacceptable to William. This gave the *Bill of Rights* a conservative appearance, yet some of its provisions went well beyond the accepted and traditional. For example, the Militia Act of 1661 had declared that 'the sole supreme government, command and disposition of the militia and of all forces by sea and land . . . is and by the laws of England ever was the undoubted right of his majesty and his royal predecessors, Kings and Queens of England, and that both or either of the Houses of Parliament cannot, nor ought, to pretend to the same', yet the *Bill of Rights* asserted parliamentary control by forbidding 'the raising or keeping a standing army within the kingdom in time of peace, unless it be with consent of Parliament'.

When it came to dealing with the succession, the *Bill* again broke fresh ground by providing 'that all and every person and persons that is, are, or shall be reconciled to, or shall hold communion with, the see or Church of Rome, or shall profess the popish religion, or shall marry a papist, shall be excluded and be for ever incapable to inherit, possess or enjoy the crown and government of this realm'. It also swept aside the principle of strict hereditary succession by ignoring James II's son – described in William's Declaration as 'the pretended Prince of Wales' – and providing that if William and Mary remained childless the throne should pass to Mary's younger sister, Anne, and her heirs.

Even when it restated existing liberties the *Bill of Rights* did so in a way that shifted the balance of the constitution significantly in favour of Parliament. The suspending power was declared illegal, while the dispensing power was to operate only in those cases where statutory provision was made for it. The Ecclesiastical Commission 'and all other commissions and courts of like nature' were declared 'illegal and pernicious'. The levying of money, except by parliamentary grant, was condemned, and the right of subjects to petition the monarch was upheld. As for Parliament, the 'election of members', it stated, 'ought to be free' and 'freedom of speech and debates or proceedings in Parliament ought not to be impeached or questioned in any court or place out of Parliament'.

Two other statutes completed the constitutional settlement. The Mutiny Act, passed for a year at a time in order to preserve the principle of parliamentary control, gave the monarch authority to impose military discipline on the armed forces which were to be raised 'during this time of danger ... for the safety of the kingdom [and] the common defence of the protestant religion'. The Triennial Act – which was not passed until 1694, because of William's unwillingness to abandon his prerogative rights – dealt with the twin perils of no parliaments and perpetual ones by stating that in future a new Parliament should meet not more than three years after the dissolution of its predecessor, and that 'no Parliament whatsoever, that shall at any time hereafter be called, assembled or held, shall have any continuance longer than for three years only at the farthest'.

The Restoration attempt to reinstate the traditional balanced constitution had been aborted by the financial arrangements which Parliament made. Put briefly, for the greater part of his reign Charles II had been too poor, but towards the end he had been, from Parliament's point of view, too rich, as was James II. Members of the Commons were determined that the new monarchs should not be over-endowed, for as one of them wryly observed, 'If you give the crown too little, you may add at any time. If once you give too much, you will never have it back again.' William expected to be treated no less generously than his immediate predecessor, but in 1689 the Commons proposed voting him an annual revenue of only £1,200,000, of which half should be spent on the civil administration. William rejected this limitation on his right to do as he pleased with his own income, but the idea of a 'civil list' remained. The 1690 Parliament voted him the excise for life but the Customs duties for only four years – another break with tradition.

The war with France which occupied the greater part of the reign reduced the yield from Customs, and William had also surrendered the unpopular hearth tax. As a consequence, his ordinary revenue rarely rose above one million pounds a year. Moreover, the war blurred the distinction between 'ordinary' and 'extraordinary' revenues, for it went on so long that it became, in effect, the norm. When the war came to a temporary halt in 1697 William was ready to accept the principle of a civil list, since it was the only way out of his increasing indebtedness. Parliament voted him taxes estimated to bring in £700,000 a year, to cover the costs of the civil administration. All other costs were to be met by direct parliamentary grant. William, then, unlike his predecessors, no longer controlled the entire expenditure of the state. Even his freedom to spend the much smaller sum at his disposal was limited by the fact that Parliament broke it down into sections, each with a maximum limit. In short, the Revolution financial settlement ensured that no monarch would be able to rule in future without Parliament. It had been intended to underpin the constitutional settlement, but in fact it went well beyond this objective and substantially reduced the power of the crown.

In the religious sphere the Revolution marked the reluctant acceptance by the political nation of the need for toleration . The dissenters and anglicans had come together during the closing years of James II's reign, in joint opposition to the King's pro-catholic policies, and prominent dissenters had made a point of visiting the Seven Bishops in the Tower, explaining that 'they could not but adhere to them as men constant in the protestant faith'. Following William's accession it was generally assumed that some measure would be passed for relieving protestant nonconformists from the penalties imposed upon them by law, but a group of high Churchmen led by the Earl of Nottingham hoped to promote the alternative policy of comprehension. This involved modifying the doctrines of the Church of England so that dissenters could once again be comprehended within it. Nottingham introduced two bills into the Lords, one designed to facilitate comprehension, the other to provide a limited measure of toleration for the minority who insisted on staying outside the Church. But there was little enthusiasm for comprehension among the anglicans, and suspicion of William's intentions – he was, after all, a Calvinist, and therefore closer in his religious attitudes to the dissenters than to the anglican establishment – made members of Parliament reluctant to abandon all discrimination against nonconformists.

Nottingham's second measure, therefore, which had been designed for a recalcitrant minority, was now turned into the Toleration Act of 1689. This freed dissenters from the operation of the penal laws as long as they took the oath of loyalty to the new monarchs and made a declaration against transubstantiation, but the penal laws themselves were not repealed and the dissenters, like the Roman Catholics, were still barred from public life. However, they were now permitted to worship freely, if they obtained a licence. In the first year of operation of the Toleration Act more than nine hundred meeting houses were licensed, and by the end of Anne's reign the figure was well above 2,500. The anglican monopoly of the religious life of the nation had gone for good, and parish priests now had to fight to maintain their congregations in the face of competition from dissenting ministers.

In its broad outlines the Revolution settlement was conservative. It did not establish parliamentary government. The King was still free to choose and dismiss his ministers as well as his judges, and he could summon, prorogue and dissolve Parliament as he thought fit, provided he did not transgress the provisions of the Triennial Act. No restraint was placed upon the use of placemen in the Commons, nor was the King's prerogative to make foreign policy called into question. Generally speaking, the framers of the settlement were trying to adhere to the principles of the ancient constitution, but experience had taught them that however carefully constitutional arrangements were worked out, kings usually managed to circumvent them. It therefore seemed prudent to weight the scales in favour of Parliament in order, eventually, to achieve and maintain equilibrium. However, by choosing to exercise the power that control of the purse strings gave it, Parliament ensured that in any future conflict of wills it was certain to prevail.

The shift in power brought about by the Revolution settlement was not necessarily irreversible, but a combination of factors made it so. William was by temperament, as well as birth, a true Stuart, and just as inclined to autocracy as Charles II or James, but he could not draw on those deep wells of loyalty which were available to hereditary monarchs. His wife,

Mary, was loved and respected, and might have recovered much of the ground the crown had lost if she had been so inclined. So might Anne in the twelve years of her reign, but neither of the two Queens regnant had the degree of political understanding and commitment required for such a task. In any case, the period from William and Mary's accession to the death of Anne was dominated by war that entailed expenditure on a scale that only Parliament could provide for. There was no constitutional provision that Parliament should meet every year, but it began doing so in order to finance the war against France, and kept up the practice; since 1689 no year has passed without a parliamentary session. Regular parliaments, controlling the flow of funds on an unprecedented scale, inevitably reduced the role of the crown. Whatever chance there had been of restoring a true balance to the constitution was lost on the battlefields of the Netherlands.

Political parties and the war

William III was a man who inspired affection in few people. His constant struggle against ill health left him short-tempered, and he concealed his feelings beneath a cold mask of indifference. The controlling passion of his life was the destruction of French power, and to this he devoted all his energy. Because England was essential to the achieving of his objective he had taken the English throne, but he had no love for the country he ruled and usually spent half of every year out of it. In his exalted view of the royal prerogative he came close to the Tories, but they could never forgive him for taking the place of the legitimate King and they could not accord him the devotion they had professed for his divinely-appointed predecessors.

The Whigs, on the other hand, though they were no great lovers of monarchy, felt that William ought to rely on them because they were wholeheartedly committed to the Revolution and its consequences. Their attitude was summed up by the Earl of Shrewsbury when he told William 'That your majesty and the government are much more safe depending upon the Whigs ... than [on] the Tories who, many of them, questionless, would bring in King James, and the very best of them I doubt [i.e. suspect] have a regency still in their heads. For although I agree them to be the properest instruments to carry the prerogative high, yet I fear they have so unreasonable a veneration for monarchy as not altogether to approve the foundation yours is built upon.'

The Tories only put up with William because they had no alternative. Mary, with her charm and vivacity, was far more popular than her husband – to whom she was devoted – and provided some of the warmth he so conspicuously lacked. The Tories comforted themselves with the thought that she was a Stuart and would be succeeded by the staunchly anglican Anne. Meanwhile, they concentrated on defending the established Church against the dangerous combination of a Calvinist King and low-Church-dissenter Whigs. The anglican clergy had accepted the change of sovereign with surprisingly little protest, in spite of the fact that they had been fervent in proclaiming the wickedness of resisting monarchical authority. Only four hundred non-jurors, including five of the Seven Bishops, gave up their livings rather than swear an oath of allegiance to the new monarchs.

William had no wish to be either a Whig or a Tory King, and his first administration was balanced between the two groupings. Halifax, who was not really a party man, held office as Lord Privy Seal, while the Tory Danby was appointed Lord President of the Council. One Secretary of State was the second Earl of Nottingham, a devout anglican, but his Tory fervour was offset by the Whiggish leanings of the other Secretary, the Duke of Shrewsbury. These ministers did not form a united 'Cabinet', with a common policy. Their job was to serve the King and proffer him advice when he called for it. Policy-making was William's prerogative and one that he exercised to the full. He was his own chief minister and used his Dutch favourite, William Bentinck, Earl of Portland, as the link between him and the administration.

In May 1689 William declared war on France and expected the country to unite behind him. But there was little enthusiasm for war at this stage, and the Whigs, who were incensed by William's lukewarm response to their offer of collaboration, spent their energies on divisive campaigns against their Tory adversaries. They pushed through a bill annulling the sentences passed against Russell and Sidney in the wake of the Rye House plot and were pressing ahead with a proposal to confine borough government to men of their own persuasion when William, disgusted by such partisan behaviour, dissolved Parliament in January 1690. Halifax resigned in the following month and Danby now became the dominant figure in an administration that was increasingly Tory.

Danby used all his old arts of parliamentary management, noting of one member 'not willing to lose his place', and of another 'I think hath a pension', and his seven 'managers' in the House of Commons kept in close touch with the 'King's men' there to ensure a reasonably smooth passage for government measures. Yet Danby never had the full support of the Tory country gentlemen, who found the heavy land tax, levied to finance the war, a crippling burden. From their stronghold in the Commons they attacked the government for fighting expensive land campaigns instead of capturing prizes at sea, for allowing corruption to divert public funds into private pockets, and for failing to bring the war to a swift and successful conclusion.

Danby suffered from this resentment and could offer little consolation in the way of victory. William, bogged down in siege warfare in the Netherlands, was unable to break the French grip on the region. In July 1692 he had to abandon Namur to the enemy, and a year later he was heavily defeated at Landen. At sea the French won command of the Channel in the summer of 1690, after a victorious encounter with the British fleet off Beachy Head, and although they were heavily defeated two years later at the battle of La Hogue – which put an end to James II's hopes of invading England – the credit for this went to the Whig admiral Russell rather than to the Tory ministry. Russell was so difficult for the administration to deal with that they replaced him with a trinity of Tory admirals, but these brought Danby's ministry into even greater discredit by failing to prevent a French attack on a convoy of ships belonging to the Levant Company in May 1693, which resulted in losses estimated at one million pounds.

What William required of his ministers was that they should maintain good relations with Parliament, so that the supply of money which kept his armies and navy in action should not dry up. Danby was at first successful in this task, but by 1693 he was finding it increasingly difficult. It was not simply a question of management. The 'court party' in the Commons was never a large group, and it flourished only while the political temperature was low. When, on the contrary, members' feelings were aroused, they were less susceptible to offers of places and pensions, or even to family ties. The country gentlemen wanted an end to heavy taxation, and the only hope of this lay in bringing the war to a conclusion. They held Danby responsible for the military and naval reverses which destroyed hopes of an early peace, and they bitterly attacked the placemen in the House who, they were convinced, were the sole reason why an inefficient, unsuccessful and corrupt administration remained in power.

Danby suffered from the effects of the Revolution settlement, which had made Parliament more powerful but left the King in charge of government. As the King's representative in Parliament he had to take the blame for William's policies, yet as Parliament's representative to the King he had to bear the brunt of royal anger at parliamentary criticism. As long as the King continued to choose his ministers without regard to their influence in the Commons the situation was bound to get worse. Matters would only improve if he limited his choice to members of the group or groups which were predominant in the Lower House, but to do so would mean restricting his prerogative, which was something William was unwilling to contemplate.

The King's use of his prerogative powers added to the resentment already being voiced in Parliament. In 1692, for instance, he vetoed a bill making the judges' tenure *Quamdiu se bene gesserint* instead of *Durante beneplacito*, though he had no objection to this in principle. In March 1693 he vetoed a Triennial Bill, and in January of the following year he refused to accept a measure aimed at excluding placemen from the Lower House. Altogether William used his veto five times, where Charles II had used it twice and James II not at all. This shows that liaison between crown and Parliament was not as good as it should have been, for better management could have ensured that discontent was diverted into relatively harmless channels before it reached the stage where the only option left was the veto.

The decline of the Privy Council was partly responsible for this unsatisfactory state of affairs. During Elizabeth's reign members of Parliament knew that Privy Councillors were in fact as well as name the Queen's counsellors. Under William they could not be so sure. The King was out of the country for half the year, and even when he was in it he confined his consultations to a handful of close advisers. During his absences a small committee called the 'Cabinet Council' dealt with government business and tendered advice to Mary, but from about 1695 this body continued meeting even when the King was in England. William himself was frequently present, and it was at these small, informal gatherings that the decisions were taken which transformed his policies into actions.

Members of Parliament knew, of course, that such meetings went on, but they resented the fact that because of the uncertain membership of these 'Cabinets' they could never be sure who to blame for measures of which they disapproved. Moreover, there were other meetings which did not have even the limited degree of formality towards which the Cabinet Council was moving. The confusion to which this situation could give rise was illustrated in 1694 when Lord Normanby claimed that William had promised him membership of *all* councils of whatever sort. The King, in reply, said 'it is true that I did promise my lord Normanby that when there was a Cabinet Council he should assist at it, but surely this does not engage either the Queen or myself to summon him to all meetings which we may order on particular occasions?'

William and the Whigs

The bill excluding placemen from the Commons which William vetoed in 1694 was the work of Tory country gentlemen in the Lower House, and a constitutional crisis was only prevented by the King's conciliatory reply to their protest, in which he assured them that 'no prince ever had a higher esteem for the constitution of the English government than myself, and . . . I shall ever have a great regard to the advice of Parliaments'. Nevertheless, the King was coming to realise that he could no longer depend upon the Tories. The Whigs might be, as he feared, neo-republicans, but at least they supported the war he was fighting, and it was this consideration that prompted him to bring more of them into his administration. He thereby began a process that, during the course of the next few months, turned a predominantly Tory ministry into one that was mainly Whig.

Although William felt he had to part with the Tories he did not wish to become the prisoner of the Whigs. What he was hoping to find, as always, was a non-party figure who would put the King's interest above every other consideration. He therefore turned to Sunderland, who had served many causes but committed himself to none, and whose attitude towards parties was summed up by the observation – delivered in the languid drawl which was his hallmark – 'What matter who saarves his majesty so long as his majesty is saarved?' Sunderland took over from Danby the task of managing the placemen in the Commons, and it was at his insistence that the King eventually agreed, in November 1693, to dispense with Nottingham's services. As for Danby, now Duke of Leeds, he was kept in office to preserve a semblance of continuity and avoid antagonising the Tories, but he was no more than a figurehead.

The key members of the reformed administration were Edward Russell, appointed First Lord of the Admiralty in May 1694; Charles Montagu, who became Chancellor of the Exchequer; and the Duke of Shrewsbury, who accepted office once again as Secretary of State. Russell and Montagu were members of the 'Junto' – the group of influential Whig leaders who were wholeheartedly in favour of the war and commanded a big following in the Commons. Other Junto members were John Somers, John Trenchard and Thomas Wharton, all of them the ideological descendants of the first Whigs of the Exclusion Crisis. For William, alliance with such men was at best a marriage of convenience, but as Sunderland pointed out 'it was very true that the Tories were better friends to monarchy than the Whigs were, but then his majesty was to consider that he was not *their* monarch'.

The reformed administration suffered from the disadvantages common to all mixed ministries. Because it contained a number of Tories, the Whigs were dissatisfied and clamoured for complete control. The Tories, on the other hand, made plain their sense of outrage that the King's government should be largely in the hands of men who were enemies to both monarchy and the established Church. If party allegiances had been clear-cut, disputes could have been settled by a mere counting of heads, but party loyalties were only one of many influences to which members of Parliament were subject. Personal feelings about major issues were of great significance in determining a member's attitude at any given time, but so also were his family ties, his involvement in one or other of the aristocratic 'connections', and his hopes of gaining office or a commission in the armed forces.

Ever since their emergence as a political entity at the time of the Exclusion Crisis the Whigs had drawn strength from the fact that they were an opposition party and could therefore appeal to 'country' sentiment. In 1694, however, they changed their nature by going over to the 'court', and becoming a party of government. This left a vacuum that was only filled by the emergence of the Harley-Foley grouping, which later became known as the New Country party. Paul Foley and Robert Harley were both Whigs, but as the Junto moved into government they moved into opposition. They became the spokesmen for 'country' suspicion of the court, and their attacks on placemen and corruption won them the support of many Tories. The New Country party thrived on resentment at the way in which men who had formerly served the cause of Stuart absolutism were now serving William III and using the same dubious methods to preserve their hold on power. In April 1695 the re-formed opposition mounted an attack on the Duke of Leeds, who was the embodiment of everything they loathed in politics, and William had to prorogue Parliament in order to prevent his minister from facing impeachment for the second time.

Fortunately for the King the war in the Netherlands had taken a turn for the better, and in August 1695 William achieved his greatest success when he recaptured the fortress of Namur. The favourable climate of opinion produced by this victory persuaded him to dissolve Parliament, in the hope that a less fractious assembly would be elected. The new Parliament was not, in fact, any friendlier towards William than the old one had been, particularly after Mary's death in 1694, which left him as sole ruler. However, in February 1696 a Jacobite plot to assassinate William was uncovered, and in the reaction against this he acquired, for the first time, a semblance of popularity. An association was formed on the model of the one set up to protect the life of Queen Elizabeth in 1584, and an act of 1696 declared that William was 'rightful and lawful King' – terms which the Tories, with their scruples about hereditary succession, had kept out of the legislation which followed the Revolution. Throughout the summer of 1696 fears of a Jacobite invasion stifled the critics of the war, and the Junto became increasingly influential. In 1696 Somers was made Lord Chancellor, Russell was created Earl of Orford, and Montagu was appointed First Lord of the Treasury.

Harley and the opposition did not abandon their attacks on the administration, but they had to concentrate on matters other than the war. One obvious target was the lavish grants of land made by the King to his Dutch favourites out of confiscated Jacobite estates in Ireland. The opposition demanded that these grants should be revoked and denounced them as examples of the way in which the wealth of the nation was being squandered while the landowners, under the burden of heavy taxation, were bleeding to death. The country gentry in the Commons strongly approved of such criticism, and they were also prepared to join with Harley and the dissident Whigs of the New Country party in attacks on the Bank of England.

The Bank had been created in 1694, and much of its capital was subscribed by City merchants and Whig financiers. These men were doing well out of the war, making big profits on the supply of weapons, ammunition and clothing to the armed forces, and the smaller landowners bitterly resented the fact that the proceeds of the land tax, which they paid at great cost to themselves, were passing, via the Bank of England, into the pockets of the Whigs. They supported Harley's demand for a Land Bank, to function in the same way as the Bank of England but with its capital provided mainly by landowners, who would share in the profits. A bill setting up the Land Bank received the royal assent in April 1696, but the scheme was stillborn. The City magnates and major landowners who had already made big investments in the Bank of England had no intention of supporting a rival institution, and the gentry alone were too poor to raise more than a few thousand pounds. The failure of the Land Bank project became just one more item in the balance sheet of gentry resentment.

The Whig Junto remained in power as long as the war lasted, but in May 1697 peace negotiations opened and in the following year the Treaty of Ryswick brought the war to a close. Both sides agreed to return their conquests, and Louis XIV announced his acceptance of William as King of England and his abandonment of the Jacobite cause. Harley and the New

Country party welcomed the end of the war and proposed that the army should be immediately reduced to seven thousand men. William, who was convinced that the Peace of Ryswick was only a truce and that Louis XIV remained a menace to the rest of Europe, struggled to preserve at least four times that number, but he could not win over the gentry in the Commons who, when they chose to unite – and they were united on this issue – could be sure of a majority. Sunderland, afraid of a revengeful Tory attack on him, insisted on leaving the King's service in December 1698, and this deprived William of a useful link between himself and the Junto ministers. The Whig leaders knew that their predominance was threatened, and demanded guarantees from William in the shape of a Secretaryship for Wharton. But William never liked being dictated to, particularly by Whigs. He was drawing close to John Churchill, now Earl of Marlborough and a favourite of Princess Anne, and felt that if need be he could dispense with the services of the Junto.

Succession problems

Under the terms of the Triennial Act, Parliament was dissolved in July 1698. In the new Commons which met in December of that year the Tories and New Country party had a majority and immediately demanded a reduction in the army. William was so disgusted at their parochial attitude that he drafted an abdication speech in which he proposed telling members of Parliament that since they had 'so little regard to my advice that you take no manner or care of your own security and expose yourselves to evident ruin by divesting yourselves of the only means for your defence, it would not be just or reasonable that I should be witness of your ruin'.

William never delivered the speech, however, for England was more than ever essential to the fulfilment of his aims. The problem of the Spanish succession still dominated European politics, and in 1698 William had concluded a secret partition treaty with France and the United Provinces. It was agreed that Louis' grandson, Philip, should have the southern Italian possessions of Spain, while the Archduke Charles, younger son of the Holy Roman Emperor, was to have northern Italy. The great bulk of the Spanish empire – Spain itself, The Netherlands and America – was to go to the Emperor's grandson, the Prince of Bavaria. In this way the enormous possessions of Spain would be prevented from falling into the hands of Louis. In January 1699, however, while William was engaged in a bitter dispute with Parliament, the Bavarian prince died, leaving the question of the Spanish succession wide open once again. It was for this reason that William decided to hold on to his crown and try to arrive at an agreement with his turbulent Parliament.

Since this body was strongly Tory in sentiment, a Tory ministry offered the best chance of harmony, but the King had first to disembarrass himself of the Junto, without giving them such offence that they would decline to serve him again if and when he needed them. The Junto ministers were therefore turned out of office one by one. Orford resigned from the Admiralty in May 1699, Montagu left the Treasury commission in the following November, but Somers remained as Lord Chancellor until April 1700. His eventual dismissal cleared the way for a Tory ministry, and only just in time, for the Commons were getting out of control. In April 1700 they passed a bill revoking all the grants William had made of Irish estates, and threatened to attaint the King's Dutch favourites. Rumours of dissolution were in the air, mobs gathered outside Parliament, and at Harley's suggestion the Commons carried on their debates behind closed doors. The King, angry and embittered, decided to accept the bill, but he prorogued Parliament rather than agree to a formal request that he should employ no foreign advisers except Prince George of Denmark, husband of Princess Anne.

This Parliament did not meet again, for William dissolved it in December 1700. Before summoning another he made approaches to the Tories and the New Country party, hoping that a ministry based upon these two groups would lead the Commons into a constructive solution of the urgent problems that had to be dealt with. In March 1700 William had secretly concluded another partition treaty, giving Spain, America and the Netherlands to the Archduke Charles, while Philip was to have all the Spanish possessions in Italy. Six months later, however, in October 1700, the King of Spain at last died, leaving all his possessions to Philip on condition that the crowns of France and Spain were never united. Louis decided to accept the will on behalf of his grandson, and there were no obvious grounds for objecting to this decision since it fulfilled the main objective of the partition treaties – namely, the continued separation of the French and Spanish empires. William, however, was convinced that Louis would ignore the provision about keeping the two crowns apart and would try to present Europe with a *fait accompli*. He could not risk another enervating struggle with Parliament while such a threat hovered on the horizon.

William also had to deal with a succession problem at home, and one that could be solved only by statute. In July 1700 the Duke of Gloucester,

Princess Anne's only surviving child, died, and since it was certain that Anne would have no more children, steps had to be taken to ensure the succession. Only William, a sick man, and Anne, a sickly woman, stood between England and the prospect of a Jacobite restoration.

By the time a new Parliament met, in January 1701, the administration had again been reformed. Rochester was now Lord Lieutenant of Ireland, while Godolphin was First Lord of the Treasury. In other words, William, in these closing years of his reign, had come to rely on the two men who had served Charles II in a similar capacity after the Exclusion Crisis. The Tories were, of course, delighted, but the Whigs could be excused for wondering why the Glorious Revolution had ever taken place.

The Rochester–Godolphin ministry was successful in pushing the Act of Settlement through Parliament, thereby ensuring – as far as statute alone could do – an undisputed succession after Anne's death. But the high Tories insisted on adding clauses to the act which reflected critically on William and the practices that had grown up during his reign. As far as the succession was concerned, the Act of Settlement provided that the crown should pass, on Anne's death, to the Electress Sophia of Hanover and her heirs. Sophia's claim derived from the fact that she was the daughter of Elizabeth of Bohemia, the 'Winter Queen', and granddaughter of James I. Roman Catholics were barred from the throne in perpetuity, and every future monarch would have to be a communicant member of the Church of England.

The last provision was an implied criticism of the Calvinist William, as were the clauses providing that 'this nation be not obliged to engage in any war for the defence of any dominions or territories which do not belong to the crown of England, without the consent of Parliament', and that no future sovereign should leave the country without obtaining prior permission from the two Houses. To prevent Dutchmen, Germans or any other aliens from playing, in succeeding reigns, the key role that foreigners had filled under William, it was ordained that no person born outside the British Isles should be eligible for 'any office or place of trust, either civil or military, or to have any grants of lands'.

As for the native Englishmen who were held to have betrayed their birthright by serving as the King's retainers in the Lower House, the triumphant Tories decreed 'that no person who has an office or place of profit under the King, or receives a pension from the crown, shall be capable of serving as a member of the House of Commons'. Government by 'Cabinets' was outlawed by the requirement that 'all matters ... which are properly cognizable in the Privy Council by the laws and customs of this realm, shall be transacted there'; and to prevent the King from inter-fering with the course of justice it was laid down that judges should be appointed *Quamdiu se bene gesserint*, and that 'no pardon under the great seal of England be pleadable to an impeachment by the Commons in Parliament'.

The passing of the Act of Settlement did not produce the harmony between the King and the two Houses for which William had hoped. News of the partition treaties had leaked out, and the Tory gentry, outraged at the way in which they had been committed behind their backs, showed their anger by proposing to impeach the leading members of the Whig Junto. But while the Commons were working themselves into a fury over the defence of their constitutional liberties, a much more substantial and dangerous threat was developing in Europe. Louis XIV had sent his troops into the Spanish Netherlands, officially to aid his grandson but in fact to annex them to France. Even a peace-lover like Harley was now talking of a 'necessary war', and the feeling of the country was indicated by a peti-tion presented to the Commons in April 1701 by representatives of the gentlemen of Kent. This called on the Lower House to vote supply to the King so that he could form his alliances before it was too late. The indig-nant members, angered by the implied criticism of their sense of priorities, committed the delegates who brought the petition to prison, but they could not so easily stifle public opinion. Robert Walpole was a member of this Parliament, and one of his Norfolk correspondents, writing in May, informed him that 'our people . . . seem pleased with the sentiments of the Grand Jury of Kent [and] think this time ought not to be neglected to make haste to secure ourselves and allies'.

The Lords refused to accept the Commons' articles of impeachment against the Junto leaders, and a violent dispute between the two Houses was only averted by William's dissolution of Parliament in November 1701. Earlier in the year he and Marlborough had been in Holland, trying to assemble a coalition against France, and their work came to fruition in September with the signing of the Grand Alliance. By the terms of this agreement England, the United Provinces and the Empire bound them-selves to force Louis to accept partition of the Spanish empire. Philip was to be left in possession of Spain and America, but the Archduke Charles was to have the Italian territories and the Spanish Netherlands. France was not to be allowed to monopolise trade with the New World, nor were the French and Spanish crowns to be united.

English opinion, which was already turning in favour of war, swung solidly behind William when, on the death of James II in September 1701,

Louis recognised his son, the Old Pretender, as King of England. This was a direct violation of the Treaty of Ryswick. It was also an insult to the English people and Parliament, since it implied that they had no right to decide the succession to the English throne. It was in the heated atmosphere created by this challenge that the general election of December 1701 took place.

When William's last Parliament met, the Commons were almost evenly balanced between the Tories and the New Country party on one wing and the adherents of the Whig Junto on the other. The Tories still felt bitter over what they regarded as William's betrayal of them, but all groups, Tory and Whig, acknowledged the need for war. The King, in his opening speech, reminded them that 'the eyes of all Europe are upon this Parliament. All matters are at a stand till your resolutions are known . . . If you do in good earnest desire to see England hold the balance of Europe and to be indeed at the head of the protestant interest, it will appear by your right improving the present opportunity'. Parliament responded to this appeal by assuring William that 'all true Englishmen, since the decay of the Spanish monarchy, have taken it for granted that the security of their religion, liberty and property, that their honour, their wealth and their trade, depend chiefly on the measures to be taken from time to time against the growing power of France'.

William, by treating foreign policy as an exclusively prerogative matter and keeping it secret from Parliament, had contributed to the insularity and narrow-mindedness of the political nation. Perhaps it was because he now recognised the need to educate his subjects in the realities of power that he made known the details of the Grand Alliance to both Houses. At the very least this would prevent members from complaining, as they had done over the partition treaties, that they had been committed to certain courses of action without their knowledge, let alone their approval. There was general support for the terms of the alliance, since they offered the prospect not only of a check to French expansion but also of security for British trade in the Mediterranean and West Indies. The Commons therefore responded to William by voting that an army of forty thousand men should be raised, and they passed an act of attainder against the Old Pretender.

William had already appointed Marlborough to command the troops being assembled in Holland and was looking forward to joining them, but as he was riding from Kensington Palace to Hampton Court in February 1702 his horse stumbled on a molehill and threw him to the ground. He died the following month, aged fifty-one – much to the delight of the followers of 'James III', who raised their glasses to toast the Jacobite mole, 'the little gentleman in black velvet'. But the mole had done his work too late. William died only after he had committed his country to war, and the reign of his successor witnessed the fulfilment of everything he had fought for.

CHAPTER TWENTY

Queen Anne

Queen Anne

Anne was the last Stuart to wear the crown of England, and she had all the pride and stubbornness that typified her family. She was only thirty-seven when she came to the throne, but youth had long ago deserted her. Anne was crippled by gout and dropsy, which made public appearances agony for her, yet she believed that God had given her the throne and she was determined not to evade the responsibilities that went with this high trust. She had disliked William, referring to him in her private correspondence as 'Mr Caliban', and proudly assured her first Parliament that 'I know my heart to be entirely English.' Yet she shared William's exalted view of the royal prerogative and struggled throughout her reign to prevent the crown from becoming the pawn of any political group or party. One of her ministers said of her, 'she will be Queen of all her subjects and would have all the parties and distinctions of former reigns ended and buried in hers', and Anne herself described her aim as that of having 'my liberty in encouraging and employing all those that concur faithfully in my service, whether they are called Whigs or Tories'.

The fact that Anne was a Stuart was not simply a matter of interest; it was a political factor of the first importance. Since 1689 – indeed, since 1685 – the Tories had been longing for a monarch to act as a true focus for their loyalty, someone who would preserve those twin pillars of their faith, the hereditary succession and the Church of England. Anne seemed to fit their requirements perfectly. In spite of her size and limited intelligence she had a natural dignity, and she emphasised her hereditary right to the throne by once again exercising those sacred functions that her predecessor had thought prudent to dispense with. She revived, for instance, the practice of 'touching' for the Queen's Evil – a type of scrofula supposed to be curable by contact with a royal body – to the benefit, it is to be hoped, of many of her subjects, including the young child who was to become famous as Dr Johnson. She also took her duties as supreme governor of the Church with great seriousness, for as she told Parliament 'my own principles must always keep me entirely firm to the interests and religion of the Church of England, and will incline me to countenance those who have the truest zeal to support it'.

Marlborough, Godolphin and the Tories

The Marlboroughs came to power with Queen Anne, for Sarah Churchill, the earl's wife, was her close personal friend. Marlborough himself was the son of Sir Winston Churchill, a royalist squire who had been impoverished by the Civil War, and he had started his career at court, as page to the future James II. He subsequently played a major part in suppressing Monmouth's rebellion, but in 1688 he deserted James and offered his services to the Prince of Orange. William, although he rewarded Marlborough with his earldom, was not disposed to take him into his confidence. He may have been jealous of Marlborough's military ability, and he certainly resented the fact that the earl was held in high esteem by Anne. The nadir of their relationship came in 1692, when Marlborough spent several months in the Tower of London on suspicion of treasonable correspondence with James, but some years before William died the two men were reconciled, and in 1702 Marlborough was ready to take over the task that William had left unfinished. His ally in the political world was Sidney Godolphin – whose son had married Marlborough's daughter – and while the earl was engaged in fighting the Queen's enemies on the continent, Godolphin looked after affairs at home and persuaded Parliament to vote the vast sums of money needed to finance war on a scale greater than anything England had yet known.

The Tories believed that with the accession of Anne they had come into the promised land, and the first administration of the reign seemed to confirm all their hopes. Rochester and Nottingham, both staunch anglicans, were appointed respectively Lord Lieutenant of Ireland and Secretary of State, while Somers, Halifax and Orford, the representatives of the Whig Junto, were deprived of their places in the Privy Council.

However, the administration was only superficially Tory, for the key figures in the government were Marlborough and Godolphin, the Lord Treasurer, who were neither of them party men. Their main concern was the prosecution of the war, and while they assumed that co-operation with

the Tories would be the best means of achieving victory they were prepared to work with the Whigs if necessary. They were far removed in their
attitudes from high-anglican Tories like Rochester and Nottingham, who
were convinced the Church was in danger and made its preservation their
overriding concern. Such fears may seem unjustified in view of the accession of a committedly anglican Queen, but the high Tories were alarmed
at the way in which nonconformists were qualifying themselves for public
office by occasionally attending anglican services and receiving the sacrament, in order to escape the penalties prescribed by the Test Act.

The practice of occasional conformity had enabled the dissenters to
retain their influence in municipal corporations. In 1697, for instance, the
Lord Mayor of London had openly attended a dissenting service, dressed
in full regalia, and by the time Anne came to the throne there were signs
that the alliance between the Whigs and the dissenters that James had originally promoted was beginning to bear fruit at local level. The prospect
that James's strategy for creating a Whig majority in Parliament might
achieve success in the reign of his daughter was too much for the high
Tories to stomach, particularly given their (quite unjustified) assumption
that all Whigs were dissenters at heart. Hence their determination to put
an end to the practice of occasional conformity.

At this stage the high Tories were not opposed in principle to a land
war, but they thought the main emphasis should be on the navy.
Nottingham told Marlborough that he was 'biast by an opinion that we
shall never have any decisive success, nor be able to hold out a war against
France, but by making it a sea war', though he added that it should be
'such a sea war as accompanies and supports attempts on land'. This view
typified the attitude of a large section of the gentry, who believed that the
costs of a naval campaign could be offset in large part by the capture of
prizes, and that they were, in any case, well below those entailed in the
maintenance of large armies. Marlborough did not reject the idea of
fighting the French at sea, but insisted that this did not rule out a major
commitment on land. He was certain in his own mind that France could
not be finally contained until her armies were defeated. He was also convinced that he was the only man who could lead the allied forces to victory.

In May 1702 Anne issued writs for a general election. The campaign
that followed was not fought on party lines. About half the total number
of seats were uncontested, and in those constituencies where an electoral
battle took place, local interests and family influence were at least as
important as national issues. In the new House of Commons the combination of the Marlborough-Godolphin connection with the high Tories

and Harley's New Country party gave the ministry a majority, but not one on which it could rely, since the coalition was based on personal relations that were inherently unstable.

War against France was formally declared by England and the United Provinces in May 1702, and Marlborough took charge of operations in The Netherlands. He was hampered by the Dutch political representatives on his staff, who were terrified of losing the war and preferred inaction to the taking of risks, but in spite of them he managed to capture a number of important strongholds and push the French out of the valleys of the Lower Rhine. His success, in striking contrast to William's early failures, made Marlborough a public hero. The Commons declared that he had 'retrieved the ancient honour and glory of the English nation', and the Queen made him a duke.

The high Tories had reservations about Marlborough's success, since it confirmed their fears that England was going to expend the wealth of her landowners in a continental war. They would have preferred an attack upon Spain, and although an expedition against Cadiz was a miserable failure, their spirits soared when the returning fleet came across some Spanish treasure-ships in Vigo Bay and sent them to the bottom. Rochester, one of the most prominent high Tories, was already on bad terms with Godolphin, whom he suspected of being lukewarm in his attitude towards occasional conformity, and an open break came in February 1703 when Godolphin persuaded the Queen to dismiss her uncle from office.

Nottingham remained a thorn in the Lord Treasurer's flesh, however, since he and Sir Edward Seymour – the leader of the high Tories in the Commons – were threatening to divide Parliament and the country by their passionate advocacy of a bill to outlaw occasional conformity. Marlborough confessed to his wife that though he felt 'bound not to wish for anybody's death ... should Sir Edward Seymour die it would be no great loss to the Queen nor the nation'. But Seymour remained obstinately alive, and in December the Commons passed the Occasional Conformity bill by a big majority. Marlborough and Godolphin felt obliged to vote for the bill in the Lords, since they knew the Queen approved of it, but they were relieved when the Upper House threw it out.

Nottingham remained a member of the administration until April 1704, when his demand for the expulsion of Whig members of the Privy Council brought matters to a head. Anne was anxious to retain the services of this pillar of the anglican establishment, but not at the cost of giving in to blackmail. When Nottingham realised that the Queen would not support him, he resigned, and Seymour went with him. The brief reign of the high Tories had come to an end, and the moderate Tories grouped round Harley were brought in to fill the vacuum. Harley himself took Nottingham's place as Secretary of State, while his protégé, Henry St John, was appointed Secretary-at-War.

The war aims of the allies had been significantly changed by the Methuen treaty signed with Portugal in May 1703. Portugal agreed to join the anti-French campaign and offered Lisbon for use as a British naval base, but she demanded, in return, that the Archduke Charles should be sent to the Peninsula with a force of allied troops, to try to establish himself on the Spanish throne. When William had signed the Grand Alliance he had not envisaged giving Spain to the Archduke, since this would have opened the way to the reunification of the Habsburg empire – a prospect almost as alarming as the union of the Spanish and French crowns. However, England could not renege on the Methuen treaty, and thereby became committed to a campaign in the Peninsula that was to keep the war dragging on long after it should have been over. The Tories at first welcomed this Peninsular involvement, but when they realised that it meant a longer, not a shorter, war they turned against it.

Hopes of a speedy end to the war rose in 1704 when Marlborough won the first of the victories which destroyed the legend of French invincibility and marked the re-emergence of Britain as a major military power. He wanted to avoid siege warfare of the sort that had hamstrung William by advancing down the Moselle river, and persuaded his reluctant Dutch allies to agree to this. But in the heart of Europe French armies were threatening Vienna, and the Emperor had sent urgent appeals for help. Marlborough knew that if Vienna fell and the Emperor was knocked out of the war the chances of allied success would be slender. He also knew that the Dutch would never consent to sending their troops hundreds of miles away from their homeland. The duke therefore resorted to deception, and allowed it to be assumed that he was preparing an attack down the Moselle while in fact he was in secret communication with the imperial commander, Prince Eugene, and planning a surprise campaign on the Danube.

Marlborough left Holland at the beginning of May with an army of over fifty thousand men, about half of whom were being paid for by Britain even though only nine thousand were actually British. For three months he marched south-east, following the Rhine, then suddenly and secretly switched course towards the Danube. On 13 August 1704 he came up against the French, who were ensconced in a defensive position near the village of Blenheim, not far from Augsburg. In a battle which lasted until late in the afternoon the French were utterly routed. Marlborough summarised his achievement in the laconic note which he scribbled to his wife. 'I have not time to say more,' he wrote, 'but beg you will give my duty to the Queen and let her know her army has had a glorious victory. Monsr. Tallard [the French commander] and two other generals are in my coach, and I am following the rest.'

Marlborough had saved Vienna and had thereby saved the Grand Alliance. He had also made British arms more feared on the continent than they had been since the days of Henry V. Even before he left England Marlborough had been a popular hero but on his return he was idolised. The Emperor made him a prince of the Empire, while Anne presented him with the royal manor of Woodstock, just outside Oxford, and commissioned Sir John Vanbrugh to build a palace for him there at her own expense.

The Godolphin–Harley ministry was enormously strengthened by Marlborough's victory, which temporarily stifled criticism. The high Tories, led by Rochester and Nottingham, looked around for another hero and found one in Admiral Rooke, who had been responsible for the capture of Gibraltar ten days before the Battle of Blenheim was fought. Marlborough himself welcomed this achievement. He was aware, like William before him, of the importance of naval operations in the Mediterranean, and appreciated that the establishment of British supremacy in this region would not only give protection to merchant shipping but also influence the outcome of the Peninsular campaign. The high Tories, however, managed to create the impression that the duke was interested only in military operations in the Netherlands and that every victory won at sea was a blow to his reputation. Daniel Defoe, who was employed by Harley as a government propagandist and sounder-out of public opinion, reported from Bury St Edmunds that Rooke was 'exalted above the Duke of Marlborough; and what can the reason of this be, but that they conceive some hopes from this that their high-Church party will revive under his patronage'.

In the winter session of 1704 the high Tories revived the Occasional Conformity bill and proposed that it should be 'tacked' to the supply bill in order to secure its passage through the Lords. The supporters of the ministry defeated this proposal, but the untacked bill passed the Commons and was sent up to the Lords, who followed the lead given by Marlborough and Godolphin and rejected it. The Commons were furious, but could hardly complain that the Upper House had acted unconstitutionally. They vented their anger by taking up the case of William White, Mayor of Aylesbury in Buckinghamshire. White, a Tory, had struck off many Whig voters from the electoral roll, confident that when the case came before the Commons – who claimed the sole right to decide disputed elections – the Tory majority in the House would uphold him. However, one of the disfranchised electors, Matthew Ashby, was encouraged by the Whigs to bring a legal action against White, and this eventually came, by way of appeal, before the Upper House. The Lords decided in Ashby's favour, on the grounds that while the Commons undoubtedly had jurisdiction over disputed elections they had no right to deprive a man of his vote, which was his property. The Commons had already decided in favour of White, and when a number of other Aylesbury men followed Ashby's example the Lower House ordered their arrest for breach of privilege. The situation became even more explosive when the prisoners appealed to the House of Lords to uphold a writ of *habeas corpus* by ordering their release. Tempers rose to such a pitch that government business came to a halt, and Anne had to put an end to the unedifying spectacle by dissolving Parliament in April 1705.

The drift towards the Whigs

The factionalism of the high Tories drove Marlborough and Godolphin towards the Whigs, but they were not yet willing to bring the Junto lords into the administration. Instead they formed an alliance with the Duke of Newcastle, a moderate Whig with vast estates and therefore considerable electoral influence, who was appointed Lord Privy Seal in April 1705. The Queen was alarmed by the implications of her government's change of course and wrote to Godolphin urging him to find a moderate Tory for the post of Lord Chancellor. 'I must own to you', she added, 'I dread the falling into the hands of either party, and the Whigs have had so many favours showed them of late that I fear a very few more will put me insensibly into their power, which is what I'm sure you would not have happen to me, no more than I . . . I do put an entire confidence in you, not doubting but you will do all you can to keep me out of the power of the merciless men of both parties.'

Godolphin shared the Queen's reservations about the Whigs, but he needed the support of the moderates in their party in order to maintain his influence in the Commons. He therefore persuaded the Queen to agree to the appointment of a Whig as Lord Keeper, but incidents such as these gradually undermined the confidence between Anne and her chief minister and led her to seek other advisers. One of these was Harley, who in 1706 expressed views that were as music to her soul. 'I have no obligation to any party', he wrote. 'I know no difference between a mad Whig and a mad Tory ... It will be very hard ever to bring the nation to submit to any other government but the Queen's. In her they will all centre.'

When Parliament met for the winter session of 1705 the high Tories temporarily abandoned the issue of occasional conformity and instead tried to embarrass the government by proposing that the Electress Sophia should be invited to take up residence in England. They knew that Anne would resent any such suggestion, since she did not wish to be constantly reminded of her own mortality. They calculated that the government would have to choose between offending the Queen by supporting the measure or alienating her successor by opposing it. Godolphin and Harley, however, aided by the Whig Junto, neatly turned the flank of the high Tories by rejecting the proposal but at the same time promoting the Regency Act to ensure the smooth succession of Sophia or her heir. The act provided that on the death of Anne the Privy Council should immediately assemble and 'with all convenient speed cause the next protestant successor entitled to the crown ... to be openly and solemnly proclaimed'. The opportunity was also taken to modify some of the provisions of the Act of Settlement. The clause requiring all government business to be dealt with by the Privy Council was repealed, while that which barred placemen from the Commons was modified by allowing members who accepted crown offices – with the exception of newly-created ones and certain named positions – to be re-elected.

Military operations had made little progress in 1705. In the Mediterranean region, Gibraltar had survived a six-month siege, and in October 'King Charles', with the assistance of allied troops, had cap tured Barcelona. In tentative peace negotiations that took place between France and the United Provinces in the summer the allies had formally committed themselves to the support of Charles's claims, and Marlborough wrote to the Dutch to remind them that 'England can like no peace but such as puts King Charles in the possession of the monarchy of Spain.'

In The Netherlands and central Europe Marlborough had been unable to exploit the victory of Blenheim. He always had difficulty in persuading the allies to sink their differences and leave him to determine strategy. When the military situation was unfavourable they were prepared to give the duke all the authority he required, but after a victory they became over-confident and stubborn in protecting their particular interests. This accounts for the two-year cycle of success followed by stagnation that pre-vented a speedy end to the war.

By the spring of 1706, however, a major French offensive on all fronts had united the allies behind Marlborough, and in May of that year he won his second great victory, at Ramillies in the Spanish Netherlands. 'The consequence of this battle', he informed Godolphin, 'is likely to be of greater advantage than that of Blenheim, for we have now the whole summer before us, and with the blessing of God I will make the best use of it'. As the allied forces swept south, capturing 'so many towns ... that it really looks more like a dream than truth', Marlborough began to hope for an early peace and told Sarah to hurry on the building of Blenheim Palace so that they could move into it as soon as the war was over. Antwerp, Brussels and Ostend were all captured, and by the time the cam-paigning season came to an end the allied armies were poised for an advance into France.

The year 1706 had also been successful for the allies in Italy, where Prince Eugene had expelled the French and proclaimed Charles as king. In the Peninsula, Barcelona held out against French attempts to retake it, while an allied force from Portugal struck into the heart of Spain and cap-tured Madrid. This provided the opportunity for 'King Charles' to win the hearts of his nominal subjects, but unfortunately he lacked the personal qualities needed for this task. The allied war aim of placing Charles securely on the Spanish throne was coming up against the difficulty that the Spaniards had accepted Philip as their sovereign and were not interested in rival claimants. Spain was highly suited to guerrilla warfare, in which the native inhabitants excelled, and the military balance moved even further against the allies when the Duke of Berwick – James II's son by Marlborough's sister, now a Marshal of France – returned to Spain to take command of the French and Spanish forces there.

The parliamentary session which opened in the winter of 1706 saw the Godolphin-Harley administration under further pressure from the high Tories. The Regency Act had settled the English succession but not the Scottish, and relations between the two countries were so bad that a full union seemed the only way out. The Whigs were in favour of such a solution, but the Tories dreaded the prospect of Scottish presbyterians sitting in the Lower House, and opposed giving formal recognition to what they regarded as the puritan Church of Scotland. Once again the uncompromising stance adopted by the high Tories drove Godolphin, against his will, into the arms of the Whigs. The Whig leaders, however, demanded that in return for their support the Queen should appoint one of their number, Charles Spencer, third Earl of Sunderland, as Secretary of State. Anne found Sunderland's person and principles repugnant, and was most unwilling to comply. 'All I desire", she declared, 'is my liberty in encouraging and employing all those that concur faithfully in my service, whether they are called Whigs or Tories; not to be tied to one nor the other.'

Unfortunately for the Queen, she was no longer free to choose her ministers as she wished. The demands of war made parliamentary co-operation essential, and this could only be achieved with the support of the Whigs. Sarah, Duchess of Marlborough, who was a close friend of Godolphin, urged Anne to set aside her personal feelings and serve the public good by appointing Sunderland. She knew that no other solution was possible, for Sunderland (who was her son-in-law) had told her that he and the Junto had 'come to our last resolution in it, that this and what other things have been promised must be done, or we and the Lord Treasurer must have nothing more to do together about business'. Anne reluctantly gave way and in December appointed Sunderland Secretary of State, but although she had bowed to the inevitable she deeply resented the pressures put upon her. Her anger was not calmed by Sarah's accurate but tactless observation that 'it looks like infatuation that one who has sense in all other things should be so blinded by the word "Tory"'.

Robert Harley, who did not approve of the drift towards the Whigs, had already established a direct link with the Queen behind Godolphin's back. He used as intermediary Abigail Hill, Mrs Masham, an acquaintance of the Duchess of Marlborough, who had originally introduced her to Anne. The ambitious Abigail set out to replace Sarah as the Queen's confidante, and by the winter of 1707 the embittered duchess was referring to 'the black ingratitude of Mrs Masham, a woman that I took out of a garret and saved from starving!' Mrs Masham was a friend of Harley, and through her good offices he built up a relationship with the Queen that undermined Godolphin's influence.

Godolphin sensed that his position was becoming less secure, especially when he learned, in the summer of 1707, that Anne had chosen two Tories as bishops without consulting him. The Junto lords were furious, because two extra Tory votes in the Upper House could make a big difference, and Godolphin was appalled by the prospect that the Whigs would retaliate by blocking the voting of supply when Parliament reassembled in the winter. 'The liberties of all Europe and the glory of your reign,' he reminded the Queen, 'depend upon the next session of Parliament. This being truly the case, what colour of reason can incline your majesty to discourage and dissatisfy those whose principles and interest lead them on with so much warmth and zeal to carry you through the difficulties of the war?'

Anne eventually agreed to cancel out the Tories' advantage by making some Whig bishops – thereby demonstrating the extent to which Church appointments had become a matter of political wrangling. The Whigs were not satisfied, however, and kept up their pressure on Godolphin, while the high Tories continued their vendetta against him. At the battle of Almanza in April 1707 the allied forces in Spain were heavily defeated by the Duke of Berwick, while in The Netherlands a combination of Dutch caution and allied bickering prevented Marlborough from taking full advantage of the situation created by Ramillies. The high Tories blamed defeat in Spain upon insufficient troops, and in December 1707 Rochester and Nottingham, in the Lords, formally proposed the transfer of several thousand men from The Netherlands to the Peninsula. Their supporters in the Commons followed up this initiative by demanding to know why fewer than nine thousand British soldiers had been present at Almanza, when Parliament had appropriated supply for thirty thousand.

By January 1708 Godolphin and Marlborough had decided to throw in their lot with the Whig Junto. They suspected Harley of treachery, they were exhausted by the endless bickering of the high Tories, and they were aware that Whig strength in the Commons had been increased by the union with Scotland brought about in 1707. The Junto had always approved of Marlborough's conduct of the war and had now openly committed itself to the principle of 'No peace without Spain.' There seemed little reason for keeping the Whigs out of the administration except Anne's dislike of party rule – which in practice seemed to mean Whig party rule. The Queen was prepared to sacrifice Godolphin rather than let the Whigs into office, and tried to persuade Marlborough to serve in an administration headed by Harley. Marlborough, however, refused to do so in view of 'the treacherous proceedings of Mr Secretary Harley to [the] Lord Treasurer and myself'. Since Anne could not possibly, at that stage, dispense with Marlborough's services, she had to let Harley go instead. Harley resigned in 1708, St John went with him, and Robert Walpole, a moderate Whig who was on good terms with the Junto, became the new Secretary-at-War.

In May 1708, after the administration had been re-formed, a general election was held. War fervour had been revived by the repulse of a French invasion attempt two months earlier, and this helped both the moderate Whigs and the Junto. Many Tories, including St John, lost their seats, and Walpole, in a letter to Marlborough, reported that 'the Whigs have had the advantage very much. I believe by the most modest computation there are near thirty more Whigs chosen in the room of Tories than Tories in the room of Whigs, which makes them in Parliament stronger by double that number'.

In July 1708 Marlborough defeated the French for the third time, at Oudenarde, but was persuaded by Prince Eugene not to advance on Paris until the great fortress of Lille had been taken. The siege lasted until December, when Lille at last capitulated, and Marlborough extended the campaigning season long beyond its normal course by capturing Ghent and Bruges in January of the following year. These victories were welcomed in England, particularly by the Whigs, but the Tory gentry were longing for peace and could not understand why, after three major triumphs, Marlborough had not been able to bring the war to a close. They suspected him of wanting to be another Cromwell, rising to supreme power through a standing army, and they convinced themselves that he was deliberately spinning out the war for his own personal advantage. In the Mediterranean theatre, Port Mahon, in Minorca, had been taken in September 1708 and provided an invaluable naval base, but the war in the Peninsula was going badly and there seemed little prospect of Charles ever establishing himself securely on the Spanish throne.

The Tories, who had earlier pressed for the Peninsular campaign to take priority over The Netherlands, had now swung into opposition to it. St John gave expression to their feelings when he told Harley that the new ministry's plan to raise yet more regiments 'is to my apprehension downright infatuation, and what I am glad of. They hasten things to a decision, and our slavery and their empire are put upon that issue. For God's sake let us be once out of Spain!'

As the Tories became more clamorous in their desire for peace, the Junto demanded a bigger role in government and insisted that Lord Somers should be given a post. Anne held out against this demand as long as she could, but in October 1708 the death of her husband left her prostrate with grief and broke her resistance. Somers was duly appointed Lord President of the Council and the Earl of Wharton was made Lord Lieutenant of Ireland. Godolphin and Marlborough were now to all intents and purposes heading a Whig administration, but public opinion was turning against the war and in favour of the Tories. Discontent was increased by the severe winter of 1708–09, when the Thames froze over and prices soared.

The strain of war was being felt in France as well as England, and in the spring of 1709 Louis XIV sued for peace. He offered to accept the transfer of the whole Spanish empire to the Archduke Charles, the *soi-disant* King of Spain, as long as his grandson Philip was compensated for the loss of the Spanish crown by being given territories elsewhere, preferably in Italy. These terms represented total defeat for France and would certainly have been acceptable to William III. But the allies insisted that Louis should join them in driving Philip out of Spain if the young man refused to leave of his own free will. Even Marlborough was shocked at such a demand, commenting that 'if I were in the place of the King of France I should venture the loss of my country much sooner than be obliged to join my troops for the forcing of my grandson', yet he did nothing to moderate it. Marlborough's enemies had some grounds for their argument that he was deliberately prolonging the war, for he was prepared to go on fighting until the French surrendered unconditionally, and his victories confirmed him in the belief that he could bring this about. He was not an opponent of peace but he was a major obstacle to a negotiated settlement.

By the summer of 1709 the allies had at last forced their way across the French border, and in September Marlborough captured Tournai. The same month saw the last of the great battles of the war, and Marlborough's final triumph, at Malplaquet. But this was a pyrrhic victory, for the allies lost more men than the French, including the flower of the Dutch infantry. If the French defended every inch of their soil with the doggedness they had shown at Malplaquet the war would turn into a holocaust, and the Tories were already talking about the 'butcher's bill'. Marlborough knew that his position was under threat, but he was convinced that nobody else could lead the allied forces to ultimate victory. The planning of strategy and negotiations with allies were long-term projects that demanded a greater measure of security than Marlborough currently enjoyed. He was therefore toying with the idea of asking to be made Captain-General for life, although he knew that his enemies would take this as proof that he aspired to be another Cromwell. In the autumn of 1709 he took the plunge and formally requested the life tenure of this high office, but Anne refused to comply. She, like the Tories, was tired of war and disillusioned with the man who seemed able to win everything except peace.

At this mid-way stage in Anne's reign English society was more deeply divided than at any time since the Exclusion Crisis. In London there were Whig coffee houses and Tory coffee houses. When Tories took over the theatre in Drury Lane, the Whigs clubbed together and built a rival to it in the Haymarket. After the lapsing of the Licensing Act in 1695 Tory and Whig news-sheets increased in number, and by 1709 there were some twenty papers circulating in London alone. The most influential Tory weekly was *The Examiner*, and so successful was it that Marlborough and Godolphin gave government patronage to Daniel Defoe, whose *Review* now became a forum for the expression of pro-Whig views. For some time the *Review* had the edge over its rival, but Defoe lost confidence after the Whig defeat in 1710 and left the field open for Jonathan Swift, who took over *The Examiner* and placed his outstanding talents at the disposal of Robert Harley.

The Tories were often referred to as the 'landed interest' and thought of themselves as such. In fact, not all landowners were Tory; a number of the biggest ones were Whig, as were a minority of the gentry. The majority, however, were fully committed to the Tories and they viewed with the utmost suspicion the growth of what they regarded as an alien 'monied interest'. This had its citadel in the Bank of England, whose major stock-holders included men of French, Dutch and Jewish extraction whom the Tories regarded as un-English and sinister. Even the smaller stockholders tended to be merchants, office-holders and professional men, mainly from London and the home counties. There were very few genuine landowners among them. The Tory gentry were paying for the war through a punitive land tax, yet the proceeds were being passed on to financiers, to businessmen who were doing well out of army and navy contracts, and to the increasing number of regular army officers. Henry St John gave voice to the Tories' feelings when he referred, in 1709, to 'a new interest ... a sort of property ... not known twenty years ago ... now increased to be almost equal to the *terra firma* of our island'.

As the gap between pro-war Whigs and anti-war Tories widened, both sides took up more and more extreme positions. The Tories prided themselves on their devotion to monarchy, in contrast to the Whigs, whom they condemned as republicans. They chose to deny the role played by Tories in the Glorious Revolution, which had been genuinely bipartisan in its initial stage, and to blame the sorry state of the country upon their failure to live up to their avowed principles of passive obedience and non-resistance. They also claimed a monopoly interest in the Church of England, conveniently ignoring the fact that the majority of Whigs were anglicans. Religious toleration was the dividing line here, for the Whigs were committed to this in principle while the Tories were in general opposed. The Tories particularly resented the degree of toleration allowed to protestant dissenters, for this, in their view, weakened the foundations of society at a time when it was already under threat from the dissenters' allies, the Whigs and the monied interest. They were also horrified at the way in which the removal of restrictions on the press had led to the appearance of a number of works highly critical not only of the established Church but of religion in general.

The deep-felt emotions and prejudices of the Tory gentry found expression when, on 5 November 1709 – Gunpowder Day and the anniversary of William of Orange's invasion – Henry Sacheverell preached a sermon in St Paul's Cathedral. Sacheverell was a noted high Tory and took as his text 'In peril among false brethren.' The Church of England, he argued, had had 'her pure doctrines corrupted and defiled; her primitive worship and discipline profaned and abused; her sacred orders denied and vilified; her priests and professors (like St Paul) calumniated, misrepresented and ridiculed'; and he implied that this tragic decline was due to the resistance that had been offered to the Stuart monarchy in 1688. The only hope of salvation lay in 'an absolute and unconditional obedience to the supreme power in all things lawful', and he insisted on 'the utter illegality of resistance upon any pretence whatsoever'.

The Whigs, who were now persuaded that they alone had carried out the Revolution, took up the challenge thrown down by Sacheverell, and all the pent-up party strife was concentrated on this single issue. The House of Commons, dominated by the Whigs, decided to impeach Sacheverell, and Walpole was one of the managers of the trial, which took place before the Lords in Westminster Hall. Sacheverell was accused of maintaining 'that the necessary means used to bring about the said happy Revolution [of 1688] were odious and unjustifiable', and Walpole, presenting the case for the prosecution, declared that 'the doctrine of unlimited, unconditional, passive obedience was first invented to support arbitrary and despotic power'.

The trial excited enormous interest. Sir Christopher Wren was commissioned to build galleries for the fashionable world and a box for the Queen, who attended daily. Outside the hall a Tory mob, in what was probably an orchestrated campaign designed to frighten the Whig government, gave itself up to the congenial task of burning down dissenters' meeting-houses. It even threatened to attack the Bank of England, the visible embodiment of Whiggery and the monied interest, and the horse guards had to be called out to protect the nation's credit.

Sacheverell was found guilty, but the punishment inflicted upon him – he was forbidden to preach for three years, and his sermon was ordered to be burned by the common hangman – was so light that it amounted to a vindication. The trial had shown the strength of Tory sentiment, and this helped persuade Anne to remodel her administration. The leading Whig ministers were gradually removed, and the Queen turned for support to the middle group of moderate Whigs and moderate Tories who looked to Harley for guidance. In April 1710 the last meeting between Anne and the Duchess of Marlborough took place, and the beginning of a new era, in which the Marlboroughs would no longer be predominant, was signalled by the appointment of the moderate Duke of Shrewsbury as Lord Chamberlain.

Godolphin complained to Anne about the way in which she had 'taken a resolution of so much consequence to all your affairs both at home and abroad, without acquainting the Duke of Marlborough and me with it till after you had taken it', but the Queen was no longer listening to him. Her policy was now formed in conjunction with Harley, via Mrs Masham, and Harley looked for support, as always, to those who put the crown's service before party loyalties. 'As soon as the Queen has shown strength and ability to give the law to both sides,' he declared, 'then will moderation be truly shown in the exercise of power without regard to parties only.' In June 1710 Sunderland, who was the link between Marlborough and the Whig Junto, was dismissed from office. Finally, on 8 August, the Queen sent a curt message to Godolphin ordering him to break his white staff of office as Lord Treasurer. In September Rochester was appointed Lord President of the Council in place of the Whig Lord Somers, and Henry St John became Secretary of State.

Harley, the Tories and peace

Only after she had given a clear indication of her preferences by dismissing the Whigs did Anne dissolve Parliament and order a general election. The result was a Tory landslide which alarmed Harley as much as it surprised him. He had hoped to build a ministry of moderates, free from the extremists of both wings, but now he was dependent for his majority upon a House of Commons in which the high Tories were extremely powerful. Marlborough made the perceptive comment that if Harley, by allying with the Whigs, could form 'a party stronger that that of the Tories, he would do it tomorrow'. But the duke was not entirely correct in deducing that because the 'Octobrists' were so numerous in the Lower House, Harley, 'who will always sacrifice everything to his ambition and private interests, will be obliged, if he is to keep his place, to devote himself to them and to embrace all their schemes'.

The 'Octobrists' were the one hundred and sixty or so high Tories who formed themselves into the October Club and demanded the dis-

missal of all Whigs from office, the impeachment of former Whig ministers, and the condemnation of occasional conformity. They were also the
voice of the 'Country', calling for an end to bribery in elections and corruption in government. They wanted a limitation on the number of
placemen allowed to sit in the Commons, and insisted that public expenditure should be brought under the scrutiny of the House. Harley
skilfully placated the high Tories by supporting a number of measures of
which they approved but opposing those he regarded as unnecessarily
divisive. The Place Bill fell into the latter category, and Harley persuaded
the Commons to reject it. But he gave his approval to an act requiring all
candidates for election to possess a minimum amount of land. The high
Tories hoped this measure would, in the words of one member, 'prevent
the monied and military men becoming lords of us who have the land',
but the act was stillborn, for temporary conveyances of property in the
period preceding an election enabled unqualified candidates to escape its
restrictive intentions.

The euphoria created among Tories by the outcome of the Sacheverell
affair had revived the hopes of all those who longed to restore the Church
of England to what they regarded as its rightful position in the life of the
nation. There were suggestions that the Church courts should be reinvigo-
rated and that all schools should be brought under the control of the
diocesan authorities. Harley deplored these attempts to put the clock back
and effectively blocked them, but by way of compensation he sponsored a
bill in January 1711 which provided funds for the construction of fifty new
churches in London. He also agreed to the setting up of a committee to
investigate the public accounts.

The main aim of the Tories was to put an end to the debilitating war
against France, and they were quite prepared to go behind their allies'
backs in order to achieve this. The Tories loathed the Dutch, in particular,
and believed that the war would not have gone on as long as it had if
English interests had been given primacy. Many of the smaller landowners
were facing bankruptcy as a result of heavy taxation and did not see why
they should be ruined for the benefit of foreign nations. The Whigs were,
in general, more outward looking and regarded the Dutch alliance as the
key to stability and security in Europe, but they were aware that they were
paying a high price, perhaps too high a price, for it. Marlborough, who
had had a close view of the Dutch, expressed his fears that 'besides the
draining our nation both of men and money almost to the last extremity,
our allies do by degrees so shift the burthen of the war upon us that, at the
rate they go on, the whole charge must at last fall on England'.

The Tories had only reluctantly accepted the Whig view that any peace settlement must include the expulsion of Louis XIV's grandson, Philip V, from the Spanish throne, and the defeat of an allied army at Madrid in December 1710 provided them with an opportunity to abandon this principle. In the secret negotiations already taking place with France, Harley had anticipated this change of attitude by letting it be known that 'we will no longer insist on the entire restoration of the monarchy of Spain to the House of Austria; or, if we do, it will be weakly and *pro forma*, and we shall be content provided France and Spain will give us good securities for our commerce. And as soon as we have got what we need and have made our bargain with the two crowns, we will tell our allies'.

In April 1711 Henry St John was made responsible for negotiating a settlement with France, and by September of that year provisional terms had been drawn up. Louis XIV was now willing to withdraw recognition from the Old Pretender, agree to the cession to Britain of Gibraltar, Port Mahon and Newfoundland, and concede English merchants a monopoly of the valuable slave trade with Spanish South America. The Netherlands, like the Italian possessions of Spain, were to go to the Emperor, except for a barrier of fortress towns to protect the Dutch against further French incursions. It was also formally agreed that the crowns of France and Spain should never be united.

These terms were highly advantageous from Britain's point of view. Port Mahon (in Majorca) and Gibraltar would give the British navy a commanding position in the Mediterranean and facilitate the expansion of British commerce in Italy and the Levant. Newfoundland would provide an invaluable base for exploitation of the valuable fishing banks, while the slave-trade monopoly, though granted initially for a period of thirty-three years, might well be extended indefinitely. Harley – who in May 1711 had been created Earl of Oxford and appointed Lord Treasurer – saw in this last provision an opportunity to free himself from dependence upon the Whig-dominated Bank of England and also to strengthen Tory ties with the City and financial interests. He therefore set up the South Sea Company and gave it a monopoly of trade with South America on condition that it took over part of the National Debt.

British pleasure at the proposed peace terms was not shared by the Emperor and the Dutch, who accused the Queen's ministers of betraying them, nor by the German princes, who wanted security against further aggression by France. Marlborough made himself the spokesman of these discontented partners, and it was to counter his powerful criticism that Oxford called on Swift to write the pamphlet which appeared in November

1711 under the title of *The Conduct of the Allies*. In this brilliant and savage piece of propaganda Swift built up a distorted but convincing interpretation of the war. It had been started, he explained, by a nation united in its determination to ensure the breaking-up of the Spanish empire. However, Marlborough and the Whigs had become intoxicated with military glory and the prospect of their continued enrichment, and had therefore turned a deaf ear to French offers conceding all their original demands. They had deliberately kept the war going, not only in the Netherlands but also in Spain, where they had committed themselves to a solution that could not be implemented. The only gainers from long years of warfare were the Whig profiteers and their foreign allies, who had bled the English squirearchy to death while they waxed fat on the proceeds.

The Conduct of the Allies sold over eleven thousand copies within a month of its appearance and provoked a pamphlet war more violent than anything seen since the days of the Exclusion Crisis. The Whigs were so determined to prevent acceptance of the proposed peace terms that they made an unholy alliance with Nottingham and the high Tories. They promised to accept the outlawing of occasional conformity on condition that the high Tories joined them in upholding the principle of 'No Peace without Spain.' In December 1711 the Occasional Conformity Act, which imposed penalties on any office-holder who attended a dissenting service, became law, and the House of Lords passed a resolution against peace without Spain. But Oxford and the moderate Tories in the Commons closed ranks in face of this danger and were ready, with the Queen's support, to counterattack. On the last day of 1711 Anne dismissed Marlborough from all his offices in a note which was so curt that the duke tossed it into the fire. In January of the following year Robert Walpole, the leader of the Whigs in the Lower House, was impeached on a charge of corruption during his time in office as Secretary-at-War. Finally, Anne created twelve new peers to ensure a majority of pro-peace members in the Upper House.

The formal peace conference opened at Utrecht in January 1712. The principal English representative was Henry St John, who was a high Tory by inclination but remained outwardly loyal to Oxford in the hope of eventually taking his place. Anne disliked and distrusted St John, and in July 1712 she refused his request for an earldom, creating him Viscount Bolingbroke instead. Bolingbroke resented this slight – 'I remain clothed with as little of the Queen's favour as she could contrive to bestow', he commented – but it only intensified his ambition and his determination to win power. 'I am afraid,' he wrote many years later, 'that the principal spring of our actions was to have the government of the state in our hands, that our principal views were the conservation of this power, great employments to ourselves and great opportunities of rewarding those who had helped to raise us, and of hurting those who stood in opposition to us ... I believe few or none of us had any very settled resolution.'

Bolingbroke, who echoed Swift's criticism of the conduct of England's allies, had no sense of obligation towards them. He was afraid that success in the field might encourage the Dutch to raise their terms, so he sent a message to Marlborough's successor in command of the British forces, giving him 'the Queen's positive command to ... avoid engaging in any siege or hazarding a battle till you have further orders from her majesty. I am at the same time directed to let your grace know that the Queen would have you disguise the receipt of this order; and her majesty thinks that you cannot want [i.e. lack] pretences for conducting yourself so as to answer her ends without owning that which might, at present, have an ill effect if it was publicly known'. He added as an afterthought, 'I had almost forgotten to tell your grace that communication is given of this order to the court of France.'

Bolingbroke was, in short, treating the French as allies and the allies as enemies. In July 1712 British troops were withdrawn from active service, leaving Prince Eugene, the imperial commander, to be heavily defeated, and in the following October Bolingbroke notified the French of Eugene's plans of attack so that they could take the necessary counter-measures. This sort of treatment drove the Dutch, who were also exhausted by the long war, to accept the Franco-British peace terms, and in April 1713 the war was formally concluded by the signing of the Treaties of Utrecht. Only the Emperor held out for another year, until he too was obliged to come to terms.

Bolingbroke and the succession

A general election held in the summer of 1713 confirmed the Tories' hold on power. Now that the war was over, the question of who would succeed Anne became the principal political concern. Legally there was no doubt, since the Act of Settlement had nominated the Electress Sophia of Hanover. Sophia, however, was a sick woman, not expected to live long, and it seemed certain that the throne of Great Britain would pass to her son, Prince George. The disadvantage of this arrangement from the Tory point of view was that George was one of the German princes who had taken a prominent part in the war against France, and he regarded the 'English Peace' as a betrayal of all he had fought for. George was in touch with Marlborough and the Whigs, and the general assumption was that his accession would open the way to a long period of Whig rule.

Such a prospect did not appeal to the Tories, and about a hundred of them, including Bolingbroke, were toying with the idea of bringing back the Stuart line in the person of James Edward, the 'warming-pan baby', called by some 'The Old Pretender' and by others 'James III.' The biggest obstacle to James's return was his religion, since he refused to renounce his faith. If 'James III' were to accede to the British throne, it would be as a catholic.

Bolingbroke was sufficient of a realist to know that the country would not accept another catholic King, yet he also knew that the accession of George of Hanover would mean the end of his political career. He therefore became engaged in a power struggle, hoping, as he later said, 'to break the body of the Whigs, to render their supports useless to them, to fill the employments of the kingdom, down to the meanest, with Tories. We imagined that such measures, joined to the advantages of our numbers and property, would secure us against all attempts during [the Queen's] reign, and that we should soon become too considerable not to make our terms in all events which might happen afterwards'.

For the fulfilment of his plan Bolingbroke needed control of royal patronage, but this was vested in Lord Treasurer Oxford. It was essential, therefore, for him to drive Oxford from office, and to do so speedily, so that he could infiltrate Tories into all the key posts before Anne died. However, Oxford, who led the somewhat smaller wing of the Tory party that was committed to the Hanoverian succession, was determined to hold on to office as long as he could in order to frustrate Bolingbroke's schemes. In June 1714 Bolingbroke made a bid for the support of the high Tories by mounting a campaign to put down the academies to which dissenters resorted, since they were barred from the universities, and to forbid anyone to teach who was not in possession of an episcopal licence. The Schism Act was introduced into the Commons to give effect to these proposals, and Bolingbroke hoped that Oxford would oppose it and thereby weaken his credit with both the Queen and the Tories. But Oxford, although he proposed amendments to the act when it reached the Lords, did not vote against it, and he turned the tables on the Jacobite Tories by persuading Anne to issue a proclamation denouncing the Old Pretender and offering a reward of £5,000 to anyone who captured him, should he attempt to land in her dominions.

Anne was slowly turning against her Lord Treasurer, but Oxford was still in office when Parliament was prorogued in July 1714. Swift compared the ministry to 'a ship's crew quarrelling in a storm, or while their enemies are within gunshot', and crisis point was reached in mid-July, when Anne fell ill and was thought unlikely to recover. Bolingbroke made frantic efforts to oust Oxford, and bitter quarrels took place between the two men in the presence of the dying Queen. At last, on 27 July, Anne dismissed her Lord Treasurer, but she did not immediately offer the post to Bolingbroke.

Before Anne could make up her mind to take this final step her condition sharply deteriorated. The Cabinet, reinforced by two Whig members who had not attended since the making of the Peace of Utrecht, recommended to the Queen, whose days were clearly numbered, that she should choose the Duke of Shrewsbury, a moderate Whig, as Oxford's replacement. Bolingbroke, hoping to make the best of a situation that was fast slipping out of his control, went along with this and headed the procession of Councillors that made its way to the Queen's bedside to add their persuasions. Anne duly gave her approval, and on 30 July Shrewsbury became Lord Treasurer. Just over a day later, on the morning of 1 August 1714, the Queen died at Kensington Palace. She had lived long enough to ensure the smooth succession of George I. Bolingbroke recorded in his diary, 'the Earl of Oxford was removed on Tuesday, the Queen died on Saturday. What a world is this, and how does fortune banter us'.

CHAPTER TWENTY-ONE

Ireland, Scotland, and overseas possessions in the seventeenth century

IRELAND

Ireland under James I

James I marked his accession to power by recalling Elizabeth's commander, Mountjoy, from Ireland and replacing him with Sir Arthur Chichester. The new Lord Deputy had no sympathy with the native Irish and obviously intended, if he could, to destroy the clan structure that made Ireland so different from England. Hugh O'Neill, Earl of Tyrone, who had led the Ulster rebellion against English rule in the closing years of Elizabeth's reign, now abandoned any lingering hope that things would be better under her successor. His fellow chieftain, Rory O'Donnell, whom James created Earl of Tyrconnell, felt the same, and the two men decided to go into exile rather than see the transformation of the Ireland they had known and loved.

The 'Flight of the Earls' provided James with the opportunity to continue and intensify the plantation policies of his predecessor. The crown took over the six northern counties, confiscating most of the land and offering it to English and Scottish 'undertakers', on condition that they restricted their choice of settlers to immigrants from the mainland.

However, like so many Stuart enterprises the plantation of Ulster was only a partial success. Ireland was in such a disturbed state and land titles so uncertain that settlers were not forthcoming in sufficient numbers. By 1628 there were only some two thousand British families in Ulster, and many of the 'undertakers' had allowed the original Irish occupants to stay on. The two most successful features of the scheme were associated with Scotland and London. Scottish emigrants, suffering from a shortage of land in their own country, were prepared to try their fortunes in Ireland, and as their numbers slowly increased they turned Ulster into a protestant enclave and gave it a flavour quite different from the rest of Ireland. The contribution of London came through the City corporation, which decided to invest money in establishing a major port in Ulster and achieved a remarkable success by creating Londonderry.

The dispossessed Irish landowners, the great majority of them Roman Catholics, were, in the words of one of their bishops, 'excluded from all hopes of restitution or compensation, and are so constituted that they would rather starve upon husks at home than fare sumptuously elsewhere. They will fight for their altars and hearths, and rather seek a bloody death near the sepulchres of their fathers than be buried as exiles in unknown earth and inhospitable sand'. The Anglo-Irish or 'Old English' landowners were not affected by the plantation of Ulster. These men, descendants of settlers who had come to Ireland in the Middle Ages, shared the Roman Catholic faith of the native Irish and had drawn much closer to them, but were not prepared at this stage to form a united front against the 'New English' – the government officials, soldiers and 'adventurers' who, with the blessing of the royal administration, were taking over Irish lands. However, their traditional dominance over Irish political life was increasingly threatened by the recent arrivals, who benefited from the creation of new parliamentary constituencies in the areas affected by settlement. When the first Irish Parliament of James's reign met in 1613 a majority of its members were protestant. The Old English had to accept that they were now a minority and would never again be able to dominate or even significantly influence parliamentary proceedings.

James had summoned the Irish Parliament in order to obtain a grant of supply, in which he was successful, but Ireland continued to be a drain on the King's resources. During the first six years of James's reign the maintenance of the army there cost him £570,000, while a further £150,000 went on restoring the quality of the Irish coinage, which had been debased under Elizabeth. As conditions became more stable, the army was reduced in size, and therefore cost, while the revenue was increased by setting up an Irish Court of Wards in 1622. The income from the Irish Customs also went up as trade expanded, but in 1618 James granted the lease of these duties to his favourite, Buckingham, on the understanding that he would split the profits with the crown. The King benefited from this arrangement, but not so much as the favourite, who used the Customs farm as a means of extending his influence in Ireland. Viscount Falkland, a client of Buckingham, was appointed Lord Deputy in 1622 and acted as his agent for collecting the Customs revenue. Another client was Sir William Parsons, the first Master of the Irish Court of Wards. Buckingham also sold Irish peerages, with James's approval, and bought up Irish estates on a substantial scale. There were rumours that he was to be appointed Lord Lieutenant, and although nothing came of these his involvement in the Irish administration added to the corruption and inefficiency for which it was already notorious. Lionel Cranfield, appointed Lord Treasurer of England in 1621, set up a commission to enquire into the workings of the Irish government and root out corruption, but he came up against the interests not only of Buckingham but also of the New English, who were well represented on the commission, and these blunted the impact of his reforming zeal.

Ireland under Charles I

The accession of Charles I in 1625 was welcomed by the Old English as a chance to demonstrate their loyalty. The King needed money for the war against Spain on which he intended to embark, and the Old English offered to subsidise the expansion of the army in return for a promise that they would not be subject, as catholics, to the penal laws. A delegation of Irish landowners was summoned to London in 1628 to work out the details of an agreement, and the King subsequently issued just over fifty 'graces', incorporating his concessions. The Old English were not granted religious toleration, exemption from the penal laws, or access to public office, but they were given security of tenure, which meant that their estates would be protected from confiscation. In return they promised to contribute three annual subsidies, each worth £40,000, towards the costs of the army that Charles was raising. This could only be done by Parliament, however, which was also the only body that could ratify the graces and give them legal standing. The Irish Parliament had already been summoned to meet in 1628, but administrative problems led to its indefinite postponement. The graces therefore remained little more than a statement of intent by the King, with no standing in law.

Falkland's period in office as Lord Deputy came to an end shortly after the assassination of his patron, Buckingham, and from April 1629, when he was recalled to England, the government of Ireland was left in the hands of the Earl of Cork and Sir Adam Loftus, who were appointed Lords Justices. These were the leaders of the New English and pursued a policy based on enforcement of the penal laws against the native Irish and Old English. The catholics had little chance of improving their condition while their sworn enemies were in power, but they welcomed the arrival in July 1633 of a new Lord Deputy, Thomas Wentworth. He made conciliatory noises, but only because he wanted to ensure a successful session of the Parliament he summoned for the following year. The Old and New English were united in their desire to gain security for their title-deeds and hoped to make certain of this by a generous grant of supply. They accordingly voted the King six subsidies, but they got very little in return. As far as the Old English were concerned, only ten of the graces secured statutory confirmation. The remainder, which included a clause giving security of title for sixty years' occupation, remained dependent on the King's goodwill.

Wentworth's refusal to concede the demands of either the Old or the New English sprang from his awareness that a great deal of property had been stolen from the crown and Church during the previous half century. He set up a Commission for Defective Titles to examine the entire structure of landholding in Ireland, and he did not want its investigations to be hampered by any statutory confirmation of existing tenures. He was thinking mainly of the New English, whose methods of acquiring land had often gone beyond the bounds of legality, but by his refusal to confirm the graces he alienated the Old English as well. The truth was that Wentworth had no love for either of the two main English groups in Ireland. He despised the Old English because they were catholic, and the New English because they were, in his own words, 'a company of men the most intent upon their own ends that ever I met with'.

Wentworth realised that the common-law courts would defend property rights in Ireland as in England. He therefore secured from the crown letters patent giving the prerogative Court of Castle Chamber authority to make final decisions in matters affecting the Church. With this weapon he prepared to embark on the process of re-endowing both the crown and the Church. No one had profited more from despoiling them than Richard Boyle, Earl of Cork, and Wentworth had a list of all his estates drawn up so that the title-deeds could be examined and, where appropriate, annulled. Some of these deeds went back to the reign of Elizabeth, when Cork had first arrived in Ireland with less than thirty pounds in his pocket, and he fought hard to preserve his property. However, he was forced to part with a great deal of it, and later informed the Long Parliament that because of Wentworth's 'oppressions and injustice' he was 'the worse by £40,000 . . . in my personal estate, and £1,200 a year in my revenue'.

Wentworth's determination to place the King's interests above all others led him to extend the plantation system into Connaught. The existing landowners, most of whom were catholic, were deprived of a quarter of their land, which now became available for settlement by protestant immigrants. Their title to the rest was confirmed, but only as tenants-in-chief of the crown, which rendered them liable to wardship and other feudal incidents. The Old English felt betrayed by Wentworth, and longed for his departure just as much as they had earlier longed for his arrival. The New English, despite their shared protestant faith, also regarded Wentworth as an enemy, while the native Irish detested him as the symbol of an unscrupulous colonising power that was depriving them of all they held dear.

Wentworth was not perturbed by criticism, particularly since he had Charles's support. He was convinced that his policy was the right one and that it would ultimately redound to the King's benefit. He also took pride in the fact that, as a result of his strong government, Irish trade was flourishing. Piracy round the coast was put down, communications were improved, and the linen industry was encouraged. Wentworth had a direct interest in the success of such measures, since he had taken over the farm of the Irish Customs and was doing well out of it. He condemned the abuse of office by other men, but he was not free from it himself – although he could claim, with some justice, that he only enriched himself by enriching his royal master.

In late 1639 Charles recalled Wentworth to England to advise him on how to deal with the looming Scottish crisis. Wentworth recommended the summoning of both an Irish and an English Parliament, and Charles therefore sent him back to Ireland in March 1640 to arrange the first of these. Wentworth returned to Dublin with hallmarks of the King's approval, for he was now Lord Lieutenant instead of merely Lord Deputy, and he had also been created Earl of Strafford. His skill as a parliamentary manager was demonstrated when the Irish Parliament voted four subsidies without any difficulty and committed itself to support the King 'with our persons and estates to the utmost of our abilities'. Strafford used the money to raise an army of nine thousand men for deployment against the rebellious Scots, but before it was ready the first Bishops' War had come to an end. So also had Strafford's term of service, for the King needed him at home. He left

Ireland convinced that his rule had been a success, and he claimed that the Irish were 'as fully satisfied and as well affected to his majesty's person and service as can possibly be wished for'.

The Irish Rebellion

Strafford had imposed order on Ireland largely through the force of his personality, but no sooner was this constraint removed than the discontent which he had held in check boiled to the surface. In October 1641 the native Irish rose in rebellion against the new settlers in Ulster and massacred them. The Old English were torn between their faith and their loyalty, but for most of them their faith proved stronger and they threw in their lot with the rebels. Successive English governments had done nothing to keep their allegiance, and they saw in the growing strength of the puritans in England a threat to their very existence.

Londonderry and a few other towns held out in Ulster, while in the Pale loyalist forces were commanded by the Earl of Ormond – head of the Butlers, one of the greatest of the Old English families, but a protestant as a result of his upbringing as a royal ward. Ormond sent urgent appeals to England for reinforcements, but the King and Parliament were too preoccupied with the political crisis there to be able to make an adequate response. Parliament proposed that ten million acres of Irish land should be confiscated and used to repay those who would advance money to the state for the suppression of the rebellion. The King accepted this proposal, but by the summer of 1642 both sides were preparing for civil war and Ireland was left to fend for itself.

The Irish rebels were guided by the Roman Catholic bishops, who set up the Confederation of Kilkenny, with a supreme council of two members from each province, pledged to carry on the war until Roman Catholicism was accepted as the official religion of Ireland. The Confederation controlled most of the country, except for pockets of resistance in Ulster and the Pale. Ormond was still the nominal commander of all the protestant forces, but his primary loyalty was to the King, and Charles was constantly urging him to come to terms with the rebels so that his army could be transferred to England. In September 1643 Ormond agreed to a cease-fire – the 'Cessation' – but little came of it. The Scots in Ulster ignored the Cessation and subscribed to the *Solemn League and Covenant*, while the Munster protestants called on the English Parliament for support. Ormond was betrayed even by the King, for Charles was engaged in secret negotiations with the rebels and gave the impression that if only they would come to his assistance he would accept their demands.

The Old English leaders in the Confederation were anxious for an agreement with the King, partly out of loyalty but also because they thought a royalist victory in the Civil War was more likely to lead to a tolerant religious settlement than a parliamentary one. They were strongly entrenched in the supreme council of the Confederation, and in early 1646 negotiated a settlement with Ormond. However, in June of that year Confederate forces in Ulster, under the leadership of Sir Phelim O'Neill, heavily defeated the Scots. O'Neill now became the principal figure in the Confederation, and one of his first acts was to dissolve the supreme council. He distrusted Charles and insisted that the demands of the Roman Catholic Church be met in full before any pact was made with the King. This did not happen until Ormond accepted the Treaty of Kilkenny in January 1649, guaranteeing religious toleration and an independent Parliament for Ireland, but his concession amounted to nothing because the King's cause was now lost.

Cromwell and Ireland

Just over six months after the signing of the treaty, Oliver Cromwell landed in Ireland with a force of twelve thousand men. He had been shocked, like all his contemporaries, by the reports of massacres and other atrocities inflicted on the protestants in Ulster and was determined to exact vengeance. In September he stormed Drogheda, and informed Parliament that 'being thus entered, we refused them quarter, having the day before summoned the town . . . I do not think thirty of the whole number escaped with their lives. Those that did are in safe custody for [exile in] Barbados'. Cromwell had no reason to anticipate criticism from a Parliament whose members thought as he did, and he was convinced 'that this is a righteous judgement of God upon those barbarous wretches who have imbrued their hands in so much innocent blood'.

Cromwell left Ireland after nine months, relying on Ireton and Ludlow to complete the conquest. Ormond fled into exile, O'Neill died, and by May 1652 Ireland lay prostrate before the English invaders. The conquerors' terms were set out in the Act for Settlement of Ireland which provided that every Irish landowner, protestant or catholic, would be liable to have his estates confiscated unless he could prove that he had shown 'constant good affection to the interests of the Commonwealth of England'. There was nothing new about this policy. It marked the extension to the whole of Ireland of the system of plantation that had hitherto been applied only to Ulster and Connaught, and it caused a seismic change in the pattern of landholding. Protestant landowners might, with luck, hold on to at least part of their estates, but the majority of the eight thousand catholic owners were expelled from their holdings. They were replaced by English soldiers, who accepted Irish land in lieu of arrears of pay, and by 'adventurers' who had financed the conquest of Ireland by making loans to the republican government. In 1641 catholics had owned some 60 per cent of cultivable Irish land, but by 1703 their share had slumped to 14 per cent.

From 1655 Ireland was under the governance of Cromwell's younger son, Henry, who was given the title of Lord Deputy in 1657. His aim was to bring together former enemies in support of his father's Protectorate. His partial success in this endeavour was demonstrated by the way in which his close associate Lord Broghill – one of the sons of the Earl of Cork – supported the Cromwellian regime in the British Parliament and promoted *The Humble Petition and Advice* (*see* p. 373). Henry Cromwell's administration was not noticeably more effective than its predecessors. Ireland remained a drain on the English Exchequer, especially since an army of thirty-five thousand men had to be kept there, and although the Protectorate Parliament contained thirty Irish representatives the majority of its members had little understanding of Irish affairs and assumed that what was best for England would ultimately be best for Ireland.

Ireland under Charles II and James II

Charles II was faced with a land problem in Ireland even more intractable than that which confronted him in England. He promised to confirm the titles of existing owners and at the same time restore to their estates all those who had been evicted for fighting on the royalist side The most realistic comment on these conflicting priorities was made by Ormond, who observed that 'there must be new discoveries of a new Ireland, for the old will not serve to satisfy these engagements'. An Irish Parliament, summoned in 1661, passed the Act of Settlement, which left existing owners secure in the possession of their lands, promised restitution for evicted protestants, and made grudging provision for Roman Catholics who could prove that they had supported the crown. As Ormond had foretold, however, there was not enough land to meet the statutory requirements, and four years later an Act of Explanation was passed requiring the

Cromwellian settlers to part with a third of their property in order to compensate land-hungry claimants. It also prescribed that in all disputes between catholics and protestants, the latter were to have the benefit of any doubt

This solution to the land problem satisfied the protestants since it confirmed their ascendancy, but the catholics had good cause to feel they had been robbed, and they kept up their agitation for repeal of the Act of Settlement. As far as religion was concerned, however, they had much to be grateful for. Ormond returned to Ireland as Lord Lieutenant, and although he was a devout anglican he was prepared to obey Charles's orders and turn a blind eye to catholic practices. Roman Catholic clergy moved freely around the country, schools and monasteries were set up, and the mass was openly celebrated. There was less tolerance of dissent, however, and in Ulster the bishops began evicting presbyterian ministers. Persecution continued on and off until the *Declaration of Indulgence* of 1672, which opened a new era for nonconformists in Ireland as well as England.

Prosperity helped keep discontent at a safe level. Cattle-raising turned out to be a profitable enterprise and became the basis of Irish wealth. English commercial jealousy resulted in the exclusion of Irish cattle from England, but continental markets remained open and a flourishing trade was built up with them. Ormond also continued Wentworth's policy of fostering the linen industry which, since it did not obviously compete with English manufactures, was relatively free from restrictive tariffs.

Ormond remained in office until 1668 and was eventually replaced by Lord Berkeley, a former royalist general and companion of Charles II in exile. He lasted only two years and was in turn replaced, in 1672, by the young Arthur Capel, Earl of Essex, who was a client of Arlington. Essex was a hard-working and successful Lord Lieutenant but spent much of his time battling with the Vice-Treasurer, Viscount Ranelagh, who treated the Irish revenue as a source of profit for himself and his friends in England, and used accounting methods which could charitably be described as unorthodox. Essex had Charles's support but was also subjected to the King's irresponsible intervention in Irish affairs. Like so many Englishmen, Charles regarded Ireland as a reservoir on which he could draw for money, patronage and gifts. In one of his many inconsiderate moments he proposed granting his mistress Barbara Villiers, Countess of Castlemaine, the extensive estate of Phoenix Park, just outside Dublin, either not knowing or not caring that this was the residence of the Lord Lieutenant. Fortunately for Essex, Charles was persuaded to change his mind, but he continued to use Ireland as a convenient way out of his English problems. Some years later, for example, he decided that the cost of maintaining the garrison in Tangier should be transferred from the English to the Irish exchequer.

Essex remained in office as long as Arlington was Charles's principal adviser, but when Arlington's power waned his position became untenable. In 1677 he was recalled to London and after much discussion Ormond was sent out again as Lord Lieutenant. The state of the Irish finances continued to create problems, but in 1682 an Irish Treasury Commission – modelled on the one set up in England after Danby's fall – assumed responsibility for this sphere. It began by deciding that the Irish revenue should be spent in Ireland and not siphoned off to London, and it took measures to reduce corruption and expand the revenue which were strikingly successful. It also secured authority from the royal government to investigate land titles, which were still causes of controversy, and to make definitive pronouncements on them. From the financial point of view, then, Ireland was better governed in Ormond's second term of office than it had been in his first.

James II, during his brief reign, began the process of turning Ireland into a catholic stronghold. In January 1687 he appointed as Lord Lieutenant the catholic Earl of Tyrconnel, with orders to weed out protestant officers from the Irish army, appoint Roman Catholic judges, and generally repeat in Ireland the policies that James was pursuing in England. Tyrconnel was so successful that when the Glorious Revolution took place in England, Ireland remained loyal – except for the Ulster protestants, who proclaimed William as their King and, when attacked by the Lord Lieutenant, took refuge in Londonderry.

Ireland under William III and Anne

After his expulsion from England, James attempted to stage a come-back by landing in Ireland, in March 1689. Two months later he met the 'Patriot Parliament', which was dominated by Roman Catholics. This passed legislation guaranteeing liberty of conscience, and also repealed the hated Act of Settlement, but little could be done to give catholics a greater share of Irish land unless and until James secured control over the whole country. In April 1689 he laid siege to Londonderry, but the city held out until it was relieved by the arrival of a British fleet. William authorised the dispatch of an expedition to Ireland in August 1689, but it was not until June of the following year that he crossed the Irish Sea to take charge of it.

The decisive encounter between the two kings came in July 1690 at the Battle of the Boyne, and it resulted in the total defeat of James, who decided to cut his losses and return to France.

By the terms of the Treaty of Limerick, which put an end to the fighting, Irish soldiers were free to take service in the armies of France, while Roman Catholic civilians were to enjoy 'such privileges as are consistent with the laws of Ireland, or as they did enjoy in the reign of King Charles II'. The military articles of the treaty were duly observed, and English ships were provided to facilitate 'the flight of the wild geese' – the departure into exile of thousands of Irish catholic soldiers. The Irish Parliament, however, once again under the control of protestant landowners, refused to ratify the civil articles. It was prepared to tolerate the open exercise of the Roman Catholic religion, but only on condition that its adherents accepted a position of permanent social and political inferiority.

During the reigns of William and Anne, Irish Parliaments passed the penal laws which confirmed the protestant ascendancy. Roman Catholics were excluded from Parliament, the civil service, the armed forces, local government and the law. They were not allowed to educate their children at universities, nor were they free to acquire land. The estates of a catholic landowner were to be divided, after his death, among all his children, unless the eldest son became a protestant, in which case he was to have the entire inheritance. These and other restrictive measures could not be rigidly enforced, but they crippled the catholic Irish and barred them from public life throughout the eighteenth century. The transformation of their position that the Tudors had started and Oliver Cromwell had accelerated was completed by the penal laws, and a legacy of hatred and violence was handed down to future generations.

SCOTLAND

Scotland under James VI & I

James VI left Edinburgh for London in April 1603, yet he remained King of Scotland and administered his native country directly, without appointing a deputy, as in Ireland. One of his first actions was to improve the postal service between London and Edinburgh, and he sent some sixty

letters a year to the Scottish Privy Council, transmitting his orders. He
had good reason to boast that as far as his northern kingdom was concerned 'here I sit and govern it with my pen. I write, and it is done, and by
a clerk of the Council I govern Scotland now, which others could not do
by the sword'. Yet messages alone were not enough. He needed to keep
his finger on the pulse of Scotland, and he did so through his old friend
Sir George Home, Earl of Dunbar and Lord Treasurer of Scotland, who
commuted regularly between Edinburgh and London.

As King of Scotland James had presided over the Church or Kirk,
and in 1595, when Richard Bancroft, at that time Bishop of London,
made dismissive remarks about Scottish presbyterianism, James
reacted by condemning the anglican form of service as nothing
more than 'an evil mass in English'. However, first-hand experience
of anglican worship, so much more formal and dignified than
its Scottish counterpart, led him to change his mind. In fact
he became such an enthusiastic advocate of the Church of England
and its practices that in 1606 he summoned a small group of leading
presbyterians, including Andrew Melville, to London, in the hope that
they would be equally impressed. However, although they were
forced to attend anglican services and to listen to sermons upholding
both episcopacy and the royal supremacy they remained intransigent.
Andrew Melville was so forthright in his condemnation that he was
imprisoned in the Tower of London for several years. Even after his
release he was forbidden to return to Scotland, and spent the rest of
his life in exile.

This was not simply vindictiveness on James's part. The King was
determined to strengthen episcopacy in Scotland and knew that Melville
would mount a formidable challenge to his policy. Episcopacy had never
died out, and by 1605 all but three of the Scottish dioceses had bishops,
but they were of little significance. The main reason for this was that they
had been stripped of their wealth by the Act of Annexation of 1587
(see p. 179), but in 1606 Dunbar, acting on James's instructions,
persuaded the Scottish Parliament to modify this act and thereby
open the way to the re-endowment of the episcopate. Two years
later, Dunbar took with him to Edinburgh his chaplain, George Abbot –
future Archbishop of Canterbury – who established good
relations with the leaders of the Kirk and persuaded them that
episcopacy did not run counter to their beliefs. Not all his new-found
friends were persuaded, but attitudes were slowly changing, as was indicated in 1609 when the Scottish Parliament passed an act restoring

bishops 'to their former authority, dignity, prerogative, privileges and jurisdiction.'

James followed up this success by persuading the General Assembly of the Scottish Church, which he summoned to Glasgow in 1610, that bishops should preside over presbyteries, synods and even the Assembly itself, which chose as its chairman or 'moderator' John Spottiswoode, whom the King had recently appointed Archbishop of Glasgow. James also set up two courts of High Commission (later combined into one), on the English model, which strengthened the bishops' disciplinary powers. The final step in restoring their spiritual authority came in 1610 when Spottiswoode and two of his colleagues travelled to London to be formally consecrated by their English brethren. On their return home they consecrated all the other Scottish bishops.

James's long-term aim was to bring the Scottish Kirk closer and closer to the English exemplar until uniformity of worship had been established throughout both kingdoms, but he moved carefully and took his time. During his return visit to his native land in 1617 he gave orders for the royal chapel to be prepared for English-style services, 'with singing of choristers, surplices, and playing on organs', and let it be known that he wished the Kirk to accept what became known as the Five Articles. These made it obligatory for communicants to kneel when receiving the sacrament, revived the practice of confirmation of children by bishops, and required Easter, Christmas and a number of other significant dates in the Christian calendar to be celebrated as feast days. Such demands outraged opinion in Scotland, and a General Assembly of the Kirk which met at St Andrews shortly after the end of James's visit refused to implement them. But James was adamant, and kept up his pressure until the next General Assembly, that convened at Perth in 1618. This time it did as James required, and three years later the Five Articles were also ratified by the Scottish Parliament. Yet public opinion remained hostile to them, and an open clash between the King and his Scottish subjects might well have ensued if James had not been distracted by the Bohemian crisis (*see* p. 288). In the event it was Charles I who bore the odium for trying to enforce James's policies.

Charles I and Scotland

One of the reasons for James's success in Scotland was that he kept the nobles and the Kirk apart by playing on the jealousies between them. Charles, however, pushed the two groups together at the outset of his reign by announcing his intention to revoke all grants of crown and Church land made since 1540. He did not mean by this that the nobles – many of whom, like their English counterparts, held former Church property – would be dispossessed. What he wanted to do, in Scotland as in Ireland, was to counter the spirit of secularism and greed which had led to the impoverishment of the monarchy and Church, and thereby re-establish the authority of both these key institutions. The ministers of the Kirk might have been expected to show gratitude for the King's support, but they were far more concerned about the doctrinal threat implied by Charles's alliance with the Arminians, and they began to regard the nobles as possible allies.

Although Charles had been born in Scotland he never identified himself with his native land in the way that James had done. In 1633 he paid a formal visit, in order to be crowned, but his party included William Laud, already regarded as the promoter of intolerant Arminianism, and his coronation service was conducted with all the ceremony and ritual of high-anglican worship. During his visit Charles summoned a meeting of the Scottish Parliament, which not only ratified James's Five Articles but also confirmed Charles's prerogative powers over the Church – including the right to prescribe what vestments should be worn by its clergy. The King insisted on the use of a surplice, but this was deeply offensive to many of his Scottish subjects, who regarded anything other than a black gown as a symbol of popery.

Among the measures James had initiated as part of his move towards uniformity of worship in England and Scotland was the drawing up of a form of service for the Scottish Church. The new liturgy, which reflected the influence of the English Book of Common Prayer, was ready by 1619, but such was the storm created by the Five Articles that James postponed publication. Charles breathed fresh life into the project, but he was not satisfied with the Jamesian prototype and instructed the Scottish bishops to produce something far closer to the English Prayer Book. They completed their task by 1635, and the liturgy was published two years later. The Scottish bishops, who included a number of Arminians or high-Churchmen, ordered the new form of service to be used for the first time in St Giles's Cathedral, Edinburgh, on 23 July 1637. This provoked a riot. One woman cried out 'The mass is entered among us', while another flung a stool at the bishop.

The revolt rapidly spread beyond Edinburgh, and all classes united in signing the *National Covenant*, binding themselves to oppose innovations in worship and calling for the election of a free Parliament. Charles decided to use force to impose his authority, especially since the

Covenanters' propaganda was now being directed towards England, where it found a responsive audience. His chief adviser in Scotland was the Marquis of Hamilton, whom the King ordered to play for time while he mustered an army. 'I expect not anything can reduce that people, but only force', he wrote. 'I give you leave to flatter them with what hopes you please . . . till I be ready to suppress them.' Suppression was out of the question, however, for Charles had no army, and he therefore instructed Hamilton to suspend the new service book – a mere formality, since it was not being used – and to summon a General Assembly of the Kirk.

The Assembly opened at Glasgow in November 1638, but the Covenanter leaders ensured that this time the moderates were excluded, instead of, as before, dominating proceedings and ensuring conformity to royal directives. Now it was the presbyterians, both ministers and lay elders, who had the upper hand, and they persuaded the Assembly to annul the Five Articles and the new service book, and to abolish the court of High Commission. They also declared that episcopacy was incompatible with the traditions of the Kirk.

Both sides were now preparing to fight, and the Scots chose as their commander Alexander Leslie, a veteran of the Thirty Years War on the continent. Charles's raw levies were no match for the well disciplined and highly motivated Scots army, and in June 1639 he agreed to the Pacification of Berwick which brought to an end what came to be known as the First Bishops' War. Under its terms both sides were to disarm, and the task of finding a long-term solution to outstanding problems was remitted to a Scottish Parliament and a General Assembly of the Kirk, which Charles promised to summon. He had little alternative at this stage, but he told the Archbishop of St Andrews that 'though perhaps we may give way for the present to that which will be prejudicial both to the Church and our own government, yet we shall not leave thinking, in time, how to remedy both'.

The two bodies met in August 1639, but showed no willingness to make concessions in order to obtain a peaceful settlement. The General Assembly confirmed the abolition of episcopacy and ordered all Scots to subscribe to the *Covenant*, while the Parliament, in which the Covenanters were strongly represented, broke with tradition by asserting its right to draw up its own agenda. Charles might have accepted a temporary abandonment of episcopacy but not the Assembly's condemnation of it as against God's will, since this had implications for his other kingdoms. The Scottish Parliament showed its approval of the Assembly's actions by ratifying its decisions. It also elected a standing committee to act as the *de facto* government of Scotland. Another meeting of Parliament, this time without a royal summons, took place in June 1640 and completed the constitutional revolution. Freedom of debate was asserted, a triennial act was passed to ensure regular meetings, the standing committee was made permanent, and a national tax was voted for the support of the war against England.

A renewal of hostilities seemed inevitable, but Charles could not rely on his troops, because their sympathies were, generally speaking, with the Scots. One informed observer reported that both officers and private soldiers 'spared not to declare ... that they would not fight to maintain the pride and power of the bishops', and many men deserted or mutinied. The Scots now took the initiative and crossed the border into England, where they captured Newcastle, thereby cutting off London's supply of coal. They also occupied the two northern counties of Northumberland and Durham, demanding £850 a day to cover their occupation costs. Peace terms were drawn up at Ripon in October, by which the King agreed to withdraw his condemnation of the *Covenant* and Covenanters, to remove his garrisons from Scotland, and to hand over Edinburgh Castle. In return the Scots promised to recall their troops from England. However, the implementation of these terms depended upon the English Parliament, which met in November, and the Covenanter leaders kept in close touch with Charles's principal critics in both Houses, urging them to promote radical measures such as 'Root and Branch' reform of the Church

Charles was now hoping to gain a party for himself in Scotland, and on his visit there in 1641 he accepted many of the Covenanters' demands. He appointed a number of them to the Scottish Privy Council, which took over responsibility for government from the parliamentary standing committee, and he distributed honours among his former enemies. Alexander Leslie, for instance, was created Earl of Leven, while Archibald Campbell, the Calvinist Earl of Argyll, was made a marquis. This policy of conciliation yielded little fruit, however. The Covenanters were not disposed to put their trust in Charles, particularly after rumours of his involvement in a plot to assassinate key figures in the Scottish opposition, including Argyll.

When civil war broke out in England the Scots took no part at first, but only because they wanted to secure the establishment of presbyterianism south of the border as well as north. The Long Parliament, having just thrown off one despotism – that of the Arminian bishops – was reluctant to subject itself to another. English puritans had never wholeheartedly accepted the political implications of Calvinism, and preferred an erastian (state-controlled) settlement to any form of theocracy (clerical domination). Only after Charles appeared to be winning the Civil War did the parliamentary leaders turn to their northern brethren for assistance, and Pym's dying contribution to the cause with which he had become identified was the negotiation of *The Solemn League and Covenant* (see p. 345). The Scots regarded this as the first step towards the creation of a presbyterian England, but for Vane and many other members of the Long Parliament it was primarily a military alliance, with doctrinal implications that were best left undefined.

In accordance with the terms of the *Solemn League* a Scottish army of twenty thousand men, under the Earl of Leven, invaded England early in 1644 and played a major part in the campaign that led to the defeat of the royalist cause. However, while the Covenanters were marching south, one of their former adherents had raised a rebellion in the highlands in the name of the King, and had won some astonishing victories. James Graham, Earl and later Marquis of Montrose, had earlier fought with the Covenanter army, but he believed in constitutional monarchy and feared that the Scottish revolt – especially under the leadership of Argyll, whom he distrusted – was moving towards republicanism. If Charles could ever have reached Montrose or sent troops to him from Ireland, the King's cause might have endured, but the war in England was now going too badly for men to be spared and Montrose had to fight on alone. His luck and skill enabled him to survive until September 1645, but in that month he was heavily beaten at Philiphaugh and fled to the continent. Nevertheless his mere presence in the highlands persuaded Leven not to move his troops south of the river Trent and thereby helped create the impression among the now-victorious English parliamentarians that the Scots were not worth what they cost.

In May 1646 the defeated King rode into the Scottish camp at Newark in Nottinghamshire and surrendered himself. He hoped to exploit the worsening relationship between the Scots and their parliamentary allies, and he could argue, with reason, that the ideal of a national Church to which both he and the Scots were committed was under increasing threat from the Independents and sectarians who dominated the New Model army. It turned out, however, that there was insufficient common ground between the King and the Covenanters to form the basis of an agreement, and in January 1647 they transferred Charles to the custody of the English Parliament, which agreed to pay their arrears, amounting to some £400,000.

Oliver Cromwell and the Scots

The Scots had sworn, in *The Solemn League and Covenant*, 'to preserve and defend the King's majesty's person and authority', and they were increasingly alarmed by the news which reached them from south of the border, where radical groups, particularly in the army, seemed to be taking matters into their own hands. When Charles escaped from Hampton Court in November 1647 and fled to Carisbrooke Castle in the Isle of Wight they accepted his invitation to reopen negotiations. The King eventually agreed to the establishment of presbyterianism in England for a term of three years in return for immediate Scottish support. This 'Engagement', as it was called, was the work of moderate Covenanters under the direction of the Duke of Hamilton, but it was opposed by Argyll and the leaders of the Kirk who regarded it as a betrayal of *The Solemn League and Covenant*. Hamilton, with the support of most of the Scottish peerage as well as a significant number of burgesses and shire representatives, persuaded the Scottish Parliament to ratify the Engagement, thereby fracturing the alliance between the nobles and the Kirk which had kept the revolution from getting out of hand. Yet there were few signs of positive enthusiasm for intervening on the King's behalf, and by the time Hamilton had gathered together an army and led it into England, Cromwell was ready to pounce. The duke's forces had got as far as Preston in Lancashire when Cromwell caught up with them, in August 1648, and put them to flight. Hamilton himself was captured and subsequently executed.

Meanwhile, back in Scotland, the Engagers' hold on power had been broken by radicals called Whiggamores, who came from the west of the country and were spurred on by harsh economic conditions and total commitment to the *Covenant*. The Engagers were hoping for support from Ireland, but Cromwell's arrival in Edinburgh ensured the restoration of the Covenanters, under the nominal leadership of Argyll. For the most part they remained supporters of monarchy, though not of Charles I. What they wanted was a monarch who would take the *Covenant* and maintain a national presbyterian Church. They saw the main threat as coming not from the anglican cavaliers but the Independents and sectarians of the New Model army, with their supporters in the Rump. In February 1649, after the execution of Charles I – about which they had not been consulted – they proclaimed his son as Charles II, and received their reward when Charles decided not only to assume his Scottish throne but also to accept the *Covenant*. The Rump sent Cromwell north again to deal with this threat, and in September 1651 he defeated the Scots at Dunbar, which gave him control over southern Scotland.

By this time the moderate Covenanters had allied with the Engagers to place Charles II on the throne of England as well as Scotland. On 1 January 1651 Charles was crowned at Scone by Argyll, but a shortage of men and money, as well as war weariness, meant that the young King had only limited resources at his disposal. He managed to push as far south as Worcester before nemesis, in the person of Cromwell, overwhelmed him. Charles became a homeless exile, while the Scots had to accept subordinate status under an occupying English army. Resistance continued in the highlands and the west, but by the end of 1654 General George Monck had established control.

The new regime was only maintained by repressive measures which made it feared and deeply unpopular. Cromwell was in favour of uniting the two countries, but the appropriate legislation was not passed until 1657. Scotland was allotted thirty seats in the Protectorate Parliament, but most of these were taken by English nominees. Cromwell left the presbyterians undisturbed in their worship while insisting that toleration should be shown towards the sects – who were few in number and without significant influence in Scotland. The ministers of the Kirk did not thank him for his lack of fanaticism, and opposition to the Protectorate was intensified by the heavy taxation needed to support the army. Monck observed in 1657 that 'the Scots are now as malignant as ever they were', and the Restoration was given as warm a welcome in Edinburgh as in London.

Scotland under Charles II and James II

The short-lived union of England and Scotland came to an end with the Restoration, since neither side wanted it to continue. The Scottish Parliament, under the influence of the nobles, passed an act annulling all legislation introduced since 1633. This confirmed that Charles I's controversial religious policies would not be revived, but more significantly it gave Charles II all the powers he could have hoped for. Parliament once again would meet only if and when he decided, and its business would be prepared beforehand by the crown-appointed Lords of the Articles. The English army was withdrawn from Scotland, though a small local one was retained, and government was placed in the hands of Scottish nobles, of whom the most important was Charles's former companion in exile, the Earl of Middleton, whom he appointed as his commissioner to the Scottish Parliament – a post which carried far more influence than its name implies.

In London the King looked for advice on Scottish matters to one of his Secretaries of State, John Maitland, Earl of Lauderdale. Middleton, an upholder of episcopacy, could count on Clarendon's support, but not on that of Lauderdale, who was sympathetic to the presbyterians even though he had renounced his earlier covenanting beliefs. Middelton tried to have Lauderdale excluded from office, but his underhand plotting was revealed to Charles II, who had an unaccountable liking for the coarse-natured, foul-mouthed Lauderdale. In the end it was Middleton who went, his influence passing to the Earl of Rothes.

There was a widespread assumption in Scotland, as in England, that Charles would do a deal with the presbyterians. However, the King had an intense dislike of the Scottish presbyterians, dating from his experiences in 1650–1, and whereas the opponents of episcopacy in Scotland were ill-prepared and divided among themselves, its proponents, led by Middleton, were well organised. In 1661, therefore, the bishops were restored, while the presbyterians were left out in the cold. In 1662 the Scottish Parliament passed an act requiring all ministers appointed since 1649 to obtain the approval of their diocesan bishop. Many ministers were unwilling to follow such a course, and were therefore evicted. In all, some 25 per cent of the entire ministry was dispossessed, and those who retained their livings were not necessarily the most conscientious or committed. The *de facto* head of the Scottish Church was James Sharp, Archbishop of St Andrews, appointed to the Scottish Privy Council in 1663. He was not only ambitious for political advancement but favoured coercive measures against presbyterian clergy who refused to attend the services of the established Church. These could have worsened the suffering of dispossessed ministers, but in practice they found refuge in the localities, among sympathetic landowners.

South-west Scotland was renowned for its radical presbyterian commitment and also for its resistance to the prevailing high level of taxation. Rothes sent the army in to impose order and collect taxes, but this provoked rebellion in November 1666. The Pentland Rising was a small-scale affair which was easily suppressed, but the brutality of the government's repression showed how nervous it was. Lauderdale placed the blame for the rising on Rothes and Archbishop Sharp, who were deprived of their defender when Clarendon fell from power in 1667. Lauderdale was now, to all intents and purposes, the King's minister for Scotland, and he took a far more relaxed line towards the presbyterians. He gave a clear indication of his new approach by persuading the King to disband the standing army and rely instead on a militia, under the control of the nobles. The *Letter of*

Indulgence of 1669 allowed ejected ministers to return to their livings as long as they accepted episcopacy, and in the same year the Act of Supremacy asserted the King's absolute control over the Scottish Church. These two measures caused deep resentment among the bishops, who were also alarmed by the increasing number of attacks on orthodox ministers by the radicals. The 1669 Scottish Parliament showed its concern by passing an act condemning such outrages.

Lauderdale now found himself in a similar position to that of Danby in England, since both men needed the support of the established Church. He made a conciliatory gesture by securing the passage of a new act against conventicles and using troops to suppress illegal assemblies. When the gentry of south-west Scotland refused to suppress the conventicles which were spreading in their region, Lauderdale and his royal master decided on a show of force. Militia elements drawn mainly from the highlands were ordered into the area, and the 'Highland Host' entered Ayrshire in January 1678. For well over a year it subjected the local inhabitants to savage repression accompanied by looting, and created so much anger that an explosion was all but inevitable. It came in May 1679 and was sparked off by the assassination of Archbishop Sharp and the publication of the *Rutherglen Declaration* upholding the *National Covenant* and condemning the way in which it had been betrayed by successive generations. Fortunately for Lauderdale the rebels were divided among themselves and were routed at the Battle of Bothwell Bridge in June. But the credit for this victory went not to Lauderdale – now a duke – but to Charles's illegitimate son, the Duke of Monmouth, who commanded the army raised to suppress the rebellion.

The King responded to the revolt by reverting to a more conciliatory policy. He pardoned many of those who had taken up arms and gave permission for conventicles to be held in private houses. This policy was maintained, however reluctantly, by James, Duke of York, whom Charles sent to Scotland in October 1679 to get him away from London, where the Exclusion Crisis was in full flood. James spent three months in his brother's northern kingdom and made a good impression on virtually everybody he met. His presence was an implied threat to Lauderdale, but the latter's dominance of Scottish affairs came to an abrupt end in March 1680 when he had a stroke. Later that year James was sent back to Scotland, since the Exclusion Crisis was far from over, and became the most influential figure in the Edinburgh government. Once again, he was remarkably successful in reconciling divergent interests and pushing through policies which he and Charles had agreed. The high point of his stay came when the Scottish Parliament formally acknowledged his right to succeed Charles on the throne of Scotland and also passed a statute requiring all office-holders to take an oath promising to preserve the existing order in Church and state.

James returned to England early in 1682, but the enforcement of the oath went ahead. Many ministers felt unable to take it with a clear conscience and were evicted from their livings. They suffered, along with their presbyterian brethren, lay and clerical, from the royalist reaction which marked the closing years of Charles II's reign. Dissent of any sort, religious or political, was not tolerated, and heavy fines as well as the forced billeting of troops were used to punish offenders. Death was the automatic penalty for anyone denying the King's authority, while those who refused to obey the bishops were liable to imprisonment. More people were executed in the 'peaceful' year of 1683 than had been after the 1679 rebellion, and the period from then until the King's death came to be known as 'the killing time'.

After James ascended the throne in 1685 there were revolts against him in both England and Scotland, but neither of them was successful. The Scottish revolt was led by Argyll – the son of the first marquis, who had been executed after the Restoration – but it was easily suppressed, and Argyll met the same fate as his father. Yet loyalty to the King did not imply any willingness to tolerate his religion. James dissolved the Scottish Parliament after it declined to annul the legislation keeping catholics out of public life, and he used his dispensing power to appoint his co-religionists to office. The most prominent example of this was his choice of the catholic Earl of Dumbarton to command the Scottish army.

After his breach with the anglicans in late 1687 James turned to the dissenters in England, and he tried to do the same in Scotland. But there was no support within the Scottish Parliament for toleration of dissent, and James therefore imposed it by virtue of his prerogative. The presbyterians were the main beneficiaries, but the Scottish bishops, with no Tory party to support them, were left high and dry. James had alienated the Churchmen, who were the traditional supporters of monarchy, without winning over the presbyterians, who continued to suspect his motives. Yet generally his rule was accepted in Scotland and might have continued had it not been for events further south.

Scotland and the Glorious Revolution

The Scots were onlookers at the Glorious Revolution, but they took advantage of it to secure their religious and constitutional liberties. A Convention of Estates, which began its deliberations in Edinburgh in March 1689, formally acknowledged William and Mary as joint sovereigns of Scotland, and, in return, secured acceptance of their *Claim of Right*. This went further than the English *Bill of Rights* by asserting that Parliament was justified in deposing any ruler who violated the law, and when the Convention was formally declared a Parliament it forced William to agree that the Lords of the Articles should cease to exist. As for the Church, episcopacy was abolished, ministers who had been ejected under Charles II and James II were restored to their livings, and a General Assembly of the Kirk was summoned for the first time since 1653.

Although the accession of the new sovereigns had been accepted by the greater part of Scotland, albeit with limited enthusiasm, the adherents of James VII and his son – known as the Jacobites, after *Jacobus*, the Latin rendering of 'James' – found support in the highlands, where a rebellion was led by James Graham of Claverhouse, Viscount Dundee. The rebels had a number of successes, including their defeat of William's troops at Killiecrankie in July 1689, where Dundee lost his life. They did not have the men or resources for a long campaign, however, and by 1690 the pacification of the highlands was well under way, with Fort William being constructed as a base from which to mount operations. Highland chiefs were offered a free pardon if they made their submission to William, but some of his advisers felt that the process should be speeded up by making an example of one of the more recalcitrant clans. The Macdonalds of Glencoe were chosen as victims, and in February 1692 troops from Fort William who had been billeted on clan members suddenly turned on their hosts and murdered them. Many of the intended victims escaped, but the clan chieftain and over thirty of his followers were slaughtered. William may not have been fully informed of the details of the plot, but the Massacre of Glencoe was laid to his charge and poisoned relations between him and his Scottish subjects.

Bad feeling was also stirred up by the English Navigation Acts, which treated the Scots as foreigners where trade was concerned. Scotland was not rich in natural resources, but in the face of English jealousy Scottish merchants looked to their own salvation. In 1695 a Bank of Scotland was successfully established, and in the same year the Scottish Parliament authorised the setting up of a company to trade with Africa and the Indies.

It was hoped that this company would be a joint venture between England and Scotland, for many English merchants who were excluded from trade with the orient by the monopoly of the East India Company saw an outlet for their capital and enterprise in the Scottish initiative. However, the English Parliament took up the matter, inspired not so much by love of the East India Company as by fear of Scottish competition, and threats of impeachment persuaded English merchants to hold back.

The Scots, smarting under a sense of betrayal, decided to go ahead on their own. Large sums of money were raised by nation-wide contributions, and it was decided to send an expedition to establish a settlement at Darien, on the Isthmus of Panama. The basic idea of establishing a new land route across the Isthmus from the Caribbean to the Pacific had much to be said for it, but insufficient account was taken of the terrible climate and the fact that Darien was claimed by the Spaniards. William was engaged in complicated diplomacy over the Spanish succession, and the last thing he wanted was an overt act of hostility against Spain. He therefore instructed neighbouring English colonies to give no assistance to the Scottish settlers, and by April 1700, after three expeditions had been decimated by disease and Spanish attacks, the Scots gave up. The money which had been subscribed, and which had meant a heavy sacrifice for a poor country like Scotland, had been dissipated without anything to show for it, and the Scots put the blame for their failure firmly on the English.

The Union

The Darien fiasco had shown up the weaknesses of William's position. As King of England he was opposed to the project, while as King of Scotland he might have been expected to support it. The only way in which to prevent the re-emergence of this split personality was to unite the legislatures of the two countries, but William died before he could bring that about. Anne took up where her predecessor had left off by appointing commissioners from both countries to work out the details of a union, but little progress was made, for the English were determined to keep the Scots out of their commercial empire, and negotiations were eventually broken off. The Scottish Parliament showed its anger by emphasising its independence. The Act anent Peace and War, passed in 1703, declared that Scotland should not be automatically committed to war or peace by English policies, but should make her own decisions. In the following year the Act of Security laid down that Scotland would not accept the Hanoverian succession unless her constitutional, economic and religious liberties were guaranteed.

The English Parliament riposted with the Aliens Act of 1705. This demanded the repeal of the Act of Security and the opening of negotiations for a full union between the two kingdoms. Failing these, all Scots in England would be treated as aliens, and all Scottish imports would be forbidden. This act aroused considerable ill feeling north of the border, but Scotland was in no position to engage in a trade war with her powerful neighbour, and the Scottish Parliament eventually agreed that the Queen should appoint commissioners to reconsider the question of union. This time the negotiations went smoothly. The commissioners were appointed in February 1706 and by July they had agreed on a draft treaty. This was ratified by the two Parliaments early in 1707, and in May of that year England and Scotland became a single state.

The union confirmed the Hanoverian succession. It also opened the trade of England to all British subjects, which meant that Scottish landowners now had access to the largest free-trade area in Europe for their corn, cattle, linen, coal and salt. Further concessions to the Scots included the right to keep their own presbyterian Church and their own systems of law, education and local government. They lost their separate Parliament, but were compensated for this by being allotted forty-five newly-created seats in the Lower House of the United Kingdom Parliament as well as sixteen in the Upper. The Scots agreed to share the burden of the national debt, but in return they received a lump sum payment of £400,000, to be used to compensate officials whose offices would no longer exist and those who had suffered from the Darien disaster.

The English government was generous in its offers of places and pensions to the Scottish nobles, and opponents of the union north of the border claimed that it had only been brought about through massive bribery. Yet the terms of the union took ample account of Scottish desires and sensibilities, which hardly suggests that the English negotiators regarded their Scottish counterparts as servile petitioners whose views could be disregarded. The union did not, of course, put an immediate end to friction between the two countries and peoples. The period of Tory rule at the end of Anne's reign placed severe strains upon the new relationship, since the government restored the rights of lay patrons in Scotland and insisted that an episcopal church should be allowed to function there. Bitterness reached such a peak that in 1713 a motion to dissolve the union was only narrowly defeated in the House of Lords, but the following year saw the triumph of the Whigs, who had framed the original agreement. The union became a fact of political life, taken largely for granted, and endured unchanged for well over two and a half centuries.

OVERSEAS POSSESSIONS

Virginia

Elizabethan attempts to found a colonial empire failed because they were given only a low priority. The resources which might have enabled infant settlements to survive were consumed in privateering expeditions and other activities which yielded a swifter and more profitable return. However, the accession of James I to the English throne was followed by the conclusion of peace with Spain and a ban on privateering. It now made more sense to use whatever monies were available from investors to establish plantations overseas. These were commercial ventures, inspired in part by economic nationalism, for it was hoped that the colonies would make England self-sufficient by providing the naval stores and 'Mediterranean' goods that she could not produce herself. Settlers were difficult to come by at first, but the economic depression which set in around 1620 created unemployment and acted as a spur to emigration. So also did the persecution of puritans, which became more acute after Laud's rise to power.

The first major attempt at colonisation in the Stuart period was directed towards Virginia, where Ralegh had pointed the way. Ralegh sold his patent to a group of London businessmen who included Sir Thomas Smythe, son of a Customs farmer and himself a member of the Merchant Adventurers and the Levant and Muscovy companies. Smythe was the moving spirit behind the formation of the Virginia Company in 1606, and it was as a result of his efforts that in December of that year three ships – the *Susan Constant, Godspeed and Discovery* – set sail from London, carrying just under 150 settlers. They arrived in Chesapeake Bay in May 1607, sailed up the river they named after King James, and established a settlement at the site that was eventually to become Jamestown.

For many years the fate of the colony hung in the balance. The swampy situation and hostile natives led to a high death rate, and the settlers were dependent on supplies reaching them from England. A royal Council of Virginia had been set up in England during the first flush of enthusiasm, but as it became clear that no easy fortunes were to be made the King lost interest and in 1609 he issued a new charter making the Virginia Company the proprietors of the colony.

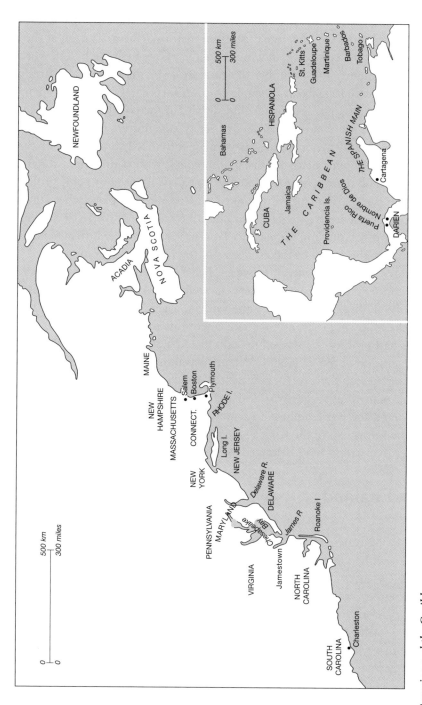

America and the Caribbean

Money for the venture came from 'adventurers' who bought shares in the company. The cost of transportation was met either by the settlers themselves, who were then free to start up their own farms as soon as they arrived, or by the company, in which case the assisted person had to work for the community for a number of years. By 1617 the colony was firmly established, with tobacco as its staple crop. Unfortunately for the company the habit of smoking developed only slowly, in face of the King's disapproval. Profits were never sufficient to repay adventurers the money they had invested, and new capital was consequently hard to attract. Smythe was unpopular with many of the shareholders, who blamed him for the poor return on their investment, and he was also criticised by some prominent figures in Parliament, who looked on Virginia as a place where their ideas on representative government could be tried out. By 1619 Smythe had been pushed out and his place as Treasurer taken by Sir Edwin Sandys, the doughty champion of the privileges of the House of Commons.

Sandys' rule lasted only a few years, but it led to the summoning of the first representative body to meet in colonial America. The general assembly of Virginia, elected by the settlers, assembled in July 1619 and again the following year, and the movement towards self-government that Sandys had promoted survived his fall. In 1624, after complaints that the administration of the Virginia Company was more concerned with politics than commerce, the crown confiscated its charter and assumed direct control. A royal governor was despatched, but he had orders to continue summoning the representative assembly, and it was also made clear that since the settlers were the King's subjects they were to enjoy the laws and liberties that would have belonged to them at home.

New England

Just over a year after the little fleet had sailed from London for Virginia a group of Nottinghamshire puritans, who could not reconcile their consciences with conformity to the established Church, emigrated to the United Provinces and set up a congregation there. However, in spite of the welcome they received from the Dutch they missed their native land and hoped that one day they might be able to live among Englishmen, if not in England itself. The Virginia Company, prompted by Sandys, gave them a licence to settle in the New World, a joint-stock company was formed, and in September 1620 the Pilgrim Fathers set sail from Plymouth in the *Mayflower*. Out of more than a hundred passengers only thirty-five were members of the original separatist congregation. The rest had come direct from England and did not necessarily share the puritan attitudes of their companions. It was assumed that the colony, when established, would come under the jurisdiction of Virginia, but since there was a possibility that the emigrants would arrive in an unknown region their leaders drew up the *Mayflower Compact*, providing for the making of laws and the establishment of a civil administration. It was as well they did so, for the Pilgrim Fathers landed far to the north of Virginia and had to establish a settlement from scratch at a place they christened Plymouth. They managed to survive, though conditions were hard, and by sending corn, timber and furs to England they made sufficient profits to buy out the home-based shareholders. They thereby created the first autonomous English community in America.

The Pilgrim Fathers had begun the colonisation of New England, and in 1629 they were followed by another puritan congregation which had obtained a separate charter under the name of 'the Company of the Massachusetts Bay'. The new arrivals founded Salem, and once securely established they resolved that 'the whole government, together with the patent for the said plantation, be ... legally transferred and established to remain with us and others which shall inhabit upon the said plantation'. In 1630 John Winthrop, who had been elected governor of the company and colony, set sail for Salem, taking with him not only the charter itself but a thousand new emigrants. These men were nearly all religious refugees, and they paid their own passage. Poor men had to go to the southern colonies and sell their labour to pay off the cost of their passage, but the New England colonists were, from the beginning, persons of substance and independent spirit.

During the reign of Charles I some sixty thousand emigrants left the shores of England, and of these about a third went to New England. The ideal of the puritan settlement in New England was not religious toleration but a different form of intolerance from that which existed in old England. In Massachusetts, for example, government was confined to elders of the Church, who constituted only about one-fifth of the adult male population, and anyone who objected to the rule of this theocratic oligarchy was expelled.

The intolerance of Massachusetts led to the foundation of a number of other colonies. One group of dissident ministers hived off and established themselves in Connecticut. Another group followed the irrepressible Roger Williams, champion of religious liberty, who was driven out of Massachusetts for declaring that the civil government had no authority in religious matters. In 1636 Williams took refuge among the native Indians and he insisted on treating them as equals and paying for the land he bought from them on which to establish a new settlement based on the principle of religious freedom. The community he set up developed eventually into the self-governing colony of Rhode Island.

By the time civil war broke out in Britain the northern colonies in America were flourishing communities which cherished the considerable degree of independence they had acquired. Further south, across the gap formed by the Dutch colony of New Netherland, Virginia had been joined by Maryland, created in 1632 by the Roman Catholic Lord Baltimore and named in honour of Charles I's Queen. The northern colonies made their living out of fish, furs and naval stores, as well as agriculture, but in Virginia and Maryland the main crops were tobacco and cotton. These were ideally suited for cultivation on big plantations, and because immigrant labour was not readily available for such work black slaves were imported from West Africa. The New England colonies built up a lucrative trade supplying the plantations with food, working in close co-operation with the Dutch merchants and shipowners of New Netherland.

The West Indies

Bermuda was the first of the islands off the American coast to be settled by the English. Sir George Somers, sailing out to Virginia with a fresh batch of emigrants in 1609, was wrecked on the 'Somers Islands' (the Bermudas), but he found life there very agreeable and sent back reports which not only inspired Shakespeare to write *The Tempest* but also encouraged the formation of the Somers Islands Company. Further south, in the Caribbean, the first English settlement was on St Kitts, discovered in 1624, but in the following year an English ship returning home came across the uninhabited island of Barbados and claimed it for King James. Sir William Courteen, partner in an Anglo-Dutch trading concern, provided the funds for the settlement of the island and began a profitable trade in tobacco, but his rights were challenged by one of James I's Scottish favourites, James Hay, Earl of Carlisle, who had been presented by the King with a patent creating him proprietor of the 'Caribee Islands'. Carlisle was not personally interested in colonisation, but he hoped that profits from the West Indian plantations would help pay off his debts, and he fought a prolonged legal battle which resulted in the confirmation of his ownership. For some years Barbados and other West Indian islands concentrated on the production of tobacco and cotton, but by the time the Civil War broke out they had begun cultivating sugar cane on a large scale.

The Colonies during the Interregnum

The colonies took no direct part in the Civil War, and although the sympathies of the New England settlers were clearly with Parliament their main objective was the preservation of their virtual independence. The victory of the puritans led to a second wave of emigration – this time of royalists, most of whom went to the southern colonies. Others settled in Barbados and Antigua, and the colonial authorities in the region showed their disapproval of the execution of Charles I by recognising his son as King. The English Parliament was not prepared to meekly relinquish control over the West Indian and southern mainland colonies, which were so valuable for English trade. In 1651 Sir George Ayscue was sent with a fleet to restore them to obedience, and this he did without any difficulty – a striking demonstration of the effectiveness of sea power.

When Cromwell took over the government of England he planned to use the navy to enforce acceptance of his rule in the colonies but also to expand their range and number. The idea of uprooting Spanish power in the region appealed to the Elizabethan in him, but he also appreciated the advantages that this would bring to English commerce. Cromwell had already been involved with the company that attempted to establish a puritan settlement on Providence Island, but this was too near the mai land and the settlers were driven out by the Spaniards in 1641. In 1654 Cromwell dispatched his own expedition with the objective of capturing Hispaniola. It failed in this, but by way of compensation it added Jamaica to England's colonial empire.

The governments of the Interregnum took the first big steps towards breaking the Dutch monopoly of trade in the American region and knitting together the commerce of England and her colonies. Early Stuart governments had not been entirely neglectful of colonial needs. The first committee of the Privy Council for foreign plantations had been set up in 1634, and as early as 1621 James I had ordered that colonial tobacco should be sent only to England, while at the same time forbidding its cultivation within the British Isles. In 1651 these *ad hoc* measures were gathered together in the Navigation Act, which laid down that 'no goods or commodities whatsoever of the growth, production or manufacture of Asia, Africa or America, or of any part thereof ... shall be imported or brought into this Commonwealth of England' except in such ships 'as do truly and without fraud belong only to the people of this Commonwealth, or the plantations thereof ... and whereof the master and mariners are also for the most part of them of the people of this Commonwealth'. The intention behind this act was clear. The growth of English shipping was to be stimulated and the Dutch were to be forced out of the dominant position they had won for themselves in international commerce.

The restoration of royal authority

The government of the restored Charles II continued the policies of its Interregnum predecessors, as was shown by the passing of another Navigation Act in 1660 and the Staple Act three years later (*see* p. 518). It also completed the process of expelling the Dutch from America by taking over the colony of New Netherland in 1664 and renaming it New York. Expansion continued to the south and north of Virginia, though the settlers for these new colonies were drawn from Europe and the existing settlements rather than from England, where the growth of trade and industry was creating a demand for labour. In 1663 a group of courtiers, including Clarendon, Albemarle and Ashley, was given proprietorship over the area which they named Carolina, in honour of the King. They planned to produce Mediterranean goods there – wine, oil and fruit – but the project was not a great success since smuggling flourished more than viticulture. By 1700 there were only two small settlements in existence, but these proved to be the seeds from which the separate colonies of North and South Carolina were to grow.

To the north of Virginia, Pennsylvania was colonised after William Penn was given proprietary rights in 1681. Penn was the quaker son of one of the admirals who had commanded Cromwell's Hispaniola expedition, and, on his father's account, was owed a considerable sum of money by the crown. Charles II granted him territory in the New World in lieu of repayment. Pennsylvania was at first settled by quakers, glad to escape from religious persecution at home, and Penn's high ideals were reflected in the framing of an elaborate constitution and rational ground-plan for Philadelphia, the 'city of brotherhood' by the Delaware river, which was to be Pennsylvania's capital. Soon, however, the quakers were outnumbered by other immigrants, who refused to accept Penn's directives and gradually took control of the colony themselves.

The great distance between England and America, and the conditions of life in the New World, promoted the growth of popular assemblies and self-government. The Navigation Acts, however, made some sort of central control imperative, in order to ensure that the regulations were not flouted, and under Charles II and James II an attempt was made to bring the colonies more directly under royal authority. The weapon of *Quo*

Warranto, which had been used to such effect against English municipal corporations, was employed to bring the American colonies to heel. In 1684 the charter of Massachusetts was declared forfeit; two years later similar action was taken against Connecticut; and in 1687 Rhode Island was turned into a crown colony. James consolidated the northern settlements into a single Dominion of New England and appointed a governor for the whole area, with orders to rule through a nominated council and suppress popular assemblies.

America and the Glorious Revolution

Autocracy, in New England as well as old, was ended by the Glorious Revolution. Most of the colonies had their charters restored, although in Massachusetts the rule of Church elders was brought to an end. The attempt at central control was abandoned, but further steps were taken to ensure that the acts regulating trade were observed. In 1697 Customs officials were given the same rights of search as their English counterparts, and governors of colonies were required to take an oath to enforce the Navigation Acts, on pain of £1,000 fine for negligence. The following year saw the setting up of Vice-Admiralty courts, which worked without juries and were therefore particularly suitable for dealing with cases involving smuggling.

The long war with France which dominated the reigns of William and Anne resulted in a number of changes in the ownership of New-World colonies. The Treaty of Utrecht, among its many other provisions, transferred to England the French settlements in Newfoundland and the Hudson Bay region and set the stage for the last act of the colonial conflict that was to take place in the eighteenth century. By the time the treaty was signed British possessions stretched unbroken along the east coast of America and included many of the more important West Indian islands. The total population of this area, including black slaves, was about 350,000 – less than the number of people living in London and only about one-fifteenth of the total population of England. Yet these figures signified an astonishing achievement on the part of a small country, and although the English colonies were usually a disappointment to the early speculators, who hoped for swift rewards, they brought enormous wealth to the Britain over which Anne ruled and confirmed Hakluyt's prediction that 'this western voyage will yield unto us all the commodities of Europe, Africa and Asia, as far as we were wont to travel, and supply the wants of all our decayed trades'.

Africa and India

The settlement of the New World led to the development of commerce with Africa, and the years that followed the Restoration saw the establishment of a number of British trading stations on the west coast. In 1664 Fort James was founded on an island in the river Gambia, and the Treaty of Breda of 1667 transferred to England the Dutch settlement at Cape Coast Castle. These posts, and others like them, served as warehouses for human cattle, where black slaves were held before being shipped, in appalling conditions, across the Atlantic. The increasing wealth of late-seventeenth and early-eighteenth century Britain was built to a large extent on unacknowledged human suffering.

Further east, English traders had set up shop in India. When Charles II resumed possession of his throne his subjects did not own any Indian territory; the various trading stations, or 'factories', were held on lease from native rulers. The situation changed after Charles's marriage to a Portuguese princess, especially since it came at a time when the rule of the Mogul emperors in India was breaking down. Catherine of Braganza brought with her, as dowry, the port of Bombay, and this possession of the King of Portugal passed into outright English ownership. Charles II found it too expensive to maintain and in 1668 handed it over to the East India Company, who later made it their headquarters.

The company had been forced out of the East Indies by the Dutch and was now concentrating on the development of its links with the Indian subcontinent. It looked for protection to the emperors, but this declined as they lost control of the great empire over which they nominally ruled, and long before Aurungzeb died in 1707 the company had taken measures for its own defence. Royal charters from Charles II and James II had already given it authority to form alliances, declare war, make peace, issue coins, and carry out many other functions which were normally the preserve of sovereign powers. The trading company, in fact, was being gradually transformed into a state in India, and in 1687 its directors ordered the governor of Surat to 'establish such a polity of civil and military power, and create and secure such a large revenue ... as may be the foundation of a large, well-grounded, sure English dominion in India for all time to come'. When it was issued, this order was little more than a statement of intent, and the years that followed saw bitter disputes between members of the old and the new East India Companies (*see* p. 517). Only after a united company was re-established, in 1708, could trade and diplomacy take advantage of the disintegration of central authority in India to establish British influence on foundations that were to endure for nearly two and a half centuries.

CHAPTER TWENTY-TWO

Late Stuart England

Population, agriculture, and the structure of society

The Tudor and early Stuart period had witnessed an unprecedented growth in the population of England. In 1524 there were some 2.3 million people living in the kingdom, but the comparable figure for 1601 was above 4 million, and by 1656 it was around 5.3 million. There followed a thirty-year period of decline until a slow growth set in again in the mid-1680s, which brought numbers up to 5.1 million by 1701.

English agriculture responded to this massive increase in population, and with the exception of brief periods when the harvest failed for several years in succession it met the demand for more food. The late Stuart period was one of consolidation but also of experimentation with new crops and new and improved techniques. In Suffolk, for example, the cultivation of turnips was being practised on a large scale by the time Charles II was restored to the throne. Turnips were planted in late summer, after the harvest had been gathered, and were used mainly as cattle feed. This made it possible to keep animals in reasonable condition throughout the winter, and the advantages of this were so apparent that the practice gradually spread into neighbouring counties. Some of these had also been pioneers in improvements. In Norfolk the use of lime, marl and manure to enrich sandy soils was already widespread, as was the growing of clover and other grasses.

Agricultural labourers, even though they were not destitute, normally lived near the poverty line. Their wages were low, their living conditions primitive, and they depended on communal grazing rights and the collection of brushwood to keep themselves going. Urban workers were no better off, and could not count even on the occasional benevolence which the country squire bestowed on his tenants. Justices of the Peace were still nominally responsible for fixing wage rates, and occasionally did so, but they were usually more concerned with holding wages down than imposing a minimum level. Strikes and combinations of workers were illegal under common law, and in 1706 the Leeds Quarter Sessions heavily fined some workers who had agreed among themselves to demand one and a half pennies an hour for their work when the official rate was only one penny [a penny was worth about 40 per cent of 1p]. Nevertheless, the poorer sections of society benefited from the fact that the expansion of trade was causing non-agricultural prices to fall. Also, the demand for more and more men to join the armed services and fight in the interminable French wars led to a scarcity of labour in certain areas, which gave the workers greater bargaining power. These factors help explain the relative quiescence of the lower levels of English society, in marked contrast to the turbulence of the mid-seventeenth century. Had it not been for this, the Glorious Revolution and the bitter party conflict of Anne's reign might have sparked off popular risings.

Life was, as always, harsh for those who had no work and depended upon the charity of their neighbours. Tudor governments had been obsessed with the problem of the migrant poor, who were travelling in search of employment, and the vagrants, who had lost their roots altogether and were perpetually on the move, since these were seen as a threat to social stability. A similar obsession was reflected in the Act of Settlement of 1662. This made the familiar assertion that 'the necessity, number, and continual increase of the poor . . . is very great and exceeding burthensome', and reiterated the long-established principle that paupers should be the responsibility of their native parishes. However, a significant change was taking place in the attitude towards migrants as the long period of population growth came to an end, and although the Act of Settlement authorised the expulsion of poor migrants who threatened to become a charge on the parish in which they had taken refuge, it implied that self-dependent ones could stay.

The pressures which led to migrancy were reduced not only by the end of population growth but also by the more effective administration of relief. The London Corporation of the Poor, originally established in 1647–9 but suppressed at the Restoration, was revived in 1698, and statutes authorised the erection of similar bodies in fourteen towns, including Bristol and Norwich. The dissenters, who were the heirs of the earlier puritans, often took the initiative in setting up these corporations, which combined charity with morality. The London Corporation, for example, declared its intention to repress 'idleness, theft, debauchery, profaneness, and other immoralities in children', and to sow 'the early seeds of industry, honesty, sobriety, piety and virtue in them'. It hoped thereby to achieve 'the reformation, happiness and welfare of the nation'.

The corporations made a promising start by building or rebuilding workhouses where the able-bodied poor were set to gainful employment, but they came up against opposition from the parishes, which resented the way in which they had been deprived of their key role in poor relief, even though they continued to meet the bill. In the end the parishes proved more durable than the corporations, and by the early eighteenth century they had resumed effective control over the system. Workhouses were fine in theory, but in practice they were not self-financing, and it seemed to make better sense to give the poor outdoor relief. This was a costly process, as was demonstrated in Bristol, where the poor rate rose 50 per cent in the period 1696–1714. In England as a whole, compulsory rates were raising some £400,000 and supporting 5 per cent of the population by the end of the seventeenth century. The role of private and institutional charities had declined, for these now contributed only £100,000 per year.

Poor rates were generally tolerated since there seemed to be no viable alternative, but they undermined the sense of moral obligation towards the poor that had been one of the mainsprings of earlier relief. Sir Matthew Hale, who published *A Discourse Touching Provision for the Poor* in 1683, was expressing an outmoded view when he declared that God had 'left the poor as his pupils, and the rich as his stewards to provide for them'. A more widely held opinion was put forward by Sir Francis Brewster in 1695. 'There is no nation I ever read of who by a compulsory law raiseth so much money for the poor as England doth ... Our charity is become a nuisance and may be thought the greatest mistake of that blessed reign [of Queen Elizabeth] in which that law passed, which is the idle and improvident man's charter.'

Brewster, and those who thought like him, were not simply being selfish and uncaring, for the richer elements in society had their own troubles, particularly if they were middle or smaller gentry dependent upon rents for their livelihood. Poor harvests in the 1690s often left tenants with insufficient money to pay their rents, yet there was little point in evicting them, since they could not be easily replaced. The gentry could theoretically meet the shortfall in their incomes by borrowing, and could use the same method to finance improvements in their estates which would pay off in the long term. But lenders were reluctant to invest in land, which offered a return of only 3 per cent, when they could get around 8 per cent from the East India Company and anything between 7 and 16 per cent from the Bank of England. Big landowners, by contrast, were not so dependent on the money market. They often had access to non-landed sources of wealth, and in any case could use profits from one part of their estates to offset losses in another.

The outlook for the gentry was not all black. For one thing the expansion of trade and the increase in the size of the armed forces meant that there were more openings available to the sons of landed families. The law offered good prospects, not only in London but also the provinces, and so did the Church, now that the social status of the clergy was rising. Medicine was another career which was becoming socially acceptable, as was government service, especially in the expanding revenue departments. Yet it remained the case that the best positions tended to go to those with most influence – which meant, in effect, to the children of the greater landowners, wealthy financiers and leading merchants. The lesser landowners lost out even in the marriage market, for they had to provide a substantial endowment for their daughters to ensure a suitable alliance, yet the cost of this could be crippling. Marriage portions, like money for improving estates, could be raised through borrowing, but with the government taking such a large share of investment funds for war purposes the interest rate was high. Officially it stood at around 5 per cent, but in practice borrowers might have to pay twice or even three times as much.

It is hardly surprising that in these circumstances the lesser landowners, most of whom were Tory, developed a vehement and at times neurotic hatred of the Whigs – whom they identified with what they condemned as the 'monied interest' – or that they adopted an intransigently 'Country' stance and denounced the corruption of ministers, courtiers and profiteers, no matter what their political affiliation.

The clergy, who from the economic point of view counted as smaller landowners, shared these Tory and 'Country' prejudices. Now that the Church had moved into alliance with the political nation there was no shortage of recruits for the ministry, and most of them were men who had received a university education. The value of livings remained low, however, and pluralism was common. Poorly paid curates were all too often left in charge of parishes while the official incumbent acted the part of a country gentleman or served as chaplain to some great household. Queen Anne showed her affection for the Church, and her appreciation of its needs, by surrendering the First Fruits and Tenths which Henry VIII had annexed to the crown. The income from this source was used, as 'Queen Anne's Bounty', to supplement the income of poorer clergy, but there was still an enormous gap between the average minister receiving about £50 a year and some of the wealthier bishops, who lived like princes on £5,000.

The greater bishops, the greater merchants, the greater landowners – these were the people who ultimately profited from the social and political changes of the sixteenth and seventeenth centuries. The Stuart and Cromwellian attempt to give the central government greater control over local affairs had ended in disaster and was not repeated. The landowners were left free to rule the areas over which their influence extended, and their mansions became the administrative centres from which their private empires were run. They could usually depend on sources other than land to swell their incomes, offset the demands of taxation, and provide capital for expansion. The profits of trade enabled Sir Josiah Child, a prosperous East India merchant, to build a magnificent house at Wanstead in Essex. The profits of six years in office as Secretary of State – amounting in this instance to £40,000 – provided Daniel Finch, first Earl of Nottingham, with the capital he required to construct a vast colonnaded mansion at Burley-on-the-Hill in Rutland. Even war could be turned to good account, as the Duke of Marlborough discovered when a grateful Queen and country presented him with Blenheim Palace and an extensive estate as a thank-offering for his services on the battlefield.

The vacuum left by the contraction of royal authority was everywhere filled by the great landowners, and their influence extended even into the former gentry stronghold of the House of Commons. Parliament met annually after 1689, and ambitious men were now prepared to devote not only much of their time but also much of their money to securing a seat. After the passing of the Triennial Act in 1694 it was illegal for a Parliament to remain in existence longer than three years, and frequent elections therefore became the rule. In the counties the right to vote was confined to forty-shilling freeholders, but because of inflation this category now included not simply most of the 'middling sort' of men but even some of their social inferiors. In boroughs there was far greater variety, for during the early Stuart period the House of Commons had used disputed elections as a means of widening the franchise in urban constituencies, and this process had continued down to the Restoration.

There were still a number of rotten boroughs, with only one or two voters, but these were counterbalanced by open boroughs, where the franchise extended to the majority of ratepayers. Taking constituencies as a whole, about a quarter of the entire adult male population of England had the right to vote in Queen Anne's reign, which was a level not reached again until the late nineteenth century. The inhabitants of newly expanding towns like Birmingham, Manchester, Sheffield and Leeds, which had no seats in the House of Commons, were deprived of an urban vote but could make their views known by participating in county elections.

Such was the intensity of political passions in late Stuart England that borough as well as county seats were bitterly contested and their electorates wooed. Candidates did not rely merely on propagating their views to attract support. They also resorted to offers of patronage or support, outright bribery, or, occasionally, threats and the use of violence. The cost of influencing a county electorate could be enormous, but even in boroughs the price of votes was rising to the point where only very rich men could afford to compete. Peers could not be members of the Commons, but by using their money and prestige they could bring considerable pressure to bear upon the electors who chose those members. By an ironic twist of fate, the gentry House of Commons, which had risked civil war in order to stifle the growth of monarchical absolutism, now found itself in danger of losing its independence to the oligarchs, whose influence extended everywhere.

Trade and industry

The years following the restoration of Charles II saw a rapid increase in the rate of expansion of English commerce. In the Tudor and early Stuart period English trade had been based upon the export of wool and woollen cloth to Europe, and by the time the Civil War broke out more distant markets had been opened up for the 'New Draperies' in India, the Levant and America. Until the Restoration, then, English industry and English trade were essentially wool and textiles. Everything else was incidental. After this date the pattern of English commerce was transformed by the exploitation of oceanic trade-routes and overseas possessions.

By 1700 nearly one-third of all imports into England came from outside Europe, and about half of these were re-exported, at a profit. The influx of overseas goods was partly due to the opening up of new sources of supply, but it would have been impossible without the lowering of prices and the consequent growth of a mass market in England. Tobacco, for instance, had been a luxury, costing at least £1 a pound in the early seventeenth century, but as the price dropped to less than a shilling [5p] it became the indulgence of all classes. There was consequently an enormous increase in the amount imported. Virginia and Maryland, which had despatched a mere twenty thousand pounds in weight to England in 1619, sent twenty-one million in the last year of the century, and colonial production was being constantly expanded to meet an apparently insatiable demand.

The same pattern was followed in the sugar trade, though its expansion was not so dramatic. The Portuguese colonies in South America had a virtual monopoly of sugar exports until the 1640s, and it was not until James II's reign that sugar from the British West Indies began pouring into London, from where it was despatched to all the major European centres. The third major item in this flourishing re-export trade was calicoes, which the East India Company began importing in considerable quantities. These fine cotton cloths, well suited to the lifestyle of an elegant age, were particularly valued by the fashionable ladies of late Stuart and early Georgian England, and their appreciation was shared by their contemporaries on the European mainland.

English governments were alarmed by the threat posed to the native woollen industry by foreign textiles, and did their best to protect the home product. The export of wool was forbidden, so that English clothmakers should have first call on the essential raw material, and in 1678 the dead were called on to aid the living by an act requiring all shrouds to be made of wool. These and other measures no doubt helped check the decline of the textile industry, but the salvation of the cloth merchants came in the end from their own efforts. They could not hope for a big expansion of their trade with hot regions like India, China and the Levant, but they exploited colder markets and sent increasing quantities of woollen goods to northern Europe and the American colonies. Although cloth no longer accounted for 90 per cent of English exports, it was still more important than any other single item.

The spice trade lost its significance as tastes changed and more fresh meat became available in winter, but tea and coffee both made their appearance in post-Restoration England and quickly became popular. The East India Company flourished as a consequence, but its monopoly was threatened by interlopers and resented by City merchants who did not belong to it. Their jealousy found expression in the decision taken by Parliament in 1698 to create a new company, but the representatives of the old one fought a stubborn battle to preserve their privileges, and in 1709 the two bodies were amalgamated into what was once again a single East India Company.

In the early seventeenth century, Parliament had been an opponent of monopoly companies, but although its power increased in the post-Restoration period it did not promote freer trade. In fact a number of new chartered companies were created. These included the Royal Africa Company, which bought slaves in West Africa and shipped them to the West Indies, where they were exchanged for sugar; and the Hudson's Bay Company, which was formed to exploit the fur trade of North America. The general assumption, in an age when first the Dutch and then the French presented a threat to the expansion of British commerce, was that only organised groups of merchants could raise the capital and provide the support that was essential if this development was to take place.

As far as trade to and from the American colonies was concerned, a monopoly was granted not to any specific company but to English merchants as a whole. The Staple Act of 1663 required the colonies to send 'enumerated' goods – of which the most important were sugar, tobacco and cotton – only to England, and forbade them to buy European goods directly, but only via England. This legislation was designed to protect English merchants against the Dutch, who were strongly entrenched in the carrying trade both from one colony to another and between the colonies and Europe. Nothing effective could be done, however, while the Dutch held colonies on the North American mainland, and in any case the number of English ships was insufficient to meet the demands made upon them.

Shortage of ships and sailors prompted the drawing-up of the 1660 Navigation Act, which closed several loopholes shown to exist in the earlier act of 1651. English-owned ships which had been built abroad now had to be registered, and all English ships had to have predominantly English crews. These measures contributed to the great expansion of English shipping after 1660, and prevented the diversion of men and capital to less protected occupations. So did the freeing of trade from official restrictions. Corn exports, for instance, which the Tudors and early Stuarts had restrained in the name of self-sufficiency, were stimulated by a government subsidy from 1673. Export duties on woollen cloth were abolished in 1699, and ten years later the duty on coal was removed. These changes had a direct effect upon British shipping, for it was bulk cargoes like corn and coal that offered the chance of big profits, as the Dutch had earlier discovered.

The freeing of trade was accompanied by the freeing of industry, though this was the result of natural changes rather than policy. In theory, industries were under the control of companies which derived their authority from official charters, and they were also shackled by the Elizabethan laws regulating apprenticeship. In practice, however, the authority of the companies was declining, and the apprenticeship laws were moribund, except where paupers were concerned. The Livery Companies survived in London, but their members were recruited by patrimony rather than occupation, and they were more concerned with social functions and City government than with the close supervision of particular manufactures.

The apprenticeship laws were the product of an age when men were plentiful and jobs were scarce. This was no longer the case in the late seventeenth century. The rise in population was slowing down, while the increasing demands of a wealthy community were an incentive for industry to expand. The use of machines such as the stocking-frame and gig-mill, which had earlier been opposed on the grounds that they put weavers out of work, was now encouraged, and experiments were taking place to harness steam power to the needs of industry. In 1712 the first steam pump, invented by Thomas Savery and Thomas Newcomen, was installed in a coal mine, and by the time George I came to the throne several more were at work. The exploitation of deeper seams was made necessary by the rising demand for coal. London alone burnt a quarter of a million tons every year, and shortage of wood encouraged manufacturers to use coal instead. The iron and steel industry remained dependent upon charcoal, because the sulphur contained in coal made the metal brittle, but even here future developments were in the making, for some time during Anne's reign a quaker ironmaster called Abraham Darby turned coal into coke, which he used to feed his blast furnaces.

Financial institutions and public administration

The growth of English commerce made London one of the focal points of world trade, and brought not only wealth but style to the capital city. The London of Pepys and Defoe was a long way removed from the city that Shakespeare had known. After the Restoration it extended westwards into the area around Piccadilly and Jermyn Street, while in the early eighteenth century Edward Harley, son of Anne's Lord Treasurer, perpetuated his family's name and fortune by building Harley Street, Oxford Street, and other elegant thoroughfares on the open spaces that surrounded Tyburn. The streets of London were broader and cleaner after the Great Fire. Hackney coaches and sedan chairs made travelling more comfortable; theatres were crowded by the *beau monde*, anxious to see the latest productions of Dryden, Congreve, Wycherly and Farquhar; and coffee-houses provided convenient places for businessmen to meet and discuss their affairs. One of these coffee-houses, started by Edward Lloyd, became a favourite haunt of ship-owners and developed into the principal European centre for maritime insurance. Other coffee-houses were associated with particular political groups or men of letters.

Lloyds was one example of the way in which London merchants were providing the financial services demanded by an expanding trading community. Commercial pressures were also behind the founding of a national bank. Ever since the Stop of the Exchequer in 1672, when Charles II had declared his inability to repay his debts but had offered regular interest on them, a national debt had existed, but public opinion was reluctant to legitimise this, since it was part of the shaky financial system of the Stuart monarchy. However, the long and enormously costly war against France after 1688 made massive government borrowing inevitable, and in 1694 an act was passed authorising the establishment of a national bank. Subscribers guaranteed to raise £1,500,000, which they would advance to the government in return for the regular payment of interest. The money was quickly raised, the bank was an immediate success, and the key role played by the City is indicated by the fact that among the first directors of the new institution were no fewer than seven future Lord Mayors of London.

The Bank of England was given permission to issue its own notes, provided the total of these did not exceed the sum originally advanced to the government. Three years later, after the attempt to set up a rival Land Bank had failed, Parliament confirmed the privileged position of the Bank of England and made the forging of its notes a felony. To ensure that the resources of the bank could not be used to finance monarchical despotism it was laid down that no advances were to be made to the government without the express approval of Parliament. This combination of parliamentary security with assurance against royal intervention persuaded the wealthier sections of English society to contribute to the needs of the state on a scale that would have been inconceivable while Charles II or his brother was on the throne.

The Bank of England did not take over the existing national debt, although from time to time government bonds were transferred to it, but it made the idea of a national debt respectable – even though it was hoped and assumed that the government would eventually return to solvency. The government in fact made a remarkable effort to meet its financial obligations through taxation, but the costs of the long war against France were so high that taxation could only go part of the way towards meeting them. It was hardly surprising, then, that by the time Anne died the national debt stood at more than £36,000,000 and that interest charges on it consumed three-fifths of the annual revenue.

The main source of government income was the land tax which, in the post-Restoration period, gradually superseded the older subsidy. It was based on the monthly assessments levied during the Civil War – which themselves owed much to Ship Money – and every county was required to provide a stated share of the total sum decided upon by the Treasury. When the land tax stood at four shillings in the pound, as it did throughout the greater part of Anne's reign, it became a major, and at times intolerable, drain on private resources. In particular it undermined the already shaky financial position of smaller property-owners, acting as the last straw which forced many of them to sell up and leave the land altogether.

When William III came to the throne, England had the lightest taxation of any major European state, but by the time he died only the United Provinces bore a heavier burden. While direct taxation remained the principal source of money for the government, indirect also played its part. Customs, as always, were a major contributor, as was the excise, which was extended from beer and cider to many other commodities and articles in daily use. By 1715 it was bringing in £2,300,000 a year, while Customs were contributing £1,700,000. The close connection between trade and revenue prompted post-Restoration governments to take an interest in commercial matters. In 1660 a Council for Trade was set up to advise the Privy Council. It collaborated with the Council for Foreign Plantations, which handled colonial business, and the two bodies survived until 1665, when their work was delegated to standing committees of the Privy Council. The fall of Clarendon brought to prominence men who were much more interested in commerce than the Chancellor had been, and in 1668 a new Council for Trade was set up, which by 1673 had also become responsible for the colonies. Anthony Ashley Cooper, Earl of Shaftesbury, was active on this body, which had John Locke as its secretary, and it began the process of collecting and interpreting statistical information. The Council for Trade lasted only two years, when it was replaced once again by committees of the Privy Council. Not until 1696 was a permanent Board of Trade set up, to keep in touch with the merchants and advise the government on commercial policy.

The increasing sophistication of government finance affected the Treasury, which not only developed more efficient book-keeping and budgeting techniques but also extended its control over other departments. These included two or three which had been of little importance hitherto but developed rapidly under the spur of war. The industrious Samuel Pepys, now famous for his diary, served as a highly efficient Secretary of the Admiralty under Charles II and James II, and created what was virtually a new department. William Blathwayt did much the same during his long tenure of office as Secretary-at-War. Men such as these were professional administrators, and their emergence was one indication of changing attitudes towards government office – although much of the work continued to be done by deputies, and old habits died hard. Another indication was the shift, which set in during Charles II's reign, from life tenures, reversionary grants, and dependence upon fees, towards reversible appointments and realistic salaries.

All departments were grossly understaffed by modern standards. The two Secretaries of State had only about a dozen clerks to serve them, and wrote most of their letters themselves, while the permanent staff of the Treasury seldom exceeded twenty. Nevertheless, the period 1660–1714 witnessed the development of an administrative machine far more complex than anything seen before. Because of its complexity it was no longer under the direct control of the King. But no single minister controlled it either, for the Lord Treasurer – or, when this office was in commission, the First Lord of the Treasury – had not yet attained the position of primacy which Walpole was to secure. Yet the collection and expenditure of public money was the most important function of government, as the Commons recognised in 1713, when they drew up a standing order giving it the sole right to initiate financial business in Parliament.

Women and English society

It was taken for granted in Tudor and Stuart England that women were, in St Peter's words, 'the weaker vessel', innately inferior to men in their capacities and potential. It was something of a paradox, therefore, that the period saw four queens regnant, one of them of outstanding ability. These ascended the throne because they embodied a right which the English regarded as sacrosanct – namely that of property. Just as private estates descended to a female heir in the absence of any males, so the crown was the rightful possession of a sovereign's daughter when she had no living brothers to take precedence.

As monarch, a woman ruler could expect to command the same unconditional obedience that would be accorded to her male counterparts, but religion proved to be a solvent in this respect. Some catholics affirmed a right to rebel against protestant rulers, and vice versa. The Scottish puritan, John Knox, was so appalled by the prospect of Mary Tudor destroying the reformed Church that had only recently been established in England that he published his *First Blast of the Trumpet against the*

Monstrous Regiment of Women. In this he asserted that the rule, or 'regiment', of a female sovereign was contrary to nature as well as God's commandment, since experience showed women to be 'inconstant, variable, cruel and lacking the spirit of counsel and regiment'. Knox chose his moment badly, for his book appeared just as the protestant Elizabeth ascended the throne, but in any case his argument, however well supported in theory, was of no practical effect, since the English preferred to accept the 'unnatural' rule of a woman rather than upset the law of succession.

While women in general were accorded only inferior status, individual ones could establish a prominent place for themselves. Mary, Countess of Pembroke, the sister of Sir Philip Sidney, was a patron of writers as well as an author in her own right. In James I's reign Lucy, Countess of Bedford, who was one of Anne of Denmark's ladies, knew most of the poets and playwrights of her day and kept open house for them. At the other end of the seventeenth century Margaret Cavendish, Duchess of Newcastle, wrote literary and philosophical works, as well as her memoirs, and became a noted blue-stocking. Some women became famous not for what they did but for who they were. Elizabeth, Countess of Shrewsbury, made four advantageous marriages, the first when she was eleven, and became so rich that she built a palace for herself in Derbyshire and has gone down in history as 'Bess of Hardwick'. Lady Anne Clifford was renowned for the way in which she proclaimed her noble lineage and defended her inheritance. Sarah Churchill was not simply the confidante of Queen Anne and the wife of the greatest soldier of his day. She was also a formidable personality in her own right and believed, with good reason, that she would have been 'the greatest hero that ever was known in the Parliament House if I had been so happy to have been a man'.

While a handful of women made a name for themselves, the vast majority fulfilled the role that society ordained for them – that of being wives and mothers. In the marriage service they were instructed to 'submit yourselves unto your own husbands as unto the Lord, for the husband is the wives' head even as Christ is the head of the Church'. No doubt some women resented their subordinate status, but many took it for granted and moulded their lives within this convention. They usually had the responsibility for bringing up their children and were often the main channel of religious instruction. The earliest surviving diary of an Englishwoman is that of the puritan Lady Margaret Hoby, who wrote it at the very end of Elizabeth's reign as a record of her readings, meditations and prayers. Puritan mothers, like catholic ones, would keep the flame of religion alight in their households and make sure that the mundane cares of their

husbands were not allowed to blunt the Christian message as they understood it.

For some women, religion was so central to their existence that it overrode all other considerations. Until Henry VIII's reign the nunneries
provided a refuge for women with a religious vocation. After the
Dissolution they had to find different outlets. Women were prominent
among the early protestants, and provided nearly 20 per cent of the
Marian martyrs. In the next reign catholic women undertook the risky
work of setting up refuges for missionary priests, and three were executed
for so doing. They were also active in keeping the old faith alive. Mary
Ward (1585–1645) was one of the most prominent. She went into temporary exile on the continent, where in 1609 she set up a missionary order
for women. By the end of the seventeenth century a further twenty such
houses had been set up, and for the first time there were more English nuns
than monks.

The growth of sects in the seventeenth century led to a brief period of
religious freedom, which profited women as much as it did men. The
quakers, in particular, made them welcome, and George Fox acknowledged that the holy spirit could 'speak in the female as well as the male'.
Margaret Fell was an early quaker, and published in 1666 a book appropriately entitled *Women's Speaking Justified*.

For most of the early modern period women married around the age of
26, while their husbands were a year or two older. The reasons for late
marriage were mainly economic, but among the upper sections of English
society, where such considerations were not so pressing, marriage tended
to take place in the early twenties. In the late sixteenth century up to a
quarter of all brides were pregnant when they got married, but this figure
had dropped to 16 per cent by the late seventeenth century, as economic
conditions improved and long engagements were not so necessary.
Illegitimacy rates were also affected by economic conditions. The overall
figure for the Tudor and Stuart period was between 1 and 2 per cent, but
in the famine years of the 1590s, when money and jobs were both in short
supply, it more than doubled. Most families consisted of the husband, wife
and children, with servants where money permitted. Aged parents might
be added at a later date, but only the richer segments of society could
afford extended households which embraced a wide range of relatives,
friends, and hangers-on. Aristocratic establishments included a large
number of servants. In the 1570s Lady Willoughby of Wollaton Hall in
Nottinghamshire had about fifty, of whom eight were women, while in the
1620s and 1630s the Earls of Salisbury had a full-time staff of forty-six at

Hatfield House, including eleven women. During the seventeenth century the proportion of women servants in great households gradually increased, but not until the mid-eighteenth did they attain parity.

Women were thought less likely to commit crime than men, and they were less liable to prosecution if, for example, they engaged in concerted action to tear down enclosures or protest against high prices. However, because of their sex they were unable to claim 'Benefit of Clergy' (*see* p. 22) and therefore suffered penalties from which men would have been exempt for the first offence. This discrimination was ended in 1624 by the enactment of a bill 'concerning women convicted of small felonies', which was passed because 'many women do suffer death for small causes'. The only major offences which concerned women in particular were infanticide and witchcraft. Infanticide was heavily punished where it could be proved, but the uncertainty surrounding the charge led to a marked decline in the number of convictions by the end of the seventeenth century. A similar decline is apparent in witchcraft trials. The vast majority of persons charged with this offence were women, usually old, poor and living alone in rural communities. Causing harm through the practice of witchcraft was a capital offence, and many innocent people were put to death as a result. But as belief in witchcraft declined, so did the number of trials, and the last conviction of a witch in the assize courts took place in Hertfordshire in 1712. The woman found guilty was subsequently reprieved.

Changing attitudes towards women in the seventeenth century were reflected in the growth of a proto-feminist movement. The prolific output of Margaret Cavendish, Duchess of Newcastle, included *The World's Olio* (1653), in which she claimed that men and women were born equal, but that men had subsequently 'usurped a supremacy to themselves'. This argument was echoed by Bathsua Makin in the 1670s. Makin, a clergyman's daughter, acquired a wide range of knowledge from her talented brother, and was subsequently a pupil of Jan Comenius, a native of Moravia who became famous throughout Europe as an educational reformer. Makin set up a school for girls at Tottenham, on the outskirts of London, where Latin and Hebrew were on the curriculum as well as more traditional subjects such as music and dancing, and she rejected any suggestion that women were inherently less intelligent than men. 'Had God intended women only as a finer sort of cattle', she declared, 'He would not have made them reasonable.' This theme was taken up by Mary Astell, a native of Newcastle writing at the very end of the seventeenth century, who asserted that women's incapacity was acquired, not natural. In other words, gender, as distinct from sex, was a largely male construct. If women were given the same education and the same opportunities as men, they would soon demonstrate that they were just as talented.

The proto-feminists were lone voices and had only a limited resonance. However, other women were taking advantage of the more liberal atmosphere of post-Restoration England to carve out careers for themselves. Women could now appear on the stage, and the more successful actresses, such as Nell Gwyn, became the talk of the town. There was at least one woman playwright, Aphra Ben (?1649–89), who was also a poet and pioneer novelist and may well have been the first woman to make a living by writing. Mary Beale (1632–99) was a disciple of Sir Peter Lely, the greatest portrait painter of his day, and established her reputation in the same field. Ben and Beale were not major figures in the arts, but they showed how a combination of talent and determination could break through the prejudices of late-Stuart society and assert a creative role for women.

Political and scientific thought

Politics and religion were the cause of such intense controversy in the late Stuart period that a casual observer might well have assumed that fanaticism and intolerance were still characteristic of English public life. In a sense this was true, but it was not the whole truth, for while the disputes between Whigs and Tories, dissenters and anglicans, were genuine, they concealed a considerable measure of agreement over fundamentals. The Tories were admittedly uneasy about the key role they had played in the Glorious Revolution, and an increasing number of them were in favour of the accession of the Old Pretender after Anne's death. But a substantial section of the Tory party remained firm in its commitment to the Hanoverian succession and was prepared to work with the Whigs to bring this about. The Tories professed their devotion to the cause of monarchy, but they did so within the context of the traditional constitution, which enshrined the liberties of the subject as well as the prerogatives of the ruler.

Similarly in religion, there was widespread acceptance of the practice, if not the principle, of toleration for protestant nonconformists. Some Tories, no doubt, would have liked to return to the days of Laud, but this was clearly out of the question. Anglican enthusiasts devoted their energies instead to such worthy causes as establishing Church schools and promoting the activities of the Society for the Reformation of Manners –

founded in 1691 to combat the immorality which, its members believed, was the inevitable result of the spread of heterodox and 'atheistical' doctrines. There was also a greater awareness on the part of Christians of all denominations of the need to evangelise the world outside Europe, and societies like those for Promoting Christian Knowledge (1698) and for the Propagation of the Gospel (1701) were founded in order to provide missionaries to convert the heathen.

One of the reasons for the grudging acceptance of toleration was the realisation that persecution was ineffective, since individual consciences could not, in the long run, be coerced. This case was argued most persuasively by John Locke who, in his *Letters on Toleration*, emphasised that true religion consisted in 'the inward and full persuasion of the mind'. 'I cannot be saved,' he added, 'by a religion that I distrust and by a worship that I abhor.' Locke's rational and dispassionate approach to controversial topics was also demonstrated in his political writings, which provided a philosophical foundation for many Whig beliefs.

Locke's immediate predecessors in the field of political philosophy had been mainly concerned with justifying absolutism, reflecting in this – as did Locke in his own time – the age in which they lived. Thomas Hobbes (1588–1679), for instance, put forward the argument in his *Leviathan* (1651) that self-preservation is the basis of society. 'The condition of man,' he wrote, 'is a condition of war of everyone against everyone,' and in the state of nature which preceded the establishment of civil society there were 'no arts, no letters, [only] continual fear and danger of violent death; and the life of man solitary, poor, nasty, brutish and short.' To free themselves from this terrible condition human beings had (so Hobbes maintained) abdicated all their rights to a ruler – whether one man or a group – and the sovereign was justified in commanding absolute obedience, since any criticism of his authority would threaten to throw society back into the condition of primitive anarchy from which it had so laboriously raised itself.

Hobbes's views shocked his contemporaries, who had not grasped the nettle of sovereignty as firmly as he had. Royalists distrusted him because he seemed to justify power no matter how it had been acquired, while parliamentarians disapproved of his apparent sanction of royal absolutism. Even Locke, who was critical of Hobbes's theories, declined to attack the *Leviathan* directly for fear that he might become involved in the unsavoury reputation of its author. Instead, he chose to target the doctrine of divine right as expounded by Sir Robert Filmer in his *Patriarcha*, written during the Interregnum but not published until 1680.

Locke took a far more optimistic view of human nature than Hobbes or Filmer. He believed that men were born with certain rights which belonged to them as individuals. They had a right to life and liberty, and because they had added their labour to the raw material provided by nature they had a right to the property so created. Locke agreed with Hobbes that the basis of society was contractual, but where Hobbes had imagined primitive men contracting to abandon their freedom of action to a sovereign power, Locke conceived of them making a bargain. They would agree to obey the sovereign because, by so doing, they could best preserve their natural rights. But if the sovereign himself became a threat to those rights, then the contract was automatically dissolved and the obligation of obedience annulled. 'A government,' he wrote, 'is not free to do as it pleases ... The law of nature stands as an eternal rule to all men, legislators as well as others.'

The even tone of Locke's writings, the absence of passion and the appeal to common sense were, like latitudinarian attitudes in religion, the heralds of the age of reason. Nothing contributed more to the triumph of reason than the progress of science, for by calling established truths into question and subjecting them to critical examination, scientists increased the prestige and self-confidence of man as a rational being.

The scientific revolution which began in the sixteenth century was a European phenomenon to which the British made a number of important contributions. They were not among the first to challenge accepted explanations of the structure of the universe, but the Scotsman John Napier produced in 1614 the earliest tables of logarithms, which were used by the German Johannes Kepler in his work on ellipses, and Queen Elizabeth's physician, William Gilbert, published a book *On the Magnet and Magnetic Bodies and that Great Magnet the Earth* which so impressed the Italian Galileo that he gave a detailed account of it in his *Dialogues*.

The first major English figure in the scientific revolution was not a practising scientist. Francis Bacon, the distinguished lawyer and essayist who became James I's Lord Chancellor, made himself the propagandist for the scientific method and constantly urged the need for experiment and research. His exalted position and his fame as a philosopher formed a shelter under which enquiring men could pursue their research, and the freedom given to scientific speculation in England may explain why by the late seventeenth century London had become the capital of the scientific as well as the commercial world. It was Bacon's hope that academies would be formed where scientists could exchange information, for he recognised the paramount importance of communication to the spread of knowledge.

No such academy was founded during his lifetime, but the Royal Society acknowledged him as its spiritual founder, and his picture appears next to the bust of Charles II in its official history.

In spite of Bacon, and of the pioneering achievements of men such as William Harvey (1578–1657), the discoverer of the circulation of the blood, English scientists did not come into their own until after the Restoration. Charles II was interested in mathematics and experimental science, and gave his patronage to the Royal Society, which was formed in 1660. Among the early members of this distinguished body were the chemist Robert Boyle – son of Strafford's old enemy, the Earl of Cork – who analysed the nature of air, gases and vacuums, and Robert Hooke, who gave the first detailed description of a microscope and of the observations he had made by using one.

Most famous of all the members of the Royal Society was Sir Isaac Newton, who fitted the isolated segments of scientific knowledge into a coherent pattern. Copernicus had shifted the earth from the centre of the universe where Ptolemy had placed it in ancient times; Galileo had confirmed by his own observations that heavenly bodies did not revolve around one fixed centre; while Kepler had discovered that the planets moved in ellipses, not circles. These men, between them, had destroyed the old picture of the universe, but had not succeeded in replacing it. As the Jacobean poet John Donne complained

'The sun is lost, and th'earth, and no man's wit
Can well direct him where to look for it.
'Tis all in pieces, all coherence gone,
All just supply and all relation.'

It was left to Newton to restore coherence to the universe. Born in 1642, the year of Galileo's death, he studied at Cambridge under the mathematician Isaac Barrow and eventually succeeded to Barrow's chair. During the Great Plague of 1665 Newton left Cambridge, as did most of his contemporaries, and returned home to Grantham in Lincolnshire. It was during this enforced vacation that he worked out the principles which were to form the basis of his system. He combined Kepler's laws and the observations of Galileo into a single theory of gravitation, and showed that the force which makes an apple fall to the ground is the same as that which sends the heavenly bodies swinging on their course.

The extension of scientific knowledge transformed older and traditional attitudes in much the same way as the Reformation and the discovery of the New World broke up the fabric of medieval Christendom.

The destruction of the old order with nothing to put in its place would almost certainly have led to a conservative reaction. The success of scientists in creating a new synthesis had the opposite effect. It encouraged criticism and experiment, and it produced a veneration for the faculty of human reason that ushered in the Enlightenment.

Further reading

This bibliography does not include works published before 1990

THE TUDOR PERIOD

BERNARD, G. W. *The Tudor Nobility*. Manchester University Press, 1992.

BERNARD, G. W. *Power and Politics in Tudor England*. Ashgate, 1992.

BRADDICK, Michael J. *The Nerves of State. Taxation and the Financing of the English State, 1558–1714*. Manchester University Press, 1996.

BRADDICK, Michael J. *State Formation in Early Modern England, c. 1550–1700*. Cambridge University Press, 2000.

BRIGDEN, Susan. *New Worlds, Lost Worlds. The Rule of the Tudors 1485–1603*. Allen Lane, The Penguin Press, 2000.

COLLINSON, Patrick and CRAIG, John (eds). *The Reformation in English Towns*. Macmillan, 1998.

CRESSY, David. *Birth, Marriage, and Death. Ritual, Religion, and the Life-Cycle in Tudor and Stuart England*. Oxford University Press, 1997.

DORAN, Susan and DURSTON, Christopher. *Princes, Pastors and People. The Church and Religion in England, 1500–1700*. Routledge, 2nd edn, 2003.

DUFFY, Eamon. *The Stripping of the Altars: Traditional Religion in England, 1400–1580*. Yale University Press, 1992.

DUFFY, Eamon. *The Voices of Morebath. Reformation and Rebellion in an English Village*. Yale University Press, 2001.

DURSTON, Christopher and EALES, Jacqueline (eds). *The Culture of English Puritanism, 1550–1700*. Macmillan, 1996.

GUY, John (ed.) *The Tudor Monarchy*. Edward Arnold, 1997.

HAIGH, Christopher. *English Reformations. Religion, Politics and Society under the Tudors*. Clarendon Press, 1993.

HAIGH, Christopher. 'Success and Failure in the English Reformation'. *Past and Present*, No. 173, 2001.

LOADES, David. *Tudor Government: Structures of Authority in the Sixteenth Century*. Blackwell, 1997.

MARSH, Christopher. *Popular Religion in Sixteenth-Century England: Holding Their Peace*. Macmillan, 1998.

SHAGAN, Ethan H. *Popular Politics and the English Reformation*. Cambridge University Press, 2003.

SPUFFORD, Margaret (ed.). *The World of Rural Dissenters, 1520–1725*. Cambridge University Press, 1998.

THURLEY, Simon. *The Royal Palaces of Tudor England: Architecture and Court Life 1460–1547*. Yale University Press, 1993.

TITTLER, Robert. *The Reformation and the Towns in England. Politics and Political Culture, c. 1540–1640*. Clarendon Press, 1998.

WILLIAMS, Penry. *The Later Tudors: England 1547–1603*. Clarendon Press, 1995

WHITE, Peter. *Predestination, Policy and Polemic: Conflict and Consensus in the English Church from the Reformation to the Civil War*. Cambridge University Press, 1992.

HENRY VII AND HENRY VIII

BERNARD, G. W. 'The Fall of Anne Boleyn'. *English Historical Review*, Vol. 106, 1991.

BERNARD, G. W. 'The making of Religious Policy 1532–46'. *Historical Journal*, Vol. 41, 1998.

BERNARD, G. W. 'Elton's Cromwell'. *History*, Vol. 83, 1998.

BUSH, Michael. 'Tax Reform and Rebellion in Early Modern England'. *History*, Vol. 76, 1991.

BUSH, Michael. *The Pilgrimage of Grace: A Study of the Rebel Armies of October 1536*. Manchester University Press, 1996.

BUSH, Michael and BOWNES, David. *The Defeat of the Pilgrimage of Grace: A Study of the Postpardon Revolts of December 1536 to March 1537 and their Effect*. Hull University Press, 1999.

GUNN, S. J. and LINDLEY, P. G. (eds). *Cardinal Wolsey: Church, state and art*. Cambridge University Press, 1991.

HOYLE, R. W. *The Pilgrimage of Grace and the Politics of the 1530s*. Oxford University Press, 2001.

LOCKYER, Roger and THRUSH, Andrew. *Henry VII*. Seminar Studies in History. Longman, 3rd edn 1997.

MACCULLOCH, Diarmaid. *Thomas Cranmer. A life*. Yale University Press, 1996.

REX, Richard. *Henry VIII and the English Reformation*. Macmillan, 1993.

EDWARD VI AND MARY

ALFORD, Stephen. *Kingship and Politics in the Reign of Edward VI.* Cambridge University Press, 2003.

LOACH, Jennifer. *Edward VI.* Yale University Press, 1999.

LOADES, David. *Revolution in Religion: The English Reformation 1530–1570.* Wales University Press, 1992.

LOADES, David. *John Dudley, Duke of Northumberland, 1504–1553.* Clarendon Press, 1996.

MACCULLOCH, Diarmaid. *Tudor Church Militant. Edward VI and the Protestant Reformation.* Allen Lane, 2000.

MAYER, Thomas F. *Reginald Pole, Prince and Prophet.* Cambridge University Press, 2001.

PETTEGREE, Andrew. *Marian Protestantism.* Scolar Press, 1996.

TUDOR ENGLAND

BARRY, Jonathan and BROOKS, Christopher (eds). *The Middling Sort of People. Culture, Society and Politics in England, 1550–1800.* Macmillan, 1994.

BRENNER, Robert. *Merchants and Revolution: Commercial change, political conflict, and London's overseas traders, 1550–1653.* Cambridge University Press, 1993.

CLARKE, Peter (ed.) *The Cambridge Urban History of Britain.* Vol. II *1540–1840.* Cambridge University Press, 2000.

FLETCHER, A. J. *Gender, Sex and Subordination in England 1500–1800.* Yale University Press, 1995.

HINDLE, Steve. *The State and Social Change in Early Modern England,* c. *1550–1640.* Macmillan, 2000.

HUTTON, Ronald. *The Rise and Fall of Merry England. The Ritual Year 1400–1700.* Oxford University Press, 1994.

JACK, Sybil M. *Towns in Tudor and Stuart England.* Macmillan, 1996.

REAY, Barry. *Popular Cultures in England 1550–1750.* Longman, 1998.

SHARPE, J. A. *Early Modern England: A social history, 1550–1760.* Edward Arnold, 2nd edn, 1997.

SLACK, Paul. *From Reformation to Improvement. Public welfare in early modern England.* Clarendon Press, 1999.

WRIGHTSON, K. 'Estates, degrees and sorts: changing perceptions of society in Tudor and Stuart England' in CORFIELD, J. P. (ed.). *Language, History and Class.* Oxford University Press, 1991.

IRELAND AND SCOTLAND IN THE TUDOR PERIOD

BRADSHAW, Brendan and MORRILL, John (eds). *The British Problem. c. 1534–1707: State formation in the Atlantic archipelago.* Macmillan, 1996.

BURNS, J. H. *The True Law of Kingship. Concepts of Monarchy in Early Modern Scotland.* Clarendon Press, 1996.

CANNY, Nicholas. *Making Ireland British 1580–1650.* Oxford University Press, 2001.

FORD, Alan. *The Protestant Reformation in Ireland, 1590–1641.* Four Courts, Dublin, 1997.

GOODARE, Julian. *State and Society in Early Modern Scotland.* Oxford University Press, 1999.

GOODARE, Julian and LYNCH, Michael (eds). *The Reign of James VI.* Tuckwell Press, 2000.

GUY, John. *My Heart is My Own: The Life of Mary Queen of Scots.* Fourth Estate, 2004.

MACDONALD, Alan R. *The Jacobean Kirk, 1567–1625: Sovereignty, Polity and Liturgy.* Ashgate, 1998.

ELIZABETH I

ALFORD, Stephen. *The Early Elizabethan Polity. William Cecil and the British Succession Crisis, 1558–1569.* Cambridge University Press, 1998.

COLLINSON, Patrick. *Elizabethan Essays.* Hambledon Press, 1996.

CROFT, Pauline (ed.). *Patronage, Culture and Power. The Early Cecils 1558–1612.* Yale University Press, 2002.

DEAN, David. *Law-Making and Society in Late Elizabethan England: The Parliament of England, 1584–1601.* Cambridge University Press, 1996.

DORAN, Susan. *Monarchy and Matrimony: The Courtships of Elizabeth I.* Routledge, 1996.

GRAVES, Michael A. R. *Burghley. William Cecil, Lord Burghley.* Longman, 1998.

GUY, John. *The Reign of Elizabeth I: Court and Culture in the Last Decade.* Cambridge University Press, 1995.

HAMMER, Paul E. J. *The Polarisation of Elizabethan Politics. The Political Career of Robert Devereux, 2nd Earl of Essex 1585–1597.* Cambridge University Press, 1999.

HARTLEY, T. E. *Elizabeth's Parliaments: Queen, Lords and Commons, 1559–1601.* Manchester University Press, 1992.

HOYLE, R. W. (ed.). *The Estates of the English Crown, 1558–1640*. Cambridge University Press, 1992.

JONES, Norman. *The Birth of the Elizabethan Age: England in the 1560s*. Blackwell, 1993.

JONES, Norman. *The English Reformation: Religion and Cultural Adaptation*. Blackwell, 2002.

MACCAFFREY, Wallace. *Elizabeth I*. Edward Arnold, 1993.

MALTBY, Judith. *Prayer Book and People in Elizabethan and Early Stuart England*. Cambridge University Press, 1998.

MCCULLOCH, Peter E. *Sermons at Court: Politics and Religion in Elizabethan and Jacobean Preaching*. Cambridge University Press, 1998.

PETTEGREE, Andrew (ed.). *The Reformation of the Parishes: The ministry and the Reformation in town and country*. Manchester University Press, 1993.

WERNHAM, R. B. *The Return of the Armadas: the last years of the Elizabethan war against Spain, 1595–1603*. Clarendon Press, 1994.

THE STUART PERIOD

BRADDICK, Michael J. *The Nerves of State. Taxation and the Financing of the English State, 1558–1714*. Manchester University Press, 1996.

BRADDICK, Michael J. *State Formation in Early Modern England, c. 1550–1700*. Cambridge University Press, 2000.

BRADSHAW, Brendon and ROBERTS, Peter (eds). *British Consciousness and Identity: The making of Britain, 1553–1707*. Cambridge University Press, 1998.

BURGESS, Glen. *The Politics of the Ancient Constitution. An Introduction to English Political Thought, 1603–1642*. Macmillan, 1993.

BURGESS, Glen. *Absolute Monarchy and the Stuart Constitution*. Yale University Press, 1996.

COLLINSON, Patrick and CRAIG, John (eds). *The Reformation in English Towns*. Macmillan, 1998.

COWARD, Barry (ed.). *A Companion to Stuart Britain*. Blackwell, 2003.

CRESSY, David. *Birth, Marriage, and Death. Ritual, Religion, and the Life-Cycle in Tudor and Stuart England*. Oxford University Press, 1997.

DURSTON, Christopher and EALES, Jacqueline (eds). *The Culture of English Puritanism: 1560–1700*. Macmillan, 1996.

FINCHAM, Kenneth (ed.). *The Early Stuart Church, 1603–1642.* Macmillan, 1993.

JONES, J. R. *The Anglo-Dutch Wars of the Seventeenth Century.* Longman, 1996.

KISHLANSKY, Mark A. *A Monarchy Transformed. Britain, 1603–1714.* Allen Lane, 1996.

LOCKYER, Roger. *The Early Stuarts. A Political History of England 1603–1642.* Longman, 2nd edn, 1999.

MALTBY, Judith. *Prayer Book and People in Elizabethan and Early Stuart England.* Cambridge University Press, 1998.

SHARPE, Kevin and LAKE, Peter (eds). *Culture and Politics in Early Stuart England.* Macmillan, 1994.

SMITH, David L. *The Stuart Parliaments 1603–1689.* Edward Arnold, 1999.

SOMMERVILLE, J. P. *Royalists and Patriots. Politics and Ideology in England 1603–1640.* Longman, 1999.

SPUFFORD, Margaret (ed.). *The World of Rural Dissenters, 1520–1725.* Cambridge University Press, 1998.

UNDERDOWN, David. *Fire from Heaven: Life in an English Town in the 17th Century.* HarperCollins, 1992.

UNDERDOWN, David. *A Freeborn People. Politics and the nation in seventeenth-century England.* Clarendon Press, 1997.

WHITE, Peter. *Predestination, Policy and Polemic: Conflict and consensus in the English Church from the Reformation to the Civil War.* Cambridge University Press, 1992.

JAMES I

CLUCAS, Stephen and DAVIES, Rosalind (eds). *The Crisis of 1614 and The Addled Parliament. Literary and Historical Perspectives.* Ashgate, 2003.

CROFT, Pauline (ed.). *Patronage, Culture and Power. The Early Cecils 1558–1612.* Yale University Press, 2002.

CROFT, Pauline. *King James.* Palgrave, 2003.

FERRELL, Lori Anne. *Government by Polemic. James I, the King's Preachers, and the Rhetorics of Conformity, 1603–1625.* Cambridge University Press, 1998.

FINCHAM, Kenneth. *Prelate as Pastor. The Episcopate of James I.* Clarendon Press, 1990.

LOCKYER, Roger. *James VI and I.* Profiles in Power. Longman, 1998.

MCCULLOCH, Peter E. *Sermons at Court: Politics and Religion in*

Elizabethan and Jacobean Preaching. Cambridge University Press, 1998.

PATTERSON, W. B. *King James VI and I and the Reunion of Christendom*. Cambridge University Press, 1998.

PECK, Linda Levy (ed.). *The Mental World of the Jacobean Court*. Cambridge University Press, 1991.

PURSELL, Brennan C. 'James I, Gondomar and the Dissolution of the Parliament of 1621'. *History*, Vol. 85, 2000.

QUESTIER, Michael C. 'The Politics of Religious Conformity and the Accession of James I'. *Historical Research*, Vol. 71, 1998.

SOMERSET, Anne. *Unnatural Murder. Poison at the court of James I*. Weidenfeld and Nicolson, 1997.

THRUSH, Andrew. 'The Personal Rule of James I' in COGSWELL, Thomas, CUST, Richard and LAKE, Peter (eds). *Politics, Religion and Popularity in Early Stuart Britain*. Cambridge University Press, 2002.

CHARLES I

DAVIES, Julian. *The Caroline Captivity of the Church: Charles I and the Remoulding of Anglicanism, 1625–1641*. Clarendon Press, 1992.

DONAGAN, Barbara. 'The York House Conference Revisited'. *Historical Research*, Vol. 64, 1991.

MERRITT, J. F. (ed.). *The Political World of Thomas Wentworth, Earl of Strafford, 1621–1641*. Cambridge University Press, 1996.

RUSSELL, Conrad. *The Fall of the British Monarchies 1637–1642*. Clarendon Press, 1991.

SHARPE, Kevin. *The Personal Rule of Charles I*. Yale University Press, 1992.

THRUSH, Andrew. 'Naval Finance and the origins and development of ship money' in FISSELL, Mark Charles (ed.). *War and Government in Britain, 1598–1650*. Manchester University Press, 1991.

WEBSTER, Tom. *Godly Clergy in Early Stuart England. The Caroline Puritan Movement, 1620–1642*. Cambridge University Press, 1997.

YOUNG, Michael. *Charles I*. Macmillan, 1997.

THE CIVIL WAR AND INTERREGNUM

ASHTON, Robert. *Counter-Revolution: The 2nd Civil War and its origins, 1646–48*. Yale University Press, 1994.

BENNETT, Martyn. *The Civil Wars in Britain and Ireland, 1638–1651*. Blackwell, 1996.

CARLIN, Norah. *The Causes of the English Civil War*. Blackwell, 1998.

CARLTON, Charles. *Going to the Wars. The Experience of the British Civil Wars, 1638–1651*. Routledge, 1992.

COLLINS, Jeffrey R. 'The Church Settlement of Oliver Cromwell'. *History*, Vol. 87, 2002.

COWARD, Barry. *Oliver Cromwell*. Profiles in Power. Longman, 1991.

COWARD, Barry. *The Cromwellian Protectorate*. Manchester University Press, 2002.

CUST, Richard and HUGHES, Ann (eds). *The English Civil War*. Edward Arnold, 1997.

DURSTON, Christopher. 'The Fall of Cromwell's Major-Generals.' *English Historical Review*, Vol. 113, 1995.

GENTLES, Ian. *The New Model Army in England, Ireland and Scotland, 1645–1653*. Blackwell, 1991.

HIRST, Derek. 'The Failure of Godly Rule in the English Republic'. *Past and Present*, No. 132, 1991.

MORRILL, John (ed.). *Revolution and Restoration: England in the 1650s*. Collins and Brown, 1992.

MORRILL, John. *The Nature of the English Revolution*. Longman, 1993.

PINCUS, Steven C. A. *Protestantism and Patriotism: Ideologies and the making of English foreign policy, 1650–1668*. Cambridge University Press, 1996.

RAYMOND, Joad. *The Invention of the Newspaper: English Newsbooks, 1641–1649*. Clarendon Press, 1990.

RICHARDSON, R. C. (ed.). *Town and Countryside in the English Revolution*. Manchester University Press, 1993.

RUSSELL, Conrad. *The Causes of the English Civil War*. Clarendon Press, 1990.

TOMLINSON, H. and GREGG, D. *Politics, Religion and Society in Revolutionary England, 1640–60*. Macmillan, 1990.

VENNING, Timothy. *Cromwellian Foreign Policy*. Macmillan, 1995.

WOOLRYCH, Austin. *Britain in Revolution 1625–1660*. Oxford University Press, 2002.

EARLY STUART ENGLAND

BARRY, Jonathan and BROOKS, Christopher (eds). *The Middling Sort of People. Culture, Society and Politics in England. 1550–1800*. Macmillan, 1994.

BRENNER, Robert. *Merchants and Revolution: Commercial change, political conflict, and London's overseas traders, 1550–1653*. Cambridge University Press, 1993.

COGSWELL, Thomas. *Home Divisions: Aristocracy, the state and provincial conflict*. Manchester University Press, 1998.

HUTTON, Ronald. *The Rise and Fall of Merry England. The Ritual Year 1400–1700*. Oxford University Press, 1994.

REAY, Barry. *Popular Cultures in England 1550–1750*. Longman, 1998.

SLACK, Paul. *From Reformation to Improvement. Public welfare in early modern England*. Clarendon Press, 1999.

WOOLF, D. R. *The Idea of History in Early Stuart England*. University of Toronto Press, 1990.

WRIGHTSON, K. 'Estates, degrees and sorts: changing perceptions of society in Tudor and Stuart England' in CORFIELD, J. P. (ed.). *Language, History and Class*. Oxford University Press, 1991.

CHARLES II

AYLMER, G. E. *The Crown's Servants: Government and Civil Service under Charles II, 1660–1685*. Oxford University Press, 2002.

GLASSEY, Lionel K. J. (ed.). *The Reigns of Charles II and James VII and II*. Macmillan, 1997.

HARRIS, Tim, SEAWARD, Paul and GOLDIE, Mark (eds). *The Politics of Religion in Restoration England*. Blackwell, 1990.

HARRIS, Tim. *Politics under the Stuarts: Party conflict in a divided society, 1660–1715*. Longman, 1993.

KEEBLE, N. H. *The Restoration: England in the 1660s*. Blackwell, 2002.

KNIGHTS, Mark. *Politics and Opinion in Crisis, 1678–81*. Cambridge University Press, 1994.

MILLER, John. *After the Civil Wars: English Politics and Government in the Reign of Charles II*. Pearson Education, 2000.

PINCUS, Steven C. A. *Protestantism and Patriotism: Ideologies and the making of English foreign policy, 1650–1668*. Cambridge University Press, 1996.

SCOTT, Jonathan. *Algernon Sidney and the Restoration Crisis, 1677–1683*. Cambridge University Press, 1991.

SEAWARD, Paul. *The Restoration*. Macmillan, 1991

SPURR, John. *The Restoration Church of England, 1646–1689*. Yale University Press, 1991.

SPURR, John. *England in the 1670s: 'This Masquerading Age'*. Blackwell, 2000.

SWATLAND, Andrew. *The House of Lords in the Reign of Charles II*. Cambridge University Press, 1996.

JAMES II, WILLIAM III AND QUEEN ANNE

BEDDARD, Robert (ed.). *The Revolutions of 1688*. Clarendon Press, 1992.

CLAYDON, Tony. *William III and the Godly Revolution*. Cambridge University Press, 1996.

CLAYDON, Tony. *William III*. Profiles in Power. Longman, 2002.

GLASSEY, Lionel K. J. (ed.). *The Reigns of Charles II and James VII and II*. Macmillan, 1997.

GRELL, Ole Peter, ISRAEL, Jonathan and TYACKE, Nicholas (eds). *From Persecution to Toleration. The Glorious Revolution and religion in England*. Clarendon Press, 1992.

HARRIS, Frances. *A Passion for Government: The Life of Sarah, Duchess of Marlborough*. Clarendon Press, 1991.

HARRIS, Tim. *Politics under the Stuarts: Party conflict in a divided society, 1660–1715*. Longman, 1993.

HOPPIT, Julian. *A Land of Liberty? England 1698–1727*. Oxford University Press, 2000.

ISRAEL, Jonathan (ed.). *The Anglo-Dutch Moment. Essays on the Glorious Revolution and its World impact*. Cambridge University Press, 1991.

MULLETT, Michael. *James II and English Politics, 1678–1688*. Lancaster Pamphlets. Routledge, 1994.

SCHWOERER, Lois G. (ed.). *The Revolution of 1688–1689: Changing Perspectives*. Cambridge University Press, 1992.

SPECK, W. A. *James II*. Profiles in Power. Longman, 2002.

IRELAND, SCOTLAND AND OVERSEAS POSSESSIONS IN THE SEVENTEENTH CENTURY

CANNY, Nicholas (ed.). *The Origins of Empire: British Overseas Enterprise to the Close of the Seventeenth Century*. Oxford University Press, 1998. Vol. I of LOUIS, W.R. (ed.). *The Oxford History of the British Empire*.

CANNY, Nicholas. *Making Ireland British 1580–1650*. Oxford University Press, 2001.

DONALD, Peter. *An Uncounselled King: Charles I and the Scottish Troubles, 1637–1641*. Cambridge University Press, 1990.

MACDONALD, Alan R. *The Jacobean Kirk, 1567–1625: Sovereignty, Polity and Liturgy*. Ashgate, 1998.

MASON, Roger A. *Scottish Political Thought and the Union of 1603*. Cambridge University Press, 1994.

OHLMEYER, Jane H. (ed.). *Ireland from Independence to Occupation, 1641–1660*. Cambridge University Press, 1995.

TREADWELL, Victor. *Buckingham and Ireland 1616–1628: A Study in Anglo-Irish Politics*. Four Courts, Dublin, 1998.

LATE STUART ENGLAND

CLIFFE, J. T. *The Puritan Gentry Besieged, 1650–1700*. Routledge, 1993.

EALES, Jacqueline. *Women in Early Modern England*. University College London, 1998.

FLETCHER, A. J. *Gender, Sex and Subordination in England 1500–1800*. Yale University Press, 1995.

HULL, Susan. *Women according to Men: The World of Tudor-Stuart women*. Sage, 1996.

HUTTON, Ronald. *The Rise and Fall of Merry England. The Ritual Year 1400–1700*. Oxford University Press, 1994.

JACK, Sybil M. *Towns in Tudor and Stuart England*. Macmillan, 1996.

MENDELSON, Sara and CRAWFORD, Patricia. *Women in Early Modern England, 1550–1720*. Clarendon Press, 1998.

PRIOR, Mary. *Women in English Society 1500–1800*. Methuen, 1985.

REAY, Barry. *Popular Cultures in England 1550–1750*. Longman, 1998.

SHARPE, James. *Instruments of Darkness: Witchcraft in England, 1550–1750*. Hamish Hamilton, 1996.

English monarchs

HOUSE OF TUDOR

Henry VII	1485–1509
Henry VIII	1509–1547
Edward VI	1547–1553
Mary I	1553–1558
Elizabeth I	1558–1603

HOUSE OF STUART

James VI and I	1603–1625
Charles I	1625–1649 (executed)
Charles II	1649–1685 (in exile until 1660)
James II	1685–1698 (fled the country in 1688)
William III and Mary II	1689–1702
Anne	1702–1714

English parliaments

HENRY VII
1485 November – 1486 March
1487 November – December
1489 January – 1490 February
1491 October – 1492 March
1495 October – December
1497 January – March
1504 January – April

HENRY VIII
1510 January – February
1512 February – 1514 March
1515 February – December
1523 April – August
1529 November – 1536 April (The Reformation Parliament)
1536 June – July
1539 April – 1540 July
1542 January – 1544 March
1545 November – 1547 January

EDWARD VI
1547 November – 1552 April
1553 March

MARY I
1553 October – December
1554 April – May
1554 November – 1555 January
1555 October – December
1558 January – November

ELIZABETH I
1559 January – May
1563 January – 1567 January
1571 April – May
1572 May – 1583 April
1584 November – 1585 September
1586 October – 1587 March
1589 February – March
1593 February – April
1597 October – 1598 February
1601 October – December

JAMES I
1604 March – 1611 February
1614 April – June (The Addled Parliament)
1621 January – 1622 February
1624 February – 1625 March

CHARLES I
1625 May – August
1626 February – June
1628 March – 1629 March
1640 April – May (The Short Parliament)
1640 November – 1660 March (The Long Parliament. Purged in December 1648 and expelled in April 1653)

CIVIL WAR AND INTERREGNUM
1644 January – October (summoned by the King to Oxford)
1653 July – December (The Nominated Assembly, Parliament of Saints, Barebones Parliament)
1654 September – 1655 January
1656 September – 1658 February
1659 January – April
1659 May – 1660 March (The recalled Rump and then the Long Parliament)

CHARLES II
1660 April – December (The Convention)
1661 May – 1679 January (The Long Parliament of the Restoration, Cavalier Parliament, Pension Parliament)
1679 March – July
1680 October – 1681 January
1681 March (The Oxford Parliament)

JAMES II
1685 May – 1687 July

WILLIAM III AND MARY II
1689 January – 1690 February (The Convention)
1690 March – 1695 October
1695 November – 1698 July
1698 August – 1700 December
1701 February – November
1701 December – 1702 July

ANNE
1702 August – 1705 April
1705 June – 1708 April (became in 1707 the first Parliament of Great Britain)
1708 July – 1710 September
1710 November – 1713 August
1713 November – 1715 January

Based on the list given in E. B. FRYDE, D. E. GREENWAY, S. PORTER and I. ROY (eds). *Handbook of British Chronology*, Royal Historical Society, 3rd edn, 1986.

Index

Canterbury 209–10,
264–5
Bank of England 448,
469, 514, 520
Baptists 431
Barbados 506, 507
Barbon, Nicholas 'Praise
God' 365
Barcelona, Treaty of
(1529) 42
Barnes, Robert 67, 77, 101
Baro, Peter 21
baronets: creation 289
Barrow, Henry 205, 206
Barrow, Isaac 529
Barton, Elizabeth ('Nun
of Kent') 58
Basilicon Doron 250
Bastwick, John 310, 311
Bate's Case (1606) 276–7,
297
Baxter, Richard 398–9
Beachy Head, Battle of
(1690) 444
Beale, Mary 526
Beaufort, Lady Margaret
7, 21, 159–60
Becket, St Thomas 59
shrine 60, 79
Ben, Aphra 526
benevolences 15
Bennett, Henry, Earl of
Arlington 403,
406–7, 408, 409, 410
Bentinck, William, Earl of
Portland 443
Berkeley, Sir Robert
319–20
Bermuda 506
Berwick, Duke of (James
II's son) 463
Berwick: pacification
(1639) 323, 491
Bess of Hardwick
(Elizabeth, Countess
of Shrewsbury) 523
Beza, Theodore 195
Bible
Authorised Version 262
control over translation
102
English 21, 60
Erasmus' New
Testament 63

Great Bible (1535,
Coverdale) 67–8
Tyndale's New
Testament 64–5
Bilney, Thomas 63–4
Bishop's Book, The
(1537) 102
Bishop's Exclusion Bill
(1641) 331, 338
Bishop, William, Bishop
of Chalcedon (RC)
272
Black Acts 179
Black Death (1348) 69
Black Rubric 119, 187
Blake, Robert 362, 371
Blaythwayt, William 522
Blenheim Palace 460
Blenheim, Battle of
(1704) 459–60
Blount, Charles, Baron
Mountjoy 172
Board of Trade 521
Boleyn, Anne 44, 55, 56,
66, 71
execution 98
Boleyn, George, Viscount
Rochester 85
Bolingbroke, Viscount *see*
St John, Henry
Bombay 406, 510
Bond of Association, The
(1584) 225
Book of Advertisements
(1565) 190–1
Book of Bounty 256
Book of Discipline (1586)
203
Book of Martyrs 13
Book of Orders 321, 383
Book of Rates 15, 137,
241, 255
borrowings: Charles II
390–1
Bosworth, Battle (1485)
1, 10
Bothwell, Lord *see*
Hepburn James, Earl
of Bothwell
Boulogne 104, 121
Bourbon, Duke of 42
Boyle, Robert 529
Boyne, Battle of the
(1690) 487

Braddock Down, Battle of
(1643) 343
Bradshaw, John 357
Brandon, Charles, Duke
of Suffolk 83–4
Bray, Sir Reginald 5, 6,
7–8, 14–15
Breda, Declaration of
(1660) 377, 398, 400
Breda, Treaty of (1667)
406
Brewster, Sir Francis:
*Discourse Touching
Provision for the
Poor, A* (1683) 513
Bristol 150, 152, 344
Broghill, Lord 372–3
Browne, Robert 198
Bucer, Martin 63, 77,
109, 110, 196
Buckingham, Dukes of
see Stafford; Villiers
Burnet, Gilbert, Bishop of
Salisbury 426
Burton, Henry 310
Butler, James, 12th Earl
of Ormond 345, 401

Cabal, The 406–7
Cabinet Council 445
Cabot, John 146
Cabot, Sebastian 146, 147
Cadiz expeditions 228,
250, 299, 382, 458
Caesar, Sir Julius 258,
259, 317
Calais: loss of 136
Calamy, Edmund 398
calicoes (fine cottons) 517
Calvin, Jean 109, 199
Calvinism/Calvinists 186,
266, 309 *see also*
Knox, John;
Presbyterians/Presbyt
erianism
Anglicans and 198–9
Netherlands 218–19
Calvert, George, Baron
Baltimore 506
Cambrai, Peace of (1529)
43
Cambridge University 28,
125, 134, 159, 160,
343, 431, 529